D1325834

Principles of Economics

PRINCIPLES

OF

ECONOMICS

BY

ALFRED MARSHALL,
PROFESSOR OF POLITICAL ECONOMY IN THE UNIVERSITY OF CAMBRIDGE,
FELLOW OF ST JOHN'S COLLEGE, CAMBRIDGE,
SOMETIME FELLOW OF BALLIOL COLLEGE, OXFORD

VOL. I.

THIRD EDITION

Natura non facit saltum

London:
MACMILLAN AND CO.
AND NEW YORK
1895

First Edition 1890. *Second Edition* 1891.
Third Edition 1895.

CAMBRIDGE: PRINTED BY J. & C. F. CLAY,
AT THE UNIVERSITY PRESS.

PREFACE TO THE THIRD EDITION.

IN this edition several chapters have been re-written; chiefly in order to meet the need, which experience has shown to exist, for fuller explanation on certain points

The most important change is in the survey of the central problem of distribution and exchange, which occupies the first two chapters of Book VI (Book VII. of the first edition). In earlier editions the reader was left to import into them the results of the preceding Books But I had underrated the difficulty of doing that, as is shown by the fact that able and careful critics both at home and abroad have raised objections to those chapters which had been anticipated in other parts of the volume. It seemed necessary therefore, to embody in those central chapters a good deal that had been said before, and to supplement by still further explanations

The first of these chapters, after reproducing a short historical introduction from the earlier editions, discusses one side of the problem of distribution, namely that on which the forces of demand work.

The following chapter deals first with the side of supply, and then with the two sides together. Some economists have treated the causes affecting the supply of the agents of production, as exercising an influence in distribution generally, not co-ordinate with, but only subordinate to that of the forces of demand, and a further attempt is made in this chapter to show that such a treatment, however appropriate to passing movements of distribution, cannot properly be applied to the broad central problem of normal distribution. The chapter ends with a fuller discussion of general wages than had been given in earlier editions; and discusses the relations between different kinds of surpluses.

The fifth and sixth chapters of Book I and the sixth chapter of Book III. have been somewhat modified and enlarged in order to make more clear how closely the economist adheres in substance to the methods of inference and judgment of ordinary life; and how thorough are the harmony and the mutual dependence between the analytical and the inductive, or historical, methods of economic study

The chapters on Capital and Income in Book II have been combined and re-written (see also Book VI. Ch I § 10, and Ch. II. § 10) in order to give effect to a long cherished design, from which I have been held back hitherto by the fear of breaking too much with tradition and especially English tradition. I have steadily grown in the conviction that there is, and from the nature of the case there must be, something artificial in every broad distinction between capital in general (or "social" capital, *i.e.* capital not regarded from the point of view of an individual) and other forms of wealth. For indeed whatever line of division be taken, the attributes assigned to capital are not present in equal degrees in all forms of capital, and they are present in some degree in other forms of wealth: such statements for instance as that capital supports, or aids, or employs labour, are not true without reserve of all things that lie within any line of demarcation that has been proposed for capital; and they are true in a measure of some forms of wealth that lie outside the line. The discussions of ordinary business life give us little guidance, and impose on us no restrictions in the matter: for they refer almost exclusively to capital from the point of view of the individual or "trade-capital". and, when they take a wider scope, they do not draw a firm and clear line between capital and other forms of accumulated wealth. Economists remain therefore free to choose their standard definition of Capital with a view to their own convenience, and it seems clear that the discussion of the distribution of the national income or dividend is that to which it is most important that their use of the term should be appropriate, and this points to the treatment of "capital" and "income" as correlative terms. Of course all wealth is designed to yield what in pure theory may be called "an income" of benefit or gain in some form or other, but the language of the market place refuses to admit so broad a use of the term Income as that It is however tolerably consistent in commonly including a certain number of forms of income, other than money income, and this consensus may well be turned to account. Labour is already defined by nearly all economists so as to include those activities, and those only, which are commonly regarded as the source of income in this broader use of the term and most if not all economists glide imperceptibly to a closely corresponding use of capital when they come to discuss the problem of distribution. It is now proposed to do this deliberately, and to define capital (from the general point of view) as wealth which yields "income" in forms that are admitted in the broader use of the term in the market place[1]

[1] Among minor changes, which often affect only one or two paragraphs, may be mentioned those on pp. 20, 21 on the economic conditions of ancient Rome; 57 *n* and 59 on Adam Smith, 118 on the name Economics, 179 and 183, 4 on variations of elasticity of demand; 192 on working men's budgets; 196, 7 on the pleasure of ownership; 214–9 on the plan of Book IV., 249, 50 on Turgot's statement of the law of diminishing return; 259 on the area of the earth's surface not yet cultivated, 263, 4 on conditions affecting birth-rate; 272, 3 on vital statistics; 280 *n* on the growth of towns, 319 on the influence of financial systems on the

The ambiguous term "determine" has been displaced, in spite of its prestige, by "govern" or "indicate" as occasion requires. Technical terms have been dispensed with, wherever it was possible to do so without great loss of clearness or brevity.

In preparing this edition I have received very great assistance from my wife, and much from Prof. Edgeworth; and helpful suggestions from Profs. Ashley, Mackenzie, Sidgwick and Taussig, and from Mr Bateson and Mr Berry.

apparent as distinguished from the real growth of wealth; 329 on the inheritance of acquired faculties through other than physical means, 426 *n*, and 427, 8 on "the long run"; 435–8 on the relation between supplementary costs and quasi-rents; 444 *n*, 445 *n* on some abnormal movements of value; 463 *n* on the doctrine of imputed value; 559–561, 563 and 565, on Ricardo's doctrine as to value, 474–6 on the phrase "rent does not enter into cost of production", 625 *n* on "task-wages"; 661–4 on the absence of any broad difference between the older and the newer doctrines of interest [the order of the following pages 665–72 has been changed, and the summary which preceded them has been distributed between Chs I II and XII of Book VI], 674 on the interest of the working classes that the purchasing power of money should increase with the progress of man's command over nature, 693 on remuneration for the net evils of risk as an element of normal profits, 710 *n* on Petty's anticipation of the independence of the doctrine of rent of any particular form of land tenure, 799–805 on mathematical versions of some parts of the theory of exchange and distribution; on the limits within which such versions are applicable, and on their use within those limits

PREFACE TO THE FIRST EDITION.

ECONOMIC conditions are constantly changing, and each generation looks at its own problems in its own way. In England, as well as on the Continent and in America, Economic studies are being more vigorously pursued now than ever before; but all this activity has only shown the more clearly that Economic science is, and must be, one of slow and continuous growth. Some of the best work of the present generation has indeed appeared at first sight to be antagonistic to that of earlier writers, but when it has had time to settle down into its proper place, and its rough edges have been worn away, it has been found to involve no real breach of continuity in the development of the science. The new doctrines have supplemented the older, have extended, developed, and sometimes corrected them, and often have given them a different tone by a new distribution of emphasis; but very seldom have subverted them.

The present treatise is an attempt to present a modern version of old doctrines with the aid of the new work, and with reference to the new problems, of our own age. Its general scope and purpose are indicated in Book I., at the end of which a short account is given of what are taken to be the chief subjects of economic inquiry, and the chief practical issues on which that inquiry has a bearing. In accordance with English traditions, it is held that the functions of the science are to collect, arrange and analyse economic facts, and to apply the knowledge, gained by observation and experience, in determining what are likely to be the immediate and ultimate effects of various groups of causes; and it is held that the Laws of Economics are statements of tendencies expressed in the indicative mood, and not ethical precepts in the imperative. Economic laws and reasonings in fact are merely a part of the material, of which Conscience and Common-sense have to make use in solving practical problems, and in laying down rules which may be a guide in life.

But ethical forces are among those of which the economist has to take account. Attempts have indeed been made to construct an abstract science with regard to the actions of an "economic man," who is under no ethical influences and who pursues pecuniary gain warily and energetically, but mechanically and selfishly But they have not been successful, nor even thoroughly carried out, for they have never really treated the economic man as perfectly selfish. No one could be relied on better than the economic man to endure toil and sacrifice with the unselfish desire to make provision for his family; and his normal motives have always been tacitly assumed to include the family affections. But if these motives are included, why not also all other altruistic motives, the action of which is so far uniform in any class at any time and place, that it can be reduced to general rule? There seems to be no good reason against including them: and in the present book normal action is taken to be that which may be expected, under certain conditions, from the members of an industrial group; and no attempt is made to exclude the influence of any motives, the action of which is regular, merely because they are altruistic. If the book has any special character of its own, that may perhaps be said to lie in the prominence which it gives to this and other applications of the Principle of Continuity.

This Principle is applied not only to the ethical quality of the motives by which a man may be influenced in choosing his ends, but also to the sagacity, the energy and the enterprise with which he pursues those ends. Thus stress is laid on the fact that there is a continuous gradation from the actions of "city men," which are based on deliberate and far-reaching calculations, and are executed with vigour and ability, to those of ordinary people who have neither the power nor the will to conduct their affairs in a business-like way. The normal willingness to save, the normal willingness to undergo a certain exertion for a certain pecuniary reward, or the normal alertness to seek the best markets in which to buy and sell, or to search out the most advantageous occupation for oneself or for one's children—all these and similar phrases must be relative to the members of a particular class at a given place and time, but, when that is once understood, the theory of normal value is applicable to the actions of the unbusiness-like classes in the same way, though not with the same precision of detail, as to those of the merchant or banker.

And as there is no sharp line of division between conduct which is normal, and that which has to be provisionally neglected as abnormal, so there is none between normal values and "current" or "market" or "occasional" values The latter are those values in which the accidents of the moment exert a preponderating influence, while normal values are those which would be ultimately attained, if the economic conditions under view had time to work out undisturbed their full effect But there is no impassable gulf between these two; they shade into one another by continuous gradations. The values which we may regard as normal if we are thinking of the changes from hour to hour on a

Produce Exchange, do but indicate current variations with regard to the year's history: and the normal values with reference to the year's history are but current values with reference to the history of the century. For the element of Time, which is the centre of the chief difficulty of almost every economic problem, is itself continuous: Nature knows no absolute partition of time into long periods and short; but the two shade into one another by imperceptible gradations, and what is a short period for one problem, is a long period for another.

Thus for instance the greater part, though not the whole, of the distinction between Rent and Interest on capital turns on the length of the period which we have in view. That which is rightly regarded as interest on "free" or "floating" capital, or on new investments of capital, is more properly treated as a sort of rent—a *Quasi-rent* it is called below—on old investments of capital And there is no sharp line of division between floating capital and that which has been "sunk" for a special branch of production, nor between new and old investments of capital; each group shades into the other gradually. And thus even the rent of land is seen, not as a thing by itself, but as the leading species of a large genus; though indeed it has peculiarities of its own which are of vital importance from the point of view of theory as well as of practice.

Again, though there is a sharp line of division between man himself and the appliances which he uses, and though the supply of, and the demand for, human efforts and sacrifices have peculiarities of their own, which do not attach to the supply of, and the demand for, material goods; yet, after all, these material goods are themselves generally the result of human efforts and sacrifices. The theories of the values of labour, and of the things made by it, cannot be separated: they are parts of one great whole; and what differences there are between them even in matters of detail, turn out on inquiry to be, for the most part, differences of degree rather than of kind. As, in spite of the great differences in form between birds and quadrupeds, there is one Fundamental Idea running through all their frames, so the general theory of the equilibrium of demand and supply is a Fundamental Idea running through the frames of all the various parts of the central problem of Distribution and Exchange[1].

Another application of the principle of Continuity is to the use of terms. There has always been a temptation to classify economic goods in clearly defined groups, about which a number of short and sharp propositions could be made, to gratify at once the student's desire for logical precision, and the popular liking for dogmas that have the air of being profound and are yet easily handled. But great mischief seems to have been done by yielding to this temptation, and drawing broad artificial lines of division where Nature has made none. The more simple and absolute an economic doctrine is, the greater will be the confusion which it brings into attempts to apply economic doctrines to practice, if the dividing lines to which it refers cannot be found in real life. There is not in real life a clear line of division between things that are and are not Capital, or that are and are not Necessaries, or again between labour that is and is not Productive

The notion of Continuity with regard to development is common to all modern schools of economic thought, whether

[1] In the *Economics of Industry* published by my wife and myself in 1879 an endeavour was made to show the nature of this fundamental unity. A short provisional account of the relations of demand and supply was given before the theory of Distribution; and then this one scheme of general reasoning was applied in succession to the earnings of labour, the interest on capital and the Earnings of Management But the drift of this arrangement was not made sufficiently clear, and on Professor Nicholson's suggestion, more prominence has been given to it in the present volume.

the chief influences acting on them are those of biology, as represented by the writings of Herbert Spencer; or of history and philosophy, as represented by Hegel's *Philosophy of History*, and by more recent ethico-historical studies on the Continent and elsewhere These two kinds of influences have affected, more than any other, the substance of the views expressed in the present book; but their form has been most affected by mathematical conceptions of Continuity, as represented in Cournot's *Principes Mathématiques de la Théorie des Richesses* He taught that it is necessary to face the difficulty of regarding the various elements of an economic problem,—not as determining one another in a chain of causation, A determining B, B determining C, and so on—but as all mutually determining one another. Nature's action is complex and nothing is gained in the long run by pretending that it is simple, and trying to describe it in a series of elementary propositions

Under the guidance of Cournot, and in a less degree of von Thunen, I was led to attach great importance to the fact that our observations of nature, in the moral as in the physical world, relate not so much to aggregate quantities, as to increments of quantities, and that in particular the demand for a thing is a continuous function, of which the "marginal"[1] increment is, in stable equilibrium, balanced against the corresponding increment of its cost of production. It is not easy to get a clear full view of Continuity in this aspect without the aid either of mathematical symbols or of diagrams The use of the latter requires no special knowledge,

[1] The term "marginal" increment is in harmony with von Thunen's methods of thought and was suggested to me by him, though he does not actually use it. It has been for some time commonly used by Austrian economists on the initiative of Prof Wieser, and it has been adopted by Mr Wicksteed When Jevons' Theory appeared, I adopted his word "final"; but I have been gradually convinced that "marginal" is the better [In the first Edition this footnote implied wrongly that the phrase, as well as the idea of, Marginal Increment could be traced to von Thunen]

and they often express the conditions of economic life more accurately, as well as more easily, than do mathematical symbols, and therefore they have been applied as supplementary illustrations in the footnotes of the present volume. The argument in the text is never dependent on them; and they may be omitted; but experience seems to show that they give a firmer grasp of many important principles than can be got without their aid; and that there are many problems of pure theory, which no one who has once learnt to use diagrams will willingly handle in any other way.

The chief use of pure mathematics in economic questions seems to be in helping a person to write down quickly, shortly and exactly, some of his thoughts for his own use: and to make sure that he has enough, and only enough, premisses for his conclusions (*i e* that his equations are neither more nor less in number than his unknowns). But when a great many symbols have to be used, they become very laborious to anyone but the writer himself And though Cournot's genius must give a new mental activity to everyone who passes through his hands, and mathematicians of calibre similar to his may use their favourite weapons in clearing a way for themselves to the centre of some of those difficult problems of economic theory, of which only the outer fringe has yet been touched; yet it seems doubtful whether anyone spends his time well in reading lengthy translations of economic doctrines into mathematics, that have not been made by himself. A few specimens of those applications of mathematical language which have proved most useful for my own purposes have, however, been added in an Appendix[1].

[1] Many of the diagrams in this book have appeared in print already and I may take this opportunity of giving their history Mr Henry Cunynghame who was attending my lectures in 1873, seeing me annoyed by being unable to draw a series of rectangular hyperbolas, invented a beautiful and original machine for the purpose It was shown at the Cambridge Philosophical Society in 1873; and,

I have to acknowledge much assistance in preparing this volume for the press. My wife has aided and advised me at every stage of the MSS. and of the proofs, and it owes a very great deal to her suggestions, her care and her judgment. Mr J. N. Keynes, and Mr L. L. Price have read all the proofs and have never returned me any without improving them much: Mr Arthur Berry and Mr A. W. Flux have given me valuable help in connection with the mathematical Appendix; and my father, Mr W. H. B. Hall and Mr C. J. Clay have assisted me on special points.

to explain its use, I read a paper (briefly reported in the *Proceedings*, Part xv pp. 318–9), in which I described the theories of Multiple Positions of Equilibrium and of Monopoly values very nearly as they are given below (Book v. Ch v and viii). In 1875–7 I nearly completed a draft of a treatise on *The Theory of Foreign Trade, with some allied problems relating to the doctrine of Laisser Faire* The first Part of it was intended for general use, while the second Part was technical, nearly all the diagrams that are now in Book v Ch v, vii and viii [Ch xi, xii, xiii of the present edition] were introduced in it, in connection with the problem of the relation of Protection to the Maximum Satisfaction of the community, and there were others relating to Foreign Trade But in 1877 I turned aside to work at the *Economics of Industry*, and afterwards was overtaken by an illness, which nearly suspended my studies for several years Meanwhile the MSS of my first projected treatise were lying idle and it is to them that Professor Sidgwick refers in the Preface to his *Political Economy*. With my consent he selected four chapters (not consecutive) out of the second Part, and printed them for private circulation These four chapters contained most of the substance of Book v Ch v and vii, but not Ch viii. [*i.e.* Ch xi and xii but not xiii. of the third edition] of the present work; together with two chapters relating to the equilibrium of foreign trade They have been sent to many economists in England and on the Continent it is of them that Jevons speaks in the Preface to the second edition of his *Theory* (p xlv), and many of the diagrams in them relating to foreign trade have been reproduced with generous acknowledgments by Prof Pantaleoni in his *Principii di Economia Pura*.

July, 1890.

CONTENTS.

[*Italics are used to give references to definitions of technical terms Asterisks denote Chapters or Sections which consist largely of new matter.*]

BOOK I.

PRELIMINARY SURVEY.

BOOK II.

SOME FUNDAMENTAL NOTIONS

BOOK III.

DEMAND AND CONSUMPTION

BOOK IV.

THE AGENTS OF PRODUCTION.

LAND, LABOUR, CAPITAL AND ORGANIZATION

BOOK V.

THE THEORY OF THE EQUILIBRIUM OF DEMAND AND SUPPLY.

BOOK VI.

VALUE, OR DISTRIBUTION AND EXCHANGE

CORRIGENDA.

Page 214, delete second marginal note

" 273, the last number in the table should be 2 2, not 12 2

" 301, ll. 4, 5, should read *the vigour of the people as a whole, if not their numbers, and both the numbers and vigour of any trade in particular*

" 435, the second marginal note should read *The income that covers supplementary costs is a part of normal profits in the long run, but for a short run it may be regarded as a Quasi-rent on investments of capital and energy.*

" 570 n last line but two, for *in the text* read *in the last note*

" 661 second marginal note, for *individual* read *fundamental*

BOOK I.

PRELIMINARY SURVEY

CHAPTER I.

INTRODUCTION

BOOK I CH I

Economics is a study of wealth and a part of the study of man

§ 1 POLITICAL ECONOMY or ECONOMICS is a study of man's actions in the ordinary business of life; it inquires how he gets his income and how he uses it. Thus it is on the one side a study of wealth, and on the other, and more important side, a part of the study of man. For man's character has been moulded by his every-day work, and by the material resources which he thereby procures, more than by any other influence unless it be that of his religious ideals; and the two great forming agencies of the world's history have been the religious and the economic. Here and there the ardour of the military or the artistic spirit has been for a while predominant. but religious and economic influences have nowhere been displaced from the front rank even for a time, and they have nearly always been more important than all others put together. Religious motives are more intense than economic; but their direct action seldom extends over so large a part of life. For the business by which a person earns his livelihood generally fills his thoughts during by far the greater part of those hours in which his mind is at its best; during them his character is being formed by the way in which he uses his faculties in his work, by the thoughts and the feelings which it suggests, and by his relations to his associates in work, his employers or his employés

Man's character formed by his daily work

And very often the influence exerted on a person's

BOOK I. CH. I

Poverty causes degradation

character by the amount of his income is hardly less, if it is less, than that exerted by the way in which it is earned. It may make little difference to the fulness of life of a family whether its yearly income is £1000 or £5000; but it makes a very great difference whether the income is £30 or £150: for with £150 the family has, with £30 it has not, the material conditions of a complete life. It is true that in religion, in the family affections and in friendship, even the poor may find scope for many of those faculties which are the source of the highest happiness. But the conditions which surround extreme poverty, especially in densely crowded places, tend to deaden the higher faculties Those who have been called the Residuum of our large towns have little opportunity for friendship; they know nothing of the decencies and the quiet, and very little even of the unity of family life; and religion often fails to reach them. No doubt their physical, mental, and moral ill-health is partly due to other causes than poverty, but this is the chief cause.

And in addition to the Residuum there are vast numbers of people both in town and country who are brought up with insufficient food, clothing, and house-room, whose education is broken off early in order that they may go to work for wages, who thenceforth are engaged during long hours in exhausting toil with imperfectly nourished bodies, and have therefore no chance of developing their higher mental faculties. Their life is not necessarily unhealthy or unhappy. Rejoicing in their affections towards God and man, and perhaps even possessing some natural refinement of feeling, they may lead lives that are far less incomplete than those of many who have more material wealth But, for all that, their poverty is a great and almost unmixed evil to them. Even when they are well, their weariness often amounts to pain, while their pleasures are few; and when sickness comes, the suffering caused by poverty increases tenfold. And though a contented spirit may go far towards reconciling them to these evils, there are others to which it ought not to reconcile them. Overworked and undertaught, weary and careworn, without quiet and without leisure, they have no chance of making the best of their mental faculties

Although then some of the evils which commonly go with poverty are not its necessary consequences; yet, broadly speaking, "the destruction of the poor is their poverty," and the study of the causes of poverty is the study of the causes of the degradation of a large part of mankind.

May we not outgrow the belief that poverty is necessary?

§ 2 Slavery was regarded by Aristotle as an ordinance of nature, and so probably was it by the slaves themselves in olden time. The dignity of man was proclaimed by the Christian religion: it has been asserted with increasing vehemence during the last hundred years. but it is only through the spread of education during quite recent times that we are beginning at last to feel the full import of the phrase. Now at last we are setting ourselves seriously to inquire whether it is necessary that there should be any so-called "lower classes" at all. that is, whether there need be large numbers of people doomed from their birth to hard work in order to provide for others the requisites of a refined and cultured life; while they themselves are prevented by their poverty and toil from having any share or part in that life.

The hope that poverty and ignorance may gradually be extinguished, derives indeed much support from the steady progress of the working classes during the present century. The steam-engine has relieved them of much exhausting and degrading toil, wages have risen, education has been improved and become more general; the railway and the printing-press have enabled members of the same trade in different parts of the country to communicate easily with one another, and to undertake and carry out broad and far-seeing lines of policy; while the growing demand for intelligent work has caused the artisan classes to increase so rapidly that they now outnumber those whose labour is entirely unskilled. A great part of the artisans have ceased to belong to the "lower classes" in the sense in which the term was originally used; and some of them already lead a more refined and noble life than did the majority of the upper classes even a century ago.

This progress has done more than anything else to give practical interest to the question whether it is really impossible that all should start in the world with a fair chance of

BOOK I CH I

leading a cultured life, free from the pains of poverty and the stagnating influences of excessive mechanical toil, and this question is being pressed to the front by the growing earnestness of the age

The question cannot be fully answered by economic science, for the answer depends partly on the moral and political capabilities of human nature, and on these matters the economist has no special means of information; he must do as others do, and guess as best he can. But the answer depends in a great measure upon facts and inferences, which are within the province of economics; and this it is which gives to economic studies their chief and their highest interest.

Need for some preliminary inquiry as to the tardy growth of economic science

§ 3. It might have been expected that a science, which deals with questions so vital for the wellbeing of mankind, would have engaged the attention of many of the ablest thinkers of every age, and be now well advanced towards maturity. But the fact is that the number of scientific economists has always been small relatively to the difficulty of the work to be done, and that the science is still almost in its infancy The chief causes of this paradoxical result are two. Firstly, the bearing of economics on the higher wellbeing of man has been overlooked; and a science which has wealth for its subject-matter, is often repugnant at first sight to many students, for indeed those who do most to advance the boundaries of knowledge, seldom care much about the possession of wealth for its own sake. And, secondly, many of those conditions of industrial life, and of those methods of production, distribution and consumption, with which modern economic science is concerned, are themselves only of recent date

The ordinary business of life is entirely different in form from what it was even a little while ago. It is indeed true that the change in substance is in some respects not so great as the change in outward form; and much more of modern economic theory than at first appears can be adapted to the conditions of backward races. But unity in substance underlying many varieties of form is not easy to detect, and the changes in form have had the effect of making writers in all ages profit less than they otherwise might have done by the work of their predecessors.

The economic conditions of modern life, though more complex, are in many ways more definite than those of earlier times. Business is more clearly marked off from other concerns, the rights of individuals as against others and as against the community are more sharply defined, and above all the emancipation from custom, and the growth of free activity, of constant forethought and restless enterprise have given a new precision and a new prominence to the causes that govern the relative values of different things and different kinds of labour The starting point of our science therefore cannot be made clear without a brief account of the growth of modern forms of industrial life, and to that we proceed next. We are however in difficulty for want of a word to express properly the special character of these modern forms.

The fundamental characteristic of modern industrial life is not competition,

§ 4 It is often said that the modern forms of industrial life are distinguished from the earlier by being more competitive But this account is not quite satisfactory. The strict meaning of competition seems to be the racing of one person against another, with special reference to bidding for the sale or purchase of anything This kind of racing is no doubt both more intense and more widely extended than it used to be but it is only a secondary, and one might almost say, an accidental consequence from the fundamental characteristics of modern industrial life

but self-reliance, independence, deliberate choice and fore-thought.

There is no one term that will express these characteristics adequately. They are, as we shall presently see, a certain independence and habit of choosing one's own course for oneself, a self-reliance; a deliberation and yet a promptness of choice and judgment, and a habit of forecasting the future and of shaping one's course with reference to distant aims They may and often do cause people to compete with one another; but on the other hand they may tend, and just now indeed they are tending, in the direction of co-operation and combination of all kinds good and evil. But these tendencies towards collective ownership and collective action are quite different from those of earlier times, because they are the

BOOK I. CH. I

result not of custom, not of any passive drifting into association with one's neighbours, but of free choice by each individual of that line of conduct which after careful deliberation seems to him the best suited for attaining his ends, whether they are selfish or unselfish.

"Competition" implies too much as well as too little. Man is not more selfish than he was

The term "competition" has gathered about it evil savour, and has come to imply a certain selfishness and indifference to the wellbeing of others. Now it is true that there is less deliberate selfishness in early than in modern forms of industry; but there is also less deliberate unselfishness. It is deliberateness, and not selfishness, that is the characteristic of the modern age.

For instance, while custom in a primitive society extends the limits of the family, and prescribes certain duties to one's neighbours which fall into disuse in a later civilization, it also prescribes an attitude of hostility to strangers. In a modern society the obligations of family kindness become more intense, though they are concentrated on a narrower area, and neighbours are put more nearly on the same footing with strangers In ordinary dealings with both of them the standard of fairness and honesty is lower than in some of the dealings of a primitive people with their neighbours, but it is much higher than in their dealings with strangers. Thus it is the ties of neighbourhood alone that have been relaxed: the ties of family are in many ways stronger than before, family affection leads to much more self-sacrifice and devotion than it used to do, and sympathy with those who are strangers to us is a growing source of a kind of deliberate unselfishness that never existed before the modern age. That country which is the birthplace of modern competition devotes a larger part of its income than any other to charitable uses, and spent twenty millions on purchasing the freedom of the slaves in the West Indies.

In every age poets and social reformers have tried to stimulate the people of their own time to a nobler life by enchanting stories of the virtues of the heroes of old. But neither the records of history nor the contemporary observation of backward races, when carefully studied, give any support to the doctrine that man is on the whole harder and harsher than he was, or that he was ever more willing than he is now to sacrifice his own happiness for the benefit of others in cases where custom and law have left him free to choose his own course. Among races whose intellectual capacity seems not to have developed in any other direction, and who have none of the originating power of the modern business man, there will be found many who show an evil sagacity in driving a hard bargain in a market even with their neighbours. No traders are more unscrupulous in taking advantage of the necessities of the unfortunate than the corn-dealers and money-lenders of the East.

Man is not more dishonest than he was

Again, the modern era has undoubtedly given new openings for dishonesty in trade. The advance of knowledge has discovered new ways of making things appear other than they are, and has rendered possible many new forms of adulteration The producer is now far removed from the ultimate consumer, and his wrong-doings are not visited with the prompt and sharp punishment which falls on the head of a person who, being bound to live and die in his native village, plays a dishonest trick on one of his neighbours. The opportunities for knavery are certainly more numerous than they were; but there is no reason for thinking that people avail themselves of a larger proportion of such opportunities than they used to do. On the contrary, modern methods of trade imply habits of trustfulness on the one side and a power of resisting temptation to dishonesty on the other, which do not exist among a backward people. Instances of simple truth and personal fidelity are met with under all social conditions: but those who have tried to establish a business of modern type in a backward country find that they can scarcely ever depend on the native population for filling posts of trust. It is even more difficult to dispense with imported assistance for work which calls for a strong moral character than for that which requires great skill and mental ability. Adulteration and fraud in trade were rampant in the middle ages to an extent that is very astonishing, when we consider the difficulties of wrong-doing without detection at that time

The term "competition" is then not well suited to

BOOK I. CH. I

describe the special characteristics of industrial life in the modern age. We need a term that does not imply any moral qualities, whether good or evil, but which indicates the undisputed fact that modern business and industry are characterized by more self-reliant habits, more forethought, more deliberate and free choice. There is not any one term adequate for this purpose but *Freedom of Industry and Enterprise*, or more shortly, *Economic Freedom*, points in the right direction, and may be used in the absence of a better. Of course this deliberate and free choice may lead to a certain departure from individual freedom when co-operation or combination seems to offer the best route to the desired end The questions how far these deliberate forms of association are likely to destroy the freedom in which they had their origin, and how far they are likely to be conducive to the public weal, will occupy a large share of our attention towards the end of this treatise.

Economic Freedom

§ 5 There is another word of which some account should be given here; because it will often occur in this Preliminary Survey; and confusion might arise from the want of a proper distinction between the different senses in which it is commonly used

Value

"The word *value*" says Adam Smith "has two different meanings, and sometimes expresses the utility of some particular object and sometimes the power of purchasing other goods which the possession of that object conveys. The one may be called value in use, the other value in exchange." In the place of "value in use" we now speak of "utility," while instead of "value in exchange" we often say "exchange-value" or simply "value." "Value" by itself always means value in exchange.

The value, that is the exchange value, of one thing in terms of another at any place and time, is the amount of that second thing which can be got there and then in exchange for the first. Thus the term value is relative, and expresses the relation between two things at a particular place and time.

Civilized countries generally adopt gold or silver or both as money. Instead of expressing the values of lead and tin, and wood, and corn and other things in terms of one another we express them in terms of money in the first instance; and call the value of each thing thus expressed its price. If we know that a ton of lead will exchange for fifteen sovereigns at any place and time, while a ton of tin will exchange for ninety sovereigns, we say that their prices then and there are £15 and £90 respectively, and we know that the value of a ton of tin in terms of lead is six tons then and there.

The price of every thing rises and falls from time to time and place to place; and with every such change the purchasing power of money changes so far as that thing goes If the purchasing power of money rises with regard to some things and at the same time falls equally with regard to equally important things, its general purchasing power (or its power of purchasing things in general) has remained stationary. It is true that this way of speaking is vague, because we have not considered how to compare the importance of different things. That is a difficulty which we shall have to deal with later on: but meanwhile we may accept the phrase in the vague but quite intelligible usage that it has in ordinary discourse Throughout the earlier stages of our work it will be best to speak of the exchange value of a thing at any place and time as measured by its price, that is, the amount of money for which it will exchange then and there, and to assume that there is no change in the general purchasing power of money[1]

[1] In this we are only following the practice of the ordinary business of life, which invariably starts by considering one change at a time and assuming for a while that "other things are equal." As Cournot points out (*Principes Mathématiques de la Théorie des Richesses*, Ch II), we get the same sort of convenience from assuming the existence of a standard of uniform purchasing power by which to measure value, that astronomers do by assuming that there is a "mean sun" which crosses the meridian at uniform intervals, so that the clock can keep pace with it, whereas the actual sun crosses the meridian sometimes before and sometimes after noon as shown by the clock

CHAPTER II.

THE GROWTH OF FREE INDUSTRY AND ENTERPRISE.

BOOK I. CH II

Individual action and race character act and react on one another: both are much influenced by physical causes

§ 1. ALTHOUGH the proximate causes of the chief events in history are to be found in the actions of individuals, yet most of the conditions which have made these events possible are traceable to the influence of inherited institutions and race qualities and of physical nature. Race qualities themselves are, however, mainly caused by the action of individuals and physical causes in more or less remote time A strong race has often sprung, in fact as well as in name, from some progenitor of singular strength of body and character. The usages which make a race strong in peace and war are often due to the wisdom of a few great thinkers who have interpreted and developed its customs and rules, perhaps by formal precepts, perhaps by a quiet and almost unperceived influence But none of these things are of any permanent avail if the climate is unfavourable to vigour: the gifts of nature, her land, her waters, and her skies, determine the character of the race's work, and thus give a tone to social and political institutions.

Savage life is ruled by custom and impulse

These differences do not show themselves clearly so long as man is still savage Scanty and untrustworthy as is our information about the habits of savage tribes, we know enough of them to be sure that they show a strange uniformity of general character, amid great variety of detail. Whatever be their climate and whatever their ancestry, we find savages living under the dominion of custom and impulse; scarcely ever striking out new lines for themselves, never forecasting the distant future, and seldom making provision even for the near future; fitful in spite of their servitude to custom, governed by the fancy of the moment; ready at times for the most arduous exertions, but incapable of keeping themselves long to steady work. Laborious and tedious tasks are avoided as far as possible, those which are inevitable are done by the compulsory labour of women.

BOOK I. CH II.

It is when we pass from savage life to the early forms of civilization that the influence of physical surroundings forces itself most on our notice. This is partly because early history is meagre, and tells us but little of the particular events and of the influences of strong individual characters by which the course of national progress has been guided and controlled, hastened onwards or turned backwards. But it is chiefly because in this stage of his progress man's power of contending with Nature is small, and he can do nothing without her generous help. Nature has marked out a few places on the earth's surface as specially favourable to man's first attempts to raise himself from the savage state, and the first growth of culture and the industrial arts was directed and controlled by the physical conditions of these favoured spots

Physical causes act most powerfully in the early stages of civilization

Even the simplest civilization is impossible unless man's efforts are more than sufficient to supply him with the necessaries of life, some surplus over them is required to support that mental effort in which progress takes its rise. And therefore nearly all early civilizations have been in warm climates where the necessaries of life are small, and where Nature makes bountiful returns even to the rudest cultivation. They have often gathered around a great river which has lent moisture to the soil and afforded an easy means of communication The rulers have generally belonged to a race that has recently come from a cooler climate in a distant country or in neighbouring mountain lands, for a warm climate is destructive of energy, and the force which enabled them to rule has almost in every case been the product of

which have necessarily taken place in warm climates

Ruling castes have given then

[1] On the general question of the influence of physical surroundings on race character, both directly and indirectly, by determining the nature of the dominant occupations, see Knies, *Politische Œkonomie*, Hegel's *Philosophy of History*, and Buckle's *History of Civilization* Compare also Aristotle's *Politics*, and Montesquieu's *Esprit des Lois*

BOOK I. CH II

energies to war and politics, not to industry

the more temperate climate of their early homes. They have indeed retained much of their energy in their new homes for several generations, living meanwhile in luxury on the surplus products of the labour of the subject races; and have found scope for their abilities in the work of rulers, warriors, and priests. Originally ignorant, they have quickly learnt all that their subjects had to teach, and have gone beyond them. But in this stage of civilization an enterprising intellectual character has almost always been confined to the ruling few, it has scarcely ever been found in those who have borne the main burden of industry.

The influence of a warm climate

The reason of this is that the climate which has rendered an early civilization possible has also doomed it to weakness[1]. In colder climates nature provides an invigorating atmosphere, and though man has a hard struggle at first, yet as his knowledge and riches increase he is able to gain plentiful food and warm clothing, and at a later stage he provides himself with those large and substantial buildings which are the most expensive requisites of a cultured life in places in which the severity of the weather makes it necessary that nearly all domestic services and meetings for social intercourse should have the protection of a roof. But the fresh invigorating air which is necessary to the fulness of life cannot be obtained at all when Nature does not freely give it[2]. The labourer may indeed be found doing hard physical work under a tropical sun; the handicraftsman may have artistic instincts; the sage, the statesman or the banker may be acute and subtle: but high temperature makes hard and sustained physical work inconsistent with a high intellectual activity. Under the combined influence of climate and luxury the

[1] Montesquieu says quaintly (Bk. xiv ch 2), that the superiority of strength caused by a cold climate produces among other effects "a greater sense of superiority—that is, less desire of revenge; and a greater opinion of security—that is, more frankness, less suspicion, policy, and cunning" These virtues are eminently helpful to economic progress

[2] This may have to be modified a little, but only a little, if Mr Galton should prove to be right in thinking that small numbers of a ruling race in a hot country, as for instance the English in India, will be able to sustain their constitutional vigour unimpaired for many generations by a liberal use of artificial ice, or of the cooling effects of the forcible expansion of compressed air. See his Presidential Address to the Anthropological Institute in 1887.

ruling class gradually lose their strength; fewer and fewer of them are capable of great things: and at last they are overthrown by a stronger race which has come most probably from a cooler climate. Sometimes they form an intermediate caste between those whom they have hitherto ruled and their new rulers; but more often they sink down among the spiritless mass of the people

In an early civilization movement is slow, but there is movement

Such a civilization has often much that is interesting to the philosophical historian. Its whole life is pervaded almost unconsciously by a few simple ideas which are interwoven in that pleasant harmony that gives their charm to Oriental carpets. There is much to be learnt from tracing these ideas to their origin in the combined influence of race, of physical surroundings, of religion, philosophy and poetry; of the incidents of warfare and the dominating influence of strong individual characters All this is instructive to the economist in many ways, but it does not throw a very direct light on the motives, which it is his special province to study For in such a civilization the ablest men look down on work. there are no bold free enterprising workmen, and no adventurous capitalists, despised industry is regulated by custom, and even looks to custom as its sole protector from arbitrary tyranny

Custom is never altogether on the side of the strong,

The greater part of custom is doubtless but a crystallized form of oppression and suppression But a body of custom which did nothing but grind down the weak could not long survive. For the strong rest on the support of the weak, their own strength cannot sustain them without that support; and if they organize social arrangements which burden the weak wantonly and beyond measure, they thereby destroy themselves. Consequently every body of custom that endures, contains provisions that protect the weak from the most reckless forms of injury[1].

and is indeed a necessary protection when the means of

In fact when there is little enterprise and no scope for effective competition, custom is a necessary shield to defend people not only from others who are stronger than themselves, but even from their neighbours in the same rank of

[1] Comp Bagehot's *Physics and Politics*, also Mr Herbert Spencer's and Sir Henry Maine's writings

BOOK I CH II

communication are small

life. If the village smith can sell his ploughshares to none but the village, and if the village can buy their shares from no one but him, it is to the interest of all that the price should be fixed at a moderate level by custom. By such means custom earns sanctity: and there is nothing in the first steps of progress that tends to break down the primitive habit of regarding the innovator as impious, and an enemy Thus the influence of economic causes is pressed below the surface. There they work surely and slowly; but they take generations instead of years to produce their effect. their action is so subtle as easily to escape observation altogether, and they can indeed hardly be traced except by those who have learnt where to look for them by watching the more conspicuous and rapid workings of similar causes in modern times[1].

Divided ownership strengthens the force of custom and resists changes

§ 2. This force of custom in early civilizations is partly a cause and partly a consequence of the limitations of individual rights in property. As regards all property more or less, but especially as regards land, the rights of the individual are generally derived from and limited by, and in every way subordinate to those of the household and the family in the narrower sense of the term. The rights of the household are in like manner subordinate to those of the village; which is often only an expanded and developed family, according to traditionary fiction if not in fact. The affairs of government have always received the careful attention of historians; and prominence has been given to the influence which the forms of government have exerted on the development of industry and commerce. But insufficient attention has been paid to that exerted by the collective ownership of property.

[1] Thus the "moderate level" at which custom fixes the price of a ploughshare will be found when analysed to mean that which gives the smith in the long run about an equal remuneration (account being taken of all his privileges and perquisites) with that of his neighbours who do equally difficult work, or in other words, that which under the régime of free enterprise, of easy communications and effective competition, we should call a normal rate of pay If a change of circumstances makes the pay of smiths, including all indirect allowances, either less or more than this, there almost always sets in a change in the substance of the custom, often almost unrecognized and generally without any change in form, which will bring it back to this level But to this point we must return later on

It is true that in an early stage of civilization few would have had much desire to depart far from the practices that were prevalent around them. However complete and sharply defined had been the rights of individuals over their own property, they would have been unwilling to face the anger with which their neighbours would regard any innovation, and the ridicule which would be poured on any one who should set himself up to be wiser than his ancestors But many little changes would occur to the bolder spirits; and if they had been free to try experiments on their own account, changes might have grown by small and almost imperceptible stages, until sufficient variation of practice had been established to blur the clear outline of customary regulations, and to give considerable freedom to individual choice. When however each head of a household was regarded as only senior partner and trustee for the family property, the smallest divergence from ancestral routine met with the opposition of people who had a right to be consulted on every detail.

And further in the background behind the authoritative resistance of the family was that of the village For though each family had sole use for a time of its cultivated ground, yet many operations were generally conducted in common, so that each had to do the same things as the others at the same time Each field when its turn came to be fallow, became part of the common pasture land; and the whole land of the village was subject to redistribution from time to time[1]. Therefore the village had a clear right to prohibit any in-

[1] Though the matter is not altogether free from controversy, there seems good reason to believe that the Teutonic Mark system was a survival of primitive customs that had prevailed, of course with endless variety in detail, among the forefathers of nearly all white races. Traces of such a plan exist even now in India and among some Sclavonic peoples, and analogies to it are found among some races of other colours In the Mark system, in its typical form, one small part, the home mark, was set aside permanently for living on, and each family retained its share in that for ever The second part or arable mark was divided into three large fields, in each of which each family had a plot Two of these were cultivated every year, and one left fallow The third and largest part was used as grazing land by the whole village in common; as was also the fallow field in the arable mark. In some cases the arable mark was from time to time abandoned to pasture, and land to make a new arable mark was cut out of the common mark, and this involved a redistribution Thus the treatment of its land by every family affected for good or ill all the members of the village

novation; for it might interfere with their plans for the collective cultivation, and it might ultimately impair the value of the land, and thus injure them when the time came for the next redistribution. In consequence there often grew up a complex network of rules, by which every cultivator was so rigidly bound, that he could not use his own judgment and discretion even in the most trivial details[1]. It is probable that this has been the most important of all the causes which have delayed the growth of the spirit of free enterprise among mankind. It may be noticed that the collective ownership of property was in harmony with that spirit of quietism which pervades many eastern religions; and that its long survival among the Hindoos has been partly due to the repose which is inculcated in their religious writings.

The influence of custom on the methods of industry is cumulative

It is probable that while the influence of custom over prices, wages and rent has been overrated, its influence over the forms of production and the general economic arrangements of society has been underrated In the one case its effects are obvious, but they are not cumulative, and in the other they are not obvious, but they are cumulative And it is an almost universal rule that when the effects of a cause, though small at any one time, are constantly working in the same direction, their influence is much greater than at first sight appears possible.

But however great was the influence of custom in early civilization the spirit of Greeks and Romans was full of enterprise, and more interest attaches to the inquiry why they knew and cared so little for those social aspects of economic problems which are of so great interest to us.

The Greeks brought Northern energy to bear on Oriental culture.

§ 3 Recent studies in biology and in philology have thrown discredit on much that was thought well-established in the early history of civilization. But there seems no reason to doubt that nearly all the chief pioneers of progress have been Aryans who, in successive waves, have spread over Europe and Asia from early homes in lands of frost and snow Some went far southwards early. early they became

[1] Compare the Duke of Argyll's account of Runrig cultivation in *Unseen Foundations of Society*, Ch IX

rulers and leaders of other nations, and early they lost their best strength under the influence of luxury and a warm climate. But others went on increasing in strength through long centuries amid the invigorating influences of a bracing climate and constant conflict; and at last a band of them, coming southwards from the Danube, found itself in a mountainous land whose many harbours opened on the Mediterranean Sea. Each harbour was cut off from its neighbours by the mountains and was united by the sea with the most suggestive thoughts and mysteries of the world The Greeks were within a few days' sail of nearly all that was best worth knowing about, whether in thought or feeling, in action or in aspiration Persia, Assyria, Phœnicia, Judæa, and Egypt, were all at the eastern end of that great sea that unites Asia, Africa, and Europe, and India was not far off.

The older civilizations had been chiefly inland

The new impulse towards freedom in thought and action came from the sea. The homes of most of the earlier civilizations had been in great river-basins, whose well-watered plains were seldom visited by famine; for in a climate in which heat is never lacking, the fertility of the soil varies almost directly with its moisture the rivers also offered means of easy communication that were favourable to simple forms of trade and division of labour, and did not hinder the movements of the large armies by which the despotic force of the central government was maintained. It is true that the Phœnicians lived on the sea. This great Semitic race did good service by preparing the way for free intercourse among many peoples, and by spreading the knowledge of writing, of arithmetic, and of weights and measures. but they gave their chief energies to commerce and manufacture It was left for the genial sympathies and the fresh spirit of the Greeks to breathe in the full breath of freedom over the sea · and to absorb into their own free lives the best thoughts and the highest art of the Old World.

The sea gave the Greeks knowledge, freedom, and the

Their numberless settlements in Asia Minor, Magna Græcia, and last of all in Hellas proper, developed freely their own ideals under the influence of the new thoughts that burst upon them, having constant intercourse with one

BOOK I. CH II

Power of variation

another, as well as with those who held the keys of the older learning; sharing one another's experiences, but fettered by no authority Energy and enterprise, instead of being repressed by the weight of traditional usage, were encouraged to found a new colony and work out new ideas without restraint

Their climate made culture inexpensive,

Their climate absolved them from the need of exhausting work; they left to their slaves what drudgery had to be done, and gave themselves up to the free play of their fancy House-room, clothing and firing cost but little, their genial sky invited them to out-of-door life, making intercourse for social and political purposes easy and without expense And yet the cool breezes of the Mediterranean so far refreshed their vigour, that they did not for many generations lose the spring and elasticity of temper which they had brought from their homes in the North. Under these conditions were matured a sense of beauty in all its forms, a subtle fancy and an originality of speculation, an energy of political life, and a delight in subordinating the individual to the state, such as the world has never again known[1]

and yet did not quickly relax their strength

Modern in many respects, they did not anticipate the economic problems which have grown up with the sense of the dignity of labour

The Greeks were more modern in many respects than the peoples of Mediæval Europe, and in some respects were even in advance of our own time. But they did not attain to the conception of the dignity of man as man; they regarded slavery as an ordinance of nature, they tolerated agriculture but they looked on all other industries as involving degradation; and they knew little or nothing of those economic problems, which are of absorbing interest to our own age[2].

They had never felt the extreme pressure of poverty. Earth and sea, and sun and sky had combined to make it

[1] Compare Neumann and Partsch, *Physikalische Geographie von Griechenland*, ch I

[2] See above p 4 Thus even Plato says —"Nature has made neither bootmakers nor blacksmiths, such occupations degrade the people engaged in them, miserable mercenaries excluded by their very position from political rights" (*Laws*, XII) And Aristotle continues —"In the state which is best governed the citizens must not lead the life of mechanics or tradesmen, for such a life is ignoble and inimical to virtue" (*Politics*, VII 9; see also III. 5.) These passages give the key-note of Greek thought with regard to business But of course there were few independent fortunes, especially in the early days of Greece, so that many of their best thinkers were compelled to take some share in business.

easy for them to obtain the material requisites for a perfect life. Even their slaves had considerable opportunities of culture. and had it been otherwise, there was nothing in the Greek temper, and nothing in the lessons that the world had up to that time learnt, to make them seriously concerned. The excellence of Greek thought has made it a touchstone by which many of the leading thinkers of after ages have tried every new inquiry and the impatience with which the academic mind has often regarded the study of economics is in a great measure due to the impatience which the Greeks felt for the anxious cares and plodding work of business.

Their impatience of the discipline of steady industry led to their fall.

And yet a lesson might have been learnt from the quick decadence of Greece; which was brought about by the want of that solid earnestness of purpose which no race has ever maintained for many generations without the discipline of steady industry Socially and intellectually they were free but they had not learnt to use their freedom well, they had no self-mastery, no steady persistent resolution. They had all the quickness of perception and readiness for new suggestions which are elements of business enterprise, but they had not its fixity of purpose and patient endurance. The genial climate gradually relaxed their physical energies, they were without that safeguard to strength of character which comes from resolute and steadfast persistence in hard work, and they sank into frivolity.

The strength of character of the Romans fitted them for business, but they generally preferred war and politics.

§ 4 Civilization still moving westwards had its next centre in Rome. The Romans were a great army, rather than a great nation. They resembled the Greeks in leaving business as much as possible to slaves· but in most other respects were a contrast to them. In opposition to the fresh fulness of the life of the Greeks, to the youthful joy with which they gave free play to all their faculties and developed their own idiosyncrasy, the Romans showed the firm will, the iron resolution, the absorption in definite serious aims of the mature man[1].

[1] This fundamental opposition between the Greek and Roman tempers was made clear by Hegel in his *Philosophy of History* "Of the Greeks in the first genuine form of their freedom we may assert that they had no conscience, the habit of living for their country without further analysis or reflection was the principle dominant among them .Subjectivity plunged the Greek world into

BOOK I. CH II

Roman economic conditions were in some respects modern in form;

Singularly free from the restraints of custom, they shaped their own lives for themselves with a deliberate choice that had never been known before They were strong and daring, steady of purpose and abundant in resource, orderly in habit, and clearsighted in judgment; and thus, though they preferred war and politics, they had in constant use all the faculties required for business enterprise.

Nor was the principle of association inactive. Trade gilds had some vigour in spite of the paucity of artisans who were free Those methods of combined action for business purposes, and of production on a large scale by slave labour in factories, in which Greece had been the pupil of the East, gained new strength when imported into Rome. The faculties and the temper of the Romans fitted them especially well for the management of joint-stock companies; and a comparatively small number of very wealthy men, with no middle class, were able with the aid of trained slaves and freedmen, to undertake large contracts by land and by sea at home and abroad They made capital hateful; but they made it powerful and efficient, they developed the appliances of money-lending with great energy, and partly in consequence of the unity of the imperial power, and the wide extent of the Roman language, there was in some important respects more freedom of commerce and of movement throughout the civilized world in the days of the Roman empire than even now.

When, then, we recollect how great a centre of wealth Rome was, how monstrous the fortunes of individual Romans (and they have only recently been surpassed), and how vast the scale of her military and civil affairs, of the provision needed for them and of the machinery of her traffic, we cannot wonder that many writers have thought they found much resemblance between her economic problems and our own.

ruin"; and the harmonious poetry of the Greeks made way for "the prose life of the Romans," which was full of subjectivity, and "a hard dry contemplation of certain voluntary aims" A generous, though discriminating tribute to the services which Hegel indirectly rendered to Historical Economics is given by Roscher, *Gesch. der Nat Œk. in Deutschland*, § 188. Compare also the chapters on Religion in Mommsen's *History*, which seem to have been much influenced by Hegel; also Kautz, *Entwickelung der National-Œkonomie*, Bk. I.

But the resemblance is superficial and illusory. It extends only to forms, and not to the living spirit of national life. It does not extend to the recognition of the worth of the life of the common people which in our own time is giving to economic science its highest interest[1].

but not at all in substance.

In ancient Rome industry and commerce lacked the vital strength which they have attained in more recent times. Her imports were won by the sword, they were not bought with the products of skilled work in which the citizens took a worthy pride, as were those of Venice or Florence or Bruges Traffic and industry alike were pursued almost with a sole eye to the money gains to be derived from them, and the tone of business life was degraded by the public disdain which showed itself in the "legal and practically effective restriction[2]" of the Senators from all forms of business except those connected with the land The Equites found their richest gains in farming the taxes, in the plunder of provinces, and, in later times, in the personal favour of the Emperors, and did not cherish that spirit of probity and thorough work which are needed for the making of a great national trade; and at length private enterprise was stifled by the ever-growing shadow of the State[3].

[1] See above Ch I § 2 The misunderstanding is in some measure attributable to the influence of the generally acute and well-balanced Roscher He took a special delight in pointing out analogies between ancient and modern problems; and though he also pointed out differences, yet the general influence of his writings tended to mislead (His position is well criticized by Knies, *Politische Œkonomie vom geschichtlichen Standpunkte* especially p 391 of the second edition)

[2] Friedlander, *Sittengeschichte Roms*, p 225 Mommsen goes so far as to say (*History*, Book IV ch XI) —"Of trades and manufactures there is nothing to be said, except that the Italian nation in this respect persevered in an inactivity bordering on barbarism ..The only brilliant side of Roman private economics was money dealing and commerce." Many passages in Cairnes' *Slave Power* read like modern versions of *Mommsen's History*. Even in the towns the lot of the poor free Roman resembled that of the "mean whits" of the Southern Slave States. *Latifundia perdidere Italiam*, but they were farms like those of the Southern States, not England The weakness of free labour, at Rome is shown in Liebenam's *Geschichte des römischen Vereinswesens*

[3] One aspect of this is described by Prof Schmoller in his short but excellent account of the Trading Companies of Antiquity. After showing how trading groups of which all the members belong to one family may thrive even among primitive peoples, he argues (*Jahrbuch für Gesetzgebung*, XVI pp 740—2) that no form of business association of the modern type could flourish long in such conditions as those of ancient Rome unless it had some exceptional privileges or advantages as the *Societates Publicanorum* had. The reason why we moderns succeed in bring-

BOOK I. CH. II.

But they founded the modern law of property.

The Stoic philosophy and the cosmopolitan experience of the later Roman lawyers

But though the Romans contributed but little directly to the progress of economic science, yet indirectly they exerted a profound influence over it, for good and evil, by laying the foundations of modern jurisprudence. What philosophic thought there was in Rome was chiefly Stoic, and most of the great Roman Stoics were of Oriental origin. Their philosophy when transplanted to Rome developed a great practical power without losing its intensity of feeling; and in spite of its severity, it had in it much that is kindred to the suggestions of modern social science Most of the great lawyers of the Empire were among its adherents, and thus it set the tone of the later Roman Law, and through it of all modern European Law. Now the strength of the Roman State had caused State rights to extinguish those of the Clan and the Tribe in Rome at an earlier stage than in Greece. But many of the primitive Aryan habits of thought as to property lingered on for a long while even in Rome. Great as was the power of the head of the family over its members, the property which he controlled was for a long time regarded as vested in him as the representative of the family rather than as an individual But when Rome had become imperial, her lawyers became the ultimate interpreters of the legal rights of many nations: and under Stoic influence they set themselves to discover the fundamental Laws of Nature, which they believed to lie in concealment at the foundation of all particular codes. This search for the universal, as opposed to the accidental elements of justice, acted as a powerful solvent on rights of common holding, for which no other reason than that of local usage could be given. The later Roman law therefore gradually but steadily enlarged the sphere of contract; gave it greater precision, greater elasticity, and greater strength At last almost all social arrangements had come under its dominion; the pro-

led them gradually to enlarge the sphere of contract

ing and keeping many people "under the same hat" to work together, which Antiquity failed in doing, "is to be sought exclusively in the higher level of intellectual and moral strength, and the greater possibility now than then of binding together men's egoistic commercial energies by the bonds of social sympathy" See also Deloume, *Les Manieurs d'Argent à Rome*; an article on *State control of Industry in the fourth century* by W A Brown in the *Political Science Quarterly*, Vol II; Blanqui's *History of Political Economy*, ch V and VI; and Ingram's *History*, ch II

perty of the individual was clearly marked out, and he could deal with it as he pleased. We see then that from the breadth and nobility of the Stoic character modern lawyers have inherited a high standard of duty: and from its austere self-determination they have derived a tendency to define sharply individual rights in property. And therefore to Roman and especially Stoic influence we may trace indirectly much of the good and evil of our present economic system, on the one hand much of the untrammelled vigour of the individual in managing his own affairs, and on the other not a little harsh wrong done under the cover of rights established by a system of law which has held its ground because its main principles are wise and just.

But a new spirit was needed

The strong sense of duty which Stoicism brought with it from its Oriental home had in it something also of Eastern quietism. The Stoic, though active in well-doing, was proud of being superior to the troubles of the world: he took his share in the turmoil of life because it was his duty to do so, but he never reconciled himself to it his life remained sad and stern, oppressed by the consciousness of its own failures. This inner contradiction, as Hegel says, could not pass away till inward perfection was recognized as an object that could be attained only through self-renunciation; and thus its pursuit was reconciled with those failures which necessarily accompany all social work. For this great change the intense religious feeling of the Jews prepared the way. But the world was not ready to enter into the fulness of the Christian spirit, till a new tone had been given to it by the deep personal affections of the German race Even among the German peoples true Christianity made its way slowly. and for a long time after the fall of Rome there was chaos in Western Europe

The Teuton slow to learn from those whom he had conquered

§ 5 The Teuton, strong and resolute as he was, found it very difficult to free himself from the bonds of custom and of ignorance The heartiness and fidelity[1] which gave him his special strength, inclined him to cherish overmuch the institutions and customs of his family and his tribe. No other

[1] Hegel (*Philosophy of History*, Part IV) goes to the root of the matter when he speaks of their energy, their free spirit, their absolute self-determination (Eigensinn), their heartiness (Gemuth), and adds, "Fidelity is their second watchword as Freedom is the first"

BOOK I
CH. II.

great conquering race has shown so little capacity as the Teutons have done for adopting new ideas from the more cultured, though weaker, people whom they conquered. They prided themselves on their rude strength and energy, and cared little for knowledge and the arts. But these found a temporary refuge on the Eastern coasts of the Mediterranean; until another conquering race coming from the south was ready to give them new life and vigour.

Our debt to the Saracens.

The Saracens learnt eagerly the best lessons that the conquered had to teach They nurtured the arts and sciences, and kept alive the torch of learning at a time when the Christian world cared little whether it went out or not; and for this we must ever owe them gratitude. But their moral nature was not so full as that of the Teutons. The warm climate and the sensuality of their religion caused their vigour rapidly to decay, and they have exercised very little direct influence on the problems of modern civilization[1]

Later on civilization moved northwards and westwards.

The education of the Teutons made slower but surer progress. They carried civilization northwards to a climate in which sustained hard work has gone hand in hand with the slow growth of sturdy forms of culture, and they carried it westwards to the Atlantic. Civilization, which had long ago left the shores of the rivers for those of the great inland sea, was ultimately to travel over the vast ocean.

and the old contest between town and country revived

But these changes worked themselves out slowly. The first point of interest to us in the new age is the re-opening of the old conflict between town and nation that had been suspended by the universal dominion of Rome; which was indeed an army with head-quarters in a town, but drawing its power from the broad land.

Without the telegraph and printing-press, freedom in a large country was confined to the aristocracy;

§ 6. Until a few years ago complete and direct self-government by the people was impossible in a great nation: it could exist only in towns or very small territories. Government was necessarily in the hands of the few, who looked upon themselves as privileged upper classes, and who treated the workers as lower classes Consequently the workers, even when permitted to manage their own local affairs, were

[1] A brilliant eulogy of their work is given by Draper, *Intellectual Development of Europe*, ch xiii

often wanting in the courage, the self-reliance, and the habits of mental activity, which are required as the basis of business enterprise. And as a matter of fact both the central Government and the local magnates did interfere directly with the freedom of industry; prohibiting migration, and levying taxes and tolls of the most burdensome and vexatious character. Even those of the lower classes who were nominally free, were plundered by arbitrary fines and dues levied under all manner of excuses, by the partial administration of justice, and often by direct violence and open pillage. These burdens fell chiefly on just those people who were more industrious and more thrifty than their neighbours, those among whom, if the country had been free, the spirit of bold enterprise would gradually have arisen to shake off the bonds of tradition and custom

but self-government by the people in the towns was not physically impossible

Far different was the state of people in the towns. There the industrial classes found strength in their numbers, and even when unable to gain the upper hand altogether, they were not, like their brethren in the country, treated as though they belonged to a different order of beings from their rulers. In Florence and in Bruges, as in ancient Athens, the whole people could hear, and sometimes did hear, from the leaders of public policy a statement of their plans and the reasons for them, and could signify their approval or disapproval before the next step was taken. The whole people could on occasion discuss together the social and industrial problems of the time, knowing each other's counsel, profiting by each other's experience, working out in common a definite resolution and bringing it into effect by their own action. But nothing of this kind could be done over a wide area till the invention of the telegraph, the railway and the cheap press.

Such as is now for the first time possible in a large country

By their aid a nation can now read in the morning what its leaders have said on the evening before; and ere another day has passed the judgment of the nation on it is pretty well known. By their aid the council of a large trades-union can at a trifling cost submit a difficult question to the judgment of their members in every part of the country and get their

BOOK I. CH. II.

decision within a few days. Even a large country can now be ruled by its people; but till now what was called "popular Government" was of physical necessity the government by a more or less wide oligarchy. Only those few who could themselves go frequently to the centre of Government, or who could at least receive constant communication from it, could take part directly in government. And though a much larger number of people would know enough of what was going on to make their will broadly effective, through their choice of representatives, yet even they were a small minority of the nation till a few years ago, and the representative system itself is only of recent date.

The case of Switzerland is exceptional

Switzerland indeed has been free: for its mountains oppose obstacles to the movements of large armies, and render cavalry almost useless; and it has nourished a sturdy race, which has been strengthened from time to time by refugees from among the bolder spirits of neighbouring lands. But the range of intercourse of those who live in mountains is generally small. Except when enriched by the lavish expenditure of tourists from more favoured lands, they live hard lives, having long hours of work during their short summer, and stagnating in close rooms during a great part of the year. They have not therefore had that mental activity and enterprise which has characterized the free cities.

The Mediæval towns were the direct precursors of modern industrial civilization.

§ 7. In the Middle Ages the history of the rise and fall of towns is the history of the rise and fall of successive waves on the tide of progress. The mediæval towns as a rule owed their origin to trade and industry, and did not despise them. And though the wealthier citizens were sometimes able to set up a close government in which the workers had no part, they seldom retained their power long; and the great body of the inhabitants frequently had the full rights of citizens, deciding for themselves the foreign and domestic policy of their city, and at the same time working with their hands and taking pride in their work. They organized themselves into Gilds, thus increasing their cohesion and educating themselves in self-government; and though the Gilds were often exclusive, and their trade-regulations ultimately retarded progress, yet they did excellent work before this deadening influence had shown itself[1]

The citizens gained culture without losing energy; without neglecting their business, they learnt to take an intelligent interest in many things besides their business They led the way in the fine arts, and they were not backward in those of war They took pride in magnificent expenditure for public purposes, and they took equal pride in a careful husbanding of the public resources, in clear and clean State budgets, and in systems of taxes levied equitably and based on sound business principles. Thus they led the way towards modern industrial civilization, and if they had gone on their course undisturbed, and retained their first love of liberty and social equality, they would probably long ago have worked out the solutions of many social and economic problems which we are only now beginning to face. But after being long troubled by tumults and war, they at last succumbed to the growing power of the countries by which they were surrounded; and indeed when they had obtained dominion over their neighbours, their own rule had often been harsh and oppressive, so that their ultimate overthrow by the country was in some degree the result of a just retribution. They have suffered for their wrong doings, but the fruit of their good work remains, and is the source of much that is best in the social and economic traditions that our age has inherited from its predecessors

Chivalry did not protect the poor

§ 8 Feudalism was perhaps a necessary stage in the development of the Teutonic race It gave scope to the political ability of the dominant class, and educated the common people in habits of discipline and order But it concealed under forms of some outward beauty much cruelty and uncleanness, physical and moral. The practices of chivalry combined extreme deference to women in public with much domestic tyranny · it combined elaborate rules of courtesy towards combatants of the knightly order with

[1] What is true of the great free towns that were practically autonomous is true in a less degree of the so-called free boroughs of England Their constitutions were even more various than the origins of their liberties; but it now seems probable that they were generally more democratic and less oligarchic than was at one time supposed See especially Gross, *The Gild Merchant*, ch. vii

BOOK I. CH. II

cruelty and extortion in dealing with the lower classes. The ruling classes were expected to discharge their obligations towards one another with frankness and generosity[1]: they had ideals of life which were not devoid of nobility; and therefore their characters will always have some attractiveness to the thoughtful historian as well as to the chronicler of wars, of splendid shows and of romantic incidents. But their consciences were satisfied when they had acted up to the code of duty which their own class required of them: and one article of that code was to keep the lower classes in their place, though they were often kind and even affectionate towards those retainers with whom they lived in daily contact.

The Church helped the growth of economic freedom in some ways,

So far as cases of individual hardship went, the Church strove to defend the weak and to diminish the sufferings of the poor. Perhaps those finer natures who were attracted to its service might often have exercised a wider and a better influence, if they had been free from the vow of celibacy, and able to mingle with the world. But this is no reason for rating lightly the benefit which the clergy, and still more the monks, rendered to the poorer classes. The monasteries were the homes of industry, and in particular of the scientific treatment of agriculture: they were secure colleges for the learned, and they were hospitals and alms-houses for the suffering. The Church acted as a peace-maker in great matters and in small: the festivals and the markets held under its authority gave freedom and safety to trade[2].

[1] But the treachery that was common in Italian cities was not very rare in northern castles. People compassed the death of their acquaintances by assassination and poison: the host was often expected to taste the food and drink which he offered to his guest. But as a painter rightly fills his canvas with the noblest faces he can find, and keeps as much in the background as possible what is ignoble, so the popular historian may be justified in exciting the emulation of the young by historical pictures in which the lives of noble men and women stand out in bold relief, while a veil is drawn over much of the surrounding depravity. When however we want to take stock of the world's progress, we must reckon the evil of past times as it really was, to be more than just to our ancestors then is to be less than just to the best hopes of our race.

[2] We are perhaps apt to lay too much stress on the condemnation by the Church of "usury" and some kinds of trade. There was then very little scope for lending capital to be used in business, and when there was, the prohibition could be evaded by many devices, some of which were indeed sanctioned by the Church itself. And though St Chrysostom said that "he who procures an article

Again, the Church was a standing protest against caste exclusiveness. It was democratic in its organization, as was the army of ancient Rome. It was always willing to raise to the highest posts the ablest men, in whatever rank they were born; its clergy and monastic orders did much for the physical and moral wellbeing of the people; and it sometimes even led them in open resistance to the tyranny of their rulers[1].

But, on the other hand, it did not set itself to help them to develop their faculties of self-reliance and self-determination, and to attain true inner freedom. While willing that those individuals who had exceptional natural talents should rise through its own offices to the highest posts, it helped rather than hindered the forces of feudalism in their endeavour to keep the working classes as a body ignorant, devoid of enterprise, and in every way dependent on those above them. Teutonic feudalism was more kindly in its instincts than the military dominion of ancient Rome, and the laity as well as clergy were influenced by the teachings, imperfectly understood as they were, of the Christian religion with regard to the dignity of man as man. Nevertheless the rulers of the country districts during the early middle ages united all that was most powerful in the oriental subtlety of theocratic caste and in the Roman force of discipline and resolution; and they used their combined strength in such a manner as on the whole to retard the growth of strength and independence of character among the lower orders of the people

but hindered it in others

to make profit by disposing of it entire and unaltered, is ejected from the temple of God," yet the Church encouraged merchants to buy and sell goods unaltered at fairs and elsewhere The authority of Church and State and the prejudices of the people combined to put difficulties in the way of those who bought up large quantities of goods in order to sell them retail at a profit But though much of the business of these people was legitimate trade, some of it was certainly analogous to the "rings" and "corners" in modern produce markets Compare the excellent chapter on the Canonist Doctrine in Ashley's *History* and the notice of it by Mr Hewins in the *Economic Review*, vol IV

[1] Indirectly it aided progress by promoting the Crusades; of which Prof Ingram well says (*History*, ch II) that they "produced a powerful economic effect by transferring in many cases the possessions of the feudal chiefs to the industrial classes, whilst by bringing different nations and races into contact, by enlarging the horizon and widening the conceptions of the populations, as well as by affording a special stimulus to navigation, they tended to give a new activity to international trade"

BOOK I. CH II

Overthrow of the Cities

The military force of feudalism was however for a long time weakened by local jealousies. It was admirably adapted for welding into one living whole the government of a vast area under the genius of a Charles the Great: but it was equally prone to dissipate itself into its constituent elements as soon as its guiding genius was gone Italy was for a long time ruled by its towns, one of which indeed, of Roman descent, with Roman ambition and hard fixity of purpose held its water-ways against all attack till quite modern times. And in the Netherlands and other parts of the Continent the free towns were long able to defy the hostility of kings and barons around them But at length stable monarchies were established in Austria, Spain and France. A despotic monarchy, served by a few able men, drilled and organized the military forces of vast multitudes of ignorant but sturdy country folk, and the enterprise of the free towns, their noble combination of industry and culture, was cut short before they had had time to outgrow their early mistakes

The invention of printing, the Reformation, and the discovery of the New World.

Then the world might have gone backwards if it had not happened that just at that time new forces were rising to break up the bonds of constraint and spread freedom over the broad land. Within a very short period came the invention of printing, the Revival of Learning, the Reformation, and the discovery of the ocean routes to the New World and to India. Any one of these events alone would have been sufficient to make an epoch in history; but coming together as they did, and working all in the same direction, they effected a complete revolution.

Thought became comparatively free, and knowledge ceased to be altogether inaccessible to the people. The free temper of the Greeks revived, the strong self-determining spirits gained new strength, and were able to extend their influence over others. And a new continent suggested new problems to the thoughtful, at the same time that it offered a new scope to the enterprise of bold adventurers.

The first benefit of the maritime discoveries went to

§ 9. The countries which took the lead in the New maritime adventure were those of the Spanish Peninsula. It seemed for a time as though the leadership of the world, having settled first in the most easterly peninsula of the Mediterranean, and thence moved to the middle peninsula, would settle again in that westerly peninsula which belonged both to the Mediterranean and the Atlantic. But the power of industry had by this time become sufficient to sustain wealth and civilization in a northern climate. And the Spanish and Portuguese could not hold their own for long against the more sustained energy and the more generous spirit of the northern people, the colonists of England, Holland, and even France demanded and obtained far more freedom than those of Spain and Portugal.

the Spanish peninsula

The early history of the people of the Netherlands is indeed a brilliant romance. Founding themselves on fishing and weaving, they built up a noble fabric of Art and Literature, of Science and Government. But Spain set herself to crush out the rising spirit of freedom, as Persia had done before. And as Persia strangled Ionia, but only raised yet higher the spirit of Greece Proper, so the Austro-Spanish Empire subdued the Belgian Netherlands, but only roused the patriotism and energy of the Dutch Netherlands and England.

But soon moved further on, to Holland;

Holland suffered from England's jealousy of her commerce, but still more from the restless military ambition of France. It soon became clear that Holland was defending the freedom of Europe against French aggression But at a critical time in her history she was deprived of the aid she might reasonably have expected from Protestant England, and though from 1688 onwards that aid was liberally given, her bravest and most generous sons had then already perished on the battle-field, and she was overburdened with debt. She has fallen into the background. but Englishmen above all others are bound to acknowledge what she did, and what more she might have done for freedom and enterprise.

France and England were thus left to contend for the empire of the Ocean France had greater natural resources than any other northern country, and more of the spirit of the new age than any southern country, and she was for some time the greatest power of the world. But she squandered in perpetual wars her wealth and the blood of the best of those citizens whom she had not already driven away by religious persecution. The progress of enlightenment brought with it

to France;

no generosity on the part of the ruling class towards the ruled, and no wisdom in expenditure

From revolutionary America came the chief impulse towards a rising of the oppressed French people against their rulers. But the French were strikingly wanting in that self-controlling freedom which had distinguished the American colonists Their energy and courage was manifested again in the great Napoleonic wars. But their ambition overleaped itself, and ultimately left to England the leadership of enterprise on the Ocean. Thus the industrial problems of the New World are being worked out under the direct influence, as to some extent those of the Old World are under the indirect influence of the English character. We may then return to trace with somewhat more detail the growth of free enterprise in England.

and to England.

CHAPTER III.

THE GROWTH OF FREE INDUSTRY AND ENTERPRISE CONTINUED.

The character of Englishmen

§ 1. ENGLAND'S geographical position caused her to be peopled by the strongest members of the strongest races of northern Europe; a process of natural selection brought to her shores those members of each successive migratory wave who were most daring and self-reliant. Her climate is better adapted to sustain energy than any other in the northern hemisphere She is divided by no high hills, and no part of her territory is more than twenty miles from navigable water, and thus there was no material hindrance to freedom of intercourse between her different parts, while the strength and wise policy of the Norman and Plantagenet kings prevented artificial barriers from being raised by local magnates

As the part which Rome played in history is chiefly due to her having combined the military strength of a great empire with the enterprise and fixedness of purpose of an oligarchy residing in one city, so England owes her greatness to her combining, as Holland had done on a smaller scale before, much of the free temper of the mediæval city with the strength and broad basis of a nation. The towns of England had been less distinguished than those of other lands, but she assimilated them more easily than any other country did, and so gained in the long run most from them.

The custom of primogeniture inclined the younger sons of noble families to seek their own fortunes; and having no special caste privileges they mixed readily with the common people. This fusion of different ranks tended to make politics business-like, while it warmed the veins of business

BOOK I. CH. III

adventure with the generous daring and romantic aspirations of noble blood. Resolute on the one hand in resistance to tyranny, and on the other in submission to authority when it is justified by their reason, the English have made many revolutions, but none without a definite purpose. While reforming the constitution they have abided by the law: they alone, unless we except the Dutch, have known how to combine order and freedom; they alone have united a thorough reverence for the past with the power of living for the future rather than in the past. But the strength of character which in later times made England the leader of manufacturing progress, showed itself at first chiefly in politics, in war, and in agriculture.

While they were still an agricultural nation they showed signs of their modern faculty for organized action

The English yeoman archer was the forerunner of the English artisan. He had the same pride in the superiority of his food and his physique over those of his Continental rivals; he had the same indomitable perseverance in acquiring perfect command over the use of his hands, the same free independence and the same power of self-control and of rising to emergencies, the same habit of indulging his humours when the occasion was fit, but, when a crisis arose, of preserving discipline even in the face of hardship and misfortune[1].

But the industrial faculties of Englishmen remained latent for a long time. They had not inherited much acquaintance with nor much care for the comforts and luxuries of civilization In manufactures of all kinds they lagged behind the Latin countries, Italy, France and Spain, as well as the free cities of northern Europe. Gradually the wealthier classes got some taste for imported luxuries, and England's trade slowly increased.

Their trade has been a consequence of their activity in production and in navigation

But there was for a long time no sign on the surface of her future commerce. That indeed is the product of her special circumstances as much as, if not more than, of any natural bias of her people They had not originally, and they have not now, that special liking for dealing and bargaining, nor for the

[1] For the purposes of statistical comparison the well-to-do yeoman must be ranked with the middle classes of to-day, not with the artisans for those who were better off than he were very few in number, while the great mass of the people were far below him, and were, even in the prosperous fifteenth century, much worse off in almost every respect than they are now.

more abstract side of financial business, which is found among the Jews, the Italians, the Greeks and the Armenians; trade with them has always taken the form of action rather than of manœuvring and speculative combination. Even now the subtlest financial speculation on the London Stock Exchange is done chiefly by those races which have inherited the same aptitude for trading which the English have for action.

The capitalist organization of agriculture pioneered the way for that of manufacture.

The qualities which have caused England in later times under different circumstances to explore the world, and to make goods and carry them for other countries, caused her even in the middle ages to pioneer the modern organization of agriculture, and thus to set the model after which most other modern business is being moulded. She took the lead in converting labour dues into money payments, a change which much increased the power of everyone to steer his course in life according to his own free choice. For good and for evil the people were set free to exchange away their rights in the land and their obligations to it. The relaxation of the bonds of custom was hastened alike by the great rise of real wages which followed the Black Death in the fourteenth century; and by the great fall of real wages which, in the sixteenth century, resulted from the depreciation of silver, the debasement of coin, the appropriation of the revenues of the monasteries to the purposes of court extravagance; and lastly by the extension of sheep farming, which set many workers adrift from their old homes, and lowered the real incomes and altered the mode of life of those who remained. The movement was further extended by the growth of the royal power in the hands of the Tudors, which put an end to private war, and rendered useless the bands of retainers which the barons and landed gentry had kept together. The habit of leaving real property to the eldest son, and distributing personal property among all the members of the family, on the one hand increased the size of landed properties, and on the other narrowed the capital which the owners of land had at their own command for working it[1].

[1] Mr Rogers says that in the thirteenth century the value of arable land was only a third of the capital required to work it; and he believes that so long as the

These causes tended to establish the relation of landlord and tenant in England: while the foreign demand for English work and the English demand for foreign luxuries led, especially in the sixteenth century, to the concentration of many holdings into large sheep-runs worked by capitalist farmers. That is, there was a great increase in the number of farmers who undertook the management and the risks of agriculture, supplying some capital of their own, but borrowing the land for a definite yearly payment, and hiring labour for wages. in like manner as, later on, the new order of English business men undertook the management and the risks of manufacture, supplying some capital of their own but borrowing the rest on interest and hiring labour for wages. Thus the English large farm, arable and pastoral, worked with borrowed capital was the forerunner of the English factory, in the same way as English archery was the forerunner of the skill of the English artisan[1]

England's industry was much influenced by the spirit of the Reformation.

§ 2. Meanwhile the English character was deepening. The natural gravity and intrepidity of the stern races that had settled on the shores of England inclined them to embrace the doctrines of the Reformation; and these reacted on their habits of life, and gave a tone to their industry. Man was, as it were, ushered straight into the presence of his Creator, with no human intermediary: life became intense and full of awe, and now for the first time large numbers of rude and uncultured people yearned towards the mysteries of absolute spiritual freedom. The isolation of each person's religious responsibility from that of his fellows, rightly understood, was a necessary condition for the highest spiritual progress[2]. But the notion was new to the world, it was bare and naked, not yet overgrown with pleasant instincts;

owner of the land was in the habit of cultivating it himself, the eldest son often used various devices for alienating a part of his land to his younger brothers in exchange for some of their capital *Six Centuries of Work and Wages*, pp 51, 2

[1] This parallelism is further developed in Book VI, see especially ch. IX § 5

[2] The Reformation "was the affirmation ...of Individuality Individuality is not the sum of life, but it is an essential part of life in every region of our nature and our work, in our work for the part and for the whole It is true, though it is not the whole truth, that we must live and die alone, alone with God" Bishop Westcott's *Social Aspects of Christianity*, p 121 Comp also Hegel's *Philosophy of History*, part IV section III ch 2

and even in kindly natures individuality showed itself with a hard sharpness of outline, while the coarser natures became self-conscious and egotistic. Among the Puritans especially, the eagerness to give logical definiteness and precision to their religious creed was an absorbing passion, hostile to all lighter thoughts and lighter amusements. When occasion arose they could take combined action, which was made irresistible by their resolute will. But they took little joy in society; they shunned public amusements, and preferred the quieter relaxations of home life; and, it must be confessed, some of them took an attitude hostile to art[1].

The first growth of strength had then something in it that was rude and ill-mannered, but that strength was required for the next stage upwards. Individualism had to be purified and softened by much tribulation, it had to become less self-assertive without becoming weaker, before new instincts could grow up around it to revive in a higher form what was most beautiful and most solid in the old collective tendencies. Individualism governed by the temper of the Reformed religion intensified family life, making it deeper and purer, and holier than it had ever been before. It is true that even the highest elements of our nature can be used wrongly, that an exclusive devotion to family cares has evils of its own. Nevertheless the family affections of those races which have adopted the Reformed religion are the richest and fullest of earthly feelings: there never has been before any material of texture at once so strong and so fine, with which to build up a noble fabric of social life.

which supplied the strength necessary for the next stage of social life

Holland and other countries shared with England the great ordeal which was thus opened by the spiritual upheaval that closed the middle ages But from many points of view,

[1] The licentiousness of some forms of art created in serious but narrow minds a prejudice against all art; and in revenge socialists now rail at the Reformation as having injured both the social and the artistic instincts of man But it may be questioned whether the intensity of the feelings which were engendered by the Reformation has not enriched art more than their austerity has injured it They have developed a literature and a music of their own; and if they have led man to think slightingly of the beauty of the works of his own hands, they have certainly increased his power of appreciating the beauties of nature It is no accident that landscape painting owes most to lands in which the Reformed religion has prevailed.

BOOK I CH III

and especially from that of the economist, England's experiences were the most instructive and the most thorough; and were typical of all the rest England led the way in the modern evolution of industry and enterprise by free and self-determining energy and will.

The economic influence of the Reformation on England was intensified through her attracting refugee artisans from the Continent

§ 3. The effects of the Reformation on England's industrial and commercial character were intensified by the fact that many of those who had adopted the new doctrines in other countries sought on her shores a safe asylum from religious persecution By a sort of natural selection, those of the French and Flemings, and others whose character was most akin to the English, and who had been led by that character to sturdy thoroughness of work in the manufacturing arts, came to mingle with them, and to teach them those arts for which their character had all along fitted them[1]. During the seventeenth and eighteenth centuries, the court and the upper classes remained more or less frivolous and licentious; but the middle class and some parts of the working class adopted a severe view of life, they took little delight in amusements that interrupted work, and they had a high standard as to those material comforts which could be obtained only by unremitting, hard work. They strove to produce things that had a solid and lasting utility, rather than those suited only for the purpose of festivities and ostentation. The tendency, when once it had set in, was promoted by the climate, for, though not very severe, it is specially unsuited to the lighter amusements, and the clothing, houseroom and other requisites for a comfortable existence in it, are of a specially expensive character.

It gave a sombre tone to her amusements, and this reacted on her industries

These were the conditions under which the modern industrial life of England was developed · the desire for material comforts tends towards a ceaseless straining to extract from every week the greatest amount of work that can be got out of it The firm resolution to submit every action to the deliberate judgment of the reason tends to make everyone constantly ask himself whether he could not improve his position by changing his business, or by changing his method

[1] Dr Smiles has shown that the debt which England owes to these immigrants is greater than historians have supposed, though they have always rated it highly.

of doing it. And, lastly, complete political freedom and security enables everyone to adjust his conduct as he has decided that it is his interest to do, and fearlessly to commit his person and his property to new and distant undertakings

In short, the same causes which have enabled England and her colonies to set the tone of modern politics, have made them also set the tone of modern business. The same qualities which gave them political freedom gave them also free enterprise in industry and commerce[1].

English free enterprise naturally tended towards division of labour,

§ 4. Freedom of industry and enterprise, so far as its action reaches, tends to cause everyone to seek that employment of his labour and capital in which he can turn them to best advantage, and this again leads him to try to obtain a special skill and facility in some particular task, by which he may earn the means of purchasing what he himself wants. And hence results a complex industrial organization, with much subtle division of labour[2].

Some sort of division of labour is indeed sure to grow up in any civilization that has held together for a long while, however primitive its form. Even in very backward countries we find highly specialized trades, but we do not find the work within each trade so divided up that the planning and arrangement of the business, its management and its risks, are borne by one set of people, while the manual work required for it is done by hired labour. This form of division of labour is at once characteristic of the modern world generally, and of the English race in particular. It may be merely a passing phase in man's development, it may be swept away by the further growth of that free enterprise which has called it into existence. But for the present it stands out for good and for evil as the chief fact in the form of modern civilization, the kernel of the modern economic problem.

The most vital changes hitherto introduced into industrial

[1] Rogers argues with great force (*Six Centuries of Work and Wages*, ch 1), that the commutation of personal for money dues was effected earlier in England than on the Continent, and was a chief cause of what is most characteristic in England's political history.

[2] This subject is studied in detail below, Book IV chs VIII—XII

BOOK I CH III.

especially in the management of business,

life, centre around this growth of business *Undertakers*[1]. We have already seen how the undertaker made his appearance at an early stage in England's agriculture. The farmer borrowed land from his landlord, and hired the necessary labour, being himself responsible for the management and risks of the business. The selection of farmers has not indeed been governed by perfectly free competition, but has been restricted to a certain extent by inheritance and by other influences, which have often caused the leadership of agricultural industry to fall into the hands of people who have had no special talents for it. But England is the only country in which any considerable play has been given to natural selection: the agricultural systems of the Continent have allowed the accident of birth to determine the part which every man should take in cultivating land or controlling its cultivation The greater energy and elasticity obtained by even this narrow play of selection in England, has been sufficient to put English agriculture in advance of all others, and has enabled it to obtain a much larger produce than is got by an equal amount of labour from similar soils in any other country of Europe[2].

and the localization of industry

But the natural selection of the fittest to undertake, to organize, and to manage has much greater scope in manufacture The tendency to the growth of undertakers in manufactures had set in before the great development of England's foreign trade, in fact traces of it are to be found in the woollen manufacture in the fifteenth century[3]. But the opening up of large markets in new countries gave a

[1] This term, which has the authority of Adam Smith and is habitually used on the Continent, seems to be the best to indicate those who take the risks and the management of business as their share in the work of organized industry

[2] In the latter half of the eighteenth century, especially, the improvements in agriculture moved very fast Implements of all kinds were improved, draining was carried out on scientific principles, the breeding of farm animals was revolutionized by Bakewell's genius; turnips, clover, rye-grass, &c came into general use, and enabled the plan of refreshing land by letting it lie fallow to be superseded by that of "alternating husbandry" These and other changes constantly increased the capital required for the cultivation of land; while the growth of fortunes made in trade increased the number of those who were able and willing to purchase their way into country society by buying large properties. And thus in every way the modern commercial spirit spread in agriculture.

[3] Comp Ochenkowski, *Englands wirthschaftliche Entwickelung*, p 112

great stimulus to the movement, both directly and through its influence on the localization of industry, that is, the concentration of particular branches of production in certain localities.

These tendencies promoted by the growth of consumers beyond the seas, who wanted goods of simple patterns.

The records of mediæval fairs and wandering merchants show that there were many things each of which was made in only one or two places, and thence distributed north and south, east and west, over the whole of Europe. But the wares whose production was localized and which travelled far, were almost always of high price and small bulk: the cheaper and heavier goods were supplied by each district for itself. In the colonies of the new world, however, people had not always the leisure to provide manufactures for themselves: and they were often not allowed to make even those which they could have made; for though England's treatment of her colonies was more liberal than that of any other country, she thought that the expense which she incurred on their behalf justified her in compelling them to buy nearly all kinds of manufactures from herself. There was also a large demand for simple goods to be sold in India and to savage races.

These causes led to the localization of much of the heavier manufacturing work. In work which requires the highly trained skill and delicate fancy of the operative, organization is sometimes of secondary importance. But the power of organizing great numbers of people gives an irresistible advantage when there is a demand for whole ship cargoes of goods of a few simple patterns. Thus localization and the growth of the system of capitalist undertakers were two parallel movements, due to the same general cause, and each of them promoting the advance of the other.

The undertakers at first merely organized supply without supervising industry that was still done by small masters.

The factory system and the use of expensive appliances in manufacture, came at a later stage. They are commonly supposed to be the origin of the power which undertakers wield in English industry; and no doubt they increased it. But it had shown itself clearly before their influence was felt. At the time of the French Revolution there was not a very great deal of capital invested in machinery whether driven by water or steam power, the factories were not large, and there were not many of them. But nearly all

BOOK I. CH III.

the textile work of the country was then done on a system of contracts. This industry was controlled by a comparatively small number of undertakers who set themselves to find out what, where and when it was most advantageous to buy and to sell, and what things it was most profitable to have made. They then let out contracts for making these things to a great number of people scattered over the country The undertakers generally supplied the raw material, and sometimes even the simple implements that were used; those who took the contract executed it by the labour of themselves and their families, and sometimes but not always by that of a few assistants[1].

As time went on, the progress of mechanical invention caused the workers to be gathered more and more into small factories in the neighbourhood of water power, and when steam came to be substituted for water power, then into larger factories in great towns Thus the great undertakers who bore the chief risks of manufacturing, without directly managing and superintending, began to give way to wealthy employers, who conducted the whole business of manufacturing on a large scale The new factories attracted the attention of the most careless observer, and this last movement was not liable to be overlooked by those who were not actually engaged in the trade, as the preceding movement had been[2]

[1] The relations in which the undertaking the risks of a business stands to the work of managing it, and superintending those who are engaged in it, are discussed below in Book IV ch XII, the causes which govern the remunerations of these several tasks are studied in Book VI. ch. VII VIII XI XII.

[2] The quarter of a century beginning with 1760 saw improvements follow one another in manufacture even more rapidly than in agriculture During that period the transport of heavy goods was cheapened by Brindley's canals, the production of power by Watt's steam engine, and that of iron by Cort's processes of puddling and rolling, and by Roebuck's method of smelting it by coal in lieu of the charcoal that had now become scarce, Hargreaves, Crompton, Arkwright, Cartwright and others invented, or at least made economically serviceable, the spinning-jenny, the mule, the carding machine, and the power-loom; Wedgwood gave a great impetus to the pottery trade that was already growing rapidly, and there were important inventions in printing from cylinders, in bleaching by chemical agents, and in other processes A cotton factory was for the first time driven directly by steam-power in 1785, the last year of the period The beginning of the nineteenth century saw steam-ships and steam printing-presses, and the use of gas for lighting towns Railway locomotion, tele

Thus at length general attention was called to the great change in the organization of industry which had long been going on; and it was seen that the system of small businesses controlled by the workers themselves was being displaced by the system of large businesses controlled by the specialized ability of capitalist undertakers. The change would have worked itself out very much as it has done, even if there had been no factories. and it will go on working itself out even if the retail distribution of force by electric or other agencies should cause part of the work that is now done in factories to be taken to the home of the workers[1]

But gradually the undertakers collected into factories large bodies of workers Henceforth manufacturing labour was hired wholesale

§ 5 The new movement both in its earlier and later forms has tended constantly to relax the bonds that used to bind nearly everyone to live in the parish in which he was born; and it developed free markets for labour, which invited people to come and take their chance of finding employment. And in consequence of this change the causes that determine the value of labour began to take a new character. Up to the eighteenth century manufacturing labour had been hired, as it were, always retail, in that century it began to be hired wholesale Up to that time its price had been in the main either nominally fixed by custom or determined by the incidents of bargaining in very small markets the bargaining had been sometimes for the hire of labour, sometimes for the sale of its products, the workman having himself undertaken the risks of production But since then its price has more and more been determined by the circumstances of supply and demand over a large area—a town, a country, or the whole world

The new organization of industry added vastly to the efficiency of production, for it went far towards securing that each man's labour should be devoted to just the highest

The new organization was accompanied by great

graphy and photography came a little later Our own age has seen numberless improvements and new economics in production, prominent among which are those relating to the production of steel, the telephone, the electric light, and the gas-engine, and the social changes arising from material progress are in some respects more rapid now than ever But the groundwork of the changes that have happened since 1785 was chiefly laid in the inventions of the years 1760 to 1785

[1] See Held's *Sociale Geschichte Englands*, Bk II ch III Compare also Mr Carroll D. Wright's vigorous defence of the Factory system, Vol II of the *U S Census for* 1880

BOOK I CH. III.

kind of work which he was capable of performing well, and that his work should be ably directed and supplied with the best mechanical and other assistance that wealth and the knowledge of the age could afford. But it brought with it great evils Which of these evils was unavoidable we cannot tell For just when the change was moving most quickly, England was stricken by a combination of calamities almost unparalleled in history. They were the cause of a great part—it is impossible to say of how great a part—of the sufferings that are commonly ascribed to the sudden outbreak of unrestrained competition. The loss of her great colonies was quickly followed by the great French war, which cost her more than the total value of the accumulated wealth she had at its commencement. An unprecedented series of bad harvests made bread fearfully dear. And worse than all, a method of administration of the poor law was adopted which undermined the independence and vigour of the people

evils, many of which were due to other causes

The first part of this century therefore saw free enterprise establishing itself in England under unfavourable circumstances, its evils being intensified and its beneficial influences being hindered by external misfortunes

There were some futile attempts to revive old ordinances regulating labour,

§ 6 The trade customs and the gild regulations by which the weak had been defended in past times, were unsuitable to the new industry. In some places they were abandoned by common consent: in others they were successfully upheld for a time. But it was a fatal success; for the new industry, incapable of flourishing under the old bonds, left those places for others where it could be more free[1]. Then the workers turned to Government for the enforcement of old laws of Parliament prescribing the way in which the trade should be carried on, and even for the revival of the regulation of prices and wages by justices of the peace.

which had done both good and evil in their time,

These efforts could not but fail. The old regulations had been the expression of the social, moral and economic ideas of the time, they had been felt out, rather than

[1] The tendency of industries to flee away from places where they were over-regulated by the gilds was of old standing, and had shown itself in the thirteenth century, though it was then comparatively feeble. See Gross' *Gild Merchant*, Vol. I pp 43 and 52

thought out; they were the almost instinctive result of the experience of generations of men who had lived and died under almost unchanged economic conditions In the new age changes came so rapidly that there was no time for this. Each man had to do what was right in his own eyes, with but little guidance from the experience of past times; those who endeavoured to cling to old traditions were quickly supplanted.

but were unfitted for the modern era of rapid change

The new race of undertakers consisted chiefly of those who had made their own fortunes, strong, ready, enterprising men: who, looking at the success obtained by their own energies, were apt to assume that the poor and the weak were to be blamed rather than to be pitied for their misfortunes Impressed with the folly of those who tried to bolster up economic arrangements which the stream of progress had undermined, they were apt to think that nothing more was wanted than to make competition perfectly free and to let the strongest have their way. They glorified individualism, and were in no hurry to find a modern substitute for the social and industrial bonds which had kept men together in earlier times

The manufacturers were chiefly strong self-made men, who saw only the good side of competition.

Meanwhile misfortune had reduced the total net income of the people of England. In 1820 a tenth of it was absorbed in paying the mere interest on the National Debt. The goods that were cheapened by the new inventions were chiefly manufactured commodities of which the working man was but a small consumer. As England had then almost a monopoly of manufactures, he might indeed have got his food cheaply if manufacturers had been allowed to change their wares freely for corn grown abroad, but this was prohibited by the landlords who ruled in Parliament The labourer's wages, so far as they were spent on ordinary food, were the equivalent of what his labour would produce on the very poor soil which was forced into cultivation to eke out the insufficient supplies raised from the richer grounds He had to sell his labour in a market in which the forces of supply and demand would have given him a poor pittance even if they had worked freely. But he had not the full advantage of economic freedom; he had no efficient union

The pressure of war taxes and the scarcity of food forced down real wages,

BOOK I. CH. III

and induced unhealthy and excessive work, which lowered the wage-earning power

with his fellows; he had neither the knowledge of the market, nor the power of holding out for a reserve price, which the seller of commodities has, and he was urged on to work and to let his family work during long hours, and under unhealthy conditions. This reacted on the efficiency of the working population, and therefore on the net value of their work, and therefore it kept down their wages. The employment of very young children for long hours was no new thing: it had been common in Norwich and elsewhere even in the seventeenth century, but the moral and physical misery and disease caused by excessive work under bad conditions reached their highest point among the factory population in the first quarter of the century; and they diminished slowly during the second quarter, and more rapidly since then.

But the new system had saved England from French armies, and the workmen accepted it

After the workmen had recognised the folly of attempts to revive the old rules regulating industry, there was no longer any wish to curtail the freedom of enterprise. The sufferings of the English people at their worst were never comparable to those which had been caused by the want of freedom in France before the Revolution; and it was argued that, had it not been for the strength which England derived from her new industries, she would probably have succumbed to a foreign military despotism, as the free cities had done before her Small as her population was she at some times bore almost alone the burden of war against a conqueror in control of nearly all the resources of the Continent; and at other times subsidized larger, but poorer countries in the struggle against him Rightly or wrongly, it was thought at the time that Europe might have fallen permanently under the dominion of France, as she had fallen in an earlier age under that of Rome, had not the free energy of English industries supplied the sinews of war against the common foe. Little was therefore heard in complaint against the excess of free enterprise, but much against that limitation of it which prevented Englishmen from obtaining food from abroad in return for the manufactures which they could now so easily produce

Change in the

And even trades-unions, which were then beginning that

brilliant though chequered career which has been more full of interest and instruction than almost anything else in English history, passed into the phase of seeking little from authority except to be left alone. They had learnt by bitter experience the folly of attempting to enforce the old rules by which Government had directed the course of industry; and they had as yet got no far-reaching views as to the regulation of trade by their own action: their chief anxiety was to increase their own economic freedom by the removal of the laws against combinations of workmen.

policy of Trades-Unions.

§ 7. It has been left for our own generation to perceive all the evils which arose from the suddenness of this increase of economic freedom Now first are we getting to understand the extent to which the capitalist employer, untrained to his new duties, was tempted to subordinate the wellbeing of his workpeople to his own desire for gain, now first are we learning the importance of insisting that the rich have duties as well as rights in their individual and in their collective capacity; now first is the economic problem of the new age showing itself to us as it really is This is partly due to a wider knowledge and a growing earnestness But however wise and virtuous our grandfathers had been, they could not have seen things as we do, for they were hurried along by urgent necessities and terrible disasters[1].

People could not see, as we can, how great are the evils of economic freedom when it degenerates into license

But we must judge ourselves by a severer standard. For we are not now struggling for national existence, and our resources have not been exhausted by great wars. on the contrary our powers of production have been immensely increased, and, what is at least as important, the repeal of the Corn Laws and the growth of steam communication have enabled a largely increased population to obtain sufficient supplies of food on easy terms The average money income

We now have greater means and must aim higher.

[1] In times of peace no one ventures openly to rank money as of high importance in comparison with human lives, but in the crisis of an expensive war money can always be used so as to save them A general who at a critical time sacrifices lives in order to protect material, the loss of which would cause the loss of many men, is held to have acted rightly, though no one would openly defend a sacrifice of soldiers' lives in order to save a few army stores in time of peace And at the beginning of this century every check to the production of wealth was likely to cause a loss of life to English soldiers, and increased the risk of their losing that national liberty which was dearer than life

BOOK I. CH III

of the people has more than doubled; while the price of almost all important commodities except animal food and houseroom has fallen by one-half or even further. It is true that even now, if wealth were distributed equally, the total production of the country would only suffice to provide necessaries and the more urgent comforts for the people[1], and that as things are, many have barely the necessaries of life. But the nation has grown in wealth, in health, in education and in morality; and we are no longer compelled to subordinate almost every other consideration to the need of increasing the total produce of industry.

The new restraints on freedom are chiefly in the interests of women and children

In particular during the present generation this increased prosperity has made us rich and strong enough to impose new restraints on free enterprise, some temporary material loss being submitted to for the sake of a higher and greater ultimate gain. But these new restraints are different from the old. They are imposed not as a means of class domination; but with the purpose of defending the weak, and especially children and the mothers of children, in matters in which they are not able to use the forces of competition in their own defence. The aim is to devise, deliberately and promptly, remedies adapted to the quickly changing circumstances of modern industry, and thus to obtain the good, without the evil, of the old defence of the weak that in other ages was gradually evolved by custom

The telegraph and printing-press enable the people now to decide on their own remedies for their evils

Even when industry remained almost unchanged in character for many generations together, custom was too slow in its growth and too blind to be able to apply pressure only when pressure was beneficial: and in this later stage custom can do but little good, and much harm But by the aid of the telegraph and the printing-press, of representative government and trade associations, it is possible for the people to think out for themselves the solution of their own problems. The growth of knowledge and self-reliance has given them that true self-controlling freedom, which enables

[1] The average income per head in the United Kingdom, which was about £15 in 1820, is about £37 now; i e. it has risen from about £75 to £185 per family of five; and its purchasing power is nearly as great as that of £400 in 1820 A few artisans' families earn about £185, and would not gain by an equal distribution of wealth but they have only enough for a healthy and many sided life.

them to impose of their own free will restraints on their own actions and the problems of collective production, collective ownership and collective consumption are entering on a new phase.

And we are gradually moving towards forms of collective action, higher than the old, because based on strong self-disciplined individuality

Projects for great and sudden changes are now, as ever, foredoomed to fail, and to cause reaction, we cannot move safely, if we move so fast that our new plans of life altogether outrun our instincts. It is true that human nature can be modified: new ideals, new opportunities and new methods of action may, as history shows, alter it very much even in a few generations, and this change in human nature has perhaps never covered so wide an area and moved so fast as in the present generation But still it is a growth, and therefore gradual; and changes of our social organization must wait on it, and therefore they must be gradual too.

But though they wait on it, they may always keep a little in advance of it, promoting the growth of our higher social nature by giving it always some new and higher work to do, some practical ideal towards which to strive Thus gradually we may attain to an order of social life, in which the common good overrules individual caprice, even more than it did in the early ages before the sway of individualism had begun. But unselfishness then will be the offspring of deliberate will, though aided by instinct individual freedom then will develop itself in collective freedom ;—a happy contrast to the old order of life, in which individual slavery to custom caused collective slavery and stagnation, broken only by the caprice of despotism or the caprice of revolution.

America is throwing much light on certain economic problems

§ 8 We have been looking at this movement from the English point of view. But other nations are taking their share in it America faces new practical difficulties with such intrepidity and directness that she is already contesting with England the leadership in economic affairs; she supplies many of the most instructive instances of the latest economic tendencies of the age, such as the growing democracy of trade and industry, and the development of speculation and trade combination in every form, and she will probably before long take the chief part in pioneering the way for the rest of the world.

BOOK I. CH III

Australia

Nor is Australia showing less signs of vigour than her elder sister; she has indeed some advantage over the United States in the greater homogeneity of her people. For, though the Australians—and nearly the same may be said of the Canadians—come from many lands, and thus stimulate one another to thought and enterprise by the variety of their experiences and their habits of thought, yet nearly all of them belong to one race: and the development of social and economic institutions can proceed in some respects more easily, and perhaps ultimately even faster than would be possible if they had to be adjusted to the capacities, the temperaments, the tastes, and the wants of peoples who have little affinity with one another.

On the Continent the power of obtaining important results by free association is less than in English speaking countries, and in consequence there is less resource and less thoroughness in dealing with industrial problems. But their treatment is not quite the same in any two nations: and there is something characteristic and instructive in the methods adopted by each of them; particularly in relation to the sphere of governmental action In this matter Germany is taking the lead. It has been a great gain to her that her manufacturing industries developed later than those of England, and she has been able to profit by England's experience and to avoid many of her mistakes[1].

Germany has special facilities for experimenting in the management of business by the Government for the people.

In Germany an exceptionally large part of the best intellect in the nation seeks for employment under Government, and there is probably no other Government which contains within itself so much trained ability of the highest order. On the other hand the energy, the originality and the daring which make the best men of business in England and America have not yet been fully developed in Germany; while the German people have a great faculty of obedience They are thus in strong contrast to the English, whose

[1] List worked out with much suggestiveness the notion that a backward nation must learn its lessons not from the contemporary conduct of more forward nations, but from their conduct when they were in the same state in which it is now. But, as Knies well shows (*Politische Œkonomie*, II 5), the growth of trade and the improvement of the means of communication are making the developments of different nations tend to synchronize.

strength of will makes them capable of thorough discipline when they see the necessity for it, but who are not naturally docile. The control of industry by Government is seen in its best and most attractive forms in Germany, and at the same time the special virtues of private industry, its vigour, its elasticity and its resource are not seen to their best advantage there. In consequence the problems of the economic functions of Government have been studied in Germany with great care, and with results that may be very instructive to English speaking people; provided they recollect that the arrangements best suited for the German character, are probably not quite the best for them; since they could not, if they would, rival the Germans in their steadfast docility, and in their easy contentment with inexpensive kinds of food, clothing, house-room and amusements

And Germany contains a larger number than any other country of the most cultivated members of that wonderful race who have been leaders of the world in intensity of religious feeling and in keenness of business speculation In every country, but especially in Germany, much of what is most brilliant and suggestive in economic practice and in economic thought is of Jewish origin. And in particular to German Jews we owe many daring speculations as to the conflict of interests between the individual and society, and as to their ultimate economic causes and their possible socialistic remedies

But we are trenching on the subject of the next chapter. In this and the previous chapter we have seen how recent is the growth of economic freedom, and how new is the substance of the problem with which economic science has now to deal, in the next chapter we have to inquire how the form of that problem has been fashioned by the progress of events and the personal peculiarities of great thinkers.

CHAPTER IV.

THE GROWTH OF ECONOMIC SCIENCE

Modern economic science owes much to ancient thought indirectly, but little directly

§ 1. We have seen how economic freedom has its roots in the past, but is in the main a product of quite recent times; we have next to trace the parallel growth of economic science. The social conditions of the present day have been developed from early Aryan and Semitic institutions by the aid of Greek thought and Roman law; but modern economic speculations have been very little under the direct influence of the theories of the ancients.

It is true that modern economics had its origin in common with other sciences at the time when the study of classic writers was reviving But an industrial system which was based on slavery, and a philosophy which regarded manufacture and commerce with contempt, had little that was congenial to the hardy burghers who were as proud of their handicrafts and their trade as they were of their share in governing the State. These strong but uncultured men might have gained much from the philosophic temper and the broad interests of the great thinkers of past times. But, as it was, they set themselves to work out their own problems for themselves, and modern economics had at its origin a certain rudeness and limitation of scope, and a bias towards regarding wealth as an end rather than a means of man's life. Its immediate concern was generally with the public revenue, and the effects and yield of taxes; and here the statesmen of the free cities and the great empires alike found their economic problems more urgent and more difficult, as trade became broader and war more expensive.

Influence of trade with the New World.

In all ages, but especially in the early middle ages, statesmen and merchants had busied themselves with endeavours to enrich the State by regulating trade. One chief object of their concern had been the supply of the precious metals, which they thought the best indication if not the chief cause of material prosperity, whether of the individual or the nation. But the voyages of Vasco de Gama and Columbus raised commercial questions from a secondary to a dominating position among the nations of Western Europe. Theories with regard to the importance of the precious metals and the best means of obtaining supplies of them, became the arbiters of public policy: they dictated peace and war, they determined alliances that issued in the rise and fall of nations and they governed the migration of peoples over the face of the globe

The early regulation of trade.

Regulations as to trade in the precious metals were but one group of a vast body of ordinances, which undertook, with varying degrees of minuteness and severity, to arrange for each individual what he should produce and how he should produce it, what he should earn and how he should spend his earnings. The natural adhesiveness of the Teutons had given custom an exceptional strength in the early middle ages. And this strength told on the side of trade gilds, of local authorities and of national Governments when they set themselves to cope with the restless tendency to change that sprang directly or indirectly from the trade with the New World In France this Teutonic bias was directed by the Roman genius for system, and paternal government reached its zenith; the trade regulations of Colbert have become a proverb. It was just at this time that economic theory first took shape and the so-called Mercantile system became prominent.

The mercantile theory tended to loosen the fetters of trade.

As years went on there set in a tendency towards economic freedom, and those who were opposed to the new ideas claimed on their side the authority of the Mercantilists of a past generation It is not therefore to be wondered at that the Mercantilists are commonly believed to have promoted the state regulation of trade and industry. But they did not. The regulations and restrictions which

BOOK I CH. IV.

are found in their systems belonged to the age; the changes which they set themselves to bring about were in the direction of the freedom of enterprise. In opposition to those who wished to prohibit absolutely the exportation of the precious metals, they argued that it should be permitted in all cases in which the trade would in the long run bring more gold and silver into the country than it took out[1].

The Mercantilists indeed did not look beyond the immediate purpose for which they were contending, they did not dream of establishing a new principle of social and political life. But by raising the question whether the State would not benefit by allowing the trader to manage his business as he liked in one particular case, they had unwittingly started a new tendency of thought, and this moved on by imperceptible steps in the direction of economic freedom, being assisted on its way by the circumstances of the time, no less than by the tone and temper of men's minds in Western Europe. A little was done here and a little there, in England and Holland, in Italy and France The steps are difficult to trace: it is not easy to tell how much each writer owes to the suggestions of others in his own and other countries (for there was much international intercourse on such subjects); nor how far he himself intended the suggestions which we with our later knowledge read into his passing hints But we know that the broadening movement did go on till, in the latter half of the eighteenth century, the time was ripe for the doctrine that the well-being of the community almost always suffers when the State attempts to oppose its own artificial regulations to the "natural" liberty of every man to manage his own affairs in his own way[2].

1 Some account of the relations between Mediæval and Mercantile Theories of money and trade will be given in the second volume of this work

2 For a sketch of the history the reader may be referred to Kautz's profound, just and suggestive *Die geschichtliche Entwickelung der National-Oekonomik*, to Travers Twiss' *View of the Progress of Political Economy*, and to the histories of Professors Ashley, Cossa, Cunningham and Ingram, to Dr Bonar's *Philosophy and Political Economy*, and to various articles by Mr Hewins, Dr Stephen Bauer and others in the *Dictionary of Political Economy* and elsewhere

The Physiocrats insisted that restriction is artificial and liberty is natural

§ 2. The first systematic attempt to form an economic science on a broad basis was made in France about the middle of the eighteenth century by a group of statesmen and philosophers under the leadership of Quesnay, the noble-minded physician to Louis XV.[1] The corner-stone of their policy was obedience to Nature[2]

They were the first to proclaim the doctrine of free trade as a broad principle of action, going in this respect beyond even such advanced English writers as Sir Dudley North; and there was much in the tone and temper of their treatment of political and social questions which was prophetic of a later age. They fell however into a confusion of thought which was common even among scientific men of their time, but which has been banished after a long struggle from the physical sciences. They confused the ethical principle of conformity to nature, which is expressed in the imperative

[1] I pass by Cantillon, whose essay *Sur la Nature de Commerce*, written in 1755, covers a wide range, and has some claims to be called systematic. It is acute and in some respects ahead of his time, though it now appears that he had been anticipated on several important points by Nicholas Barbon, who wrote sixty years earlier. Kautz was the first to recognize the importance of Cantillon's work; and Jevons declared he was the true founder of Political Economy. For a well balanced estimate of his place in economics, see an article by Mr Higgs in the *Quarterly Journal of Economics*, Vol VI

[2] In the two preceding centuries writers on economic questions had continually appealed to Nature, each disputant claiming that his scheme was more natural than that of others, and the philosophers of the eighteenth century, some of whom exercised a great influence on economics, were wont to find the standard of right in conformity to Nature In particular Locke anticipated much of the work of the French economists in the general tone of his appeals to Nature, and in some important details of his theory But Quesnay and the other French economists who worked with him, were drawn to the pursuit of natural laws of social life by several forces in addition to those which were at work in England

The luxury of the French court, and the privileges of the upper classes which were ruining France, showed the worst side of an artificial civilization, and made thoughtful men yearn for a return to a more natural state of society The lawyers, among whom much of the best mental and moral strength of the country was to be found, were full of the Law of Nature which had been developed by the Stoic lawyers of the later Roman Empire, and as the century wore on, the sentimental admiration for the "natural" life of the American Indians which Rousseau had kindled into flame, began to influence the economists Before long they were called Physiocrats or adherents of the rule of Nature, this name being derived from the title of Dupont de Nemours' *Physiocratie ou Constitution Naturelle du Gouvernement le plus avantageux au Genre Humain* published in 1768 It may be mentioned that their enthusiasm for agriculture and for the naturalness and simplicity of rural life was in part derived from their Stoic masters

BOOK I CH IV.

mood, and prescribes certain laws of action, with those causal laws which science discovers by interrogating Nature, and which are expressed in the indicative mood. For this and other reasons their work has but little direct value.

They gave to economics its modern philanthropic tone

But its indirect influence on the present position of economics has been very great. For, firstly, the clearness and logical consistency of their arguments have caused them to exercise a great influence on later thought. And, secondly, the chief motive of their study was not, as it had been with most of their predecessors, to increase the riches of merchants and fill the exchequers of kings[1]; it was to diminish the suffering and degradation which was caused by extreme poverty. They thus gave to economics its modern aim of seeking after such knowledge as may help to raise the quality of human life[2].

Adam Smith's genius.

§ 3. The next great step in advance, the greatest step that economics has ever taken, was the work, not of a school but of an individual. Adam Smith was not indeed the only great English economist of his time. Shortly before he wrote, important additions to economic theory had been made by Hume and Steuart, and excellent studies of economic facts had been published by Anderson and Young. But Adam Smith's breadth was sufficient to include all that was best in all his contemporaries, French and English; and, though he undoubtedly borrowed much from others, yet the more one compares him with those who went before and those who came after him, the finer does his genius appear, the broader his knowledge and the more well balanced his judgment.

He resided a long time in France in personal converse

[1] Even the generous Vauban (writing in 1717) had to apologize for his interest in the well-being of the people, arguing that to enrich them was the only way to enrich the king—Pauvres paysans, pauvre Royaume, pauvre Royaume, pauvre Roi.

[2] Their favourite phrase *Laissez faire, laissez aller*, is commonly misapplied now *Laissez faire* means that anyone should be allowed to make what things he likes, and as he likes; that all trades should be open to everybody; that Government should not, as the Colbertists insisted, prescribe to manufacturers the fashions of their cloth *Laissez aller* (or *passer*) means that persons and goods should be allowed to travel freely from one place to another, and especially from one district of France to another, without being subject to tolls and taxes and vexations regulations. It may be noticed that *laissez aller* was the signal used in the Middle Ages by the Marshals to slip the leash from the combatants at a Tournament.

with the Physiocrats; he made a careful study of the English and French philosophy of his time, and he got to know the world practically by wide travel and by intimate association with Scotch men of business. To these advantages he added unsurpassed powers of observation, judgment and reasoning The result is that wherever he differs from his predecessors, he is more nearly right than they; while there is scarcely any economic truth now known of which he did not get some glimpse And since he was the first to write a treatise on wealth in all its chief social aspects, he might on this ground alone have a claim to be regarded as the founder of modern economics[1]

But the area which he opened up was too vast to be thoroughly surveyed by one man, and many truths of which at times he caught sight escaped from his view at other times It is therefore possible to quote his authority in support of many errors; though, on careful examination, he is always found to be working his way towards the truth[2].

He greatly developed the doctrine of free trade;

He developed the Physiocratic doctrine of Free Trade with so much practical wisdom, and with so much knowledge of the actual conditions of business, as to make it a great force in real life, and he is most widely known both here

[1] Compare the short but weighty statement of Adam Smith's claims to supremacy in Wagner's *Grundlegung*, Ed. 3, pp 6, &c ; also Hasbach's *Untersuchungen uber Adam Smith* (in which the notice of the influence of Dutch thought on both English and French is of special interest); and L L Price's *Adam Smith and his relations to Recent Economics* in the *Economic Journal*, Vol III Prof. Cunningham's *History*, § 306, argues forcibly that his great achievement lay in isolating the conception of national wealth, while previous writers had treated it in conscious subordination to national power". but perhaps each half of this contrast is drawn with too sharp outlines

[2] For instance, he had not quite got rid of the confusion prevalent in his time between the laws of economic science and the ethical precept of conformity to nature "Natural" with him sometimes means that which the existing forces actually produce or tend to produce, sometimes that which his own human nature makes him wish that they should produce In the same way, he sometimes regards it as the province of the economist to expound a science, and at others to set forth a part of the art of government. But loose as his language often is, we find on closer study that he himself knows pretty well what he is about When he is seeking for causal laws, that is, for laws of nature in the modern use of the term, he uses scientific methods; and when he utters practical precepts he generally knows that he is only expressing his own views of what ought to be, even when he seems to claim the authority of nature for them

and abroad for his argument that Government generally does harm by interfering in trade. While giving many instances of the ways in which self-interest may lead the individual trader to act injuriously to the community, he contended that even when Government acted with the best intentions, it nearly always served the public worse than the enterprise of the individual trader, however selfish he might happen to be. So great an impression did he make on the world by his defence of this doctrine that most German writers have it chiefly in view when they speak of *Smithianismus*[1].

but his chief work was to find in the theory of value a common centre that gave unity to economic science

But after all, this was not his chief work. His chief work was to combine and develop the speculations of his French and English contemporaries and predecessors as to value. His highest claim to have made an epoch in thought is that he was the first to make a careful and scientific inquiry into the manner in which value measures human motive, on the one side measuring the desire of purchasers to obtain wealth, and on the other the efforts and sacrifices (or "Real Cost of Production") undergone by its producers[2].

Possibly the full drift of what he was doing was not seen by him, certainly it was not perceived by many of his followers But for all that, the best economic work which came after the *Wealth of Nations* is distinguished from that which went before, by a clearer insight into the balancing and weighing, by means of money, of the desire for the possession of a thing on the one hand, and on the other

[1] The popular use of this term in Germany implies not only that Adam Smith thought that the free play of individual interests would do more for the public weal than Government interference could, but further that it almost always acted in the ideally best way But the leading German economists are well aware that he steadily insisted on the frequent opposition that there is between private interests and the public good. and the old use of the term *Smithianismus* is becoming discredited See for instance a long list of such conflicts quoted from the *Wealth of Nations* by Knies, *Politische Oekonomie*, Ch. III. § 3 See also Feilbogen's *Smith und Turgot* and Zeyss' *Smith und der Eigennutz*

[2] The relations of Value to Cost of Production had been indicated by the Physiocrats and by many earlier writers, among whom may be mentioned Harris, Cantillon, Locke, Barbon, Petty, and even Hobbes who hinted, though vaguely, that plenty dependeth on labor and abstinence applied by man to working up and accumulating the gifts of nature by land and by sea—*proventus terræ et aquæ, labor et parsimonia*

BOOK I. CH IV

of all the various efforts and self-denials which directly and indirectly contribute towards making it. Important as had been the steps that others had taken in this direction, the advance made by him was so great that he really opened out this new point of view, and by so doing made an epoch In this he and the economists, who went before and came after him, were not inventing a new academic notion, they were merely giving definiteness and precision to notions that are familiar in common life. In fact the ordinary man, without analytical habits of mind, is apt to regard money as measuring motive and happiness more closely and exactly than it actually does; and this is partly because he does not think out the manner in which the measurement is effected. Economic language seems technical and less real than that of common life. But in truth it is more real, because it is more careful and takes more account of differences and difficulties[1].

The study of facts

§ 4. None of Adam Smith's contemporaries and immediate successors had a mind as broad and well balanced as his But they did excellent work, each giving himself up to some class of problems to which he was attracted by the natural bent of his genius, or the special events of the time in which he wrote During the remainder of the eighteenth century the chief economic writings were historical and descriptive, and bore upon the condition of the working classes, especially in the agricultural districts. Arthur Young continued the inimitable records of his tour, Eden wrote a history of the poor which has served both as a basis and as a model for all succeeding historians of industry, while Malthus showed by a careful investigation of history what were the forces which had as a matter of fact controlled the growth of population in different countries and at different times

[1] See below Ch. v Adam Smith saw that while economic science is based on a study of facts, the facts are so complex, that they generally can teach nothing directly, they must be interpreted by careful reasoning and analysis And as Hume said, the *Wealth of Nations* "is so much illustrated with curious facts that it must take the public attention" This is exactly what Adam Smith did he seldom attempted to prove anything by detailed induction or history. The data of his proofs were chiefly facts that were within everyone's knowledge, facts physical, mental and moral But he illustrated his proofs by curious and instructive facts; he thus gave them life and force, and made his readers feel that they were dealing with problems of the real world, and not with abstractions; and his book, though not well arranged, is a model of method

Bentham's opposition to customary restrictions on trade for which no valid reason could be given, greatly influenced English economists early in this century.

But on the whole the most influential of the immediate successors of Adam Smith was Bentham. He wrote little on economics himself, but he went far towards setting the tone of the rising school of English economists at the beginning of the nineteenth century. He was an uncompromising logician and averse to all restrictions and regulations for which no clear reason could be given, and his pitiless demands that they should justify their existence received support from the circumstances of the age. England had won her unique position in the world by her quickness in adapting herself to every new economic movement; while by their adherence to old-fashioned ways the nations of Central Europe had been prevented from turning to account their great natural resources. The business men of England therefore were inclined to think that the influence of custom and sentiment in business affairs was harmful, that in England at least it had diminished, was diminishing, and would soon vanish away: and the disciples of Bentham were not slow to conclude that they need not concern themselves much about custom It was enough for them to discuss the tendencies of man's action on the supposition that everyone was always on the alert to find out what course would best promote his own interest, and was free and quick to follow it[1].

There is then some justice in the charges frequently brought against the English economists of the beginning of this century, that they neglected to inquire with sufficient care whether a greater range might not be given to collective as opposed to individual action in social and economic affairs; that they exaggerated the strength of competition and its rapidity of action: and there is some ground, though a very slight one, for the charge that their work is marred

1 Another way in which he influenced the young economists around him was through his passionate desire for security. He was indeed an ardent reformer. He was an enemy of all artificial distinctions between different classes of men; he declared with emphasis that any one man's happiness was as important as any other's, and that the aim of all action should be to increase the sum total of happiness; he admitted that other things being equal this sum total would be the greater, the more equally wealth was distributed. Nevertheless so full was his mind of the terror of the French revolution, and so great were the evils which he attributed to the smallest attack on security that, daring analyst as he was, he felt himself and he fostered in his disciples an almost superstitious reverence for the existing institutions of private property.

by a certain hardness of outline and even harshness of temper. These faults were partly due to Bentham's direct influence, partly to the spirit of the age of which he was an exponent But they were partly also due to the fact that economic study had again got a good deal into the hands of men whose strength lay in vigorous action rather than in philosophical thought

Many of whom had a bias towards rapid generalization.

§ 5. Statesmen and merchants again threw themselves into problems of money and foreign trade with even more energy than they used to do when these questions were first started in the earlier period of the great economic change at the end of the Middle Ages It might at first sight seem probable that their contact with real life, their wide experience, and their vast knowledge of facts would have led them to take a wide survey of human nature and to found their reasonings on a broad basis But the training of practical life often leads to a too rapid generalization from personal experience.

Their work was excellent so long as they treated of money,

So long as they were well within their own province their work was excellent. The theory of currency is just that part of economic science in which but little harm is done by neglecting to take much account of any human motives except the desire for wealth; and the brilliant school of deductive reasoning which Ricardo led was here on safe ground[1].

[1] He is often spoken of as a representative Englishman but this is just what he was not His strong constructive originality is the mark of the highest genius in all nations But that quality by which he is distinguished from most other scientific geniuses is his aversion to inductions and his delight in abstract reasonings And this quality is due, not to his English education, but, as Bagehot points out, to his Semitic origin Nearly every branch of the Semitic race has had some special genius for dealing with abstractions, and several of them have had a bias towards the abstract calculations connected with the trade of money dealing, and its modern developments There is no truly English economist whose method resembles that of Ricardo, his power of threading his way without slip through intricate paths to new and unexpected results has never been surpassed But it is difficult even for an Englishman to follow his track, and his foreign critics have, as a rule, failed to detect the real drift and purpose of his work. Even the ablest of them frequently undertake to refute him by establishing propositions which are consistent with his and often even involved in them For he never explains himself he never shows what his purpose is in working first on one hypothesis and then on another, nor how by properly combining the results of his different hypotheses it is possible to cover a great variety of practical questions See the Note at the end of Book v It is to be remembered

BOOK I CH. IV

and foreign trade,

The economists next addressed themselves to the theory of foreign trade and cleared away many of the flaws which Adam Smith had left in it. There is no other part of economics except the theory of money, which so nearly falls within the range of pure deductive reasoning. It is true that a full discussion of a free trade policy must take account of many considerations that are not strictly economic; but most of these, though important for agricultural countries, and especially for new countries, had little bearing in the case of England.

nor did they neglect statistics

During all this time the study of economic facts was not neglected in England. The statistical studies of Petty, Arthur Young, Eden, and others were ably continued by Tooke, M'Culloch and Porter And though it may be true that an undue prominence is given in their writings to those facts which were of direct interest to merchants and other capitalists, the same cannot be said of the admirable series of Parliamentary inquiries into the condition of the working classes, which were brought about by the influence of the economists. In fact, the public and private collections of statistics and the economic histories that were produced in England at the end of the last century and the beginning of this, may fairly be regarded as the origin of systematic historical and statistical studies in economics.

and inquiries into the condition of the working classes

But they lacked a knowledge of the Comparative Method

Nevertheless there was a certain narrowness in their work: it was truly historical; but for the greater part it was not "comparative." Hume, Adam Smith, Arthur Young and others had been led by their own instinctive genius and the example of Montesquieu occasionally to compare social facts of different ages and different countries, and to draw lessons from the comparison. But no one had grasped the notion of the comparative study of history on a systematic plan. In consequence the writers of that time, able and earnest as they were in their search for the actual facts of life, worked rather at haphazard. They overlooked whole groups of facts which we now see to be of vital importance, and they

however that his *Principles* was not originally designed for publication It consists of terse notes, written for the benefit of himself and perhaps a few friends, on points of special difficulty.

often failed to make the best use of those which they collected. And this narrowness was intensified when they passed from the collection of facts to general reasonings about them

Their desire for simplicity led them sometimes to argue as though all mankind had the same habits of mind as city men

§ 6. For the sake of simplicity of argument, Ricardo and his followers often spoke as though they regarded man as a constant quantity, and they never gave themselves enough trouble to study his variations. The people whom they knew most intimately were city men; and they sometimes expressed themselves so carelessly as almost to imply that other Englishmen were very much like those whom they knew in the city

They were aware that the inhabitants of other countries had peculiarities of their own that deserved study; but they seemed to regard such differences as superficial and sure to be removed, as soon as other nations had got to know that better way which Englishmen were ready to teach them The same bent of mind that led our lawyers to impose English civil law on the Hindoos, led our economists to work out their theories on the tacit supposition that the world was made up of city men. And though this did little harm so long as they were treating of money and foreign trade, it led them astray as to the relations between the different industrial classes It caused them to speak of labour as a commodity without staying to throw themselves into the point of view of the workman, and without dwelling upon the allowances to be made for his human passions, his instincts and habits, his sympathies and antipathies, his class jealousies and class adhesiveness, his want of knowledge and of the opportunities for free and vigorous action. They therefore attributed to the forces of supply and demand a much more mechanical and regular action than is to be found in real life: and they laid down laws with regard to profits and wages that did not really hold even for England in their own time[1]

[1] As regards wages there were even some logical errors in the conclusions they deduced from their own premises These errors when traced back to their origin are little more than careless modes of expression. But they were seized upon eagerly by those who cared little for the scientific study of economics, and cared only to quote its doctrines for the purpose of keeping the working classes in their place, and perhaps no other great school of thinkers has ever suffered so

BOOK I CH IV.

They did not allow enough for the dependence of man's character on his circumstances The Socialists

But their most vital fault was that they did not see how liable to change are the habits and institutions of industry. In particular they did not see that the poverty of the poor is the chief cause of that weakness and inefficiency which are the causes of their poverty. they had not the faith that modern economists have in the possibility of a vast improvement in the condition of the working classes.

The perfectibility of man had indeed been asserted by the socialists. But their views were based on little historic and scientific study; and were expressed with an extravagance that moved the contempt of the business-like economists of the age. The socialists did not study the doctrines which they attacked; and there was no difficulty in showing that they had not understood the nature and efficiency of the existing economic organization of society. The economists therefore did not trouble themselves to examine carefully any of their doctrines, and least of all their speculations as to human nature[1]

But the socialists were men who had felt intensely, and who knew something about the hidden springs of human action of which the economists took no account Buried among their wild rhapsodies there were shrewd observations and pregnant suggestions from which philosophers and economists had much to learn And gradually their influence began to tell Comte's debts to them were very great; and the crisis of John Stuart Mill's life, as he tells us in his autobiography, came to him from reading them

The growing tendency of economists to take

§ 7 When we come to compare the modern view of the vital problem of the Distribution of Wealth with that which prevailed at the beginning of the century we shall find that

much from the way in which its "parasites" (to use a term that is commonly applied to them in Germany), professing to simplify economic doctrines, really enunciated them without the conditions required to make them true

[1] A partial exception must be made for Malthus, whose studies of population were suggested by Godwin's essay But he did not properly belong to the Ricardian school and he was not a man of business Half a century later Bastiat, a lucid writer but not a profound thinker, maintained the extravagant doctrine that the natural organization of society under the influence of competition is the best not only that can be practically effected, but even that can be theoretically conceived.

over and above all changes in detail and all improvements in scientific accuracy of reasoning, there is a fundamental change in treatment; for, while the earlier economists argued as though man's character and efficiency were to be regarded as a fixed quantity, modern economists keep constantly in mind the fact that it is a product of the circumstances under which he has lived. This change in the point of view of economics is partly due to the fact that the changes in human nature during the last fifty years have been so rapid as to force themselves on the attention; partly to the direct influence of individual writers, socialists and others; and partly to the indirect influence of a similar change in some branches of natural science

account of the pliability of human nature

At the beginning of this century the mathematico-physical group of sciences were in the ascendant, and these sciences, widely as they differ from one another, have this point in common, that their subject-matter is constant and unchanged in all countries and in all ages The progress of science was familiar to men's minds but the development of the subject-matter of science was strange to them As the century wore on the biological group of sciences were slowly making way, and people were getting clearer ideas as to the nature of organic growth They were learning that if the subject-matter of a science passes through different stages of development, the laws which apply to one stage will seldom apply without modification to others, the laws of the science must have a development corresponding to that of the things of which they treat The influence of this new notion gradually spread to the sciences which relate to man. and showed itself in the works of Goethe, Hegel, Comte and others

is partly due to the influence of biological studies

At last the speculations of biology made a great stride forwards its discoveries fascinated the attention of the world as those of physics had done in earlier years, and there was a marked change in the tone of the moral and historical sciences Economics has shared in the general movement, and is getting to pay every year a greater attention to the pliability of human nature, and to the way in which the character of man affects and is affected by

BOOK I. CH IV

John Stuart Mill

the prevalent methods of the production, distribution and consumption of wealth. The first important indication of the new movement was seen in John Stuart Mill's admirable *Principles of Political Economy*[1].

Recent English economists

Mill's followers have continued his movement away from the position taken up by the immediate followers of Ricardo; and the human as distinguished from the mechanical element is taking a more and more prominent place in economics The new temper is shown in Cliffe Leslie's historical inquiries, and in the many-sided work of Bagehot, Cairnes and other writers yet living, but above all in that of Jevons, which has secured a permanent and notable place in economic history by its rare combination of many various qualities of the highest order.

Characteristics of modern English work

A higher notion of social duty is spreading everywhere In Parliament, in the press and in the pulpit, the spirit of humanity speaks more distinctly and more earnestly. Mill and the economists who have followed him have helped onwards this general movement, and they in their turn have been helped onwards by it. Partly for this reason, partly in consequence of the modern growth of historical science, their study of facts has been broader and more philosophic It is true that the historical and statistical work of some of the earlier economists has seldom if ever been surpassed But much information which was beyond their reach, is now accessible to everyone; and economists who have

[1] James Mill had educated his son in the straitest tenets of Bentham and Ricardo, and had implanted in his mind a zeal for clearness and definiteness And in 1830 John Mill wrote an essay on economic method in which he proposed to give increased sharpness of outline to the abstractions of the science. He faced Ricardo's tacit assumption that no motive of action except the desire for wealth need be much considered by the economist, he held that it was dangerous so long as it was not distinctly stated, but no longer, and he half promised a treatise which should be deliberately and openly based on it But he did not redeem the promise A change had come over his tone of thought and of feeling before he published in 1848 his great economic work He called it *Principles of Political Economy, with some of their Applications to Social Philosophy* [it is significant that he did not say *to other branches of Social Philosophy*, comp Ingram's *History*, p 154], and he made in it no attempt to mark off by a rigid line those reasonings which assume that man's sole motive is the pursuit of wealth from those which do not The change in his attitude was a part of the great changes that were going on in the world around him, though he was not fully aware of their influence on himself.

neither McCulloch's familiarity with practical business, nor his vast historical learning, are enabled to get a view of the relations of economic doctrine to the true facts of life which is both broader and clearer than his. In this they have been helped by the general improvement which has taken place in the methods of all sciences, including that of history

The abandonment of dogma, the development of analysis

Thus in every way economic reasoning is now more exact than it was: the premisses assumed in any inquiry are stated with more rigid precision than formerly. But this greater exactness of thought is partly destructive in its action, it is showing that many of the older applications of general reasoning were invalid, because no care had been taken to think out all the assumptions that were implied and to see whether they could fairly be made in the special cases under discussion. As a result, many dogmas have been destroyed which appeared to be simple only because they were loosely expressed; but which, for that very reason, served as an armoury with which partisan disputants (chiefly of the capitalist class) have equipped themselves for the fray This destructive work might appear at first sight to have diminished the value of processes of general reasoning in economics: but really it has had the opposite result. It has cleared the ground for newer and stronger machinery, which is being steadily and patiently built up. It has enabled us to take broader views of life, to proceed more surely though more slowly, to be more scientific and much less dogmatic than those good and great men who bore the first brunt of the battle with the difficulties of economic problems, and to whose pioneering work we owe our own more easy course.

The change may, perhaps, be regarded as a passing onward from that early stage in the development of scientific method, in which the operations of Nature are represented as conventionally simplified for the purpose of enabling them to be described in short and easy sentences, to that higher stage in which they are studied more carefully, and represented more nearly as they are, even at the expense of some loss of simplicity and definiteness, and even apparent lucidity.

BOOK I CH IV

And in consequence general reasoning in economics has made more rapid progress, and established a firmer position in this generation in which it is subject to hostile criticism at every step, than when it was at the height of its popularity and its authority was seldom challenged.

So far we have looked at recent progress from the point of view of England only: but progress in England has been only one side of a broader movement which has extended over the whole western world.

French economists

§ 8 English economists have had many followers and many critics in foreign countries. The French school has had a continuous development from its own great thinkers in the eighteenth century, and has avoided many errors and confusions, particularly with regard to wages, which have been common among the second rank of English economists From the time of Say downwards it has done a great deal of useful work In Cournot it has had a constructive thinker of the highest genius, while Fourier, St Simon, Proudhon and Louis Blanc have made many of the most valuable, as well as many of the wildest suggestions of Socialism

American School.

A generation ago, the "American school" of economists was supposed to consist of the group of Protectionists who followed Carey's lead But there are now growing up in America new schools of thinkers, who are studying the science for its own sake; and there are many signs that America is on the way to take the same leading position in economic thought, that she has already taken in economic practice.

Economic science is showing signs of renewed vigour in two of its old homes, Holland and Italy. And more especially is the vigorous analytical work of the Austrian economists attracting much attention in all countries

German economists

But on the whole the most important economic work that has been done on the Continent in this century is that of Germany. While recognizing the leadership of Adam Smith, the German economists have been irritated more than any others by what they have regarded as the insular narrowness and self-confidence of the Ricardian school In particular they resented the way in which the English advocates of free trade tacitly assumed that a proposition which had been established with regard to a manufacturing country, such as England was, could be carried over without modification to agricultural countries. The brilliant genius and national enthusiasm of List overthrew this presumption; and showed that the Ricardians had taken but little account of the indirect effects of free trade. No great harm might be done in neglecting them so far as England was concerned, because there they were in the main beneficial and thus added to the strength of its direct effects But he showed that in Germany and still more in America, many of its indirect effects were evil; and he contended that these evils outweighed its direct benefits. Many of his arguments were invalid, but some of them were not, and as the English economists scornfully refused them a patient discussion, able and public-spirited men, impressed by the force of those which were sound, acquiesced in the use for the purposes of popular agitation of other arguments which were unscientific, but which appealed with greater force to the working classes.

List

American manufacturers adopted List as their advocate· and the beginning of his fame, as well as of the systematic advocacy of protectionist doctrines in America, was in the wide circulation by them of a popular treatise which he wrote for them[1]

The Germans are fond of saying that the Physiocrats and the school of Adam Smith underrated the importance of national life; that they tended to sacrifice it on the one

The Germans press the claims of national-

[1] It has already been observed that List overlooked the tendency of modern inter-communication to make the development of different nations synchronize His patriotic fervour perverted in many ways his scientific judgment· but Germans listened eagerly to his argument that every country had to go through the same stages of development that England had gone through, and that she had protected her manufactures when she was in transition from the agricultural to the manufacturing stage. He had a genuine desire for truth, his method was in harmony with the comparative method of inquiry which is being pursued with vigour by all classes of students in Germany, but especially by her historians and lawyers; and the direct and indirect influence of his thought has been very great His *Outlines of a New System of Political Economy* appeared in Philadelphia in 1827, and his *Das nationale System der Politischen Oekonomie* in 1840 It is a disputed point whether Carey owed much to List. As to the general relations between their doctrines, see Knies, *Pol Oek*, 2nd edition, pp 440, &c

BOOK I. CH. IV.

ism against those of individualism on the one hand and cosmopolitanism on the other.

hand to a selfish individualism and on the other to a limp philanthropic cosmopolitanism They urge that List did great service in stimulating a feeling of patriotism, which is more generous than that of individualism, and more sturdy and definite than that of cosmopolitanism. It may be doubted whether the cosmopolitan sympathies of the Physiocrats and of the English economists have been as strong as the Germans think. But there is no question that the recent political history of Germany has influenced the tone of her economists in the direction of nationalism Surrounded by powerful and aggressive armies Germany can exist only by the aid of an ardent national feeling, and German writers have insisted eagerly, perhaps too eagerly, that altruistic feelings have a more limited scope in the economic relations between countries than in those between individuals

Their great work in the study of economic history by the comparative method, and in relation to general history and jurisprudence.

But though national in their sympathies, the Germans are nobly international in their studies They have taken the lead in the "comparative" study of economic, as well as of general history They have brought side by side the social and industrial phenomena of different countries and of different ages, have so arranged them that they throw light upon and interpret one another, and have studied them all in connection with the suggestive history of jurisprudence[1] The work of a few members of this school is tainted by exaggeration, and even by a narrow contempt for the reasonings of the Ricardian school, the drift and purpose of which they have themselves failed to understand · and this has led to much bitter and dreary controversy But with scarcely an exception, the leaders of the school have been free from this narrowness. It would be difficult to overrate the value of the work which they and their fellow workers in other countries have done in tracing and explaining the history of economic habits and institutions It is one of the great achievements of our age, and an important addition to our real wealth. It has done more

[1] The excellence of this work may perhaps partly be attributed to the union of legal and economic studies in the avenues to many careers in Germany as in other countries of the Continent A splendid instance is to be found in Prof Wagner's contributions to economics

than almost anything else to broaden our ideas, to increase our knowledge of ourselves, and to help us to understand the central plan, as it were, of the Divine government of the world.

Their work in economic theory and analysis

They have given their chief attention to the historical treatment of the science, and to its application to the conditions of German social and political life, especially to the economic duties of the German bureaucracy. But led by the brilliant genius of Hermann they have made careful and profound analyses which add much to our knowledge, and they have greatly extended the boundaries of economic theory[1]

German Socialism

German thought has also given an impetus to the study of socialism and the functions of the State. It is from German writers, some of whom have been of Jewish origin, that the world has received the greater part of the most thoroughgoing of recent propositions for utilizing the property of the world for the benefit of the community with but little reference to the existing incidents of ownership It is true that on closer investigation their work turns out to be less original as well as less profound than at first sight appears but it derives great power from its dialectic ingenuity, its brilliant style, and in some cases from its wide-reaching though distorted historical learning.

Besides the revolutionary socialists, there is a large body of thinkers in Germany who are setting themselves to insist on the scantiness of the authority which the institution of private property in its present form can derive from history, and to urge on broad scientific and philosophic grounds a reconsideration of the rights of society as against the individual The political and military institutions of the German people have recently increased their natural ten-

Germans and English

[1] In such matters, the English, the Germans, the Austrians, and indeed every nation claim for themselves more than others are willing to allow them. This is partly because each nation has its own intellectual virtues, and misses them in the writings of foreigners; while it does not quite understand the complaints which others make as to its shortcomings But the chief reason is that, since a new idea is generally of gradual growth, and is often worked out by more than one nation at the same time; each of those nations is likely to claim it, and thus to underestimate the originality of the others

have much to learn from one another

dency to rely more on Government and less on individual enterprise than Englishmen do. And in all questions bearing on social reforms the English and German nations have much to learn from one another.

There is some danger that the severe and less popular task of careful scientific reasoning may be neglected

But amid all the historical learning and reforming enthusiasm of the age there is danger that a difficult but important part of the work of economic science may be neglected The popularity of economics has tended in some measure to the neglect of careful and rigorous reasoning. The growing prominence of what has been called the biological view of the science has tended to throw the notions of economic law and measurement into the background, as though such notions were too hard and rigid to be applied to the living and ever-changing economic organism. But biology itself teaches us that the vertebrate organisms are the most highly developed The modern economic organism is vertebrate; and the science which deals with it should not be invertebrate It should have that delicacy and sensitiveness of touch which are required for enabling it to adapt itself closely to the real phenomena of the world, but none the less must it have a firm backbone of careful reasoning and analysis.

CHAPTER V.

THE SCOPE OF ECONOMICS[1]

BOOK I. CH V

A unified Social Science, however desirable, is unattainable,

§ 1 THERE are some who hold, with Comte, that the scope of any profitable study of man's action in society must be coextensive with the whole of social science. They argue that all the aspects of social life are so closely connected, that a special study of any one of them must be futile; and they urge on economists to abandon their distinctive *rôle* and to devote themselves to the general advancement of a unified and all embracing social science But the whole range of man's actions in society is too wide and too various to be analysed and explained by a single intellectual effort. Comte himself and Mr Herbert Spencer have brought to the task unsurpassed knowledge and great genius, they have made epochs in thought by their broad surveys and their suggestive hints, but they can hardly be said even to have made a commencement with the construction of a unified social science[2].

as is shown by experience,

The physical sciences made slow progress so long as the brilliant but impatient Greek genius insisted on searching after a single basis for the explanation of all physical phenomena, and their rapid progress in the modern age is due to a breaking up of broad problems into their component parts Doubtless there is a unity underlying all the forces of nature, but whatever progress has been made towards

and as may be inferred from the history of Physical Science

[1] The reader is referred to Dr Keynes' *Scope and Method of Political Economy* for a more full and detailed investigation of many of the subjects of this and the next chapters

[2] A less ambitious aim has been more nearly attained in the *Bau und Leben des Socialen Körpers* of the eminent economist Professor Schaffle

BOOK I CH V

discovering it, has depended on knowledge obtained by persistent specialized study, no less than on occasional broad surveys of the field of nature as a whole. And similar patient detailed work is required to supply the materials which may enable future ages to understand better than we can the forces that govern the development of the social organism

Comte showed well the evils of extreme specialization,

But on the other hand it must be fully conceded to Comte that, even in the physical sciences, it is the duty of those who are giving their chief work to a limited field, to keep up close and constant correspondence with those who are engaged in neighbouring fields. Specialists who never look beyond their own domain are apt to see things out of true proportion, much of the knowledge they get together is of comparatively little use; they work away at the details of old problems which have lost most of their significance and have been supplanted by new questions rising out of new points of view, and they fail to gain that large illumination which the progress of every science throws by comparison and analogy on those around it. Comte did good service therefore by insisting that the solidarity of social phenomena must render the work of exclusive specialists even more futile in social than in physical science. Mill

but failed to prove that there should be none

conceding this continues.—"A person is not likely to be a good economist who is nothing else. Social phenomena acting and reacting on one another, they cannot rightly be understood apart; but this by no means proves that the material and industrial phenomena of society are not themselves susceptible of useful generalizations, but only that these generalizations must necessarily be relative to a given form of civilization and a given stage of social advancement[1]."

[1] Mill, *On Comte*, p. 82 His controversy with Comte is still worth studying. Comte's arguments have recently been restated with great force and eloquence by Dr Ingram but they do not appear to have shaken Mill's position that Comte, though right when he affirmed, was wrong when he denied And this remark may be extended it would seem that in the long controversy which has been waged in England, Germany, and more recently in America, as to the right method of economic study, nearly every one has been right when he has affirmed that a certain method is useful, it has generally been the one best adapted for that part of the many-sided work of economics in which he has had the most interest But he has been wrong in denying that other methods are useful· they may be un

§ 2. This is a valid answer to Comte's denial of the utility of an independent science of economics. But it does not show that the scope assigned to economics by Mill and his predecessors was exactly the right one. Any widening of that scope must no doubt result in some sacrifice of definiteness and precision, and the resulting loss may be greater than the gain But it need not necessarily be so; and what is wanted is a general principle which shall determine the point in the widening of the scope of economics, at which the growing loss of scientific precision would begin to outweigh the gain of increasing reality and philosophic completeness.

But the limits assigned to their science by the older economists were too narrow

We must then inquire what are the advantages which have enabled economics, though far behind the more advanced physical sciences, yet to outstrip every other branch of social science. For it would seem reasonable to conclude that any broadening of the scope of the science which brings it more closely to correspond with the facts, and to take account of the higher aims of life, will be a gain on the balance provided it does not deprive the science of those advantages: but that any further extension beyond that limit would cause more loss than gain.

§ 3 The advantage which economics has over other branches of social science appears to arise from the fact that it concerns itself chiefly with those desires, aspirations and other affections of human nature, the outward manifestations of which appear as incentives to action in a form which is easily measurable, and which therefore are specially amenable to treatment by scientific machinery An opening is made for the methods and the tests of science as soon as the force of a person's motives can be measured by the sum of money which he will just give up in order to secure a desired satisfaction, or again the sum which is just required to induce him to undergo a certain fatigue[1].

Economics concerns itself chiefly with motives that are easily measurable

suited for those purposes of which he has been chiefly thinking; but they may probably be better suited than his own favourite methods for other and equally important purposes But more of this in the next chapter.

[1] J S Mill had himself indicated the centre of the strength of economics when he says (*Logic*, Book VI. Ch. IX § 3) that in economic phenomena "the psychological law mainly concerned is the familiar one that a greater gain is preferred to

But here a little explanation is needed. We cannot measure any affection of the mind directly, the utmost we can do is to measure it indirectly through its effect No one can compare and measure accurately against one another even his own mental states at different times: and no one can measure the mental states of another at all except indirectly and conjecturally by their effects.

Even common pleasures and pains can be compared only through the strength of the incentives which they supply to action,

It is not merely that some affections belong to man's higher nature and others to his lower, and are thus different in kind. But further, there is no means of comparing directly with one another mere physical pleasures and pains they can only be compared indirectly by their effects; and even this comparison is necessarily to some extent conjectural, unless they occur to the same person at the same time. We cannot directly compare the pleasures which two persons derive from smoking, nor even those which the same person derives from it at different times But if we find a man in doubt whether to spend a few pence on a cigar, or a cup of tea, or on riding home instead of walking home, then we may follow ordinary usage, and say that he expects from them equal pleasures On another day he may have neither more nor less money to spare, but his mood may be different, and perhaps there may be several ways in which he can get more pleasure from spending the money than he could have got on the earlier day from any way of spending it[1].

If then we wish to compare even physical gratifications, we must do it not directly, but indirectly by the incentives which they afford to action. If the desires to secure either of two pleasures will induce people in similar circumstances each to do just an hour's extra work, or will induce men in the same rank of life and with the same means each to pay a shilling for it, we then may say that those pleasures are

a smaller," and argues that science gets a better hold in economic than in other social phenomena because it deals with motives that can be easily measured one against another

[1] For simplicity this illustration refers to things consumed in a single use But most of the material objects of desire are more or less enduring sources of gratification· and of course the desire for such an object is not generally accompanied by a conscious anticipation of the particular pleasures to be derived from its use, among which a prominent place must often be given to the mere pleasure of possession We must return to these points.

equal for our purposes, because the desires for them are equally strong incentives to action for persons who are *primâ facie* similar and similarly situated[1]

and this indirect comparison can be applied to all classes of desire

Thus measuring a mental state, as men do in ordinary life, by its motor-force or the incentive which it affords to action, no new difficulty is introduced by the fact that some of the motives of which we have to take account belong to man's higher nature, and others to his lower.

For suppose that the person whom we saw doubting between several little gratifications for himself had thought after a while of a poor invalid whom he would pass on his way home, and had spent some time in making up his mind whether he would choose a physical gratification for himself, or would do a kindly act and rejoice in another's joy. As his desires turned now towards the one, now the other, there would be change in the quality of his mental states, which it is the function of the psychologist to analyse. But the economist studies mental states rather through their manifestations than in themselves; and if he finds they afford evenly balanced incentives to action, he treats them *primâ facie* as for his purpose equal. No doubt his concern with them does not end there. Even for the narrower uses of economic studies, it is important to know whether the desires which prevail are such as will help to build up a strong and righteous character And in the broader uses of those studies, when they are being applied to practical problems, the economist, like every one else, must concern himself with the ultimate aims of man, and take account of differences in real value between gratifications that are equally powerful incentives to action and have therefore equal economic measures. A study of these measures is only the starting-point of economics but it is the starting-point[2]

[1] The objections raised by some philosophers to speaking of two pleasures as equal, under any circumstances, seem to apply only to uses of the phrase other than those with which the economist is concerned

[2] It has however unfortunately happened that the customary uses of economic terms have sometimes suggested the belief that economists are adherents of the philosophical system of Hedonism or of Utilitarianism For, while they have generally taken for granted that the greatest pleasures are those which come with the endeavour to do one's duty, they have spoken of "pleasures" and "pains" as supplying the motives to all action and have thus brought themselves under the

BOOK I
CH. V

§ 4 There are several other limitations of the measurement of motive by money to be discussed The first of these arises from the necessity of taking account of the variations in the amount of pleasure, or other satisfaction, represented by the same sum of money to different persons and under different circumstances

censure of those philosophers, with whom it is a matter of principle to insist that the desire to do one's duty is a different thing from a desire for the pleasure which, if one happens to think of the matter at all, one may expect from doing it, though perhaps it may be not incorrectly described as a desire for "self-satisfaction" or "the satisfaction of the permanent self."

Thus T H Green (*Prolegomena to Ethics*, pp 165-6) says —The pleasure to be derived from doing one's duty "cannot be the exciting cause of the desire, any more than the pleasure of satisfying hunger can be the exciting cause of hunger .. When the idea of which the realisation is sought is not that of enjoying any pleasure, the fact that self-satisfaction is sought in the effort to realize the idea of the desired object does not make pleasure the object of the desire The man who calmly faces a life of suffering in the fulfilment of what he conceives to be his mission could not bear to do otherwise So to live is his good If he could attain the consciousness of having accomplished, if he could count himself to have apprehended—and probably just in proportion to the elevation of his character he is unable to do so—he would find satisfaction in the consciousness and with it a certain pleasure But supposing this pleasure to be attained, only the exigencies of a theory could suggest the notion that, as so much pleasure, it makes up for the pleasures foregone and the pains endured in the life through which it has been reached" While to others it appears obvious that the pain of deliberately refusing to do his duty, and so to live "as is his good," is less than the pains which he would endure in so living

It is true that this large use of "pain and pleasure" has sometimes served as a bridge by which to pass from individualistic Hedonism to a complete ethical creed, without recognizing the necessity for the introduction of an independent major premiss, and for such a premiss the necessity would appear to be absolute, although opinions will perhaps always differ as to its form Some will regard it as the Categorical Imperative; while others will regard it as a simple belief that, whatever be the origin of our moral instincts, their indications are borne out by a verdict of the experience of mankind to the effect that true happiness is not to be had without self-respect, and that self-respect is to be had only on the condition of endeavouring so to live as to promote the progress of the human race

It is clearly not the part of economics to appear to take a side in ethical controversy and since there is a general agreement that all incentives to action, in so far as they are conscious desires at all, may without impropriety be spoken of shortly as desires for "satisfaction," it may perhaps be well to use this word instead of "pleasure," when occasion arises for referring to the aims of all desires, whether appertaining to man's higher or lower nature The simple antithesis to satisfaction is "dissatisfaction" but perhaps it may be well to use the shorter and equally colourless word "detriment" in its place

Reference may also be made to Prof Mackenzie's interesting discussion of "The relations between Ethics and Economics" in the *International Journal of Ethics*, vol III, and in his *Introduction to Social Philosophy* but his position appears to be even more uncompromising than Green's

A shilling may measure a greater pleasure (or other satisfaction) at one time than at another even for the same person; because money may be more plentiful with him, or because his sensibility may vary[1] And persons whose antecedents are similar, and who are outwardly like one another, are often affected in very different ways by similar events. When, for instance, a band of city school children are sent out for a day's holiday in the country, it is probable that no two of them derive from it enjoyment exactly the same in kind, or equal in intensity. The same surgical operation causes different amounts of pain to different people. Of two parents who are, so far as we can tell, equally affectionate, one will suffer much more than the other from the loss of a favourite son Some who are not very sensitive generally are yet specially susceptible to particular kinds of pleasure and pain, while differences in nature and education make one man's total capacity for pleasure or pain much greater than another's

The same price measures different satisfactions even to persons with equal incomes,

It would therefore not be safe to say that any two men with the same income derive equal benefit from its use, or that they would suffer equal pain from the same diminution of it Although when a tax of £1 is taken from each of two persons having an income of £300 a-year, each will give up that £1 worth of pleasure (or other satisfaction) which he can most easily part with, i e., each will give up what is measured to him by just £1, yet the intensities of the satisfaction given up may not be nearly equal.

Nevertheless, if we take averages sufficiently broad to cause the personal peculiarities of individuals to counterbalance one another, the money which people of equal incomes will give to obtain a benefit or avoid an injury is a good measure of the benefit or injury. If there are a thousand persons living in Sheffield, and another thousand in Leeds, each with about £100 a-year, and a tax of £1 is levied on all of them, we may be sure that the loss of pleasure or other injury which the tax will cause in Sheffield is of about equal importance with that which it will cause in Leeds · and anything that increased all the incomes by £1 would give

but these differences may generally be neglected when we consider the average of large numbers of people

[1] Compare Prof Edgeworth's *Mathematical Psychics*

BOOK I CH V

command over equivalent pleasures and other benefits in the two towns This probability becomes greater still if all of them are adult males engaged in the same trade, and therefore presumably somewhat similar in sensibility and temperament, in taste and education Nor is the probability much diminished, if we take the family as our unit, and compare the loss of pleasure that results from diminishing by £1 the income of each of a thousand families with incomes of £100 a-year in the two places

The significance of a given price is greater for the poor than the rich.

Next we must take account of the fact that a stronger incentive will be required to induce a person to pay a given price for anything if he is poor than if he is rich. A shilling is the measure of less pleasure to a rich man than to a poor one. A rich man in doubt whether to spend a shilling on a single cigar, is weighing against one another smaller pleasures than a poor man, who is doubting whether to spend a shilling on a supply of tobacco that will last him for a month The clerk with £100 a year will walk to business in a much heavier rain than the clerk with £300 a year; for a sixpenny omnibus fare measures a greater pleasure to the poorer man than to the richer If the poorer man spends the money, he will suffer more from the want of it afterwards than the richer would The pleasure that is measured in the poorer man's mind by sixpence is greater than that measured by it in the richer man's mind.

But this is not important in comparing two groups composed of rich and poor in like proportions

But this source of error also is lessened when we are able to consider the actions and the motives of large groups of people. If we know, for instance, that a bank failure has taken £200,000 from the people of Leeds and £100,000 from those of Sheffield, we may fairly assume that the suffering caused in Leeds has been about twice as great as in Sheffield, unless indeed we have some special reason for believing that the shareholders of the bank in the one town were a richer class than those in the other; or that the loss of employment caused by it pressed in uneven proportions on the working classes in the two towns.

Increase of material means sometimes

By far the greater number of the events with which economics deals affect in about equal proportions all the different classes of society, so that if the money measures of the happiness caused by two events are equal, it is reasonable and in accordance with common usage to regard the amounts of the happiness in the two cases as equivalent. And further as money is likely to be turned to the higher uses of life in about equal proportions, by any two large groups of people taken without special bias from any two parts of the western world, there is even some *primâ facie* probability that equal additions to their material resources will make about equal additions to the fulness of life, and the true progress of the human race.

a fair measure of real progress

Action is largely ruled by habit

§ 5 To pass to another point. When we speak of the measurement of desire by the action to which it forms the incentive, it is not to be supposed that we assume every action to be deliberate, and the outcome of calculation For in this, as in every other respect, economics takes man just as he is in ordinary life · and in ordinary life people do not weigh beforehand the results of every action, whether the impulses to it come from their higher nature or their lower[1]

But habit itself is largely based on deliberate choice.

Some people are of wayward temperament, and could give no good account even to themselves of the motives of their action But if a man is steadfast and thoughtful, even his impulses are the products of habits which he has adopted more or less deliberately And, whether they are an expression of his higher nature or not whether they are the mandates of his conscience, the pressure of social connection, or the claims of his bodily wants, he yields a certain relative precedence to them without reflection now, because on previous occasions he has decided deliberately to yield that relative precedence the predominant attractiveness of one course of action over others, even when not the result of calculation at the time, is the product of more or less deliberate decisions made by him before in somewhat similar cases[2]

[1] This is specially true of that group of gratifications, which is sometimes named "the pleasures of the chase" They include not only the light-hearted emulation of games and pastimes, of hunts and steeplechases, but the more serious contests of professional and business life and they will occupy a good deal of our attention in discussions of the causes that govern wages and profits, and forms of industrial organization

[2] Some reference to these characteristics of habit and custom has been made in Ch II, and we shall need to return to them towards the end of the treatise

BOOK I
CH. V.

especially as regards business conduct

Now the side of life with which economics is specially concerned is that in which man's conduct is most deliberate, and in which he most often reckons up the advantages and disadvantages of any particular action before he enters on it And further it is that side of his life in which, when he does follow habit and custom, and proceed for the moment without calculation, the habits and customs themselves are most nearly sure to have proceeded from a close and careful watching the advantages and disadvantages of different courses of conduct[1]

It is true that when a habit or a custom which has grown up under one set of conditions, influences action under other conditions, there is so far no exact relation between the effort and the end which is attained by it. But in business matters in the modern world such habits quickly die away[2].

Thus business work has generally a money measure

Thus then the most systematic part of people's lives is generally that by which they earn their living. The work of all those engaged in any one occupation can be carefully observed; general statements can be made about it, and tested by comparison with the results of other observations, and numerical estimates can be framed as to the amount of money or general purchasing power that is required to supply a sufficient motive for them.

Again, the unwillingness to postpone enjoyment, and thus to save for future use, is measured by the interest on accumulated wealth which just affords a sufficient incentive to save for the future. This measurement presents however some special difficulties, the study of which must be postponed.

[1] There will not in general have been any formal reckoning up of two sides of a balance-sheet but men going home from their day's work, or in their social meetings, will have said to one another, "It did not answer to do this, it would have been better to do that," and so on. What makes one course answer better than another, will not necessarily be a selfish gain, nor any material gain; and it will often have been argued that "though this or that plan saved a little trouble or a little money, yet it was not fair to others," and "it made one look mean," or "it made one feel mean"

[2] In backward countries there are still many habits and customs similar to those that lead a beaver in confinement to build himself a dam. They are full of suggestiveness to the historian, and must be reckoned with by the legislator

And, lastly, the desire to obtain anything that is ordinarily bought and sold for money, is for that very reason measurable by the price that people are willing to pay for it.

The motives that lead to the pursuit of money may themselves be noble

§ 6. But here, as elsewhere, we must ever bear in mind that the desire to make money does not itself necessarily proceed from motives of a low order, even when it is to be spent on oneself. Money is a means towards ends, and if the ends are noble, the desire for the means is not ignoble. The lad who works hard and saves all he can, in order to be able to pay his way afterwards at a University, is eager for money; but his eagerness is not ignoble. In short, money is general purchasing power, and is sought as a means to all kinds of ends, high as well as low, spiritual as well as material[1].

And there is no truth in the common opinion that economics regards man as absorbed in a selfish pursuit of wealth

Thus though it is true that "money" or "general purchasing power" or "command over material wealth," is the centre around which economic science clusters; this is so, not because money or material wealth is regarded as the main aim of human effort, nor even as affording the main subject-matter for the study of the economist, but because in this world of ours it is the one convenient means of measuring human motive on a large scale. If the older economists had made this clear, they would have escaped many grievous misrepresentations; and the splendid teachings of Carlyle and Ruskin as to the right aims of human endeavour and the right uses of wealth, would not then have been marred by bitter attacks on economics, based on the mistaken belief that that science had no concern with any motive except the selfish desire for wealth, or even that it inculcated a policy of sordid selfishness[2].

[1] See an admirable essay by Cliffe Leslie on *The Love of Money*. We do indeed hear of people who pursue money for its own sake without caring for what it will purchase, especially at the end of a long life spent in business: but in this as in other cases the habit of doing a thing is kept up after the purpose for which it was originally done has ceased to exist. The possession of wealth gives such people a feeling of power over their fellow-creatures, and insures them a sort of envious respect in which they find a bitter but strong pleasure.

[2] The fact that the predominant position which money holds in economics, results rather from its being a measure of motive than an aim of endeavour, may be illustrated by the reflection that the almost exclusive use of money as a measure of motive is, so to speak, an accident, and perhaps an accident that is not found in

BOOK I CH V

The desire for money does not exclude other influences, such as the pleasure afforded by the work itself and the instinct of power

Again, when the motive to a man's action is spoken of as supplied by the money which he will earn, it is not meant that his mind is closed to all other considerations save those of gain. For even the most purely business relations of life assume honesty and good faith; while many of them take for granted, if not generosity, yet at least the absence of meanness, and the pride which every honest man takes in acquitting himself well. Again, much of the work by which people earn their living is pleasurable in itself; and there is truth in the contention of socialists that more of it might be made so Indeed even business work, that seems at first sight unattractive, often yields a great pleasure by offering scope for the exercise of men's faculties, and for their instincts of emulation and of power For just as a racehorse

other worlds than ours When we want to induce a man to do anything for us we generally offer him money It is true that we might appeal to his generosity or sense of duty; but this would be calling into action latent motives that are already in existence, rather than supplying new motives If we have to supply a new motive we generally consider how much money will just make it worth his while to do it Sometimes indeed the gratitude, or esteem, or honour which is held out as an inducement to the action may appear as a new motive particularly if it can be crystallized in some definite outward manifestation, as for instance in the right to make use of the letters C B , or to wear a star or a garter Such distinctions are comparatively rare and connected with but few transactions, and they would not serve as a measure of the ordinary motives that govern men in the acts of every-day life But political services are more frequently rewarded by such honours than in any other way so we have got into the habit of measuring them not in money but in honours We say, for instance, that A's exertions for the benefit of his party or of the State, as the case may be, were fairly paid for by knighthood, while knighthood was but shabby pay for B, he had earned a baronetcy

It is quite possible that there may be worlds in which no one ever heard of private property in material things, or wealth as it is generally understood, but public honours are meted out by graduated tables as rewards for every action that is done for others' good. If these honours can be transferred from one to another without the intervention of any external authority they may serve to measure the strength of motives just as conveniently and exactly as money does with us In such a world there may be a treatise on economic theory very similar to the present, even though there be little mention in it of material things, and no mention at all of money.

It may seem almost trivial to insist on this, but it is not so For a misleading association has grown up in people's minds between that measurement of motives which is prominent in economic science, and an exclusive regard for material wealth to the neglect of other and higher objects of desire The only conditions required in a measure for economic purposes are that it should be something definite and transferable Its taking a material form is practically convenient, but is not essential

or an athlete strains every nerve to get in advance of his competitors, and delights in the strain; so a manufacturer or a trader is often stimulated much more by the hope of victory over his rivals than by the desire to add something to his fortune[1].

Economists have always

§ 7. It has indeed always been the practice of economists to take careful account of all the advantages which attract

[1] German economists have done good service by dwelling on this class of considerations also, but they seem to be mistaken in supposing that it was overlooked by the older English economists It is an English habit to leave much to be supplied by the common sense of the reader, in this case reticence has been carried too far, and has led to frequent misunderstanding at home as well as abroad

Thus prominence has been given to Mill's statement, that "Political Economy considers man as occupied solely in acquiring and consuming wealth" (*Essays*, p 138, and again, *Logic*, Bk VI Ch IX § 3). But it is forgotten that he is there referring to an abstract treatment of economic questions, which he once indeed contemplated, but which he never executed, preferring to write on "Political Economy, with some of its applications to Social Philosophy" It is forgotten also that he goes on to say, "There is, perhaps, no action of a man's life in which he is neither under the immediate nor under the remote influence of any impulse but the mere desire of wealth," and it is forgotten that his treatment of economic questions took constant account of many motives besides the desire for wealth (see above, Ch IV § 7) His discussions of economic motives are, however, inferior both in substance and in method to those of his German contemporaries, and notably Hermann An instructive argument that non-purchasable, non-measurable pleasures vary at different times and tend to increase with the progress of civilization is to be found in Knies' *Political Economy*, III. 3, and the English reader may be referred to Syme's *Outlines of an Industrial Science*

But it may be well to give here the heads of the analysis of economic motives (*Motive im wirthschaftlichen Handeln*) in the third edition of Prof Wagner's monumental treatise. He divides them into Egoistic and Altruistic The former are four in number The first and least intermittent in its action is the striving for one's own economic advantage, and the fear of one's own economic need Next comes the fear of punishment, and the hope of reward The third group consists of the feeling of honour, and the striving for recognition (*Geltungsstreben*), including the desire for the moral approbation of others, and the fear of shame and contempt And the last of the egoistic motives is the craving for occupation, the pleasure of activity; and the pleasure of the work itself and its surroundings, including "the pleasures of the chase" The altruistic motive is "the impelling force (*Trieb*) of the inward command to moral action, the pressure of the feeling of duty, and the fear of one's own inward blame, that is, of the gnawings of conscience In its pure form this motive appears as the 'Categorical Imperative,' which one follows because one feels in one's soul the command to act in this or that manner, and feels the command to be right The following of the command is no doubt regularly bound up with feelings of pleasure (*Lustgefühlen*), and the not following it with feelings of pain Now it may be, and often is, that these feelings act as strongly as the Categorical Imperative, or even more strongly, in driving us, or in taking part in driving us on to do or to leave undone. And in so far as this is the case this motive also has in it an egoistic element, or at least itself merges into one"

BOOK I CH V

reckoned for advantages of an occupation other than material gain;

people generally towards an occupation, whether they appear in a money form or not. Other things being equal, people will prefer an occupation in which they do not need to soil their hands, in which they enjoy a good social position, and so on; and since these advantages affect, not indeed every one exactly in the same way, but most people in nearly the same way, their attractive force can be estimated and measured by the money wages to which they are regarded as equivalent.

and they have allowed for class sympathies,

Again, the desire to earn the approval, to avoid the contempt of those around one is a stimulus to action which often works with some sort of uniformity in any class of persons at a given time and place; though local and temporary conditions influence greatly not only the intensity of the desire for approval, but also the range of persons whose approval is desired A professional man, for instance, or an artisan will be very sensitive to the approval or disapproval of those in the same occupation, and care little for that of other people, and there are many economic problems, the discussion of which would be altogether unreal, if care were not taken to watch the direction and to estimate pretty closely the force of motives such as these.

and family affections

As there may be a taint of selfishness in a man's desire to do what seems likely to benefit his fellow-workers, so there may be an element of personal pride in his desire that his family should prosper during his life and after it But still the family affections generally are so pure a form of altruism, that their action might have shown little semblance of regularity, had it not been for the uniformity in the family relations themselves. As it is, their action is fairly regular; and it has always been fully reckoned with by economists, especially in relation to the distribution of the family income between its various members, the expenses of preparing children for their future career, and the accumulation of wealth to be enjoyed after the death of him by whom it has been earned.

It is then not the want of will but the want of power, that prevents economists from reckoning in the action of motives such as these; and they welcome the fact that some kinds of philanthropic action can be described in statistical returns, and can to a certain extent be reduced to law, if sufficiently broad averages are taken. For indeed there is scarcely any motive so fitful and irregular, but that some law with regard to it can be detected by the aid of wide and patient observation. It would perhaps be possible even now to predict with tolerable closeness the subscriptions that a population of a hundred thousand Englishmen of average wealth will give to support hospitals and chapels and missions; and, in so far as this can be done, there is a basis for an economic discussion of supply and demand with reference to the services of hospital nurses, missionaries and other religious ministers. It will however probably be always true that the greater part of those actions, which are due to a feeling of duty and love of one's neighbour, cannot be classed, reduced to law and measured; and it is for this reason, and not because they are not based on self-interest, that the machinery of economics cannot be brought to bear on them.

The motives to collective action are of great and growing importance

§ 8. Perhaps the earlier English economists confined their attention too much to the motives of individual action. But in fact economists, like all other students of social science, are concerned with individuals chiefly as members of the social organism. As a cathedral is something more than the stones of which it is made, as a person is something more than a series of thoughts and feelings, so the life of society is something more than the sum of the lives of its individual members. It is true that the action of the whole is made up of that of its constituent parts; and that in most economic problems the best starting-point is to be found in the motives that affect the individual, regarded not indeed as an isolated atom, but as a member of some particular trade or industrial group; but it is also true, as German writers have well urged, that economics has a great and an increasing concern in motives connected with the collective ownership of property and the collective pursuit of important aims. The growing earnestness of the age, the growing intelligence of the mass of the people, and the growing power of the telegraph, the press, and other means of communication are ever widening the scope of collective action for the public good; and these changes, together with the spread of the co-operative movement, and other kinds of voluntary association are growing up under the influence of various motives besides that of pecuniary gain; and they are ever opening to the economist new opportunities of measuring motives whose action it had seemed impossible to reduce to any sort of law.

But in fact the variety of motives, the difficulties of measuring them, and the manner of overcoming those difficulties are among the chief subjects with which we shall be occupied during the remainder of this treatise. Almost every point touched in the present chapter will need to be discussed in fuller detail with reference to some one or more of the leading problems of economics.

Economists study the individual as a member of an industrial group;

§ 9. To conclude provisionally: economists study the actions of individuals, but study them in relation to social rather than individual life; and therefore concern themselves but little with personal peculiarities of temper and character. They watch carefully the conduct of a whole class of people, sometimes the whole of a nation, sometimes only those living in a certain district, more often those engaged in some particular trade at some time and place and by the aid of statistics, or in other ways, they ascertain how much money on the average the members of the particular group they are watching, are just willing to pay as the price of a certain thing which they desire, or how much must be offered to them to induce them to undergo a certain effort or abstinence that they dislike. The measurement of motive thus obtained is not indeed perfectly accurate, for if it were, economics would rank with the most advanced of the physical sciences, and not as it actually does with the least advanced.

and measure the play of motives in demand and supply at first in simple cases,

But yet the measurement is accurate enough to enable experienced persons to forecast fairly well the extent of the results that will follow from changes in which motives of this kind are chiefly concerned. Thus, for instance, they can estimate very closely the payment that will be required to produce an adequate supply of labour of any grade, from the lowest to the highest, for a new trade which it is proposed to start in any place When they visit a factory of a kind that they have never seen before, they can tell within a shilling or two a week what any particular worker is earning, by merely observing how far his is a skilled occupation and what strain it involves on his physical, mental and moral faculties. And they can predict with tolerable certainty what rise of price will result from a given diminution of the supply of a certain thing, and how that increased price will react on the supply.

and afterwards in more complex cases

And, starting from simple considerations of this kind, economists go on to analyse the causes which govern the local distribution of different kinds of industry, the terms on which people living in distant places exchange their goods with one another, and so on: and they can explain and predict the ways in which fluctuations of credit will affect foreign trade; or again the extent to which the burden of a tax will be shifted from those on whom it is levied, on to those for whose wants they cater, and so on.

They deal mainly with one side of man's life, but it is always the life of a real man not of a fictitious being

In all this they deal with man as he is: not with an abstract or "economic" man; but a man of flesh and blood; influenced by egoistic motives and shaping his business life to a great extent with reference to them; but not above the frailties of vanity or recklessness, and not below the delight of doing his work well for its own sake, nor below the delight in sacrificing himself for the good of his family, his neighbours, or his country, and not below the love of a virtuous life for its own sake. They deal with man as he is. But being concerned chiefly with those actions in which the action of motive is so regular that it can be predicted, and the estimate of the motor-forces can be verified by results, they have established their work on a scientific basis.

The claims of economics to be a science, are its power of appeal to definite external tests, and its internal homogeneity

For in the first place, they deal with facts which can be observed, and quantities which can be measured and recorded, so that when differences of opinion arise with regard to them, the differences can be brought to the test of public and well-established records; and thus science obtains a solid basis on which to work. In the second place, the problems, which are grouped as economic, because they relate specially to man's conduct under the influence of motives that are measurable by a money price,

BOOK I. CH. V.

are found to make a fairly homogeneous group. Of course they have a great deal of subject-matter in common: that is obvious from the nature of the case. But, though not so obvious *à priori*, it will also be found to be true that there is a fundamental unity of form underlying all the chief of them, and that in consequence, by studying them together, the same kind of economy that is gained, as by sending a single postman to deliver all the letters in a certain street, instead of each one entrusting his letters to a separate messenger. For the analyses and organized processes of reasoning that are wanted for any one group of them, will be found generally useful for other groups.

The less then we trouble ourselves with scholastic inquiries as to whether a certain consideration comes within the scope of economics, the better If the matter is important let us take account of it as far as we can. If it is one as to which there exist divergent opinions, such as cannot be brought to the test of exact and well-ascertained knowledge; if it is one on which the general machinery of economic analysis and reasoning cannot get any grip, then let us leave it aside in our purely economic studies. But let us do so, simply because the attempt to include it would lessen the certainty and the exactness of our economic knowledge without any commensurate gain; and remembering always that some sort of account of it must be taken by our ethical instincts and our common sense, when they as ultimate arbiters come to apply to practical issues the knowledge obtained and arranged by economics and other sciences

CHAPTER VI.

METHODS OF STUDY. THE NATURE OF ECONOMIC LAW

BOOK I CH VI

Economics uses both induction and deduction

§ 1 It is the function of economics, as of almost every other science, to collect facts, to arrange and interpret them, and to draw inferences from them. "Observation and description, definition and classification are the preparatory activities. But what we desire to reach thereby is a knowledge of the interdependence of economic phenomena....Induction and deduction are both needed for scientific thought as the right and left foot are both needed for walking[1]" The methods required for this twofold work are not peculiar to economics, they are the common property of all sciences All the devices for the discovery of the relations between cause and effect, which are described in treatises on scientific method, have to be used in their turn by the economist· there is not any one method of investigation which can properly be called the method of economics, but every method must be made serviceable in its proper place, either singly or in combination with others And as the number of combinations that can be made on the chess board, is so great that probably no two games exactly alike were ever played, so no two games which the student plays with nature to wrest from her her hidden truths, which were worth playing at all, ever made use of quite the same methods in quite the same way

[1] Prof Schmoller in the article on *Volkswirtschaft* in Conrad's *Handwörterbuch*

BOOK I CH VI

but in different proportions for different purposes

But in some branches of economic inquiry and for some purposes, it is more urgent to ascertain new facts, than to trouble ourselves with the mutual relations and explanations of those which we already have. While in other branches there is still so much uncertainty as to whether those causes of any event which lie on the surface and suggest themselves at first are both *true* causes of it and the *only* causes of it, that it is even more urgently needed to scrutinize our reasonings about facts which we already know, than to seek for more facts.

Analytical and historical schools are both needed and supplement each other

For this and other reasons, there always has been and there probably always will be a need for the existence side by side of workers with different aptitudes and different aims, some of whom give their chief attention to the ascertainment of facts, while others give their chief attention to discovering obscure causal connections between individual facts or classes of facts and to developing the machinery, or organon, of scientific analysis It is to be hoped that these two schools will always exist side by side; each doing its own work thoroughly, and each making use of the work of the other. Let us look at the work of each[1].

[1] The discussions of the last twenty years have gradually proved that those who are doing the most genuine and original work in any part of the large field of economic investigation, are agreed in fundamental principle as to the right use of various scientific methods for various parts of the work and that what real differences exist between them, are mainly differences of emphasis. It is now generally admitted that the severe criticism which the founders of the German Historical School sometimes made on the older economists if quoted by itself, gives a misleading impression of their true position Roscher and Knies not only spoke often with generous appreciation of the work of their predecessors, but, especially in their later years, they themselves made habitual use of the analytical methods which had come down to them from the "classical" economists And on the other hand even those who rate highly the importance of analytical methods are glad to acknowledge the great services which the historical method, in the hands of really able men, renders to economics generally, and even to economic analysis

The most notable controversy on method of recent times is that between Prof Carl Menger and Prof Schmoller It was conducted with great acumen, but perhaps with some slight exaggeration on either side. Prof Wagner, who was one of the earliest leaders of the historical movement in economics, and whose unsurpassed learning gives a singular weight to his judgment, took a view of the controversy which seems just and well balanced (Part of his criticism is accessible to English readers in the first number of the Harvard *Journal of Economics*) And the account which he has recently published (*Grundlegung*, Ed III Book I ch II) of the services to be rendered by the historical and analytical

§ 2. To begin with, there is no scope in economics for long chains of reasoning; that is for chains in which each link is supported, wholly or mainly, by that which went before, and without obtaining further support and guidance from observation and the direct study of real life. Such chains might indeed afford interesting speculation in the closet but they could not correspond to nature closely enough to be of use as a guide in action The classical economists treated economics not as an academic diversion, but as a means towards attaining important public ends, and none of them, not even Ricardo, indulged in long chains of deductive reasoning without reference to direct observation.

The work of deduction in economics does not extend to forging long chains of reasoning

It is true that the forces with which economics deals have one advantage for deductive treatment in the fact that their method of combination is, as Mill observed, that of mechanics rather than of chemistry. That is to say, when we know the action of two economic forces separately—as for instance the influences which an increase in the rate of wages and a diminution in the difficulty of the work in a trade will severally exert on the supply of labour in it—we can predict fairly well their conjoint action, without waiting for specific experience of it[1].

though economic forces combine mechanically rather than chemically

But even in mechanics long chains of deductive reasoning are directly applicable only to the occurrences of the laboratory By themselves they are seldom a sufficient guide for

methods, and of their mutual interdependence, is a masterpiece of subtle and sound exposition

But meanwhile it has become apparent that Prof Schmoller's part of the controversy had been somewhat misunderstood He is now the recognized leader of the specially historical tendencies of German economics, and as his manifesto, in the article already quoted, formally disavows the narrow and contentious doctrines that have been put forward by some of the younger adherents of the school in Germany and elsewhere; it may be hoped that at last the time has come for the cessation of barren controversy and the devotion of all the energies of economists to various forms of constructive work, each supplementing the other See also Prof Ashley "On the Study of Economic History" in the Harvard *Journal of Economics*, Vol. VII

[1] Mill exaggerated the importance of this fact and was led by it to make excessive claims for the deductive method in economics See the last of his *Essays;* Book VI of his *Logic*, and especially its ninth chapter, also pp. 157—161 of his *Autobiography* His practice, like that of many other writers on economic method of all shades of opinion, was less extreme than his profession. But see above, pp 65, 6

BOOK I. CH VI

dealing with the heterogeneous materials and the complex and uncertain combination of the forces of the real world For that purpose they need to be supplemented by specific experience, and applied in harmony with, and often in subordination to, a ceaseless study of new facts, a ceaseless search for new inductions[1]

The complexity of economic phenomena

But the forces of which economics has to take account are more numerous, less definite, less well known, and more diverse in character than those of mechanics; while the material on which they act is more uncertain and less homogeneous. Again the cases in which economic forces combine with more of the apparent arbitrariness of chemistry than of the simple regularity of pure mechanics, are neither rare nor unimportant. And further, though unexpected combinations of forces are less likely to produce startling results in economics than in chemistry, yet they are far more difficult to exclude[2].

[1] Long chains of deductive reasoning are indeed directly serviceable in astronomy, in which nature herself has given practically exclusive possession to a few definite forces, and the astronomer's predictions of the movements of the solar system are subject to only one hypothesis, namely that nature will not bring into it any large external body for which he has not reckoned

When the calculations of theoretical mechanics are applied in an engineering problem in which the forces of nature are few and definite, and the materials simple and homogeneous, they correspond roughly to nature—somewhat as does a view seen through a window-pane of inferior glass The engineer for instance can calculate with fair precision the angle at which an ironclad will lose its stability in still water; but before he predicts how she would behave in a storm, he will avail himself of the observations of experienced sailors who have watched her movements in an ordinary sea If her lines are new, but specific experience has been had of the speed of ships with nearly similar lines, he may perhaps calculate fairly well what her speed will be But partly because rushing water lays aside all pretence of being a frictionless fluid, his theory will not enable him to give a good guess under conditions at all far away from specific experience nor can he even now quite understand why a torpedo is so much more wasteful of propelling force than a fish at an equal distance below the surface And throughout the whole of his work he has to be guided by specific observation more than by deductive reasoning as to the allowance to be made for flaws of material, and for the fitful action of natural forces

[2] A knowledge of the actions of an elastic string under tensions of ten and twenty pounds may not tell us how it will act under a tension of thirty for then it may not stretch further, but break and spring back And two economic forces acting in the same direction may introduce changes into men's habits and aims in life; and produce results different in kind, perhaps even partly opposed to, those which would result from either alone For instance a small addition to a man's income will generally increase his purchases a little in almost every direction·

Lastly, while the matter with which the chemist deals is the same always, economics, like biology, deals with a matter, of which the inner nature and constitution, as well as the outer form, is constantly changing[1].

Thus if we look at the history of such strictly economic relations as those of business credit and banking, of trade-unionism or co-operation, we see that modes of working, that have been generally successful at some times and places, have uniformly failed at others. The difference may sometimes be explained simply as the result of variations in general enlightenment, or of moral strength of character and habits of mutual trust But often the explanation is more difficult. At one time or place men will go far in trust of one another and in sacrifice of themselves for the common well-being, but only in certain directions; and at another time or place there will be a similar limitation, but the directions will be different, and every variation of this kind limits the range of deduction in economics[2].

but a large addition may alter his habits, perhaps increase his self-respect and make him cease to care for some things altogether. The spread of a fashion from a higher social grade to a lower may destroy the fashion among the higher grade And again increased earnestness in our care for the poor may make charity more lavish, or may destroy some of its forms altogether

[1] The chemist's predictions all rest on the latent hypothesis that the specimen operated upon is what it is supposed to be, so at least that the impurities in it are only such as may be neglected. The economist's predictions involve the further hypothesis that the nature of man is substantially the same as when those facts were observed on which his reasonings are mainly based Even the chemist, when he deals not with inanimate matter but with living beings can seldom sail safely any considerable way out of sight of the firm land of specific experience He must rely mainly on that to tell him how a new drug will affect a person in health, and again how it will affect a person with a certain disease; and even after some general experience he may find unexpected results in its action on persons of different constitutions or in a new combination with other drugs But by patient interrogation of nature and the progress of analysis, the reign of law is being made to invade new fields in both therapeutics and economics and some sort of prediction, independent of specific experience is becoming possible as to the separate and combined action of an ever increasing variety of agencies

[2] Compare above, ch. I § 4 and ch. IV § 7 For our present purpose the pliability of the race is more important than the pliability of the individual It is true that individual character changes, partly in an apparently arbitrary way, and partly according to well known rules It is true for instance that the average age of the workmen engaged in a labour dispute is an important element in any forecast of the lines on which it will run But as, generally speaking, young and old, people of a sanguine and a despondent temperament are found in about like proportions at one place as at another, and at one time as at another, individual

BOOK I CH. VI

The nature of the work of analysis and deduction in economics

§ 3. The function then of analysis and deduction in economics is not to forge a few long chains of reasoning, but to forge rightly many short chains and single connecting links. This however is no trivial task. If the economist reasons rapidly and with a light heart, he is apt to make bad connections at every turn of his work. He needs to make careful use of analysis and deduction, because only by their aid can he select the right facts, group them rightly, and make them serviceable for suggestions in thought and guidance in practice; and because, as surely as every deduction must rest on the basis of inductions, so surely does every inductive process involve and include analysis and deduction.

Explanation and prediction are the same operation in opposite directions

Or to put the same thing in another way the explanation of the past and the prediction of the future are not different operations, but the same worked in opposite directions, the one from effect to cause, the other from cause to effect. For to obtain "a knowledge of individual causes" we need "induction, the final conclusion of which is indeed nothing but the inversion of the syllogism which is employed in deduction.... Induction and deduction rest on the same tendencies, the same beliefs, the same needs of our reason[1]."

peculiarities of character and changes of character are a less hindrance to the general application of the deductive method, than at first sight appears. Compare above, ch. v. § 4. For similar reasons the philosophic questions relating to the freedom of the will, do not concern the economist as such: his reasonings do not assume any particular answers to those questions.

[1] It may be well to quote the whole passage, which occurs in Prof. Schmoller's article on *Volkswirtschaft* already mentioned:—"What we call the inductive process starts from the particular, from observation, and seeks the rule which declares what has been observed, which declares to be true of a class what has been found to be true of the observed instances. The more complex a phenomenon, and the even more imperfect our observation of the complex conditions, resulting as they do from a combination of the most various causes, the more difficult is it to discover the true rule, the more often do we get no further than hypotheses, and provisional guesses as to the uniformity of the result. But we apply even these to obtain further conclusions.

Deduction, which rests on the same tendencies, the same beliefs, the same needs of our reason as induction, consists in the wider application of those rules as to causality which have been obtained by induction. What was true in accurately observed cases must be true in all exactly similar cases; the rule is sought for only in order to apply it further. Every rule attributes a predicate, a mode of action, a characteristic to a class of things; an analysis of the notion of the subject and predicate shows what is contained in the rule in question, to what purposes it applies, what cases come under it, what it can account for."

BOOK I CH VI

We can explain an event completely only by first discovering all the events which can have affected it, and the ways in which they can severally have done so. In so far as our analysis of any of these facts or relations is imperfect, in so far is our explanation liable to error; and the inference latent in it is already on its way to build up an induction which, though probably plausible, is false. While in so far as our knowledge and analysis are complete, we are able by merely inverting our mental process to deduce and predict the future almost as certainly as we could have explained the past on a similar basis of knowledge. It is only when we go beyond a first step that a great difference arises between the certainty of prediction and the certainty of explanation: for any error made in the first step of prediction, will be accumulated and intensified in the second; while in interpreting the past, error is not so likely to be accumulated, for observation or recorded history will probably bring a fresh check at each step[1].

The difficulty of interpreting facts.

It must then always be remembered that though observation or history may tell us that one event happened at the same time as another, or after it, they cannot tell us whether the first was the cause of the second That can be done only

[1] The science of the tides presents many close analogies to economics. In either science one set of leading forces exercises a visible influence over almost every movement, and a predominating influence over some. in the science of the tides, it is the attractions of the moon and sun, in economics it is the desire to obtain comfort at the least cost In either case a merely deductive study of the action of the leading forces either by themselves, or in conjunction with forces less universal in their action, would give results that might have a scientific interest but would be useless for guidance But in either case such deductions are useful in giving life to observed facts, in connecting them with one another, and thus helping to build up the secondary laws of the science

It is true for instance that even now no knowledge of sea-currents and of the action of the wind on the water would enable a man to say exactly what difference there would be between the tides in the ports of Guernsey and Jersey, nor the exact limits of the points on the English coast at which there are four tides every day, nor how strong a gale in the North Sea would be required to make the water at the London Docks fall a couple of feet in the middle of a time of rising tide. And yet a study of general principles has aided in the selection of the right facts for observation, and in connecting them with one another by secondary laws, which aid both in explaining known facts and predicting results of known causes The same processes, both inductive and deductive, are used in nearly the same way in the explanation of a known fact in the history of the tides, and in the prediction of an unknown fact (Compare Mill, *Logic*, Book VI ch III)

by reason acting on the facts. When it is said that a certain event in history teaches this or that, formal reckoning is never made for all the conditions which were present when the event happened, some are tacitly, if not unconsciously, assumed to be irrelevant. This assumption may be justifiable in any particular case; but it may not. Wider experience, more careful inquiry, may show that the causes to which the event is attributed could not have produced it unaided; perhaps even that they hindered the event, which was brought about in spite of them by other causes that have escaped notice.

This difficulty has been made prominent by recent controversies as to contemporary events in our own country. Whenever a conclusion is drawn from them that meets with opposition, it has to stand a sort of trial, rival explanations are offered; new facts are brought to light, the old facts are tested and rearranged, and in some cases shown to support the opposite conclusion from that on behalf of which they were at first invoked

Both the difficulty of analysis and the need for it are increased by the fact that no two economic events are seldom alike in all respects Of course there may be a close resemblance between two simple incidents: the terms of the leases of two farms may be governed by nearly the same causes: two references of wages questions to Boards of Arbitration may raise substantially the same question. But there is no exact repetition even on a small scale. However nearly two cases correspond, we have to decide whether the difference between the two may be neglected as practically unimportant; and this may not be very easy, even if the two cases refer to the same place and time.

The untrustworthiness of *primâ facie* evidence drawn from the distant past.

And if we are dealing with the facts of remote times we must allow for the changes that have meanwhile come over the whole character of economic life: however closely a problem of to-day may resemble in its outward incidents another recorded in history, it is probable that a closer examination will detect a fundamental difference between their real characters. Till this has been made, no valid argument can be drawn from one case to the other.

§ 4. This brings us to consider the relation in which economics stands to the facts of distant times.

The aid of subtle analysis is not needed for all the work of the economic historian:

The study of economic history may have various aims, and correspondingly various methods. Regarded as a branch of general history it may aim at helping us to understand "what has been the institutional framework of society at the several periods, what has been the constitution of the various social classes and their relation to one another". it may "ask what has been the material basis of social existence; how have the necessities and conveniences of life been produced, by what organization has labour been provided and directed; how have the commodities thus produced been distributed; what have been the institutions resting on this direction and distribution"; and so on[1].

And for this work, interesting and important as it is on its own account, not very much analysis is essential; and most of what is needed may be supplied for himself by a man of active and inquiring mind. Saturated with a knowledge of the religious and moral, the intellectual and aesthetic, the political and social environment, the economic historian may extend the boundaries of our knowledge and may suggest new and valuable ideas, even though he may have contented himself with observing those affinities and those causal relations which lie near the surface.

but it is needed for deriving guidance from the past for the present.

But even in spite of himself, his aims will surely run beyond these limits, and will include some attempt to discover the inner meaning of economic history, to unveil the mysteries of the growth and decay of custom, and other phenomena which we are not any longer contented to take as ultimate and insoluble facts given by nature. nor is he likely altogether to withhold himself from suggesting inferences from the events of the past for guidance in the present. And indeed the human mind abhors a vacuum in its notions of the causal relations between the events that are presented vividly to it. By merely placing things together in a certain order, and consciously or unconsciously

[1] Ashley, *On the Study of Economic History*.

BOOK I CH. VI

suggesting *post hoc ergo propter hoc*, the historian takes on himself some responsibility as a guide[1].

And if this is his main aim, if his interests lie chiefly in the attempt to discover the hidden springs of the economic order of the world, and to obtain light from the past for guidance in the present, then he should avail himself of every resource that may help him to detect real differences that are disguised by a similarity of name or outward appearance, and real similarities that are obscured by a superficial difference, to select the true causes of each event and assign to each its proper weight; and above all to detect the remoter causes of change

An analogy from naval history

An analogy may be borrowed from naval affairs. The details of a battle with appliances that have passed away

[1] For example —the introduction of long leases at fixed money rents in North Britain was followed by a great improvement in agriculture, and in the general condition of the people there, but before inferring that it was the sole, or even the chief cause of the improvement, we must inquire what other changes were taking place at the same time, and how much of the improvement is to be referred to each of them. We must, for instance, allow for the effects of changes in the prices of agricultural produce, and of the establishment of civil order in the border provinces To do this requires care and scientific method, and till it has been done, no trustworthy inference can be drawn as to the general tendency of the system of long leases And even when it has been done, we cannot argue from this experience to a proposal for a system of long leases in, say, Ireland now, without allowing for differences in the character of local and world markets for various kinds of agricultural produce, for probable changes in the production and consumption of gold and silver, and so on The history of Land Tenures is full of antiquarian interest; but until carefully analysed and interpreted by the aid of economic theory it throws no trustworthy light on the question what is the best form of land tenure to be adopted now in any country Thus some argue that since primitive societies usually held their land in common, private property in land must be an unnatural and transitional institution Others with equal confidence contend that, since private property in land has extended its range with the progress of civilization, it is a necessary condition for further progress. But to wrest from history her true teaching on the subject requires the effects of the common holding of land in the past to be analysed so as to discover how far each of them is likely to act always in the same way, how far to be modified by changes in the habits, the knowledge, the wealth, and the social organization of mankind

Even more interesting and instructive is the history of the professions, made by Gilds and other Corporations and Combinations in industry and in domestic and foreign trade, that they used their privileges on the whole for the benefit of the public But to bring in a complete verdict on the question, and still more to deduce from it sound guidance for our own time, needs not only the wide general knowledge and subtle instincts of the practised historian, but also a grasp of many of the most difficult analyses and reasonings relating to monopolies, to foreign trade, to the incidence of taxation, etc may be of great interest to the student of the general history of those times, but they may afford little useful guidance for the naval commander of to-day, who has to deal with a wholly different material of war. And therefore, as Captain Mahan has admirably shown, the naval commander of to-day will give more attention to the *strategy* than to the *tactics* of past times[1].

It is only recently, and to a great extent through the wholesome influence of the criticisms of the historical school, that prominence has been given to that distinction in economics which corresponds to the distinction between strategy and tactics in warfare. Corresponding to tactics are those details and outward forms of economic organization which depend on temporary or local aptitudes, customs and relations of classes; on the influence of individuals; or on the changing appliances and needs of production. While to strategy corresponds that more fundamental substance of economic organization, which depends mainly on such wants and activities, such preferences and aversions as are found in man everywhere: they are not indeed always the same in form, nor even quite the same in substance; but yet they have a sufficient element of permanence and universality to enable them to be brought in some measure under general statements, whereby the experiences of one time and one age may throw light on the difficulties of another. This distinction

[1] He will concern himself not so much with the incidents of particular combats, as with practical illustrations of those leading principles of action which will enable him to hold his whole force in hand, and yet give to each part of it adequate initiative, to keep up wide communication, and yet to be able to concentrate quickly, and select a point of attack at which he can bring an overwhelming force. A man saturated with the general history of a period, may give a vivid picture of the tactics of a battle, which will be true in its main outlines, and almost harmless even if occasionally wrong: for no one is likely to copy tactics, the appliances of which have passed away. But to comprehend the strategy of a campaign, to separate the real from the apparent motives of a great general of past times, a man must be a strategist himself. And if he is to make himself responsible for suggesting, however unobtrusively, the lessons which the strategists of to-day have to learn from the story which he records; then he is bound to have analysed thoroughly the naval conditions of to-day, as well those of the time about which he is writing; and he must neglect no aid for this end that is to be had from the work of many minds in many countries studying the difficult problem of strategy. As it is with naval history, so it is with economic

BOOK I. CH. VI

was probably seldom present in Ricardo's mind: it is certainly not prominent in his writings: and when attention is paid, not to the principles which are embodied in his method of working, but to particular conclusions which he reaches, when these are converted into dogmas and applied crudely to the conditions of times or places other than his own, then no doubt they are almost unmixed evils. His thoughts are like sharp chisels with which it is specially easy to cut one's fingers, because they have such awkward handles.

But modern economists distilling his crude expressions; extracting their essence, and adding to it; rejecting dogmas, but developing principles of analysis and reasoning, are finding the Many in the One and the One in the Many: they are showing for instance that the principles of his analysis of rent are not applicable to much that commonly goes by the name of rent to-day, but that they are applicable with proper care to much that has the outward form of rent, in the economic conditions of almost every stage of civilization as well as to much that does not appear at first sight to be of the nature of rent at all[1].

Common-sense and

§ 5 It is doubtless true that much of this work has less need of elaborate analytical methods, than of a shrewd

[1] Of course no student of strategy can ignore tactics And, though no one life will reach out to a study in detail of the tactics of every fight which man has waged with his economic difficulties; yet no study of the broad problems of economic strategy is likely to be worth much unless it is combined with an intimate knowledge of the tactics as well as the strategy of man's struggles against his difficulties in some particular age and country And further every student should make by personal observation a minute study of some particular set of details, not necessarily for publication, but for his own training; and this will help him much to interpret and weigh the evidence which he obtains in print or writing, whether with regard to present or past times Of course every thoughtful and observant man is always obtaining, from conversation and current literature, a knowledge of the economic facts of his own time, and especially in his own neighbourhood, and the store of facts which he thus imperceptibly gets is sometimes more full and thorough in certain special regards than is to be distilled from all the records in existence as to some classes of facts in remote places and times But independently of this, the direct and formal study of facts, perhaps mainly those of his own age, will much exceed the study of mere analysis and "theory," in its demands on the time of any serious economist, even though he may be one of those who rank most highly the importance of ideas relatively to facts, even though he may think that it is not so much the collection of new facts as the better study of those already collected, that is our most urgent need now, or that will help us most in improving the tactics as well as the strategy of man's contests with his difficulties

mother-wit, of a sound sense of proportion, and of a large experience of life But on the other hand there is much work that is not easily to be done without such machinery. Natural instinct will select rapidly and combine justly, considerations which are relevant to the issue in hand; but it will select chiefly from those which are familiar; it will seldom lead a man far below the surface or far beyond the limits of his personal experience.

mother-wit can go far in analysis,

And it happens that in economics, neither those effects of known causes, nor those causes of known effects which are most patent, are generally the most important. "That which is not seen" is often better worth studying than that "which is seen" Especially is this the case if we are not dealing with some question of merely local or temporary interest, but are seeking guidance in the construction of a far-reaching policy for the public good, or if, for any other reason, we are concerned less with immediate causes, than with causes of causes,—*causae causantes.* For experience shows, as might have been anticipated, that common sense, and instinct, are inadequate for this work, that even a business training does not always lead a man to search far for those causes of causes, which lie beyond his immediate experience; and that it does not always direct that search well, even when he makes the attempt. For help in doing that, everyone must perforce rely on the powerful machinery of thought and knowledge that has been gradually built up by past generations For indeed the part which systematic scientific reasoning plays in the production of knowledge resembles that which machinery plays in the production of goods.

but not far enough for all purposes

When the same operation has to be performed over and over again in the same way, it generally pays to make a machine to do the work; though when there is so much changing variety of detail that it is unprofitable to use machines, the goods must be made by hand. Similarly in knowledge, when there are any processes of investigation or reasoning in which the same kind of work has to be done over and over again in the same kind of way, then it is worth while to reduce the processes to system, to organize methods of reasoning and to formulate general propositions

Analogy between the machinery of science and that of material production, to be used as machinery for working on the facts and as vices for holding them firmly in position for the work And though it be true that economic causes are intermingled with others in so many different ways, that exact scientific reasoning will seldom bring us very far on the way to the conclusion for which we are seeking, yet it would be foolish to refuse to avail ourselves of its aid, so far as it will reach —just as foolish as would be the opposite extreme of supposing that science alone can do all the work, and that nothing will remain to be done by practical instinct and trained common sense. An architect without practical wisdom and æsthetic instincts will build but a poor house however thorough his knowledge of mechanics: but without any knowledge of it he will build insecurely or wastefully[1].

For mental faculties, like manual dexterity, die with those who possess them: but the improvement which each generation contributes to the machinery of manufacture or to the organon of science is handed down to the next. There may be no abler sculptors now than those who worked on the Parthenon, no thinker with more mother-wit than Aristotle. But the appliances of thought develop cumulatively as do those of material production[2].

[1] A Brindley, without academic instruction, may do some engineering work better than a man of inferior mother-wit, however well he may have been trained A wise nurse, who reads her patients by instinctive sympathy, may give better counsel on some points than a learned physician But yet the study of analytical mechanics should not be neglected by the engineer, nor that of physiology by the medical man

[2] Ideas, whether those of art and science, or those embodied in practical appliances, are the most "real" of the gifts that each generation receives from its predecessors. The world's material wealth would quickly be replaced if it were destroyed, but the ideas by which it was made were retained. If however the ideas were lost, but not the material wealth, then that would dwindle and the world would go back to poverty And most of our knowledge of mere facts could quickly be recovered if it were lost, but the constructive ideas of thought remained; while if the ideas perished, the world would enter again on Dark Ages Thus the pursuit of ideas is not less "real" work in the highest sense of the word than is the collection of facts, though the latter may in some cases properly be called in German a *Realstudium*, that is, a study specially appropriate to *Realschulen*. In the highest use of the word, that study of any field of the wide realm of economics is most "real" in which the collection of facts, and the analysis and construction of ideas connecting them are combined in those proportions which are best calculated to increase knowledge and promote progress in that particular field. And what this is, cannot be settled offhand, but only by careful study and by specific experience

§ 6. This brings us to consider the nature of *Economic Laws*. Some have said that the term is inappropriate, because there are no definite and universal propositions in economics which can compare with the Laws of Gravitation and of Conservation of Energy in physics. But the objection would appear to be irrelevant. For though there are no economic laws of that class, there are many which may rank with the secondary laws of those natural sciences, which resemble economics in dealing with the complex action of many heterogeneous and uncertain causes. The laws of biology, for instance, or—to take an example from a purely physical science—the laws of the tides, like those of economics vary much in definiteness, in range of application and in certainty[1]

Economic laws correspond to secondary natural laws relating to the action of heterogeneous forces.

An economic law is then nothing but a general proposition, or statement of uniformity, more or less certain, more or less definite. A countless number of such statements might be made. but there are not very many of which it is necessary to make a formal statement· and there are fewer still to which it is worth while to give a special name[2].

Thus a law of social science, or a *Social Law*, is a statement that a certain course of action may be expected under certain conditions from the members of a social group

Definition of *law*, *social*,

[1] There is indeed a sense in which all physical laws, including even that of gravitation, are but schemes for holding ascertained uniformities and tendencies in a convenient grip; while they derive their prestige partly from the number and certainty of the facts which they hold within their grip, and partly from the number and cogency of the chains of inductive and deductive reasoning which connect them with other laws.

[2] The selection is directed less by purely scientific considerations than by practical convenience If there is any general statement which one wants to bring to bear so often, that the trouble of quoting it at length, when needed, is greater than that of burdening this discussion with an additional formal statement and an additional technical name, then it receives a special name, otherwise not

The term Rule (German *Regel*) has been suggested as a substitute for Law but the objections to it, in English, at all events, seem very great. It seems however to be the only possible short substitute for Law; and brevity is essential.

The relation of "natural and economic laws," is exhaustively discussed by Neumann (*Zeitschrift für die gesamte Staatswissenschaft*, 1892) who concludes (p 464) that there is no other word than Law (*Gesetz*) to express those statements of tendency, which play so important a part in natural as well as economic science And Prof. Wagner (*Grundlegung*, §§ 86—91) comes to the same conclusion after a somewhat similar analysis of the different kinds of laws See also Keynes, *Scope and Method*, and an article by Prof Ritchie, "What are economic Laws," in the second volume of the *Economic Review*.

BOOK I CH. VI.

and *economic*

Economic laws are those social laws which relate to branches of conduct in which the strength of the motives chiefly concerned can be measured by a money price.

There is thus no hard and sharp line of division between those social laws which are, and those which are not, to be regarded also as economic laws: for there is a continuous gradation from social laws concerned almost exclusively with motives that can be measured by price, to social laws in which such motives have little place, and which are therefore generally as much less precise and exact than economic laws, as those are than the laws of the more exact physical sciences[1].

Corresponding to the substantive "law" is the adjective "legal" But this term is used only in connection with "law" in the sense of an ordinance of government; not in the sense of a scientific statement of connection between cause and effect. The adjective used for this purpose is derived from "norma," a term which is nearly equivalent to "law," and might perhaps with advantage be substituted for it in scientific discussions. And following our definition of an economic law, we may say that the course of action which may be expected under certain conditions from the members of an industrial group is the *normal* action of the members of that group[2].

Definition of *normal*

1 The term Economic Law is also given for convenience to some laws of physical science of which economics makes use The best known of these is the Law of Diminishing Return (Book IV Ch. III), which, at all events in its simplest form, is properly a statement of physical facts and belongs to agricultural science.

2 It will be noticed that this use of the word Normal is broader than that which is often adopted Thus it is frequently said that those results only are normal which are due to the undisturbed action of free competition But the term has often to be applied to conditions in which perfectly free competition does not exist, and can hardly even be supposed to exist, and even where free competition is most dominant, the normal conditions of every fact and tendency will include vital elements that are not a part of competition nor even akin to it. Thus, for instance, the normal arrangement of many transactions in retail and wholesale trade, and on Stock and Cotton Exchanges, rests on the assumption that verbal contracts, made without witnesses, will be honourably discharged; and in countries in which this assumption cannot legitimately be made, some parts of the Western doctrine of normal value are inapplicable Again, the prices of various Stock Exchange securities are affected "normally" by the patriotic feelings not only of the ordinary purchasers, but of the brokers themselves: and so on

The use of the term now proposed is more in accordance with its etymological meaning, as well as with the ordinary language of everyday life. An objection may

BOOK I CH VI

Normal action is not always morally right, very often it is action which we should use our utmost efforts to stop. For instance, the normal condition of many of the very poorest inhabitants of a large town is to be devoid of enterprise, and unwilling to avail themselves of the opportunities that may offer for a healthier and less squalid life elsewhere; they have not the strength, physical, mental and moral, required for working their way out of their miserable surroundings. The existence of a considerable supply of labour ready to make match-boxes at a very low rate is normal in the same way that a contortion of the limbs is a normal result of taking strychnine. It is one result, a deplorable result, of the action of those laws which we have to study[1].

Normal action is not always right action

[The phrase just used—*the action of a law*—is sanctioned by authority, and is convenient on account of its brevity. But it is elliptical: for a law itself does not take action, it merely records action. When we speak of the action of a law, what we mean is *the action of those causes, the results or tendencies of which are described by the law.*]

Explanation of the phrase *the action of a law*

It is sometimes said that the laws of economics are "hypothetical." Of course, like every other science, it undertakes to study the effects which will be produced by certain causes, not absolutely, but subject to the condition that *other things are equal,* and that the causes are able to work out their effects undisturbed Almost every scientific doctrine, when carefully and formally stated, will be found to contain some proviso to the effect that other things are equal. the action of the causes in question is supposed to be isolated;

All scientific doctrines tacitly or implicitly assume certain conditions and are in this sense hypothetical

be raised that it has not a sufficiently definite and rigid outline but it will be found that the difficulties arising from this source are not very great, and that the use now proposed will help to bring the doctrines of economics into closer connection with real life.

[1] This indicates one peculiarity which economics shares with a few other sciences, the nature of the material of which can be modified by human effort It may be a moral or practical precept to modify that nature and thus modify laws of nature; as for instance by substituting capable workers for those who can only do such work as matchbox making; or again by modifying the breeds of cattle so that they mature early, and carry much flesh on light frames Jonah's prophecy of the fall of Nineveh saved it (See Venn, *Empirical Logic*, ch xxv.) And the laws of the fluctuation of credit and prices have been much altered by increased powers of prediction

BOOK I. CH. VI

certain effects are attributed to them, but only *on the hypothesis* that no cause is permitted to enter except those distinctly allowed for[1].

But in economics the implied conditions must be emphasized

These conditioning clauses are not continually repeated, but the common sense of the reader supplies them for himself In economics it is necessary to repeat them oftener than elsewhere, because its doctrines are more apt than those of any other science to be quoted by persons who have had no scientific training, and who perhaps have heard them only at second hand and without their context[2].

Limitations of economic law

It is however true that an economic law may be applicable only to a very narrow range of circumstances which may exist together at one particular place and time, but quickly pass away. When they are gone the law has no practical bearing, because the particular set of causes with which it deals are nowhere to be found acting together without important disturbance from other causes. Though economic analysis and general reasoning are of wide application, we cannot insist too urgently that every age and every country has its own problems, and that every change in social conditions is likely to require a new development of economic doctrines

The distinction between *pure* and *applied* Sciences is not absolute

§ 7. But in all this much turns on the extent to which we are treating economics as an *applied* science The contrast between pure and applied sciences is not absolute, but one of degree. For instance mechanics is an applied science relatively to geometry; but a pure science relatively to

[1] It is true that on account of the changing material of economics, special difficulty is often caused by the condition that time must be allowed for causes to produce their effects. For meanwhile the material on which they work, and perhaps even the causes themselves, will have changed, and the tendencies which are being described will not have a sufficiently "long run" in which to work themselves out fully This difficulty will occupy our attention later on. See especially Book v ch xi

[2] One reason why ordinary conversation is simpler in form than a scientific treatise, is that in conversation we can safely omit conditioning clauses; because, if the hearer does not supply them for himself, we quickly detect the misunderstanding, and set it right. Adam Smith and many of the earlier writers on economics attained seeming simplicity by following the usages of conversation, and omitting conditioning clauses But this has caused them to be constantly misunderstood, and has led to much waste of time and trouble in profitless controversy, they purchased apparent ease at too great a cost even for that great gain

engineering · while engineering itself is often spoken of as a pure science by men, who devote their lives to the applied science of railway development. Now in a sense the whole of economics is an applied science; because it always deals more or less with the uncertain and irregular conditions of life as they actually exist

but one of degree

But some parts of it are relatively *pure,* because they are concerned mainly with broad general propositions For, in order that a proposition may be of broad application it must necessarily contain few details: it cannot adapt itself to particular cases, and if it points to any prediction, that must be governed by a strong conditioning clause in which a very large meaning is given to the phrase "other things being equal." (In logical phrase a proposition can gain in Extension, only by sacrificing Intension.)

And other parts of the science are relatively *applied,* because they deal with narrower questions more in detail; they take more account of local and temporary elements, and they consider economic conditions in fuller and closer relation to other conditions of life Thus we may have a pure science of credit and an applied science of credit. The applied science of credit will include the science of banking And even the science of banking itself may be treated in two ways, either as general and relatively *pure,* or as particular and *applied* to special circumstances of individual districts

There may be but a short step from an applied Science to an Art

Now in such a matter as banking or taxation, in which the economic element predominates over all others, there may be but a short step from the laws of the applied science in the indicative mood to the precepts of practice, or Art, in the imperative mood. There may be but a short step from the applied science of banking in its more general sense, to broad rules or precepts of the general Art of banking: while the step from a particular local problem of the applied science of banking to the corresponding rule of practice or precept of Art may be shorter still.

But it is best to regard economics only as a Science

Of course an economist retains the liberty, common to all the world, of expressing his opinion that a certain course of action is the right one under given circumstances, and if the difficulties of the problem are chiefly economic, he may speak with a certain authority. But on the whole, though the matter is one on which opinions differ, it seems best that he should do so rather in his private capacity, than as claiming to speak with the authority of economic science.

In spite of much good authority to the contrary among continental writers, and the earlier English writers, and even some recent English writers, there seems to be a balance of advantage in avoiding the use of the phrase, the Art of Economics, or of Political Economy. It seems better to regard the science as pursuing its inquiries with more or less direct reference to certain practical issues, and as pointing the way towards solutions of them, than to make pretension to the authority of an Art, complete and self-contained, and responsible for the entire direction of conduct in certain matters But we shall return to this point in the next chapter.

CHAPTER VII.

SUMMARY AND CONCLUSION

BOOK I. CH VII.

Summary of Book I.

§ 1 We have traced the growth of economic freedom and enterprise, and have seen that the chief features of modern economic problems, and the chief incentives to economic study are of quite recent date Till not very long ago the Distribution and Exchange of wealth were governed in the main by conditions which changed but slowly, and by institutions which had the authority of custom and prescription, and which most people were content to take as they found them. Even where there was no slavery and no rigid system of caste, the governing classes seldom took much thought for the material well-being of the great mass of the workers; while the workers had not the habits of mind nor the opportunities of thought and action required for thinking out the problems of their own lives. Much of modern economics might indeed have been anticipated in the towns of the Middle Ages, in which an intelligent and daring spirit was for the first time combined with patient industry, but they were not left to work out their career in peace; and the world had to wait for the dawn of the new economic era till a whole nation was ready for the ordeal of economic freedom

We have seen how England especially was prepared for the task, but how towards the end of last century, the changes which had so far been slow and gradual, suddenly became rapid and violent. Mechanical inventions, the concentration of industries, and a system of manufacturing on a large scale for distant markets broke up the old traditions of industry, and left everyone to bargain for himself as best he might; and at the same time stimulated a rapid increase of population for which no provision had been made beyond standing-room in factories and workshops. Thus free competition, or

BOOK I CH VII

Summary of Book I

rather, freedom of industry and enterprise, was set loose to run, like a huge untrained monster, its wayward course. The abuse of their new power by able but uncultured business men led to evils on every side, it unfitted mothers for their duties, it weighed down children with overwork and disease; and in many places it degraded the race. Meanwhile the kindly meant recklessness of the poor law did even more to lower the moral and physical energy of Englishmen than the hard-hearted recklessness of the manufacturing discipline; for by depriving the people of those qualities which would fit them for the new order of things, it increased the evil and diminished the good caused by the advent of free enterprise.

And yet the time at which free enterprise was showing itself in an unnaturally harsh form, was the very time in which economists were most lavish in their praises of it This was partly because they saw clearly, what we of this generation have in a great measure forgotten, the cruelty of the yoke of custom and rigid ordinance which it had displaced, partly because the general tendency of thought in England was that freedom in all matters, political and social, was worth having at every cost except the loss of security: but partly also it was that the productive force which free enterprise was giving to the nation, was the only means by which, weakened as it was by a series of bad harvests, it could offer a successful resistance to Napoleon. Economists therefore treated free enterprise not indeed as an unmixed good, but as the natural state of things, and they regarded its evils as of secondary importance

Adhering to the lines of thought that had been started chiefly by mediæval traders, and continued by French and English philosophers in the latter half of the eighteenth century, Ricardo and his followers developed a theory of the action of free enterprise (or, as they said, free competition) which contained many truths that will be of high importance so long as the world exists. Their work was wonderfully complete within the narrow area which it covered; but much of the best of it consists of problems relating to rent and the value of corn, problems on the solution of which the fate of England just then seemed to depend, but which,

Summary of Book I

in the particular form in which they were worked out by Ricardo, have very little direct bearing on the present state of things. A good deal of the rest of their work was narrowed and almost spoiled by its regarding too exclusively the peculiar condition of England at that time, and this narrowness has caused a reaction.

So that now, when more experience and leisure, and greater material resources have enabled us to bring free enterprise somewhat under control, to diminish its power of doing evil and increase its power of doing good, there is growing up among many economists a sort of spite against it. Some German economists in particular seem to exaggerate its evils, attributing to it the ignorance and suffering, which are the results either of tyranny and oppression in past ages, or of the misunderstanding and mismanagement of economic freedom

Intermediate between these two extremes are the great body of economists who, in Germany, England, America, and other countries, are bringing to the study of economic questions an unbiassed desire to ascertain the truth, and a willingness to go through with the long and heavy work by which alone scientific results of any value can be obtained. Varieties of mind, of temper, of training and of opportunities lead them to work in different ways, and to give their chief attention to different parts of the problem Some set themselves to collect and arrange facts and statistics relating either to past or to present times; while others occupy themselves chiefly with analysis and reasoning on the basis of those facts which are ready at hand. This division of labour, however, implies not opposition, but harmony of purpose. The work of all adds something or other to that knowledge, which enables us to understand the influences exerted on the quality and tone of man's life by the manner in which he earns his livelihood and by the character of that livelihood.

The economist must be greedy of facts, but facts by themselves teach nothing History tells of sequences and coincidences, but reason alone can interpret and draw lessons from them. The work to be done is so various that much

BOOK I. CH VII.

Summary of Book I.

of it must be left to be dealt with by trained common sense, which is the ultimate arbiter in every practical problem. Economic science is but the working of common sense aided by appliances of organized analysis and general reasoning, which facilitate the task of collecting, arranging, and drawing inferences from particular facts Though its scope is always limited, though its work without the aid of common sense is always vain, yet in almost every difficult problem it will enable common sense to go further than would otherwise be possible. Its chief work is connected with the measurement of motives by the price which, as a "normal" or general rule, is sufficient to induce a person of a particular class under given conditions to undertake a certain task or undergo a certain sacrifice. A statement with regard to man's normal action, or in other words an economic law, is hypothetical only in the same sense as are the laws of the physical sciences: for they also contain or imply conditions. But there is more difficulty in making the conditions clear, and more danger in any failure to do so, in economics than in physics. The laws of human action are not indeed as simple, as definite or as clearly ascertainable as the law of gravitation, but many of them may rank with the laws of those natural sciences which deal with complex subject-matter. The *raison d'être* of economics as a separate science is that it deals chiefly with that part of man's action which is most under the control of measurable motives; and which therefore lends itself better than any other to systematic reasoning and analysis.

The study of theory must go hand and hand with that of facts. and for dealing with most modern problems it is modern facts that are of the greatest use. For the economic records of the distant past are in some respects slight and untrustworthy; and the economic conditions of early times are wholly unlike those of the modern age of free enterprise, of general education, of true democracy, of steam, of the cheap press and the telegraph.

Scientific inquiries are to be arranged with reference

§ 2 Economics has then as its purpose firstly to acquire knowledge for its own sake, and secondly to throw light on practical issues. But though we are bound, before entering on any study, to consider carefully what are its uses, we should not plan out our work with direct reference to them. For by so doing we are tempted to break off each line of thought as soon as it ceases to have an immediate bearing on that particular aim which we have in view at the time: the direct pursuit of practical aims leads us to group together bits of all sorts of knowledge, which have no connection with one another except for the immediate purposes of the moment; and which throw but little light on one another. Our mental energy is spent in going from one to another; nothing is thoroughly thought out, no real progress is made

BOOK I CH VII

not to the practical aims which they subserve but to the nature of the subjects with which they are concerned

The best grouping, therefore, for the purposes of science is that which collects together all those facts and reasonings which are similar to one another in nature: so that the study of each may throw light on its neighbour By working thus for a long time at one set of considerations, we get gradually nearer to those fundamental unities which are called nature's laws: we trace their action first singly, and then in combination, and thus make progress slowly but surely. The practical uses of economic studies should never be out of the mind of the economist, but his special business is to study and interpret facts and to find out what are the effects of different causes acting singly and in combination.

§ 3. Economics is then the science which investigates man's action in the ordinary business of life. It pursues the inquiries:—

Questions to be investigated by the economist

How does economic freedom tend, so far as its influence reaches, to arrange the demand and supply of wealth, distribution and exchange? What organization of industry and trade does economic freedom tend to bring about; what forms of division of labour; what arrangements of the money market, of wholesale and retail dealing, and what relations between employer and employed? How does it tend to adjust values, that is, the prices of material things whether produced on the spot or brought from a distance, rents of all kinds, interest on capital and the earnings of all forms of work, including that of undertaking and managing business enterprises? How does it affect the course of foreign trade? Subject to what limitations is the price of anything a measure of its real utility? What increase of happiness is

BOOK I CH. VII

primâ facie likely to result from a given increase in the wealth of any class of society? How far is the industrial efficiency of any class impaired by the insufficiency of its income? How far would an increase of the income of any class, if once effected, be likely to sustain itself through its effects in increasing their efficiency and earning power?

How far does, as a matter of fact, the influence of economic freedom reach (or how far has it reached at any particular time) in any place, in any rank of society, or in any particular branch of industry? What other influences are most powerful there, and how is the action of all these influences combined? In particular, how far does economic freedom tend of its own action to build up combinations and monopolies, and what are their effects? How are the various classes of society likely to be affected by its action in the long run; what will be the intermediate effects while its ultimate results are being worked out; and, account being taken of the time over which they will spread, what is the relative importance of these two classes of ultimate and intermediate effects? What will be the incidence of any system of taxes? What burdens will it impose on the community, and what revenue will it afford to the State?

Practical issues which stimulate the inquiries of the English economist at the present time, though they do not lie wholly within the range of his science

§ 4. The above are the main questions with which economic science has to deal directly, and with reference to which its main work of collecting facts, of analysing them and reasoning about them should be arranged. The practical issues which, though lying for the greater part outside the range of economic science, yet supply a chief motive in the background to the work of the economist, vary from time to time, and from place to place, even more than do the economic facts and conditions which form the material of his studies The following problems seem to be of special urgency now in our own country:—

How should we act so as to increase the good and diminish the evil influences of economic freedom, both in its ultimate results and in the course of its progress? If the first are good and the latter evil, but those who suffer the evil, do not reap the good; how far is it right that they should suffer for the benefit of others?

Taking it for granted that a more equal distribution of wealth is to be desired, how far would this justify changes in the institutions of property, or limitations of free enterprise even when they would be likely to diminish the aggregate of wealth? In other words, how far should an increase in the income of the poorer classes and a diminution of their work be aimed at, even if it involved some lessening of national material wealth? How far could this be done without injustice, and without slackening the energies of the leaders of progress? How ought the burdens of taxation to be distributed among the different classes of society?

Ought we to rest content with the existing forms of division of labour? Is it necessary that large numbers of the people should be exclusively occupied with work that has no elevating character? Is it possible to educate gradually among the great mass of workers a new capacity for the higher kinds of work; and in particular for undertaking co-operatively the management of the business in which they are themselves employed?

What are the proper relations of individual and collective action in a stage of civilization such as ours? How far ought voluntary association in its various forms, old and new, to be left to supply collective action for those purposes for which such action has special advantages? What business affairs should be undertaken by society itself acting through its Government, imperial or local? Have we, for instance, carried as far as we should the plan of collective ownership and use of open spaces, of works of art, of the means of instruction and amusement, as well as of those material requisites of a civilized life, the supply of which requires united action, such as gas and water, and railways?

When Government does not itself directly intervene, how far should it allow individuals and corporations to conduct their own affairs as they please? How far should it regulate the management of railways and other concerns which are to some extent in a position of monopoly, and again of land and other things the quantity of which cannot be increased by man? Is it necessary to retain in their full force all the existing rights of property; or have the original necessities

BOOK I CH VII

for which they were meant to provide, in some measure passed away?

Are the prevailing methods of using wealth entirely justifiable? What scope is there for the moral pressure of social opinion in constraining and directing individual action in those economic relations in which the rigidity and violence of Government interference would be likely to do more harm than good?

In what respect do the duties of one nation to another in economic matters differ from those of members of the same nation to one another?

The dominant aim of economics in the present generation is to contribute to a solution of social problems

Economics is thus taken to mean a study of the economic aspects and conditions of man's political, social and private life, but more especially of his social life. The aims of the study are to gain knowledge for its own sake, and to obtain guidance in the practical conduct of life, and especially of social life. The need for such guidance was never so urgent as now; a later generation may have more abundant leisure than we for researches that throw light on obscure points in abstract speculation, or in the history of past times, but do not afford immediate aid in present difficulties

But though thus largely directed by practical needs, economics avoids as far as possible the discussion of those exigencies of party organization, and those diplomacies of home and foreign politics of which the statesman is bound to take account in deciding what measures that he can propose will bring him nearest to the end that he desires to secure for his country. It aims indeed at helping him to determine not only what that end should be, but also what are the best methods of a broad policy devoted to that end. But it shuns many details of political tactics, which the practical man cannot ignore: and it is therefore a Science, Pure and Applied, rather than a Science and an Art. And it is better described as Social Economics, or as Economics simply, than as Political Economy.

BOOK II.

SOME FUNDAMENTAL NOTIONS.

CHAPTER I.

INTRODUCTORY.

Economics regards wealth as satisfying Wants and as the result of Efforts

§ 1. We have seen that economics is, on the one side, a Science of Wealth; and, on the other, that part of the Social Science of man's action in society, that deals with his Efforts to satisfy his Wants, in so far as the efforts and wants are capable of being measured in terms of wealth, or its general representative, *i.e.* money. We shall be occupied during the greater part of this volume with these wants and efforts, and the causes by which the prices that measure the wants are brought into equilibrium with those that measure the efforts. For this purpose we shall have to study in Book III. wealth in relation to the diversity of man's wants which it has to satisfy, and in Book IV. wealth in relation to the diversity of man's efforts by which it is produced.

But it is best to make a preliminary study of wealth itself

But in the present Book, we have to inquire which of all the things that are the result of man's efforts, and are capable of satisfying man's wants, are to be counted as Wealth; and into what groups or classes these are to be divided. For there is a compact group of terms connected with Wealth itself, and with Capital, the study of each of which throws light on the others; while the study of the whole together is a direct continuation, and in some respects a completion, of that inquiry as to the scope and methods of

BOOK II. CH. I

economics on which we have just been engaged. And, therefore, instead of taking what may seem the more natural course of starting with an analysis of wants, and of wealth in direct relation to them, it seems on the whole best to deal with this group of terms at once.

In doing this we shall of course have to take some account of the variety of wants and efforts; but we shall not want to assume anything that is not obvious and a matter of common knowledge. The real difficulty of our task lies in another direction; being the result of the need under which economics, alone among sciences, lies of making shift with a few terms in common use to express a great number of subtle distinctions.

Principles of classification.

§ 2 As Mill says[1]:—"The ends of scientific classification are best answered when the objects are formed into groups respecting which a greater number of general propositions can be made, and those propositions more important, than those which could be made respecting any other groups into which the same things could be distributed." But we meet at starting with the difficulty that those propositions which are the most important in one stage of economic development, are not unlikely to be among the least important in another, if indeed they apply at all.

The difficulties of classifying things which are changing their characters and their uses

In this matter economists have much to learn from the recent experiences of biology: and Darwin's profound discussion of the question[2] throws a strong light on the difficulties before us He points out that those parts of the structure which determine the habits of life and the general place of each being in the economy of nature, are as a rule not those which throw most light on its origin, but those which throw least. The qualities which a breeder or a gardener notices as eminently adapted to enable an animal or a plant to thrive in its environment, are for that very reason likely to have been developed in comparatively recent times And in like manner those properties of an economic institution which play the most important part in fitting it for the

[1] *Logic*, Bk IV. ch VII. Par. 2.

[2] *Origin of Species*, ch XIV.

work which it has to do now, are for that very reason likely to be in a great measure of recent growth[1].

But on the other hand we must keep constantly in mind the history of the terms which we use. For, to begin with, this history is important for its own sake, and because it throws side lights on the history of the economic development of society. And further, even if the sole purpose of our study of economics were to obtain knowledge that would guide us in the attainment of immediate practical ends, we should yet be bound to keep our use of terms as much as possible in harmony with the traditions of the past; in order that we might be quick to perceive the indirect hints and the subtle and subdued warnings, which the experiences of our ancestors offer for our instruction.

In its use of terms economics must follow as closely as possible the practice of every-day life

§ 3 Our task is difficult In physical sciences indeed, whenever it is seen that a group of things have a certain set of qualities in common, and will often be spoken of together, they are formed into a class with a special name; and as soon as a new notion emerges, a new technical term is invented to represent it But economics cannot venture to follow this example Its reasonings must be expressed in language that is intelligible to the general public, it must therefore endeavour to conform itself to the familiar terms of every-day life, and so far as possible must use them as they are commonly used.

But that is not always consistent,

In common use almost every word has many shades of meaning, and therefore needs to be interpreted by the context And, as Bagehot has pointed out, even the most formal writers on economic science are compelled to follow this course; for otherwise they would not have enough words at their disposal. But unfortunately they do not always

[1] Instances are found in many of the relations between employer and employed, between middleman and producer, between bankers and their two classes of clients, those from whom they borrow and those to whom they lend The substitution of the term "interest" for "usury" corresponds to a general change in the character of loans, which has given an entirely new key-note to our analysis and classification of the different elements into which the cost of production of a commodity may be resolved. Again, the general scheme of division of labour into skilled and unskilled is undergoing a gradual change, the scope of the term "rent" is being broadened in some directions and narrowed in others; and so on.

BOOK II. CH. I.

avow that they are taking this freedom; sometimes perhaps they are scarcely even aware of the fact themselves. The bold and rigid definitions, with which their expositions of the science begin, lull the reader into a false security. Not being warned that he must often look to the context for a special interpretation clause, he ascribes to what he reads a meaning different from that which the writers had in their own minds, and perhaps misrepresents them and accuses them of folly of which they had not been guilty. Misunderstandings of this kind have been a frequent source of controversies that have diverted energy from constructive work, and have hindered the progress of the science[1].

or definite.

Again, most of the chief distinctions marked by economic terms are differences not of kind but of degree At first sight they appear to be differences of kind, and to have sharp outlines which can be clearly marked out, but a more careful study has shown that there is no real breach of continuity It is a remarkable fact that the progress of economics has discovered hardly any new real differences in kind, while it is continually resolving apparent differences in kind into differences in degree. We shall meet with many instances of the evil that may be done by attempting to draw broad, hard and fast lines of division, and to formulate

[1] We ought "to write more as we do in common life, where the context is a sort of unexpressed 'interpretation clause,' only as in Political Economy we have more difficult things to speak of than in ordinary conversation, we must take more care, give more warning of any change; and at times write out 'the interpretation clause' for that page or discussion lest there should be any mistake I know that this is difficult and delicate work, and all that I have to say in defence of it is that in practice it is safer than the competing plan of inflexible definitions. Any one who tries to express various meanings on complex things with a scanty vocabulary of fastened senses, will find that his style grows cumbrous without being accurate, that he has to use long periphrases for common thoughts, and that after all he does not come out right, for he is half the time falling back into the senses which fit the case in hand best, and these are sometimes one, sometimes another, and almost always different from his 'hard and fast' sense In such discussions we should learn to vary our definitions as we want, just as we say 'let x, y, z, mean' now this, and now that, in different problems; and this, though they do not always avow it, is really the practice of the clearest and most effective writers" (Bagehot's *Postulates of English Political Economy*, pp. 78, 9) Cairnes also (*Logical Method of Political Economy*, Lect. VI) combats "the assumption that the attribute on which a definition turns ought to be one which does not admit of degrees;" and argues that "to admit of degrees is the character of all natural facts"

definite propositions with regard to differences between things which nature has not separated by any such lines.

Each term must have a definition corresponding to its leading use, supplemented by an interpretation clause when necessary

§ 4. We must then analyze carefully the real characteristics of the various things with which we have to deal; and we shall thus generally find that there is some use of each term which has distinctly greater claims than any other to be called its leading use, on the ground that it represents a distinction that is more important for the purposes of modern science than any other that is in harmony with ordinary usage. This may be laid down as the meaning to be given to the term whenever nothing to the contrary is stated or implied by the context[1]. When the term is wanted to be used in any other sense, whether broader or narrower, the change must be indicated, and a formal interpretation clause must be supplied, if there is the slightest danger of a misunderstanding[2]

[1] Even among the most careful thinkers there will always remain differences of opinion as to the exact places in which some at least of the lines of definition should be drawn The questions at issue must in general be solved by judgments as to the practical convenience of different courses, and such judgments cannot always be established or overthrown by scientific reasoning there must remain a margin of debatable ground. But there is no such margin in the analysis itself if two people differ with regard to that, they cannot both be right And the progress of the science may be expected gradually to establish this analysis on an impregnable basis

[2] When it is wanted to narrow the meaning of a term (that is, in logical language, to diminish its extension by increasing its intension) a qualifying adjective will generally suffice, but a change in the opposite direction cannot as a rule be so simply made Contests as to definitions are often of this kind —A and B are qualities common to a great number of things, many of these things have in addition the quality C, and again many the quality D, while some have both C and D It may then be argued that on the whole it will be best to define a term so as to include all things which have the qualities A and B, or only those which have the qualities A, B, C, or only those which have the qualities, A, B, D; or only those which have A, B, C, D The decision between these various courses must rest on considerations of practical convenience, and is a matter of far less importance than a careful study of the qualities A, B, C, D, and of their mutual relations But unfortunately this study has occupied a much smaller space in English economics than controversies as to definitions; which have indeed occasionally led indirectly to the discovery of scientific truth, but always by roundabout routes, and with much waste of time and labour.

CHAPTER II.

WEALTH.

BOOK II CH II

Wealth consists of desirable things or *Goods*.

ALL wealth consists of things that satisfy wants, directly or indirectly. All wealth consists of desirable things, or things that satisfy human wants; but not all desirable things are reckoned as wealth. The affection of friends, for instance, is an important element of well-being, but it is not reckoned as wealth, except by a poetic licence. Let us then begin by classifying desirable things, and then consider which of them should be accounted as elements of wealth.

§ 1. In the absence of any short term in common use to represent all desirable things, or things that satisfy human wants, we may for brevity sometimes use the term *Goods* for that purpose[1].

Material goods.

Desirable things or goods are Material, or Personal and Immaterial. *Material Goods* consist of useful material things, and of all rights to hold, or use, or derive benefits from material things, or to receive them at a future time. Thus they include the physical gifts of nature, land and water, air and climate; the products of agriculture, mining, fishing, and manufacture; buildings, machinery, and implements, mortgages and other bonds, shares in public and private companies, all kinds of monopolies, patent-rights, copyrights; also rights of way and other rights of usage. Lastly, opportunities of travel, access to good scenery, museums, etc. ought strictly speaking to be reckoned under this head.

Personal Goods

A man's *Personal Goods* fall into two classes. Under the

[1] The term *Commodity* has also been used for it; but *Good* is shorter, and is in correspondence with the German *Gut*.

first come the benefits he derives from other persons, such as labour dues and personal services of all kinds, property in slaves, the organization of his business, and his business connection generally. The second class consists of his own qualities and faculties for action and for enjoyment.

External and Internal

The former of these two classes is to be classed as *External*, and the latter *Internal*[1].

Transferable and non-transferable Goods

Again, goods may be *Transferable* or *Non-transferable*. Among the latter are to be classed a person's qualities and faculties for action and enjoyment (*i.e.* his internal goods); also such part of his business connection as depends on personal trust in him, and cannot be transferred as part of his vendible good will; also the advantages of climate, light, air, and his privileges of citizenship and rights and opportunities of making use of public property[2].

[1] For, in the words in which Hermann begins his masterly analysis of wealth, "Some Goods are *internal*, others *external*, to the individual. An internal good is that which he finds in himself given to him by nature, or which he educates in himself by his own free action, such as muscular strength, health, mental attainments. Everything that the outer world offers for the satisfaction of his wants is an external good to him."

[2] The above classification of goods may be expressed thus:—

Goods are
- external
  - material
    - transferable
    - non-transferable
  - personal
    - transferable
    - non-transferable
- internal-personal-non-transferable.

Or to adopt another arrangement which is more convenient for some purposes, thus:—

Goods are
- material-external
  - transferable
  - non-transferable
- personal
  - external
    - transferable
    - non transferable
  - internal non-transferable

The land in its original state was a free gift of nature. But in settled countries it is not a free good from the point of view of the individual. Wood is still free in some Brazilian forests: the fish of the sea are free generally: but some sea fisheries are jealously guarded for the exclusive use of members of a certain nation, and may be classed as national property. Oyster beds that have been planted by man are not free in any sense; those that have grown naturally are free in every sense if they are not appropriated; if they are private property they are still free gifts from the point of view of the nation, but since the nation has allowed its rights in them to become vested in individuals they are not free from the point of view of the individual, and the same is true of private rights of fishing in many rivers. But the wheat grown on free land and the fish caught in free fisheries are not free: for they have been acquired by labour.

BOOK II CH. II.

Those goods are *Free*, which are not appropriated and are afforded by Nature without requiring the effort of man.

Free goods Exchangeable goods.

Exchangeable goods are all those transferable goods which are limited in quantity and not free. This distinction is however not very important practically, because there are not many goods which are transferable, but being free, have no exchange value.

A person's *Wealth*

§ 2. We may now pass to the question which classes of a man's goods are to be reckoned as part of his wealth. The question is one as to which there is some difference of opinion, but the balance of argument as well as of authority seems clearly to incline in favour of the following answer:—

consists of two classes of goods,

When a man's *Wealth* is spoken of simply, and without any interpretation clause in the context, it is to be taken to consist of two classes of goods

material goods,

In the first class are those material goods to which he has (by Law or Custom) private rights of property, and which are therefore transferable and exchangeable. These it will be remembered include not only such things as land and houses, furniture and machinery, and other material things which may be in his single private ownership, but also any shares in public companies, debenture bonds, mortgages and other obligations which he may hold from others to pay goods to him. On the other hand, the debts which he owes to others may be regarded as negative wealth, and they must be subtracted from his gross possessions before his true net wealth can be found. It is perhaps hardly necessary to say specially that services and other goods, which pass out of existence in the same instant that they come into it, do not contribute to the stock of wealth, and may therefore be left out of our account[1].

and such immaterial external goods as are used to obtain material goods.

In the second class are those immaterial goods which belong to him, are external to him, and serve directly as the means of enabling him to acquire material goods. Thus it excludes all his own personal qualities and faculties, even those which enable him to earn his living; because they are

[1] That part of the value of the share in a trading company which is due to the personal reputation and connection of those who conduct its affairs ought properly to come under the next head as external personal goods. But this point is not of much practical importance

Internal. And it excludes his personal friendships, in so far as they have no direct business value. But it includes his business and professional connections, the organization of his business, and—where such things exist—his property in slaves, labour dues, &c.

The two classes together constitute *Economic Goods*

This use of the term Wealth is in harmony with the usage of ordinary life. and, at the same time, it includes those goods, and only those, which come clearly within the scope of economic science, as defined in Book I.; and which may therefore be called *Economic Goods*. For it includes all those things, external to a man, which (i) belong to him, and do not belong equally to his neighbours, and therefore are distinctly his; and (ii) which are directly capable of a money measure,—a measure that represents on the one side the efforts and sacrifices by which they have been called into existence, and, on the other, the wants which they satisfy[1]

A broader use of the term *wealth* is sometimes required

§ 3. A broader view of wealth has indeed to be taken for some purposes, but then recourse must be had to a special interpretation clause, to prevent confusion. Thus, for instance, the carpenter's skill is as direct a means of enabling him to satisfy other people's material wants, and therefore indirectly his own, as are the tools in his work-basket, and therefore it is convenient to have a term which will include it as part of wealth in a broader use Pursuing the lines indicated by Adam Smith[2], and followed by most continental economists, we may define *Personal Wealth* so as to include

Personal wealth.

[1] It is not implied that the owner of Transferable goods, if he transferred them, could always realize the whole money value, which they have for him A well fitting coat, for instance, may be worth the price charged for it by an expensive tailor to its owner, because he wants it and cannot get it made for less but he could not sell it for half that sum The successful financier who has spent £50,000 on having a house and grounds made to suit his own special fancy, is from one point of view right in reckoning them in the inventory of his property at their cost price but, should he fail, they will not form an asset to his creditors of anything like that value

And in the same way from one point of view we may count the business connection of the solicitor or physician, the merchant or the manufacturer, at the full equivalent of the income he would lose if he were deprived of it, while yet we must recognize that its exchange value, i e the value which he could get for it by selling it, is much less than that

[2] Comp *Wealth of Nations*, Book II Ch II

BOOK II. CH II

all those energies, faculties, and habits which directly contribute to making people industrially efficient; together with those business connections and associations of any kind, which we have already reckoned as part of wealth in the narrower use of the term. Industrial faculties have a claim to be regarded as economic, not only on account of their importance as factors in the production of wealth, but because their value is as a rule capable of some sort of indirect measurement[1].

A broad term to include all forms of private wealth

But confusion would be caused by using the term "wealth" simply when we desire to include a person's industrial qualities. For this purpose it will be best to use the more explicit phrase "material and personal wealth." "Wealth" simply should always mean external wealth only.

But we still have to take account of the individual's share of the common wealth

§ 4. But we still have to take account of those material goods which are common to him with his neighbours, and which therefore it would be a needless trouble to mention when comparing his wealth with theirs; though they may be important for some purposes, and especially for comparisons between the economic conditions of distant places or distant times.

These goods consist of the benefits which he derives from living in a certain place at a certain time, and being a member of a certain state or community; they include civil and military security, and the right and opportunity to make use of public property and institutions of all kinds, such as roads, gaslight, etc., and rights to justice or to a free education The townsman and the countryman have each of them

[1] "The bodies of men are without doubt the most valuable treasure of a country," said Davenant in the seventeenth century; and similar phrases have been common whenever the trend of political development has made men anxious that the population should increase fast.

Many curious, but practically unimportant, subtleties are met with in developing the definition of personal wealth; for instance, in so far as a person uses his faculties to do things for his own enjoyment, the benefit that he derives from them, though certainly part of his well-being, is perhaps best excluded from the estimate of his wealth. But the line of partition here is very thin For instance, the faculties of an opera singer are part of his wealth in so far as he uses them for hire, but are only elements of his well-being and not of his wealth in so far as he uses them to sing in private for his own pleasure When, however, a dressmaker makes a dress for herself, her dressmaking faculties may be regarded as wealth in the broad use of that term

for nothing many advantages which the other either cannot get at all, or can get only at great expense Other things being equal, one person has more real wealth in its broadest sense than another, if the place in which the former lives has a better climate, better roads, better water, more wholesome drainage; and again better newspapers, books, and places of amusement and instruction. House-room, food and clothing, which would be insufficient in a cold climate, may be abundant in a warm climate: on the other hand, that warmth which lessens men's physical needs, and makes them rich with but a slight provision of material wealth, makes them poor in the energy that procures wealth.

Collective Goods

Many of these things are *Collective Goods*; *i.e* goods which are not in private ownership. And this brings us to consider wealth from the Social, as opposed to the Individual point of view.

In a broad view of national wealth account must be taken of free goods and of the organization of society or the State

§ 5 Let us then look at those elements of the wealth of a nation which are commonly ignored when estimating the wealth of the individuals composing it. The most obvious forms of such wealth are public material property of all kinds, such as roads and canals, buildings and parks, gas-works and waterworks; though unfortunately many of them have been secured not by public savings, but by public borrowings, and there is the heavy "negative" wealth of a large debt to be set against them.

But the Thames has added more to the wealth of England than all its canals, and perhaps even than all its railroads. And though the Thames is a free gift of nature, except in so far as its navigation has been improved, while the canal is the work of man, we ought for many purposes to reckon the Thames a part of England's wealth.

German economists often lay stress on the non-material elements of national wealth; and it is right to do this in some problems relating to national wealth, but not in all. Scientific knowledge indeed, wherever discovered, soon becomes the property of the whole civilized world, and may be considered as cosmopolitan rather than as specially national wealth The same is true of mechanical inventions and of many other improvements in the arts of production; and it

BOOK II CH. II.

is true of music. But those kinds of literature which lose their force by translation, may be regarded as in a special sense the wealth of those nations in whose language they are written. And the organization of a free and well-ordered State is to be regarded for some purposes as an important element of national wealth.

But national wealth includes the individual as well as the collective property of its members. And in estimating the aggregate sum of their individual wealth, we may save some trouble by omitting all debts and other obligations due to one member of a nation from another. For instance, so far as the English national debt and the bonds of an English railway are owned within the nation, we can adopt the simple plan of counting the railway itself as part of the national wealth, and neglecting railway and Government bonds altogether. But we still have to deduct for those bonds etc. issued by the English Government or by private Englishmen, and held by foreigners; and to add for those foreign bonds etc. held by Englishmen[1].

Debts from one member of a nation to another may be omitted

[1] The value of a business may be to some extent due to its having a monopoly, either a complete monopoly, secured perhaps by a patent; or a partial monopoly, owing to its wares being better known than others which are really equally good; and in so far as this is the case the business does not add to the real wealth of the nation. If the monopoly were broken down, the diminution of national wealth due to the disappearance of its value would generally be more than made up, partly by the increased value of rival businesses, and partly by the increased purchasing power of the money representing the wealth of other members of the community (It should, however, be added that in some exceptional cases, the price of a commodity may be lowered in consequence of its production being monopolized. but such cases are very rare, and may be neglected for the present)

Again, business connections and trade reputations add to the national wealth, only in so far as they bring purchasers into relation with those producers who will meet their real wants most fully for a given price, or in other words, only in so far as they increase the extent to which the efforts of the community as a whole meet the wants of the community as a whole. Nevertheless when we are estimating national wealth, not directly but indirectly as the aggregate of individual wealth, we must allow for these businesses at their full value, even though this partly consists of a monopoly which is not used for the public benefit For the injury they do to rival producers was allowed for in counting up the values of the businesses of those rivals; and the injury done to consumers by raising the price of the produce, which they buy, was allowed for in reckoning the purchasing power of their means, so far as this particular commodity is concerned.

A special case of this is the organization of credit It increases the efficiency of production in the country, and thus adds to national wealth. And the power of obtaining credit is a valuable asset to any individual trader. If, however, any

Cosmopolitan wealth differs from national wealth much as that differs from individual wealth. In reckoning it, debts due from members of one nation to those of another may conveniently be omitted from both sides of the account. Again, just as rivers are important elements of national wealth, the ocean is one of the most valuable properties of the world. The notion of cosmopolitan wealth is indeed nothing more than that of national wealth extended over the whole area of the globe.

Cosmopolitan wealth

Individual and national rights to wealth rest on the basis of civil and international law, or at least of custom that has the force of law. An exhaustive investigation of the economic conditions of any time and place requires therefore an inquiry into law and custom, and economics owes much to those who have worked in this direction. But its boundaries are already wide; and the historical and juridical bases of the conceptions of property are vast subjects which may best be discussed in separate treatises[1].

The juridical basis of rights to wealth

accident should drive him out of business, the injury to national wealth is something less than the whole value of that asset, because some part at least of the business, which he would have done, will now be done by others with the aid of some part at least of the capital which he would have borrowed

There are similar difficulties as to how far money is to be reckoned as part of national wealth; but to treat them thoroughly would require us to anticipate a good deal of the Theory of Money

[1] Here again special reference may be made to Wagner's *Volkswirthschaftslehre*, which throws much light on the connection between the economic concept of wealth and the juridical concept of rights in private property.

CHAPTER III.

PRODUCTION. CONSUMPTION. LABOUR. NECESSARIES

BOOK II CH. III.

Man cannot produce matter, but only utilities inherent in matter

§ 1 MAN cannot create material things. In the mental and moral world indeed he may produce new ideas; but when he is said to produce material things, he really only produces utilities; or in other words, his efforts and sacrifices result in changing the form or arrangement of matter to adapt it better for the satisfaction of wants. All that he can do in the physical world is either to readjust matter so as to make it more useful, as when he makes a log of wood into a table; or to put it in the way of being made more useful by nature, as when he puts seed where the forces of nature will make it burst out into life[1].

The trader produces utilities

It is sometimes said that traders do not produce: that while the cabinet-maker produces furniture, the furniture-dealer merely sells what is already produced But there is no scientific foundation for this distinction. They both produce utilities, and neither of them can do more: the furniture-dealer moves and rearranges matter so as to make it more serviceable than it was before, and the carpenter does nothing more. The sailor or the railway-man who carries coal above ground produces it, just as much

[1] As James Mill has said, "The distinction between what is done by labour and what is done by nature is not always observed Labour produces its effects only by consistency with the laws of nature It is found that the agency of man can be traced to very simple elements. He does nothing but produce motion. He can move things towards one another, and he can separate them from one another. The properties of matter perform the rest" (*Elements of Political Economy*, Ch I) Dr Bonar (*Philosophy and Political Economy*, p 249) quotes from Bacon, *Novum Organon* IV., "Ad opera nil aliud potest homo quam ut corpora naturalia admoveat et amoveat, reliqua natura intus agit."

as the miner who carries it underground, the dealer in fish helps to move on fish from where it is of comparatively little use to where it is of greater use, and the fisherman does no more. It is true that if there are more traders than are necessary there is a waste. But there is also waste if there are two men to a plough which can be well worked by one man, in both cases all those who are at work produce, though they may produce but little. Some American and other writers have revived the mediæval attacks on trade on the ground that it does not produce But they have not aimed at the right mark They should have attacked the imperfect organization of trade, particularly of retail trade[1].

Man can consume, as he can produce, only utilities

Consumption may be regarded as negative production. Just as man can produce only utilities, so he can consume nothing more. He can produce services and other immaterial products, and he can consume them But as his production of material products is really nothing more than a rearrangement of matter which gives it new utilities, so his consumption of them is nothing more than a disarrangement of matter, which diminishes or destroys its utilities. Often indeed when he is said to consume things, he does nothing more than to hold them for his use, while, as Senior says, they "are destroyed by those numerous gradual agents which we call collectively *time*[2]." As the "producer" of wheat is he who puts seed where nature will make it grow, so the "consumer" of pictures, of curtains, and even of a house or a yacht does little to wear them out himself; but he uses them while time wastes them.

Consumers' and Producers' goods.

Goods have been divided into *Consumers' goods* (called also *Consumption goods*, or again *goods of the first Order*), such as food, clothes, &c., which satisfy wants *directly*; and *Producers' goods* (called also *Production goods*, or again *Instrumental*, or again *Intermediate goods*), such as ploughs and looms and raw cotton, which satisfy wants *indirectly* by contributing towards the production of the first class of goods.

[1] Production, in the narrow sense, changes the form and nature of products Trade and transport change their external relations.

[2] *Political Economy*, p. 54 Senior would like to substitute the verb "to use" for the verb "to consume"

BOOK II. CH III

The line of division between the two classes is however vague, is drawn in different places by different writers; and the terms can seldom be used safely without special explanation[1].

Nearly all labour is in some sense productive

§ 2. All labour is directed towards producing some effect. For though some exertions are taken merely for their own sake, as when a game is played for amusement, they are not counted as labour. We may define *labour* as any exertion of mind or body undergone partly or wholly with a view to some good other than the pleasure derived directly from the work[2]. And if we had to make a fresh start it would be best to regard all labour as productive except that which failed to promote the aim towards which it was directed, and so produced no utility But in all the many changes which the meaning of the word "productive" has undergone, it has had special reference to stored-up wealth, to the comparative neglect and sometimes even to the exclusion of immediate and transitory enjoyment[3]; and an almost

[1] Thus flour to be made into a cake when already in the house of the consumer, is treated by some as a Consumers' good; while not only the flour, but the cake itself is treated as a Producers' good when in the hand of the confectioner. Prof. Carl Menger (*Volkswirthschaftslehre*, ch. i § 2) says bread belongs to the first order, flour to the second, a flour mill to the third order and so on It appears that a railway train carrying people on a pleasure excursion, also some tins of biscuits, and milling machinery and some machinery that is used for making milling machinery, is at one and the same time a good of the first, second and fourth orders But such subtleties are of little use

[2] This is Jevons' definition (*Theory of Political Economy*, ch v), except that he includes only painful exertions. But he himself points out how painful idleness often is Most people work more than they would if they considered only the direct pleasure resulting from the work; but in a healthy state, pleasure predominates over pain in a great part even of the work that is done for hire. Of course the definition is elastic, an agricultural labourer working in his garden in the evening thinks chiefly of the fruit of his labours; a mechanic returning home after a day of sedentary toil finds positive pleasure in his garden work, but he too cares a good deal about the fruit of his labour; while a rich man working in like manner, though he may take a pride in doing it well, will probably care little for any pecuniary saving that he effects by it.

[3] Thus the Mercantilists who regarded the precious metals, partly because they were imperishable, as wealth in a fuller sense than anything else, regarded as unproductive or "sterile" all labour that was not directed to producing goods for exportation in exchange for gold and silver. The Physiocrats thought all labour sterile which consumed an equal value to that which it produced; and regarded the agriculturist as the only productive worker, because his labour alone (as they thought) left behind it a net surplus of stored-up wealth. Adam Smith softened down the Physiocratic definition; but still he considered that agricultural labour was more productive than any other His followers discarded

unbroken tradition compels us to regard the central notion of the word as relating to the provision for the wants of the future rather than those of the present. It is true that all wholesome enjoyments, whether luxurious or not, are legitimate ends of action both public and private: and it is true that the enjoyment of luxuries affords an incentive to exertion, and promotes progress in many ways. But if the efficiency and energy of industry are the same, the true interest of a country is generally advanced by the subordination of the desire for transient luxuries to the attainment of those more solid and lasting resources which will assist industry in its future work, and will in various ways tend to make life larger. This general idea has been in solution, as it were, in all stages of economic theory, and has been precipitated by different writers into various hard and fast distinctions by which certain trades have been marked off as productive and certain others as unproductive.

But that labour is generally said to be specially productive which provides for the wants of the future rather than the present

For instance, many writers even of recent times have adhered to Adam Smith's plan of classing domestic servants as unproductive. There is doubtless in many large houses a superabundance of servants, some of whose energies might with advantage to the community be transferred to some other direction: but the same is true of the greater part of those who earn their livelihood by distilling whisky, and yet no economist has proposed to call them unproductive There is no distinction in character between the work of the baker who provides bread for a family, and that of the cook who boils potatoes If the baker should be a confectioner, or fancy baker, it is probable that he spends at least as much of his time as the domestic cook does, on labour that is unproductive in the popular sense of providing transitory and unnecessary enjoyments.

The work of domestic servants is not necessarily unproductive

this distinction, but they have generally adhered, though with many differences in points of detail, to the notion that productive labour is that which tends to increase accumulated wealth; a notion which is implied rather than stated in the celebrated chapter of *The Wealth of Nations* which bears the title, "On the Accumulation of Capital, or on Productive and Unproductive Labour." (Comp. Travers Twiss, *Progress of Political Economy*, Sect VI, and the discussions on the word Productive in J S. Mill's *Essays*, and in his *Principles of Political Economy*)

BOOK II CH. III.

Productive is a transitive adjective. When precision is necessary the implied substantive must be supplied

There seems to be a way of escaping from most of these ambiguities and confusions. It would indeed be unsafe to invent a number of new terms to correspond to the various uses of "productive." But recollecting that it is a transitive adjective, we can avoid all difficulties by the simple plan of considering what is the implied substantive which it governs, and supplying that substantive explicitly. When it means *productive of accumulated wealth* in any form, let us write in the phrase at length and the ambiguity disappears; when it means *productive of capital* either in general or only in the particular form of *Wage capital* (to anticipate the use of terms which we are just about to define), let us say so.

Provisional definition of *productive*

But while frequently applied in each of these senses, it is still more often used to mean *productive of the means of production, and of lasting sources of enjoyment.* Whenever we use the word *productive* by itself, this is the sense in which it is to be understood. Among the means of production are included the necessaries of labour but not ephemeral luxuries; and the maker of ices is thus classed as unproductive whether he is working for a pastry-cook, or as a private servant in a country house But a bricklayer engaged in building a theatre is classed as productive.

There is no hard and fast line of division in nature and we seldom want an artificial one

No doubt the dividing line between permanent and ephemeral sources of enjoyment cannot be drawn rigidly But this is a difficulty which exists in the nature of things and cannot be evaded by any device of words We can speak of an increase of tall men relatively to short, without deciding whether all those above five feet nine inches are to be classed as tall, or only those above five feet ten. And we can speak of the increase of productive labour at the expense of unproductive without fixing on any rigid, and therefore arbitrary line of division between them. If such an artificial line is required for any particular purpose, it must be drawn explicitly for the occasion. But in fact such occasions seldom or never occur.

Productive consumption

Productive consumption is commonly defined as the use of wealth in the production of further wealth. But this definition is ambiguous. For it is sometimes taken to include everything that is actually consumed by people engaged in productive work, even though it may not conduce at all to their efficiency as workers. But *productive consumption*, strictly so called, must be taken to include only such consumption by productive workers as is necessary for their work; under which head may be reckoned the necessary consumption of children who will hereafter be productive workers as well as that of adults during sickness[1].

Necessaries are things which meet wants that *must* be satisfied. But this account is ambiguous

§ 3. This brings us to consider the term Necessaries. It is common to divide wealth into Necessaries, Comforts, and Luxuries; the first class including all things required to meet wants which *must* be satisfied, while the latter consist of things that meet wants of a less urgent character. But here again there is a troublesome ambiguity. When we say that a want *must* be satisfied, what are the consequences which we have in view if it is not satisfied? Do they include death? Or do they extend only to the loss of strength and vigour? In other words are Necessaries the things which are necessary for life, or those which are necessary for efficiency?

The term Necessaries is elliptical

The term Necessaries like the term Productive has been used elliptically, the subject to which it refers being left to be supplied by the reader; and since the implied subject has varied, the reader has often supplied one which the writer did not intend, and thus misunderstood his drift. In this, as in the preceding case, the chief source of confusion can be

[1] All the distinctions in which the word Productive is used are very thin and have a certain air of unreality It would hardly be worth while to introduce them now but they have a long history; and it is probably better that they should dwindle gradually out of use, rather than be suddenly discarded.

The attempt to draw a hard and fast line of distinction where there is no real discontinuity in nature has often done more mischief, but has perhaps never led to more quaint results, than in the rigid definitions which have been sometimes given of this term Productive Some of them for instance lead to the conclusion that a singer in an opera is unproductive, that the printer of the tickets of admission to the opera is productive, while the usher who shows people to their places is unproductive, unless he happens to sell programmes, and then he is productive. Senior points out that "a cook is not said to *make* roast meat but to *dress* it; but he is said to *make* a pudding . . . A tailor is said to *make* cloth into a coat, a dyer is not said to *make* undyed cloth into dyed cloth The change produced by the dyer is perhaps greater than that produced by the tailor, but the cloth in passing through the tailor's hands changes its name; in passing through the dyer's it does not the dyer has not produced a *new name*, nor consequently a *new thing*." *Pol. Econ* pp 51—2.

BOOK II. CH. III.

removed by supplying explicitly in every critical place that which the reader is intended to understand

Necessaries for existence, and for efficiency

The older use of the term Necessaries was limited to those things which were sufficient to enable the labourers, taken one with another, to support themselves and their families. Adam Smith and the more careful of his followers observed indeed variations in the standard of comfort at different times and places: they recognized that differences of climate and differences of custom make things necessary in some cases, which are superfluous in others. But Adam Smith's view was much influenced by that of the Physiocrats, and their reasonings were based on the condition of the French people in the eighteenth century, the great mass of whom had no notion of any necessaries beyond those which were required for mere existence In happier times, however, a more careful analysis has brought into prominence the distinction between the necessaries for efficiency and the necessaries for existence, and has made it evident that there is for each rank of industry, at any time and place, a more or less clearly defined income which is necessary for merely sustaining its members; while there is another and larger income which is necessary for keeping it in full efficiency[1].

Account must be taken of the conditions of place and time and of the habits of living

It may be true that the wages of any industrial class might have sufficed to maintain a higher efficiency, if they had been spent with perfect wisdom But every estimate of necessaries must be relative to a given place and time; and unless there be a special interpretation clause to the contrary, it may be assumed that the wages will be spent with just

[1] Thus in the South of England population has increased during the present century at a fair rate, allowance being made for migration But the efficiency of labour, which in earlier times was as high as that in the North of England, has sunk relatively to the North; so that the low-waged labour of the South is often dearer than the more highly-paid labour of the North. We cannot thus say whether the labourers in the South have been supplied with necessaries, unless we know in which of these two senses the word is used They have had the bare necessaries for existence and the increase of numbers, but apparently they have not had the necessaries for efficiency It must however be remembered that the strongest labourers in the South have constantly migrated to the North; and that the energies of those in the North have been raised by their larger share of economic freedom and of the hope of rising to a higher position. See Mr Mackay in *Charity Organization Journal*, Feb 1891.

that amount of wisdom, forethought, and unselfishness, which prevails in fact among the industrial class under discussion. With this understanding we may say that the income of any class in the ranks of industry is below its *necessary* level, when any increase in their income would in the course of time produce a more than proportionate increase in their efficiency. Consumption may be economized by a change of habits, but any stinting of necessaries is wasteful[1].

Necessaries

§ 4. Some detailed study of the necessaries for efficiency of different classes of workers will have to be made, when we come to inquire into the causes that determine the supply of efficient labour. But it will serve to give some definiteness to our ideas, if we consider here what are the necessaries for the efficiency of an ordinary agricultural or of an unskilled town labourer and his family, in England, in this generation. They may be said to consist of a well-drained dwelling with several rooms, warm clothing, with some changes of underclothing, pure water, a plentiful supply of cereal food, with a moderate allowance of meat and milk, and a little tea, &c., some education and some recreation, and lastly, sufficient freedom for his wife from other work to enable her to perform properly her maternal and her household duties. If in any district unskilled labour is deprived of any of these things, its efficiency will suffer in the same way as that of a horse that is not properly tended, or a steam-engine that has an inadequate supply of coals. All consumption up to this limit is strictly productive consumption: any stinting of this consumption is not economical, but wasteful.

Illustration. Necessaries of unskilled labour

There is waste when any one consumes less than is necessary.

[1] If we considered an individual of exceptional abilities we should have to take account of the fact that there is not likely to be the same close correspondence between the real value of his work for the community and the income which he earns by it, that there is in the case of an ordinary member of any industrial class. And we should have to say that all his consumption is strictly productive and necessary, so long as by cutting off any part of it he would diminish his efficiency by an amount that is of more real value to him or the rest of the world than he saved from his consumption. If a Newton or a Watt could have added a hundredth part to his efficiency by doubling his personal expenditure, the increase in his consumption would have been truly productive. As we shall see later on, such a case is analogous to additional cultivation of rich land that bears a high rent: it may be profitable though the return to it is less than in proportion to the previous outlay.

BOOK II. CH. III.

Conventional necessaries.

In addition, perhaps, some consumption of alcohol and tobacco, and some indulgence in fashionable dress are in many places so habitual, that they may be said to be *conventionally necessary*, since in order to obtain them the average man and woman will sacrifice some things which are necessary for efficiency. Their wages are therefore less than are practically necessary for efficiency, unless they provide not only for what is strictly necessary consumption, but include also a certain amount of conventional necessaries[1].

The consumption of conventional necessaries by productive workers is commonly classed as productive consumption, but strictly speaking it ought not to be; and in critical passages a special interpretation clause should be added to say whether or not they are included

It should however be noticed that many things which are rightly described as superfluous luxuries, do yet, to some extent, take the place of necessaries; and to that extent their consumption is productive when they are consumed by producers[2].

[1] Compare the distinction between "Physical and Political Necessaries" in Sir James Steuart's *Inquiry*, II xxi

[2] Thus a dish of green peas in March, costing perhaps ten shillings, is a superfluous luxury but yet it is wholesome food, and does the work perhaps of three pennyworth of cabbage, or even, since variety undoubtedly conduces to health, a little more than that So it may be entered perhaps at the value of fourpence under the head of necessaries, and at that of nine shillings and eightpence under that of superfluities; and its consumption may be regarded as strictly productive to the extent of one fortieth In exceptional cases, as for instance when the peas are given to an invalid, the whole ten shillings may be well spent, and reproduce their own value

For the sake of giving definiteness to the ideas it may be well to venture on estimates of necessaries, rough and random as they must be. Perhaps at present prices the strict necessaries for an average agricultural family are covered by fifteen or eighteen shillings a week, the conventional necessaries by about five shillings more For the unskilled labourer in the town a few shillings must be added to the strict necessaries For the family of the skilled workman living in a town we may take twenty-five or thirty shillings for strict necessaries, and ten shillings for conventional necessaries. For a man whose brain has to undergo great continuous strain the strict necessaries are perhaps two hundred or two hundred and fifty pounds a year if he is a bachelor: but more than twice as much if he has an expensive family to educate His conventional necessaries depend on the nature of his calling

CHAPTER IV.

CAPITAL INCOME

BOOK II CH IV

The term capital has many different uses. We may not venture to invent a separate term for each of them

§ 1. It is customary to divide wealth into that which is capital and that which is not. But there are many different purposes for which the division is wanted; and in consequence the term Capital has many different uses both in the language of the market-place and in the writings of economists. In fact there is no other part of economics in which the temptation is so strong to invent a completely new set of technical terms; each of which should have a precise and fixed meaning, while between them they should cover all the various significations which are given to the one term Capital in the language of the market-place. But this would throw the science out of touch with real life; and formal precision would be obtained at too great a cost. We must then first seek for the central notions that underlie all these various uses, and consider generally their relations to one another, and afterwards must follow the practice of ordinary life in allowing ourselves some elasticity in the use of the term, but taking care always to say explicitly how we are using it whenever there is room for doubt.

Productiveness and prospectiveness of capital

In almost every use, the conception of capital involves two fundamental attributes, that of "productiveness," and that of "prospectiveness" or the subordination of present desires to future enjoyments and these two attributes have much in common For, as we saw in the last chapter, that labour is commonly said to be employed productively which provides for wants of the future rather than the present

BOOK II. CH IV.

Similarly with regard to wealth: that also is commonly said to be employed productively, when it is devoted to providing for the future rather than the present. And further these two fundamental notions supplement one another, ranging themselves one on either side of the problem of interest; that is, of the value of the command over ready capital. This point can be touched but lightly now, for indeed to touch it at all is to anticipate: but without some reference to it, no true notion can be had of the inner relations of the fundamental attributes of capital.

control the demand for it and the supply of it

The chief *demand* for capital arises from its productiveness, from the services which it renders, for instance, in enabling wool to be spun and woven more easily than by unaided hand, or in causing water to flow freely wherever it is wanted instead of being carried laboriously in pails, (though there are other uses of capital, as for instance when it is lent to a spendthrift, which cannot easily be brought under this head). And on the other hand the *supply* of capital is controlled by the fact that in order to accumulate it, men must act prospectively: they must "wait" and "save," they must sacrifice the present to the future. And, as we shall see, the exchange value of the services rendered by capital is governed in the long run by the pressure of the eagerness of demand against the sluggishness of supply[1].

Differences between capital and other

§ 2. The task of finding a good definition of capital is however not so easy as would appear from the fact that these two attributes of productiveness and prospectiveness

[1] The connection of the productiveness of capital with the demand for it, and of its prospectiveness with the supply of it has long been latent in men's minds, though much overlaid by other considerations, many of which appear now to be based on misconceptions. Some writers have laid more stress on the supply side and others on the demand side: but the difference between them has often been little more than a difference of emphasis. Those who have laid stress on the productivity of capital, have not been ignorant of man's unwillingness to save and sacrifice the present for the future. And on the other hand, those who have given their thought mainly to the nature and extent of the sacrifice involved in this postponement, have regarded as obvious such facts as that a store of the implements of production gives mankind a largely increased power of satisfying their wants. In short there is no reason to believe that the accounts which Prof. Böhm-Bawerk has given of the "naive productivity theories," the "use theories" &c of capital and interest would have been accepted by the older writers themselves as well balanced and complete presentations of their several positions.

belong to it in all its various uses. For they belong also in some degree to every form of accumulated wealth. They both belong for instance to cooking utensils and to clothes; and yet when these things are being used by their owners for their own purposes, they are counted as capital only by those who draw no distinction between wealth and capital. To make any consistent distinction betweem them, we must emphasize differences of degree Similar differences of degree will be found in the various uses of the term Income, and this suggests a solution of our difficulty.

forms of wealth are mainly differences of degree

For Adam Smith said that a person's capital is *that part of his stock from which he expects to derive an income*; and in fact each use of the term capital has corresponded more or less closely to one of the uses of the term Income. The significations of the two terms have varied in breadth together. in almost every use, capital has been that part of a man's stock from which he expects to derive an income

Capital yields income.

In ordinary life capital is commonly regarded from the point of view of the individual; and economists are much bound by the customs of the market-place in their uses of the term *Individual capital.* But they have a freer hand in dealing with *Social capital,* that is capital regarded from the point of view of the nation, or the world, or indeed any social group[1]. We will begin with the former and work up to the latter, having regard throughout to the relativity of capital and income.

§ 3. In a primitive community no distinction is made between capital and other forms of wealth each family is nearly self-sufficing, and provides most of its own food and clothing and even household furniture. Only a very small part of the income, or comings in, of the family are in the form of money; when one thinks of their income at all one reckons in the benefits which they get from their cooking utensils just as much as those which they get from their plough: one draws no distinction between their capital and the rest of their accumulated stock, to which the cooking utensils and plough alike belong[2].

Income in its broad use

[1] Compare the discussion of individual and social wealth in Chapter II

[2] This and similar facts have led some people to suppose not only that some

BOOK II CH. IV.

Corresponding to *money-income*,

But with the growth of a money economy there has been a strong tendency to confine the notion of income to those comings in which are in the form of money; or else—like the free use of a house, the free coals, gas, water of some employés—take the place of things on which most people spend a part of their money income.

we have *trade capital*

In harmony with this meaning of Income, the language of the market-place commonly regards a man's capital as that part of his wealth which he devotes to acquiring an income in the form of money, or, more generally, to acquisition (*Erwerbung*) by means of trade. It may be convenient sometimes to speak of this as his *Trade capital*; which may be defined to consist of those external goods which a person uses in his trade, either holding them to be sold for money or applying them to produce things that are to be sold for money Among its conspicuous elements are such things as the factory and the business plant of a manufacturer; that is, his machinery, his raw material, any food, clothing, and house-room that he may hold for the use of his employés, and the goodwill of his business[1].

Its most conspicuous elements

To the things in his possession must be added those to which he has a right and from which he is drawing income· including loans which he has made on mortgage or in other ways, and all the command over capital which he may hold under the complex forms of the modern "money market." On the other hand debts owed by him must be deducted from his capital[2].

parts of the modern analysis of distribution and exchange are inapplicable to a primitive community; which is true but also that there are no important parts of it that are applicable, which is not true This is a striking instance of the dangers that arise from allowing ourselves to become the servants of words, avoiding the hard work that is required for discovering unity of substance underlying variety of form

[1] Under this head are to be reckoned fancy ball dresses that are let out for hire, but not the house in which a frugal working man lives if he happens to own it himself; ices in the hands of a pastry-cook, but not the store of wheat for his own use which a man has grown on his allotment; and not even the sewing-machine with which his wife makes clothes for the family M Gide has used the term *Lucrative capital* to denote that part of Trade capital which "does not really serve to produce new wealth, but merely yields an income to its owner"

[2] When we come to discuss the intricacies of the modern money market we shall have to consider the limitations under which coined money, bank notes, bank

This use of Capital has great prestige in spite of its disadvantages

§ 4. The dominant use of the term Capital for ordinary purposes is undoubtedly that to which the name of Trade capital has been given: and we may look at the causes which have given it this prestige, in spite of its disadvantages.

Its disadvantages are indeed great and obvious. For instance it compels us to regard as capital the yachts, but not the carriage, belonging to a yacht builder. If therefore he had been hiring a carriage by the year, and instead of continuing to do so, sold a yacht to a carriage builder who had been hiring it, and bought a carriage for his own use, the result would be that the total stock of capital in the country would be diminished by a yacht and a carriage. And this, though nothing had been destroyed, and though there remained the same products of saving, themselves productive of as great benefits to the individuals concerned and to the community as before, and probably even of greater benefits.

Trade capital not the only form of wealth which gives employment to labour

Nor can we avail ourselves here of the notion that capital is distinguished from other forms of wealth by its superior power of giving employment to labour. For in fact, when yachts and carriages are in the hands of dealers and are thus counted as capital, less employment is given to labour by a given amount of yachting or carriage driving than when the yachts and carriages are in private hands and are not counted as capital[1].

But such facts as these are often overlooked; and here lies a part of the explanation of the prestige of this use of the term Capital.

But it does specially affect the policy of the Labour Market

Again, the relations between private employers and their employed seldom enter into the strategical and tactical movements of the conflicts between employers and employed;

deposits, bank credit accounts, &c. may properly be regarded as capital, firstly from the point of view of the individual, and secondly from that of the community

[1] The employment of labour would not be increased but lessened by the substitution of professional cookshops and bakeries (where all the appliances are reckoned as capital) for private kitchens (where nothing is reckoned as capital) Under a professional employer, the workers may possibly have more personal freedom: but they almost certainly have less material comfort, and lower wages in proportion to the work they do than under the laxer régime of a private employer

BOOK II. CH IV

or, as is commonly said, between capital and labour. This point has been emphasized by Karl Marx and others: who have avowedly made the definition of capital turn on it[1].

and it has a special place in the Money Market

But further, this use of capital is prominent in the Money Market as well as in the Labour Market. Loans are indeed made on houses and furniture, on yachts and carriages in private ownership: but they are relatively rare. And Trade capital is habitually connected with loans. No one hesitates to borrow in order to increase the trade capital at his command, when he can see a good opening for its use. and for doing this he can pledge his own trade capital more easily, and more regularly in the ordinary course of business transactions, than he could his furniture or his private carriage. Lastly, a man makes up the accounts of his trade capital carefully; he allows for depreciation as a matter of course: and thus he keeps his stock intact[2].

In estimating social capital

§ 5 When we pass to the social point of view we are at liberty to neglect many rights of individual ownership, and to lay more exclusive stress on purely economic considerations. But experience shows that there is great difficulty in making good use of this liberty[3].

internal debts may be neglected

Something is indeed clearly gained in matters of detail. For instance, mortgages and other debts between persons of the same nation (or other social group) can be omitted, since the entries made for them on the creditor and debtor side of the national capital would cancel one another.

1 Their point of view is, that only that is capital which is a means of production owned by one person (or group of persons) and used to produce things for the benefit of another, generally by means of the hired labour of a third, in such wise that the first has the opportunity of plundering or exploiting the others

2 A man who has been hiring a carriage by the year, can buy it with the produce of the sale of railway stock that yields very much less interest than he has paid as hire If he lets the annual income accumulate till the carriage is worn out, it will more than suffice to buy him a new one and thus his total stock of capital will have been increased by the change But there is a chance that he will not do this. whereas, so long as the carriage was owned by the dealer, he provided for replacing it in the ordinary course of his business

3 Rodbertus emphasized the distinction between individual rights in capital in a historic-juristic sense (*Kapital im historisch-rechtlichen Sinne*, *Kapital-vermogen*, *Kapital-besitz*) and the social view of pure capital. And this distinction has been developed by Knies, Neumann, Wagner and others

Again, though the balance of usage and convenience is in favour of reckoning rights to land as part of individual capital, it is best to put under separate heads those of the nation's resources which were made by men, and those which were not; and to separate the capital which is the result of labour and saving from those things which nature has given freely[1].

and land omitted.

But when we try to go further, and to apply clear-cut principles to the line of demarcation of capital, we meet a great divergence of opinion; and that divergence is the result, not of accident, but of causes which are not to be removed.

Opinions differ as to the relative importance of its chief attributes.

[For the notion of social capital enters into many veins of economic thought; and whatever definition a writer takes at starting, he finds that the various elements of which capital is composed differ more or less from one another in the way in which they enter into the different problems with which he has successively to deal; and he is compelled to supplement his standard definition by an explanation of the bearing of each several element of capital on the point at issue.] Thus the divergence at starting turns out to be a less evil than it seemed. For ultimately there is a general convergence; and the reader is brought to very much the same conclusion by whatever route he travels; though it may indeed require a little trouble to discern the unity in substance, underlying the differences in the words which are used by various schools of economists to express their doctrines.

But in spite of this divergence,

For instance, whatever definition of capital be taken, it will be found to be true that a general increase of capital augments the demand for labour and raises wages: and whatever definition be taken it is not true that all kinds of capital act with equal force in this direction, or that it is possible to say how great an effect any given increase in the total amount of capital will have in raising wages, without specially inquiring as to the particular form which the increase has taken This inquiry is the really important part of the work · it has to be made, and it is made by all

there is substantial agreement on practical issues

[1] This separation is not indeed always very easy. See Book IV. ch. II , Book V. ch VIII , IX., Book VI ch. X , XI.

BOOK II CH IV

careful writers in very much the same manner, and it comes to the same result, whatever be the definition of capital with which we have started.

We may pass quickly in review the leading notions on which various writers have endeavoured to base precise definitions.

Capital regarded mainly as the result of labour and saving.

§ 6. For some purposes it is important to insist on the notion of prospectiveness, and to regard capital as a store of things the result of human efforts and sacrifices, devoted mainly to securing benefits in the future rather than in the present. But those who have tried to take their stand definitely on this notion have found themselves on an inclined plane· and have not reached a stable resting-place till they have included all accumulated wealth as capital[1]

[1] It may be said that a stone house, which will last many hundred years, is more truly capital than a wooden house, which on the whole gives equal accommodation in the present, but lasts only a short time and that costly but thoroughly efficient machinery, and other plant of the Western World, are more truly capital than the slight and wasteful appliances of poorer and less prospective countries. But this rather helps to elucidate the notion of capital than to define the term We shall return to this point in Book III ch. V and Book IV. ch VII.

It may be noted that nearly all the earlier French Economists have followed in the lines laid down by the Physiocrats before Adam Smith wrote, and used the term "capital" very much in the sense in which he and his immediate followers used the word "stock," to include all accumulated wealth (*valeurs accumulées*); i e all the result of the excess of production over consumption And although in recent years they have shown a decided tendency to use the term in the narrower English sense, there is at the same time a considerable movement on the part of some of the profoundest thinkers in Germany and England in the direction of the older and broader French definition The Physiocrats were undoubtedly led in this direction by their bias towards mathematical habits of thought; because it is possible to represent by a clear cut mathematical formula the elements of past labours that were devoted to providing for the needs of the future, each multiplied by compound interest for the time during which its fruits were in abeyance This formula has great attractions, but it does not correspond closely to the conditions of real life For instance it takes no account of the different rates of depreciation of different products of past labour, according as the purposes for which they were originally intended have retained their ground, or have become obsolete. And when corrections of this class are introduced the formula loses its one great merit of simplicity combined with exactness

It was probably Hermann's mathematical bias that inclined him to say (*Staatswirthschaftliche Untersuchungen*, Chs III and V) that capital consists of goods "which are a lasting source of satisfaction that has exchange value"

Again, Walras (*Éléments d'Économie Politique*, p. 197) defines capital as "every kind of social wealth which is not consumed at all, or is consumed but slowly; every utility limited in quantity, that survives the first use which is made

§ 7. Accordingly most of the attempts to define capital from a purely economic point of view, whether in England or other countries, have turned on its productivity: and have regarded social capital as a means for acquisition (*Erwerbs-kapital*), or as a supply of the requisites of production (*Productions-mittel-Vorrath*) But this general notion has been treated in different ways.

Capital regarded mainly as a means of production;

According to the older English traditions capital consists of those things which *aid or support* labour in production; or, as has been said more recently, it consists of those things

and firstly as both supporting and aiding labour

of it; in one word, which can be used more than once a house, a piece of furniture"

The American Astronomer, Newcomb (*Principles of Political Economy*, Book II ch. V), defines capital as "wealth desired not for its own sake, but for the sake of the Sustenance [*i.e* Consumption-wealth] which it will enable us to produce," and proposes that we should debit a person who lives in a hired house with *negative capital* to the amount of the value of that house He thus carries out to its logical conclusion a proposal that has often been made (as for instance by Mr Macleod) with regard to the loan of capital His plan simplifies the relation in which social capital stands to individual capital, and it avoids the difficulty, which has been noticed in the text, of having to say that when a boat builder hires his carriage from a carriage builder, who meanwhile hires his yacht from the boat builder, the capital of each would be diminished if each were to buy the thing that he has been hiring But his plan still fails to exhibit clearly the increased provision for the future which is made when a durable stone house is substituted for a perishable wooden one, which gave for the time equal accommodation

The same mathematical bias has led Jevons to a very similar conclusion (see in particular his "Quantitative Notions concerning Capital," and his argument that "Articles in the consumer's hands are capital," in ch VII of his *Theory of Political Economy*) His position is thus admirably described by M Gide — "Stanley Jevons asserts that stores of food are typical capital, and are its essential and primordial manifestations whence all the other forms have sprung. Indeed his premise is that the true function of capital is to support the worker while waiting for the moment when his labour can give good results. This definition of the function of capital necessarily requires it to exist under the shape of means of subsistence, of *advances*. Of these, all tools, machines, railways, etc. would be only derivative forms, for their production takes some time, perhaps a considerable period; and hence they must have required a previous amount of advances in the shape of stores of food It is to this primary form, therefore, that we have always to return." It will be seen that Prof. Böhm-Bawerk has mistaken its drift, when he says (*Positive Capital*, Book I. ch V) that "if it were correct every land would be rich in capital in proportion as its wages were high and its means of subsistence cheap."

Knies defines capital as the existing stock of goods "which is ready to be applied to the satisfaction of demand in the future." And Nicholson says —"The line of thought suggested by Adam Smith and developed by Knies is found to lead to this result Capital is wealth set aside for the satisfaction—directly or indirectly—of future needs" But the term "set aside" does not seem to give a clue to a solution of the difficulties mentioned in the text

without which production could not be carried on with equal efficiency, but which are not free gifts of nature. From this point of view it has been divided into Consumption capital and Auxiliary capital

Consumption capital. *Consumption capital* consists of goods in a form to satisfy wants directly; that is, goods which afford a direct sustenance to the workers, such as food, clothes, house-room, &c.

Auxiliary capital *Auxiliary capital* is so called because it consists of all the goods that aid labour in production. Under this head come tools, machines, factories, railways, docks, ships, &c.; and raw materials of all kinds[1].

Unfortunately capital regarded from this point of view has often been taken to include all the things which employers directly or indirectly provide in payment for the work of their employees—*Wage capital* or *Remuneratory capital,* as it is called; but yet not to include any of the things needed for their own support, or that of architects, engineers, and other professional men. To complete this notion of capital we should include the necessaries for efficiency of all classes of workers; and ought, strictly speaking, to exclude the luxuries of the manual labour classes as well as of other workers. But if it had been pushed to this logical conclusion, it would not have played the prominent part which it did in the discussion of the relations of employers and employed in the first half of the century[2].

[1] See above, p 133

[2] Of course there is a fringe of debateable ground at the margin of each definition A factory is Auxiliary capital simply; a weaver's cottage in which he plies his trade is partly Auxiliary and partly Consumption capital. The private dwelling house of a rich man engaged in business is Consumption capital to the extent of that accommodation which directly contributes to the health and efficiency of himself and his family but beyond that, it is not capital at all, in the use of the term which we are adopting

Held laid stress on the relation between the definition of capital and the practical problems which were then prominent People were anxious to insist that the welfare of the working classes depended on a provision of the means of employment and sustenance made beforehand and to emphasize the dangers of attempting to make employment for them artificially under the extravagance of the Protective system and the old Poor-law. (Held's point of view has been developed with great acumen in Mr Cannan's suggestive and interesting *Production and Distribution*, 1776—1848 though some of the utterances of the earlier economists seem capable of interpretation quite as obvious as those which

Capital regarded mainly as a means of production, and as aiding but not supporting labour

§ 8. In other countries however, and especially in Germany and Austria, there has been some tendency to confine capital (from the social point of view) to that which English writers have called Auxiliary capital, and which is now sometimes called Instrumental capital. It is argued that in order to keep clear the contrast between production and consumption, nothing which enters directly into consumption should be regarded as a means to production. But there appears no good reason why a thing should not be regarded in a twofold capacity, if it be found convenient to do so[1]

It is further argued that those things which render their services to man not directly, but through the part which they play in preparing other things for his use, form a compact class, because their value is derived from that of the things which they help to produce. There is much to be said for having a name for this group. But there is room for doubt whether capital is a good name for it, and also for doubt whether the group is as compact as it appears at first sight[2].

Mr Cannan attaches to them, and more consistent with the belief that they were not greatly deficient in common sense)

The following are among the chief definitions of capital by Adam Smith's English followers —Ricardo says —"Capital is that part of the wealth of a country which is employed in production and consists of food, clothing, tools, raw materials, machinery, etc necessary to give effect to labour." Malthus says — "Capital is that portion of the stock of a country which is kept or employed with a view to profit in the production and distribution of wealth" Senior says — "Capital is an article of wealth, the result of human exertion, employed in the production or distribution of wealth" John Stuart Mill says —"What capital does for production, is to afford the shelter, protection, tools and materials which the work requires, and to feed and otherwise maintain the labourers during the process Whatever things are destined for this use are capital." We shall have to return to this conception of capital in connection with the so-called Wages Fund doctrine

[1] An argument to this effect is given by Wagner (*Grundlegung*, Ed III pp 315—6); who includes Consumer's capital in his excellent and almost exhaustive discussion of the subject

[2] Thus we may define instrumental goods so as to include tramways and other things which derive their value from the personal services which they render; or we may follow the example of the old use of the phrase productive labour, and insist that those things only are properly to be regarded as instrumental goods the work of which is directly embodied in a material product. The former definition brings this use of the term rather close to that discussed in the last section and shares with it the demerit of vagueness The latter is a little more

BOOK II. CH IV

No one definition convenient for all purposes

§ 9 Thus we finally arrive at the conclusion foreshadowed at the beginning of this chapter. There are several more or less precise definitions of capital, which are useful for certain special purposes: and there may be something to be said for inventing separate terms for each of them. But there is no one rigid definition which is universally available. Something must be left for explanation by the context.

Standard use of individual capital

Whenever capital is being discussed from the individual point of view, it will be taken in this treatise to mean trade capital unless the contrary is explicitly stated.

Social capital may be defined as wealth which yields income as commonly understood.

But we shall be much occupied in considering the way in which the three agents of production, land (that is, natural agents), labour and capital, contribute to producing the national income (or the National Dividend, as it will be called later on), and the way in which this is distributed between the three agents.

Now there is a tacit, but thorough agreement among all writers on economics, to treat this income in its broad outlines only, and not to trouble about petty details So far as scientific considerations go, we should be quite at liberty to count as part of that income all the income of benefit that everyone derives from the use of his own clothes, furniture, &c. If we did that, we should need to count everyone to this extent as a capitalist, and to credit him under this head with the share of the total national income which corre-

definite but seems to make an artificial distinction where nature has made none, and to be as unsuitable for scientific purposes as the old use of productive labour.

Prof Böhm Bawerk defines Social capital "as a group of products destined to serve towards further production, or briefly a group of Intermediate products" He formally excludes (Book I ch. VI) "dwelling houses and other kinds of buildings such as serve immediately for any purpose of enjoyment or education or culture," and perhaps he would exclude all things that are intermediate to the performance of personal services, as distinguished from material goods; but if so he must exclude hotels, tramways, passenger ships, trains, &c ; and perhaps even plant for supplying the electric light for private dwellings, and that would deprive the notion of capital of all practical interest Further there seems no good ground for excluding the public theatre while including the tramcar, which would not justify the inclusion of mills engaged in making home-spun and excluding those engaged in making lace.

sponds to the use value of his own goods But in ordinary life no one ever thinks of doing this[1].

It will be found that except in this problem of Distribution it is important practically seldom to define clearly the limits of social capital: and that even in this problem, a precise definition is needed chiefly for the purpose of securing that we do not count in some parts of the true national income twice and others not at all.

The ordinary practice of life, as exemplified in the rules of the income tax commissioners, is governed by the same considerations as that of economists in this matter. For the purposes of both, it is expedient to count in everything which is commonly regarded as a means of income and treated in a business fashion; even though it may happen, like a dwelling-house inhabited by its owner, to yield its income of comfort directly: and this partly because of its intrinsic importance, and partly because the real income accruing from it can easily be separated off and estimated.

In all discussions of Distribution therefore, in the present treatise, capital (regarded from the social point of view) will be taken to consist of those kinds of wealth (other than the free gifts of nature) which yield income that is generally reckoned as such in common discourse · together with similar things in public ownership, such as government factories.

Thus it will include all things held for trade purposes, whether machinery, raw material or finished goods, theatres and hotels, home farms and houses: but not furniture or clothes owned by those who use them. For the former are and the latter are not commonly regarded as yielding income by the world at large, as is shown by the practice of the income tax commissioners.

It will be found that nearly every broad proposition which is commonly made as to the relations between national or social well-being and national or social capital is true of capital thus defined.

There remain some minor points to be noticed firstly in relation to Capital, and secondly in relation to Income.

[1] As has been already intimated however the application of mathematical phrases to the problem of Distribution tends towards doing it.

BOOK II CH IV

Circulating and *Fixed capital*

§ 10 We may follow Mill in distinguishing *Circulating capital* "which fulfils the whole of its office in the production in which it is engaged, by a single use," from *Fixed capital* "which exists in a durable shape and the return to which is spread over a period of corresponding duration[1]."

Specialized capital.

Sometimes again we have to distinguish certain kinds of capital as *Specialized* because having been designed for use in one trade they cannot easily be diverted to another.

A caution against a source of confusion.

Mill and others have used fixed capital sometimes in the sense that we have retained for it, sometimes in the senses that we have given to specialized and to auxiliary capital But there is much fixed capital which is not specialized, such as buildings and some kinds of machinery which are adapted to many different trades: while materials of manufacture and some other kinds of circulating capital are specialized. Again much fixed capital is also consumption capital, as for instance workmen's cottages.

Personal capital

We have already defined personal wealth to consist firstly of those energies, faculties and habits which directly contribute to making people industrially efficient, and secondly of their business connections and associations of every kind All these are productive, and therefore if they are to be reckoned as wealth at all, they are also to be reckoned as capital. Thus personal wealth and personal capital are convertible; and it seems best to follow here the same course as in the case of wealth, and for the same reasons. That is, it is best to assume that the term "capital" when taken alone includes none but external goods; but yet to raise no

1 Adam Smith's distinction between fixed and circulating capital turned on the question whether the goods "yield a profit without changing masters" or not. Ricardo made it turn on whether they are "of slow consumption or require to be frequently reproduced;" but he truly remarks that this is "a division not essential and in which the line of demarcation cannot be accurately drawn." Mill's modification of Ricardo's definitions of these terms is generally accepted by modern economists

The notion of the fixedness of capital is like to, and yet different from, the mediæval notion of capital as the *caput* or head of a loan. (See Ashley's *History*, Book II ch VI ; but also Hewins' review of it in the *Economic Review*, vol. III. pp 396 &c) The caput is a fixed stock of "pure capital," in Prof. Clark's phrase, for goods may "circulate" through it, as water does through a reservoir that is kept at a constant height

objection to an occasional broad use of the term, in which it is explicitly stated to include personal capital.

Net Income

§ 11 If a person is engaged in business, he is sure to have to incur certain outgoings for raw material, the hire of labour &c. And, in that case, his true or *Net Income* is found by deducting from his gross income "the outgoings that belong to its production[1]."

Elements of real income which do not appear in the form of money are in some danger of being overlooked.

Anything which a person does for which he is paid directly or indirectly in money, helps to swell his money income, while no services that he performs for himself are reckoned as adding to his nominal income, though they may be a very important part of his total real income if they are of a kind which people commonly pay for having done for them. Thus a woman who makes her own clothes or a man who digs in his own garden or repairs his own house, is earning income just as would the dressmaker, gardener or carpenter who might be hired to do the work.

It would be a great convenience if there were two words available: one to represent a person's total income and another his money income, i.e. that part of his total income which comes to him in the form of money. For scientific purposes it would be best that the word income when occurring alone should always mean total real income. But as this plan is inconsistent with general usage we must, whenever there is any danger of misunderstanding, say distinctly whether the term is to be taken in its narrower or its broader use.

Provisional definition of *Net Advantages.*

§ 12 In this connection we may introduce a term of which we shall have to make frequent use hereafter The need for it arises from the fact that every occupation involves other disadvantages besides the fatigue of the work required in it, and every occupation offers other advantages besides the receipt of money wages. The true reward which an occupation offers to labour has to be calculated by deducting the money value of all its disadvantages from that of all its advantages; and we may describe this true reward as the *Net Advantages* of the occupation.

[1] See a report of a Committee of the British Association, 1878

BOOK II. CH IV.

Usance of wealth corresponds to Interest of capital

Another convenient term is the *Usance* of wealth. It consists of the benefits which a person derives from the ownership of wealth whether he uses it as capital or not Thus it includes the benefits which he gets from the use of his own piano, equally with those which a piano dealer would win by letting out a piano on hire. Thus it includes, as a special case, the money income which is derived from capital. This income is most easily measured when it takes the form of a payment made by a borrower for the use of a loan for, say, a year; it is then expressed as the ratio which that payment bears to the loan, and is called *Interest*

This is one of a group of notions of which provisional definitions may conveniently be introduced here.

Profits,

When a man is engaged in business, his *Profits* for the year are the excess of his receipts from his business during the year over his outlay for his business; the difference between the value of his stock and plant at the end and at the beginning of the year being taken as part of his receipts or as part of his outlay, according as there has been an increase or decrease of value. What remains of his profits after deducting interest on his capital at the current rate may be called his *Earnings of Undertaking* or *Management.*

Earnings of Management,

and Rent

The income derived from the ownership of land and other free gifts of nature is called *Rent*; the term is commonly stretched, so as to include the income derived from houses and other things the supply of which is limited and cannot quickly be increased, and we shall need to stretch it yet further.

Social income.

§ **13.** Social income may be estimated by adding together the incomes of the individuals in the society in question, whether it be a nation or any other larger or smaller group of persons But to reckon it directly is for most purposes simplest and best. Everything that is produced in the course of a year, every service rendered, every fresh utility brought about is a part of the national income

Thus it includes the benefit derived from the advice of a physician, the pleasure got from hearing a professional singer, and the enjoyment of all other services which one person may be hired to perform for another. It includes the services rendered not only by the omnibus driver, but also by the coachman who drives a private carriage. It includes the services of the domestic servant who makes or mends or cleans a carpet or a dress, as well as the results of the work of the upholsterer, the milliner, and the dyer.

Elements of social income that are in danger of being omitted

We must however be careful not to count the same thing twice. If we have counted a carpet at its full value, we have already counted the values of the yarn and the labour that were used in making it; and these must not be counted again. But if the carpet is cleaned by domestic servants or at steam scouring works, the value of the labour spent in cleaning it must be counted in separately; for otherwise the results of this labour would be altogether omitted from the inventory of those newly-produced commodities and conveniences which constitute the real income of the country.

Again, suppose a landowner with an annual income of £10,000 hires a private secretary at a salary of £500, who hires a servant at wages of £50 It may seem that if the incomes of all these three persons are counted in as part of the net income of the country, some of it will be counted twice over, and some three times. But this is not the case. The landlord transfers to his secretary, in return for his assistance, part of the purchasing power derived from the produce of land; and the secretary again transfers part of this to his servant in return for his assistance. The farm produce the value of which goes as rent to the landlord, the assistance which the landlord derives from the work of the secretary, and that which the secretary derives from the work of the servant are independent parts of the real net income of the country, and therefore the £10,000 and the £500 and the £50 which are their money measures, must all be counted in when we are estimating the income of the country[1].

National income is a better mea-

§ 14. The money income of a nation gives a measure of its economic prosperity, which, untrustworthy as it is,

[1] But if the landlord makes an allowance of £500 a year to his son, that must not be counted as an independent income; because no services are rendered for it And it would not be assessed to the income tax.

BOOK II CH. IV.

is yet in some respects better than that afforded by the money value of its wealth.

sure of general economic prosperity than national wealth.

For income consists chiefly of commodities in a form to give pleasure directly, while the greater part of national wealth consists of the means of production, which are of service to the nation only in so far as they contribute to producing commodities ready for consumption. And further, though this is a minor point, consumable commodities, being more portable, have more nearly uniform prices all the world over than the things used in producing them: the prices of an acre of good land in Manitoba and Kent differ more than those of a bushel of wheat in the two places.

But if we look chiefly at the income of a country we must allow for the depreciation of the sources from which it is derived. More must be deducted from the income derived from a house if it is made of wood, than if it is made of stone; a stone house counts for more towards the real richness of a country than a wooden house which gives equally good accommodation. Again, a mine which yields for a time a large income, but will be exhausted in a few years, must be counted as equivalent to a field, or a fishery, which yields a much smaller annual income but will yield that income permanently[1].

[1] All estimates of a nation's richness based on a mere money measure are necessarily misleading, chiefly for the reasons which have been indicated in the chapter on wealth and the present chapter. But since they are frequently made, it may be well to point out that even if we agree for any special purpose to regard the richness of a nation as represented by its money income the question which of two nations is richer than another is still ambiguous. Is the richness of a nation to be measured by the aggregate money income of its inhabitants or by their average income? If the former, India is richer than Holland, if the latter, Holland is far richer than India. The latter is generally the more important measure for the purposes of the student of social science, the former for those of the diplomatist If, however, we are considering a nation's power of bearing a long-continued financial strain of war, we may measure its richness roughly by the excess of the sum total of the incomes of its inhabitants over what is required to supply them with the necessaries of life A rough notion of the economic strength of a nation, for the purpose of comparison with that of others, may be got by multiplying the aggregate income of its inhabitants by their average income

BOOK III.

DEMAND OR CONSUMPTION.

CHAPTER I.

INTRODUCTORY.

The relation in which the present Book stands to the remainder of the Volume

§ 1. THE older definitions of economics described it as the science which is concerned with the Production, the Distribution, the Exchange, and the Consumption of Wealth. Later experience has shown that the problems of Distribution and Exchange are so closely connected, that it is doubtful whether anything is to be gained by the attempt to keep them separate. There is however a good deal of general reasoning with regard to the relation of Demand and Supply which is required as a basis for the practical problems of Value, and which acts as an underlying backbone, giving unity and consistency to the main body of economic reasoning. Its very breadth and generality mark it off from the more concrete problems of Distribution and Exchange to which it is subservient; and therefore it is put together in a separate Book on "The General Theory of Demand and Supply" which (together with a supplementary discussion of some points of difficulty in the relation of Cost of Production to Value) prepare the way for "Distribution and Exchange, or Value." But first of all come "Demand or Consumption," *i.e* the Theory of Wants, and "Production or Supply," *i.e.* the Theory of the Efforts and Sacrifices devoted to the satisfaction of Wants.

BOOK III CH. I.

The latter of these two Books corresponds in general character to that discussion of Production to which a large place has been given in nearly all English treatises on general economics during the last two generations; although its relation to the problems of Demand and Supply has not been made sufficiently clear.

Very little attention has been paid till recently to the subject of Demand or Consumption

§ 2. But until recently the subject of Demand or Consumption has been somewhat neglected[1]. For important as is the inquiry how to turn our resources to the best account, it is not one which lends itself, so far as the expenditure of private individuals is concerned, to the methods of economics. The common sense of a person who has had a large experience of life will give him more guidance in such a matter than he can gain from subtle economic analyses; and until recently economists said little on the subject, because they really had not much to say that was not the common property of all sensible people. But recently several causes have combined to give the subject a greater prominence in economic discussions.

But several causes are now bringing it into greater prominence

The first cause.

The first of these is the growing belief that harm was done by Ricardo's habit of laying disproportionate stress on the side of cost of production, when analysing the causes that determine exchange value. For although he and his chief followers were aware that the conditions of demand played as important a part as those of supply in determining value, yet they did not express their meaning with sufficient clearness, and they have been misunderstood by all but the most careful readers.

The second cause

Secondly, the growth of exact habits of thought in economics is making people more careful to state distinctly the premises on which they reason. This increased care is partly due to the application by some writers of mathematical language and mathematical habits of thought. It is indeed doubtful whether much has been gained by the use of complex mathematical formulæ. But the application of mathematical habits of thought has been of great service,

[1] James Mill indeed called a large part of his *Elements of Political Economy* by the title "Consumption," but it is really occupied almost exclusively with an inquiry into the principles of Taxation

for it has led people to refuse to consider a problem until they are quite sure what the problem is; and to insist on knowing what is, and what is not intended to be assumed, before proceeding further. This has in its turn compelled a more careful analysis of all the leading conceptions of economics, and especially of demand; for the mere attempt to state clearly how the demand for a thing is to be measured opens up new aspects of the main problems of economics And though the theory of demand is yet in its infancy, we can already see that it may be possible to collect and arrange statistics of consumption in such a way as to throw light on difficult questions of great importance to public well-being.

The third cause

Lastly, the spirit of the age induces a closer attention to the question whether our increasing wealth may not be made to go further than it does in promoting the general well-being; and this again compels us to examine how far the exchange value of any element of wealth, whether in collective or individual use, represents accurately the addition which it makes to happiness and well-being.

We will begin with a study of wants in relation to efforts

We will begin this Book with a short study of the variety of human wants, considered in their relation to human efforts and activities For the progressive nature of man is one whole. It is only temporarily and provisionally that we can with profit isolate for study the economic side of his life; and we ought to be careful to take together in one view the whole of that side. There is a special need to insist on this just now, because the reaction against the comparative neglect of the theory of wants by Ricardo and his followers shows signs of being carried to the opposite extreme, and resulting in some neglect of the great truth on which they insisted rightly, though too exclusively, that while wants are the rulers of life among the lower animals, it is to changes in the forms of efforts and activities that we must turn when in search for the keynotes of the history of mankind

CHAPTER II.

WANTS IN RELATION TO ACTIVITIES.

The wants of the savage are few;

§ 1 HUMAN wants and desires are countless in number and very various in kind The uncivilized man indeed has not many more than the brute animal; but every step in his progress upwards increases the variety of his needs together with the variety in his methods of satisfying them. He desires not merely larger *quantities* of the things he has been accustomed to consume, but better qualities of those things, he desires a greater choice of things, and things that will satisfy new wants growing up in him.

but civilization brings with it a desire for variety for its own sake

Thus though the brute and the savage alike have their preferences for choice morsels, neither of them cares much for variety for its own sake. As, however, man rises in civilization, as his mind becomes developed, and even his animal passions begin to associate themselves with mental activities, his wants become rapidly more subtle and more various; and in the minor details of life he begins to desire change for the sake of change, long before he has consciously escaped from the yoke of custom. The first great step in this direction comes with the art of making a fire: gradually he gets to accustom himself to many different kinds of food and drink cooked in many different ways, and before long monotony begins to become irksome to him, and he finds it a great hardship when accident compels him to live for a long time exclusively on one or two kinds of food.

Man's capacity for food is limited,

As a man's riches increase his food and drink become more various and costly; but his appetite is limited by nature, and when his expenditure on food is extravagant it is more often to gratify the desires of hospitality and display than to indulge his own senses.

but profuse hospitality is a means of social distinction. Man's craving for distinction.

This brings us to remark with Senior that "Strong as is the desire for variety, it is weak compared with the desire for distinction a feeling which if we consider its universality, and its constancy, that it affects all men and at all times, that it comes with us from the cradle and never leaves us till we go into the grave, may be pronounced to be the most powerful of human passions." This great half-truth is well illustrated by a comparison of the desire for choice and various food with that for choice and various dress

It is a chief source of the desire for costly dress

§ 2. That need for dress which is the result of natural causes varies with the climate and the season of year, and a little with the nature of a person's occupations But in dress conventional wants overshadow those which are natural. Thus in many of the earlier stages of civilization the sumptuary mandates of Law and Custom have rigidly prescribed to the members of each caste or industrial grade, the style and the standard of expense up to which their dress must reach and beyond which they may not go; and part of the substance of these mandates remains now, though subject to rapid change In Scotland, for instance, in Adam Smith's time many persons were allowed by custom to go abroad without shoes and stockings who may not do so now; and many may still do it in Scotland who might not in England Again, in England now a well-to-do labourer is expected to appear on Sunday in a black coat and, in some places, in a silk hat; though these would have subjected him to ridicule but a short time ago. In all the lower ranks of life there is a constant increase both in that variety and expensiveness which custom requires as a minimum, and in that which it tolerates as a maximum; and the efforts to obtain distinction by dress are extending themselves throughout the lower grades of English society.

But in the upper grades, though the dress of women is still various and costly, that of men is simple and inexpensive as compared with what it was in Europe not long ago, and is to-day in the East. For those men who are most truly distinguished on their own account, have a natural dislike to

BOOK III. CH. II

seem to claim attention by their dress; and they have set the fashion[1].

Abundant house room is desired less for the sake of direct enjoyment,

§ 3. House room satisfies the imperative need for shelter from the weather but that need plays very little part in the effective demand for house room. For though a small but well-built cabin gives excellent shelter, its stifling atmosphere, its necessary uncleanliness, and its want of the decencies and the quiet of life are great evils It is not so much that they cause physical discomfort as that they tend to stunt the faculties, and limit people's higher activities. With every increase in these activities the demand for larger house room becomes more urgent[2]

than as a means towards efficiency and as a mark of distinction

And therefore relatively large and well-appointed house room is, even in the lowest social ranks, at once a "necessary for efficiency[3]," and the most convenient and obvious way of advancing a material claim to social distinction And even in those grades in which everyone has house room sufficient for the higher activities of himself and his family, a yet further and almost unlimited increase is desired as a requisite for the exercise of many of the higher social activities.

Wants resulting from scientific æsthetic activities

§ 4 It is again the desire for the exercise and development of activities, spreading through every rank of society, which leads not only to the pursuit of science, literature and art for their own sake, but to the rapidly increasing demand for the work of those who pursue them as professions.

Athletic activities;

Leisure is used less and less as an opportunity for mere

[1] A woman may display wealth, but she may not display only her wealth, by her dress; or else she defeats her ends. She must also suggest some distinction of character as well as of wealth for though her dress may owe more to her dress-maker than to herself, yet there is a traditional assumption that, being less busy than man with external affairs, she can give more time to taking thought as to her dress. Even under the sway of modern fashions, to be "well dressed"—not "expensively dressed"—is a reasonable minor aim for those who desire to be distinguished for their faculties and abilities; and this will be still more the case if the evil dominion of the wanton vagaries of fashion should pass away For to arrange costumes beautiful in themselves, various and well-adapted to their purposes, is an object worthy of high endeavour, it belongs to the same class, though not to the same rank in that class, as the painting of a good picture.

[2] It is true that many active minded working men prefer cramped lodgings in a town to a roomy cottage in the country; but that is because they have a strong taste for those activities for which a country life offers little scope.

[3] See Book II. ch III. § 3.

stagnation, and there is a growing desire for those amusements, such as athletic games and travelling, which develop activities, rather than indulge any sensuous craving[1]

the desire for travel.

Gradations of the desire for excellence.

For indeed the desire for excellence for its own sake, is almost as wide in its range as the lower desire for distinction. As that graduates down from the ambition of those who may hope that their names will be in men's mouths in distant lands and in distant times, to the hope of the country lass that the new ribbon she puts on for Easter may not pass unnoticed by her neighbours, so the desire for excellence for its own sake graduates down from that of a Newton, or a Stradivarius, to that of the fisherman who, even when no one is looking and he is not in a hurry, delights in handling his craft well, and in the fact that she is well built and responds promptly to his guidance Desires of this kind exert a great influence on the supply of the highest faculties and the greatest inventions; and they are not unimportant on the side of demand For a large part of the demand for the most highly skilled professional services and the best work of the mechanical artisan, arises from the delight that people have in the training of their own faculties, and in exercising them by aid of the most delicately adjusted and responsive implements.

In a healthy state new activities pioneer the way for new wants,

Speaking broadly therefore, although it is man's wants in the earliest stages of his development that give rise to his activities, yet afterwards each new step upwards is to be regarded rather as the development of new activities giving rise to new wants, than that of new wants giving rise to new activities.

but not in an unhealthy state

We see this clearly if we look away from healthy conditions of life, where new activities are constantly being developed; and watch the West Indian negro, using his new freedom and wealth not to get the means of satisfying new wants, but in idle stagnation that is not rest, or again look at that rapidly lessening part of the English working classes,

[1] As a minor point it may be noticed that those drinks which stimulate the mental activities are largely displacing those which merely gratify the senses The consumption of tea is increasing very fast while that of alcohol is stationary, and there is in all ranks of society a diminishing demand for the grosser and more immediately stupefying forms of alcohol.

BOOK III CH. II

who have no ambition and no pride or delight in the growth of their faculties and activities, and spend on drink whatever surplus their wages afford over the bare necessaries of a squalid life.

The theory of wants can claim no supremacy over the theory of efforts

It is not true therefore that "the Theory of Consumption is the scientific basis of economics[1]" For much that is of chief interest in the science of wants, is borrowed from the science of efforts and activities. These two supplement one another; either is incomplete without the other. But if either, more than the other, may claim to be the interpreter of the history of man, whether on the economic side or any other, it is the science of activities and not that of wants, and M'Culloch indicated their true relations when, discussing "the Progressive Nature of Man[2]," he said·—"The gratification of a want or a desire is merely a step to some new pursuit. In every stage of his progress he is destined to contrive and invent, to engage in new undertakings; and, when these are accomplished to enter with fresh energy upon others"

From this it follows that such a discussion of demand as is possible at this stage of our work, must be confined to an elementary analysis of an almost purely formal kind. The higher study of consumption must come after, and not before, the main body of economic analysis, and, though it may have its beginning within the proper domain of economics, it cannot find its conclusions there, but must extend far beyond[3].

[1] This doctrine is laid down by Banfield, and adopted by Jevons as the key of his position It is unfortunate that here as elsewhere Jevons' delight in stating his case strongly has led him to a conclusion, which not only is inaccurate, but does mischief by implying that the older economists were more at fault than they really were Banfield says "the first proposition of the theory of consumption is that the satisfaction of every lower want in the scale creates a desire of a higher character" And if this were true, the above doctrine, which he bases on it, would be true also But, as Jevons points out (*Theory*, 2nd Ed p 59), it is not true and he substitutes for it the statement that the satisfaction of a lower want permits a higher want to manifest itself That is a true and indeed an identical proposition but it affords no support to the claims of the Theory of Consumption to supremacy

[2] *Political Economy*, ch II

[3] The formal classification of Wants is a task not without interest; but it is not needed for our purposes. The basis of most modern work in this direction is to be found in Hermann's *Staatswirthschaftliche Untersuchungen*, Ch II, where

he classified wants as "absolute and relative, higher and lower, urgent and capable of postponement, positive and negative, direct and indirect, general and particular, constant and interrupted, permanent and temporary, ordinary and extraordinary, present and future, individual and collective, private and public"

Some analysis of wants and desires is to be found in the great majority of French and other Continental treatises on economics even of the last generation but the rigid boundaries which English writers have ascribed to their science, has excluded such discussions And it is a characteristic fact that there is no allusion to them in Bentham's *Manual of Political Economy*, although his profound analysis of them in the *Principles of Morals and Legislation* and in the *Table of the Springs of Human Action* has exercised a wide-spread influence Hermann had studied Bentham, and on the other hand Banfield, whose lectures were perhaps the first ever given in an English University that owed much directly to German economic thought, acknowledges special obligations to Hermann In England the way was prepared for Jevons' excellent work on the Theory of Wants, by Bentham himself, by Senior, whose short remarks on the subject are pregnant with far reaching hints, by Banfield, and by the Australian Hearn Hearn's *Plutology or Theory of the Efforts to satisfy Human Wants* is at once simple and profound it affords an admirable example of the way in which detailed analysis may be applied to afford a training of a very high order for the young, and to give them an intelligent acquaintance with the economic conditions of life, without forcing upon them any particular solution of those more difficult problems on which they are not yet able to form an independent judgment And at about the same time as Jevons' *Theory* appeared, Prof Carl Menger initiated the subtle and interesting studies of Wants and Utilities by the Austrian school of economists

CHAPTER III.

THE LAW OF DEMAND.

BOOK III. CH. III

The Law of Satiable Wants or Diminishing Utility.

§ 1. WE have seen that each several want is limited, and that with every increase in the amount of a thing which a man has, the eagerness of his desire to obtain more of it diminishes; until it yields place to the desire for some other thing, of which perhaps he hardly thought, so long as his more urgent wants were still unsatisfied. There is an endless variety of wants, but there is a limit to each separate want. This familiar and fundamental law of human nature may pass by the name of the *Law of Satiable Wants* or the *Law of Diminishing Utility.*

It may be written thus:—

Total Utility

The *Total Utility* of a commodity to a person (that is, the total benefit or satisfaction yielded to him by it) increases with every increment in his stock of it, but not as fast as his stock increases. If his stock of it increases at a uniform rate the benefit derived from it increases at a diminishing rate.

In other words, the additional benefit which a person derives from a given increment of his stock of anything, diminishes with every increase in the stock that he already has.

Marginal Increment.

Marginal Utility

The increment of the commodity which he is only just induced to acquire (whether by his direct labour or by purchase) may be called its *Marginal Increment*, because he is on the margin of doubt whether it is worth his while to incur the outlay required to obtain it. And the benefit-giving power, or Utility, of that increment to him may be called the *Marginal Utility* of the commodity to him. It is the marginal increment of the total utility of his whole stock of the commodity. And thus the law may be worded:—

The marginal utility of a commodity to anyone diminishes with every increase in the amount of it he already has[1].

It is implied that the consumer's character is unchanged

There is however an implicit condition in this law which should be made clear. It is that we do not suppose time to be allowed for any alteration in the character or tastes of the man himself. It is therefore no exception to the law that the more good music a man hears, the stronger is his taste for it likely to become; that avarice and ambition are often insatiable; or that the virtue of cleanliness and the vice of drunkenness alike grow on what they feed upon. For in such cases our observations range over some period of time; and the man is not the same at the beginning as at the end of it. If we take a man as he is, without allowing time for any change in his character, the marginal utility of a thing to him diminishes steadily with every increase in his supply of it[2].

Translation of the law into terms of price

§ 2. Now let us translate this law of diminishing utility into terms of price Let us take an illustration from the case of a commodity such as tea, which is in constant demand and which can be purchased in small quantities Suppose, for instance, that tea of a certain quality is to be

[1] See Note I in the Mathematical Appendix at the end of the Volume This law holds a priority of position to the *Law of Diminishing Return* from land; which however has the priority in time; since it was the first to be subjected to a rigid analysis of a semi mathematical character And if by anticipation we borrow some of its terms, we may say that the *Return* of pleasure which a person gets from each additional *Dose* of a commodity diminishes till at last a Margin is reached at which it is no longer worth his while to acquire any more of it

[2] It may be noticed here, though the fact is of but little practical importance, that a small quantity of a commodity may be insufficient to meet a certain special want; and then there will be a more than proportionate increase of pleasure when the consumer gets enough of it to enable him to attain the desired end Thus, for instance, anyone would derive less pleasure in proportion from ten pieces of wall paper than from twelve, if the latter would, and the former would not, cover the whole of the walls of his room Or again a very short concert or a holiday may fail of its purpose of soothing and recreating and one of double length might be of more than double total utility This case corresponds to the fact, which we shall have to study in connection with the law of diminishing return, that the capital and labour already applied to any piece of land may be so inadequate for the development of its full powers, that some further expenditure on it even with the existing arts of agriculture would give a more than proportionate return; and in the fact that an improvement in the arts of agriculture may suspend the operation of that law, we shall find an analogy to the condition just mentioned in the text as implied in the law of diminishing utility.

had at 2*s.* per lb. A person might be willing to give 10*s.* for a single pound once a year rather than go without it altogether; while if he could have any amount of it for nothing he would perhaps not care to use more than 30 lbs. in the year. But as it is, he buys perhaps 10 lbs. in the year; that is to say, the difference between the happiness which he gets from buying 9 lbs and 10 lbs. is just enough for him to be willing to pay 2*s.* for it: while the fact that he does not buy an eleventh pound, shows that he does not think that it would be quite worth an extra 2*s.* to him. That is, 2*s* a pound measures the utility to him of the tea which lies at the margin or terminus or end of his purchases; it measures the marginal utility to him. If the price which he is just willing to pay for any pound be called his *Demand Price,* then 2*s* is his *Marginal Demand Price.* And our law may be worded:—

Marginal Demand Price

An increase in the amount of a thing that a person has will, other things being equal (*i e.* the purchasing power of money, and the amount of money at his command being equal) diminish his marginal demand price for it.

Account must be taken of possible changes in the marginal utility of money

§ 3 This last sentence reminds us that we have as yet taken no account of changes in the marginal utility of money, or general purchasing power At one and the same time, a person's material resources being unchanged, the marginal utility of money to him is a fixed quantity, so that the prices he is just willing to pay for two commodities are to one another in the same ratio as the utility of those two commodities.

It is greater for the poor than the rich

Of course a greater utility will be required to induce him to buy a thing if he is poor than if he is rich. We have seen[1] how a shilling is the measure of less benefit to a rich man, than to a poor one, how a rich man in doubt whether to spend a shilling on a single cigar, is weighing against one another smaller benefits than a poor man, who is doubting whether to spend a shilling on a supply of tobacco that will last him for a month, and how the clerk with £100 a year will walk into business in a heavier rain than the clerk with £300 a year

[1] Above, p 80

But although the utility, or the benefit, that is measured in the poorer man's mind by sixpence is greater than that measured by it in the richer man's mind, yet if the richer man rides a hundred times in the year and the poorer man twenty times, then the utility of the hundredth ride which the richer man is only just induced to take is measured to him by sixpence; and the utility of the twentieth ride which the poorer man is only just induced to take is measured to him by sixpence. For each of them the marginal utility is measured by sixpence, but this marginal utility is greater in the case of the poorer man than in that of the richer.

In other words the richer a man becomes, the less is the marginal utility of money to him, every increase in his resources increases the price which he is willing to pay for any given benefit. And in the same way every diminution of his resources increases the marginal utility of money to him, and diminishes the price that he is willing to pay for any benefit[1].

A more definite expression for the demand of an individual.

§ 4. When then we say that a person's demand for anything increases, we mean that he will buy more of it than he would before at the same price, and that he will buy as much of it as before at a higher price To complete our knowledge of his demand for it, we should have to ascertain how much of it he would be willing to purchase at each of the prices at which it is likely to be offered; and the circumstances of his demand for, say, tea can be best expressed by a list of the prices which he is willing to pay; that is, by his several demand prices for different amounts of it[2]

Thus for instance we may find that he would buy

6 lbs.	at the price of		50*d.*	per lb.
7	"	"	40	"
8	"	"	33	"
9	"	"	28	"
10	"	"	24	"
11	"	"	21	"
12	"	"	19	"
13	"	"	18	"

[1] See Note II. in the Appendix.

[2] This may be called his *Demand Schedule*

If corresponding prices were filled in for all intermediate amounts we should have an exact statement of his demand[1].

The meaning of the term an Increase of Demand

We see then that a person's demand for a thing is indeterminate so long as nothing is said as to the price at which the thing is to be had. There is no use in trying to measure his demand as some writers have done merely by the "amount he is willing to buy" or merely by the "intensity of his eagerness to buy a certain amount." Nothing is gained by representing a notion, which is really complex, as though it were simple. Wherever precision is required, we must speak of a person's demand for a thing as represented by the schedule of the prices at which he is willing to buy different amounts of it[2]. An increase in his demand for the commodity

[1] Such a demand schedule may be translated, on a plan now coming into familiar use, into a curve that may be called his *Demand Curve*. Let *Ox* and *Oy* be drawn the one horizontally, the other vertically. Let an inch measured along *Ox* represent 10 lbs. of tea, and an inch measured along *Oy* represent 40*d*.

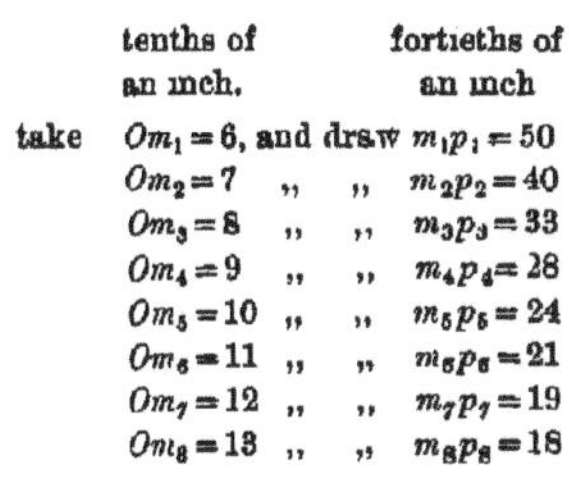

	tenths of an inch.		fortieths of an inch
take	$Om_1 = 6$,	and draw	$m_1p_1 = 50$
	$Om_2 = 7$	,, ,,	$m_2p_2 = 40$
	$Om_3 = 8$	,, ,,	$m_3p_3 = 33$
	$Om_4 = 9$	,, ,,	$m_4p_4 = 28$
	$Om_5 = 10$	,, ,,	$m_5p_5 = 24$
	$Om_6 = 11$	,, ,,	$m_6p_6 = 21$
	$Om_7 = 12$	,, ,,	$m_7p_7 = 19$
	$Om_8 = 13$	,, ,,	$m_8p_8 = 18$

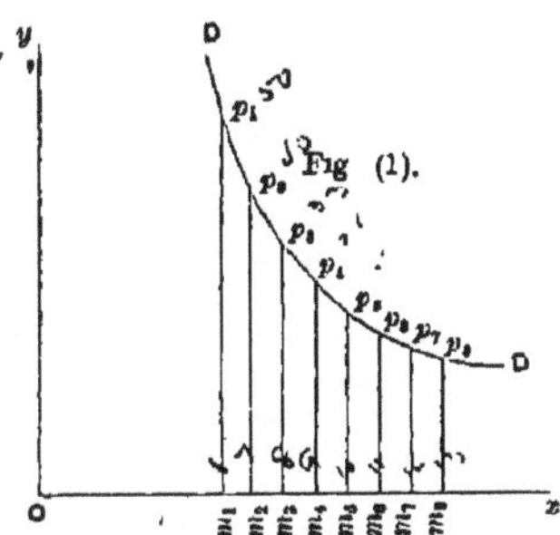

m_1 being on *Ox* and m_1p_1 being drawn vertically from m_1, and so for the others. Then p_1p_2 . . p_8 are points on his demand curve for tea, or as we may say *Demand Points*. If we could find demand points in the same manner for every possible quantity of tea, we should get the whole continuous curve *DD'* as shown in the figure.

This account of the demand schedule and curve is provisional. several difficulties connected with it are deferred to chapter v.

[2] Thus Mill says that we must "mean by the word demand, the quantity demanded, and remember that this is not a fixed quantity, but in general varies according to the value" (*Principles*, Book III ch II § 4). This account is scientific in substance, but it is not clearly expressed and it has been much misunderstood. Cairnes prefers to represent "demand as the desire for commodities and services, seeking its end by an offer of general purchasing power, and supply as the desire for general purchasing power, seeking its end by an offer of specific commodities or services." He does this in order that he may be able to speak of a

means generally an increase throughout the whole list of prices at which he is willing to purchase different amounts of it, and not merely that he is willing to buy more of it at the current prices[1].

BOOK III. CH III

Transition to the demand of a group of persons or market

§ 5. So far we have looked at the demand of a single individual. And in the particular case of such a thing as tea, the demand of a single person is fairly representative of the general demand of a whole market: for the demand for tea is a constant one, and, since it can be purchased in small quantities, every variation in its price is likely to affect the amount which he will buy. But even among those things which are in constant use, there are many for which the demand on the part of any single individual cannot vary continuously with every small change in price, but can move only by great leaps For instance a small fall in the price of hats or watches will not affect the action of everyone, but it will induce a few persons, who were in doubt whether or not to get a new hat or a new watch, to decide in favour of doing so.

The demand on the part of any individual for some things is discontinuous

ratio, or equality, of demand and supply But the quantities of two desires on the part of two different persons cannot be compared directly, their measures may be compared, but not they themselves And in fact Cairnes is himself driven to speak of supply as "limited by the quantity of specific commodities offered for sale, and demand by the quantity of purchasing power offered for their purchase" But sellers have not a fixed quantity of commodities which they offer for sale unconditionally at whatever price they can get buyers have not a fixed quantity of purchasing power which they are ready to spend on the specific commodities, however much they pay for them Account must then be taken in either case of the relation between quantity and price, in order to complete Cairnes' account, and when this is done it is brought back to the lines followed by Mill. He says, indeed, that "Demand, as defined by Mill, is to be understood as measured, not, as my definition would require, by the quantity of purchasing power offered in support of the desire for commodities, but by the quantity of commodities for which such purchasing power is offered" It is true that there is a great difference between the statements, "I will buy twelve eggs," and "I will buy a shilling's worth of eggs" But there is no substantive difference between the statement, "I will buy twelve eggs at a penny each, but only six at three halfpence each," and the statement, "I will spend a shilling on eggs at a penny each, but if they cost three halfpence each I will spend ninepence on them" But while Cairnes' account when completed becomes substantially the same as Mill's, its present form is even more misleading (See an article by the present writer on *Mill's Theory of Value* in the *Fortnightly Review* for April, 1876)

[1] We may sometimes find it convenient to speak of this as *a raising of his demand schedule* Geometrically it is represented by raising his demand curve, or, what comes to the same thing, moving it to the right, with perhaps some modification of its shape

BOOK III CH III

And there are many classes of things the need for which on the part of any individual is inconstant, fitful, and irregular. There can be no list of individual demand prices for wedding-cakes, or the services of an expert surgeon.

And indeed the special province of the economist is the study—not of particular incidents in the lives of individuals but—of general laws relating to "the course of action that may be expected under certain conditions from the members of an industrial group," in so far as the motives of that action are measurable by a money price, the facts which he collects and applies are chiefly those in which the variety and the fickleness of the individual is merged in the comparatively regular aggregate of the action of a large number of people

But the aggregate demand of a great many persons has a continuous schedule, showing a fall of demand price corresponding to every increase in the quantity demanded.

In large markets then—where rich and poor, old and young, men and women, persons of all varieties of tastes, temperaments and occupations are mingled together—the peculiarities in the wants of individuals will compensate one another in a comparatively regular gradation of total demand. Every fall however slight in the price of a commodity in general use, will, other things being equal, increase the total sales of it; just as an unhealthy autumn increases the mortality of a large town, though many persons are uninjured by it And therefore if we had the requisite knowledge, we could make a list of prices at which each amount of it could find purchasers in a given place during, say, a year.

The total demand in the place for, say tea, is the sum of the demands of all the individuals there. Some will be richer and some poorer than the individual consumer whose demand we have just written down; some will have a greater and others a smaller liking for tea than he has. Let us suppose that there are in the place a million purchasers of tea, and that their average consumption is equal to his at each several price. Then the demand of that place is represented by the same list of prices as before, if we write a million pounds of tea instead of one pound[1].

[1] The demand is represented by the same curve as before, only an inch measured along Ox now represents ten million pounds instead of ten pounds. And

The Law of Demand

There is then one *Law of Demand*, which is common to all demands, viz. that the greater the amount to be sold, the smaller will be the price at which it will find purchasers; or in other words, that the amount demanded increases with a fall in price, and diminishes with a rise in price.

There will not be any exact relation between the fall in price and the increase of demand. A fall of one-tenth in the price may increase the sales by a twentieth or by a quarter, or it may double them. But as the numbers in the left-hand column of the demand schedule increase, those in the right-hand column will always diminish[1].

The price will measure the marginal utility of the commodity to each purchaser: but as the purchasers are likely to be some rich and others poor, we cannot speak of price as measuring marginal utility in general, but only with reference to some individual purchaser.

The influence on demand of the growth of a rival commodity

§ 6 It must be remembered that the demand schedule gives the prices at which various quantities of a thing can be sold in a market during a given time and under given conditions If the conditions vary in any respect the figures of the schedule will probably require to be changed, and this has constantly to be done when the desire for anything is materially altered by a variation of custom, or by a cheapening of the supply of a rival commodity, or by the invention of a new one. For instance, the list of demand prices for tea is drawn out on the assumption that the price of coffee is known; but a failure of the coffee harvest would

a formal definition of the demand curve for a market may be given thus:—The demand curve for any commodity in a market during any given unit of time is the locus of demand points for it That is to say, it is a curve such that if from any point P on it, a straight line PM be drawn perpendicular to Ox, PM represents the price at which purchasers will be forthcoming for an amount of the commodity represented by OM

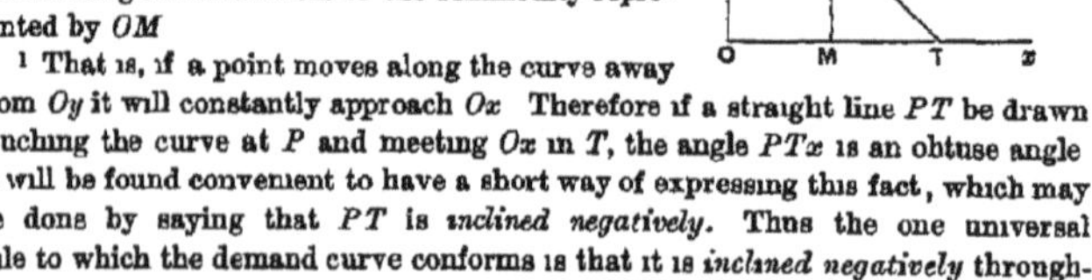

Fig. (2).

[1] That is, if a point moves along the curve away from Oy it will constantly approach Ox Therefore if a straight line PT be drawn touching the curve at P and meeting Ox in T, the angle PTx is an obtuse angle It will be found convenient to have a short way of expressing this fact, which may be done by saying that PT is *inclined negatively*. Thus the one universal rule to which the demand curve conforms is that it is *inclined negatively* throughout the whole of its length.

BOOK III CH III

raise the prices throughout the demand schedule for tea. The demand for gas is liable to be reduced by an improvement in electric lighting[1]; and in the same way a fall in the price of a particular kind of tea may cause it to be substituted for an inferior but cheaper variety.

Other points to be postponed

Again, a commodity may be simultaneously demanded for several uses (for instance there may be a "composite demand" for leather for making shoes and portmanteaus); the demand for a thing may be conditional on there being a supply of some other thing without which it would not be of much service (thus there may be a "joint demand" for raw cotton and cotton-spinners' labour). Again, the demand for a commodity on the part of dealers who buy it only with the purpose of selling it again, though governed by the demand of the ultimate consumers in the background, has some peculiarities of its own But all such points may best be discussed at a later stage.

Relation of the following to the preceding chapter

Our next step will be to consider the general character of demand in the cases of some important commodities ready for immediate consumption. We shall thus be continuing the inquiry made in the preceding chapter as to the variety and satiability of wants; but we shall be treating it from a rather different point of view, viz. that of price-statistics[2].

[1] It is even conceivable, though not probable, that a simultaneous and proportionate fall in the price of all teas may diminish the demand for some particular kind of it; if it happens that those whom the increased cheapness of tea leads to substitute a superior kind for it are less numerous than those who are led to take it in the place of an inferior kind The question where the lines of division between different commodities should be drawn must be settled by the convenience of the particular question under discussion For some purposes it may be best to regard Chinese and Indian teas, or even Souchong and Pekoe teas, as different commodities; and to have a separate demand schedule for each of them. While for other purposes it may be best to group together commodities as distinct as beef and mutton, or even as tea and coffee, and to have a single schedule to represent the demand for the two combined, but in such a case of course some convention must be made as to the number of ounces of tea which are taken as equivalent to a pound of coffee

[2] A great change in the manner of economic thought has been brought about during the present generation by the general adoption of semi mathematical language for expressing the relation between small increments of a commodity on the one hand, and on the other hand small increments in the aggregate price that will be paid for it· and by formally describing these small increments of price

as measuring corresponding small increments of pleasure The former, and by far the more important, step was taken by Cournot (*Recherches sur les Principes Mathématiques de la Théorie des Richesses*, 1838); the latter by Dupuit (*De la Mesure d'utilité des travaux publics* in the *Annales des Ponts et Chaussées*, 1844), and by Gossen (*Entwickelung der Gesetze des menschlichen Verkehrs*, 1854). But their work was forgotten, and part of it was done over again and published almost simultaneously by Jevons and by Prof. Carl Menger in 1871 Jevons almost at once arrested public attention by his brilliant lucidity and interesting style He applied the new name *Final Utility* so ingeniously as to enable people who knew nothing of mathematical science to get clear ideas of the general relations between the small increments of two things that are gradually changing in causal connection with one another His success was aided even by his faults For under the honest belief that Ricardo and his followers had rendered their account of the causes that determine value hopelessly wrong by omitting to lay stress on the Law of Satiable Wants, he led many to think he was correcting great errors; whereas he was really only adding very important explanations He did excellent work in insisting on a fact which is none the less important, because his predecessors, and even Cournot, thought it too obvious to be explicitly mentioned, viz that the diminution in the amount of a thing demanded in a market indicates a diminution in the intensity of the desire for it on the part of individual consumers, whose wants are becoming satiated But he has led many of his readers into a confusion between the provinces of Hedonics and Economics, by exaggerating the applications of his favourite phrases, and speaking (*Theory*, 2nd Edn p 105) without qualification of the price of a thing as measuring its final utility not only to an individual, which it can do, but also to "a trading body" which it cannot do [These points are developed later on in a Note on Ricardo's Theory of cost of production in relation to value at the end of Book V]

Dr Carl Menger's *Grundsatze der Volkswirthschaftslehre*, which, though not making use of mathematical language, is distinctly mathematical in tone, and appears to be in some respects, though not in all, further advanced than Jevons' work, and it is better balanced A mathematical tone is even more clearly pronounced, though the use of mathematical formulæ is still avoided, in the writings of Profs Böhm-Bawerk, Wieser, and other members of the brilliant Austrian School as well as those of Profs Clark, Giddings, Patten, Greene and other Americans Among the many recent writers on mathematical aspects of economics, special reference may be made to Prof Walras, who was almost as early in the field as Jevons and Menger, to Profs Pantaleoni, Pareto, Edgeworth, and Wicksteed, to Drs Auspitz, Lieben, Launhardt, and Fisher

CHAPTER IV.

LAW OF DEMAND CONTINUED ELASTICITY OF DEMAND

BOOK III CH IV.

Definition of *Elasticity of demand*

§ 1. We have seen that the only universal law as to a person's desire for a commodity is that it diminishes, other things being equal, with every increase in his supply of that commodity But this diminution may be slow or rapid. If it is slow the price that he will give for the commodity will not fall much in consequence of a considerable increase in his supply of it, and a small fall in price will cause a comparatively large increase in his purchases. But if it is rapid, a small fall in price will cause only a very small increase in his purchases In the former case his willingness to purchase the thing stretches itself out a great deal under the action of a small inducement. the elasticity of his demand, we may say, is great. In the latter case the extra inducement given by the fall in price causes hardly any extension of his desire to purchase · the elasticity of his demand is small.

And as with the demand of one person so with that of a whole market. The *Elasticity of demand* in a market is great or small according as the amount demanded increases much or little for a given fall in price, and diminishes much or little for a given rise in price[1].

[1] Speaking more exactly we may say that the elasticity of demand is one, if a fall of one per cent. in price will make an increase of one per cent in the amount demanded, that it is two or a half, if a fall of one per cent in price makes an increase of two or one half per cent. respectively in the amount demanded, and so on. The elasticity of demand can be best traced in the demand curve with the aid of the following rule Let a straight line touching the curve at any point P meet Ox in T and Oy in t, then *the measure of the elasticity at the point P is the ratio of PT to Pt.*

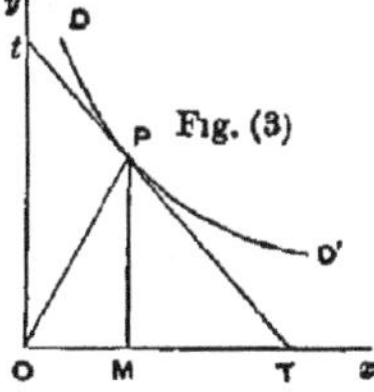

The general law of variation of the elasticity of demand

§ 2. The price which is so high relatively to the poor man as to be almost prohibitive, may be scarcely felt by the rich; the poor man for instance never tastes wine, but the very rich man may drink as much of it as he has a fancy for, without giving himself a thought of its cost. We shall therefore get the clearest notion of the law of the elasticity of demand, by considering one class of society at a time Of course there are many degrees of richness among the rich, and of poverty among the poor, but for the present we may neglect these minor subdivisions.

When the price of a thing is very high relatively to any class, they will buy but little of it, and in some cases custom and habit may prevent them from using it freely even after its price has fallen a good deal. It may still remain set apart for a limited number of special occasions, or for use in extreme illness, &c But such cases, though not infrequent, will not form the general rule, and anyhow as soon as it has been taken into common use, any considerable fall in its price will cause a great increase in the demand for it. The elasticity of demand will be great for high prices, and great, or at least considerable, for medium prices; but it will decline as the price falls, and gradually fades away if the fall goes so far that satiety level is reached.

This rule appears to hold with regard to nearly all commodities and with regard to the demand of every class; save only that the level at which high prices end and low prices begin, is different for different classes; and so again is the level at which low prices end and very low prices begin There are however many varieties in detail; arising chiefly from the fact that there are some commodities with which people are easily satiated, and others—chiefly things

If PT were twice Pt, a fall of 1 per cent in price would cause an increase of 2 per cent, in the amount demanded; the elasticity of demand would be two If PT were one third of Pt, a fall of 1 per cent in price would cause an increase of $3\frac{1}{3}$ per cent. in the amount demanded, the elasticity of demand would be one-third, and so on Another way of looking at the same result is this —the elasticity at the point P is measured by the ratio of PT to Pt, that is of MT to MO (PM being drawn perpendicular to Om); and therefore *the elasticity is equal to one when the angle TPM is equal to the angle OPM, and it always increases when the angle TPM increases relatively to the angle OPM, and vice versâ.* See Note III. in Appendix

BOOK III CH IV

used for display—for which their desire is almost unlimited. For the latter the elasticity of demand remains considerable, however low the price may fall, while for the former the demand loses nearly all its elasticity as soon as a low price has once been reached[1].

[1] Let us illustrate by the case of the demand for, say, green peas in a town in which all vegetables are bought and sold in one market Early in the season perhaps 100 lb a day will be brought to market and sold at 1s per lb., later on 500 lb will be bought and sold at 6d, later on 1,000 lb at 4d, later still 5,000 at 2d, and later still 10,000 at 1½d Thus demand is represented in fig. (4), an inch along Ox representing 5,000 lb and an inch along Oy representing 10d Then a curve through $p_1 p_2 \cdot p_5$, found as shown above, will be the total demand curve But this total demand will be made up of the demands of the rich, the middle class and the poor. The amounts that they will severally demand may perhaps be represented by the following schedules:—

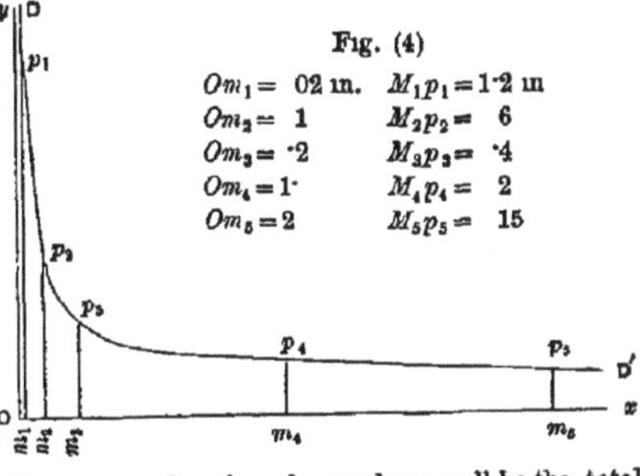

At price in pence per lb.	Number of lbs bought by			
	rich	middle class	poor	total
12	100	0	0	100
6	300	200	0	500
4	500	400	100	1,000
2	800	2,500	1,700	5,000
1½	1,000	4,000	5,000	10,000

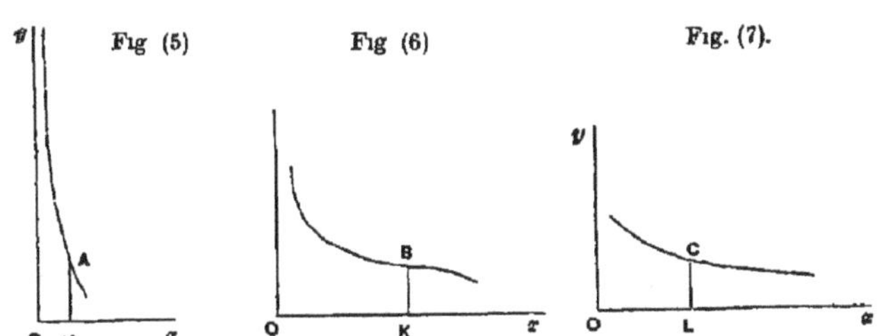

These schedules are translated into curves fig (5), (6), (7), showing the demands of the rich, the middle class and the poor represented on the same scale as fig. (4). Thus for instance AH, BK and CL each of them represents a price of 2d and is 2 inches in length, OH = ·16 in representing 800 lb, OK = ·5 in. representing 2,500 lb. and OL = ·34 in representing 1,700 lbs while $OH + OK + OL$ = one inch i e = Om_4 in fig (4) as they should do This may serve as an example of the way in which several partial demand curves, drawn to the same scale, can

Illustrations drawn from the demand for particular commodities.

§ 3 There are some things the current prices of which in this country are very low relatively even to the poorer classes; such are for instance salt, and many kinds of savours and flavours, and also cheap medicines. It is doubtful whether any fall in price would induce a considerable increase in the consumption of these

The current prices of meat, milk and butter, wool, tobacco, imported fruits, and of ordinary medical attendance, are such that every variation in price makes a great change in the consumption of them by the working classes, and the lower half of the middle classes, but the rich would not much increase their own personal consumption of them however cheaply they were to be had. In other words the direct demand for these commodities is very elastic on the part of the working and lower middle classes, though not on the part of the rich. But the working class is so numerous that their consumption of such things as are well within their reach is much greater than that of the rich; and therefore the aggregate demand for all things of the kind is very elastic. A little while ago sugar belonged to this group of commodities. but its price in England has now fallen so far as to be low relatively even to the working classes, and the demand for it is therefore not elastic[1].

The current prices of wall-fruit, of the better kinds of fish and other moderately expensive luxuries are such as to make the consumption of them by the middle class increase much with every fall in price, in other words, the middle class demand for them is very elastic· while the demands on the

be superimposed horizontally on one another to make the total demand curve representing the aggregate of the partial demands.

[1] We must however remember that the character of the demand schedule for any commodity depends in a great measure on whether the prices of its rivals are taken to be fixed or to alter with it. If we separated the demand for beef from that for mutton, and supposed the price of mutton to be held fixed while that for beef was raised, then the demand for beef would become extremely elastic For any slight fall in the price of beef would cause it to be used largely in the place of mutton and thus lead to a very great increase of its consumption while on the other hand even a small rise in price would cause many people to eat mutton to the almost entire exclusion of beef But the demand schedule for all kinds of fresh meat taken together, their prices being supposed to retain always about the same relation to one another, and to be not very different from those now prevailing in England, shows only a modern elasticity. And similar remarks apply to beet root and cane sugar Compare the first note on p 176.

part of the rich and on the part of the working class is much less elastic, the former because it is already nearly satiated, the latter because the price is still too high.

The current prices of such things as rare wines, fruit out of season, highly skilled medical and legal assistance, are so high that there is but little demand for them except from the rich. but what demand there is, often has considerable elasticity. Part of the demand for the more expensive kinds of food is really a demand for the means of obtaining social distinction, and is almost insatiable[1].

The demand for necessaries

§ 4. The case of necessaries is exceptional. When the price of wheat is very high, and again when it is very low, the demand has very little elasticity. at all events if we assume that wheat, even when scarce, is the cheapest food for man, and that, even when most plentiful, it is not consumed in any other way We know that a fall in the price of the quartern loaf from 6*d.* to 4*d.* has scarcely any effect in increasing the consumption of bread. With regard to the other end of the scale it is more difficult to speak with certainty, because there has been no approach to a scarcity in England since the repeal of the corn laws. But, availing ourselves of the experience of a less happy time, we may suppose that deficits in the supply of 1, 2, 3, 4, or 5 tenths would cause a rise in price of 3, 8, 16, 28, or 45 tenths respectively[2] Much greater variations in prices indeed than

[1] See above ch II § 1 In April 1894, for instance, six plovers' eggs, the first of the season, were sold in London at 10*s* 6*d.* each The following day there were more, and the price fell to 5*s*, the next day to 3*s* each; and a week later to 4*d*

[2] This is the famous estimate quoted by Gregory King. Its bearing on the law of demand is admirably discussed by Lord Lauderdale (*Inquiry*, pp 51—3). It is represented in fig (8) by the curve *DD'*, the point *A* corresponding to the ordinary price If we take account of the fact that where the price of wheat is very low, it may be used, as it was for instance in 1834, for feeding cattle and sheep and pigs and for brewing and distilling, the lower part of the curve would take a shape somewhat like that of the dotted line in the figure And if we assume that when the price is very high, cheaper substitutes can be got for it, the upper part of the curve would take a shape similar to that of the upper dotted line.

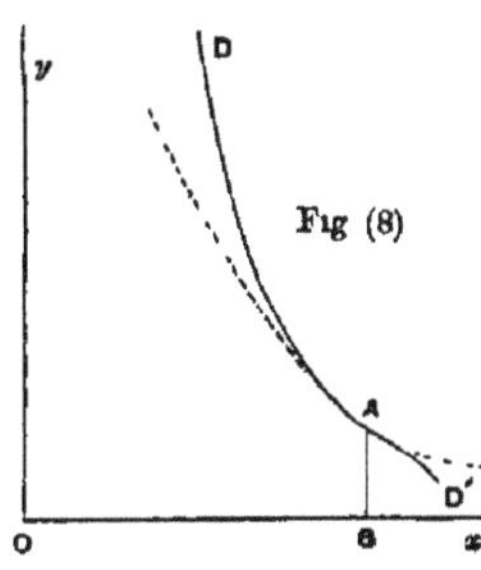

Fig (8)

this have not been uncommon. Thus wheat sold in London for ten shillings a bushel in 1335, but in the following year it sold for ten pence.

There may be even more violent changes than this in the price of a thing which is not necessary, if it is perishable and the demand for it is inelastic thus fish may be very dear one day, and sold for manure two or three days later.

Commodities some part of the consumption of which is necessary

Water is one of the few things the consumption of which we are able to observe at all prices from the very highest down to nothing at all. At moderate prices the demand for it is very elastic. But the uses to which it can be put are capable of being completely filled· and as its price sinks towards zero the demand for it loses its elasticity Nearly the same may be said of salt Its price in England is so low that the demand for it as an article of food is very inelastic but in India the price is comparatively high and the demand is comparatively elastic.

The price of house-room on the other hand has never fallen very low except when a locality is being deserted by its inhabitants. Where the condition of society is healthy, and there is no check to general prosperity, there seems always to be an elastic demand for house-room, on account both of the real conveniences and the social distinction which it affords The desire for those kinds of clothing which are not used for the purpose of display, is satiable: when their price is low the demand for them has scarcely any elasticity.

Influence of sensibility and acquired tastes and distastes

The demand for things of a higher quality depends much on sensibility· some people care little for a refined flavour in their wine provided they can get plenty of it: others crave a high quality, but are easily satiated. In the ordinary working class districts the inferior and the better joints are sold at nearly the same price· but some well-paid artisans in the north of England have developed a liking for the best meat, and will pay for it nearly as high a price as can be got in the west end of London, where the price is kept artificially high by the necessity of sending the inferior joints away for sale elsewhere. Use also gives rise to acquired distastes as well as to acquired tastes. Illustrations

BOOK III. CH IV

which make a book attractive to many readers, will repel those whose familiarity with better work has rendered them fastidious. A person of high musical sensibility in a large town will avoid bad concerts: though he might go to them gladly if he lived in a small town, where no good concerts are to be heard, because there are not enough persons willing to pay the high price required to cover their expenses. The effective demand for first-rate music is elastic only in large towns; for second-rate music it is elastic both in large and small towns.

Influence of variety of uses

Generally speaking those things have the most elastic demand, which are capable of being applied to many different uses. Water for instance is needed first as food, then for cooking, then for washing of various kinds and so on When there is no special drought, but water is sold by the pailful, the price may be low enough to enable even the poorer classes to drink as much of it as they are inclined, while for cooking they sometimes use the same water twice over, and they apply it very scantily in washing. The middle classes will perhaps not use any of it twice for cooking, but they will make a pail of water go a good deal further for washing purposes than if they had an unlimited supply at command. When water is supplied by pipes, and charged at a very low rate by meter, many people use as much of it even for washing as they feel at all inclined to do; and when the water is supplied not by meter but at a fixed annual charge, and is laid on in every place where it is wanted, the use of it for every purpose is carried to the full satiety limit[1].

[1] Thus the general demand of any one person for such a thing as water is the aggregate (or *Compound*, see Book V. Ch VI § 3) of his demand for it for each use; in the same way as the demand of a group of people of different orders of wealth for a commodity, which is serviceable in only one use, is the aggregate of the demands of each member of the group Again, just as the demand of the rich for peas is considerable even at a very high price, but loses all elasticity at a price that is still high relatively to the consumption of the poor; so the demand of the individual for water to drink is considerable even at a very high price, but loses all elasticity at a price that is still high relatively to his demand for it for the purpose of cleaning up the house And as the aggregate of a number of demands on the part of different classes of people for peas retains elasticity over a larger range of price than will that of any one individual, so the demand of an individual for water for many uses retains elasticity over a larger range of prices than his demand for it for any one use Compare an article by Prof J B Clark on *A Universal Law of Economic Variation* in the *Harvard Journal of Economics*, Vol. VIII.

§ 5. So far we have taken no account of the difficulties of getting exact lists of demand prices, and interpreting them correctly. The first which we have to consider arises from the element of *Time*, the source of many of the greatest difficulties in economics.

Difficulties to be overcome; firstly the element of Time

The list of demand prices represents the changes in the price at which a commodity can be sold consequent on changes in the amount offered for sale, *other things being equal* But in fact other things seldom are equal over periods of time sufficiently long for the collection of full and trustworthy statistics There are always occurring disturbing causes whose effects are commingled with, and cannot easily be separated from, the effects of that particular cause which we desire to isolate. This difficulty is aggravated by the fact that in economics the full effects of a cause seldom come at once, but often spread themselves out after it has ceased to exist.

Changes in the purchasing power of money

To begin with, the purchasing power of money is continually changing, and rendering necessary a correction of the results obtained on our assumption that money retains a uniform value. This difficulty can however be overcome fairly well, since we can ascertain with tolerable accuracy the broader changes in the purchasing power of money.

whether permanent, or temporary

Next come the changes in the general prosperity and in the total purchasing power at the disposal of the community at large. The influence of these changes is important, but perhaps less so than is generally supposed. For when the wave of prosperity is descending, prices fall, and this increases the resources of those with fixed incomes at the expense of those whose incomes depend on the profits of business. The downward fluctuation of prosperity is popularly measured almost entirely by the conspicuous losses of this last class, but the statistics of the total consumption of such commodities as tea, sugar, butter, wool, &c prove that the total purchasing power of the people does not meanwhile fall very fast. Still there is a fall, and the allowance to be made for it must be ascertained by comparing the prices and the consumption of as many things as possible

Next come the changes due to the gradual growth of

population and wealth. For these an easy numerical correction can be made when the facts are known[1].

Gradual changes in habits and in the familiarity with new things and new ways of using them.

§ 6. Next, allowance must be made for changes in fashion, and taste and habit[2], for the opening out of new uses of a commodity, for the discovery or improvement or cheapening of other things that can be applied to the same uses with it In all these cases there is great difficulty in allowing for the time that elapses between the economic cause and its effect. For time is required to enable a rise in the price of a commodity to exert its full influence on consumption. Time is required for consumers to become familiar with substitutes that can be used instead of it, and perhaps for producers to get into the habit of producing them in sufficient quantities. Time may be also wanted for the growth of habits of familiarity with the new commodities and the discovery of methods of economizing them

Illustrations

For instance when wood and charcoal became dear in England, familiarity with coal as a fuel grew slowly, fireplaces were but slowly adapted to its use, and an organized traffic in

[1] When a statistical table shows the gradual growth of the consumption of a commodity over a long series of years, we may want to compare the percentage by which it increases in different years This can be done pretty easily with a little practice But when the figures are expressed in the form of a statistical diagram, it cannot easily be done, without translating the diagram back into figures; and this is a cause of the disfavour in which many statisticians hold the graphic method. But by the knowledge of one simple rule the balance can be turned, so far as this point goes, in favour of the graphic method The rule is as follows —Let the quantity of a commodity consumed (or of trade carried, or of tax levied etc), be measured by horizontal lines parallel to Ox, fig (9), while the corresponding years are in the usual manner ticked off in descending order at equal distances along Oy To measure the rate of growth at any point P, put a ruler to touch the curve at P Let it meet Oy in t, and let N be the point on Oy at the same vertical height as P then the number of years marked off along Oy by the distance Nt is the inverse of the fraction by which the amount is increasing annually That is, if Nt is 20 years the amount is increasing at the rate of $\frac{1}{20}$ i e. of 5 per cent annually, if Nt is 25 years, the increase is $\frac{1}{25}$ or 4 per cent annually, and so on See a paper by the present writer in the Jubilee number of the *Journal of the London Statistical Society*, June 1855; also Note IV in the Appendix

Fig (9)

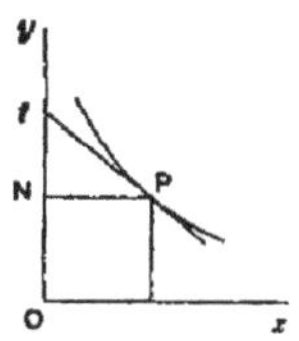

[2] For illustrations of the influence of fashion see articles by Miss Foley in the *Economic Journal*, Vol III and Miss Heather Bigg in the *Nineteenth Century*, Vol XXIII

it did not spring up quickly even to places to which it could be easily carried by water: the invention of processes by which it could be used as a substitute for charcoal in manufacture went even more slowly, and is indeed hardly yet complete. Again, when in recent years the price of coal became very high, a great stimulus was given to the invention of economies in its use, especially in the production of iron and steam, but few of these inventions bore much practical fruit till after the high price had passed away. Again, when a new line of tramways or of suburban railways is opened, even those who live near the line do not get into the habit of making the most of its assistance at once; and a good deal more time elapses before many of those whose places of business are near one end of the line change their homes so as to live near the other end. Again, when petroleum first became plentiful few people were ready to use it freely, gradually petroleum and petroleum lamps have become familiar to all classes of society: too much imfluence would therefore be attributed to the fall in price which has occurred since then, if it were credited with all the increase of consumption.

Some demands can be more easily postponed than others

Another difficulty of the same kind arises from the fact that there are many purchases which can easily be put off for a short time, but not for a long time. This is often the case with regard to clothes and other things which are worn out gradually, and which can be made to serve a little longer than usual under the pressure of high prices. For instance, at the beginning of the cotton famine the recorded consumption of cotton in England was very small. This was partly because retail dealers reduced their stock, but chiefly because people generally made shift to do as long as they could without buying new cotton goods. In 1864 however many found themselves unable to wait longer, and a good deal more cotton was entered for home consumption in that year, though the price was then much higher, than in either of the preceding years. For commodities of this kind then a sudden scarcity does not immediately raise the price fully up to the level, which properly corresponds to the reduced supply. Similarly after the great commercial depression in the United States in 1873 it was noticed that the boot trade revived before the general clothing trade; because there is a great deal of reserve wear in the coats and hats that are thrown aside in prosperous times as worn out, but not so much in the boots.

Difficulties in the way of obtaining the requisite statistics

§ 7. The above difficulties are fundamental: but there are others which do not lie deeper than the more or less inevitable faults of our statistical returns.

Firstly the imperfections of the market

A demand schedule is supposed to present a series of prices at which different amounts of a commodity can find purchasers during a given time in a market. A perfect Market is a district, small or large, in which there are many buyers and many sellers all so keenly on the alert and so well acquainted with one another's affairs that the price of a commodity is always practically the same for the whole of the district. But independently of the fact that those who buy for their own consumption, and not for the purposes of trade, are not always on the look out for every change in the market, there is no means of ascertaining exactly what prices are paid in many transactions Again the geographical limits of a market are seldom clearly drawn, except when they are marked out by the sea or by custom-house barriers; and no country has accurate statistics of commodities produced in it for home consumption

and its want of definite boundaries

Secondly an increase of dealers' stocks is apt to be mistaken for an increase of consumption

Again, there is generally some ambiguity even in such statistics as are to be had. They commonly show goods as entered for consumption as soon as they pass into the hands of dealers, and consequently an increase of dealers' stocks cannot easily be distinguished from an increase of consumption. But the two are governed by different causes. A rise of prices tends to check consumption, but if the rise is expected to continue, it will probably, as has already been noticed, lead dealers to increase their stocks[1].

[1] In examining the effects of taxation, it is customary to compare the amounts entered for consumption just before and just after the imposition of the tax But this is untrustworthy For dealers anticipating the tax lay in large stocks just before it is imposed, and need to buy very little for some time afterwards And *vice versâ* when a tax is lowered Again, high taxes lead to false returns For instance, the nominal importation of molasses into Boston increased fiftyfold in consequence of the tax being lowered by the Rockingham Ministry in 1766, from 6*d* to 1*d* per gallon But this was chiefly due to the fact that with the tax at 1*d*, it was cheaper to pay the duty than to smuggle.

Changes of quality

Next it is difficult to insure that the commodities referred to are always of the same quality After a dry summer what wheat there is, is exceptionally good, and the prices for the next harvest year appear to be higher than they really are. It is possible to make allowance for this, particularly now that dry Californian wheat affords a standard. But it is almost impossible to allow properly for the changes in quality of many kinds of manufactured goods This difficulty occurs even in the case of such a thing as tea the substitution in recent years of the stronger Indian tea for the weaker Chinese tea has made the real increase of consumption greater than that which is shown by the statistics.

Note on Statistics of Consumption

General Statistics of consumption are published by many Governments with regard to certain classes of commodities But partly for the reasons just indicated they are of very little service in helping us to trace either a causal connection between variations in prices and variations in the amounts which people will buy, or in the distribution of different kinds of consumption among the different classes of the community

As regards the first of these objects, viz. the discovery of the laws connecting variations in consumption consequent on variations in price, there seems much to be gained by working out a hint given by Jevons (*Theory*, pp 11, 12) with regard to shopkeepers' books

A shopkeeper in the working man's quarter of a manufacturing town has often the means of ascertaining with tolerable accuracy the financial position of the great body of his customers. He can find out how many factories are at work, and for how many hours in the week, and he can hear about all the important changes in the rate of wages · in fact he makes it his business to do so And as a rule his customers are quick in finding out changes in the price of things which they commonly use He will therefore often find cases in which an increased consumption of a commodity is brought about by a fall in its price, the cause acting quickly, and acting alone without any admixture of disturbing causes Even where disturbing causes are present, he will often be able to allow for their influence For instance, he will know that as the winter comes on, the prices of butter and vegetables rise; but the cold weather makes people desire butter more and vegetables less than before: and therefore when the prices of both vegetables and butter rise towards the winter, he will expect a greater falling off of consumption in the case of vegetables than should properly be attributed to the rise in price taken alone, but a less falling off in the case of butter If however in two neighbouring winters his customers have been about equally numerous, and in receipt of about the same rate of wages, and if in the one the price of butter was a good deal higher than in the other, then a comparison of his books for the two winters will afford a very accurate indication of the influence of changes in price on consumption.

Such a shopkeeper's book affords good opportunities for the application of "the Method of Difference." It may be hoped that, as the knowledge of economic science is diffused, local statistical societies will do important work in this and similar directions Above all this may be hoped from the great co-operative stores. Shopkeepers who supply other classes of society must occasionally be in a position to furnish similar facts relating to the consumption of their customers. And if a sufficient number of tables of demand by different sections of society could be obtained, they would afford the means of estimating indirectly the variations in total demand that would result from extreme variations in price, and thus attaining an end which is inaccessible by any other route For, as a general rule, the price of a commodity fluctuates within but narrow limits, and therefore statistics afford us no direct means of guessing what the consumption of it would be, if its price were either fivefold or a fifth part of what it actually is. But we know that its consumption would be confined almost entirely to the rich if its price were very high; and that, if its price were very low, the great body of its consumption would in most cases be among the working classes If then the present price is very high relatively to the middle or to the working classes, we may be able to infer from the laws of their demand at the present prices what would be the demand of the rich if the price were so raised so as to be very high relatively even to their means On the other hand, if the present price is moderate relatively to the means of the rich, we may be able to infer from their demand what would be the demand of the working classes if the price were to fall to a level which is moderate relatively to their means. It is only by thus piecing together fragmentary laws of demand that we can hope to get any approach to an accurate law relating to widely different prices (That is to say the general demand curve for a commodity cannot be drawn with confidence except in the immediate neighbourhood of the current price, until we are able to piece it together out of the fragmentary demand curves of different classes of society Compare the second Section of this Chapter.)

When some progress has been made in reducing to definite law the demand for commodities that are destined for immediate consumption, then, but not till then, will there be use in attempting a similar task with regard to those secondary demands which are dependent on these —the demands namely for the labour of artisans and others who take part in the production of things for sale; and again the demand for machines, factories, railway material and other instruments of production. The demand for the work of medical men, of domestic servants and of all those whose services are rendered direct to the consumer is similar in character to the demand for commodities for immediate consumption, and its laws may be investigated in the same manner

It is a very important, but also difficult task to ascertain the proportions in which the different classes of society distribute their expenditure between necessaries, comforts and luxuries, between things that provide only present pleasure, and those that build up stores of physical and moral strength, and lastly between those which gratify the lower wants and those which stimulate and educate the higher wants Several endeavours have been made in this direction on the Continent during the last fifty years, and latterly the subject has been investigated with increasing vigour not only there but also in America and in England.

A single table made out by the great statistician Dr Engel for the consumption of the lower, middle and working classes in Saxony in 1857, may be quoted here, because it has acted as a guide and a standard of comparison to later inquiries. It is as follows —

Items of Expenditure.	Proportions of the Expenditure of the Family of—		
	1. Workman with an Income of 45*l* to 60*l* a Year	2. Workman with an Income of 90*l* to 120*l*	3. Middle-Class person with an Income of 150*l* to 200*l*
1 Food only . . .	62 0 per cent	55 0 per cent	50·0 per cent
2. Clothing	16 0 ,,	18 0 ,,	18 0 ,,
3 Lodging	12 0 ,,	12 0 ,,	12 0 ,,
4 Light and Fuel	5 0 ,,	5 0 ,,	5 0 ,,
5 Education . . .	2 0 ,,	3 5 ,,	5 5 ,,
6. Legal Protection	1 0 ,,	2·0 ,,	3 0 ,,
7 Care of health . .	1 0 ,,	2 0 ,,	3 0 ,,
8 Comfort and recreation	1 0 ,,	2 5 ,,	3 5 ,,
Totals .	100 0 per cent	100 0 per cent	100 0 per cent

Working-men's budgets have often been collected and compared. But like all other figures of the kind they suffer from the facts that those who will take the trouble to make such returns voluntarily are not average men, that those who keep careful accounts are not average men; and that when accounts have to be supplemented by the memory, the memory is apt to be biassed by notions as to how the money ought to have been spent, especially when the accounts are put together specially for another's eye This border-ground between the provinces of domestic and public economy is one in which excellent work may be done by many who are disinclined for more general and abstract speculations[1].

[1] Working men's budgets were collected by Eden at the end of the last century; and there is much miscellaneous information on the expenditure of the working classes in the Reports of Commissions on Poor-relief, Factories, &c during the whole of this century See also an article on wages and prices in the Companion to the British Almanack for 1834, *Workmen's Budgets in Manchester*, in the Statistical Journal, 1841—2; Tuckett's *Labouring Population*, 1846; Sargant's *Economy of the Working Classes* in 1857; Reports by her Majesty's Consuls *On the Condition of the Working Classes in Foreign Countries*, 1872; the inquiry for the Board of Trade in 1887, *Workmen's Budgets* by Higgs in Statistical Journal 1893, Reports of Subcommissioners on Agriculture to the Labour Commission 1893, 4, some articles in Vols IV and V. of the *Bulletin de l'Institut International de Statistique*, in the latter of which a compendious view is given of the results of M le Play's monumental *Les Ouvriers Européens*, while an abstract of many continental inquiries is presented in a convenient form in Dr Gruber's *Die Haushaltung der arbeitenden Klassen* Much work has been done in the same direction in the United States, see Young's *Labour in Europe and America*, and the reports of various American Labour Bureaux, especially those of the United States Commissioner of Labour for 1886, and 1891; and Prof Falkner's introduction to the Report on Wholesale Prices, &c to the Senate in 1893.

The method of M le Play is the *intensive* study of all the details of the domestic life of a few carefully chosen families. To work it well requires a rare combination of judgment in selecting cases, and of insight and sympathy in interpreting them At its best, it is the best of all but in ordinary hands it is likely to suggest more untrustworthy general conclusions, than those obtained by the *extensive* method of collecting more rapidly very numerous observations, reducing them as far as possible to statistical form, and obtaining broad averages in which inaccuracies and idiosyncracies may be trusted to counteract one another to some extent

Information bearing on the subject was collected by Harrison, Petty, Cantillon (whose lost Supplement seems to have contained some workmen's budgets), Arthur Young, Malthus and others Part of the work is now being taken over by the younger sciences of Anthropology and Demography, and there is much to be gleaned from the *Descriptive Sociology* of various nations compiled under the direction of Herbert Spencer, which, though too ambitious, may be of service to the economist if used with care. See also Lavollée, *Classes ouvrières en Europe*, Barbaret, *Le travail en France*, Symonds, *Arts and Artisans at Home and Abroad*, Mayhew, *London Labour*, and Charles Booth, *Life and Labour in London* and *Condition of the Aged Poor*

CHAPTER V.

THE CHOICE BETWEEN DIFFERENT USES OF THE SAME THING. IMMEDIATE AND DEFERRED USES.

BOOK III CH. V

The distribution of a person's means between the gratification of different wants

§ 1. THE primitive housewife finding that she has a limited number of hanks of yarn from the year's shearing, considers all the domestic wants for clothing and tries to distribute the yarn between them in such a way as to contribute as much as possible to the family well-being. She will think she has failed if, when it is done, she has reason to regret that she did not apply more to making, say, socks, and less to vests. That would mean that she had miscalculated the points at which to suspend the making of socks and vests respectively, that she had gone too far in the case of vests, and not far enough in that of socks; and that therefore at the points at which she actually did stop, the utility of yarn turned into socks was greater than that of yarn turned into vests. But if, on the other hand, she hit on the right points to stop at, then she made just so many socks and vests that she got an equal amount of good out of the last bundle of yarn that she applied to socks, and the last she applied to vests This illustrates a general principle, which may be expressed thus:—

If a person has a thing which he can put to several uses, he will distribute it between these uses in such a way that it has the same marginal utility in all. For if it had a greater marginal utility in one use than another, he would gain by taking away some of it from the second use and applying it to the first[1].

[1] Our illustration belongs indeed properly to domestic production rather than to domestic consumption But that was almost inevitable; for there are very

BOOK III. CH V

But a person may have too much of one thing for all uses, and too little of another

One great disadvantage of a primitive economy, in which there is but little free exchange, is that a person may easily have so much of one thing, say wool, that when he has applied it to every possible use, its marginal utility in each use is low: and at the same time he may have so little of some other thing, say wood, that its marginal utility for him is very high. Meanwhile some of his neighbours may be in great need of wood, and have more wool than they can turn to good account. If each gives up that which has for him the lower utility and receives that which has the higher, each will gain by the exchange. But to make such an adjustment by barter, would be tedious and difficult

Barter is a partial remedy.

The difficulty of barter is indeed not so very great where there are but a few simple commodities each capable of being adapted by domestic work to several uses, the weaving wife and the spinster daughters adjusting rightly the marginal utilities of the different uses of the wool, while the husband and the sons do the same for the wood.

Money can be distributed so as to have equal marginal utilities in each use

§ 2 But when commodities have become very numerous and highly specialized, there is an urgent need for the free use of money, or general purchasing power; for that alone can be applied easily in an unlimited variety of purchases. And in a money-economy, good management is shown by so adjusting the margins of suspense on each line of expenditure that the marginal utility of a shilling's worth of goods on each line shall be the same. And this result each one will attain by constantly watching to see whether there is any thing on which he is spending so much that he would gain by taking a little away from that line of expenditure and putting it on some other line

Illustrations

Thus for instance the clerk who is in doubt whether to ride to town, or to walk and have some little extra indulgence at his lunch, is weighing against one another the (marginal) utilities of two different modes of spending his money And when an experienced housekeeper urges on a young couple

A chief use of domestic accounts.

few things ready for immediate consumption which are available for many different uses And the doctrine of the Distribution of means between different uses has less important and less interesting applications in the Science of Demand than in that of Supply; where one particular form of it—the Law of Substitution—will occupy us a great deal

BOOK III. CH V.

the importance of keeping accounts carefully; a chief motive of the advice is that they may avoid spending impulsively a great deal of money on furniture and other things, for, though some quantity of these is really needful, yet when bought lavishly they do not give high (marginal) utilities in proportion to their cost. And when the young pair look over their year's budget at the end of the year, and find perhaps that it is necessary to curtail their expenditure somewhere, they compare the (marginal) utilities of different items, weighing the loss of utility that would result from taking away a pound's expenditure here, with that which they would lose by taking it away there they strive to adjust their parings down so that the aggregate loss of utility may be a minimum, and the aggregate of utility that remains to them may be a maximum[1].

The balancing of future benefits against present

§ 3 The different uses between which a commodity is distributed need not all be present uses; some may be present and some future A prudent person will endeavour to distribute his means between all their several uses present and future in such a way that they will have in each the same marginal utility. But in estimating the present marginal utility of a distant source of pleasure a twofold allowance must be made; firstly, for its uncertainty (this is an *objective* property which all well-informed persons would estimate in the same way), and secondly, for its difference in the value to them of a distant as compared with a present pleasure (this is a *subjective* property which different people would estimate in different ways according to their individual characters, and their circumstances at the time).

1 The working-class budgets which were mentioned in the Note at the end of the last chapter may render most important services in helping people to distribute their resources wisely between different uses, so that the marginal utility for each purpose shall be the same But the vital problems of domestic economy relate as much to wise action as to wise spending. The English and the American housewife make limited means go a much less way towards satisfying wants than the French housewife does, not because they do not know how to buy, but because they cannot produce as good finished commodities out of the raw material of inexpensive joints, vegetables &c, as she can Domestic economy is often spoken of as belonging to the Science of Consumption but that is only half true The greatest faults in domestic economy, among the sober portion of the Anglo-Saxon working-classes at all events, are faults of Production rather than of Consumption

BOOK III. CH V

Future benefits are "discounted," at different rates

If people regarded future benefits as equally desirable with similar benefits at the present time, they would probably endeavour to distribute their pleasures and other satisfactions evenly throughout their lives They would therefore generally be willing to give up a present pleasure for the sake of an equal pleasure in the future, provided they could be certain of having it But in fact human nature is so constituted that in estimating the "present value" of a future benefit most people generally make a second deduction from its future value, in the form of what we may call a "discount," that increases with the period for which the benefit is deferred One will reckon a distant benefit at nearly the same value which it would have for him if it were present; while another who has less power of realizing the future, less patience and self-control, will care comparatively little for any benefit that is not near at hand. And the same person will vary in his mood, being at one time impatient, and greedy for present enjoyment, while at another his mind dwells on the future, and he is willing to postpone all enjoyments that can conveniently be made to wait Sometimes he is in a mood to care little for anything else: sometimes he is like the children who pick the plums out of their pudding to eat them at once, sometimes like those who put them aside to be eaten last. And, in any case, when calculating the rate at which a future benefit is discounted, we must be careful to make allowance for the pleasures of expectation.

Desire for lasting sources of enjoyment and for ownership

The rates at which different people discount the future affect not only their tendency to save, as the term is ordinarily understood, but also their tendency to buy things which will be a lasting source of pleasure rather than those which give a stronger but more transient enjoyment; to buy a new coat rather than to indulge in a drinking bout, or to choose simple furniture that will wear well, rather than showy furniture that will soon fall to pieces.

It is in regard to these things especially that the pleasure of possession makes itself felt Many people derive from the mere feeling of ownership a stronger satisfaction than they derive from ordinary pleasures in the narrower sense of the term: for example, the delight in the possession of land will often induce people to pay for it so high a price that it yields them but a very poor return on their investment. There is a delight in ownership for its own sake; and there is a delight in ownership on account of the distinction it yields. Sometimes the latter is stronger than the former, sometimes weaker; and perhaps no one knows himself or other people well enough to be able to draw the line quite certainly between the two.

But we cannot really estimate the *quantity* of a future benefit.

§ 4 As has already been urged, we cannot compare the *quantities* of two benefits, which are enjoyed at different times even by the same person. When a person postpones a pleasure-giving event he does not postpone the pleasure; but he gives up a present pleasure and takes in its place another, or an expectation of getting another at a future date: and we cannot tell whether he expects the future pleasure to be greater than the one which he is giving up, unless we know all the circumstances of the case. And therefore, even though we know the rate at which he discounts future pleasurable events, such as spending £1 on immediate gratifications, we yet do not know the rate at which he discounts future pleasures[1].

[1] In classifying some pleasures as more *urgent* than others, it is often forgotten that the postponement of a pleasurable event may alter the circumstances under which it occurs, and therefore alter the character of the pleasure itself. For instance it may be said that a young man discounts at a very high rate the pleasure of the Alpine tours which he hopes to be able to afford himself when he has made his fortune. He would much rather have them now, partly because they would give him much greater pleasure now.

Again, it may happen that the postponement of the pleasurable event involves an unequal distribution in Time of a certain good, and that the Law of Diminution of Marginal Utility acts strongly in the case of this particular good. For instance, it is sometimes said that the pleasures of eating are specially urgent, and it is undoubtedly true that if a man goes dinnerless for six days in the week and eats seven dinners on the seventh, he loses very much; because when postponing six dinners, he does not postpone the pleasures of eating six separate dinners, but substitutes for them the pleasure of one day's excessive eating. Again, when a person puts away eggs for the winter he does not expect that they will be better flavoured then than now, he expects that they will be scarce, and that therefore their utility will be higher than now. This shows the importance of drawing a clear distinction between discounting a future pleasure, and discounting the pleasure derived from the future enjoyment of a certain amount of a commodity. For in the latter case we must make separate allowance for differences between the marginal utilities of the commodity at the two times: but in the latter this has been allowed for once in estimating the amount of the pleasure, and it must not be allowed for again.

BOOK III CH V

An artificial measure of the rate of discount of future benefits

We can however get an artificial measure of the rate at which he discounts future benefits by making two assumptions. These are, firstly, that he expects to be about as rich at the future date as he is now; and secondly, that his capacity for deriving benefit from the things which money will buy will on the whole remain unchanged, though it may have increased in some directions and diminished in others. On these assumptions, if he is willing, but only just willing, to spare a pound from his expenditure now with the certainty of having (for the disposal of himself or his heirs) a guinea one year hence, we may fairly say that he discounts future benefits that are perfectly secure (subject only to the conditions of human mortality) at the rate of five per cent. per annum And on these assumptions the rate at which he discounts future (certain) benefits, will be the rate at which he can discount money in the money market[1].

[1] It is important to remember that, except on these assumptions there is no direct connection between the rate of discount on the loan of money, and the rate at which future pleasures are discounted A man may be so impatient of delay that a certain promise of a pleasure ten years hence will not induce him to give up one close at hand which he regards as a quarter as great. And yet if he should fear that ten years hence money may be so scarce with him (and its marginal utility therefore so high) that half-a crown then may give him more pleasure or save him more pain than a pound now, he will save something for the future even though he have to hoard it, on the same principle that he might store eggs for the winter But we are here straying into questions that are more closely connected with Supply than with Demand. We shall have to consider them again from different points of view in connection with the Accumulation of Wealth, and later again in connection with the causes that determine the Rate of Interest

We may however consider here how to measure numerically the present value of a future pleasure, on the supposition that we know, (i) its amount, (ii) the date at which it will come, if it comes at all, (iii) the chance that it will come, and (iv) the rate at which the person in question discounts future pleasures

If the probability that a pleasure will be enjoyed is three to one, so that three chances out of four are in its favour, the value of its expectation is three-fourths of what it would be if it were certain if the probability that it will be enjoyed were only seven to five, so that only seven chances out of twelve are in its favour, the value of its expectation is only seven-twelfths of what it would be if the event were certain, and so on [This is its actuarial value but further allowance may have to be made for the fact that the true value to anyone of an uncertain gain is generally less than its actuarial value (see the second note on p 187)] If the anticipated pleasure is both uncertain and distant we have a two-fold deduction to make from its full value We will suppose, for instance, that a person would give 10*s* for a gratification if it were present and certain, but that it is due a year hence, and the probability of its happening then is three to one

So far we have considered each pleasure singly; but a great many of the things which people buy are durable, i e. are not consumed in a single use, a durable good, such as a piano, is the probable source of many pleasures, more or less remote, and its value to a purchaser is the aggregate of the value to him of all these pleasures, allowance being made for their uncertainty and for their distance[1]

Future pleasures expected from the ownership of durable commodities

Suppose also that he discounts the future at the rate of twenty per cent. per annum Then the value to him of the anticipation of it is $\frac{3}{4} \times \frac{80}{100} \times 10s$ i e. 6s Compare the Introductory chapter of Jevons' *Theory of Political Economy*

[1] Of course this estimate is formed by a rough instinct; and in any attempt to reduce it to numerical accuracy (see Note V in the Appendix), we must recollect what has been said, in this and the preceding Section, as to the impossibility of comparing accurately pleasures or other satisfactions that do not occur at the same time, and also as to the assumption of uniformity involved in supposing the discount of future pleasures to obey the exponential law

CHAPTER VI.

VALUE AND UTILITY.

BOOK III. CH VI.

Price and Utility

§ 1 WE may now turn to consider how far the price which is actually paid for a thing represents the benefit that arises from its possession This is a wide subject on which economic science has very little to say, but that little is of some importance

We have already seen that the price which a person pays for a thing can never exceed, and seldom comes up to that which he would be willing to pay rather than go without it· so that the satisfaction which he gets from its purchase generally exceeds that which he gives up in paying away its price, and he thus derives from the purchase a surplus of satisfaction. The excess of the price which he would be willing to pay rather than go without it, over that which he actually does pay is the economic measure of this surplus satisfaction · and, for reasons which will appear later on, may be called *Consumers' Rent*

Consumers' Rent

It is obvious that the Consumers' Rents derived from some commodities are much greater than from others. There are many comforts and luxuries of which the prices are very much below those which many people would pay rather than go entirely without them, and which therefore afford a very great Consumers' Rent Good instances are matches, salt, a penny newspaper, or a postage-stamp.

is part of the benefit a man derives from his

This benefit, which he gets from purchasing at a low price things which he would rather pay a high price for than go without, may be called the benefit which he derives from his *Opportunities*, or from his *Environment*, or, to recur to a word that was in common use a few generations ago, from his *Conjuncture* Our aim in the present is to apply the notion of Consumers' Rent as an aid in estimating roughly some of the benefits which a person derives from his Environment or his Conjuncture[1]

Environment or Conjuncture

§ 2 In order to give definiteness to our notions, let us consider the case of tea purchased for domestic consumption. Let us take the case of a man, who, if the price of tea were 20*s* a pound, would just be induced to buy one pound annually; who would just be induced to buy two pounds if the price were 14*s*, three pounds if the price were 10*s*, four pounds if the price were 6*s*, five pounds if the price were 4*s*, six pounds if the price were 3*s*., and who, the price being actually 2*s*., does purchase seven pounds. We have to investigate the Consumers' Rent which he derives from his power of purchasing tea at 2*s*. a pound

Consumers' Rent in relation to the demand of an individual.

The fact that he would just be induced to purchase one pound if the price were 20*s*, proves that the total enjoyment or satisfaction which he derives from that pound is as great as that which he could obtain by spending 20*s* on other things. When the price falls to 14*s*, he could if he chose, continue to buy only one pound. He would then get for 14*s* what was worth to him at least 20*s*., and he will obtain a surplus satisfaction worth to him at least 6*s*, or in other words a Consumers' Rent of at least 6*s*. But in fact he buys a second pound of his own free choice, thus showing that he regards it as worth to him at least 14*s*. He obtains for 28*s*. what is worth to him at least 20*s*. + 14*s*., i.e. 34*s*. His surplus satisfaction is at all events not diminished by buying it, but remains worth at least 6*s*. to him The total utility of

[1] This term is a familiar one in German Economics, and meets a need which is much felt in English Economics For opportunity and environment, the only available substitutes for it, are sometimes rather misleading By *Conjunctur*, says Wagner (*Grundegung* Ed III p 387), "we understand the sum total of the technical, economic, social and legal conditions, which, in a mode of national life (*Volkswirthschaft*) resting upon Division of Labour and Private Property,—especially private property in land and other material means of production—determine the demand for and supply of goods, and therefore their exchange value this determination being as a rule, or at least in the main, *independent* of the will of the owner, of his activity and his remissness

BOOK III CH VI

the two pounds is worth at least 34*s.*, his Consumers' Rent is at least 6*s.*[1]

When the price falls to 10*s*, he might, if he chose, continue to buy only two pounds, and obtain for 20*s.* what was worth to him at least 34*s.*, and derive a surplus satisfaction worth at least 14*s.* But in fact he prefers to buy a third pound: and as he does this freely, we know that he

[1] The first pound was probably worth to him more than 20*s*. All that we know is that it was not worth less to him He probably got some small surplus even on that Again, the second pound was probably worth more than 14*s* to him. All that we know is that it was worth at least 14*s* and not worth 40*s* to him. He would get therefore at this stage a surplus satisfaction of at least 6*s*, probably a little more A ragged edge of this kind, as mathematicians are aware, always exists when we watch the effects of considerable changes, as that from 20*s* to 14*s* a pound. If we had begun with a very high price, had descended by practically infinitesimal changes of a farthing per pound, and watched infinitesimal variations in his consumption of a small fraction of a pound at a time, this ragged edge would have disappeared

The significance of the condition in the text that he buys the second pound of his own free choice is shown by the consideration that if the price of 14*s.* had been offered to him on the condition that he took two pounds, he would then have to elect between taking one pound for 20*s.* or two pounds for 28*s* and then his taking two pounds would not have proved that he thought the second pound worth more than 8*s* to him But as it is, he takes a second pound paying 14*s* unconditionally for it, and that proves that it is worth at least 14*s* to him (If he can get buns at a penny each but seven for sixpence, and he elects to buy seven, we know that he is willing to give up his sixth penny for the sake of the sixth and the seventh buns · but we cannot tell how much he would pay rather than go without the seventh bun only)

It is sometimes objected that as he increases his purchases, the urgency of his need for his earlier purchases is diminished, and their utility falls, therefore we ought to continually redraw the earlier parts of our list of demand prices at a lower level, as we pass along it towards lower prices (i e to redraw at a lower level our demand curve as we pass along it to the right) But this misconceives the plan on which the list of prices is made out. The objection would have been valid, if the demand price set against each number of pounds of tea represented the *average* utility of that number For it is true that, if he would pay just 20*s* for one pound, and just 14*s* for a second, then he would pay just 34*s* for the two; i e 17*s* each on the average And if our list had had reference to the *average* prices he would pay, and had set 17*s* against the second pound; then no doubt we should have had to redraw the list as we passed on For when he has bought a third pound the average utility to him of each of the three will be less than that of 17*s*; being in fact 14*s* 8*d* if, as we go on to assume, he would pay just 10*s.* for a third pound But this difficulty is entirely avoided on the plan of making out demand prices which is here adopted, according to which his second pound is credited, not with the 17*s* which represents the average value per pound of the two pounds; but with the 14*s*, which represents the *additional* utility which a second pound has for him For that remains unchanged when he has bought a third pound, of which the additional utility is measured by 10*s*

does not diminish his surplus satisfaction by doing it He now gets for 30s. three pounds, of which the first is worth to him at least 20s., the second at least 14s., and the third at least 10s. The total utility of the three is worth at least 44s, his Consumers' Rent is at least 14s, and so on

When at last the price has fallen to 2s he buys seven pounds, which are severally worth to him not less than 20, 14, 10, 6, 4, 3, and 2s or 59s. in all This sum measures their total utility to him, and his Consumers' Rent is (at least) the excess of this sum over the 14s. he actually does pay for them, i e. 45s This is the excess value of the satisfaction he gets from buying the tea over that which he could have got by spending the 14s. in extending a little his purchase of other commodities, of which he had just not thought it worth while to buy more at their current prices, and any further purchases of which therefore would not yield him any Consumers' Rent. In other words, he derives this 45s. worth of surplus enjoyment from his Conjuncture, from the adaptation of the environment to his wants in the particular matter of tea. If that adaptation ceased, and tea could not be had at any price, he would have incurred a loss of satisfaction at least equal to that which he could have got by spending 45s. more on extra supplies of things that were worth to him only just what he paid for them[1]

Demand of a market

§ 3 In the same way if we were to neglect for the moment the fact that the same sum of money represents

[1] Prof. Nicholson (*Principles of Political Economy*, Vol. I and *Economic Journal*, Vol IV.), apparently under some misapprehension as to the drift of the doctrine of consumers' rent, has raised several objections to it, which have been answered by Prof Edgeworth in the same Journal. Prof Nicholson says —"Of what avail is it to say that the utility of an income of say £100 a year is worth (say) £1000 a year?" There would be no avail in saying that But there might be use, when comparing life in Central Africa with life in England, in saying that, though the things which money will buy in Central Africa may on the average be as cheap there as here, yet there are so many things which cannot be bought there at all, that a person with a thousand a year there is not so well off as a person with three or four hundred a year here If a man pays 1*d* toll on a bridge, which saves him an additional drive that would cost a shilling, we do not say that the penny is worth a shilling, but that the penny together with the advantage offered him by the bridge (the part it plays in his Conjuncture) is worth a shilling for that day Were the bridge swept away on a day on which he needed it, he would be in at least as bad a position as if he had been deprived of eleven pence

BOOK III. CH. VI. different amounts of pleasure to different people, we might measure the surplus satisfaction which the sale of tea affords, say, in the London market, by the aggregate of the sums by which the prices shown in a complete list of demand prices for tea exceeds its selling price[1].

[1] Let us then consider the demand curve DD' for tea in any large market. Let OH be the amount which is sold there at the price HA annually, a year being taken as our unit of time. Taking any point M in OH let us draw MP vertically upwards to meet the curve in P and cut a horizontal line through A in R. We will suppose the several lbs numbered in the order of the eagerness of the several purchasers: the eagerness of the purchaser of any lb being measured by the price he is just willing to pay for that lb. The figure informs us that OM can be sold at the price PM, but that at any higher price not quite so many lbs can be sold. There must be then some individual who will buy more at the price PM, than he will at any higher price; and we are to regard the OMth lb as sold to this individual. Suppose for instance that PM represents 4*s.*, and that OM represents a million lbs. The purchaser described in the text is just willing to buy his fifth lb of tea at the price 4*s.*, and the OMth or millionth lb may be said to be sold to him. If AH and therefore RM represent 2*s.*, the Consumers' Rent derived from the OMth lb is the excess of PM or 4*s.* which the purchaser of that lb would have been willing to pay for it over RM the 2*s.* which he actually does pay for it. Let us suppose that a very thin vertical parallelogram is drawn of which the height is PM and of which the base is the distance along Ox that measures the single unit or lb of tea. It will be convenient henceforward to regard price as measured not by a mathematical straight line without thickness, as PM, but by a very thin parallelogram, or as it may be called a thick straight line, of which the breadth is in every case equal to the distance along Ox which measures a unit or lb of tea. Thus we should say that the total satisfaction derived from the OMth lb of tea is represented (or, on the assumption made in the last paragraph of the text is measured) by the thick straight line MP; that the price paid for this lb is represented by the thick straight line MR and the Consumers' Rent derived from this lb by the thick straight line RP. Now let us suppose that such thin parallelograms, or thick straight lines, are drawn for all positions of M between O and H, one for each lb of tea. The thick straight lines thus drawn, as MP is, from Ox up to the demand curve will each represent the aggregate of the satisfaction derived from a lb of tea, and taken together thus occupy and exactly fill up the whole area $DOHA$. Therefore we may say that the area $DOHA$ represents the aggregate of the satisfaction derived from the consumption of tea. Again, each of the straight lines drawn, as MR is, from Ox upwards as far as AC represents the price that actually is paid for a lb of tea. These straight lines together make up the area $COHA$, and therefore this area represents the total price paid for tea. Finally each of the straight lines drawn as RP is from AC upwards as far as the demand curve, represents the Consumers' Rent derived from the corresponding lb of tea. These straight lines together make up the area DCA; and therefore this area represents the total Consumers' Rent that is derived from tea when the price is

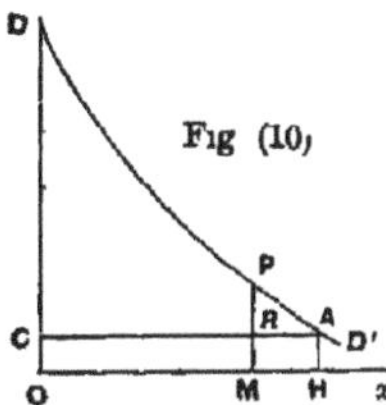

BOOK III CH. VI

This analysis aims only at giving definite expression to familiar notions

This analysis, with its new names and elaborate machinery, appears at first sight laboured and unreal. But on closer study it will be found to introduce no new difficulties and to make no new assumptions; but only to bring to light difficulties and assumptions that are latent in the common language of the market-place For in this, as in other cases, the apparent simplicity of popular phrases veils a real complexity, and it is the function of analysis to bring out that latent complexity, to face it, and to reduce it as far as possible: so that in later stages we may handle firmly difficulties that could not be grasped with a good grip by the vague thought and language of ordinary life.

It is a common saying in ordinary life that the real value of things to us is not gauged by the price we pay for them: that, though we spend for instance much more on tea than on salt; yet salt is of greater real value to us; and that this would be clearly seen, if we were entirely deprived of it. This line of argument implies that we cannot trust the marginal utility of a commodity to indicate its total utility for though, when a person spends sixpence on a quarter of a pound of tea instead of on a stone of salt, he does so because he prefers the tea. yet he would not prefer the tea if he did not know that he could easily get whatever salt he needed for his more urgent requirements. And if an attempt were made to give this vague saying greater definiteness, the ordinary course would be to estimate first the price that people would pay for a small quantity of tea, rather than go without it; and next what they would pay for further supplies, if it became a little more plentiful, and next what they

AH But it must be repeated that this geometrical measurement is only an aggregate of the measures of benefits which are not all measured on the same scale except on the assumption just made in the text. Unless that assumption is made the area only represents an aggregate of satisfactions, the several amounts of which are not exactly measured. On that assumption only, its area measures the volume of the total *net* satisfaction derived from the tea by its various purchasers

The notion of an exact measurement of Consumers' Rent was published by Dupuit in 1844 But his work was forgotten, and the first to publish a clear analysis of the relation of total to marginal (or final) utility in the English language was Jevons in 1871, when he had not read Dupuit The notion of Consumers' Rent was suggested to the present writer by a study of the mathematical aspects of demand and utility under the influence of Cournot, von Thunen and Bentham

BOOK III CH VI

would pay for further supplies, and so on: and the whole would be added up. And then the like would be done for salt, and the two would be compared The process would be the same as in our analysis; but it would remain vague; or if an attempt were made to be definite and exact, there would be much waste of labour in the absence of appropriate phrases and machinery[1].

Allowance has to be made where necessary for differences of sensibility;

In any such reasoning in ordinary life it would be assumed that a pound's worth of gratification to one Englishman might be taken as equivalent with a pound's worth to another, "to start with," and "until cause to the contrary were shown." But every one would know that this was a reasonable course only on the supposition that the consumers of tea and those of salt belonged to the same classes of people, and included people of every variety of temperament[2].

and for differences of wealth

A much more important point practically is that a pound's worth of satisfaction to an ordinary poor man is a much greater thing than a pound's worth of satisfaction to an ordinary rich man · and if instead of comparing tea and salt, which are both used largely by all classes, we compared either of them with champagne or pineapples, the correction

[1] The outlines of this notion are given in the following passage from Harris *On Coins* 1757, which was followed closely by Adam Smith, while the analysis was carried further by Ricardo (see below, Note at the end of Book V) Harris says (p 5), "Things in general are valued, not according to their real uses in supplying the necessities of men; but rather in proportion to the land, labour and skill that are requisite to produce them It is according to this proportion nearly, that things or commodities are exchanged one for another, and it is by the said scale, that the intrinsic values of most things are chiefly estimated Water is of great use, and yet ordinarily of little or no value; because in most places, water flows spontaneously in such great plenty, as not to be withheld within the limits of private property, but all may have enough, without other expense than that of bringing or conducting it, when the case so requires On the other hand, diamonds being very scarce, have upon that account a great value, though they are but little use"

[2] There might conceivably be persons of high sensibility who would suffer specially from the want of either salt or tea or who were generally sensitive, and would suffer more from the loss of a certain part of their income than others in the same station of life But it would be assumed that such differences between individuals might be neglected, since we were considering in either case the average of large numbers of people, though of course it might be necessary to consider whether there were some special reason for believing, say, that those who laid most store by tea were a specially sensitive class of people If it could, then a separate allowance for this would have to be made before applying the results of economical analysis to practical problems of ethics or politics

to be made on this account would be more than important: it would change the whole character of the estimate In earlier generations many statesmen, and even some economists, neglected to make adequate allowance for considerations of this class, especially when constructing schemes of taxation; and their words or deeds seemed to imply a want of sympathy with the sufferings of the poor; though more often they were due simply to want of thought.

but it is seldom needed in considering large groups of people

On the whole however it happens that by far the greater number of the events with which economics deals, affect in about equal proportions all the different classes of society; so that if the money measures of the happiness caused by two events are equal, there is not in general any very great difference between the amounts of the happiness in the two cases. And it is on account of this fact that the exact measurement of the Consumers' Rent in a market has already much theoretical interest, and may become of high practical importance.

It will be noted however that the demand prices of each commodity, on which our estimates of its total utility and consumers' rent are based, assume that *other things remain equal*, while its price rises to scarcity value· and when the total utilities of two commodities which contribute to the same purpose are calculated on this plan, we cannot say that the total utility of the two together is equal to the sum of the total utilities of each separately[1].

[1] Some ambiguous phrases in earlier editions appear to have suggested to some readers the opposite opinion. But the task of adding together the total utilities of all commodities, so as to obtain the aggregate of the total utility of all wealth, is beyond the range of any but the most elaborate mathematical formulæ. An attempt to treat it by them some years ago convinced the present writer that even if the task be theoretically feasible, the result would be encumbered by so many hypotheses as to be practically useless.

Attention has already (pp. 176, 181) been called to the fact that for some purposes such things as tea and coffee must be grouped together as one commodity and it is obvious that, if tea were inaccessible, people would increase their consumption of coffee, and vice versa The loss that people would suffer from being deprived both of tea and coffee would be greater than the sum of their losses from being deprived of either alone and therefore the total utility of tea and coffee is greater than the sum of the total utility of tea calculated on the supposition that people can have recourse to coffee, and that of coffee calculated on a like supposition as to tea. This difficulty can be theoretically evaded by grouping the two "rival" commodities together under a common demand schedule

BOOK III CH VI

It is seldom necessary to take account of changes in the purchasers' command of money.

§ 4. The substance of our argument would not be affected if we took account of the fact that, the more a person spends on anything the less power he retains of purchasing more of it or of other things, and the greater is the value of money to him, (in technical language every fresh expenditure increases the marginal value of money to him) But though its substance would not be altered, its form would be made more intricate without any corresponding gain; for there are very few practical problems, in which the corrections to be made under this head would be of any importance[1].

There are however some exceptions. For instance, as Mr Giffen has pointed out, a rise in the price of bread makes so large a drain on the resources of the poorer labouring families and raises so much the marginal utility of money to them, that they are forced to curtail their consumption of meat and the more expensive farinaceous foods and, bread being still the cheapest food which they can get and will take, they consume more, and not less of it But such cases are rare, when they are met with they must be treated separately.

We can seldom obtain a complete list of demand

It has already been remarked that we cannot guess at all accurately how much of anything people would buy at prices very different from those which they are accustomed to pay for it or in other words, that the demand prices for

On the other hand, if we have calculated the total utility of fuel with reference to the fact that without it we could not obtain hot water to obtain the beverage tea from tea leaves, we should count something twice over if we added to that utility the total utility of tea leaves, reckoned on a similar plan Other aspects of these two difficulties are examined in Book V ch VI

Prof Patten has insisted on the latter of them in various writings, and in particular in some suggestive articles in Vol. III of the *Annals of the American Academy* His own attempt to express the aggregate utility of all forms of wealth is ingenious but does not appear to take account of all the difficulties of the task

[1] In mathematical language the neglected elements would generally belong to the second order of small quantities, and the legitimacy of the familiar scientific method by which they are neglected would have seemed beyond question, had not Prof Nicholson challenged it A short reply to him has been given by Prof Edgeworth in the *Economic Journal* for March 1894, and a fuller reply by Sig Barone in the *Giornale degli Economisti* for Sept 1884, of which some account is given by Mr Sanger in the *Economic Journal* for March 1895

As is indicated in Note VI in the appendix, formal account could be taken of changes in the marginal utility of money, if it were desired to do so; and if we attempted to add together the total utilities of all commodities, we should be bound to do so.

BOOK III. CH VI

it would be for amounts very different from those which are commonly sold. Our list of demand prices is therefore highly conjectural except in the neighbourhood of the customary price, and the best estimates we can form of the whole amount of the utility of anything are liable to large error. But this difficulty is not important practically. For the chief applications of the doctrine of consumers' rent are concerned with such changes in it as would accompany changes in the price of the commodity in question in the neighbourhood of the customary price: that is, they require us to use only that information with which we are fairly well supplied. These remarks apply with special force to necessaries[1].

prices nor do we often need them.

Elements of collective wealth are apt to be overlooked

§ 5. There remains another class of considerations which are apt to be overlooked in estimating the dependence of well-being upon material wealth. Not only does a person's happiness often depend more on his own physical, mental and moral health than on his external conditions: but even among these conditions many that are of chief importance

[1] The notion of consumers' rent may help us a little now; and, when our statistical knowledge is further advanced, it may help us a great deal, to decide how much injury would be done to the public by an additional tax of $6d$. a pound on tea, or by an addition of ten per cent. to the freight charges of a railway: and the value of the notion is but little diminished by the fact that it would not help us much to estimate the loss that would be caused by a tax of $30s$. a pound on tea, or a tenfold rise in freight charges.

Reverting to our last diagram, we may express this by saying that, if A is the point on the curve corresponding to the amount that is wont to be sold in the market, data can be obtained sufficient for drawing the curve with tolerable correctness for some distance on either side of A; though the curve can seldom be drawn with any approach to accuracy right up to D. But this is practically unimportant, because in the chief practical applications of the theory of value, we should seldom make any use of a knowledge of the whole shape of the demand curve if we had it. We need just what we can get, that is a fairly correct knowledge of its shape in the neighbourhood of A. We seldom require to ascertain the total area DCA, it is sufficient for most of our purposes to know the changes in this area that would be occasioned by moving A through small distances along the curve in either direction. Nevertheless it will save trouble to assume provisionally, as in pure theory we are at liberty to do, that the curve is completely drawn.

There is however a special difficulty in estimating the whole of the utility of commodities some supply of which is necessary for life. If any attempt is made to do it, the best plan is perhaps to take that necessary supply for granted, and estimate the total utility only of that part of the commodity which is in excess of this amount. But we must recollect that the desire for anything is much dependent on the difficulty of getting substitutes for it. (See Note VI in Appendix.)

BOOK III CH VI.

for his real happiness are apt to be omitted from an inventory of his wealth. Some are free gifts of nature; and these might indeed be neglected without great harm if they were always the same for everybody; but in fact they vary much from place to place. More of them however are elements of collective wealth which are often omitted from the reckoning of individual wealth; but which become important when we compare different parts of the modern civilized world, and even more important when we compare our own age with earlier times.

So-called consumers' associations belong to the subject of Production.

Collective action for the purposes of securing common well-being, as for instance in lighting and watering the streets, will occupy us much towards the end of our inquiries. Cooperative associations for the purchase of things for personal consumption have made more progress in England than elsewhere: but those for purchasing the things wanted for trade purposes by farmers and others, have until lately been backward in England. Both kinds are sometimes described as Consumers' associations; but they are really associations for economizing effort in certain branches of business, and belong to the subject of Production rather than Consumption.

We are here concerned with large incomes rather than large possessions

§ 6 When we speak of the dependence of well-being on material wealth, we of course refer to the flow or stream of well-being as measured by the flow or stream of incoming wealth and the consequent power of using and consuming it. A person's stock of wealth yields by its usance and in other ways an income of happiness: but there is little direct connection between the aggregate amount of that stock and his aggregate happiness. And it is for that reason that we have throughout this and preceding chapters spoken of the rich, the middle classes and the poor as having respectively large, medium and small incomes—not possessions[1].

Bernouilli's suggestion

In accordance with a suggestion made by Daniel Bernouilli, we may perhaps suppose that the satisfaction which a person derives from his income may be regarded as commencing when he has enough to support life and afterwards as increasing by equal amounts with every equal

[1] See Note VII. in the Appendix

successive percentage that is added to his income, and *vice versâ* for loss of income[1].

The edge of enjoyment is blunted by familiarity

But after a time new riches often lose a great part of their charms. Partly this is the result of familiarity, which makes people cease to derive much pleasure from accustomed comforts and luxuries, though they suffer greater pain from their loss. Partly it is due to the fact that with increased riches there often comes either the weariness of age, or at least an increase of nervous strain; and perhaps even habits of living that lower physical vitality, and diminish the capacity for pleasure.

The value of leisure and rest.

In every civilized country there have been some followers of the Buddhist doctrine that a placid serenity is the highest

[1] That is to say, if £30 represent necessaries, a person's satisfaction from his income will begin at that point, and when it has reached £40, an additional £1 will add a tenth to the £10 which represents its happiness-yielding power. But if his income were £100, that is £70 above the level of necessaries, an additional £7 would be required to add as much to his happiness as £1 if his income were £40 while if his income were £10,030, an additional £1000 would be needed to produce an equal effect (compare Note VIII in the Appendix). Of course such estimates are very much at random, and unable to adapt themselves to the varying circumstances of individual life. As we shall see later, the systems of taxation which are now most widely prevalent follow generally on the lines of Bernoulli's suggestion. Earlier systems took from the poor very much more than would be in accordance with that plan; while the systems of graduated taxation, which are being foreshadowed in several countries, are in some measure based on the assumption that the addition of one per cent to a very large income adds less to the well-being of its owner than an addition of one per cent to smaller incomes would, even after Bernoulli's correction for necessaries has been made.

It may be mentioned in passing that from the general law that the utility to anyone of an additional £1 diminishes with the number of pounds he already has, there follow two important practical principles. The first is that gambling involves an economic loss, even when conducted on perfectly fair and even terms. For instance, a man who having £600 makes a fair even bet of £100, has now an expectation of happiness equal to half that derived from £700, and half that derived from £500, and this is less than the certain expectation of the happiness derived from £600, because by hypothesis the difference between the happiness got from £600 and £500 is greater than the difference between the happiness got from £700 and £600. (Compare Jevons, *l. c.* Ch. IV and see Note IX in the Appendix.) The second principle, the direct converse of the first, is that a theoretically fair insurance against risks is always an economic gain. But of course every insurance office, after calculating what is a theoretically fair premium, has to charge in addition to it enough to pay profits on its own capital, and to cover its own expenses of working, among which are often to be reckoned very heavy items for advertising and for losses by fraud. The question whether it is advisable to pay the premium which insurance officers practically do charge, is one that must be decided for each case on its own merits.

BOOK III. CH. VI.

ideal of life; that it is the part of the wise man to root out of his nature as many wants and desires as he can, that real riches consist not in the abundance of goods but in the paucity of wants. At the other extreme are those who maintain that the growth of new wants and desires is always beneficial because it stimulates people to increased exertions They seem to have made the mistake, as Mr Herbert Spencer says, of supposing that life is for working, instead of working for life[1].

The excellence of a moderate income obtained by moderate work

The truth seems to be that as human nature is constituted, man rapidly degenerates unless he has some hard work to do, some difficulties to overcome; and that some strenuous exertion is necessary for physical and moral health. The fulness of life lies in the development and activity of as many and as high faculties as possible. There is intense pleasure in the ardent pursuit of any aim, whether it be success in business, the advancement of art and science, or the improvement of the condition of one's fellow-beings. The highest constructive work of all kinds must often alternate between periods of over-strain and periods of lassitude and stagnation, but for ordinary people, for those who have no strong ambitions, whether of a lower or a higher kind, a moderate income earned by moderate and fairly steady work offers the best opportunity for the growth of those habits of body, mind, and spirit in which alone there is true happiness.

Expenditure for the sake of display

There is some misuse of wealth in all ranks of society. And though, speaking generally, we may say that every increase in the wealth of the working classes adds to the fulness and nobility of human life, because it is used chiefly in the satisfaction of real wants; yet even among the artisans in England, and perhaps still more in new countries, there are signs of the growth of that unwholesome desire for wealth as a means of display which has been the chief bane of the well-to-do classes in every civilized country. Laws against luxury have been futile; but it would be a gain if the moral sentiment of the community could induce people to avoid all sorts of display of individual wealth. There are indeed

[1] See his lecture on *the Gospel of Relaxation*

true and worthy pleasures to be got from wisely ordered magnificence: but they are at their best when free from any taint of personal vanity on the one side and envy on the other; as they are when they centre round public buildings, public parks, public collections of the fine arts, and public games and amusements. So long as wealth is applied to provide for every family the necessaries of life and culture, and an abundance of the higher forms of enjoyment for collective use, so long the pursuit of wealth is a noble aim; and the pleasures which it brings are likely to increase with the growth of those higher activities which it is used to promote.

The superior nobility of the collective over the private use of wealth.

When the necessaries of life are once provided, everyone should seek to increase the beauty of things in his possession rather than their number or their magnificence. An improvement in the artistic character of furniture and clothing trains the higher faculties of those who make them, and is a source of growing happiness to those who use them. But if instead of seeking for a higher standard of beauty, we spend our growing resources on increasing the complexity and intricacy of our domestic goods, we gain thereby no true benefit, no lasting happiness. The world would go much better if everyone would buy fewer and simpler things, and would take trouble in selecting them for their real beauty, being careful of course to get good value in return for his outlay, but preferring to buy a few things made well by highly paid labour rather than many made badly by low paid labour. But we are exceeding the proper scope of the present Book; the discussion of the influence on general well-being which is exerted by the mode in which each individual spends his income is one of the more important of those applications of economic science to the art of living which will find their place at the end of this treatise.

The tasteful purchaser educates the producer.

We thus approach the fringe of broad inquiries, which must be deferred.

BOOK IV.

THE AGENTS OF PRODUCTION.

LAND, LABOUR, CAPITAL AND ORGANIZATION.

CHAPTER I.

INTRODUCTORY.

The agents of production may be classed under three heads,

§ 1. THE agents of production are commonly classed as Land, Labour and Capital. By Land is meant the material and the forces which Nature gives freely for man's aid, in land and water, in air and light and heat. By Labour is meant all the economic work of man, whether with the hand or the head: but such labour with the head as does not tend directly or indirectly to promote material production is left out of account, so long as we are confining our attention to production in the common and natural sense of the term[1]. By Capital is meant all stored-up provision for the production of material goods, and for the attainment of those benefits which are commonly reckoned as part of income.

capital has two main forms;

Capital consists in a great part of knowledge and organization: and of this some part is private property and other part is not. The distinction between the public and private property in knowledge and organization is of great and growing importance: in some respects of more importance than that between public and private property in material things: it cannot be fully examined till a much later stage in our inquiry: but something has to be said of it in the present Book. And partly for that reason it seems best

[1] Labour is classed as economic when it is "undergone partly or wholly with a view to some good other than the pleasure directly derived from it." See p. 134 and footnote

sometimes to reckon Organization apart as a distinct Agent of production.

but for some purposes under two.

In a sense there are only two agents of production, Nature and Man. Capital and Organization are the result of the work of man aided by nature, and directed by his power of forecasting the future and his willingness to make provision for it. If the character and powers of nature and of man be given, the growth of wealth and knowledge and organization follow from them as effect from cause. But on the other hand man is himself largely formed by his surroundings, in which nature plays a great part: and thus from every point of view man is the centre of the problem of Production as well as that of Consumption, and also of that further problem of the relations between the two, which goes by the twofold name of Distribution and Exchange.

Man both the end and an agent of production

The growth of mankind in numbers, in health and strength, in knowledge, ability, and in richness of character is the end of all our studies: but it is an end to which economics can do no more than contribute some important elements In its broader aspects therefore the study of this growth belongs to the end, if to any part of a treatise on economics. but does not properly belong even there Meanwhile we cannot avoid taking account of the direct agency of man in production, and of the conditions which govern his efficiency as a producer And on the whole it is perhaps the most convenient course, as it certainly is that most in accordance with English tradition, to include some account of the growth of population in numbers and character as a part of the general discussion of Production[1].

[1] The objections to the English practice are well stated by Prof Wagner (*Harvard Journal of Economics*, Vol. v pp. 332—3); but nothing much is gained by a compact and thorough treatment of Population, unless it is on a scale which would make the treatise far too long for English readers In the present work the simpler aspects of agriculture are treated early; partly on account of their historical connection with the doctrine of population, partly to make way for a gradual development of the notion of industrial organization in the remainder of the Book. In the great treatise edited, and for the greater part written by Prof. Wagner, Agriculture (*Agrarwesen und Agrarpolitik*) by Prof Buchenberger fills a large volume, the second of the whole treatise The first volume is given to Foundations (*Grundlegung*), the first half of it being occupied with Fundamental Notions and Method, the second with Population, Industrial Organization and the economic aspects of the State

BOOK IV CH I

Provisional antithesis of demand and supply,

§ 2. It is not possible at this stage to do more than indicate very slightly the general relations between Demand and Supply, between Consumption and Production. But it may be well, while the discussion of utility and value is fresh in our minds, to take a short glance at the relations between value and the disutility or discommodity that has to be overcome in order to obtain those goods which have value because they are at once desirable and difficult of attainment. All that can be said now must be provisional; and may even seem rather to raise difficulties than to solve them: but there will be an advantage in having before us a map, in however slight and broken outline, of the ground to be covered.

ordinary labour being selected for illustration

While demand is based on the desire to obtain commodities, supply depends mainly on the overcoming of the unwillingness to undergo "discommodities." These fall generally under two heads:—labour, and the sacrifice involved in putting off consumption It must suffice here to give a sketch of the part played by ordinary labour in supply. It will be seen hereafter that remarks similar, though not quite the same, might have been made about the work of management and the sacrifice which is involved (sometimes, but not always) in that waiting which is involved in accumulating the means of production.

The discommodities of labour are various,

The discommodity of labour may arise from bodily or mental fatigue, or from its being carried on in unhealthy surroundings, or with unwelcome associates, or from its occupying time that is wanted for pastime, or for social or intellectual pursuits But whatever be the form of the discommodity, its intensity nearly always increases with the severity and the duration of labour

as are its motives.

Of course much exertion is undergone for its own sake, as for instance in mountaineering, in playing games and in the pursuit of literature, of art, and of science, and much hard work is done under the influence of a desire to benefit others But the chief motive to most labour, in our use of the term, is the desire to obtain some material advantage; which in the present state of the world appears generally in the form of the gain of a certain amount of money. It is true that even when a man is working for hire he often finds pleasure in his work: but he generally gets so far tired before it is done that he is glad when the hour for stopping arrives. Perhaps after he has been out of work for some time, he might, as far as his immediate comfort is concerned, rather work for nothing than not work at all; but he will probably prefer to store up his strength till he can get paid for his work. In most occupations even that part of the work which affords him more pleasure than pain must as a rule be paid for at the same rate as the rest; the price of the whole therefore is determined by that part of the labour which he gives most unwillingly, and is on the verge of refusing to give, or as we may say by the *Marginal disutility* of labour[1].

Marginal disutility.

As with every increase in the amount of a commodity offered for sale, its marginal utility falls, and as with every fall in the marginal utility, there is a fall in the price that can be got for the whole of the commodity, and not for the last part only; so it is with regard to the supply of labour. On the one hand if a person makes the whole of his purchases at the price which he would be just willing to pay for his last purchases, he gains a Surplus or Rent of satisfaction on his earlier purchases; since he gets them for less than he would have paid rather than go without them. And on the other hand, if the price paid to him for doing any work is an adequate reward for that part which he does most unwillingly, and if, as generally happens, the same payment is given for that part of the work which he does less unwillingly and at less real cost to himself; then from that part he obtains a Producer's Surplus or Rent

Labour's permanent Surplus or Rent corresponding to Consumer's Surplus.

The unwillingness of anyone already in an occupation to increase his exertions depends, under ordinary circumstances, on fundamental principles of human nature which economists have to accept as ultimate facts As Jevons remarks[2], there is often some resistance to be overcome before setting to work. Some little painful effort is often involved at starting; but this gradually diminishes to zero, and is succeeded by

Though much labour is pleasurable,

[1] See above p 84, also Note X. in the Appendix.

[2] *Theory of Political Economy*, Ch v This doctrine has been emphasized and developed in much detail by Austrian and American economists.

BOOK IV. CH I

pleasure; which increases for a while until it attains a certain low maximum; after which it diminishes to zero, and is succeeded by increasing weariness and craving for relaxation and change. In intellectual work, however, the pleasure and excitement, after they have once set in, often go on increasing till progress is stopped of necessity or by prudence. Everyone in health has a certain store of energy on which he can draw, but which can only be replaced by rest; so that if his expenditure exceed his income for long, his health becomes bankrupt; and employers often find that in cases of great need a temporary increase of pay will induce their workmen to do an amount of work which they cannot long keep up, whatever they are paid for it One reason of this is that with every increase in the hours of labour beyond a certain limit the need for relaxation and the craving for it increase, at all events among those who are in a healthy condition. The marginal disutility of labour increases; partly because, as the time left for rest and other activities diminishes, the marginal utility of free time increases

the willingness to do it is governed by the price to be got for it.

Subject to these and some other qualifications, it is broadly true that the exertions which any set of workers will make, rise or fall with a rise or fall in the remuneration which is offered to them As the price required to attract purchasers for any given amount of a commodity, was called the Demand price for that amount, so the price required to call forth the exertion necessary for producing any given amount of a commodity, may be called the *Supply price* for that amount. And if for the moment we assumed that production depended solely upon the exertions of a certain number of workers, already in existence and trained for their work, we should get a list of supply prices (a *Supply Schedule*) corresponding to the list of demand prices (or Demand Schedule) which we have already considered. This list would set forth theoretically in one column of figures various amounts of exertion and therefore of production; and in a parallel column the prices which must be paid to induce the available workers to put forth these amounts of exertion

Supply price.

Forecasts of difficul-

But this simple method of treating the supply of labour of any kind, and consequently the supply of goods made by

BOOK IV CH I

ties in the relations of demand and supply

that labour, assumes that the number of those who are qualified for it is fixed; and that assumption can be made only for short periods of time In the long run the supply of labour in any trade is adapted more or less closely to the demand for it · parents bring up their children to the most advantageous occupations to which they have access, that is to those that offer the best reward, in wages and other advantages, in return for labour that is not too severe in quantity or character, and for skill that is not too hard to be acquired. But this adjustment between demand and supply can never be perfect; fluctuations of demand may make it much greater or much less for a while, even for many years, than would have been just sufficient to induce parents to select that trade rather than some other of the same class for their children. Although therefore the reward to be had for any kind of work at any time does stand in some relation to the difficulty of acquiring the necessary skill combined with the exertion, the disagreeableness, the waste of leisure, etc. involved in the work itself, yet this correspondence is liable to great disturbances. The study of these disturbances is a difficult task, and it will occupy us much in later stages of our work, and especially in the fifth and sixth Books But the present Book is mainly descriptive and raises few difficult problems[1].

[1] It may be observed, however, that this income of labour, together with a similar income of capital, varying as it does with changes in opportunity or conjuncture, will be called hereafter a Quasi-rent, and that it is of a different nature from that permanent surplus discussed earlier in this section and corresponds rather to the income derived from land in a new country, which sometimes gives the settler a better reward than he had expected.

CHAPTER II.

THE FERTILITY OF LAND.

BOOK IV CH. II

The notion that land is a free gift of nature while the produce of land is due to man's work is a loose one but there is a truth underlying it

§ 1. THE requisites of production are commonly spoken of as land, labour and capital those material things which owe their usefulness to human labour being classed under capital, and those which owe nothing to it being classed as land. The distinction is obviously a loose one: for bricks are but pieces of earth slightly worked up; and the soil of old settled countries has for the greater part been worked over many times by man, and owes to him its present form. There is however a scientific principle underlying the distinction. While man has no power of creating matter, he creates utilities by putting things into a useful form[1]; and the utilities made by him can be increased in supply if there is an increased demand for them. they have a supply price. But there are other utilities over the supply of which he has no control, they are given as a fixed quantity by nature and have therefore no supply price. The term "land" has been extended by economists so as to include the permanent sources of these utilities[2]; whether they are found in land, as the term is commonly used, or in seas and rivers, in sunshine and rain, in winds and waterfalls.

When we have inquired what it is that marks off land from those material things which we regard as products

[1] See Book II Chapter III.

[2] In Ricardo's famous phrase "the original or indestructible properties of the soil" Von Thunen, in a noteworthy discussion of the basis of the theory of rent, and of the positions which Adam Smith and Ricardo took with regard to it, speaks of "Der Boden an sich", a phrase which unfortunately cannot be translated, but which means the soil as it would be by itself, if not altered by the action of man (*Der Isolirte Staat*, I I. 5)

of the land, we shall find that the fundamental attribute of land is its extension. The right to use a piece of land gives command over a certain space—a certain part of the earth's surface The area of the earth is fixed: the geometric relations in which any particular part of it stands to other parts are fixed. Man has no control over them; they are wholly unaffected by demand, they have no cost of production, there is no supply price at which they can be produced.

The use of a certain area of the earth's surface is a primary condition of anything that man can do, it gives him room for his own actions, with the enjoyment of the heat and the light, the air and the rain which nature assigns to that area; and it determines his distance from, and in a great measure his relations to, other things and other persons. We shall find that it is this property of "land" which, though as yet insufficient prominence has been given to it, is the ultimate cause of the distinction which all writers on economics are compelled to make between land and other things. It is the foundation of much that is most interesting and most difficult in economic science

Some parts of the earth's surface contribute to production chiefly by the services which they render to the navigator: others are of chief value to the miner, others—though this selection is made by man rather than by nature—to the builder. But when the productiveness of land is spoken of our first thoughts turn to its agricultural use

§ 2 To the agriculturist an area of land is the means of supporting a certain amount of vegetable, and perhaps ultimately of animal, life For this purpose the soil must have certain mechanical and chemical qualities.

Mechanical conditions of fertility

Mechanically, it must be so far yielding that the fine roots of plants can push their way freely in it; and yet it must be firm enough to give them a good hold. It must not err as some sandy soils do by affording water too free a passage: for then it will often be dry, and the plant food will be washed away almost as soon as it is formed in the soil or put into it. Nor must it err, as stiff clays do, by not allowing the water a fairly free passage For constant supplies of

BOOK IV. CH. II.

fresh water, and of the air that it brings with it in its journey through the soil, are essential they convert into plant food the minerals and gases that otherwise would be useless or even poisonous. The action of fresh air and water and of frosts are nature's tillage of the soil, and even unaided they will in time make almost any part of the earth's surface fairly fertile if the soil that they form can rest where it is, and is not torn away down-hill by rain and torrents as soon as it is formed. But man gives great aid in this mechanical preparation of the soil The chief purpose of his tillage is to help nature to enable the soil to hold plant roots gently but firmly, and to enable the air and water to move about freely in it. Even when he manures the ground he has this mechanical preparation in view For farmyard manure benefits clay soils by subdividing them and making them lighter and more open, no less than by enriching them chemically, while to sandy soils it gives a much needed firmness of texture, and helps them, mechanically as well as chemically, to hold the materials of plant food which would otherwise be quickly washed out of them.

Chemical conditions of fertility.

Chemically the soil must have the inorganic elements that the plant wants in a form palatable to it The greater part of the bulk of the plant is made up of so-called "organic compounds", that is, compounds of carbon chiefly with oxygen, hydrogen and nitrogen[1], and of these it obtains by far the greater part from air and water. Only a small fraction (somewhere about a twentieth on an average) of its dry bulk consists of mineral matter that it cannot get except from the soil And as most soils have given them by nature at least some small quantities of all the mineral substances that are necessary for plant life, they can support some sort of vegetation without human aid. Often however they have but very scanty provision of one or two necessary elements; phosphoric acid, potash and lime being those of which the

[1] They are called organic, not because they really are organized, but because they are found in vegetable and animal organisms; and because at one time chemists thought that none of them could be made except as a process of organic growth. But Liebig showed that it was a mistake to suppose that plants can absorb organized matter It must become unorganized before it can be plant food.

supplies are most apt to run short It may indeed happen that the deficient food is one of which some kinds of plants require only a little, and then there may be a fairly good growth of just those plants; but such cases are rare; and the vegetation generally is poor and thin whenever the soil is deficient in one of the mineral constituents of plant life. If however it be well provided in other respects, and in a good condition mechanically, there is an opportunity for man to make a great change with but little labour. He can then turn a barren into a very fertile soil by adding a small quantity of just those things that are needed; using in most cases either lime in some of its many forms, or those artificial manures which modern chemical science has provided in great variety.

Manures.

Again, these special manures are of the highest importance to supply particular mineral elements of plant food of which the soil is robbed by the animal and vegetable products which are sold away from the land. It is true that the soil itself has often large "dormant" stores of many of these things They are dormant because they are not in a fit chemical and mechanical condition to be consumed by the plant To bring them into that condition and make them "active" food, they must be well plied with oxygen and carbonic acid gas. This may be effected by proper tillage, even the subsoil being forced to give up its stores of dormant food, if it has them; and in that case the land may be kept fertile with very little aid from special manures, particularly if it receives a general return of its lost constituents in the form of farmyard manure[1]

[1] Farmyard manure contains everything that plant life wants, but in unequal proportions. It has the advantage of aiding the distribution over the whole of the soil of small particles of everything that the plant wants each rootlet in contact with decaying vegetable matter finds ready to it all that it needs, nothing is left out. But the mineral elements form only a small part of farmyard manure The great bulk of it, exclusive of water, consists of organic compounds. The plant draws its chief supply of these, and can in case of necessity get all, from the atmosphere, though it prefers to obtain some through its roots The supply of mineral elements in the soil is therefore of primary importance· its supply of nitrogen is the chief chemical factor of its "condition," that is, of its readiness to meet any immediate demand on it; while its supplies of phosphoric acid, potash and lime are the chief chemical factors of its permanent fertility. But the organic compounds in farmyard manure and other decaying

BOOK IV CH. II.

Man's power of altering the character of the soil

§ 3. By all these means the fertility of the soil can be brought under man's control He can by sufficient labour make almost any land bear large crops. He can prepare the soil mechanically and chemically for whatever crops he intends to grow next. He can adapt his crops to the nature of the soil and to one another; selecting such a rotation that each will leave the land in such a state, and at such a time of year, that it can be worked up easily and without loss of time into a suitable seed bed for the coming crop[1]. He can even

vegetable matter in the soil are of great use even in this respect; for they work the dormant mineral plant food in the soil up into an active form, and hold stores of it ready for the plant. Certain crops absorb an exceptionally large amount of certain minerals and these may happen not to come back in manure to the particular land from which they are taken; and of course any such special deficiency cannot be made good by farmyard manure without giving the soil more than it wants of some other things Lime for instance sometimes runs short, and potash is often in great demand on sandy soils, particularly when root crops are grown on them But the most important case is that of phosphoric acid Of this the soil has scarcely ever any large quantity, while plants, particularly cereals, require a good deal of it In fact it is believed that there is very little near the surface of the ground which has not already been many times absorbed into vegetable and thence into animal life, and it has nearly always to be supplied by special manures to land that is required to grow continuous heavy crops, particularly of cereals Farmyard manure generally contains little of it unless the cattle have been fed largely on grain Human excrements are rich in it and are of great assistance in this way to most peasant proprietors, but our modern habit of washing sewage out to sea makes the use of artificial manures much more necessary than it was There is however at last, after many disappointments, some prospect of a remedy for this waste

[1] The basis of most of the modern English rotations is the Norfolk course, which was adapted by Mr Coke (Lord Leicester) to enable light, and so-called "poor," soils to bear good wheat crops The first crop on his plan is turnips they do not require to be sown till May or June, and therefore the winter and spring following the wheat crop, with which the preceding rotation closes, can be spent in tilling, cleaning and manuring In the spring of the second year barley and clover are sown together in the third year the clover is consumed the land can be ploughed up in time for autumn-sown wheat, which finds the soil strengthened mechanically by the clover roots and improved chemically by the nitrogen which these venturesome explorers have brought up from the subsoil. On these lines an immense variety of rotations have been adapted to various soils and conditions of farming, many of them extending over six or seven years. (A list of the chief of them is given in the *Memoir of the Agriculture of England and Wales prepared by the Royal Agricultural Society of England for the International Agricultural Congress* 1878. Pages 316—354) At present rather more than half the cultivated land of the United Kingdom is in permanent pasture; and of the rest, one-half is in corn crops, rather less than a quarter in green crops, chiefly roots, and rather more than a quarter in clover and grasses under rotation. In England the permanent pasture is proportionately less and the corn crops are greater than in Ireland and Scotland

permanently alter the nature of the soil by draining it, or by mixing with it other soil that will supplement its deficiencies[1]

All these changes are likely to be carried out more extensively and thoroughly in the future than in the past. But even now the greater part of the soil in old countries owes much of its character to human action, all that lies just below the surface has in it a large element of capital, the produce of man's past labour: the inherent, or indestructible, properties of the soil, the free gifts of nature, have been largely modified; partly robbed and partly added to by the work of many generations of men

But it is different with that which is above the surface Every acre has given to it by nature an annual income of heat and light, of air and moisture; and over these man has but little control. He may indeed alter the climate a little by extensive drainage works or by planting forests, or cutting them down[2] But, on the whole, the action of the sun and the wind and the rain are an annuity fixed by nature for each plot of land Ownership of the land gives possession of this annuity and it also gives the space required for the life and action of vegetables and animals, the value of this space being much affected by its geographical position.

Original and artificial properties of land

We may then continue to use the ordinary distinction between the original or inherent properties, which the land derives from nature, and the artificial properties which it owes to human action; provided we remember that the first include the space-relations of the plot in question, and the annuity that nature has given it of sunlight and air and

[1] Hitherto this has been done only on a small scale, chalk and lime, clay and marl have been but thinly spread over the fields, a completely new soil has seldom been made except in gardens and other favoured spots. But it is possible, and even as some think probable, that at some future time the mechanical agencies used in making railways and other great earthworks may be applied on a large scale to creating a rich soil by mixing two poor soils with opposite faults. (See Mr Scott Burn's *Directory for the Improvement of Landed Property*, p. 239) As it is, when the subsoil is known to contain important elements which the surface soil has lost, or perhaps has never had, the enterprising owner will stir it deeply so that the air and fresh water may act on it, and after a time bring some of it up to mix with the surface soil

[2] See in particular "The Influence of Trees on Climate and Productiveness" in Appendix I to the *Report of the Indian Famine Commission*, 1881

BOOK IV CH II.

rain, and that in many cases these are the chief of the inherent properties of the soil It is chiefly from them that the ownership of agricultural land derives its peculiar significance, and the Theory of Rent its special character[1]. But

[1] There is some interest in the attempt to distinguish that part of the value of land which is the result of man's labour, from that which is due to the original bounty of nature. Part of its value is caused by highways and other general improvements that were made for the general purposes of the country, and are not a special charge on its agriculture. Counting these in, List, Carey, Bastiat and others contend that the expense of bringing land from the state in which man found it to its present condition would exceed the whole value it has now; and hence they argue that all of its value is due to man's labour Their facts may be disputed, but they are really not relevant to their conclusions What is wanted for their argument is that the present value of land should not exceed the expense, in so far as it can properly be charged to agricultural account, of bringing the land from the state in which man found it to a condition in which it would be as fertile and generally useful for agricultural purposes as it now is Many of the changes wrought in it were made to suit agricultural methods that are long since obsolete; and some of them even deduct from, rather than add to, the value of the land And further, the expenses of making the change must be the net expenses after adding indeed interest on the gradual outlay, but also after deducting the aggregate value of the extra produce which has, from first to last, been attributable to the improvement The value of land in a well-peopled district is generally much greater than these expenses, and often many times as great

The following table, taken from the above-quoted *Memoir of the Royal Agricultural Society*, shows the investments of capital per acre on four typical English farms —

	Total value	Cost of farm buildings and labourers' cottages.	Fencing and local roads.	Drainage.	Leaving for value of land in its natural condition.	Tenant's capital.	Rent.
	£ s	£ s	£ s d	£ s	£ s d	£ s d	£ s.
Dairy farm	75 0	12 15	2 10 0	5 0	54 15 0	12 0 0	2 10
Mixed arable and pasture	45 0	8 0	2 0 0	0 0	35 0 0	12 0 0	1 10
Ditto upland	30 0	6 7	1 0 0	0 0	22 13 0	10 0 0	1 0
Pasture farm	94 10	7 0	1 13 4	0 0	85 16 8	12 0 0	3 3

But the fall in all agricultural values which had begun before 1878, when the Memoir was written, has continued at an increasing rate since then, and there are many who think that the rise in the value of English land during the past generation is a bare return to the capital invested in permanent improvements, that is, they think there has been no rise in the real value of the original properties of the soil for agricultural purposes M Leroy Beaulieu (*Repartition des Richesses*, Ch II.) holds that this has been the case at all events in Belgium and France; and Mr Pell supports a similar opinion with regard to England by some instructive statistical instances (see an Article on *The Making of the Land in England* in Vol XXIII of the Journal of the Royal Agricultural Society) The values of the farms in the United States were $6,645,000,000 in 1860, they rose to

the question how far the fertility of any soil is due to the original properties given to it by nature, and how far to the changes in it made by man, cannot be fully discussed without taking account of the kind of produce raised from it.

The original qualities count for more and the artificial for less in some cases than in others

§ 4. Human agency can do much more to promote the growth of some crops than of others At one end of the scale are forest trees, an oak well planted and with plenty of room has very little to gain from man's aid: there is no way of applying labour to it so as to obtain any considerable return. Nearly the same may be said of the grass on some rich river bottoms which are endowed with a rich soil and good natural drainage, wild animals feeding off this grass without man's care will farm it nearly as well as he does; and much of the richest farm land in England (paying a rent of £6 an acre and upwards) would give to unaided nature almost as great a return as is got from it now[1]. Next comes land which, though not quite so rich, is still kept in permanent pasture; and after this comes arable land on which man does not trust to nature's sowing, but prepares for each crop a seed bed to suit its special wants, sows the seed himself and weeds away the rivals to it. The seeds which he sows are selected for their habit of quickly maturing and fully developing just those parts which are most useful to him; and though the habit of making this selection carefully is only quite modern, and is even now far from general, yet the continued work of thousands of years has given him plants that have but little resemblance to their wild ancestors[2]. Lastly, the kinds of produce which

$7,500,000,000 (estimated in gold) in 1870, and to $10,197,000,000 in 1880 But as General Walker points out (*Tenth Census*, Vol VII p 23), "It is a familiar feature of paper money inflations that real estate, especially rural real estate, seldom begins to rise so early or continues to rise so long as the prices of commodities" Allowing therefore for only half the premium on gold he gets the value for 1870 at $8,250,000,000 and thus arrives at an increase of about 24 % in each of the two decades

[1] Of course wherever the grass is mown, manure should be returned It has moreover recently been found that manuring permanent pasture enriches it for a long time to come, for then the richest and finest grasses find within their reach as much food as they can consume, and are thus able to beat out of the field the poorer and coarser sorts

[2] Perhaps it is not unreasonable to hope that in time plants may be obtained every part of which will serve an important purpose Just as in the Arctic

BOOK IV. CH II

owe most to man's labour and care are the choicer kinds of fruits, flowers and vegetables, and of animals, particularly those which are used for improving their own breeds. For while nature left to herself would select those that are best able to take care of themselves and their offspring, man selects those which will provide him most quickly with the largest supplies of the things he most wants; and many of the choicest products could not hold their own at all without his care.

In any case the extra return to additional capital and labour diminishes sooner or later.

Thus various then are the parts which man plays in aiding nature to raise the different kinds of agricultural produce In each case he works on till the extra *Return* got by extra capital and labour has so far *diminished* that it will no longer remunerate him for applying them. Where this limit is soon reached he leaves nature to do nearly all the work; where his share in the production has been great, it is because he has been able to work far without reaching this limit. We are thus brought to consider the Law of Diminishing Return

regions every fragment of the reindeer's body is turned to account, so it may become possible to use as food, or for some other important purpose, both root and leaves, both stem and fruit of our plants. At present we eat the root of the potato, but the rest of the plant is useless except as food for other plants: we eat the leaves of the cabbage, but root and stalk are useless The wood of the beech tree, the wood and the fruit of the pear tree are turned to good account but their leaves are left to decay Possibly (as Mr Moore Ede has suggested to me) chemical science may enable us to use as food many of those vegetable materials which we now throw away

CHAPTER III.

THE FERTILITY OF LAND, CONTINUED. THE LAW OF DIMINISHING RETURN.

BOOK IV. CH III

§ 1. *The Law of Diminishing Return* may be provisionally stated thus:

Provisional statement of the Law,

An increase in the capital and labour applied in the cultivation of land causes *in general* a less than proportionate increase in the amount of produce raised, unless it happens to coincide with an improvement in the arts of agriculture.

which is founded on general experience.

We learn from history and by observation that every agriculturist in every age and clime desires to have the use of a good deal of land, and that when he cannot get it freely, he will pay for it, if he has the means. If he thought that he would get as good results by applying all his capital and labour to a very small piece, he would not pay for any but a very small piece.

Land may be under-cultivated, and then extra capital and labour will give an Increasing Return until a maximum rate has been reached, after which it will diminish again.

When land that requires no clearing is to be had for nothing, everyone uses just that quantity which he thinks will give his capital and labour the largest return. His cultivation is "extensive," not "intensive." He does not aim at getting many bushels of corn from any one acre, for then he would cultivate only a few acres. His purpose is to get as large a total crop as possible with a given expenditure of seed and labour, and therefore he sows as many acres as he can manage to bring under a light cultivation. Of course he may go too far: he may spread his work over so large an area that he would gain by concentrating his capital and labour on a smaller space; and under these circumstances if he could get command over more capital and labour so as to apply more to each acre, the land would give him an *Increasing Return*;

BOOK IV. CH. III.

that is, an extra return larger in proportion than it gives to his present expenditure. But if he has made his calculations rightly, he is using just so much ground as will give him the highest return; and he would lose by concentrating his capital and labour on a smaller area. If he had command over more capital and labour and were to apply more to his present land, he would gain less than he would by taking up more land; he would get a *Diminishing Return*, that is, an extra return smaller in proportion than he gets for the last applications of capital and labour that he now makes, provided of course that there is meanwhile no perceptible improvement in his agricultural skill. As his sons grow up they will have more capital and labour to apply to land, and in order to avoid obtaining a Diminishing Return, they will want to cultivate more land. But perhaps by this time all the neighbouring land is already taken up, and in order to get more they must buy it or pay a rent for the use of it, or migrate where they can get it for nothing.

Were it otherwise every farmer would save most of his rent by applying all his capital and labour to a small part of his land.

This tendency to a Diminishing Return was the cause of Abraham's parting from Lot[1], and of most of the migrations of which history tells. And wherever the right to cultivate land is much in request, we may be sure that the tendency to a Diminishing Return is in full operation. Were it not for this tendency every farmer could save nearly the whole of his rent by giving up all but a small piece of his land, and bestowing all his capital and labour on that. If all the capital and labour which he would in that case apply to it, gave as good a return in proportion as that which he now applies to it, he would get from that plot as large a produce as he now gets from his whole farm, and he would make a net gain of all his rent save that of the little plot that he retained.

It may be conceded that the ambition of farmers often leads them to take more land than they can properly manage: and indeed almost every great authority on agriculture from Arthur Young downwards, has inveighed against this mistake. But when they tell a farmer that he would gain by

[1] "The land was not able to bear them, that they might dwell together: for their substance was great, so that they could not dwell together." Genesis xiii. 6.

applying his capital and labour to a smaller area, they do not necessarily mean that he would get a larger gross produce. It is sufficient for their argument that the saving in rent would more than counterbalance any probable diminution of the total returns that he got from the land. If a farmer pays a fourth of his produce as rent, he would gain by concentrating his capital and labour on less land, provided the extra capital and labour applied to each acre gave anything more than three-fourths as good a return in proportion, as he got from his earlier expenditure.

Improved methods may enable more capital and labour to be profitably applied

Again, it may be granted that much land, even in a country as advanced as England, is so unskilfully cultivated that it could be made to give more than double its present gross produce if twice the present capital and labour were applied to it skilfully. Very likely those are right who maintain that if all English farmers were as able, wise and energetic as the best are, they might profitably apply twice the capital and labour that is now applied. Assuming rent to be one-fourth of the present produce, they might get seven hundredweight of produce for every four that they now get: it is conceivable that with still more improved methods they might get eight hundredweight, or even more But this does not prove that, *as things are*, further capital and labour could obtain from land an Increasing Return. The fact remains that, taking farmers as they are with the skill and energy which they actually have, we find as the result of universal observation that there is not open to them a short road to riches by giving up a great part of their land, by concentrating all their capital and labour on the remainder, and saving for their own pockets the rent of all but that remainder. The reason why they cannot do this is told in the Law of Diminishing Return.

The Law relates to the amount of the produce, not its value

It is important to remember that the Return to capital and labour of which the Law speaks, is measured by the *amount* of the produce raised independently of any changes that may meanwhile take place in the *price* of produce, such, for instance, as might occur if a new railway had been made in the neighbourhood, or a new town population had grown up close by. Such changes will be of vital importance when we come to draw inferences from the Law of Diminishing Return, and particularly when we discuss the pressure of increasing population on the means of subsistence. But they have no bearing on the Law itself, because that has to do not with the value of the produce raised, but only with its amount.

We may now state distinctly the limitations which were implied under the words "in general" in our provisional statement of the Law. The Law is a statement of a tendency which may indeed be held in check for a time by improvements in the arts of production and by the fitful course of the development of the full powers of the soil; but which must ultimately become irresistible if the demand for produce should increase without limit. Our final statement of the Law may then be divided into two parts, thus —

Final statement of the Law.

Although an improvement in the arts of agriculture may raise the rate of return which land generally affords to any given amount of capital and labour; and although the capital and labour already applied to any piece of land may have been so inadequate for the development of its full powers, that some further expenditure on it even with the existing arts of agriculture would give a more than proportionate return, yet these conditions are rare in an old country. and, except when they are present, the application of increased capital and labour to land will add a less than proportionate amount to the produce raised, unless there be meanwhile an increase in the skill of the individual cultivator. Secondly, whatever may be the future developments of the arts of agriculture, a continued increase in the application of capital and labour to land must ultimately result in a diminution of the extra produce which can be obtained by a given extra amount of capital and labour.

A *Dose* of capital and labour.

§ 2 Making use of a term suggested by James Mill, we may regard the capital and labour applied to land as consisting of equal successive *Doses*[1]. As we have seen, the return to the first few doses may perhaps be small and a greater number of doses may get a larger proportionate

[1] Some difficulties in the interpretation of this term are considered in a Note at the end of the chapter.

return; the return to successive doses may even in exceptional cases alternately rise and fall But our law states that sooner or later (it being always supposed that there is meanwhile no change in the arts of cultivation) a point will be reached after which all further doses will obtain a less proportionate return than the preceding doses

Marginal dose, marginal return, margin of cultivation

The dose which only just remunerates the cultivator may be said to be the *marginal dose*, and the return to it the *marginal return*. If there happens to be in the neighbourhood land that is cultivated but only just pays its expenses, and so gives no surplus for rent, we may suppose this dose applied to it. We can then say that the dose applied to it is applied to land on the *margin of cultivation*, and this way of speaking has the advantage of simplicity. But it is not necessary for the argument to suppose that there is any such land: what we want to fix our minds on is the return to the marginal dose· whether it happens to be applied to poor land or to rich does not matter; all that is necessary is that it should be the last dose which can profitably be applied to that land[1].

The marginal dose is not necessarily the last in time

When we speak of the marginal. or the "last" dose applied to the land, we do not mean the last in time, we mean that dose which is on the margin of profitable expenditure; that is, which is applied so as just to give the ordinary returns to the capital and labour of the cultivator, without affording any surplus To take a concrete instance, we may suppose a farmer to be thinking of sending the hoers over a field once more; and after a little hesitation he decides that it is worth his while, but only just worth his while to do it. The dose of capital and labour spent on doing it, is then the last dose in our present sense, though there are many doses still to be applied in reaping the crop. Of course the return to this last dose cannot be separated from the others, but we ascribe to it all that part of the produce which we believe would not have been produced if the farmer had decided against the extra hoeing[2].

[1] Ricardo was well aware of this though he did not emphasize it enough Those opponents of his doctrine who have supposed that it has no application to places where all the land pays a rent, have mistaken the nature of his argument

[2] An illustration from recorded experiments may help to make clearer the

BOOK IV CH III

Since the return to the dose on the margin of cultivation just remunerates the cultivator, it follows that he will be just remunerated for the whole of his capital and labour by as many times the marginal return as he has applied doses in all Whatever he gets in excess of this is the *Surplus Produce* of the land This surplus is retained by the cultivator if he owns the land himself[1]

Surplus Produce

notion of the Return to a marginal dose of capital and labour The Arkansas Experimental Station (see *The Times*, 18 Nov. 1889) reported that four plots of an acre each were treated exactly alike except in the matter of ploughing and harrowing, with the following result —

Plot	Cultivation.	Crop yields bushels per acre
1	Ploughed once . . .	16
2	Ploughed once and harrowed once	$18\frac{1}{2}$
3	Ploughed twice and harrowed once .	$21\frac{2}{3}$
4	Ploughed twice and harrowed twice .	$23\frac{1}{4}$

This would show that the dose of capital and labour applied in harrowing a second time an acre which had already been ploughed twice gave a Return of $1\frac{7}{12}$ bushels And if the value of these bushels, after allowing for expenses of harvesting, &c *just* replaced that dose with profits, then that dose was a *marginal* one, even though it was not the last in point of time, since those spent on harvesting must needs come later

[1] Let us seek a graphical illustration If on any given field there were expended a capital of £50, a certain amount of produce would be raised from it a certain amount larger than the former would be raised if there were expended on it a capital of £51 The difference between these two amounts may be regarded as the produce due to the fifty-first pound; and if we suppose the capital to be applied in successive doses of £1 each we may speak of this difference as the produce due to the fifty first dose Let the doses be represented in order by successive equal divisions of the line *OD* Let there now be drawn from the division of this line representing the fifty-first dose *M*, a line *MP* at right angles to *OD*, in thickness equal to the length of one of the divisions, and such that its length represents the amount of the produce due to the fifty first dose Suppose this done for each separate division up to that corresponding to the last dose which it is found profitable to put on the land Let this last dose be the 110th at *D*, and *DC* the corresponding return that only just remunerates the farmer The extremities of such lines will lie on a curve *APC* The gross produce will be represented by the sum of these lines *i e*, since the thickness of each line is equal to the length of the division on which it stands, by the area *ODCA* Let *CGH* be drawn parallel to *DO*, cutting *PM* in *G*, then *MG* is equal to *CD*, and since *DC* just remunerates the farmer for one dose, *MG* will just remunerate him for another and so for all the portions of the thick vertical lines cut off

Fig (11)

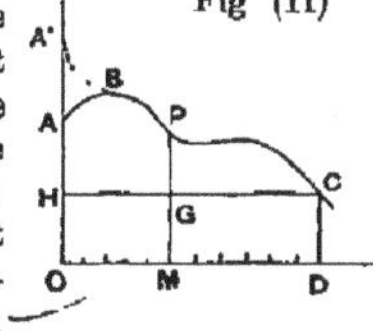

(This Surplus Produce may, under certain conditions, become the rent which the owner of the land can exact from the tenant for its use. But, as we shall see hereafter, the full rent of a farm in an old country is made up of three elements: the first being due to the value of the soil as it was made by Nature; the second to improvements made in it by man, and the third, which is often the most important of all, to the growth of a dense and rich population, and to facilities of communication by public roads, railroads, &c)

Its relation to rent

In an old country it is seldom possible to discover what was the original state of the land before it was first cultivated The results of some of man's work are for good and evil fixed in the land, they cannot be distinguished from the results of nature's work, but must be counted with them. The line of division between nature's work and man's work is blurred, and must be drawn more or less arbitrarily But for most purposes it is best to regard the first difficulties of coping with nature as pretty well conquered before we begin to reckon the farmer's cultivation Thus the returns that we count as due to the first doses of capital and labour are generally the largest of all, and the tendency of the return to diminish shows itself at once Having English agriculture chiefly in view, we may fairly take, as Ricardo did, this as the typical case[1].

Ricardo confined his attention to the circumstances of an old country

between *OD* and *HC* Therefore the sum of these, that is, the area *ODCH*, represents the share of the produce that is required to remunerate him, while the remainder, *AHGCPA*, is the Surplus Produce, which under certain conditions becomes the rent

[1] That is, we may substitute (fig 11) the dotted line *BA'* for *BA* and regard *A'BPC* as the typical curve for the return to capital and labour applied in English agriculture. No doubt crops of wheat and some other annuals cannot be raised at all without some considerable labour But natural grasses which sow themselves will yield a good return of rough cattle to scarcely any labour.

It has already been noticed (Book III ch III. § 1), the law of Diminishing Return bears a close analogy to the law of Demand The return which land gives to a dose of capital and labour may be regarded as the price which land offers for that dose Land's return to capital and labour is, so to speak, her effective demand for them her return to any dose is her demand price for that dose, and the list of returns that she will give to successive doses may thus be regarded as her demand schedule: but to avoid confusion we shall call it her "Return Schedule" Corresponding to the case of the land in the text is that of a man who may be willing to pay a larger proportionate price for a paper that would cover the whole of the walls of his room than for one that would go only half way; and then his

BOOK IV CH. III.

The schedule of nature's return to increased applications of capital and labour shows great variety of detail, according to the character of the land and of the crops raised from it

§ 3 Let us next inquire on what depends the *rate* of diminution or of increase of the returns to successive doses of capital and labour We have seen that there are great variations in the share of the produce which man may claim as the additional result of his own work over what unaided nature would have produced; and that man's share is much larger with some crops and soils and methods of cultivation than with others. Thus broadly speaking it increases as we pass from forest to pasture land, from pasture to arable, and from plough land to spade land; and this is because the rate of diminution of the return is as a rule greatest in forests, rather less in pasture, still less in arable land, and least of all in spade land.

But the order of relative fertility of different pieces of land may change with circumstances

There is no absolute measure of the richness or fertility of land Even if there be no change in the arts of production, a mere increase in the demand for produce may invert the order in which two adjacent pieces of land rank as regards fertility. The one which gives the smaller produce, when both are uncultivated, or when the cultivation of both is equally slight, may rise above the other and justly rank as the more fertile when both are cultivated with equal thoroughness In other words, many of those lands which are the least fertile when cultivation is merely extensive, become among the most fertile when cultivation is intensive For instance, self-drained pasture land may give a return large in proportion to a very slight expenditure of capital and labour, but a rapidly diminishing return to further expenditure: as population increases it may gradually become profitable to break up some of the pasture and introduce a mixed cultivation of roots and grains and grasses; and then

demand schedule would at one stage show an increase and not a diminution of demand price for an increased quantity. But in the aggregate demand of many individuals these unevennesses destroy one another; so that the aggregate demand schedule of a group of people always shows the demand price as falling steadily with every increase in the amount offered In the same way, by grouping together many pieces of land we might obtain a Return Schedule that would show a constant diminution for every increase of capital and labour applied But it is more easy to ascertain, and in some ways more important to take note of, the variations of individual demand in the case of plots of land than in the case of people And therefore our typical return schedule is not drawn out so as to show as even and uniform a diminution of return as our typical demand schedule does of demand price the return to further doses of capital and labour may diminish less quickly[1]

Other land makes poor pasture, but will give more or less liberal returns to a great deal of capital and labour applied in tilling and in manuring it, its returns to the early doses are not very high, but they diminish slowly[2].

Again, other land is marshy. It may, as did the fens of East England, produce little but osiers and wild fowl. Or, as is the case in many tropical districts, especially on the American Continent, it may be prolific of vegetation, but so shrouded with malaria that it is difficult for man to live there, and still more to work there. In such cases the returns to capital and labour are at first small, but as drainage progresses, they increase; afterwards perhaps they again fall off[3]. But when improvements of this kind have once

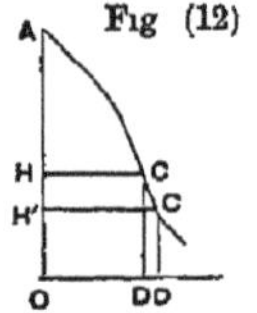

1 This case is illustrated by fig. 12, for when produce has risen in real value in the ratio of OH' to OH (so that the amount required to remunerate the farmer for a dose of capital and labour has fallen from OH to OH',) the Surplus Produce rises only to $AH'C'$, which is not very much greater than its old amount AHC

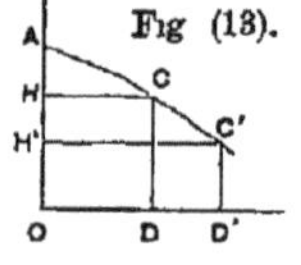

2 This case is represented in fig 13, when a similar change in the price of produce makes the new Surplus Produce $AH'C'$ about three times as large as the old Surplus, AHC

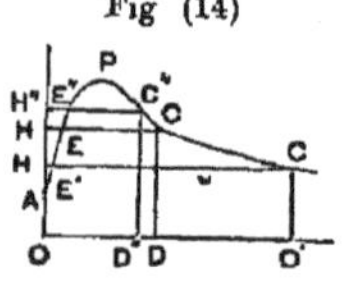

3 This case is represented in fig 14 The earliest doses of capital and labour applied to the land give so poor a return, that it would not be worth while to apply them unless it were intended to carry the cultivation further But later doses give an increasing return which culminates at P, and afterwards diminishes If the price to be got for produce is so low that an amount OH'' is required to remunerate the cultivator for a dose of capital and labour, it will then be only just profitable to cultivate the land For then cultivation will be carried as far as D''; there will be a deficit on the earlier doses represented by the area $H''AE''$, and a surplus on the later doses represented by the area $E''PC''$ and as these two are about equal, the cultivation of the land so far will only just pay its way But if the price of produce rises till OH is sufficient to remunerate the cultivator for a dose of capital and labour, the deficit on the earlier doses will sink to HAE, and the surplus on the later doses will rise to EPC: the net surplus (the true rent in case the land is hired out) will be the excess of EPC over HAE Should the price rise further till OH' is sufficient to remunerate the cultivator for a dose of capital and labour,

BOOK IV CH III

been made, the capital invested in the soil cannot be removed; the early history of the cultivation is not repeated; and the produce due to further applications of capital and labour conforms to the Law of Diminishing Return[1].

Similar though less conspicuous changes may occur on land already well cultivated. For instance, without being marshy, it may be in need of a little drainage to take off the stagnant water from it, and to enable fresh water and air to stream through it. Or the subsoil may happen to be naturally richer than the soil at the surface: or again, though not itself rich, it may have just those properties in which the surface soil is deficient, and then a thorough system of deep steam-ploughing may permanently change the character of the land.

Thus we need not suppose that when the return to extra capital and labour has begun to diminish, it will always continue to do so. Improvements in the arts of production may, it has always been understood, raise generally the return which can be got by any amount of capital and labour, but this is not what is meant here. The point is that, independently of any increase in his knowledge, and using only those methods with which he has long been familiar, a farmer finding extra capital and labour at his command, may sometimes obtain an increasing return even at a late stage in his cultivation. His return may diminish and then increase and then diminish again, and yet again increase when he is in a position to carry out some further extensive change[2].

It has been well said that as the strength of a chain is that of its weakest link, so fertility is limited by that element

this net surplus will rise to the very large amount represented by the excess of $E'PC'$ over $H'AE'$.

[1] In such a case as this the earlier doses are pretty sure to be sunk in the land, and the actual rent paid, if the land is hired out, will then include profits on them in addition to the Surplus Produce or true rent thus shown. Of course provision can be made in the diagrams for the returns due to the landlord's capital.

[2] This case was represented by fig. 11. But more extreme instances, of the kind represented by fig 15, are not very rare.

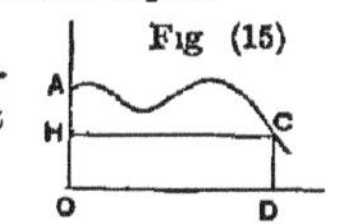

Fig (15)

in which it is most deficient. Those who are in a hurry, will reject a chain which has one or two very weak links, however strong the rest may be; and prefer to it a much slighter chain that has no flaw. But if there is heavy work to be done, and they have time to make repairs, they will set the larger chain in order, and then its strength will exceed that of the other. In this we find the explanation of much that is apparently strange in agricultural history.

Land which gave the best returns to the early settlers is not always that which gives the best returns to modern farmers, especially when good markets have grown up near them

The first settlers in a new country generally avoid land which does not lend itself to immediate cultivation. They are often repelled by the very luxuriance of natural vegetation, if it happens to be of a kind that they do not want. They do not care to plough land that is at all heavy, however rich it might become if thoroughly worked. They will have nothing to do with water-logged land. They generally select light land which can easily be worked with a double plough, and then they sow their seed broadly, so that the plants when they grow up may have plenty of light and air, and may collect their food from a wide area.

When America was first settled, many farming operations that are now done by horse machinery were still done by hand, and though now the farmers have a strong preference for flat prairie land, free from stumps and stones, where their machines can work easily and without risk, they had then no great objection to a hill-side. Their crops were light in proportion to their acreage, but heavy in proportion to the capital and labour expended in raising them.

Thus any measure of fertility must be relative to the circumstances of the place and time

We cannot then call one piece of land more fertile than another till we know something about the skill and enterprise of its cultivators, and the amount of capital and labour at their disposal, and till we know whether the demand for produce is such as to make intensive cultivation profitable with the resources at their disposal. If it is, those lands will be the most fertile which give the highest average returns to a large expenditure of capital and labour, but if not, those will be the most fertile which give the best returns to the first few doses. The term fertility has no meaning except with reference to the special circumstances of a particular time and place.

But even when so limited there is some uncertainty as to the usage of the term. Sometimes attention is directed chiefly to the power which land has of giving adequate returns to intensive cultivation and so bearing a large total produce per acre; and sometimes to its power of yielding a large surplus produce or rent, even though its gross produce is not very large: thus in England now rich arable land is very fertile in the former sense, rich meadow in the latter. For many purposes it does not matter which of these senses of the term is understood: in the few cases in which it does matter, an interpretation clause must be supplied in the context[1].

Other causes of change in the relative values of different pieces of land

§ 4. But further, the order of fertility of different soils is liable to be changed by changes in the methods of cultivation and in the relative values of different crops. Thus when at the end of last century Mr Coke showed how to grow wheat well on light soils by preparing the way with clover, they rose relatively to clay soils, and now though they are still sometimes called from old custom "poor," some of them have a higher value, and are really more fertile, than much of the land that used to be carefully cultivated while they were left in a state of nature.

Again, the increasing demand in Central Europe for wood to be used as fuel and for building purposes, has raised the value of the pine-covered mountain slopes relatively to almost every other kind of land. But in England this rise has been prevented by the substitution of coal for wood as fuel, and of iron for wood as a material for ship-building, and lastly by England's special facilities for importing wood.

[1] If the price of produce is such that an amount of it *OH* (figs 12, 13, 14) is required to pay the cultivator for one dose of capital and labour, the cultivation will be carried as far as *D*, and the produce raised, *AODC* will be greatest in fig 12, next greatest in fig 13, and least in fig 14. But if the demand for agricultural produce so rises that *OH'* is enough to repay the cultivator for a dose, the cultivation will be carried as far as *D'*, and the produce raised will be *AOD'C'*, which is greatest in fig 14, next in fig. 13, and least in fig 12. The contrast would have been even stronger if we had considered the surplus produce which remains after deducting what is sufficient to repay the cultivator, and which becomes under some conditions the rent of the land. For this is *AHC* in figs. 12 and 13 in the first case and *AH'C'* in the second, while in fig 14 it is in the first case the excess of *AODCPA* over *ODCH*, i e the excess of *PEC* over *AHE*, and in the second case the excess of *PE'C'* over *AH'E'*.

BOOK IV. CH III

Again, the cultivation of rice and jute often gives a very high value to lands that are too much covered with water to bear most other crops. And again, since the repeal of the Corn Laws the prices of meat and dairy produce have risen in England relatively to that of corn. Those arable soils that would grow rich forage crops in rotation with corn, rose relatively to the cold clay soils, and permanent pasture recovered part of that great fall in value relatively to arable land, which had resulted from the growth of population[1].

As a rule the poorer soils rise in value relatively to the richer as the pressure of population increases

Independently of any change in the suitability of the prevailing crops and methods of cultivation for special soils, there is a constant tendency towards equality in the value of different soils In the absence of any special cause to the contrary, the growth of population and wealth will make the poorer soils gain on the richer. Land that was at one time entirely neglected is made by much labour to raise rich crops; its annual income of light and heat and air, is probably as good as those of richer soils: while its faults can be much lessened by labour[2]. Conversely, the depression

[1] Mr Rogers (*Six Centuries of Work and Wages*, p 73) calculates that while rich meadow had about the same value, estimated in corn five or six centuries ago as it has now, the value estimated in corn of arable land has increased about fivefold in the same time. This is partly due to the great importance of hay at a time when roots and other modern kinds of winter food for cattle were unknown

[2] Thus we may compare two pieces of land represented in figs 16 and 17, with regard to which the Law of Diminishing Return acts in a similar way, so that their produce curves have similar shapes, but the former has a higher fertility than the other for all degrees of intensity of cultivation. The value of the land may generally be represented by its surplus produce or rent, which is in each case represented by AHC when OH is required to repay a dose of capital and labour, and by $AH'C'$ when the growth of numbers and wealth have made OH' sufficient It is clear that $AH'C'$ in fig 17 bears a more favourable comparison with $AH'C'$ in fig 16 than does AHC in fig 17 with AHC in fig 16 In the same way, though not to the same extent, the total produce $AOD'C'$ in fig. 17 bears a more favourable comparison with $AOD'C'$ in fig 16, than does $AODC$ in fig 17 with $AODC$ in fig 16 (Prof. Wicksteed argues ingeniously (*Coordination of Laws of Distribution*, pp 51–2) that rent may be negative Of course taxes may absorb rent but land which will not reward the plough will grow trees or rough grass See above, p 235)

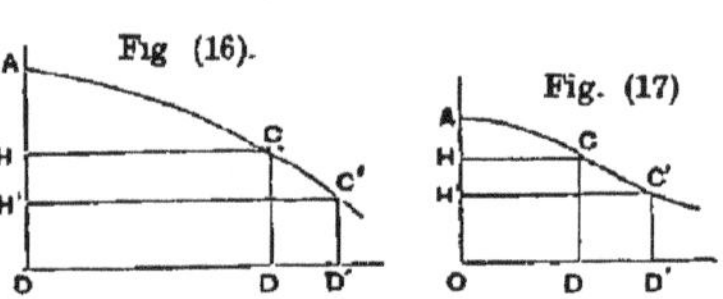

M Leroy Beaulieu (*Repartition des Richesses*, chap II) has collected several facts illustrating this tendency of poor lands to rise in value relatively to rich He

BOOK IV CH III.

of English agriculture, through which we are now passing in consequence of American competition, is lowering the value of poor lands relatively to that of rich lands of the same character; and especially it is lowering the values of those lands which return good crops to a very high cultivation; but which quickly relapse into a poor condition, unless a great deal of capital and labour is constantly spent on them.

There is no absolute standard of good cultivation.

As there is no absolute standard for fertility, so there is none of good cultivation. The best cultivation in the richest parts of the Channel Islands, for instance, involves a lavish expenditure of capital and labour on each acre· for they are near good markets and have a monopoly of an equable and early climate. If left to nature the land would not be very fertile, for though it has many virtues, it has two weak links (being deficient in phosphoric acid and potash). But, partly by the aid of the abundant seaweed on its shores, these links can be strengthened, and the chain thus becomes exceptionally strong. Intense, or as it is ordinarily called in England "good" cultivation, will thus raise £100 worth of early potatoes from a single acre But an equal expenditure per acre by the farmer in Western America would ruin him, relatively to his circumstances it would not be good, but bad cultivation.

Ricardo's statement of the law was inaccurately worded

§ 5 Ricardo's statement of the Law of Diminishing Return was inexactly worded It is however probable that the inaccuracy was due not to careless thinking but only to careless writing. There are strong reasons for holding that he had not overlooked the conditions which were necessary to make the law true, he seems here, as elsewhere, to have made the great error of taking for granted that his readers would supply those conditions which were present in his own mind In any case he would have been justified in thinking that these conditions were not of great importance in the peculiar circumstances of England at the time at which he

quotes from M H Passy the following figures, showing the rental in francs per hectare ($2\frac{1}{2}$ acres) of five classes of land in several communes of the Départements de l'Eure et de l'Oise in 1829 and 1852 respectively —

	Class I	Class II	Class III	Class IV	Class V.
A D 1829	58	48	34	20	8
A D. 1852	80	78	60	50	40

BOOK IV. CH III.

wrote, and for the special purposes of the particular practical problems he had in view. Of course he could not anticipate the great series of inventions which were about to open up new sources of supply, and, with the aid of free trade, to revolutionize English agriculture, but the agricultural history of England and other countries might have led him to lay greater stress on the probability of a change[1].

Ricardo said that the richest lands were cultivated first; this is true in the sense in which he meant it:

He stated that the first settlers in a new country invariably chose the richest lands, and that as population increased, poorer and poorer soils were gradually brought under cultivation, speaking carelessly as though there were an absolute standard of fertility But as we have already seen, where land is free, everyone chooses that which is best adapted for his own purpose, and that which will give him, all things considered, the best return for his capital and labour. He looks out, therefore, for land that can be cultivated at once, and passes by land that has any weak links in the chain of its elements of fertility, however strong it may be in some other links. But besides having to avoid malaria, he must think of his communication with his markets and the base of his resources, and in some cases the need for security against the attacks of enemies and wild beasts outweighs all

[1] Had he done this, he would have helped his readers to supply the premises that were present in his own mind if they do that they will find nothing of importance in his statement of the law of diminishing return, or in his deductions from it, which is not true as far as it goes As Roscher says (*Political Economy*, Sect CLV), "In judging Ricardo, it must not be forgotten that it was not his intention to write a text-book on the science of Political Economy, but only to communicate to those versed in it the result of his researches in as brief a manner as possible Hence he writes so frequently making certain assumptions, and his words are to be extended to other cases only after due consideration, or rather re-written to suit the changed case" The followers of Ricardo have accepted John Stuart Mill's re-statement of the law in which the conditions necessary to make it exact were introduced Nevertheless these conditions are habitually ignored even now by some critical writers, they persist in putting forward what they call refutations of the law, but what are really either arguments that these conditions ought not to be overlooked or else attacks on inferences or deductions that have been made rightly or wrongly from it. For instance, some people have inferred from the law of diminishing return that the English people now would be better off if their numbers did not increase so fast This doctrine is a fair matter for argument; and some of those who have denied it have thought that they were denying the law of diminishing return. But really they were denying something quite different from it The truth of the law has probably never been questioned by any one who has interpreted it right

BOOK IV. CH III

other considerations. It is therefore not to be expected that the lands which were first chosen, should turn out always to be those which ultimately come to be regarded as the most fertile. Ricardo did not consider this point, and thus laid himself open to attacks by Carey and others, which, though for the greater part based on a misinterpretation of his position, have yet some solid substance in them.

but it is apt to be misunderstood, as it was by Carey

Of course it often happens that soils which an English farmer would regard as poor, are cultivated before neighbouring soils which he would regard as rich The facts on which the law of diminishing return is based lead us *a priori* to expect such cases to occur sometimes. Their occasional occurrence is not inconsistent, as some foreign writers have supposed, with the general tenor of Ricardo's doctrines on the contrary, many of these cases really afford instructive illustrations of those doctrines when rightly understood, though some of them are to be explained, as has already been said, by the necessity of providing for military safety. By insisting on such facts as these Carey did nothing to invalidate the statement that the returns which a farmer will get by applying extra doses of capital and labour to land already well cultivated will be less than those which he got for the earlier doses, other things being equal; that is, there being no change in his methods of cultivation, in his markets, or in the other conditions by which he is surrounded. The practical importance of his doctrine lies in its bearing on the conditions under which the growth of population tends to cause increased pressure on the means of subsistence[1]

[1] Carey claims to have proved that "in every quarter of the world cultivation has commenced on the sides of the hills where the soil was poorest, and where the natural advantages of situation were the least With the growth of wealth and population, men have been seen descending from the high lands bounding the valley on either side, and coming together at its feet" (*Principles of Social Science*, Chap IV § 4) He had been brought up in the tenets of Ricardo, by a father who had emigrated from Ireland to America, and he began to write as an advocate of Free Trade; but after a while he was struck by the facts that the soil of New England is nearly the poorest in America, and that whenever he saw ruined houses and the traces of abandoned cultivation he found the soil exceptionally barren This set him to inquire into the history of the occupation of the earth's surface; and he has collected a great mass of evidence in support of his proposition that the general progress of cultivation has been from lands which would be regarded as poor in an old and settled country, to those which would be

BOOK IV CH. III

But Carey has shown that Ricardo underrated the indirect advantages which a dense population offer to agriculture,

§ 6. Ricardo, and the economists of his time generally, were too hasty in deducing this inference from the law of diminishing return; and they did not allow enough for the increase of strength that comes from organization. But in fact every farmer is aided by the presence of neighbours whether agriculturists or townspeople[1]. Even if most of them are engaged like himself in agriculture, they gradually supply him with good roads, and other means of communication: they give him a market in which he can buy at reasonable terms what he wants, necessaries, comforts and luxuries for himself and his family, and all the various requisites for his farm work: they surround him with knowledge: medical aid, instruction and amusement are brought to his door, his mind becomes wider, and his efficiency is in many ways increased And if the neighbouring market town expands into a large industrial centre, his gain is much

regarded as rich He has even argued that whenever a thickly peopled country is laid waste, "whenever population, wealth, and the power of association decline, it is the rich soil that is abandoned by men who fly again to the poor ones" (*Ib* ch v § 3), the rich soils being rendered difficult and dangerous by the rapid growth of jungles which harbour wild beasts and banditti, and perhaps by malaria.

His facts are drawn chiefly from warm if not tropical regions; and with regard to them his conclusions are perhaps true in the main But much of the apparent attractiveness of tropical countries is delusive: they would give a very rich return to hard work, but hard work in them is impossible A cool refreshing breeze is as much a necessary of vigorous life, as food itself Food can be imported but fresh air cannot, land that offers plenty of food but whose climate destroys energy, is not more productive of the raw material of human well being, than land that supplies less food but has an invigorating climate.

Again, the importance of many of Carey's facts diminishes on investigation The choice of New England by the early settlers was an accident, houses on the hills were often, in early times as they are now, the homes of those who cultivate the rich but unhealthy valleys a few miles off Passing down the Missouri Valley to St Louis some years ago, the present writer saw it bearing everywhere crops of unsurpassed richness, but the farmers' houses were on the river bluffs several miles away It may be said that this explanation may account for the absence of houses in comparatively narrow river valleys, but not in broad rich plains If, however, we follow the maps which show the distribution of population in the United States at each successive census, we find that broad river valleys, such as those of the Lower Mississippi and the Lower Red River, were as a rule peopled in advance of the neighbouring uplands

A well-balanced account of Mr Carey's position is given by Mr Levermore in the *Political Science Quarterly*, Vol v

[1] In a new country an important form of this assistance is to enable him to venture on rich land that he would have otherwise shunned, through fear of enemies or of malaria

BOOK IV. CH. III. greater. All his produce is worth more; some things which he used to throw away fetch a good price. He finds new openings in dairy farming and market gardening, and with a larger range of produce he makes use of rotations that keep his land always active without denuding it of any one of the elements that are necessary for its fertility.

Of the way in which organization promotes production, particularly in manufactures, we shall have to speak hereafter. But we have already seen enough to be sure that even as regards agriculture the law of diminishing return does not apply to the total capital and labour spent in a district as sharply as to that on a single farm Even when cultivation has reached a stage after which each successive dose applied to a field would get a less return than the preceding dose, it may be possible for an increase in the population to cause a more than proportional increase in the means of subsistence. It is true that the evil day is only deferred: but it is deferred. The growth of population, if not checked by other causes, must ultimately be checked by the difficulty of obtaining raw produce, but in spite of the law of diminishing return, the pressure of population on the means of subsistence may be restrained for a long time to come by the opening up of new fields of supply, by the cheapening of railway and steamship communication, and by the growth of organization and knowledge

and this has an important bearing on the doctrine of population.

The value of fresh air, light, water, and beautiful scenery

In the following chapters we shall have much to say about the evil effects of local congestions of population in making it difficult to get fresh air and light, and in some cases fresh water. Again, natives of New England who have gone to the fertile plains of the West, would often be willing to barter part of their heavy crops for the pure water which the barren granite soil of their old homes supplied; and even in England there are many places, particularly at the sea-side which are kept poor by the want of drinking water Again, the natural beauties of a place of fashionable resort have a direct money value which cannot be overlooked, but it requires some effort to realize the true value to men, women and children of being able to stroll amid beautiful and various scenery

The fertility of fisheries

§ 7 As has already been said the land in economic phrase includes rivers and the sea. In river-fisheries, the extra return to additional applications of capital and labour shows a rapid diminution. As to the sea, opinions differ. Its volume is vast, and fish are very prolific; and some think that a practically unlimited supply can be drawn from the sea by man without appreciably affecting the numbers that remain there; or in other words, that the law of diminishing return scarcely applies at all to sea-fisheries, that the schedule of the sea's return to additional capital and labour shows no signs of any appreciable diminution On the other hand it is contended that modern methods of fishing, especially trawling, destroy much spawn, and that experience shows a falling-off in the productiveness of those fisheries that have been vigorously worked. The question is important, for there is no doubt that the future population of the world will be appreciably affected as regards both quantity and quality, by the available supply of fish.

A mine does not give a diminishing return in the same sense as a farm does

The produce of mines again, among which may be reckoned quarries and brickfields, is said to conform to the law of diminishing return; but this statement is misleading It is true that we find continually increasing difficulty in obtaining a further supply of minerals, except in so far as we obtain increased power of nature's stores through improvements in the arts of mining, and through better knowledge of the contents of the earth's crust, and there is no doubt that, other things being equal, the continued application of capital and labour to mines will result in a diminishing rate of yield. But this yield is not a *net* yield, like the return of which we speak in the law of diminishing return. That return is part of a constantly recurring income, while the produce of mines is merely a giving up of their stored-up treasures The produce of the field is something other than the soil; for the field, properly cultivated, retains its fertility. But the produce of the mine is part of the mine itself[1].

[1] For the rate of growth of minerals in the earth is so slow, that it may almost be neglected It has indeed been asserted that the earth is producing petroleum fast by using for the purpose some of its internal heat If this were true, it would have a great influence on the future of the world; but there seems to be no good ground for hoping that it is

BOOK IV. CH. III.

To put the same thing in another way, the supply of agricultural produce and of fish is a perennial stream; mines are as it were nature's reservoir The more nearly a reservoir is exhausted, the greater is the labour of pumping from it, but if one man could pump it out in ten days, ten men could pump it out in one day: and when once empty, it would yield no more. So the mines that are being opened this year might just as easily have been opened many years ago: if the plans had been properly laid in advance, and the requisite specialized capital and skill got ready for the work, ten years' supply of coal might have been raised in one year without any increased difficulty, and when a vein had once given up its treasure, it could produce no more. This difference is illustrated by the fact that the rent of a mine is calculated on a different principle from that of a farm. The farmer contracts to give back the land as rich as he found it a mining company cannot do this; and while the farmer's rent is reckoned by the year, mining rent consists chiefly of "royalties" which are levied in proportion to the stores that are taken out of nature's storehouse[1].

But building land does give a diminishing return of convenience as increased capital is spent on it.

On the other hand, services which land renders to man in giving him space and light and air in which to live and work, do conform strictly to the law of diminishing return. It is advantageous to apply a constantly increasing capital to land that has any special advantages of situation, natural or acquired. Buildings tower up towards the sky, natural light and ventilation are supplemented by artificial means, and the steam lift reduces the disadvantages of the highest floors, and for this expenditure there is a return of extra convenience, but it is a diminishing return. However great the ground rent may be, a limit is at last reached after which it is better to pay more ground rent for a larger area than to go on piling up storey on storey any further; just as

[1] As Ricardo says, *Principles*, Chap II, "The compensation given (by the lessee) for the mine or quarry is paid for the value of the coal or stone which can be removed from them, and has no connection with the original or indestructible powers of the land" But both he and others seem sometimes to lose sight of these distinctions in discussing the law of diminishing return in its application to mines Especially is this the case in Ricardo's criticism of Adam Smith's theory of rent. *Principles*, Chap XXIV.

the farmer finds that at last a stage is reached at which more intensive cultivation will not pay its expenses, and it is better to pay more rent for extra land, than to face the diminution in the return which he would get by applying more capital and labour to his old land[1]. From this it results that the theory of ground rents is substantially the same as that of farm rents. This and similar facts will presently enable us to simplify and extend the theory of value as given by Ricardo and Mill.

Note on the Law of Diminishing Return.

Ricardo, Anderson and Turgot.

There has been a long controversy as to the authorship of the law of diminishing return. As has been already observed, the fundamental idea, which it expresses, has been the common property of every one who has had experience of agriculture, whether arable or pastoral, since the world began What economists did for the law a century ago, was not to discover it, but to give it definiteness, and to deduce inferences from it; which, if sometimes too hasty, yet contained important elements of suggestive and constructive truth. So far as these inferences go undoubtedly the first place must be assigned to Ricardo while Mr Cannan has shown that Turgot can claim priority over Anderson, Ricardo and other English writers in the clear statement of the law In some observations written about 1768 (*Oeuvres*, ed. Daire, Vol. I pp 420–1) he says —"Granting that where ordinary good cultivation prevails, the annual advances bring in 250 to the hundred, it is more than probable that if the advances were increased by degrees from this point up to that at which they would bring in nothing, each increment would be less and less fruitful. In this case the fertility of the earth would be like a spring which is forced to bend by being loaded with a number of equal weights in succession This comparison is not perfectly exact, but it is sufficient to show how, when the soil approaches near to returning all that it can produce, a very great expense may augment the production very

[1] Of course the return to capital spent in building increases for the earlier doses. Even where land can be had for almost nothing, it is cheaper to build houses two stories high than one, and hitherto it has been thought cheapest to build factories about four stories high But a belief is growing up in America, that where land is not very dear factories should be only two stories high, partly in order to avoid the evil effects of vibration, or of the expensive foundations and walls required to prevent it in a high building that is, it is found that the return of accommodation diminishes perceptibly after the capital and labour required to raise two stories have been spent on the land

BOOK IV. CH III

little. Seed thrown on a soil naturally fertile but totally unprepared would be an advance almost entirely lost. If it were once tilled the produce would be greater; tilling it a second, a third time, might not merely double and triple, but quadruple or decuple the produce, which will thus augment in a much larger proportion than the advances increase, and that up to a certain point, at which the produce will be as great as possible compared with the advances. Past this point if the advances be still increased, the produce will still increase, but less, and always less and less"

Difficulties of measuring off equal amounts of capital and labour,

Turgot, like practical agriculturists, implicitly refers to successive applications of capital and labour. He assumes things to be measured by their money prices, and implicitly regards a dose of capital and labour as the outlay of the equivalent of a certain sum of money distributed, according to the convenience of the case, between the earnings of labour of different kinds (including that of management), the price of seed and other materials, the cost of repair and replacement of machinery, etc., and lastly, interest on all the capital employed. This assumption may fairly be made when we are confining our attention to one place, and time, and method of cultivation.

But this resource fails us if we want to bring to a common standard the productiveness of lands in distant times or places. We shall then have to fall back on rough, and more or less arbitrary modes of measurement, which make no aim at numerical precision, but will yet suffice for the broader purposes of history. This difficulty is closely connected with that of finding a common standard of purchasing power, which we shall have to discuss later on. But it has some features peculiar to itself. For one thing there are great variations in the relative amounts of capital and labour that enter into a dose. Interest on capital is generally a much less important item in backward than in advanced stages of agriculture, in spite of the fact that the rate of interest is generally much lower in the latter. For most purposes however it is probably best to take as a common standard a day's unskilled labour of given efficiency. We thus regard the dose as made up of so much labour of different kinds, and such charges for the use and replacement of capital, as will together make up the value of, say, ten days' such labour, the relative proportions of these elements and their several values in terms of such labour being fixed according to the special circumstances of each problem.

and of reducing various produce to a common unit.

A similar difficulty is found in comparing the returns obtained by capital and labour applied under different circumstances. So long as the crops are of the same kind, the quantity of one return can be measured off against that of another but when they are of different kinds they cannot be compared till they are reduced to a common measure of value. When, for instance, it is said that land would give better returns to the capital and labour expended on it with one crop or rotation of crops than with another, the statement must be understood to hold only on the basis of the prices at the time. much error has arisen from losing sight of this limitation.

In the case of land cultivated on a system of rotating crops, we must take the whole period of rotation together, reckoning for the land being in the same condition at the beginning and the end of the rotation, and counting on the one hand all the capital and labour applied during the whole period, and on the other the aggregate returns of all the crops.

Different methods of book-keeping may class the same thing as capital or produce, but each must be consistent with itself.

It must be remembered that the return due to a dose of capital and labour is not here taken to include the value of the capital itself For instance, if part of the capital on a farm consists of two year old oxen, then the returns to a year's capital and labour will include not the full weight of these oxen at the end of the year, but only the addition that has been made to it during the year. Again, when a farmer is said to work with a capital of £10 to the acre, this includes the value of everything that he has on the farm. As has been already explained, however, a dose of capital and labour applied to a farm, does not include the whole value of the fixed capital, such as machinery and horses, but only the value of their use after allowing for depreciation and repairs; though it does include the whole value of the circulating capital, such as seed.

But although this is the method of measuring capital which is most generally adopted by economists, and the one which is to be taken for granted if nothing is said to the contrary; there are yet some exceptional cases in which it is best to adopt another. Sometimes it is convenient to speak as though all the capital applied were circulating capital applied at the beginning of the year or during it and in that case everything that is on the farm at the end of the year is part of the produce Thus, young cattle are regarded as a sort of raw material which is worked up in the course of time into fat cattle ready for the butcher The farm implements may even be treated in the same way, their value at the beginning of the year being taken as so much circulating capital applied to the farm, and at the end of the year as so much produce. This plan enables us to avoid a good deal of repetition of conditioning clauses as to depreciation, etc., and to save the use of words in many ways It is often the best plan for general reasonings of an abstract character, particularly if they are expressed in a mathematical form

CHAPTER IV.

THE GROWTH OF POPULATION.

Population and production

§ 1. THE production of wealth is but a means to the sustenance of man; to the development of his activities physical, mental, and moral; and the satisfaction of his wants. But yet, as has already been observed[1], man himself is the chief means of the production of that wealth of which he is the ultimate aim, and it seems best to make at this stage some study of the growth of population in numbers and in strength and in character.

The growth of numbers among animals is governed by present conditions, among men it is affected by traditions of the past and forecasts of the future

In the animal and vegetable world the growth of numbers is governed by the tendency of individuals to propagate their species on the one hand, and on the other hand by the struggle for life which thins out the young before they arrive at maturity. In the human race alone the conflict of these two opposing forces is complicated by other influences. On the one hand regard for the future induces many individuals to control their natural impulses, sometimes with the purpose of worthily discharging their duties as parents; sometimes, as for instance at Rome under the Empire, for mean motives. And on the other hand society exercises pressure on the individual by religious, moral and legal sanctions, sometimes with the object of quickening, and sometimes with that of retarding, the growth of population.

The problems of population are older than civilization

The study of the growth of population is often spoken of as though it were a modern one. But in a more or less vague form it has occupied the attention of thoughtful men in all ages of the world. To its influence often unavowed,

[1] Book IV Ch I § 1

sometimes not even clearly recognized, we can trace a great part of the rules, customs and ceremonies that have been enjoined in the Eastern and Western world by law-givers, by moralists, and those nameless thinkers, whose far-seeing wisdom has left its impress on national habits. Among vigorous races, and in times of great military conflict, they aimed at increasing the supply of males capable of bearing arms; and in the higher stages of progress they have inculcated a great respect for the sanctity of human life, but in the lower stages, they have encouraged and even compelled the ruthless slaughter of the infirm and the aged, and sometimes of a certain proportion of the female children

Fluctuations of opinion on State encouragement of large families.

In ancient Greece and Rome, with the safety-valve of the power of planting colonies, and in the presence of constant war, an increase in the number of citizens was regarded as a source of public strength, and marriage was encouraged by public opinion, and in many cases even by legislation though thoughtful men were even then aware that action in the contrary sense might be necessary if the responsibilities of parentage should ever cease to be burdensome[1] In later times there may be observed, as Roscher says[2], a regular ebb and flow of the opinion that the State should encourage the growth of numbers It was in full flow in England under the first two Tudors, but in the course of the sixteenth century it slackened and turned, and it began to ebb, when the abolition of the celibacy of the religious orders, and the more settled state of the country had had time to give a perceptible impetus to population; the effective demand for labour having meanwhile been diminished by the increase of sheep runs, and by the collapse of that part of the industrial system which had been organized by the monastic establishments.

[1] Thus Aristotle (*Politics*, II 6) objects to Plato's scheme for equalizing property and abolishing poverty on the ground that it would be unworkable unless the State exercised a firm control over the growth of numbers And as Professor Jowett points out, Plato himself was aware of this (see *Laws* V 740 also Aristotle, *Politics*, VII 16) The population of Greece is said to have declined from the seventh century B C, and that of Rome from the third (See Zumpt, *Bevölkerung im Alterthum* quoted by Rumelin in Schonberg's *Handbuch*. Comp. also Hume's essay on *The populousness of ancient nations*)

[2] *Political Economy*, § 254

BOOK IV CH. IV

Later on the growth of population was checked by that rise in the standard of comfort which took effect in the general adoption of wheat as the staple food of Englishmen during the first half of the eighteenth century. At that time there were even fears, which later inquiries showed to be unfounded, that the population was actually diminishing. Petty[1] had forestalled some of Carey's and Wakefield's arguments as to the advantages of a dense population. Child had argued that "whatever tends to the depopulating of a country tends to the impoverishment of it;" and that "most nations in the civilized parts of the world, are more or less rich or poor proportionably to the paucity or plenty of their people, and not to the sterility or fruitfulness of their land[2]." And by the time that the world-struggle with France had attained its height, when the demands for more and more troops were ever growing, and when manufacturers were wanting more men for their new machinery, the bias of the ruling classes was strongly flowing in favour of an increase of population. So far did this movement of opinion reach that in 1796 Pitt declared that a man who had enriched his country with a number of children had a claim on its assistance. An act, passed amid the military anxieties of 1806, which granted exemptions from taxes to the fathers of more than two children born in wedlock, was repealed as soon as Napoleon had been safely lodged in St Helena[3].

[1] He argues that Holland is richer than it appears to be relatively to France, because its people have access to many advantages that cannot be had by those who live on poorer land, and are therefore more scattered "Rich land is better than coarse land of the same Rent" *Political Arithmetick*, Ch. I

[2] *Discourse on Trade*, Chap. x. Harris, Essay on *Coins*, pp. 32—3, argues to a similar effect, and proposes to "encourage matrimony among the lower classes by giving some privileges to those who have children" &c.

[3] "Let us," said Pitt, "make relief, in cases where there are a large number of children, a matter of right and an honour, instead of a ground for opprobrium and contempt This will make a large family a blessing and not a curse, and this will draw a proper line of distinction between those who are able to provide for themselves by labour, and those who after having enriched their country with a number of children have a claim on its assistance for their support." Of course he desired "to discourage relief where it was not wanted" Napoleon the First had offered to take under his own charge one member of any family which contained seven male children and Louis XIV, his predecessor in the slaughter of men, had exempted from public taxes all those who married before the age of 20 or had more than ten legitimate children A comparison of the rapid increase in the

The doctrines of recent economists The Physiocrats

§ 2. But during all this time there had been a growing feeling, among those who thought most seriously on social problems, that an inordinate increase of numbers, whether it strengthened the State or not, must necessarily cause great misery: and that the rulers of the State had no right to subordinate individual happiness to the aggrandizement of the State In France in particular a reaction was caused, as we have seen, by the cynical selfishness with which the Court and its adherents sacrificed the well-being of the people for the sake of their own luxury and military glory. If the humane sympathies of the Physiocrats had been able to overcome the frivolity and harshness of the privileged classes of France, the eighteenth century would probably not have ended in tumult and bloodshed, the march of freedom in England would not have been arrested, and the dial of progress would have been more forward than it is by the space of at least a generation As it was, but little attention was paid to Quesnay's guarded but forcible protest:—"one should aim less at augmenting the population than at increasing the national income, for the condition of greater comfort which is derived from a good income, is preferable to that in which a population exceeds its income and is ever in urgent need of the means of subsistence[1]."

population of Germany with that of France was a chief motive of the order of the French Chamber in 1885 that education and board should be provided at the public expense for every seventh child in all necessitous families. In 1890 the Académie des Sciences was much occupied with similar proposals, of which one may be noted as characteristic of our Age: it would give to the father of a family two, three, or four votes according to its size

[1] The Physiocratic doctrine with regard to the tendency of population to increase up to the margin of subsistence may be given in Turgot's words.—the employer "since he always has his choice of a great number of working men, will choose that one who will work most cheaply Thus then the workers are compelled by mutual competition to lower their price, and with regard to every kind of labour the result is bound to be reached—and it is reached as a matter of fact—that the wages of the worker are limited to that which is necessary to procure his subsistence" (*Sur la formation et la distribution des richesses*, § VI)

Similarly Sir James Steuart says, *Inquiry* (Bk I Ch III), "The generative faculty resembles a spring loaded with a weight, which always exerts itself in proportion to the diminution of resistance when food has remained some time without augmentation or diminution, generation will carry numbers as high as possible, if then food comes to be diminished the spring is overpowered, the force of it becomes less than nothing, inhabitants will diminish at least in proportion to the overcharge If, on the other hand, food be increased, the spring which stood

Adam Smith

Adam Smith said but little on the question of population, for indeed he wrote at one of the culminating points of the prosperity of the English working classes, but what he does say is wise and well balanced and modern in tone. Accepting the Physiocratic doctrine as his basis, he corrected it by insisting that the necessaries of life are not a fixed and determined quantity, but have varied much from place to place and time to time; and may vary more[1]. But he did not work out this hint fully. And there was nothing to lead him to anticipate the second great limitation of the Physiocratic doctrine, which has been made prominent in our time by the carriage of wheat from the centre of America to Liverpool for less than what it used to cost to carry it across England.

The eighteenth century ended and the nineteenth began in gloom

The eighteenth century wore on to its close and the next century began, year by year the condition of the working classes in England became more gloomy An astonishing series of bad harvests[2], a most exhausting war[3], a change in the methods of industry that dislocated old ties combined with an injudicious poor law to bring the working classes into the greatest misery they have ever suffered, at all events since the beginning of trustworthy records of English social history[4] And to crown all, well-meaning enthusiasts, chiefly under French influence, were proposing communistic schemes

at 0, will begin to exert itself in proportion as the resistance diminishes, people will begin to be better fed, they will multiply, and in proportion as they increase in numbers the food will become scarce again" Sir James Steuart was much under the influence of the Physiocrats, and was indeed in some respects imbued with Continental rather than English notions of government and his artificial schemes for regulating population seem very far off from us now See his *Inquiry*, Bk I Ch XII, "*Of the great advantage of combining a well-digested Theory and a perfect Knowledge of Facts with the practical Part of Government in order to make a People multiply*"

[1] See *Wealth of Nations*, Bk I. Ch VIII and Bk V Ch. II See also *supra*, Bk II. Ch IV

[2] The average price of wheat in the decade 1771–1780 in which Adam Smith wrote was 34*s* 7*d*, in 1781–1790 it was 37*s* 1*d*, in 1791–1800 it was 63*s* 6*d*., in 1801–1810 it was 83*s* 11*d*, and in 1811–1820 it was 87*s* 6*d*

[3] Early in the present century the Imperial taxes—for the greater part war taxes—amounted to one-fifth of the whole income of the country, whereas now they are not much more than a twentieth, and even of this a great part is spent on education and other benefits which Government did not then afford.

[4] See below § 7 and above Bk I Ch III §§ 5, 6

which would enable people to throw on society the whole responsibility for rearing their children[1]. BOOK IV CH. IV

Thus while the recruiting sergeant and the employer of labour were calling for measures tending to increase the growth of population, more far-seeing men began to inquire whether the race could escape degradation if the numbers continued long to increase as they were then doing. Of these inquirers the chief was Malthus, and his *Essay on the Principle of Population* is the starting point of all modern speculations on the subject

Malthus.

§ 3. Malthus' reasoning consists of three parts, which must be kept distinct. The first relates to the supply of labour. By a careful study of facts he proves that every people, of whose history we have a trustworthy record, has been so prolific that the growth of its numbers would have been rapid and continuous if it had not been checked either by a scarcity of the necessaries of life, or some other cause, that is, by disease, by war, by infanticide, or lastly by voluntary restraint.

His argument has three stages The first.

His second position relates to the demand for labour Like the first it is supported by facts, but by a different set of facts. He shows that up to the time at which he wrote no country (as distinguished from a city, such as Rome or Venice) had been able to obtain an abundant supply of the necessaries of life after its territory had become very thickly peopled The produce which Nature returns to the work of man is her effective demand for population: and he shows that up to this time a rapid increase in population when already thick had not led to a proportionate increase in this demand[2]

The second.

[1] Especially Godwin in his *Inquiry concerning Political Justice* (1792). It is interesting to compare Malthus' criticism of this Essay (Bk III Ch II.) with Aristotle's comments on Plato's *Republic* (see especially *Politics*, II 6)

[2] But many of his critics suppose him to have stated their position much less unreservedly than he did; they have forgotten such passages as this —"From a review of the state of society in former periods compared with the present I should certainly say that the evils resulting from the principle of population have rather diminished than increased, even under the disadvantage of an almost total ignorance of their real cause. And if we can indulge the hope that this ignorance will be gradually dissipated, it does not seem unreasonable to hope that they will be still further diminished. The increase of absolute population, which will of

BOOK IV CH. IV

The third

Thirdly, he draws the conclusion that what had been in the past, was likely to be in the future; and that the growth of population would be checked by poverty or some other cause of suffering unless it were checked by voluntary restraint. He therefore urges people to use this restraint, and, while leading lives of moral purity, to abstain from very early marriages[1]

course take place, will evidently tend but little to weaken this expectation, as everything depends on the relative proportions between population and food, and not on the absolute number of the people. In the former part of this work it appeared that the countries which possessed the fewest people often suffered the most from the effects of the principle of population." *Essay*, Bk. IV Ch XII.

[1] In the first edition of his essay, 1798, Malthus gave his argument without any detailed statement of facts, though from the first he regarded it as needing to be treated in direct connection with a study of facts, as is shown by his having told Pryme (who afterwards became the first Professor of Political Economy at Cambridge) "that his theory was first suggested to his mind in an argumentative conversation which he had with his father on the state of some other countries" (Pryme's *Recollections*, p 66). American experience showed that population if unchecked would double at least once in twenty-five years. He argued that a doubled population might, even in a country as thickly peopled as England was with its seven million inhabitants, conceivably though not probably double the subsistence raised from the English soil. but that labour doubled again would not suffice to double the produce again "Let us then take this for our rule, though certainly far beyond the truth, and allow that the whole produce of the Island might be increased every twenty-five years [that is with every doubling of the population] by a quantity of subsistence equal to that which it at present produces"; or in other words, in an arithmetical progression. His desire to make himself clearly understood made him, as Wagner says in his excellent introduction to the study of Population (*Grundlegung*, Ed. III p 453), "put too sharp a point on his doctrine, and formulate it too absolutely" Thus he got into the habit of speaking of population as capable of increasing in an arithmetical ratio and many writers, including even so acute a critic as Mr Cannan (*Production and Distribution* 1776—1848, p 143), think that he attached importance to the phrase itself. whereas it was really only a short way of stating the utmost that he thought any reasonable person could ask him to concede. What he meant, stated in modern language, was that the Law of Diminishing Return, which underlies the whole of his argument, would begin to operate sharply after the produce of the island had been doubled Doubled labour might give doubled produce but quadrupled labour would hardly treble it octupled labour would not quadruple it

In the second edition, 1803, he based himself on so wide and careful a statement of facts as to claim a place among the founders of historical economics; he softened and explained away many of the "sharp points" of his old doctrine, though he did not abandon (as was implied in earlier editions of this work) the use of the phrase "arithmetical ratio" In particular he took a less despondent view of the future of the human race; and dwelt on the hope that moral restraint might hold population in check, and that "vice and misery," the old checks, might thus be kept in abeyance Francis Place, who was not blind to his many faults, wrote in 1822 an apology for him, excellent in tone and judgment Good accounts of his

Later events affect the validity of his second and third stages, but not of his first

His position with regard to the supply of population, with which alone we are directly concerned in this chapter, remains substantially valid. The changes which the course of events has introduced into the doctrine of population relate chiefly to the second and third steps of his reasoning. We have already noticed that the English economists of the earlier half of this century overrated the tendency of an increasing population to press upon the means of subsistence, and it was not Malthus' fault that he could not foresee the great developments of steam transport by land and by sea, which have enabled Englishmen of the present generation to obtain the products of the richest lands of the earth at comparatively small cost.

But the fact that he did not foresee these changes makes the second and third steps of his argument antiquated in form; though they are still in a great measure valid in substance. It remains true that unless the checks on the growth of population in force at the end of the nineteenth century are on the whole increased (they are certain to change their form in places that are as yet imperfectly civilized) it will be impossible for the habits of comfort prevailing in Western Europe to spread themselves over the whole world and maintain themselves for many hundred years. But of this more hereafter[1].

§ 4. The growth in numbers of a people depends firstly

work are given in Prof Nicholson's *Political Economy*, Book I Ch XII, Dr Bonar's *Malthus and his Work*, and Mr Cannan's book just mentioned Prof Ashley has edited in a convenient form leading passages of his first and second editions

[1] Taking the present population of the world at one and a half thousand millions; and assuming that its present rate of increase (about 8 per 1000 annually, see Mr Ravenstein's paper before the British Association in 1890) will continue, we find that in less than two hundred years it will amount to six thousand millions, or at the rate of about 200 to the square mile of fairly fertile land (Mr Ravenstein reckons 28 million square miles of fairly fertile land, and 14 millions of poor grass lands The first estimate is thought by many to be too high but, allowing for this, if the less fertile land be reckoned in for what it is worth, the result will be about thirty million square miles as assumed above). Meanwhile there will probably be great improvements in the arts of agriculture, and, if so, the pressure of population on the means of subsistence may not be much felt, even in two hundred years But if the same rate of increase be continued till the year 2400, the population will then be 1000 for every mile of fairly fertile land: and, so far as we can see now, the diet of such a population must needs be in the main vegetarian.

BOOK IV CH. IV

on the *Natural Increase*, that is, the excess of their births over their deaths; and secondly on migration.

Natural Increase

The number of births depends chiefly on habits relating to marriage, the early history of which is full of instruction; but we must confine ourselves here to the conditions of marriage in modern civilized countries

Marriage affected by the climate,

The age of marriage varies with the climate. In warm climates where child bearing begins early, it ends early, in colder climates it begins later and ends later[1]; but in every case the longer marriages are postponed beyond the age that is natural to the country, the smaller is the birth-rate; the age of the wife being of course much more important in this respect than that of the husband[2]. Given the climate, the average age of marriage depends chiefly on the ease with which young people can establish themselves, and support a family according to the standard of comfort that prevails among their friends and acquaintances; and therefore it is different in different stations of life.

and the difficulty of supporting a family

Middle classes marry late and unskilled labourers early

In the middle classes a man's income seldom reaches its maximum till he is forty or fifty years old, and the expense of bringing up his children is heavy and lasts for many years The artisan earns nearly as much at twenty-one as he ever does, unless he rises to a responsible post, but he does not earn much before he is twenty-one · his children are likely to be a considerable expense to him till about the age of fifteen; unless they are sent into a factory, where they may pay their way at a very early age, and lastly the labourer earns nearly full wages at eighteen, while his children begin

[1] Of course the length of a generation has itself some influence on the growth of population. If it is 25 years in one place and 20 in another; and if in each place population doubles once in two generations during a thousand years, the increase will be a million-fold in the first place, but thirty million-fold in the second

[2] Dr Ogle (*Statistical Journal*, Vol. 53) calculates that if the average age of marriage of women in England were postponed five years, the number of children to a marriage, which is now 4 2 would fall to 3 1 Prof Korosi, basing himself on the facts of the relatively warm climate of Buda Pest, finds 18—20 the most prolific age for women, 24—26 that for men But he concludes that a slight postponement of weddings beyond these ages is advisable mainly on the ground that the vitality of the children of women under 20 is generally small See *Proceedings of Congress of Hygiene and Demography*, London 1892, and *Statistical Journal*, Vol 57 Compare also the International Statistics at the end of this chapter

to pay their own expenses very early. In consequence, the average age at marriage is highest among the middle classes: it is low among the artisans and lower still among the unskilled labourers[1].

Unskilled labourers, when not so poor as to suffer actual want and not restrained by any external cause, have seldom, if ever, shown a lower power of increase than that of doubling in thirty years; that is, of multiplying a million-fold in six hundred years, a billion-fold in twelve hundred: and hence it might be inferred *a priori* that their increase has never gone on without restraint for any considerable time. This inference is confirmed by the teaching of all history. Throughout Europe during the Middle Ages, and in some parts of it even up to the present time, unmarried labourers have usually slept in the farmhouse or with their parents: while a married pair have generally required a house for themselves: when a village has as many hands as it can well employ, the number of houses is not increased, and young people have to wait as best they can

[1] The term marriage in the text must be taken in a wide sense so as to include not only legal marriages, but all those informal unions which are sufficiently permanent in character to involve for several years at least the practical responsibilities of married life They are often contracted at an early age, and not unfrequently lead up to legal marriages after the lapse of some years For this reason the average age at marriage in the broad sense of the term, with which alone we are here concerned, is below the average age at legal marriage The allowance to be made on this head for the whole of the working classes is probably considerable, but it is very much greater in the case of unskilled labourers than of any other class The following statistics must be interpreted in the light of this remark, and of the fact that all English industrial statistics are vitiated by the want of sufficient care in the classification of the working classes in our official returns The Registrar-General's forty-ninth Annual Report states that in certain selected districts the returns of marriages for 1884—5 were examined with the following results, the number after each occupation being the average age of bachelors in it at marriage, and the following number, in brackets, being the average age of spinsters who married men of that occupation —Miners 24 06 (22 46); Textile hands 24 38 (23 43), Shoemakers, Tailors 24 92 (24 31); Artisans 25 35 (23 70); Labourers 25 56 (23 66), Commercial Clerks 26 25 (24 43); Shopkeepers, Shopmen 26 67 (24 22), Farmers and sons 29 23 (26 91); Professional and Independent Class 31 22 (26 40).

Dr Ogle, in the paper already referred to, shows that the marriage-rate is greatest generally in those parts of England in which the percentage of those women between 15 and 25 years of age who are industrially occupied is the greatest. This is no doubt due, as he suggests, partly to the willingness of men to have their money incomes supplemented by those of their wives, but it may be partly due also to an excess of women of a marriageable age in those districts.

BOOK IV. CH IV

Hindrances to early marriage in stationary rural districts.

There are many parts of Europe even now in which custom exercising the force of law prevents more than one son in each family from marrying, he is generally the eldest, but in some places the youngest: if any other son marries he must leave the village. When great material prosperity and the absence of all extreme poverty are found in old-fashioned corners of the Old World, the explanation generally lies in some such custom as this with all its evils and hardships[1]. It is true that the severity of this custom may be tempered by the power of migration, but in the Middle Ages the free movement of the people was hindered by stern regulations. The free towns indeed often encouraged immigration from the country: but the rules of the gilds were in some respects almost as cruel to people who tried to escape from their old homes as were those enforced by the feudal lords themselves[2].

The birth-rate is often low among present proprietors,

§ 5. In this respect the position of the hired agricultural labourer has changed very much. The towns are now always open to him and his children; and if he betakes himself to the New World he is likely to succeed better than any other class of emigrants. But on the other hand the gradual rise in the value of land and its growing scarcity is tending to check the increase of population in some districts in which the system of peasant properties prevails, in which there is not much enterprise for opening out new trades or for emigration, and parents feel that the social position of their children will depend on the amount of their land. They incline to limit artificially the size of their families and to treat marriage very much as a business contract, seeking always to marry their sons to heiresses. Mr Francis Galton has pointed out that, though the families of English peers are generally large, the habit of marrying the eldest son to

[1] A typical instance is that of the valley Jachenau in the Bavarian Alps There the custom is rigidly enforced and there are scarcely any small cottages in the valley Aided by a great recent rise in the value of their woods, with regard to which they have pursued a farseeing policy, the inhabitants live prosperously in large houses, the younger brothers and sisters acting as servants in their old homes or elsewhere They are of a different race from the work people in the neighbouring valleys, who live poor and hard lives, but seem to think that the Jachenau purchases its material prosperity at too great a cost.

[2] See *e g* Rogers, *Six Centuries*, pp 106—7

an heiress, who is presumably not of a fertile stock, and sometimes dissuading the younger sons from marriage, has led to the extinction of a great many peerages; and in like manner among the French peasants this habit combined with their preference for small families keeps their numbers almost stationary.

BOOK IV. CH IV.

On the other hand there seem to be no conditions more favourable to the rapid growth of numbers than those of the agricultural districts of new countries Land is to be had in abundance, railways and steamships carry away the produce of the land and bring back in exchange implements of advanced types, and many of the comforts and luxuries of life. The "farmer," as the peasant proprietor is called in America, finds therefore that a large family is not a burden, but an assistance to him. He and they live healthy out-of-door lives, there is nothing to check but everything to stimulate the growth of numbers The natural increase is aided by immigration; and thus, in spite of the fact that some classes of the inhabitants of large cities in America are, it is said, reluctant to have many children, the population has increased sixteen-fold in the last hundred years[1]

but not among American farmers

[1] The extreme prudence of peasant proprietors under stationary conditions was noticed by Malthus; see his account of Switzerland (*Essay*, Bk. II Ch v) Adam Smith remarked that poor Highland women frequently had twenty children of whom not more than two reached maturity (*Wealth of Nations*, Bk I Ch VIII); and the notion that want stimulated fertility was insisted on by Doubleday, *True Law of Population* See also Sadler, *Law of Population* Malthus' remark, that the reproductive power is less in barbarous than in civilized races, has been extended by Darwin to the animal and vegetable kingdom generally Mr Herbert Spencer seems to think it probable that the progress of civilization will of itself hold the growth of population completely in check

Mr Charles Booth (*Statistical Journal*, 1893) has divided London into 27 districts (chiefly Registration districts), and arranged them in order of poverty, of overcrowding, of high birth-rate and of high death-rate He finds that the four orders are generally the same The excess of birth-rate over death rate is lowest in the very rich and the very poor districts

Mr Brownell (*Annals of American Academy*, Vol v) has shown that the birth-rate is generally highest in those parts of America in which population is scanty, that it decreases generally with an increase of agricultural wealth, and even more generally with an increase of manufacturing wealth, and with an increase in the number of deaths from nervous diseases There are many exceptions, some of which can be explained away by the race differences, which are so disturbing an element in American Statistics. (Possibly also the fashion of describing diseases as nervous may not spread as fast in the rural as in the urban parts of America) But on the whole the facts seem to support Mr Herbert Spencer's position.

BOOK IV. CH IV

General conclusion

On the whole it seems proved that the birth-rate is generally lower among the well-to-do than among those who make little expensive provision for the future of themselves and their families, and who live an active life: and that fecundity is diminished by luxurious habits of living. Probably it is also diminished by severe mental strain, that is to say, given the natural strength of the parents, their expectation of a large family is diminished by a great increase of mental strain. Of course those who do high mental work, have as a class more than the average of constitutional and nervous strength, and Dr Galton has shown that they are not as a class unprolific. But they commonly marry late.

Population in England.

§ 6. The growth of population in England has a more clearly defined history than that in the United Kingdom, and we shall find some interest in noticing its chief movements.

In Belgium also race differences are disturbing but the figures arranged by M. Leroy Beaulieu (*Statistical Journal* for 1891, p. 377) show that the birth-rate is highest in those provinces in which wages and education are lowest

The movements of the population of France have been studied with exceptional care and the last great work on the subject by M Levasseur, *La Population Française*, is a mine of valuable information as regards other nations besides France Montesquieu, reasoning perhaps rather *a priori*, accused the law of primogeniture which ruled in his time in France of reducing the number of children in a family and le Play brought the same charge against the law of compulsory division. M Levasseur (*l c.* Vol III pp 171—7) calls attention to the contrast, and remarks that Malthus' expectations of the effect of the Civil Code on population were in harmony with Montesquieu's rather than le Play's diagnosis But in fact the birth-rate varies much from one part of France to another. It is generally lower where a large part of the population owns land than where it does not If however the Departments of France be arranged in groups in ascending order of the property left at death (*valeurs successorales par tête d'habitant*), the corresponding birth-rate descends almost uniformly, being 23 per hundred married women between 15 and 50 years for the ten Departments in which the property left is 48—57 fr ; and 13 2 for the Seine, where it is 412 fr And in Paris itself the arrondissements inhabited by the well-to-do show a smaller percentage of families with more than two children than the poorer arrondissements show There is much interest in the careful analysis which M. Levasseur gives of the connection between economic conditions and birth-rate; his general conclusion being that it is not direct but indirect, through the mutual influence of the two on manners and the habit of life (*mœurs*) He appears to hold that, however much the decline in the numbers of the French relatively to surrounding nations (see the tables at the end of this chapter) may be regretted from the political and military points of view, there is much good mixed with the evil in its influences on material comfort and even social progress

The Middle Ages.

The restraints on the increase of numbers during the Middle Ages were the same in England as elsewhere. In England as elsewhere the religious orders were a refuge to those for whom no establishment in marriage could be provided, and religious celibacy while undoubtedly acting in some measure as an independent check on the growth of population, is in the main to be regarded rather as a method in which the broad natural forces tending to restrain population expressed themselves, than as an addition to them. Infectious and contagious diseases, both endemic and epidemic, were caused by dirty habits of life which were even worse in England than in the South of Europe; and famines by the failures of good harvests and the difficulties of communication; though this evil was less in England than elsewhere.

Country life was, as elsewhere, rigid in its habits; young people found it difficult to establish themselves until some other married pair had passed from the scene and made a vacancy in their own parish; for migration to another parish was seldom thought of by an agricultural labourer under ordinary circumstances. Consequently whenever plague or war or famine thinned the population, there were always many waiting to be married, who filled the vacant places, and, being perhaps younger and stronger than the average of newly married couples, had larger families[1].

There was however some movement even of agricultural labourers towards districts which had been struck more heavily than their neighbours by pestilence, by famine or the sword Moreover artisans were often more or less on the move, and this was especially the case with those who were engaged in the building trades, and those who worked in metal and wood, though no doubt the "wander years" were chiefly those of youth, and after these were over the wanderer was likely to settle down in the place in which he was born. Again, there seems to have been a good deal of migration on the part of the retainers of the landed gentry, especially of the greater barons who had seats in several parts of the

[1] Thus we are told that after the Black Death of 1349 most marriages were very fertile (Rogers, *History of Agriculture and Prices*, Vol I p. 301).

BOOK IV CH IV.

country. And lastly, in spite of the selfish exclusiveness which the gilds developed as years went on, the towns offered in England as elsewhere a refuge to many who could get no good openings for work and for marriage in their own homes In these various ways some elasticity was introduced into the rigid system of mediæval economy; and population was able to avail itself in some measure of the increased demand for labour which came gradually with the growth of knowledge, the establishment of law and order, and the development of oceanic trade[1].

Settlement Laws.

In the latter half of the seventeenth and the first half of the eighteenth century the central government exerted itself to hinder the adjustment of the supply of population in different parts of the country to the demand for it by Settlement Laws, which made any one chargeable to a parish who had resided there forty days, but ordered that he might be sent home by force at any time within that period[2] Land-

[1] There is no certain knowledge to be had as to the density of population in England before the eighteenth century Prof Rogers while agreeing with Mr Seebohm that the Black Death of 1349 destroyed one-half of the population, is inclined to take considerably lower estimates than Mr Seebohm's for the whole of the Middle Ages and to think that population doubled during the seventeenth century. (*History of Agriculture and Prices*, I pp 55 &c, IV pp 132 &c., VI pp 782 &c) Nevertheless Mr Seebohm's estimates (*Fortnightly Review*, Vol VII N S) probably give us a fairly trustworthy general view The figures in square brackets are "merely conjectural"

	Agricultural	Non-agricultural	Total.
1086	1½ millions	½ million	2 millions
1348	3 ,,	1 ,,	4 ,,
1377	1½ ,,	½ ,,	2 ,,
1500	[2¼] ,,	[¾] ,,	[3] ,,
1630	[3] ,,	[1] ,,	[4] ,,
1700	[3½] ,,	[2] ,,	5½ ,,

If we are to trust Harrison (*Description of England*, Bk II Ch XVI), the muster of men able for service in 1574 amounted to 1,172,674

The Black Death was England's only very great calamity She was not, like the rest of Europe, liable to devastating wars, such as the Thirty Years' War, which destroyed more than half the population of Germany, a loss which it required a full century to recover (See Rümelin's instructive article on *Bevölkerungslehre* in Schonberg's *Handbuch*)

[2] Adam Smith is justly indignant at this. (See *Wealth of Nations*, Bk I Ch X. Part II. and Book IV Ch II) The Act recites (14 Charles II c 12, A D 1662) that "by reason of some defects in the law, poor people are not restrained from going from one parish to another, and thereby do endeavour to settle themselves in those parishes where there is the best stock, the largest

Slow growth of population and rise in the standard of living in the first half of the eighteenth century,

lords and farmers were so eager to prevent people from getting a "settlement" in their parish that they put great difficulties in the way of building cottages, and sometimes even razed them to the ground. In consequence the agricultural population of England was stationary during the hundred years ending with 1760, while the manufactures were not yet sufficiently developed to absorb large numbers. This retardation in the growth of numbers was partly caused by, and partly a cause of, a rise in the standard of living; a chief element of which was an increased use of wheat in the place of inferior grains as the food of the common people[1]

changes in the second half

From 1760 onwards those who could not establish themselves at home found little difficulty in getting employment in the new manufacturing or mining districts, where the demand for workers often kept the local authorities from enforcing the removal clauses of the Settlement Act. To these districts young people resorted freely, and the birth-rate in them became exceptionally high, but so did the death-rate also; the net result being a fairly rapid growth of population At the end of the century, when Malthus wrote, the Poor Law again began to influence the age of marriage, but this time in the direction of making it unduly early. The sufferings of the working classes caused by a series of famines and by the French War made some measure of relief necessary, and the need of large bodies of recruits for the army and navy was an additional inducement to tender-hearted people to be somewhat liberal in their allowances to a large family, with the practical effect of making the father of many children often able to procure more indulgences for himself without working than he could have

wastes or commons to build cottages, and the most woods for them to burn and destroy etc" and it is therefore ordered "that upon complaint made . within forty days after any such person or persons coming, so as to settle as aforesaid, in any tenement under the yearly value of ten pounds... it shall be lawful for any two justices of the Peace to remove and convey such person or persons to such parish where he or they were last legally settled" Several Acts purporting to soften its harshness had been passed before Adam Smith's time, but they had been ineffective In 1795 however it was ordered that no one should be removed until he became actually chargeable

[1] Some interesting remarks on this subject are made by Eden, *History of the Poor*, I pp 560—4

BOOK IV. CH. IV.

got by hard work if he had been unmarried or had only a small family Those who availed themselves most of this bounty were naturally the laziest and meanest of the people, those with least self-respect and enterprise. So although there was in the manufacturing towns a fearful mortality, particularly of infants, the quantity of the people increased fast; but its quality improved little, if at all, till the passing of the New Poor Law in 1834. Since that time the rapid growth of the town population has, as we shall see in the next chapter, tended to increase mortality, but this has been counteracted by the growth of temperance, of medical knowledge, of sanitation and of general cleanliness. Emigration has increased, the age of marriage has been slightly raised and a somewhat less proportion of the whole population are married; but, on the other hand, the ratio of births to a marriage has risen[1]; with the result that population has been growing very nearly steadily[2] Let us examine the course of recent changes a little more closely.

Since the reform of the poor law the growth of population has been fairly steady

[1] But this increase in the figures shown is partly due to improved registration of births (Farr, *Vital Statistics*, p 97)

[2] The following tables show the growth of the population of England and Wales from the beginning of last century The figures for the last century are computed from the registers of births and deaths, and the poll and hearth tax returns those since 1801 from Census returns. It will be noticed that the numbers increased nearly as much in the twenty years following 1760 as in the preceding sixty years The pressure of the great war and the high price of corn is shown in the slow growth between 1790 and 1801, and the effects of indiscriminate poor law allowances, in spite of greater pressure, is shown by the rapid increase in the next ten years, and the still greater increase when that pressure was removed in the decade ending 1821. The third column shows the percentage which the increase during the preceding decade was of the population at the beginning of that decade

Year	Population 000s omitted	Increase per cent	Year	Population 000s omitted	Increase per cent.
1700	5,475		1801	8,892	2 5
10	5,240	-4 9*	11	10,164	14 3
20	5,565	6 2	21	12,000	18 1
30	5,796	4 1	31	13,897	15 8
40	6,064	4 6	41	15,909	14 5
50	6,467	6 6	51	17,928	12 7
60	6,736	4·1	61	20,066	11 9
70	7,428	10·3	71	22,712	13 2
80	7,953	7·1	81	25,974	14 4
90	8,675	9 1	91	29,002	11·7

* Decrease.

The great growth of emigration during recent years makes it important to

BOOK IV CH IV

§ 7 Early in this century, when wages were low and wheat was dear, the working classes generally spent more than half their income on bread and consequently a rise in the price of wheat diminished marriages very much among them: that is, it diminished very much the number of marriages by banns. But it raised the income of many members of the well-to-do classes, and therefore often increased the number of marriages by license[1]. Since however these were but a small part of the whole, the net effect was to lower the marriage-rate[2]. But as time went on, the price of wheat fell and wages rose, till now the working classes spend on the average less than a quarter of their incomes on bread; and in consequence the variations of commercial prosperity have got to exercise a preponderating influence on the marriage-rate[3].

In the earlier part of the century the marriage rate varied with the goodness of the harvest

Later on the influence of commercial fluctuations predominated

correct the figures for the last three decades so as to show the "natural increase," viz that due to the excess of births over deaths

Decade ending	mean annual birthrate per 1000	mean annual deathrate per 1000	average annual natural increment per thousand	average annual actual increment per thousand	net emigration in thousands
1861	34 15	22 25	12 61	11·93	122
71	35 24	22 50	13·58	13 19	79
81	35 35	21 27	15 09	14 36	164
91			13 97	11 66	601

The last column is obtained by comparing the census returns with those of births and deaths, for there is no independent record of the net emigration from England and Wales. The following figures show the gross emigration (000s omitted) from the United Kingdom in the decades ending with the years named

Decade ending	emigration	Decade ending	emigration
1831	247,	1871	1,967,
1841	703,	1881	2,228,
1851	1,685,	1891	3,572,
1861	2,287,		

The net emigration from the United Kingdom during the two last of these decades was 1,480,000, and 1,747,000 respectively

1 See Dr Farr's 17th Annual Report for 1854 as Registrar-General, or the abstract of it in *Vital Statistics* (pp 72—5)

2 For instance, representing the price of wheat in shillings and the number of marriages in England and Wales in thousands, we have for 1801 wheat at 119 and marriages at 67, for 1803 wheat at 59 and marriages at 94; for 1805 the numbers are 90 and 80, for 1807 they are 75 and 84, for 1812 they are 126 and 82, for 1815 they are 66 and 100, for 1817 they are 97 and 88, for 1822 they are 45 and 99

3 Since 1820 the average price of wheat has seldom exceeded 60*s*. and never 75*s* . and the successive inflations of commerce which culminated and broke in 1826, 1836—9, 1848, 1856, 1866 and 1873 exercised an influence on the marriage-rate

BOOK IV. CH IV.

Since 1873 though the average real income of the population of England has indeed been increasing, its rate of increase has been less than in the preceding years, and meanwhile there has been a continuous fall of prices, and consequently a continuous fall in the money-incomes of many classes of society. Now people are governed in their calculations as to whether they can afford to marry or not, more by the money income which they expect to be able to get, than by elaborate calculations of changes in its purchasing power. And therefore the standard of living among the working classes has been rising rapidly, perhaps more rapidly than at any other time in English history: their household expenditure measured in money has remained about stationary, and measured in goods has increased very fast. The English marriage-rate fell from 8·8 per 1000 in 1873, to 7·1 in 1886, the lowest rate that has occurred since civil registration began. It has since risen to 7·8 in 1891 and fallen to 7·4 in 1893.

The price of wheat and the marriage-rate now sometimes fall together

Meanwhile the price of wheat has also fallen very much, and a marked fall in the marriage-rate for the whole country has often accompanied a marked fall in the price of wheat The statistics even seem to suggest that this is not a merely casual coincidence, but that the price of bread is now so low that a further fall in its price does not perceptibly and at once affect the marriage-rate among the population at large; and that its more rapid influence in checking marriages among the agricultural population and those directly de-

about equal with changes in the price of corn. When the two causes act together the effects are very striking thus between 1829 and 1834, there was a recovery of prosperity accompanied by a steady fall in the price of wheat and marriages rose from a hundred and four to a hundred and twenty-one thousand. The marriage-rate rose again rapidly between 1842 and 1845 when the price of wheat was a little lower than in the preceding years, and the business of the country was reviving; and again under similar circumstances between 1847 and 1853 and between 1862 and 1865

A comparison of the marriage-rate with the harvests in Sweden for the years 1749 to 1883 is given by Sir Rawson Rawson in the *Statistical Journal* for December 1885. The harvest does not declare itself till part of the year's tale of marriages is made up, and further the inequalities of harvests are to some extent compensated for by the storage of grain; and therefore the individual harvest figures do not correspond closely with the marriage-rate. But when several good or bad harvests come together, the effect in increasing or diminishing the marriage rate is very clearly marked

pendent on them is sufficient to lower the average marriage-rate for the kingdom[1]. Again, it must be remembered that those alternate inflations and contractions of credit which more chiefly govern the fluctuations in the employment, and therefore in the marriage-rate of the people, tend to raise and lower respectively general prices, and the price of wheat among others, though less than most others[2].

Scotland

There is much to be learnt from the history of population in Scotland and in Ireland. In the lowlands of Scotland a high standard of education, the development of mineral resources, and close contact with their richer English neighbours have combined to afford a great increase of average income to a rapidly increasing population. On the other hand, the inordinate growth of population in Ireland before the potato-famine in 1847, and its steady diminution since that time, will remain for ever landmarks in economic history.

Ireland

Note on International Vital Statistics.

The adjoining tables show the main movements of population in some of the chief countries of the world. [They are compiled chiefly from figures arranged by Signor Bodio in *Movimento del Stato Civile, Confronti Internazionali*, 1884, and *Bulletin de l'Institut International de Statistique*, Vol. VII.; while the last three columns are taken mainly from M Levasseur's *La Population Française*, III 240—1. See also his diagram on p. 248.]

Comparing the habits of different nations with the aid of the adjoining tables, we find that in the Teutonic countries of Central and Northern Europe, the age of marriage is kept late, partly in consequence of the early years of manhood being spent in the army; but that it has been very early in Russia, where, at all events under the old régime, the family group insisted on the son's bringing a wife to help in the work of the household as early as possible, even if he had to leave her for a time and go to earn his living elsewhere. In the United Kingdom

[1] But the statistical problem suggested by a comparison of marriage-rates and prices of wheat, as for instance in the Reports of the Registrar-General, is not so simple as it appears; and it may be questioned whether its true solution has yet been reached.

[2] Statistics of exports are among the best indications of commercial prosperity, and in the article already quoted, Dr Ogle has shown a correspondence between the marriage-rate and the exports per head. Compare diagrams in Vol II p 12 of Levasseur's *La Population Française;* and with regard to Massachusetts by Mr Willcox in the *Political Science Quarterly*, Vol. VIII pp 76—82.

Countries.	1 Marriages per 1000 living		2 Percentage of bride-grooms not over 25 years.		3 Percentage of brides not over 20 years.		4 Births per 1000 living.		5 Births to a marriage.
	1865 to 83.	1887 to 91.	1865 to 83.	1887 to 91.	1865 to 83.	1887 to 91	1865 to 83.	1887 to 91	1865 to 83.
Europe	8 3 –	—	39 3	—	24 0	—	38 7 –	—	4 7
England & Wales	8 1 –	7 5	51 3	45 6	14 4	11 1	35 1 –	31·3	4·3
Scotland ...	7 2 –	6 6	42·3	38 2	13 4	11 6	34 7 –	31·1	4·8
Ireland........	4 8 –	4 4	32 6	33 6	13 5	11 8	26 4 –	22 8	5 5
Sweden ...	6 5 +	6 0	23 3	26 8	5 6	6 4	30 2 –	28 4	4 6
Holland ...	8 0 –	7 0	26·6	31·0	—	10 ?	35 9 –	33 4	4 5
Belgium ...	7 2 –	7 2	22 6	27 0	6 4	8·?	31 5 –	29 3	4 4
France	7 8 –	7 3	27 0	27 3	21 2	20 5	25 4 –	23 0	3 3
Prussia	8 6 –	8·1	—	—	10 3	8 1	38 8 –	37 2	4 5
Saxony.. ...	9 2 –	9 3	34 7	39·0	10 7	7 6	42·4 –	41 8	4·6
Bavaria	8 5 –	7·0	18 9	29·4	6 4	10 7	39 5 +	35·9	4 7
Switzerland	7 4 –	7 1	26 5	27 3	8 8	7 2	30 2 –	27 7	4 1
Austria	8 4 –	7 7	—	—	18 1	17·3	38 4 +	38 0	4 5
Hungary	10 3 –	8 6	31 7	—	36·0	36 7	43 0 +	42 8	4 2
Spain ..	7 3	5 6	38 4	41 9	—	—	33 9 –	36 3	4 6
Italy	7 7 +	7 7	26 0	—	16 9	23 4	36 8 –	37 6	4 8
Russia	9 4 –	—	68 5	64 1	58 0	56 3	49 4 +	—	5 3
United States	—	—	—	—	—	—	—	—	—
Massachusetts ...	9 4 –	9 3	40 0	37 5	18 9	16 1	25 7 –	25 8	2 7

and America there is no compulsory service, and men marry early. In France, contrary to general opinion, early marriages on the part of men are not rare, while on the part of women they are more common than in any country for which we have statistics, except the Sclavonic countries (among which we may reckon Hungary), where they are much the highest

The marriage-rate is generally highest where the number of early marriages is the greatest; and so also is the fecundity of marriages But there are some striking exceptions Thus the number of children to a marriage is exceptionally low in France, and even lower in Massachusetts, though the age of marriage is not particularly high in either of these countries, and it is not very low in Sweden, where very few women marry under twenty.

The marriage-rate, the birth-rate and the death-rate are diminishing in almost every country, in spite of the unexpected fact that the percentage of bridegrooms who are not over twenty-five years of age is increasing in nearly every country, for which the figures are given. (The exceptions are Great Britain, Russia and Massachusetts. Nearly the same is true of the percentage of bridegrooms not over thirty years of age; see *Bulletin de Statistique*, Vol. VII p. 16) The percentage of brides who are not over twenty years of age seems to be on the whole nearly stationary, though it is falling rapidly in some countries, and notably in the United Kingdom and the same seems to be true of those who are not over twenty-five.

6 Deaths per 1000 living 1865 to 83	1890	7 Deaths percentage under five years of age.	8 Annual percentage increase 1860 to 1880. natural	actual	9 Population in millions (partly estimated) 1801	1840.	1890	Countries.
28 1 –	—	32 3	10 6	—	175 0	250·6	360 9	Europe
21·4 –	19 5	24·9	13 7	13 2	8 9	15 7	28 8	England & Wales
21 4 –	19 7	28 1	13 3	10·2	1 6	2 6	4 0	Scotland
17 8 +	18 2	16 5	8 6	– 6 9*	?	8 0	4·7	Ireland
18·9 –	17·1	22 2	11·3	7·7	2 8	8·1	4 8	Sweden
24 6 –	20 5	—	11 3	10 2	2 0	2·9	4 5	Holland
22 4 –	20 8	25 3	9 1	8 4	—	4 1	6 1	Belgium
23 8 –	22 8	25 8	1 6	2 5	33 1	34 1	38 5	France
26 5 –	24 2	32·4	12 3	9 4	8 7	15 1	29 9	Prussia
29 0 –	26 9	—	13 4	14 9	—	—	3 5	Saxony
30 6 +	27 3	39 3	8 9	7 1	—	—	5 6	Bavaria
23 1 –	20 9	24 9	7 1	6 2	1 8	2 2	2·9	Switzerland
31 0 –	29 4	39 0	7 4	7 7	} 25 8	35 8	41 0	Austria
38 2 +	32 0	—	4 8	4 8				Hungary
29 1 –	—	—	4 8	3 3	11 0	12 0	17·2	Spain
29 1 –	26 4	37 8	7 7	6 8	—	—	30·2	Italy
35 7 –	—	42 3	13 7	12 9	35 0	54·6	98 6	Russia
—	—	—	—	23·6	5 4	17 1	62·6	United States
19 2 +	—	27 9	6 5	18 7	4	7	12·2	Massachusetts

The general mortality is high where the birth-rate is high. For instance, both are high in Russia and Hungary, both are low in Sweden, France and Massachusetts

In France and in Massachusetts the "natural" increase is very small; but there is an excess of immigration over emigration, which raises the actual rate of increase In all other countries of Europe except France, Saxony and Austria proper, emigration exceeds immigration: the natural rate of increase is greater than the actual

In comparing the aggregates of population shown in the last three tables, it must be recollected that the areas of Russia and the United States were much larger in 1890 than in 1801, those of Prussia and the Austrian Empire rather larger while that of France was much smaller; for in 1801 it had included Belgium, and part of Germany and Italy.

The signs + and – in the first column of division 1 indicate that the corresponding figures for the last five years of the period were respectively greater or less than those for the first five years of the period 1865—1883, that is, that the marriage-rate was tending to increase or to diminish; and similarly for divisions 4 and 6 It will be noted that they generally point in the same direction as the subsequent changes shown by the second columns of those divisions.

The groups of years for which the figures are collected differ slightly in some cases from those given at the heads of the various columns

CHAPTER V.

THE HEALTH AND STRENGTH OF THE POPULATION.

BOOK IV CH V

The basis of industrial efficiency.

§ 1. We have next to consider the conditions on which depend health and strength, physical, mental and moral. They are the basis of industrial efficiency, on which the production of material wealth depends; while conversely the chief importance of material wealth lies in the fact that, when wisely used, it increases the health and strength, physical, mental and moral of the human race.

Physical exertion

In many occupations industrial efficiency requires little else than physical vigour; that is, muscular strength, a good constitution and energetic habits In estimating muscular, or indeed any other kind of strength for industrial purposes, we must take account of the number of hours in the day, of the number of days in the year, and the number of years in the lifetime, during which it can be exerted. But with this precaution we can measure a man's muscular exertion by the number of feet through which his work would raise a pound weight, if it were applied directly to this use; or in other words by the number of "foot pounds" of work that he does[1].

[1] This measure can be applied directly to most kinds of navvies' and porters' work, and indirectly to many kinds of agricultural work. In a controversy that was waged after the great agricultural lock-out as to the relative efficiency of unskilled labour in the South and North of England, the most trustworthy measure was found in the number of tons of material that a man would load into a cart in a day Other measures have been found in the number of acres reaped or mown, or the number of bushels of corn reaped &c but these are unsatisfactory, particularly for comparing different conditions of agriculture: since the implements used, the nature of the crop and the mode of doing the work all vary widely Thus nearly all comparisons between mediæval and modern work and

requires nervous as well as muscular strength

Although the power of sustaining great muscular exertion seems to rest on constitutional strength and other physical conditions, yet even it depends also on force of will, and strength of character. Energy of this kind, which may perhaps be taken to be the strength of the man, as distinguished from that of his body, is moral rather than physical; but yet it depends on the physical condition of nervous strength. This strength of the man himself, this resolution, energy and self-mastery, or in short this "vigour" is the source of all progress: it shows itself in great deeds, in great thoughts and in the capacity for true religious feeling[1].

Vigour works itself out in so many forms, that no simple measure of it is possible. But we are all of us constantly estimating vigour, and thinking of one person as having more "backbone," more "stuff in him," or as being "a stronger man" than another. Business men even in different trades, and University men even when engaged in different studies,

wages based on the wages of reaping, mowing &c are valueless until we have found means to allow for the effects of changes in the methods of agriculture It costs for instance less labour than it did to reap by hand a crop that yields a hundred bushels of corn, because the implements used are better than they were but it may not cost less labour to reap an acre of corn; because the crops are heavier than they were

In backward countries, particularly where there is not much use of horses or other draught animals, a great part of men's and women's work may be measured fairly well by the muscular exertion involved in it But in England less than one-sixth of the industrial classes are now engaged on work of this kind; while the force exerted by steam-engines alone is more than twenty times as much as could be exerted by the muscles of all Englishmen

[1] This must be distinguished from nervousness, which, as a rule, indicates a general deficiency of nervous strength; though sometimes it proceeds from nervous irritability or want of balance A man who has great nervous strength in some directions may have but little in others, the artistic temperament in particular often develops one set of nerves at the expense of others but it is the weakness of some of the nerves, not the strength of the others, that leads to nervousness The most perfect artistic natures seem not to have been nervous Leonardo da Vinci and Shakespeare for example The term "nervous strength" corresponds in some measure to *Heart* in Dr Engel's great division of the elements of efficiency into (*a*) Body, (*b*) Reason, and (*c*) Heart (*Leib, Verstand und Herz*), and he classifies activities according to the permutations *a*, *ab*, *ac*, *abc*, *acb*; *b*, *ba*, *bc*, *bca*, *bac*, *c*, *ca*, *cb*, *cab*, *cba* the order in each case being that of relative importance, and a letter being omitted where the corresponding element plays only a very small part.

In the war of 1870 Berlin University students, who seemed to be weaker than the average soldier, were found to be able to bear fatigue better

BOOK IV CH V

get to estimate one another's strength very closely It soon becomes known if less strength is required to get a "first class" in one study than another.

The influence of climate, and race.

§ 2 In discussing the growth of numbers a little has been said incidentally of the causes which determine length of life. but they are in the main the same as those which determine constitutional strength and vigour, and they will occupy our attention again in the present chapter.

The first of these causes is the climate. In warm countries we find early marriages and high birth-rates, and in consequence a low respect for human life: this has probably been the cause of a great part of the high mortality that is generally attributed to the insalubrity of the climate[1].

Vigour depends partly on race qualities: but these, so far as they can be explained at all, seem to be chiefly due to climate[2].

The necessaries of life Food

§ 3. Climate has also a large share in determining the necessaries of life, the first of which is food Much depends on the proper preparation of food; and a skilled housewife

[1] A warm climate impairs vigour. It is not altogether hostile to high intellectual and artistic work but it prevents people from being able to endure very hard exertion of any kind for a long time More sustained hard work can be done in the cooler half of the temperate zone than anywhere else; and most of all in places such as England and her counterpart New Zealand, where sea-breezes keep the temperature nearly uniform. The summer heats and winter colds of many parts of Europe and America, where the mean temperature is moderate, have the effect of shortening the year for working purposes by about two months. Extreme and sustained cold is found to dull the energies, partly perhaps it causes people to spend much of their time in close and confined quarters inhabitants of the Arctic regions are generally incapable of long-continued severe exertion. In England popular opinion has insisted that a "warm Yule-tide makes a fat churchyard,' but statistics prove beyond question that it has the opposite effect the average mortality is highest in the coldest quarter of the year, and higher in cold winters than in warm But in warm climates the autumn is generally the most unhealthy part of the year. In India moisture is more hurtful to health and strength than either heat or cold: while the dry cold of Colorado, Canada and the Alps is often beneficial to those who are well fed, clothed and housed

[2] Race history is a fascinating but disappointing study for the economist. for conquering races generally incorporated the women of the conquered, they often carried with them many slaves of both sexes during their migrations, and slaves were less likely than freemen to be killed in battle or to adopt a monastic life. In consequence nearly every race had much servile, that is mixed blood in it and as the share of servile blood was largest in the industrial classes, a race history of industrial habits seems impossible.

with ten shillings a week to spend on food will often do more for the health and strength of her family than an unskilled one with twenty The great mortality of infants among the poor is largely due to the want of care and judgment in preparing their food, and those who do not entirely succumb to this want of motherly care often grow up with enfeebled constitutions

Scarcity that increases mortality;

In all ages of the world except the present, want of food has caused wholesale destruction of the people. Even in London in the seventeenth and eighteenth centuries the mortality was eight per cent greater in years of dear corn than in years of cheap corn[1] But gradually the effects of increased wealth and improved means of communication are making themselves felt nearly all over the world; the severity of famines is mitigated even in such a country as India, and they are unknown in Europe and in the New World In England now want of food is scarcely ever the direct cause of death: but it is a frequent cause of that general weakening of the system which renders it unable to resist disease, and it is a chief cause of industrial inefficiency

We have already seen that the necessaries for efficiency vary with the nature of the work to be done, but we must now examine this subject a little more closely

and scarcity that lowers vigour

As regards muscular work in particular there is a close connection between the supply of food that a man has, and his available strength. If the work is intermittent, as that of some dock labourers, a cheap but nutritious grain diet is sufficient But for very heavy continuous strain such as is involved in puddlers' and the hardest navvies' work, food is required which can be digested and assimilated even when the body is tired This quality is still more essential in the food of the higher grades of labour, whose work involves great nervous strain; though the quantity required by them is generally small.

Clothing, house-room and firing

After food, the next necessaries of life and labour, are clothing, house-room and firing. When they are deficient,

[1] This was proved by Farr, who eliminated disturbing causes by an instructive statistical device (*Vital Statistics*, p 139)

BOOK IV. CH. V.

the mind becomes torpid, and ultimately the physical constitution is undermined. When clothing is very scanty, it is generally worn night and day, and the skin is allowed to be enclosed in a crust of dirt. A deficiency of house-room, or of fuel, causes people to live in a vitiated atmosphere which is injurious to health and vigour; and not the least of the benefits which English people derive from the cheapness of coal, is the habit, peculiar to them, of having well-ventilated rooms even in cold weather. Badly-built houses with imperfect drainage cause diseases which even in their slighter forms weaken vitality in a wonderful way, and overcrowding leads to moral evils which diminish the numbers and lower the character of the people.

Rest.

Rest is as essential for the growth of a vigorous population as the more material necessaries of food, clothing, &c. Overwork of every form lowers vitality, but anxiety, worry, and excessive mental strain have a fatal influence in undermining the constitution, in impairing fecundity and diminishing the vigour of the race.

Hopefulness, freedom and change.

§ 4. Next come three closely allied conditions of vigour, namely, hopefulness, freedom, and change. All history is full of the record of inefficiency caused in varying degrees by slavery, serfdom, and other forms of civil and political oppression and repression. Freedom and hope increase not only man's willingness but also his power for work; physiologists tell us that a given exertion consumes less of the store of nervous energy if done under the stimulus of pleasure than of pain: and without hope there is no enterprise. Security of person and property are two conditions of this hopefulness and freedom; but security always involves restraints on freedom, and it is one of the most difficult problems of civilisation to discover how to obtain the security which is a condition of freedom without too great a sacrifice of freedom itself. Changes of work, of scene, and of personal associations bring new thoughts, call attention to the imperfections of old methods, stimulate a "divine discontent," and in every way develop creative energy.

In all ages colonies have been apt to outstrip their mother countries in vigour and energy. This has been due partly to the abundance of land and the cheapness of necessaries at their command; partly to that natural selection of the strongest characters for a life of adventure, and partly to physiological causes connected with the mixture of races: but perhaps the most important cause of all is to be found in the hope, the freedom and the changefulness of their lives[1]

The influence of mothers,

Freedom so far has been regarded as freedom from external bonds. But that higher freedom, which comes of self-mastery, is an even more important condition for the highest work. The elevation of the ideals of life on which this depends, is due on the one side to political and economic causes, and on the other to personal and religious influences; among which the influence of the mother in early childhood is supreme.

and of occupation

§ 5. Bodily and mental health and strength are much influenced by occupation[2] At the beginning of this century

[1] By converse with others who come from different places, and have different customs, travellers learn to put on its trial many a habit of thought or action which otherwise they would have always acquiesced in as though it were a law of nature Moreover, a shifting of places enables the more powerful and original minds to find full scope for their energies and to rise to important positions whereas those who stay at home are often over much kept in their places Few men are prophets in their own land; neighbours and relations are generally the last to pardon the faults and to recognize the merits of those who are less docile and more enterprising than those around them It is doubtless chiefly for this reason that in almost every part of England a disproportionately large share of the best energy and enterprise is to be found among those who were born elsewhere

But change may be carried to excess, and when population shifts so rapidly, that a man is always shaking himself loose from his reputation, he loses some of the best external aids to the formation of a high moral character The extreme hopefulness and restlessness of those who wander to new countries lead to much waste of effort in half acquiring technical skill, and half finishing tasks which are speedily abandoned in favour of some new occupation

[2] The rate of mortality is low among ministers of religion and schoolmasters, among the agricultural classes, and in some other industries such as those of wheelwrights, shipwrights and coal-miners It is high in lead and tin mining, in file-making and earthenware manufacture. But neither these nor any other regular trade show as high a rate of mortality as is found among London general labourers and costermongers, while the highest of all is that of servants in inns. Such occupations are not directly injurious to health, but they attract those who are weak in physique and in character and they encourage irregular habits A good account of the influence of occupation on death-rates is given in the supplement to the forty-fifth (1885) Annual Report of the Registrar-General, pp xxv. to lxiii. See also Farr's *Vital Statistics*, pp 392—411, Mr Humphreys' paper on *Class Mortality Statistics* in the *Statistical Journal* for June, 1887, and the literature of the Factory Acts generally

BOOK IV. CH. V

the conditions of factory work were needlessly unhealthy and oppressive for all, and especially for young children. But Factory and Education Acts have removed the worst of these evils from factories, though many of them still linger about domestic industries and the smaller workshops.

The higher wages, the greater intelligence, and the better medical facilities of townspeople should cause infant mortality to be much lower among them than in the country. But it is generally higher, especially where there are many mothers who neglect their family duties in order to earn money wages.

Influence of town life.

§ 6. In almost all countries there is a constant migration towards the towns[1]. The large towns and especially London absorb the very best blood from all the rest of England; the most enterprising, the most highly gifted, those with the highest *physique* and the strongest characters go there to find scope for their abilities. But by the time their children and children's children have grown up without healthy play, and without fresh air, there is often little trace left of their original vigour.

[1] Davenant (*Ballance of Trade*, A D 1699, p. 20), following Gregory King, proves that according to official figures London has an excess of deaths over births of 2000 a year, but an immigration of 5000, which is more than half of what he calculates, by a rather risky method, to be the true net increase of the population of the country He reckons that 530,000 people live in London, 870,000 in the other cities and market towns, and 4,100,000 in villages and hamlets Compare these figures with the census of 1891; where we find London with a population of over 4,000,000, five more towns with an average of over 400,000 and fifty-six more ranging from 250,000 down to 50,000 with an average of 100,000 Nor is this all for many suburbs whose population is not counted in, are often really parts of the big towns, and in some cases the suburbs of several adjacent towns run into one another, making them all into one gigantic, though rather scattered town. The suburbs of Liverpool are growing so fast at the expense of the city, that its actual increase is less than its excess of births over deaths; those who go out from it exceed in numbers those who emigrate into it, as was shown by Mr Cannan in the *Economic Journal*, vol IV. A suburb of Manchester is counted as a large town with 200,000 inhabitants; and the same is true of West Ham, a suburb of London

Similar changes are taking place elsewhere Thus the population of Paris has grown twelve times as fast during the present century as that of France. The towns of Germany are increasing at the expense of the country by one half per cent of the population yearly. In the United States there was in 1800 no town with more than 75,000 inhabitants; and now there are three with more than 1,000,000 each, and thirteen more with above 200,000 each. More than a third of the population of Victoria are collected in Melbourne

We shall presently need to discuss the causes of the growth of great cities,

It is sometimes urged that the death-rate in some large towns, and especially in London, is not as high as might have been anticipated if town life is really injurious to health and vigour. But this argument seems untrustworthy, partly because many of the town influences which lower vigour, do not much affect mortality, and partly because the majority of immigrants into the towns are in the full strength of youth, and of more than average energy and courage; while young people whose parents live in the country generally go home when they become seriously ill[1].

It is not to be concluded from this that the race is degenerating physically, nor even that its nervous strength is on the whole decaying On the contrary the opposite is plainly true of those boys and girls who are able to enter freely into modern outdoor amusements, who frequently spend holidays in the country and whose food, clothing and medical care are abundant, and governed by the best

especially in English speaking countries On the growth of modern cities generally see Longstaff's *Studies in Statistics* and Levasseur's *La Population Française*, Book II ch xv

It must be recollected that the characteristics of town life increase in intensity for good and for evil with every increase in the size of a town, and its suburbs Fresh country air has to pass over many more sources of noisome vapour before it reaches the average Londoner than before it reaches the average inhabitant of a small town The Londoner has generally to go far before he can reach the freedom and the restful sounds and sights of the country London therefore with 4,000,000 inhabitants adds to the urban character of England's life far more than a hundred times as much as a town of 40,000 inhabitants

[1] The mortality of females in London between the ages of fifteen and thirty-five is, chiefly for this reason, abnormally low. If however a town has a stationary population its vital statistics are more easily interpreted; and selecting Coventry as a typical town, Mr Galton has calculated that the adult children of artisan townsfolk are little more than half as numerous as those of labouring people who live in healthy country districts When a place is decaying, the young and strong and hearty drift away from it, leaving the old and the infirm behind them, and consequently the birth-rate is generally low On the other hand, a centre of industry that is attracting population is likely to have a very high birth-rate, because it has more than its share of people in the full vigour of life. This is especially the case in the coal and iron towns, partly because they do not suffer, as the textile towns do, from a deficiency of males; and partly because miners as a class marry early In some of them, though the death-rate is high, the excess of the birth-rate over it exceeds 20 per thousand of the population. The death-rate is generally highest in towns of the second order, chiefly because their sanitary arrangements are not yet as good as those of the very largest towns

BOOK IV. CH V

modern knowledge[1] But until quite recently the children of the working classes in large towns have had a bad time: and it is doubtful whether the recent diminution of their hours of labour, the advances of sanitation and medical science, improvement of their food and clothing, of their education and even in some cases their playgrounds quite makes up for the evils inherent in town life[2].

Nature left to herself tends to weed out the weak, but man has interfered

§ 7. And there are yet other causes for anxiety. For there is some partial arrest of that selective influence of struggle and competition which in the earlier stages of civilization caused those who were strongest and most vigorous to leave the largest progeny behind them; and to which, more than any other single cause, the progress of the human race is due. In the later stages of civilization the rule has indeed long been that the upper classes marry late, and in consequence have fewer children than the working classes. but this has been compensated for by the fact that among the working classes themselves the old rule has held, and the vigour of the nation that is tending to be damped out among the upper classes is thus replenished by the fresh stream of strength that is constantly welling up

[1] See an excellent article by Prof Clifford Allbutt in the *Contemporary Review*, Feb 1895 Prof Haycraft (*Darwinism and Race Progress*) argues in the opposite direction He lays just stress on the dangers to the human race which would result from a diminution of those diseases, such as phthisis and scrofula, which attack chiefly people of weak constitution, and thus exercise a selective influence on the race, unless it were accompanied by corresponding improvements in other directions. But phthisis does not kill all its victims, there is some net gain in a diminution of its power of weakening them

[2] There is therefore no better use for public and private money than in providing public parks and playgrounds in large cities, in contracting with railways to increase the number of the workmen's trains run by them, and in helping those of the working classes who are willing to leave the large towns to do so, and to take their industries with them, while money spent on reducing the cost of living in large towns by building workmen's houses at a loss or in other ways, is likely to do almost as much harm as good, and sometimes even more. If the numbers of the working classes in the large towns are reduced to those whose work must be carried on there, the scarcity of their labour will enable them to command high wages, and therefore if sanitary laws and rules against overcrowding are rigidly enforced, and space enough is secured to provide opportunities of healthy play for their children, those who live in large towns will have a better chance of leaving a healthy progeny behind them, and meanwhile some check will be given to the migration from the country to the towns See an article on *Where to House the London Poor* by the present writer in the *Contemporary Review*, Feb 1884

from below. But in France for a long time, and recently in America, and England, some of the abler and more intelligent of the working class population have shown signs of a disinclination to have large families, and this is a source of danger

Thus there are increasing reasons for fearing, that while the progress of medical science and sanitation is saving from death a continually increasing number of the children of those who are feeble physically and mentally; many of those who are most thoughtful and best endowed with energy, enterprise and self-control are tending to defer their marriages and in other ways to limit the number of children whom they leave behind them The motive is sometimes selfish, and perhaps it is best that hard and frivolous people should leave but few descendants of their own type But more often it is a desire to secure a good social position for their children This desire contains many elements that fall short of the highest ideals of human aims, and in some cases, a few that are distinctly base; but after all it has been one of the chief factors of progress, and those who are affected by it include many of those whose children would probably be among the best and strongest of the race[1]

[1] It has already been noticed that the celibacy of the religious orders probably did not affect the growth of numbers very much it gave a particular direction to the forces tending to keep that growth in check, but it probably did not add much to their effects Its main influence was not on the quantity but on the quality of the population "Whenever a man or woman was possessed of a gentle nature that fitted him or her to deeds of charity, to meditation, to literature or to art, the social condition of the time was such that they had no refuge elsewhere than in the bosom of the Church But the Church chose to preach and enact celibacy .. She practised those arts which breeders would use who aimed at creating ferocious, churlish, and stupid natures No wonder that club law prevailed for centuries in Europe" Meanwhile by her persecutions of those who were "the most fearless, truthseeking, and intelligent in their modes of thought and therefore the most suitable parents of a high civilisation, she put a strong check, if not a direct stop, to their progeny" (Galton, *Hereditary Genius*, p. 356)

In modern times the same evil on a larger scale was seen in the Southern States of America, where manual work became disgraceful to the white man, so that if unable to have slaves himself he led a paltry degenerate life, and seldom married Again, on the Pacific Slope, there were at one time just grounds for fearing that all but highly skilled work would be left to the Chinese, and that the white men would live in an artificial way in which a family became a great expense In this case Chinese lives would have been substituted for American, and the average quality of the human race would have been lowered

BOOK IV. CH. V

The State gains much from large families of healthy children.

It must be remembered that the members of a large family educate one another, they are usually more genial and bright, often more vigorous in every way than the members of a small family. Partly, no doubt, this is because their parents were of unusual vigour; and for a like reason they in their turn are likely to have large and vigorous families. The progress of the race is due to a much greater extent than appears at first sight to the descendants of a few exceptionally large and vigorous families.

The evils of infant mortality

But on the other hand there is no doubt that the parents can often do better in many ways for a small family than a large one. Other things being equal, an increase in the number of children who are born causes an increase of infantile mortality, and that is an unmixed evil The birth of children who die early from want of care and adequate means is a useless strain to the mother and an injury to the rest of the family[1]. And though these evils may be reduced within small compass by those parents who are exceptionally good managers, yet example is always more potent than precept, and habits of prudence will not spread among the people, so long as the natural leaders of the people marry early and have larger families than they can expect to bring up well if they should meet with any considerable misfortunes in their own career[2].

Practical conclusion

§ 8 There are other considerations of which account ought to be taken; but so far as the points discussed in this chapter are concerned, it seems *primâ facie* advisable that people should not bring children into the world till they can see their way to giving them at least as good an education both physical and mental as they themselves had; and that

[1] The extent of the infant mortality that arises from preventable causes may be inferred from the facts that while the annual death-rate of children under five years of age is only about two per cent. in the families of peers and is less than three per cent for the whole of the upper classes, it is between six and seven per cent. for the whole of England For the upper classes the expectation of life at birth is 53 years, and at ten years of age it is 52 years but for the whole of England the expectation of life at birth is only 41 years, while at ten years of age, instead of being lower, it rises to 47 years (See Mr Humphreys' paper in the *Statistical Journal* for June, 1883)

[2] On the other hand M Leroy Beaulieu says that in France the parents of but one or two children are apt to indulge them, and be over-careful about them to the detriment of their boldness, enterprise and endurance (See *Statistical Journal*, Vol 54, pp. 378—9)

it is best to marry moderately early provided there is sufficient self-control to keep the family within the requisite bounds without transgressing moral laws. The general adoption of these principles of action, combined with an adequate provision of fresh air and of healthy play for our town populations, could hardly fail to cause the strength and vigour of the race to improve. And we shall presently find reasons for believing that if the strength and vigour of the race improves, the increase of numbers will not for a long time to come cause a diminution of the average real income of the people.

The swaying to-and-fro of the forces of good and evil.

Thus then the progress of knowledge, and in particular of medical science, the ever-growing activity and wisdom of Government in all matters relating to health, and the increase of material wealth, all tend to lessen mortality and to increase health and strength, and to lengthen life. On the other hand, vitality is lowered and the death-rate raised by the rapid increase of town life, and by the tendency of the higher strains of the population to marry later and to have fewer children than the lower. If the former set of causes were alone in action, but so regulated as to avoid the danger of over-population, it is probable that man would quickly rise to a physical and mental excellence superior to any that the world has yet known; while if the latter set acted unchecked, he would speedily degenerate

The former slightly preponderate

As it is, the two sets hold one another very nearly in balance, the former slightly preponderating While the population of England is growing nearly as fast as ever, those who are out of health in body or mind are certainly not an increasing part of the whole; and the rest are much better fed and clothed, and with a few exceptions are stronger than they were[1].

[1] The old English Life Table, based on the figures of the years 1838—54, shows one-half of the males dying before they are 45, and of the females before they are 47, while the New Table, based on the figures of 1871—80, raises these ages to 47 and 52 respectively The death-rate is much lower than it was in the earlier years of life, though higher in the later years and of the total number of years added to life by the greater longevity, two-thirds fall within the most important period of 25 to 65 years of age See Supplement to the 45th Annual Report of the Registrar-General, and Mr Humphreys' paper in the *Statistical Journal* for June, 1883 On the comparative length of life in different countries, see Dr Bodio's work already referred to, and Dr Perozzo's *Sulla Classificazione per Eta*, &c

CHAPTER VI.

INDUSTRIAL TRAINING.

BOOK IV. CH. VI.

§ 1. Having discussed the causes which determine the growth of a numerous and vigorous population, we have next to consider the training that is required to develop its industrial efficiency.

The form which natural vigour takes depends largely on training

The natural vigour that enables a man to attain great success in any one pursuit would generally have served him in good stead in almost any other. But there are exceptions. Some people, for instance, seem to be fitted from birth for an artistic career, and for no other; and occasionally a man of great practical genius is found to be almost devoid of artistic sensibility. But a race that has great nervous strength seems generally able, under favourable conditions, to develop in the course of a few generations ability of almost any kind that it holds in specially high esteem A race that has acquired vigour in war or in the ruder forms of industry sometimes gains intellectual and artistic power of a high order very quickly, and nearly every literary and artistic epoch of classical and mediæval times has been due to a people of great nervous strength, who have been brought into contact with noble thoughts before they have acquired much taste for artificial comforts and luxuries.

The defects of our own age are apt to be overestimated

The growth of this taste in our own age has prevented us from taking full advantage of the opportunities our largely increased resources give us of consecrating the greater part of the highest abilities of the race to the highest aims. But perhaps the intellectual vigour of the age appears less than it really is, in consequence of the growth of scientific pursuits.

For in art and literature success is often achieved while genius still wears the fascinating aspect of youth; but in modern science so much knowledge is required for originality, that before a student can make his mark in the world, his mind has often lost the first bloom of its freshness; and further the real value of his work is not often patent to the multitude as that of a picture or poem generally is[1] In the same way the solid qualities of the modern machine-tending artisan are rated more cheaply than the lighter virtues of the mediæval handicraftsman. This is partly because we are apt to regard as commonplace those excellences which are common in our own time; and to overlook the fact that the term "unskilled labourer" is constantly changing its meaning.

Skilled and unskilled labour

§ 2 Very backward races are unable to keep on at any kind of work for a long time; and even the simplest forms of what we regard as unskilled work is skilled work relatively to them; for they have not the requisite assiduity, and they can acquire it only by a long course of training. But where education is universal, an occupation may fairly be classed as unskilled, though it requires a knowledge of reading and writing Again, in districts in which manufactures have long been domiciled, a habit of responsibility, of carefulness and promptitude in handling expensive machinery and materials becomes the common property of all, and then much of the work of tending machinery is said to be entirely mechanical and unskilled, and to call forth no human faculty that is worthy of esteem But in fact it is probable that not one-tenth of the present populations of the world have the mental and moral faculties, the intelligence, and the self-control that are required for it· perhaps not one-half could

Skill with which we are familiar we often do not recognize as skill.

[1] In this connection it is worth while to notice that the full importance of an epoch making idea is often not perceived in the generation in which it is made. it starts the thoughts of the world on a new track, but the change of direction is not obvious until the turning-point has been left some way behind In the same way the mechanical inventions of every age are apt to be underrated relatively to those of earlier times For a new discovery is seldom fully effective for practical purposes till many minor improvements and subsidiary discoveries have gathered themselves around it an invention that makes an epoch is very often a generation older than the epoch which it makes. Thus it is that each generation seems to be chiefly occupied in working out the thoughts of the preceding one, while the full importance of its own thoughts is as yet not clearly seen

BOOK IV. CH. VI

be made to do the work well by steady training for two generations. Even of a manufacturing population only a small part are capable of doing many of the tasks that appear at first sight to be entirely monotonous. Machine-weaving, for instance, simple as it seems, is divided into higher and lower grades; and most of those who work in the lower grades have not "the stuff in them" that is required for weaving with several colours. And the differences are even greater in industries that deal with hard materials, wood, metals, or ceramics.

Mere manual skill is losing importance relatively to general intelligence and vigour of character.

Some kinds of manual work require long-continued practice in one set of operations, but these cases are not very common, and they are becoming rarer: for machinery is constantly taking over work that requires manual skill of this kind. It is indeed true that a general command over the use of one's fingers is a very important element of industrial efficiency; but this is the result chiefly of nervous strength, and self-mastery. It is of course developed by training, but the greater part of this may be of a general character and not special to the particular occupation; just as a good cricketer soon learns to play tennis well, so a skilled artisan can often move into other trades without any great and lasting loss of efficiency.

Manual skill that is so specialized that it is quite incapable of being transferred from one occupation to another is becoming steadily a less and less important factor in production. Putting aside for the present the faculties of artistic perception and artistic creation, we may say that what makes one occupation higher than another, what makes the workers of one town or country more efficient than those of another, is chiefly a superiority in general sagacity and energy which is not specialized to any one trade.

To be able to bear in mind many things at a time, to have everything ready when wanted, to act promptly and show resource when anything goes wrong, to accommodate oneself quickly to changes in details of the work done, to be steady and trustworthy, to have always a reserve of force which will come out in emergency, these are the qualities which make a great industrial people. They are not peculiar to any occupation, but are wanted in all; and if they cannot always be easily transferred from one trade to other kindred trades, the chief reason is that they require to be supplemented by some knowledge of materials and familiarity with special processes

General and Specialized ability

We may then use the term *general ability* to denote those faculties and that general knowledge and intelligence which are in varying degrees the common property of all the higher grades of industry: while that manual dexterity and that acquaintance with particular materials and processes which are required for the special purposes of individual trades may be classed as *specialized ability*

The causes that determine the supply of general ability

§ 3. General ability depends largely on the surroundings of childhood and youth In this the first and far the most powerful influence is that of the mother[1]. Next comes the influence of the father, of other children, and in some cases of servants[2] As years pass on the child of the working man learns a great deal from what he sees and hears going on around him; and when we inquire into the advantages for starting in life which children of the well-to-do classes have over those of artisans, and which these in their turn have over the children of unskilled labourers, we shall have to consider these influences of home more in detail But at present we may pass to consider the more general influences of school education

The home

School.

Little need be said of general education, though the influence even of that on industrial efficiency is greater than

[1] According to Mr Galton the statement that all great men have had great mothers goes too far but that shows only that the mother's influence does not outweigh all others; not that it is not greater than any one of them He says that the mother's influence is most easily traceable among theologians and men of science, because an earnest mother leads her child to feel deeply about great things, and a thoughtful mother does not repress, but encourages that childish curiosity which is the raw material of scientific habits of thought

[2] There are many fine natures among domestic servants But those who live in very rich houses are apt to get self-indulgent habits, to overestimate the importance of wealth, and generally to put the lower aims of life above the higher, in a way that is not common with independent working people The company in which the children of some of our best houses spend much of their time, is less ennobling than that of the average cottage Yet in these very houses, no servant who is not specially qualified is allowed to take charge of a young pointer or a young horse

BOOK IV. CH. VI.

it appears. It is true that the children of the working classes must very often leave school, when they have but learnt the elements of reading, writing, arithmetic and drawing, and it is sometimes argued that part of the little time spent on these subjects would be better given to practical work. But the advance made during school-time is important not so much on its own account, as for the power of future advance which a school education gives. Reading and writing afford the means of that wider intercourse which leads to breadth and elasticity of mind, and which is enabling the working man of to-day to be as capable a citizen as was the country gentleman of last century[1].

The functions of liberal education.

The absence of a careful general education for the children of the working classes, has been hardly less detrimental to industrial progress than the narrow range of the old grammar-school education of the middle classes. Till recently indeed it was the only one by which the average schoolmaster could induce his pupils to use their minds in anything higher than the absorption of knowledge It was therefore rightly called liberal, because it was the best that was to be had. But it failed in its aim of familiarizing the citizen with the great thoughts of antiquity, it was generally forgotten as soon as school-time was over, and it raised an injurious antagonism between business and culture Now however the advance of knowledge is enabling us to use science and art to supplement the curriculum of the grammar-school, and to give to those who can afford it an education that develops their best faculties, and starts them on the track of thoughts which will most stimulate the higher activities of their minds in after-life.

But while a truly liberal general education adapts the mind to use its best faculties in business and to use business itself as a means of increasing culture, it does not concern itself with the details of particular trades. That task is left for technical education.

[1] It is true that learning to spell does not educate the faculties to any considerable extent, and that the time spent on it is nearly wasted If spelling and pronunciation could be brought into harmony in the English language, as they are in most other languages, children would, it has been estimated, be able to read fluently a year earlier than they can now

Technical education.

§ 4. Technical education has in like manner raised its aims in recent years. It used to mean little more than imparting that manual dexterity and that elementary knowledge of machinery and processes which an intelligent lad quickly picks up for himself when his work has begun; though if he has learnt it beforehand, he can perhaps earn a few shillings more at starting than if he had been quite ignorant. But such so-called education does not develop faculties; it rather hinders them from being developed. A lad, who has picked up the knowledge for himself has educated himself by so doing; and he is likely to make better progress in the future than one who has been taught in a school of this old-fashioned kind. Technical education is however outgrowing its mistakes; and is aiming, firstly, at giving a general command over the use of eyes and fingers[1] (though there are signs that this work is being taken over by general education, to which it properly belongs); and secondly at imparting artistic skill and knowledge, and methods of investigation, which are useful in particular occupations, but are seldom properly acquired in the course of practical work[1].

[1] As Mr Nasmyth says, if a lad having dropped two peas at random on a table, can readily put a third pea midway in a line between them, he is on the way to become a good mechanic. Command over eye and hand is gained in the ordinary English games, no less than in the playful work of the Kinder-garten. Drawing has always been on the border line between work and play.

[2] Continental systems of technical education give habits of order, assiduity and docility, they store the mind with useful information, and the German system, in particular, has produced a race of men who are better fitted in some respects to do the work required of the middle ranks of industry than any that the world has ever seen. Aided by their knowledge of modern languages German clerks, commercial agents and scientific advisers are gaining ground in many countries, partly no doubt because they have more energy than most of their countrymen who have stayed at home. They also make excellent administrators under Government, and that is a chief reason why business under the control of Government compares so much more favourably with that under private management in Germany than in England. But the balance of evidence seems to show that the German system, excellent as it is in many ways, is not in all respects well suited for developing that daring energy and restless enterprise which go to the root of the hardest difficulties. For this purpose the existing English system is already superior in some respects, and its deficiencies, though still great, are rapidly being filled up.

On the whole we may say that at present England is very much behindhand as regards the provision for the commercial as well as the technical education of the proprietors and principal managers of industrial works, but that, chiefly through the influence of the Science and Art Department of South Kensington,

BOOK IV. CH VI

The aims of English education reform.

According to the best English opinions, technical education for the higher ranks of industry should keep the aim of developing the faculties almost as constantly before it as general education does. It should rest on the same basis as a thorough general education, but should go on to work out in detail special branches of knowledge for the benefit of particular trades[1]. Our aim should be to add the scientific training in which the countries of Western Europe are ahead of us to that daring and restless energy and those practical instincts, which seldom flourish unless the best years of youth are spent in the workshop; recollecting always that whatever a youth learns for himself by direct experience in well-conducted works, teaches him more and stimulates his mental activity more than if it were taught him by a master in a technical school with model instruments[2].

Apprenticeships, their past,

The old apprenticeship system is not exactly suited to modern conditions and it has fallen into disuse; but a sub-

elementary (or lower secondary) scientific and technical education covers a wider area in this than in any other country Unfortunately, however, these advantages are prevented from being turned to the best account by the still backward condition of our elementary schools Compare Sir Bernhard Samuelson's Preface to Mr Montague's excellent summary of the Report of the Commission on Technical Education

[1] See the *Report* 1884 *of the Commissioners on Technical Instruction*, Vol. I pp. 506, 514, also the opinions of Sir Lowthian Bell, Prof. Huxley, Dr Siemens and others in Vol. III of the Report, also Scott Russell's *Technical Education* See also the various publications of the National Association for the Promotion of Technical Education One of the weakest points of technical education is that it does not educate the sense of proportion and the desire for simplicity of detail. The English, and to an even greater extent, the Americans, have acquired in actual business the faculty of rejecting intricacies in machinery and processes, which are not worth what they cost, and practical instinct of this kind often enables them to succeed in competition with Continental rivals who are much better educated

[2] A good plan is that of spending the six winter months of several years after leaving school in learning science in College, and the six summer months as articled pupils in large workshops. The present writer introduced this plan several years ago at University College, Bristol, and it has also been adopted in Japan (See the Report above quoted, Vol III p. 140) But it has practical difficulties which can be overcome only by the cordial and generous co-operation of the heads of large firms with the College authorities Another excellent plan is that adopted in the school attached to the works of Messrs Mather and Platt at Manchester "The drawings made in the school are of work actually in progress in the shops. One day the teacher gives the necessary explanations and calculations, and the next day the scholars see, as it were on the anvil, the very thing which has been the subject of his lecture"

stitute for it is wanted Within the last few years many of the ablest manufacturers have begun to set the fashion of making their sons work through every stage in succession of the business they will ultimately have to control, but this splendid education can be had only by a few. So many and various are the branches of any great modern industry that it would be impossible for the employers to undertake, as they used to do, that every youth committed to their care should learn all; and indeed a lad of ordinary ability would be bewildered by the attempt But it does not seem impracticable to revive the apprenticeship system in a modified form[1].

and their possible future

Inventions in England and other countries.

The great epoch-making inventions in industry came till recently almost exclusively from England. But now other nations are joining in the race. The excellence of the common schools of the Americans, the variety of their lives, the interchange of ideas between different races among them, and the peculiar conditions of their agriculture have developed a restless spirit of inquiry, while technical education is now being pushed on with great vigour[2]. On the other hand, the diffusion of scientific knowledge among the middle and even the working classes of Germany, combined

[1] The employer binds himself to see that the apprentice is thoroughly taught in the workshop all the subdivisions of one great division of his trade, instead of letting him learn only one of these subdivisions, as too often happens now The apprentice's training would then often be as broad as if he had been taught the whole of the trade as it existed a few generations ago, and it might be supplemented by a theoretical knowledge of all branches of the trade, acquired in a technical school Something resembling the old apprenticeship system has recently come into vogue for young Englishmen who desire to learn the business of farming under the peculiar conditions of a new country and there are some signs that the plan may be extended to the business of farming in this country, for which it is in many respects admirably adapted But there remains a great deal of education suitable to the farmer and to the farm-labourer which can best be given in agricultural colleges and dairy schools.

Meanwhile many great agencies for the technical education of adults are being rapidly developed, such as public exhibitions, trade associations and congresses, and trade journals Each of them has its own work to do; in agriculture and some other trades the greatest aid to progress is perhaps found in public shows; but those industries which are more advanced and in the hands of persons of studious habits owe more to the diffusion of practical and scientific knowledge by trade journals, which, aided by changes in the methods of industry and also in its social conditions, are breaking up trade secrets and helping men of small means in competition with their richer rivals

[2] The splendid Massachusetts Institute of Technology is under the direction of the economist, General Walker

BOOK IV CH. VI.

with their familiarity with modern languages and their habits of travelling in pursuit of instruction, has enabled them to keep up with English and American mechanics and to take the lead in many of the applications of chemistry to business[1].

A high education will increase the efficiency of the lower grades of industry indirectly rather than directly

§ 5. It is true that there are many kinds of work which can be done as efficiently by an uneducated as by an educated workman: and that the higher branches of education are of little direct use except to employers and foremen and a comparatively small number of artisans. But a good education confers great indirect benefits even on the ordinary workman. It stimulates his mental activity; it fosters in him a habit of wise inquisitiveness, it makes him more intelligent, more ready, more trustworthy in his ordinary work; it raises the tone of his life in working hours and out of working hours, it is thus an important means towards the production of material wealth; at the same time that, regarded as an end in itself, it is inferior to none of those which the production of material wealth can be made to subserve.

We must however look in another direction for a part, perhaps the greater part, of the immediate economic gain which the nation may derive from an improvement in the general and technical education of the mass of the people. We must look not so much at those who stay in the rank and file of the working classes, as at those who rise from a humble birth to join the higher ranks of skilled artisans, to become foremen or employers, to advance the boundaries of science, or possibly to add to the national wealth in art and literature.

Much of the best natural ability in the nation is born

The laws which govern the birth of genius are inscrutable. It is probable that the percentage of children of the working classes who are endowed with natural abilities of the highest order is not so great as that of the

[1] The heads of almost every progressive firm on the Continent have carefully studied processes and machinery in foreign lands. The English are great travellers; but partly perhaps on account of their ignorance of other languages they seem hardly to set enough store on the technical education that can be gained by the wise use of travel. See the Report quoted above, Vol. I. p. 281 and *passim*.

children of people who have attained or have inherited a higher position in society. But since the manual labour classes are four or five times as numerous as all other classes put together, it is not unlikely that more than half the best natural genius that is born into the country belongs to them, and of this a great part is fruitless for want of opportunity. There is no extravagance more prejudicial to the growth of national wealth than that wasteful negligence which allows genius that happens to be born of lowly parentage to expend itself in lowly work. No change would conduce so much to a rapid increase of material wealth as an improvement in our schools, and especially those of the middle grades, provided it is combined with an extensive system of scholarships, which will enable the clever son of a working man to rise gradually from school to school till he had the best theoretical and practical education which the age can give

among the working classes, and too often runs to waste now.

To the abilities of children of the working classes may be ascribed the greater part of the success of the free towns in the Middle Ages and of Scotland in recent times. Even within England itself there is a lesson of the same kind to be learnt progress is most rapid in those parts of the country in which the greatest proportion of the leaders of industry are the sons of working men. For instance, the beginning of the manufacturing era found social distinctions more closely marked and more firmly established in the South than in the North of England. In the South something of a spirit of caste has held back the working men and the sons of working men from rising to posts of command, and the old established families have been wanting in that elasticity and freshness of mind which no social advantages can supply, and which comes only from natural gifts. This spirit of caste, and this deficiency of new blood among the leaders of industry, have mutually sustained one another; and there are not a few towns in the South of England whose decadence within living memory can be traced in a great measure to this cause.

§ 6. Education in art stands on a somewhat different footing from education in hard thinking: for while the latter

Education in art

BOOK IV CH VI.

nearly always strengthens the character, the former not unfrequently fails to do this Nevertheless the development of the artistic faculties of the people is in itself an aim of the very highest importance, and is becoming a chief factor of industrial efficiency.

We are here concerned almost exclusively with those branches of art which appeal to the eye. For though literature and music contribute as much and more to the fulness of life, yet their development does not directly affect, and does not depend upon, the methods of business, the processes of manufacture and the skill of artisans.

Among peoples who change their habits slowly, art is guided by well matured instincts,

The artisan of Europe in the Middle Ages, and of eastern countries now, has perhaps obtained credit for more originality than he has really possessed. Eastern carpets, for instance, are full of grand conceptions: but if we examine a great many examples of the art of any one place, selected perhaps from the work of several centuries, we often find very little variety in their fundamental ideas. In fact every designer in a primitive age is governed by precedent· only very daring people depart from it, even they do not depart far, and their innovations are subjected to the test of experience, which, in the long run, is infallible. For though the crudest and most ridiculous fashions in art and in literature will be accepted by the people for a time at the bidding of their social superiors, nothing but true artistic excellence has enabled a ballad or a melody, a style of dress or a pattern of furniture to retain its popularity among a whole nation for many generations together. Those innovations, then, which were inconsistent with the true spirit of art were suppressed, and those that were on the right track were retained, and became the starting-point for further progress; and thus traditional instincts played a great part in preserving the purity of the industrial arts in Oriental countries, and to a less extent in mediæval Europe. But in the modern era of rapid changes—some caused by fashion and some by the beneficial movements of industrial and social progress—everyone feels free to make a new departure, everyone has to rely in the main on his own resources. there is no slowly matured public criticism to guide him.

But this is not the only, perhaps not the chief disadvantage under which artistic design labours in our own age. There is no good reason for believing that the children of ordinary workmen in the Middle Ages had more power of artistic origination than those of ordinary village carpenters or blacksmiths of to-day; but if one among ten thousand happened to have genius, it found vent in his work and was stimulated by the competition of the gilds and in other ways. But the modern artisan is apt to be occupied in the management of machinery; and though the faculties which he develops may be more solid and may help more in the long run towards the highest progress of the human race, than did the taste and fancy of his mediæval predecessor, yet they do not contribute directly towards the progress of art And if he should find in himself a higher order of ability than among his fellows, he will probably endeavour to take a leading part in the management of a trades-union or some other society, or to collect together a little store of capital and to rise out of that trade in which he was educated. These are not ignoble aims; but his ambition would perhaps have been nobler and more fruitful of good to the world, if he had stayed in his old trade and striven to create works of beauty which should live after he had gone

and often attracts a large share of natural genius

It must however be admitted that he would have great difficulties in doing this The shortness of the time which we allow ourselves for changes in the arts of decoration is scarcely a greater evil than the width of the area of the world over which they are spread; for that causes a further distraction of the hasty and hurried efforts of the designer, by compelling him to be always watching the world movements of the supply of and demand for art products. This is a task for which the artisan, who works with his own hands, is not well fitted; and in consequence now-a-days the ordinary artisan finds it best to follow and not to lead. Even the supreme skill of the Lyons weaver shows itself now almost exclusively in an inherited power of delicate

But in modern times design is almost limited to a narrow profession;

BOOK IV. CH. VI

manipulation, and fine perception of colour, that enable him to carry out perfectly the ideas of professional designers.

which is forced to pay court to fashion

Increasing wealth is enabling people to buy things of all kinds to suit the fancy, with but a secondary regard to their powers of wearing; so that in all kinds of clothing and furniture it is every day more true that it is the pattern which sells the things. And, so great is the hold which French taste has on the average consumer, that many English manufacturers who hold their own against the world would, it is said, be driven out of the market if they had to depend on English patterns. This is however partly due to the fact that Paris having got the lead in fashions, a Parisian design is likely to be in harmony with the coming fashions and to sell better than a design of equal intrinsic worth from elsewhere[1].

It is probably true, though opinion is still somewhat divided on the subject, that schools of artistic design are not so urgently needed in England, as a more efficient and cheaper system of popular education in art proper For in this respect perhaps more than any other, the child of the English workman has less opportunities than his continental rivals, and especially those of France. If we could secure that all who have a natural turn for it should receive a fairly good education in art proper, the applications of art to design and decoration might perhaps be left pretty much to take care of themselves[2]

[1] French designers find it best to live in Paris if they stay for long out of contact with the central movements of fashion they seem to fall behindhand. Most of them have been educated as artists, but have failed of their highest ambition It is only in exceptional cases, as for instance for the Sèvres china, that those who have succeeded as artists find it worth their while to design Englishmen can, however, hold their own in designing for Oriental markets, and there is evidence that the English are at least equal to the French in originality, though they are inferior in quickness in seeing how to group forms and colours so as to obtain an effective result (See the *Report on Technical Education*, Vol I pp. 256, 261, 324, 325 and Vol III pp 151, 152, 202, 208, 211 and *passim*) It is probable that the profession of the modern designer has not yet risen to the best position which it is capable of holding For it has been to a disproportionate extent under the influence of one nation, and that nation is one whose works in the highest branches of art have seldom borne to be transplanted. They have indeed often been applauded and imitated at the time by other nations, but they have as yet seldom struck a key note for the best work of later generations

[2] The highest branches of art escape indeed many of the disadvantages under which artistic design labours in our modern age For he who designs a picture

Technical education then, though it cannot add much directly to the supply of genius in art, any more than it can in science or in business, can yet save much natural artistic genius from running to waste, and it is called on to do this all the more because the training that was given by the older forms of handicraft can never be revived on a large scale.

Education a national investment.

§ 7. We may then conclude that the wisdom of expending public and private funds on education is not to be measured by its direct fruits alone. It will be profitable as a mere investment, to give the masses of the people much greater opportunities than they can generally avail themselves of For by this means many, who would have died unknown, are enabled to get the start needed for bringing out their latent abilities And the economic value of one great industrial genius is sufficient to cover the expenses of the education of a whole town; for one new idea, such as Bessemer's chief invention, adds as much to England's productive power as the labour of a hundred thousand men Less direct, but not less in importance, is the aid given to production by medical discoveries such as those of Jenner or Pasteur, which increase our health and working power; and again by scientific work such as that of mathematics or biology, even though many generations may pass away before it bears visible fruit in greater material well-being. All that is spent during many years in opening the means of higher education to the masses would be well paid for if it called out one more Newton or Darwin, Shakespeare or Beethoven.

There are few practical problems in which the economist has a more direct interest than those relating to the principles on which the expense of the education of children should be divided between the State and the parents. But we

executes it with his own hands, there is not in painting nor even in sculpture that divorce between design and technical familiarity with the material which is so great an obstacle to the progress of our metal and wood work

But the painters themselves have put on record in the portrait galleries the fact that in mediæval times, and even later, their art attracted a larger share of the best intellect than it does now, when the ambition of youth is tempted by the excitement of modern business, when its zeal for imperishable achievements finds a noble field in the romantic discoveries of modern science, and, lastly, when a great deal of excellent talent is insensibly diverted from high aims by the ready pay to be got by hastily writing half thoughts for periodical literature

BOOK IV. CH. VI. must now consider the conditions that determine the power and the will of the parents to bear their share of the expense, whatever it may be.

and a duty of parents. Most parents are willing enough to do for their children what their own parents did for them; and perhaps even to go a little beyond it if they find themselves among neighbours who happen to have a rather higher standard. But to do more than this requires, in addition to the moral qualities of unselfishness and a warmth of affection that are perhaps not rare, a certain habit of mind which is as yet not very common. It requires the habit of distinctly realizing the future, of regarding a distant event as of nearly the same importance as if it were close at hand (discounting the future at a low rate of interest), this habit is at once a chief product and a chief cause of civilization, and is seldom fully developed except among the middle and upper classes of the more cultivated nations.

Mobility between grades and within grades § 8 Parents generally bring up their children to occupations in their own grade, and therefore the total supply of labour in any grade in one generation is in a great measure determined by the numbers in that grade in the preceding generation, yet within the grade itself there is greater mobility If the advantages of any one occupation in it rise above the average, there is a quick influx of youth from other occupations into the grade. The vertical movement from one grade to another is seldom very rapid or on a very large scale, but, when the advantages of a grade have risen relatively to the difficulty of the work required of it, many small streams of labour, both youthful and adult, will begin to flow towards it; and though none of them may be very large, they will together have a sufficient volume to satisfy before long the increased demand for labour in that grade

Provisional conclusion. We must defer to a later stage a fuller discussion of the obstacles which the conditions of any place and time oppose to the free mobility of labour, and also of the inducements which they offer to anyone to change his occupation or to bring up his son to an occupation different from his own But we have seen enough to conclude that, other things being equal, an increase in the earnings that are to be got by labour increases its rate of growth; or, in other words, a rise in its demand price increases the supply of it If the state of knowledge, and of social and domestic habits be given; then the numbers, if not vigour of the people as a whole, and in a yet greater degree the numbers of any trade in particular, may be said to have a supply price in this sense, that there is a certain level of the demand price which will keep them stationary, that a higher price would cause them to increase, and that a lower price would cause them to decrease[1].

[1] Mill was so much impressed by the difficulties that beset a parent in the attempt to bring up his son to an occupation widely different in character from his own, that he said —"So complete, indeed, has hitherto been the separation, so strongly marked the line of demarcation, between the different grades of labourers, as to be almost equivalent to an hereditary distinction of caste; each employment being chiefly recruited from the children of those already employed in it, or in employments of the same rank with it in social estimation, or from the children of persons who, if originally of a lower rank, have succeeded in raising themselves by their exertions The liberal professions are mostly supplied by the sons of either the professional or the idle classes the more highly skilled manual employments are filled up from the sons of skilled artisans or the class of tradesmen who rank with them: the lower classes of skilled employments are in a similar case; and unskilled labourers, with occasional exceptions, remain from father to son in their pristine condition. Consequently the wages of each class have hitherto been regulated by the increase of its own population, rather than that of the general population of the country" But he goes on, "The changes, however, now so rapidly taking place in usages and ideas are undermining all these distinctions"

His prescience has been vindicated by the progress of change since he wrote The broad lines of division which he pointed out have been almost obliterated by the rapid action of those causes which, as we saw earlier in the chapter, are reducing the amount of skill and ability required in some occupations and increasing it in others We cannot any longer regard different occupations as distributed among four great planes, but we may perhaps think of them as resembling a long flight of steps of unequal breadth, some of them being so broad as to act as landing stages Or even better still we might picture to ourselves two flights of stairs, one representing the "hard-handed industries" and the other "the soft-handed industries", because the vertical division between these two is in fact as broad and as clearly marked as the horizontal division between any two grades

Mill's classification had lost a great part of its value when Cairnes adopted it (*Leading Principles*, p 72) A classification more suited to our existing conditions is offered by Mr Giddings (*Political Science Quarterly*, Vol II pp 69—71) It is open to the objection that it draws broad lines of division where Nature has made no broad lines, but it is perhaps as good as any division of industry into four grades can be His divisions are (i) *automatic manual labour*, including common labourers and machine tenders; (ii) *responsible manual labour*, including those who can be entrusted with some responsibility and labour of self-direction, (iii) *automatic brain workers*, such as bookkeepers, and (iv) *responsible brain workers*, including the superintendents and directors

CHAPTER VII.

THE GROWTH OF CAPITAL AND OTHER FORMS OF WEALTH.

BOOK IV CH VII

Forms of wealth among barbarous peoples.

§ 1. The earliest forms of wealth were probably implements for hunting and fishing, and personal ornaments; and, in cold countries, clothing and huts[1]. During this stage the domestication of animals began, but at first they were probably cared for chiefly for their own sake, because they were beautiful, and it was pleasant to have them; they were, like articles of personal ornament, desired because of the immediate gratification to be derived from their possession rather than as a provision against future needs[2]. Gradually the herds of domesticated animals increased; and during the pastoral stage they were at once the pleasure and the pride of their possessors, the outward emblems of social rank, and by far the most important store of wealth accumulated as a provision against future needs

Forms of wealth in early stages of civilization

As numbers thickened and the people settled down to agriculture, cultivated land took the first place in the inventory of wealth; and that part of the value of the land which was due to improvements (among which wells held a conspicuous place) became the chief element of capital, in the

[1] A short but suggestive study of the growth of wealth in its early forms, and of the arts of life, is given in Tylor's *Anthropology*

[2] Bagehot (*Economic Studies*, pp 163—5) after quoting the evidence which Mr Galton has collected on the keeping of pet animals by savage tribes, points out that we find here a good illustration of the fact that however careless a savage race may be for the future, it cannot avoid making some provision for it A bow, a fishing-net, which will do its work well in getting food for to day, must be of service for many days to come. a horse or a canoe that will carry one well to-day, must be a stored-up source of many future enjoyments The least provident of barbaric despots may raise a massive pile of buildings, because it is the most palpable proof of his present wealth and power.

narrower sense of the term. Next in importance came houses, domesticated animals, and in some places boats and ships; but the implements of production, whether for use in agriculture or in domestic manufactures, remained for a long time of little value. In some places, however, precious stones and the precious metals in various forms became early a leading object of desire and a recognized means of hoarding wealth, while, to say nothing of the palaces of monarchs, a large part of social wealth in many comparatively rude civilizations took the form of edifices for public purposes, chiefly religious, and of roads and bridges, of canals and irrigation works. For many thousands of years these remained the chief forms of accumulated wealth. In towns indeed houses and household furniture took the first place, and stocks of the more expensive of raw materials counted for a good deal, but though the inhabitants of the towns had often more wealth per head than those of the country, their total numbers were small, and their aggregate wealth was very much less than that of the country. During all this time the only trade that used very expensive implements was the trade of carrying goods by water: the weaver's looms, the husbandman's ploughs and the blacksmith's anvils were of simple construction and were of little account beside the merchant's ships. But in the eighteenth century England inaugurated the era of expensive implements

Until recently there was little use of expensive forms of auxiliary capital.

The implements of the English farmer had been rising slowly in value for a long time, but the progress was quickened in the eighteenth century After a while the use first of water power and then of steam power caused the rapid substitution of expensive machinery for inexpensive hand tools in one department of production after another. As in earlier times the most expensive implements were ships and in some cases canals for navigation and irrigation, so now they are the means of locomotion in general;—railways and tramways, canals, docks and ships, telegraph and telephone systems and water-works: even gas-works might almost come under this head, on the ground that a great part of their plant is devoted to distributing the gas. After these come mines and iron and chemical works, ship-building yards,

But in recent years they have increased very fast.

BOOK IV. CH. VII.

printing-presses, and other large factories full of expensive machinery.

On whichever side we look we find that the progress and diffusion of knowledge are constantly leading to the adoption of new processes and new machinery which economize human effort on condition that some of the effort is spent a good while before the attainment of the ultimate ends to which it is directed. It is not easy to measure this progress exactly, because many modern industries had no counterpart in ancient times. But let us compare the past and present conditions of the four great industries the products of which have not changed their general character: viz. agriculture, the building, the cloth-making, and the carrying trades. In the first two of these hand work still retains an important place: but even in them there is a great development of expensive machinery. Compare for instance the rude implements of an Indian Ryot even of to-day with the equipment of a progressive Lowland farmer[1]; and consider the brickmaking, mortar-making, sawing, planing, moulding and slotting machines of a modern builder, his steam cranes and his electric light. And if we turn to the textile trades, or at least to those of them which make the simpler products, we find each operative in early times content with implements the cost of which was equivalent to but a few months of his labour, while in modern times it is estimated that for each man, woman and child employed there is a capital in plant alone of about £200, or say the equivalent of five years' labour.

[1] The farm implements for a first class Ryot family, including six or seven adult males, are a few light ploughs and hoes chiefly of wood, of the total value of about 13 rupees (Sir G Phear, *Aryan Village*, p 233) or the equivalent of their work for about a month, while the value of the machinery alone on a well equipped large modern arable farm amounts to £3 an acre (*Equipment of the Farm*, edited by J. C. Morton) or say a year's work for each person employed They include steam-engines, trench, subsoil and ordinary ploughs, some to be worked by steam and some by horse power; various grubbers, harrows, rollers, clod-crushers, seed and manure drills, horse hoes, rakes, hay-making, mowing and reaping machines, steam or horse threshing, chaff cutting, turnip cutting, hay-pressing machines and a multitude of others. Meanwhile there is an increasing use of silos and covered yards, and constant improvements in the fittings of the dairy and other farm buildings, all of which give great economy of effort in the long run, but require a larger share of it to be spent in preparing the way for the direct work of the farmer in raising agricultural produce.

Again the cost of a steam-ship is perhaps equivalent to the labour for ten years or more of those who work her, while a capital of about £900,000,000 invested in railways in England and Wales is equivalent to the work for perhaps twenty years of the 300,000 people employed on them.

And they are likely to continue to increase

§ 2. As civilization has progressed, man has always been developing new wants, and new and more expensive ways of gratifying them. The rate of progress has sometimes been slow, and occasionally there has even been a great retrograde movement; but now we are moving on at a rapid pace that grows quicker every year; and we cannot guess where it will stop. On every side further openings are sure to offer themselves, all of which will tend to change the character of our social and industrial life, and to enable us to turn to account vast stores of capital in providing new gratifications and new ways of economizing effort by expending it in anticipation of distant wants. There seems to be no good reason for believing that we are anywhere near a stationary state in which there will be no new important wants to be satisfied, in which there will be no more room for profitably investing present effort in providing for the future, and in which the accumulation of wealth will cease to have any reward. The whole history of man shows that his wants expand with the growth of his wealth and knowledge[1].

[1] For instance, improvements which have recently been made in some American cities indicate that by a sufficient outlay of capital each house could be supplied with what it does require, and relieved of what it does not, much more effectively than now, so as to enable a large part of the population to live in towns and yet be free from many of the present evils of town life. The first step is to make under all the streets large tunnels, in which many pipes and wires can be laid side by side, and repaired when they get out of order, without any interruption of the general traffic and without great expense. Motive power, and possibly even heat, might then be generated at great distances from the towns (in some cases in coal-mines), and laid on wherever wanted. Soft water and spring water, and perhaps even sea water and ozonized air, might be laid on in separate pipes to nearly every house, while steam-pipes might be used for giving warmth in winter, and compressed air for lowering the heat of summer, or the heat might be supplied by gas of great heating power laid on in special pipes, while light was derived from gas specially suited for the purpose or from electricity; and every house might be in electric communication with the rest of the town. All unwholesome vapours, including those given off by any domestic fires which were still used, might be carried away by strong draughts through long conduits, to be purified by passing through large furnaces and thence away through huge

BOOK IV. CH. VII.

And meanwhile there has been and probably will be a parallel increase in the power to accumulate

And with the growth of openings for the investment of capital there is a constant increase in that surplus of production over the necessaries of life, which gives the power to save. When the arts of production were rude, there was very little surplus, except where a strong ruling race kept the subject masses hard at work on the bare necessaries of life, and where the climate was so mild that those necessaries were small and easily obtained. But every increase in the arts of production, and in the capital accumulated to assist and support labour in future production, increased the surplus out of which more wealth could be accumulated. After a time civilization became possible in temperate and even in cold climates, the increase of material wealth was possible under conditions which did not enervate the worker, and did not therefore destroy the foundations on which it rested[1]. Thus from step to step wealth and knowledge have grown, and with every step the power of saving wealth and extending knowledge has increased

The slow and fitful development of the habit of providing for the future.

§ 3. The habit of distinctly realizing the future and providing for it has developed itself slowly and fitfully in the course of man's history. Travellers tell us of tribes who might double their resources and enjoyments without increasing their total labour, if they would only apply a little in advance the means that lie within their power and their knowledge; as, for instance, by fencing in their little plots of vegetables against the intrusion of wild animals.

But even this apathy is perhaps less strange than the wastefulness that is found now among some classes in our own country. Cases are not rare of men who alternate between earning two or three pounds a week and being reduced to the verge of starvation: the utility of a shilling to them when they are in employment is less than that of a penny when they are out of it, and yet they never attempt to make

chimneys into the higher air To carry out such a scheme in the towns of England would require the outlay of a much larger capital than has been absorbed by our railways This conjecture as to the ultimate course of town improvement may be wide of the truth, but it serves to indicate one of very many ways in which the experience of the past foreshadows broad openings for investing present effort in providing the means of satisfying our wants in the future.

[1] Comp Bk I. Ch. II.

provision for the time of need[1]. At the opposite extreme there are misers, in some of whom the passion for saving borders on insanity; while, even among peasant proprietors and some other classes, we meet not unfrequently with people who carry thrift so far as to stint themselves of necessaries, and to impair their power of future work. Thus they lose every way. they never really enjoy life, while the income which their stored-up wealth brings them is less than they would have got from the increase of their earning power, if they had invested in themselves the wealth that they have accumulated in a material form.

In India, and to a less extent in Ireland, we find people who do indeed abstain from immediate enjoyment and save up considerable sums with great self-sacrifice, but spend all their savings in lavish festivities at funerals and marriages. They make intermittent provision for the near future, but scarcely any permanent provision for the distant future: the great engineering works by which their productive resources have been so much increased, have been made chiefly with the capital of the much less self-denying race of Englishmen

Thus the causes which control the accumulation of wealth differ widely in different countries and different ages. They are not quite the same among any two races, and perhaps not even among any two social classes in the same race They depend much on social and religious sanctions, and it is remarkable how, when the binding force of custom has been in any degree loosened, differences of personal character will cause neighbours brought up under like conditions to differ from one another more widely and more frequently in their habits of extravagance or thrift than in almost any other respect.

Security as a condition of saving.

§ 4. The thriftlessness of early times was in a great measure due to the want of security that those who made provision for the future would enjoy it · only those who were already wealthy were strong enough to hold what they had saved; the laborious and self-denying peasant who had heaped up a little store of wealth only to see it taken from him by a

[1] They "discount" future benefits (comp Book III ch v § 3) at the rate of many thousands per cent. per annum.

stronger hand, was a constant warning to his neighbours to enjoy their pleasure and their rest when they could. The border country between England and Scotland made little progress so long as it was liable to incessant forays; there was very little saving by the French peasants in the last century when they could escape the plunder of the tax-gatherer only by appearing to be poor, or by Irish cottiers, who, on many estates, even a generation ago, were compelled to follow the same course in order to avoid the landlords' claims of exorbitant rents.

Insecurity of this kind has nearly passed away from the civilized world But we are still suffering in England from the effects of the Poor-law which ruled at the beginning of the century, and which introduced a new form of insecurity for the working classes. For it arranged that part of their wages should, in effect, be given in the form of poor relief; and that this should be distributed among them in inverse proportion to their industry and thrift and forethought, so that many thought it foolish to make provision for the future. The traditions and instincts which were fostered by that evil experience are even now a great hindrance to the progress of the working classes; and the principle which nominally at least underlies the present Poor-law, that the State should take account only of destitution and not at all of merit, acts in the same direction though with less force.

Insecurity of this kind also is being diminished: the growth of enlightened views as to the duties of the State and of private persons towards the poor, is tending to make it every day more true that those who have helped themselves and endeavoured to provide for their own future will be cared for by society better than the idle and the thoughtless. But the progress in this direction remains slow, and there remains much to be done yet.

The growth of a money economy gives new temptations to extravagance

§ 5. The growth of a money-economy and of modern habits of business does indeed hinder the accumulation of wealth by putting new temptations in the way of those who are inclined to live extravagantly. In old times if a man wanted a good house to live in he must build it himself; now he finds plenty of good houses to be hired at a rent.

Formerly, if he wanted good beer he must have a good brew-house, now he can buy it more cheaply and better than he could brew it. Now he can borrows books from a library instead of buying them; and he can even furnish his house before he is ready to pay for his furniture. Thus in many ways the modern systems of buying and selling, and lending and borrowing, together with the growth of new wants, lead to new extravagances, and to a subordination of the interests of the future to those of the present

but also a new certainty that savings will really provide what is wanted in the future.

But on the other hand, a money-economy increases the variety of the uses between which a person can distribute his future expenditure. A person who in a primitive state of society stores up some things against a future need, may find that after all he does not need those things as much as others which he has not stored up; and there are many future wants against which it is impossible to provide directly by storing up goods. But he who has stored up capital from which he derives a money income can buy what he will to meet his needs as they arise[1].

And it has enabled people who have no faculty for business to reap the full fruits of saving

Again, modern methods of business have brought with them opportunities for the safe investment of capital in such ways as to yield a revenue to persons who have no good opportunity of engaging in any business,—not even in that of agriculture, where the land will under some conditions act as a trustworthy savings-bank. These new opportunities have induced some people who would not otherwise have attempted it to put by something for their own old age And, what has had a far greater effect on the growth of wealth, it has rendered it far easier for a man to provide a secure income for his wife and children after his death. for, after all, family affection is the main motive of saving.

A few people save for their own sakes

§ 6 There are indeed some who find an intense pleasure in seeing their hoards of wealth grow up under their hands, with scarcely any thought for the happiness that may be got from its use by themselves or by others. They are prompted partly by the instincts of the chase, by the desire to outstrip their rivals; by the ambition to have shown ability

[1] Comp Book III. Ch. v. § 2.

in getting the wealth, and to acquire power and social position by its possession. And sometimes the force of habit, started when they were really in need of money, has given them, by a sort of reflex action, an artificial and unreasoning pleasure in amassing wealth for its own sake. But were it not for the family affections, many who now work hard and save carefully, would not exert themselves to do more than secure a comfortable annuity for their own lives; either by purchase from an insurance company, or by arranging to spend every year, after they had retired from work, part of their capital as well as all their income In the one case they would leave nothing behind them: in the other only provision for that part of their hoped-for old age, from which they had been cut off by death. That men labour and save chiefly for the sake of their families and not for themselves, is shown by the fact that they seldom spend, after they have retired from work, more than the income that comes in from their savings, preferring to leave their stored-up wealth intact for their families; while in this country alone twenty millions a year are saved in the form of insurance policies and are available only after the death of those who save them.

but the chief motive of saving is family affection

A man can have no stronger stimulus to energy and enterprise than the hope of rising in life, and leaving his family to start from a higher round of the social ladder than that on which he began. It may even give him an overmastering passion which reduces to insignificance the desire for ease, and for all ordinary pleasures, and sometimes even destroys in him the finer sensibilities and nobler aspirations But, as is shown by the marvellous growth of wealth in America during the present generation, it makes him a mighty producer and accumulator of riches; unless indeed he is in too great a hurry to grasp the social position which his wealth will give him: for his ambition may then lead him into as great extravagance as could have been induced by an improvident and self-indulgent temperament

The greatest savings are made by those who have been brought up on narrow means to stern hard work, who have retained their simple habits, in spite of success in business, and who nourish a contempt for showy expenditure and a desire to be found at their death richer than they had been thought to be. This type of character is frequent in the quieter parts of old but vigorous countries, and it was very common among the middle classes in the rural districts of England for more than a generation after the pressure of the great French war and the heavy taxes that lingered in its wake

The source of accumulation is surplus income; whether that derived from capital,

§ 7. Next, as to the sources of accumulation. The power to save depends on an excess of income over necessary expenditure; and this is greatest among the wealthy In this country, most of the larger incomes, but only a few of the smaller, are chiefly derived from capital And, early in the present century, the commercial classes in England had much more saving habits than either the country gentlemen or the working classes. These causes combined to make English economists of the last generation regard savings as made almost exclusively from the profits of capital

or rent, the earnings of professional men, and of hired workers

But even in modern England rent and the earnings of professional men and hired workers are an important source of accumulation · and they have been the chief source of it in all the earlier stages of civilization[1]. Moreover, the middle and especially the professional classes have always denied themselves much in order to invest capital in the education of their children, while a great part of the wages of the working classes is invested in the physical health and strength of their children The older economists took too little account of the fact that human faculties are as important a means of production as any other kind of capital; and we may conclude, in opposition to them, that any change in the distribution of wealth which gives more to the wage receivers and less to the capitalists is likely, other things being equal, to hasten the increase of material production, and that it will not perceptibly retard the storing-up of material wealth Of course other things would not be equal if the change were brought about by violent methods which gave a shock to public security But a slight and temporary check to the accumulation of material wealth need not necessarily be an evil, even from a purely economic point of view, if, being made quietly and without disturbance, it provided better oppor-

[1] Comp *Principles of Political Economy*, by Richard Jones

BOOK IV. CH VII

tunities for the great mass of the people, increased their efficiency, and developed in them such habits of self-respect as to result in the growth of a much more efficient race of producers in the next generation. For then it might do more in the long-run to promote the growth of even material wealth than great additions to our stock of factories and steam-engines.

The public accumulations of democracies

A people among whom wealth is well distributed, and who have high ambitions, are likely to accumulate a great deal of public property; and the savings made in this form alone by some well-to-do democracies form no inconsiderable part of the best possessions which our own age has inherited from its predecessors. The growth of the co-operative movement in all its many forms, of building societies, friendly societies, trades unions, of working men's savings-banks &c, shows that, even so far as the immediate accumulation of material wealth goes, the resources of the country are not, as the older economists assumed, entirely lost when they are spent in paying wages[1].

Co-operation

We must call to mind the study already made of the distribution of a commodity between present and deferred uses

§ 8. Having looked at the development of the methods of saving and the accumulation of wealth, we may now return to that analysis of the relations between present and deferred pleasures, which we began from another point of view in our study of Demand[2].

We there saw that anyone who has a stock of a commodity which is applicable to several uses will endeavour to distribute it between them all in such a way, that if he had thought he could increase his happiness by transferring some of it from one use to another he would have done so, and that therefore, if he has made his distribution rightly, he stopped in applying it to each several use at such a point that he got an equal amount of good out of his last, or marginal, appli-

[1] It must however be admitted that what passes by the name of public property is often only nothing more than private wealth borrowed on a mortgage of future public revenues. Municipal gas works for instance are not generally the results of public accumulations. They were built with wealth saved by private persons, and borrowed on public account

[2] Book III ch. v

cation—i.e. on the application that he was only just induced to make of it—to each separate use: or in other words, he distributes it between the different uses in such a way that it has the same marginal utility in each.

We saw, further, that the principle remains the same whether all the uses are present, or some are present and others deferred: but that in this latter case some new considerations enter, of which the chief are that the deferring of a pleasure necessarily introduces some uncertainty as to its ever being enjoyed, and secondly, that, as human nature is constituted, a present pleasure is generally, though not always, preferred to a pleasure that is expected to be equal to it, and is as certain as anything can be in human life.

A person may save even though he prefers present pleasures to future, and he reaps no increment of his means by waiting

A prudent person who thought that he would derive equal pleasures from equal means at all stages of his life, would perhaps endeavour to distribute his means equally over his whole life: and if he thought that there was a danger that his power of earning income at a future date would run short, he would certainly save some of his means for a future date. He would do this not only if he thought that his savings would increase in his hands, but even if he thought they would diminish. He would put by a few fruit and eggs for the winter, because they would then be scarce, though they would not improve by keeping. If he did not see his way to investing his earnings in trade or on loan, so as to derive interest or profits from them, he would follow the example of some of our own forefathers who accumulated small stores of guineas which they carried into the country, when they retired from active life. They reckoned that the extra gratification which they could get by spending a few more guineas while money was coming in fast, would be of less service to them than the comfort which those guineas would buy for them in their old age. The care of the guineas cost them a great deal of trouble, and no doubt they would have been willing to pay some small charge to anyone who would have relieved them from the trouble without occasioning them any sort of risk.

Some saving might

We can therefore imagine a state of things in which stored-up wealth could be put to but little good use, in which

BOOK IV CH. VII.

therefore conceivably be made even if interest were negative,

many persons wanted to make provision for their own future; while but few of those who wanted to borrow goods, were able to offer good security for returning them, or equivalent goods, at a future date. In such a state of things the postponement of, and waiting for enjoyments would be an action that incurred a penalty rather than reaped a reward: by handing over his means to another to be taken care of, a person could only expect to get a sure promise of something less, and not of something more than that which he lent: the rate of interest would be negative[1].

but it is equally true that some work would be done even if there were a penalty for it.

Such a state of things is conceivable. But it is also conceivable, and almost equally probable, that people may be so anxious to work that they will undergo some penalty as a condition of obtaining leave to work. For, as deferring the consumption of some of his means is a thing which a prudent person would desire on its own account, so doing some work is a desirable object on its own account to a healthy person. Political prisoners, for instance, generally regard it as a favour to be allowed to do a little work. And human nature being what it is, we are justified in speaking of the interest on capital as the reward of the sacrifice involved in the waiting for the enjoyment of material resources, because few people would save much without reward, just as we speak of wages as the reward of labour, because few people would work hard without reward[2].

We may therefore call interest the reward of waiting

not of abstinence

The sacrifice of present pleasure for the sake of future, has been called *abstinence* by economists. But this term has been misunderstood: for the greatest accumulators of wealth are very rich persons, some of whom live in luxury, and certainly do not practise abstinence in that sense of the term in which it is convertible with abstemiousness. What economists meant was that, when a person abstained from consuming anything which he had the power of consuming, with the purpose of increasing his resources in the future, his absti-

[1] The suggestion that the rate of interest may conceivably become a negative quantity has been discussed by Prof. Foxwell in a paper on *Some Social Aspects of Banking*, read before the Bankers' Institute in January, 1886.

[2] A Producer's Surplus or Rent is yielded by those waitings which need little or no reward, but are yet rewarded at the market rate, as it is by labour in a like case. See above, p. 217. But we must return to this point.

nence from that particular act of consumption increased the accumulation of wealth. Since, however, the term is liable to be misunderstood, we may with advantage avoid its use, and say that the accumulation of wealth is generally the result of a postponement of enjoyment, or of a *waiting* for it[1].

The "demand price" of accumulation, that is the future pleasure which his surroundings enable a person to obtain by working and waiting for the future, takes many forms: but the substance is always the same The extra pleasure which a peasant who has built a weather-proof hut derives from its usance while the snow is drifting into those of his neighbours who have spent less labour on building theirs, is the price earned by his working and waiting and is similar in all fundamental respects to the interest which the retired physician derives from the capital he has lent to a factory or a mine to enable it to improve its machinery. And on account of the numerical definiteness of the form in which it is expressed, we may take this interest to be the type of and to represent the usance of wealth in other forms

It matters not for our immediate purpose whether the power over the enjoyment for which the person waits, was earned by him directly by labour, which is the original source of nearly all enjoyment, or was acquired by him from others, by exchange or by inheritance, by legitimate trade or by unscrupulous forms of speculation, by spoliation or by fraud the only points with which we are just now concerned are that the growth of wealth involves in general a deliberate waiting for a pleasure which a person has (rightly or wrongly) the power of commanding in the immediate present, and that his willingness so to wait depends on his habit of vividly realizing the future and providing for it.

§ 9. But let us look more closely at the statement that, as human nature is constituted, an increase in the future pleasure

The greater the rate of gain from

[1] Karl Marx and his followers have found much amusement in contemplating the accumulations of wealth which result from the abstinence of Baron Rothschild, which they contrast with the extravagance of a labourer who feeds a family of seven on seven shillings a week, and who, living up to his full income, practises no economic abstinence at all The argument that it is Waiting rather than Abstinence, which is rewarded by Interest and is a factor of production, was given by Prof Macvane in the Harvard *Journal of Economics* for July, 1887

which can be secured by a present given sacrifice will in general increase the amount of present sacrifice that people will make. Suppose, for instance, that villagers have to get timber for building their cottages from the forests; the more distant these are, the smaller will be the return of future comfort got by each day's work in fetching the wood, the less will be their future gain from the wealth accumulated probably by each day's work: and this smallness of the return of future pleasure, to be got at a given present sacrifice, will tend to prevent them from increasing the size of their cottages; and will perhaps diminish on the whole the amount of labour they spend in getting timber. But this rule is not without exception. For, if custom has made them familiar with cottages of only one fashion, the further they are from the woods, and the smaller the usance to be got from the produce of one day's work, the more days' work will they give.

present sacrifice the greater will often be the saving,

but not always

So the higher the rate of interest the greater the saving as a rule,

And similarly if a person expects, not to use his wealth himself, but to let it out on interest, the higher the rate of interest the higher his reward for saving. If the rate of interest on sound investments is 4 per cent, and he gives up £100 worth of enjoyment now, he may expect an annuity of £4 worth of enjoyment: but he can expect only £3 worth, if the rate is 3 per cent And a fall in the rate of interest will generally lower the margin at which a person finds it just not worth while to give up present pleasures for the sake of those future pleasures that are to be secured by saving some of his means It will therefore generally cause people to consume a little more now, and to make less provision for future enjoyment But this rule is not without exception

but there are exceptions to the rule

For indeed Sir Josiah Child remarked two centuries ago, that in countries in which the rate of interest is high, merchants "when they have gotten great wealth, leave trading" and lend out their money at interest, "the gain thereof being so easy, certain and great; whereas in other countries where interest is at a lower rate, they continue merchants from generation to generation, and enrich themselves and the state" And it is as true now, as it was then, that many men retire from business when they are yet almost in the prime of life, and when their knowledge of men and things might enable them to conduct their business more efficiently than ever. Again, as Mr Sargant has pointed out, if a man has decided to go on working and saving till he has provided a certain income for his old age, or for his family after his death, he will find that he has to save more if the rate of interest is low than if it is high Suppose, for instance, that he wishes to provide an income of £400 a year on which he may retire from business, or to insure £400 a year for his wife and children after his death: if then the current rate of interest is 5 per cent, he need only put by £8,000, or insure his life for £8,000, but if it is 4 per cent., he must save £10,000, or insure his life for £10,000

But in spite of exceptions, a fall in the rate of interest tends to make saving less than it otherwise would be

It is then possible that a continued fall in the rate of interest may be accompanied by a continued increase in the yearly additions to the world's capital But none the less is it true that a fall in the distant benefits to be got by a given amount of working and waiting for the future does tend on the whole to diminish the provision which people make for the future, or in more modern phrase, that a fall in the rate of interest tends to check the accumulation of wealth. For though with man's growing command over the resources of nature, he may continue to save much even with a low rate of interest, yet while human nature remains as it is every fall in that rate is likely to cause many more people to save less than to save more than they would otherwise have done.

The causes which govern the accumulation of wealth and its relation to the rate of interest have so many points of contact with various parts of economic science that the study of them cannot easily be brought together in one part of our inquiry Something needed to be said of them before going further; but we must return to them again and discuss them from a more advanced standpoint when we treat of Demand and Supply in relation to Capital. Meanwhile we may sum up provisionally the results of the present chapter.

Provisional conclusion.

§ 10 The accumulation of wealth is governed by a great variety of causes by custom, by habits of self-control and realizing the future, and above all by the power of family affection. Security is a necessary condition for it,

BOOK IV. CH. VII. and the progress of knowledge and intelligence furthers it in many ways

A rise in the rate of interest, or demand price, for saving tends to increase the volume of saving. For in spite of the fact that a few people who have determined to secure an income of a certain fixed amount for themselves or their family will save less with a high rate of interest than with a low rate, it is a nearly universal rule that a rise in the rate increases the *desire* to save; and it often increases the *power* to save, or rather it is often an indication of an increased efficiency of our productive resources but the older economists went too far in suggesting that a rise of interest (or of profits) at the expense of wages always increased the power of saving they forgot that from the national point of view the investment of wealth in the child of the working man is as productive as its investment in horses or machinery.

It must however be recollected that the annual investment of wealth is a small part of the already existing stock, and that therefore the stock would not be increased perceptibly in any one year by even a considerable increase in the annual rate of saving

Note on the Statistics of the Growth of Wealth.

The statistical history of the growth of wealth is singularly poor and misleading This is partly due to difficulties inherent in any attempt to give a numerical measure of wealth which shall be applicable to different places and times, partly to the absence of systematic attempts to collect the necessary facts. The Government of the United States does indeed ask for returns of every person's property, and though the results thus obtained are not very satisfactory, yet they are probably the best we have.

Estimates of the wealth of other countries have to be based almost exclusively on estimates of income, which are capitalized at various numbers of years' purchase, this number being chosen with reference (i) to the general rate of interest current at the time, (ii) to the extent to which the income derived from the use of wealth in any particular form is to be credited (*a*) to the permanent income-yielding power of the wealth itself; and (*b*) to either the labour spent in applying it, or the using up of the capital itself This last head is specially important in the case of ironworks which depreciate rapidly, and still more in the case of such mines as are likely to be speedily exhausted; both must be capitalized at only a few years' purchase. On the other hand, the income-yielding power of land is likely to increase; and where that is the case, the income from land has to be capitalized at a great number of years' purchase (which may be regarded as making a negative provision under the head of ii b)

Land, houses, and live stock are the three forms of wealth which have been in the first rank of importance always and everywhere But land differs from other things in this, that an increase in its value is often chiefly due to an increase in its scarcity, and is therefore a measure rather of growing wants, than of growing means of meeting wants. Thus the land of the United States in 1880 counted as of about equal value with the land of the United Kingdom, and about half that of France Its money value was insignificant a hundred years ago; and if the density of population two or three hundred years hence is nearly the same in the United States as in the United Kingdom, the land of the former will then be worth at least twenty times as much as that of the latter

In the early middle ages the whole value of the land of England was much less than that of the few large-boned but small-sized animals that starved through the winter on it now, though much of the best land is entered under the heads of houses, railways, &c , though the live stock is now probably more than ten times as heavy in aggregate weight, and of better quality, and though there is now abundant farming capital of kinds which were then unknown, yet agricultural land is now worth more than three times as much as the farm stock. The few years of the pressure of the great French war nearly doubled the nominal value of the land of England, and the free trade which has enriched the people has checked the rise in the value of that part of the land which is devoted to agriculture. Thus various causes, of which her free trade policy is the chief, have made the general purchasing power of money rise in England relatively to the continent Early in this century 25 fr would buy more, and especially more of the things needed by the working classes, in France than £1 would in England But now the advantage is the other way: and even if it were true (as Mr Harris argues by methods otherwise open to criticism in the *Statistical Journal*, Vol 57) that the money wealth of France is rising faster than that of England, it might yet be true that the real wealth of England is rising faster than that of France

When account is taken of facts of this class, and also of the fact that a fall in the rate of interest increases the number of years' purchase at which any income has to be capitalized, and therefore increases the value of a property which yields a given income, we see that the estimates of national wealth would be very misleading, even if the

BOOK IV CH VII.

statistics of income on which they were based were accurate. But still such estimates are not wholly without value

Mr Giffen's *Growth of Capital* contains suggestive discussions on many of the figures in the following table

Country and Author of Estimate.	Land. £ million.	Houses, &c. £ million.	Farm-capital. £ million.	Other wealth. £ million.	Total wealth £ million.	Wealth per cap. £
ENGLAND						
1679 (Petty) . .	144	30	36	40	250	42
1690 (Gregory King)	180	45	25	70	320	58
1812 (Colquhoun)	750	300	143	653	1,846	180
1885 (Giffen) . .	1,333	1,700	382	3,012	6,427	315
UNITED KINGDOM						
1812 (Colquhoun) .	1,200	400	228	908	2,736	160
1855 (Edleston) .	1,700	550	472	1,048	3,760	130
1865 (Giffen) . .	1,864	1,031	620	2,598	6,113	200
1875 — . .	2,007	1,420	668	4,453	8,548	260
1885 — .	1,691	1,927	522	5,897	10,037	270
UNITED STATES						
1880 (Census) .	2,040	2,000	480	4,208	8,728	175
1890 — .					13,200	200
FRANCE						
1892 (de Foville)	3,000	2,000	400	4,000	9,400	247
ITALY						
1884 (Pantaleoni) .	1,160	360			1,920	65

An instructive history of changes in the relative wealth of different parts of England has been deduced by Rogers from the assessment of the several counties for the purpose of taxation Le Vicomte d'Avenel's great work *L'Histoire Economique de la Propriété &c* 1200—1800 contains a rich store of materials as to France, and excellent comparative studies of the growth of wealth in France and other nations have been made by MM. Levasseur, Leroy Beaulieu, Neymarck and de Foville; see especially a paper by the last, translated in the *Statistical Journal*, Vol. 56.

CHAPTER VIII.

INDUSTRIAL ORGANIZATION.

BOOK IV CH VIII

The doctrine that organization increases efficiency is old

§ 1. WRITERS on social science from the time of Plato downwards have delighted to dwell on the increased efficiency which labour derives from organization But in this, as in other cases, Adam Smith gave a new and larger significance to an old doctrine by the philosophic thoroughness with which he explained it, and the practical knowledge with which he illustrated it After insisting on the advantages of the division of labour, and pointing out how they render it possible for increased numbers to live in comfort on a limited territory, he argued that the pressure of population on the means of subsistence tends to weed out those races who through want of organization or for any other cause are unable to turn to the best account the advantages of the place in which they live.

Biologists and economists have studied the influence which the struggle for survival exerts on organization

Before Adam Smith's book had yet found many readers, biologists were already beginning to make great advances towards understanding the real nature of the differences in organization which separate the higher from the lower animals, and before two more generations had elapsed, Malthus' historical account of man's struggle for existence started Darwin on that inquiry as to the effects of the struggle for existence in the animal and vegetable world, which issued in his discovery of the selective influence constantly played by it. Since that time biology has more than repaid her debt, and economists have in their turn owed much to the many profound analogies which have been discovered between social and especially industrial organiza-

BOOK IV CH VIII.

tion on the one side and the physical organization of the higher animals on the other In a few cases indeed the apparent analogies disappeared on closer inquiry: but many of those which seemed at first sight most fanciful, have gradually been supplemented by others, and have at last established their claim to illustrate a fundamental unity of action between the laws of nature in the physical and in the moral world. This central unity is set forth in the general rule, to which there are not very many exceptions, that the development of the organism, whether social or physical, involves an increasing subdivision of functions between its separate parts on the one hand, and on the other a more intimate connection between them[1]. Each part gets to be less and less self-sufficient, to depend for its well-being more and more on other parts, so that any disorder in any part of a highly-developed organism will affect other parts also

Differentiation and Integration

This increased subdivision of functions, or "differentiation" as it is called, manifests itself with regard to industry in such forms as the division of labour, and the development of specialized skill, knowledge and machinery: while "integration," that is, a growing intimacy and firmness of the connections between the separate parts of the industrial organism, shows itself in such forms as the increase of security of commercial credit, and of the means and habits of communication by sea and road, by railway and telegraph, by post and printing-press.

The doctrine that those organisms which are the most highly developed, in the sense in which we have just used the phrase, are those which are most likely to survive in the struggle for existence, is itself in process of development. It is not yet completely thought out either in its biological or its economic relations. But we may pass to consider the main bearings in economics of the law that the struggle for existence causes those organisms to multiply which are best fitted to derive benefit from their environment.

[1] Besides the writings of Herbert Spencer on this subject, and Bagehot's *Physics and Politics*, see a brilliant paper by Hackel on *Arbeitstheilung in Menschen- und Thierleben* Reference may also be made to Schaffle's *Bau und Leben des socialen Körpers*, and to Hearn's *Plutology*.

The law of struggle for survival requires to be carefully interpreted.

The law requires to be interpreted carefully: for the fact that a thing is beneficial to its environment will not by itself secure its survival either in the physical or in the moral world. The law of "survival of the fittest" states that those organisms tend to survive which are best fitted to utilize the environment for their own purposes. Now those that utilize the environment most, may turn out to be those that benefit those around them most. But it must not be assumed in any particular case that they are thus beneficial, without special study of the case.

Its harshest features softened by the principle of heredity.

In order therefore that the demand for any industrial arrangement may be certain to call forth a supply, it must be something more than a mere desire for the arrangement, or a need for it, such as a desire on the part of employés for a share in the management and the profits of the factory in which they work, or the need on the part of clever youths for a good technical education. It must be an *efficient demand*; that is, it must take effect by offering payment or some other benefit to those who supply it[1]; otherwise it is not a demand in the sense in which the term is used when it is said that supply naturally and surely follows demand. This seems a hard truth: but some of its harshest features are softened down by the fact that those races, of which the members render unrequited services to other members, are not only the most likely to flourish for the time, but most likely to rear a large number of descendants who inherit their beneficial habits.

Influence of parental care on survival of the species.

§ 2. Even in the vegetable world a species of plants, however vigorous in its growth, which should be neglectful of the interests of its seeds, would soon perish from the earth. The standard of family and race duty is often high in the animal kingdom; and even those predatory animals which we are accustomed to regard as the types of cruelty, which fiercely utilize the environment and do nothing for it in return, must yet be willing as individuals to exert themselves

[1] Like all other doctrines of the same class, this requires to be interpreted in the light of the fact that the effective demand of a purchaser depends on his means, as well as on his wants: a small want on the part of a rich man often has more effective force in controlling the business arrangements of the world than a great want on the part of a poor man.

BOOK IV CH VIII

for the benefit of their offspring. And going beyond the narrower interests of the family to those of the race, we find that among so-called social animals, such as bees and ants, those races survive in which the individual is most energetic in performing varied services for the society without the prompting of direct gain to himself.

In man self-sacrifice becomes deliberate and is the basis of the strength of the race.

But when we come to human beings, endowed with reason and speech, the influence of a tribal sense of duty in strengthening the tribe takes a more varied form. It is true that in the ruder stages of human life many of the services rendered by the individual to others are nearly as much due to hereditary habit and unreasoning impulse, as are those of the bees and ants. But deliberate, and therefore moral, self-sacrifice soon makes its appearance; it is fostered by the far-seeing guidance of prophets and priests and legislators, and is inculcated by parable and legend. Gradually the unreasoning sympathy, of which there are germs in the lower animals, extends its area and gets to be deliberately adopted as a basis of action: tribal affection, starting from a level hardly higher than that which prevails in a pack of wolves or a horde of banditti, gradually grows into a noble patriotism, and religious ideals are raised and purified. The races in which these qualities are the most highly developed are sure, other things being equal, to be stronger than others in war and in contests with famine and disease, and to prevail in the long run Thus the struggle for existence causes in the long run those races of men to survive in which the individual is most willing to sacrifice himself for the benefit of those around him; and which are consequently the best adapted collectively to make use of their environment.

But evil is mixed with the good,

Unfortunately however not all the qualities which enable one race to prevail over another benefit mankind as a whole. It would no doubt be wrong to lay very much stress on the fact that warlike habits have often enabled half-savage races to reduce to submission others who were their superiors in every peaceful virtue, for such conquests have in the long run increased the physical vigour of the world, and its capacity for great things, and ultimately perhaps have done more good than harm But there is no such qualification to the statement that a race does not establish its claim to deserve well of the world by the mere fact that it flourishes in the midst or on the surface of another race. For, though biology and social science alike show that parasites sometimes benefit in unexpected ways the race on which they thrive, yet in many cases they turn the peculiarities of that race to good account for their own purposes without giving any good return. The fact that there is an economic demand for the services of Jewish and Armenian money-dealers in Eastern Europe and Asia, or for Chinese labour in California, is not by itself a proof, nor even a very strong ground for believing, that such arrangements tend to raise the quality of human life as a whole. For, though a race entirely dependent on its own resources can scarcely prosper unless it is fairly endowed with the most important social virtues, yet a race, which has not these virtues and which is not capable of independent greatness, may be able to thrive on its relations with another race. But on the whole, and subject to grave exceptions, those races survive and predominate in which the best qualities are most strongly developed.

especially in the case of a parasitic race.

§ 3. This influence of heredity shows itself nowhere more markedly than in social organization. For that must necessarily be a slow growth, the product of many generations: it must be based on those customs and aptitudes of the great mass of the people which are incapable of quick change In early times when religious, ceremonial, political, military and industrial organization were intimately connected, and were indeed but different sides of the same thing, nearly all those nations which were leading the van of the world's progress were found to agree in having adopted a more or less strict system of caste and this fact by itself proved that the distinction of castes was well suited to its environment, and that on the whole it strengthened the races or nations which adopted it. For since it was a controlling factor of life, the nations which adopted it could not have generally prevailed over others, if the influence exerted by it had not been in the main beneficial. Their pre-eminence proved not that it was free from defects, but that its ex-

The predominance of the caste system in early times proves that it was useful, but not that it was free from drawbacks even then

cellencies, relatively to that particular stage of progress, outweighed its defects

We know that in the animal or vegetable kingdom a species may differ from its competitors by having two qualities, one of which is of great advantage to it, while the other is unimportant, perhaps even slightly injurious, and that the former of these qualities will make the species succeed in spite of its having the latter: the survival of which will then be no proof that it is beneficial Thus the struggle for existence has kept alive many qualities and habits in the human race which were in themselves of no advantage, but which are associated by a more or less permanent bond with others that are great sources of strength. Such instances are found in the tendency to an overbearing demeanour and a scorn for patient industry among nations that owe their advance chiefly to military victories; and again in the tendency among commercial nations to think too much of wealth and to use it for the purposes of display. But the most striking instances are found in matters of organization, the excellent adaptation of the system of caste for the special work which it had to do, enabled it to flourish in spite of its great faults, the chief of which were its rigidity, and its sacrifice of the individual to the interests of society, or rather to certain special exigencies of society.

The same is true of the relations between different industrial classes in the modern Western world

Passing over intermediate stages and coming at once to the modern organization of the Western world, we find it offering a striking contrast, and a no less striking resemblance, to the system of caste. On the one hand, rigidity has been succeeded by plasticity the methods of industry which were then stereotyped, now change with bewildering quickness; the social relations of classes, and the position of the individual in his class, which were then definitely fixed by traditional rules, are now perfectly variable and change their forms with the changing circumstances of the day. But on the other hand, the sacrifice of the individual to the exigencies of society as regards the production of material wealth seems in some respects to be a case of atavism, a reversion to conditions which prevailed in the far-away times of the rule of caste For the division of labour between the different ranks of industry and between different individuals in the same rank is so thorough and uncompromising, that the real interests of the producer are sometimes in danger of being sacrificed for the sake of increasing the addition which his work makes to the aggregate production of material wealth.

Adam Smith's caution on this subject,

§ 4 Adam Smith while insisting on the general advantages of that minute division of labour and of that subtle industrial organization which were being developed with unexampled rapidity in his time, was yet careful to indicate many points in which the system failed, and many incidental evils which it involved[1]. But many of his followers with less philosophic insight, and in some cases with less real knowledge of the world, argued boldly that whatever is, is right They were not contented with insisting that the new industrial organization was spreading rapidly and obtaining victories over its rivals in every direction, and that this very fact proved that it met a want of the times, and had a good balance of advantages over disadvantages But they went further and applied the same argument to all its details; they did not see that the very strength of the system as a whole enabled it to carry along with it many incidents which were in themselves evil. For a while they fascinated the world by their romantic accounts of the flawless proportions of that "natural" organization of industry which had grown from the rudimentary germ of self-interest, each man selecting his daily work with the sole view of getting for it the best pay he could, but with the inevitable result of choosing that in which he could be of most service to others. They argued for instance that, if a man had a talent for managing business, he would be surely led to use that talent for the benefit of mankind that meanwhile a like pursuit of their own interests would lead others to provide for his use such capital as he could turn to best account; and that his own interest would lead him so to arrange those in his employment that everyone should do the highest work of which he was capable, and no other; and that it would lead him to purchase and use all machinery and other aids to

the extravagance of some of his followers

[1] Reference has already been made (Bk I. Ch IV § 3) to the inaccurate use of the term *Smithianismus* in Germany

BOOK IV CH VIII.

production, which could in his hands contribute more than the equivalent of their own cost towards supplying the wants of the world

They were right in contending that these were important problems which could not be properly understood without a much more careful study than was given to them by those ready writers who, then as now, attained an easy popularity by indiscriminate attacks on the existing state of society. But their own defence of it, though more intelligent, was almost equally open to the charge of partisan bias. The romantic subtilty of this "natural organization of industry" had a fascination for earnest and thoughtful minds; it prevented them from seeing and removing the evil that was intertwined with the good in the changes that were going on around them; and it hindered them from inquiring whether many even of the broader features of modern industry may not be transitional, having indeed good work to do in their time, as the caste system had in its time: but like it chiefly serviceable in leading the way towards better arrangements for a happier age.

They took too little account of the development of faculties by use

§ 5. Moreover the doctrine took no account of the manner in which organs are strengthened by being used. Mr Herbert Spencer has done more than anyone else to establish the truth and the significance of the law that if any physical or mental exercise gives pleasure, and is therefore frequent, those physical or mental organs which are used in it are likely to grow rapidly. Among the lower animals indeed the action of this law is so intimately interwoven with that of the survival of the fittest, that the distinction between the two need not often be emphasized. For as it may have been guessed *a priori*, and as seems to be well proved by observation, the struggle for survival tends to prevent animals from taking much pleasure in the exercise of functions which do not contribute to their well-being

But man, with his strong individuality, has greater freedom. He delights in the use of his faculties for their own sake; sometimes using them nobly, whether with the abandon of the great Greek burst of life, or under the control of a deliberate and steadfast striving towards important ends; sometimes ignobly, as in the case of a morbid development of the taste for drink. The physical superiority of the English race over all others that have lived a town life, as largely as we are doing, is due to a great extent to the games in which our youth exercises its physical faculties for the sake of exercising them: the religious, the moral, the intellectual and the artistic faculties on which the progress of industry depends, are not acquired solely for the sake of the things that may be got by them; but are developed by exercise for the sake of the pleasure and the happiness which they themselves bring: and, in the same way, that great factor of economic prosperity, the organization of a well-ordered state, is the product of an infinite variety of motives, many of which have no direct connection with the pursuit of national wealth[1].

No doubt it is true that physical peculiarities acquired by the parents during their life time are seldom if ever transmitted to their offspring. But there seems no good reason for doubting that the children of those who have led healthy lives, physically and morally, will be born with a firmer fibre than they would have been had the same parents grown up under unwholesome influences which had enfeebled the fibre of their bodies and their minds And it is certain that in the former case the children are likely after birth to be better nourished, and better trained, to acquire more wholesome instincts; and to have more of that regard for others and that self-respect, which are the mainsprings of human progress, than in the former case[2].

Conclusion

It is needful then diligently to inquire whether the present industrial organization might not with advantage be so modified as to increase the opportunities which the lower grades of industry have for using their mental faculties, for deriving pleasure from their use, and for strengthening them

[1] Man with his many motives, as he may set himself deliberately to encourage the growth of one peculiarity, may equally set himself to check the growth of another. the slowness of progress during the Middle Ages was partly due to a deliberate detestation of learning.

[2] On these grounds we may admit the embryological doctrines on which Mr Kidd bases so large a part of his doctrine of social evolution, and yet decline to accept his conclusions.

by use; since the argument that if such a change had been beneficial, it would have been already brought about by the struggle for survival, must be rejected as invalid. No doubt development would of itself tend in that direction, but its action would be slow; and it is the prerogative of man to hasten the progress of development by forecasting and preparing the way for its next step.

We may then proceed to study provisionally the present forms of the organization of industry, and the part which they play in governing the supply of material wealth, remembering always that changes, which add but little to the immediate efficiency of production, may be worth having if they make mankind ready and fit for a higher organization, which will be more effective in the production of wealth and more equal in its distribution; and that every system which allows the higher faculties of the lower grades of industry to go to waste, is open to grave suspicion. But a final judgment as to the good and evil effects of any system must be deferred until we are able to take a broader survey.

CHAPTER IX.

INDUSTRIAL ORGANIZATION, CONTINUED DIVISION OF LABOUR. THE INFLUENCE OF MACHINERY.

BOOK IV CH. IX

The course of inquiry in this and the two following chapters.

§ 1. THE first condition of an efficient organization of industry is that it should keep everyone employed at such work as his abilities and training fit him to do well, and should equip him with the best machinery and other appliances for his work. We shall leave on one side for the present the distribution of functions between those who carry out the details of production on the one hand, and those who manage its general arrangement and undertake its risk on the other; and confine ourselves to the division of labour between different classes of operatives, with special reference to the influence of machinery In the following chapter we shall consider the reciprocal effects of division of labour and localization of industry, in a third chapter we shall inquire how far the advantages of division of labour depend upon the aggregation of large capitals into the hands of single individuals or firms, or, as is commonly said, on production on a large scale, and lastly, we shall examine the growing specialization of the work of business management

Practice makes perfect

Physiological explanation.

Everyone is familiar with the fact that "practice makes perfect," that it enables an operation, which at first seemed difficult, to be done after a time with comparatively little exertion, and yet much better than before, and physiology in some measure explains this fact. For it gives reasons for believing that the change is due to the gradual growth of new habits of more or less "reflex" or automatic action. Perfectly reflex actions, such as that of breathing during sleep, are performed by the responsibility of the local nerve

BOOK IV CH IX

centres without any reference to the supreme central authority of the thinking power, which is supposed to reside in the cerebrum But all deliberate movements require the attention of the chief central authority: it receives information from the nerve centres or local authorities and perhaps in some cases direct from the sentient nerves, and sends back detailed and complex instructions to the local authorities, or in some cases direct to the muscular nerves, and so co-ordinates their action as to bring about the required results[1].

Knowledge and intellectual ability

The physiological basis of purely mental work is not yet well understood; but what little we do know of the growth of brain structure seems to indicate that practice in any kind of thinking develops new connections between different parts of the brain. Anyhow we know for a fact that practice will

[1] For instance, the first time a man attempts to skate he must give his whole attention to keeping his balance, his cerebrum has to exercise a direct control over every movement, and he has not much mental energy left for other things But after a good deal of practice the action becomes semi-automatic, the local nerve centres undertake nearly all the work of regulating the muscles, the cerebrum is set free, and the man can carry on an independent train of thought; he can even alter his course to avoid an obstacle in his path, or recover his balance, after it has been disturbed by a slight unevenness, without in any way interrupting the course of his thoughts. It seems that the exercise of nerve force under the immediate direction of the thinking power residing in the cerebrum has gradually built up a set of connections, involving probably distinct physical change, between the nerves and nerve centres concerned, and these new connections may be regarded as a sort of capital of nerve force There is probably something like an organized bureaucracy of the local nerve centres the medulla, the spinal axis, and the larger ganglia generally acting the part of provincial authorities, and being able after a time to regulate the district and village authorities without troubling the supreme government. Very likely they send up messages as to what is going on but if nothing much out of the way has happened, these are very little attended to When however a new feat has to be accomplished, as for instance learning to skate backwards, the whole thinking force will be called into requisition for the time, and will now be able by aid of the special skating-organization of the nerves and nerve centres to do what would have been altogether impossible without such aid

To take a higher instance when an artist is painting at his best, his cerebrum is fully occupied with his work his whole mental force is thrown into it, and the strain is too great to be kept up for a long time together In a few hours of happy inspiration he may give utterance to thoughts that exert a perceptible influence on the character of coming generations, but his power of expression had been earned by numberless hours of plodding work in which he had gradually built up an intimate connection between eye and hand, sufficient to enable him to make good rough sketches of things with which he is tolerably familiar, even while he is engaged in an engrossing conversation and is scarcely conscious that he has a pencil in his hand

enable a person to solve quickly, and without any considerable exertion, questions which he could have dealt with but very imperfectly a little while before, even by the greatest effort. The mind of the merchant, the lawyer, the physician, and the man of science, becomes gradually equipped with a store of knowledge and a faculty of intuition, which can be obtained in no other way than by the continual application of the best efforts of a powerful thinker for many years together to one more or less narrow class of questions. Of course the mind cannot work hard for many hours a day in one direction and a hard-worked man will sometimes find recreation in work that does not belong to his business, but would be fatiguing enough to a person who had to do it all day long.

Change of activity often a form of relaxation

Some social reformers have indeed maintained that those who do the most important brain work might do a fair share of manual work also, without diminishing their power of acquiring knowledge or thinking out hard questions. But experience seems to show that the best relief from overstrain is in occupations taken up to suit the mood of the moment and stopped when the mood is passed, that is, in what popular instinct classes as "relaxation" Any occupation which is so far business-like that a person must sometimes force himself by an effort of the will to go on with it, draws on his nervous force and is not perfect relaxation and therefore it is not economical from the point of view of the community unless its value is sufficient to outweigh a considerable injury to his main work[1].

In the higher grades of

§ 2 It is a difficult and unsettled question how far specialization should be carried in the highest branches of

[1] J S. Mill went so far as to maintain that his occupations at the India Office did not interfere with his pursuit of philosophical inquiries. But it seems probable that this diversion of his freshest powers lowered the quality of his best thought more than he was aware; and though it may have diminished but little his remarkable usefulness in his own generation, it probably affected very much his power of doing that kind of work which influences the course of thought in future generations It was by husbanding every atom of his small physical strength that Darwin was enabled to do so much work of just that kind and a social reformer who had succeeded in exploiting Darwin's leisure hours in useful work on behalf of the community, would have done a very bad piece of business for it

BOOK IV CH IX

work extreme specialization does not always increase efficiency

work. In science it seems to be a sound rule that the area of study should be broad during youth, and should gradually be narrowed as years go on. A medical man who has always given his attention exclusively to one class of diseases, may perhaps give less wise advice even in his special subject than another who, having learnt by wider experience to think of those diseases in relation to general health, gradually concentrates his study more and more on them, and accumulates a vast store of special experiences and subtle instincts. But there is no doubt that greatly increased efficiency can be attained through division of labour in those occupations in which there is much demand for mere manual skill.

But it is easy to acquire a high manual skill in a narrow range of work

Adam Smith pointed out that a lad who had made nothing but nails all his life could make them twice as quickly as a first-rate smith who only took to nail-making occasionally Anyone who has to perform exactly the same set of operations day after day on things of exactly the same shape, gradually learns to move his fingers exactly as they are wanted, by almost automatic action and with greater rapidity than would be possible if every movement had to wait for a deliberate instruction of the will. One familiar instance is seen in the tying of threads by children in a cotton mill. Again, in a clothing or a boot factory, a person who sews, whether by hand or machinery, just the same seam on a piece of leather or cloth of just the same size, hour after hour, day after day, is able to do it with far less effort and far more quickly than a worker with much greater quickness of eye and hand, and of a much higher order of general skill, who was accustomed to make the whole of a coat or the whole of a boot[1].

[1] The best and most expensive clothes are made by highly skilled and highly paid tailors, each of whom works right through first one garment and then another while the cheapest and worst clothes are made for starvation wages by unskilled women who take the cloth to their own homes and do every part of the sewing themselves But clothes of intermediate qualities are made in workshops or factories, in which the division and subdivision of labour are carried as far as the size of the staff will permit, and this method is rapidly gaining ground at both ends at the expense of the rival method Lord Lauderdale, (*Inquiry*, p 282,) quotes Xenophon's argument that the best work is done when each confines himself to one simple department, as when one man makes shoes for man, and another for

The uniformity of many processes in the wood and metal trades

Again, in the wood and the metal industries, if a man has to perform exactly the same operations over and over again on the same piece of material, he gets into the habit of holding it exactly in the way in which it is wanted, and of arranging the tools and other things which he has to handle in such positions that he is able to bring them to work on one another with the least possible loss of time and of force in the movements of his own body. Accustomed to find them always in the same position and to take them in the same order, his hands work in harmony with one another almost automatically: and with increased practice his expenditure of nervous force diminishes even more rapidly than his expenditure of muscular force

The provinces of manual labour and machinery

But when the action has thus been reduced to routine it has nearly arrived at the stage at which it can be taken over by machinery. The chief difficulty to be overcome is that of getting the machinery to hold the material firmly in exactly the position in which the machine tool can be brought to bear on it in the right way, and without wasting too much time in taking grip of it. But this can generally be contrived when it is worth while to spend some labour and expense on it, and then the whole operation can often be controlled by a worker who, sitting before a machine, takes with the left hand a piece of wood or metal from a heap and puts it in a socket, while with the right he draws down a lever, or in some other way sets the machine tool at work, and finally with his left hand throws on to another heap the material which has been cut or punched or drilled or planed exactly after a given pattern It is in these industries especially that we find the reports of modern trades unions to be full of complaints that unskilled labourers, and even their wives and children, are put to do work which used to require the skill and judgment of a trained mechanic, but which has been reduced to mere routine by the improvement

women, or better when one man only sews shoes or garments, another cuts them out the king's cooking is much better than anybody else's, because he has one cook who only boils, another who only roasts meat; one who only boils fish, another who only fries it there is not one man to make all sorts of bread but a special man for special qualities.

BOOK IV CH IX

of machinery and the ever-increasing minuteness of the subdivision of labour

The division of labour in relation to the growth of machinery

§ 3 We are thus led to a general rule, the action of which is more prominent in some branches of manufacture than others, but which applies to all. It is, that any manufacturing operation that can be reduced to uniformity, so that exactly the same thing has to be done over and over again in the same way, is sure to be taken over sooner or later by machinery. There may be delays and difficulties, but if the work to be done by it is on a sufficient scale, money and inventive power will be spent without stint on the task till it is achieved[1].

Thus the two movements of the improvement of machinery and the growing subdivision of labour have gone together and are in some measure connected. But the connection is not so close as is generally supposed. It is the largeness of markets, the increased demand for great numbers of things of the same kind, and in some cases of things made with great accuracy, that leads to subdivision of labour; the chief effect of the improvement of machinery is to cheapen and make more accurate the work which would anyhow have been subdivided. For instance, "in organizing the works at Soho, Boulton and Watt found it necessary to carry division of labour to the furthest practicable point

Machinery displaces purely manual skill,

[1] One great inventor is rumoured to have spent £300,000 on experiments relating to textile machinery, and his outlay is said to have been abundantly returned to him some of his inventions were of such a kind as can be made only by a man of genius, and however great the need, they must have waited till the right man was found for them He charged not unreasonably £1000 as royalty for each of his combing machines; and a worsted manufacturer, being full of work, found it worth his while to buy an additional machine, and pay this extra charge for it, only six months before the expiry of the patent But such cases are exceptional, as a rule patented machines are not very dear In some cases the economy of having them all produced at one place by special machinery has been so great that the patentee has found it to his advantage to sell them at a price lower than the old price of the inferior machines which they displaced · for that old price gave him so high a profit, that it was worth his while to lower the price still further in order to induce the use of the machines for new purposes and in new markets In almost every trade many things are done by hand, though it is well known that they could easily be done by some adaptations of machines that are already in use in that or some other trade, and which are not made only because there would not as yet be enough employment for them to remunerate the trouble and expense of making them

There were no slide-lathes, planing machines or boring tools, such as now render mechanical accuracy of construction almost a matter of certainty. Everything depended on the individual mechanic's accuracy of hand and eye, yet mechanics generally were much less skilled then than they are now. The way in which Boulton and Watt contrived partially to get over the difficulty was to confine their workmen to special classes of work, and make them as expert in them as possible. By continued practice in handling the same tools and fabricating the same articles, they thus acquired great individual proficiency[1]" Thus machinery constantly supplants and renders unnecessary that purely manual skill, the attainment of which was, even up to Adam Smith's time, the chief advantage of division of labour But this influence is more than countervailed by its tendency to increase the scale of manufactures and to make them more complex; and therefore to increase the opportunities for division of labour of all kinds, and especially in the matter of business management.

and thus diminishes some of the advantages of division of labour but increases the scope for it

§ 4. The powers of machinery to do work that requires too much accuracy to be done by hand are perhaps best seen in some branches of the metal industries in which the system of Interchangeable Parts is being rapidly developed. It is only after long training and with much care and labour that the hand can make one piece of metal accurately to resemble or to fit into another and after all the accuracy is not perfect. But this is just the work which a well made machine can do most easily and most perfectly. For instance, if sowing and reaping machines had to be made by hand, their first cost would be very high, and when any part of them was broken, it could be replaced only at great cost by sending the machine back to the manufacturer or by bringing a highly skilled mechanic to the machine. But as it is, the manufacturer keeps in store many facsimiles of the broken part, which were made by the same machinery, and are therefore interchangeable with it. A farmer in the North-West of America, perhaps a hundred miles away from any good mechanic's shop, can yet use complicated ma-

Machine-made machinery is introducing the new era of Interchangeable Parts

[1] Smiles' *Boulton and Watt*, pp 170—1

chinery with confidence; since he knows that by telegraphing the number of the machine and the number of any part of it which he has broken, he will get by the next train a new piece which he can himself fit into its place The importance of this principle of interchangeable parts has been but recently grasped, there are however many signs that it will do more than any other to extend the use of machine-made machinery to every branch of production, including even domestic and agricultural work[1].

Illustration from the history of the watch-making trade

The influences which machinery exerts over the character of modern industry are well illustrated in the manufacture of watches. A few years ago the chief seat of this business was in French Switzerland, where the subdivision of labour was carried far, though a great part of the work was done by a more or less scattered population. There were about fifty distinct branches of trade each of which did one small part of the work. In almost all of them a highly specialized manual skill was required, but very little judgment, the earnings were generally low, because the trade had been established too long for those in it to have anything like a monopoly, and there was no difficulty in bringing up to it any child with ordinary intelligence. But this industry is now yielding ground to the American system of making watches by machinery, which requires very little specialized manual skill. In fact the machinery is becoming every year more and more automatic, and is getting to require less and less assistance from the human hand But the more delicate the machine's power, the greater is the judgment and carefulness which is called for from those who see after it Take for instance a beautiful machine which feeds itself with steelwire at one end, and delivers at the other tiny screws of exquisite form, it displaces a great many operatives who had indeed acquired a very high and specialized manual skill, but who lived sedentary lives, straining their eyesight through microscopes, and finding in

Complex machinery increases the demand for judgment and general intelligence,

1 The system owes its origin in great measure to Sir Joseph Whitworth's standard gauges; but it has been worked out with most enterprise and thoroughness in America. There is a good account of it by Mr Trowbridge in Vol II of the Report of the tenth census for the United States

their work very little scope for any faculty except a mere command over the use of their fingers. But the machine is intricate and costly, and the person who minds it must have an intelligence, and an energetic sense of responsibility, which go a long way towards making a fine character; and which, though more common than they were, are yet sufficiently rare to be able to earn a very high rate of pay No doubt this is an extreme case; and the greater part of the work done in a watch factory is much simpler But much of it requires higher faculties than the old system did, and those engaged in it earn on the average higher wages; at the same time that it has already brought the price of a trustworthy watch within the range of the poorest classes of the community, and it is showing signs of being able soon to accomplish the very highest class of work[1].

and in some cases weakens the barriers that divide different trades

Those who finish and put together the different parts of a watch must always have highly specialized skill: but most of the machines which are in use in a watch factory, are not different in general character from those which are used in any other of the lighter metal trades. in fact many of them are mere modifications of the turning lathes and of the slotting, punching, drilling, planing, shaping, milling machines and a few others, which are familiar to all engineering trades. This is a good illustration of the fact that while there is a constantly increasing subdivision of labour, many of the lines of division between trades which are nominally distinct are becoming narrower and less difficult to be passed. In old times it would have been very small comfort to watch-makers, who happened to be suffering from a diminished demand for their wares, to be told that the gun-making trade was in want of extra hands; but most of the operatives in a watch factory would find machines very similar to those with which they were familiar, if they

[1] The perfection which the machinery has already attained is shown by the fact that at the Inventions Exhibition recently held in London, the representative of an American watch factory took to pieces fifty watches before some English representatives of the older system of manufacture, and after throwing the different parts into different heaps, asked them to select for him one piece from each heap in succession; he then set these pieces up in one of the watch-cases and handed them back a watch in perfect order

BOOK IV. CH IX

strayed into a gun-making factory or sewing-machine factory, or a factory for making textile machinery A watch factory with those who worked in it could be converted without any overwhelming loss into a sewing-machine factory almost the only condition would be that in the new factory no one should be put to work which required a higher order of general intelligence, than that to which he was already accustomed

Illustration from the printing trade.

§ 5. The printing trade affords another instance of the way in which an improvement of machinery and an increase in the volume of production causes an elaborate subdivision of labour. Everyone is familiar with the pioneer newspaper editor of newly settled districts of America, who sets up the type of his articles as he composes them; and with the aid of a boy prints off his sheets and distributes them to his scattered neighbours. When however the mystery of printing was new, the printer had to do all this for himself, and in addition to make all his own appliances[1]. These are now provided for him by separate "subsidiary" trades, from whom even the printer in the backwoods can obtain everything that he wants to use. But in spite of the assistance which it thus gets from outside, a large printing establishment has to find room for many different classes of workers within its walls To say nothing of those who organize and superintend the business, of those who do its office work and keep its stores, of the skilled "readers" who correct any errors that may have crept into the "proofs," of its engineers and repairers of machinery, of those who cast, and who correct and prepare its stereotype plates; of the warehousemen and the boys and girls who assist them, and several other minor classes, there are the two great groups of the compositors who set up the type, and the machinists and pressmen who print impressions from them Each of these two groups is divided into many smaller groups, especially in the large

Instance of the multiplication in

[1] "The type-founder was probably the first to secede from the concern, then printers delegated to others the making of presses; afterwards the ink and the rollers found separate and distinct manufacturers, and there arose a class of persons who, though belonging to other trades, made printing appliances a specialty, such as printers' smiths, printers' joiners and printers' engineers" (Mr Southward in the Article on *Typography* in the *Encyclopædia Britannica*)

centres of the printing trade. In London, for instance, a minder who was accustomed to one class of machine, or a compositor who was accustomed to one class of work, if thrown out of employment would not willingly abandon the advantage of his specialized skill, and falling back on his general knowledge of the trade seek work at another kind of machine or in another class of work[1]. These barriers between minute subdivisions of a trade count for a great deal in many descriptions of the modern tendency towards specialization of industry, and to some extent rightly, because though many of them are so slight that a man thrown out of work in one subdivision could pass into one of its neighbours without any great loss of efficiency, yet he does not do so until he has tried for a while to get employment in his old lines, and therefore the barriers are as effective as stronger ones would be so far as the minor fluctuations of trade from week to week are concerned. But they are of an altogether different kind from the deep and broad partitions which divided one group of mediæval handicraftsmen from another, and which caused the lifelong suffering of the handloom-weavers when their trade had left them[2].

Modern industry of thin lines of division, which can be passed without great difficulty.

[1] For instance, Mr Southward tells us "a minder may understand only book machines or only news machines; he may know all about" machines that print from flat surfaces or those that print from cylinders; "or of cylinders he may know only one kind Entirely novel machines create a new class of artisans There are men perfectly competent to manage a Walter press who are ignorant how to work two-colour or fine book-work machines. In the compositor's department division of labour is carried out to a still minuter degree An old fashioned printer would set up indifferently a placard, a title-page, or a book. At the present day we have jobbing hands, book hands and news hands, the word 'hand' suggesting the factory-like nature of the business There are jobbing hands who confine themselves to posters Book hands comprise those who set up the titles and those who set up the body of the work Of these latter again, while one man composes, another, the 'maker-up,' arranges the pages"

[2] Let us follow still further the progress of machinery in supplanting manual labour in some directions and opening out new fields for its employment in others Let us watch the process by which large editions of a great newspaper are set up and printed off in a few hours To begin with, a good part of the type-setting is itself often done by a machine, but in any case the types are in the first instance on a plane surface, from which it is impossible to print very rapidly The next step therefore is to make a papier-maché cast of them, which is bent on to a cylinder, and is then used as the mould from which a new metal plate is cast that fits the cylinders of the printing machine. Fixed on these it rotates alternately against the inking cylinders and the paper. The paper is arranged in a huge roll

BOOK IV CH IX

Instance of the increased demand for faculties of a high order caused by machinery

In the printing trades, as in the watch trade, we see mechanical and scientific appliances attaining results that would be impossible without them, at the same time that they persistently take over work that used to require manual skill and dexterity, but not much judgment, while they leave for man's hand all those parts which do require the use of judgment, and open up all sorts of new occupations in which there is a great demand for it. Every improvement and cheapening of the printer's appliances increases the demand for the judgment and discretion and literary knowledge of the reader, for the skill and taste of those who know how to set up a good title-page, or how to make ready a sheet on which an engraving is to be printed, so that light and shade will be distributed properly. It increases the demand for the gifted and highly-trained artists who draw or engrave on wood and stone and metal, and for those who know how to give an accurate report in ten lines of the substance of a speech that occupied ten minutes—an intellectual feat the difficulty of which we underrate, because it is so frequently performed And again, it tends to increase the work of photographers and electrotypers, and stereotypers, of the makers of printer's machinery, and many others who get a higher training and a higher income from their work than did those layers on and takers off, and those folders of newspapers who have found their work taken over by iron fingers and iron arms

Machinery relieves the strain on human muscles

§ 6 We may now pass to consider the effects which machinery has in relieving that excessive muscular strain which a few generations ago was the common lot of more than half the working men even in such a country as England. The most marvellous instances of the power of machinery are seen in large iron-works, and especially in those for making armour plates, where the force to be exerted is so great that man's muscles count for nothing, and where every movement, whether horizontal or vertical, has to be effected by

at the bottom of the machine and unrolls itself automatically, first against the damping cylinders and then against the printing cylinders, the first of which prints it on one side, and the second on the other thence to the cutting cylinders, which cut it into equal lengths, and thence to the folding apparatus, which folds it ready for sale When the machinery has been got ready, one man can manage it entirely and it will print off 12,000 copies in an hour

hydraulic or steam force, and man stands by ready to govern the machinery and clear away ashes or perform some such secondary task.

Machinery of this class has increased our command over nature, but it has not directly altered the character of man's work very much, for that which it does he could not have done without it. But in other trades machinery has lightened man's labours The house carpenters, for instance, make things of the same kind as those used by our forefathers, with much less toil for themselves. They now give themselves chiefly to those parts of the task which are most pleasant and most interesting; while in every country town and almost every village there are found steam mills for sawing, planing and moulding, which relieve them of that grievous fatigue which not very long ago used to make them prematurely old[1].

Machinery takes over sooner or later all monotonous work in manufacture

New machinery, when just invented, generally requires a great deal of care and attention. But the work of its attendant is always being sifted; that which is uniform and monotonous is gradually taken over by the machine, which thus becomes steadily more and more automatic and self-acting, till at last there is nothing for the hand to do, but to supply the material at certain intervals and to take away the work when finished There still remains the responsibility for seeing that the machinery is in good order and working smoothly; but even this task is often made light by the introduction of an automatic movement, which brings the machine to a stop the instant anything goes wrong

[1] The jack plane, used for making smooth large boards for floors and other purposes, was the worst enemy of the carpenter All but specially skilled men were compelled to spend a great part of their time with the jack-plane, and this brought on heart disease, making them as a rule old men by the time they were forty But now those who become prematurely old through overwork are to be found almost exclusively among the professional classes, among those engaged in the more anxious kinds of business, and in some agricultural districts in which the rate of wages is still very low and the people are habitually underfed Adam Smith tells us that "workmen, when they are liberally paid, are very apt to over work themselves and to ruin their health and constitution in a few years A carpenter in London, and in some other places, is not supposed to last in his utmost vigour above eight years. .Almost every class of artificers is subject to some particular infirmity occasioned by excessive application to their peculiar species of work" *Wealth of Nations*, Book I Chapter VII

BOOK IV. CH. IX

Illustration from the textile industries

Nothing could be more narrow or monotonous than the occupation of a weaver of plain stuffs in the old time. But now one woman will manage four or more looms, each of which does many times as much work in the course of the day as the old hand-loom did, and her work is much less monotonous and calls for much more judgment than his did So that for every hundred yards of cloth that are woven, the purely monotonous work done by human beings is probably not a twentieth part of what it was [1].

It thus prevents monotony of work from involving monotony of life.

Facts of this kind are to be found in the recent history of many trades and they are of great importance when we are considering the way in which the modern organization of industry is tending to narrow the scope of each person's work, and thereby to render it monotonous. For those trades in which the work is most subdivided are those in which the chief muscular strain is most certain to be taken off by machinery; and thus the chief evil of monotonous work is much diminished As Roscher says, it is monotony of life much more than monotony of work that is to be dreaded. monotony of work is an evil of the first order only when it involves monotony of life. Now when a person's employment requires much physical exertion, he is fit for nothing after his work, and unless his mental faculties are called forth in his work, they have little chance of being developed at all But the nervous force is not very much exhausted in the ordinary work of a factory, at all events where there is not excessive noise, and where the hours of labour are not too long The social surroundings of factory life stimulate mental activity in and out of working hours, and even those factory workers whose occupations are seemingly the most monotonous have more intelligence and mental resource than has been shown by the English agricultural labourer whose employment has more variety [2].

[1] The efficiency of labour in weaving has been increased twelve-fold and that in spinning six-fold during the last seventy years In the preceding seventy years the improvements in spinning had already increased the efficiency of labour two-hundred-fold (see Ellison's *Cotton Trade of Great Britain*, ch IV. and V)

[2] Perhaps the textile industries afford the best instance of work that used to be done by hand and is now done by machinery. They are especially prominent in England, where they give employment to nearly half a million males and more

It is true that the American agriculturist is an able man, and that his children rise rapidly in the world But partly because land is plentiful, and he generally owns the farm that he cultivates, he has better social conditions than the English; he has always had to think for himself, and has long had to use and to repair complex machines. The English agricultural labourer has many great disadvantages to contend with, but he is steadily improving his position.

The economic use of specialized skill and machinery requires that they should be fully occupied

§ 7. We must now proceed to consider what are the conditions under which the economies in production arising from division of labour can best be secured It is obvious that the efficiency of specialized machinery or specialized skill is but one condition of its economic use; the other is that sufficient work should be found to keep it well employed As Babbage pointed out, in a large factory "the master manufacturer by dividing the work to be executed into different processes, each requiring different degrees of skill or force, can purchase exactly that precise quantity of both which is necessary for each process, whereas if the whole work were executed by one workman that person must possess sufficient skill to perform the most difficult and

than half a million females, or more than one in ten of those persons who are earning independent incomes The strain that is taken off human muscles in dealing even with those soft materials is shown by the fact that for every one of these million operatives there is used about one horse-power of steam, that is, about ten times as much as they would themselves exert if they were all strong men, and the history of these industries will serve to remind us that many of those who perform the more monotonous parts of manufacturing work are as a rule not skilled workers who have come down to it from a higher class of work, but unskilled workers who have risen to it A great number of those who work in the Lancashire cotton mills have come there from poverty-stricken districts of Ireland, while others are the descendants of paupers and people of weak physique, who were sent there in large numbers early in the century from the most miserable conditions of life in the poorest agricultural districts, where the labourers were fed and housed almost worse than the animals whom they tended. Again, when regret is expressed that the cotton factory hands of New England have not the high standard of culture which prevailed among them a century ago, we must remember that the descendants of those factory workers have moved up to higher and more responsible posts, and include many of the ablest and wealthiest of the citizens of America Those who have taken their places are in the process of being raised, they are chiefly French Canadians and Irish, who though they may learn in their new homes some of the vices of civilization, are yet much better off and have on the whole better opportunities of developing the higher faculties of themselves and their children than they had in their old homes.

BOOK IV. CH IX

sufficient strength to execute the most laborious of the operations into which the work is divided." The economy of production requires not only that each person should be employed constantly in a narrow range of work, but also that, when it is necessary for him to undertake different tasks, each of these tasks should be such as to call forth as much as possible of his skill and ability Just in the same way the economy of machinery requires that a powerful turning-lathe when specially arranged for one class of work should be kept employed as long as possible on that work, and if after all it is necessary to employ it on other work, that should be such as to be worthy of the lathe, and not such as could have been done equally well by a much smaller machine.

But the most economic use of man as an agent of production is wasteful if he is not himself developed by it

Here then, so far as the economy of production goes, men and machines stand on much the same footing · but while machinery is a mere implement of production, man's welfare is also its ultimate aim. We have already been occupied with the question whether the human race as a whole gains by carrying to an extreme that specialization of function which causes all the most difficult work to be done by a few people: but we have now to consider it more nearly with special reference to the work of business management The main drift of the next three chapters is to inquire what are the causes which make different forms of business management the fittest to profit by their environment, and the most likely to prevail over others, but it is well that meanwhile we should have in our minds the question, how far they are severally fitted to benefit their environment.

Many of those economies in the use of specialized skill and machinery which are commonly regarded as within the reach of very large establishments, do not depend on the size of individual factories. Some depend on the aggregate volume of production of the kind in the neighbourhood, while others again, especially those connected with the growth of knowledge and the progress of the arts, depend chiefly on the aggregate volume of production in the whole civilized world. And here we may introduce two technical terms.

We may divide the economies arising from an increase in

BOOK IV CH. IX

External and Internal Economies

the scale of production of any kind of goods, into two classes —those dependent on the general development of the industry and those dependent on the resources of the individual houses of business engaged in the efficiency of their management. And we may call the former *External Economies*, and the latter *Internal Economies*. In the present chapter we have been chiefly discussing Internal economies; but we now proceed to examine those very important External economies which can often be secured by the concentration of many small businesses of a similar character in particular localities: or, as is commonly said, by the localization of industry.

CHAPTER X.

INDUSTRIAL ORGANIZATION CONTINUED. THE CONCENTRATION OF SPECIALIZED INDUSTRIES IN PARTICULAR LOCALITIES

Even in early stages of civilization the production of some light and valuable wares has been localized.

§ 1. In an early stage of civilization every place had to depend on its own resources for most of the heavy wares which it consumed, unless indeed it happened to have special facilities for water carriage. But the slowness with which customs changed, made it easy for producers to meet the wants even of consumers with whom they had little communication; and it enabled comparatively poor people to buy a few expensive goods from a distance, in the security that they would add to the pleasure of festivals and holidays during a life-time, or perhaps even during two or three life-times Consequently the lighter and more expensive articles of dress and personal adornment, together with spices and some kinds of metal implements used by all classes, and many other things for the special use of the rich, often came from astonishing distances. Some of these were produced only in a few places, or even only in one place; and they were diffused all over Europe partly by the agency of fairs[1] and professional pedlers, and partly by the producers themselves, who would vary their work by travelling on foot for many thousand miles to sell their goods and see the world These sturdy travellers took on themselves the risks of their little businesses; they enabled the production of certain classes of

[1] Thus in the records of the Stourbridge Fair held near Cambridge we find an endless variety of light and precious goods from the older seats of civilization in the East and on the Mediterranean, some having been brought in Italian ships, and others having travelled by land as far as the shores of the North Sea

goods to be kept on the right track for satisfying the needs of purchasers far away; and they created new wants among consumers, by showing them at fairs or at their own houses new goods from a distant land. An industry concentrated in certain localities is commonly, though perhaps not quite accurately, described as a Localized Industry[1].

This elementary localization of industry gradually prepared the way for many of the modern developments of division of labour in the mechanical arts and in the task of business management Even now we find industries of a primitive fashion localized in retired villages of central Europe, and sending their simple wares even to the busiest haunts of modern industry. In Russia the expansion of a family group into a village has often been the cause of a localized industry, and there are an immense number of villages each of which carries on only one branch of production, or even only a part of one[2].

The various origins of localized industries; physical conditions,

§ 2 Many various causes have led to the localization of industries, but the chief causes have been physical conditions, such as the character of the climate and the soil, the existence of mines and quarries in the neighbourhood, or within easy access by land or water. Thus metallic industries have generally been either near mines or in places where fuel was cheap. The iron industries in England first sought those districts in which charcoal was plentiful, and

[1] Not very long ago travellers in Western Tyrol could find a strange and characteristic relic of this habit in a village called Imst The villagers had somehow acquired a special art in breeding canaries and their young men started for a tour to distant parts of Europe each with about fifty small cages hung from a pole over his shoulder, and walked on till they had sold all

[2] There are for instance over 500 villages devoted to various branches of woodwork, one village makes nothing but spokes for the wheels of vehicles, another nothing but the bodies and so on, and indications of a like state of things are found in the histories of oriental civilizations and in the chronicles of mediæval Europe Thus for instance we read (Rogers' *Six Centuries of Work and Wages*, Ch IV) of a lawyer's handy book written about 1250, which makes note of scarlet at Lincoln, blanket at Bligh; burnet at Beverley, russet at Colchester; linen fabrics at Shaftesbury, Lewes, and Aylsham; cord at Warwick and Bridport, knives at Marstead, needles at Wilton, razors at Leicester, soap at Coventry; horse girths at Doncaster; skins and furs at Chester and Shrewsbury and so on.

The localization of trades in England at the beginning of the eighteenth century is well described by Defoe, *Place of English Commerce*, 85—7, *English Tradesman*, II 282—3

afterwards they went to the neighbourhood of collieries[1]. Staffordshire makes many kinds of pottery, all the materials of which are imported from a long distance, but she has cheap coal and excellent clay for making the heavy "seggars" or boxes in which the pottery is placed while being fired. Straw plaiting has its chief home in Bedfordshire, where straw has just the right proportion of silex to give strength without brittleness, and Buckinghamshire beeches have afforded the material for the Wycombe chairmaking. The Sheffield cutlery trade is due chiefly to the excellent grit of which its grindstones are made.

the patronage of courts,

Another chief cause has been the patronage of a court. The rich folk there assembled make a demand for goods of specially high quality, and this attracts skilled workmen from a distance, and educates those on the spot. When an Eastern potentate changed his residence—and, partly for sanitary reasons, this was constantly done—the deserted town was apt to take refuge in the development of a specialized industry, which had owed its origin to the presence of the court. But very often the rulers deliberately invited artisans from a distance and settled them in a group together Thus the mechanical faculty of Lancashire is said to be due to the influence of Norman smiths who were settled at Warrington by Hugo de Lupus in William the Conqueror's time. And the greater part of England's manufacturing industry before the era of cotton and steam had its course directed by settlements of Flemish and Huguenot artisans, many of which were made under the immediate direction of Plantagenet and Tudor kings These immigrants taught us how to weave woollen and worsted stuffs, though for a long time we sent our cloths to the Netherlands to be fulled and dyed. They taught us how to cure herrings, how to manufacture silk, how to make lace, glass, and paper, and to provide for many other of our wants[2].

the deliberate invitation of rulers

[1] The later wanderings of the iron industry from Wales, Staffordshire and Shropshire to Scotland and the North of England are well shown in the tables submitted by Sir Lowthian Bell to the recent Commission on the Depression of Trade and Industry See their Second Report, Part I p 320

[2] Fuller says that Flemings started manufactures of cloths and fustians in Norwich, of baizes in Sudbury, of serges in Colchester and Taunton, of cloths in

The industrial development of nations waits upon opportunities and upon character.

But how did these immigrants learn their skill? Their ancestors had no doubt profited by the traditional arts of earlier civilizations on the shores of the Mediterranean and in the far East for nearly all important knowledge has long deep roots stretching downwards to distant times; and so widely spread have been these roots, so ready to send up shoots of vigorous life, that there is perhaps no part of the old world in which there might not long ago have flourished many beautiful and highly skilled industries, if their growth had been favoured by the character of the people, and by their social and political institutions This accident or that may have determined whether a particular industry flourished in any one town; the industrial character of a whole country even may have been largely influenced by the richness of her soil and her mines, and her facilities for commerce Such natural advantages may themselves have stimulated free industry and enterprise: but it is the existence of these last, by whatever means they may have been promoted, which has been the supreme condition for the growth of noble forms of the arts of life. In sketching the history of free industry and enterprise we have already incidentally traced the outlines of the causes which have localized the industrial leadership of the world now in this country and now in that We have seen how physical nature acts on man's energies, how he is stimulated by an invigorating climate, and how he is encouraged to bold ventures by the opening out of rich fields for his work . but we have also seen how the use he makes of these advantages depends on his ideals of life, and how inextricably therefore the religious, political and economic threads of the world's history are interwoven; while together they have been bent this way or that by great political events and the influence of the strong personalities of individuals

The causes which determine the economic progress of nations will require further study when we come to discuss

Kent, Gloucestershire, Worcestershire, Westmoreland, Yorkshire, Hants, Berks and Sussex, of kerseys in Devonshire and of Levant cottons in Lancashire Smiles' *Huguenots in England and Ireland*, p 109 See also Lecky's *History of England in the eighteenth century*, Ch II.

BOOK IV CH. X.

the problems of international trade[1]. But for the present we must turn aside from these broader movements of the localization of industry, and follow the fortunes of groups of skilled workers who are gathered within the narrow boundaries of a manufacturing town or a thickly peopled industrial district.

The advantages of localized industries, hereditary skill;

§ 3. When an industry has thus chosen a locality for itself, it is likely to stay there long: so great are the advantages which people following the same skilled trade get from near neighbourhood to one another The mysteries of the trade become no mysteries, but are as it were in the air, and children learn many of them unconsciously Good work is rightly appreciated, inventions and improvements in machinery, in processes and the general organization of the business have their merits promptly discussed: if one man starts a new idea, it is taken up by others and combined with suggestions of their own; and thus it becomes the source of further new ideas. And presently subsidiary trades grow up in the neighbourhood, supplying it with implements and materials, organizing its traffic, and in many ways conducing to the economy of its material.

the growth of subsidiary trades;

the use of highly specialized machinery;

Again, the economic use of expensive machinery can sometimes be attained in a very high degree in a district in which there is a large aggregate production of the same kind, even though no individual capital employed in the trade be very large. For subsidiary industries devoting themselves each to one small branch of the process of production, and working it for a great many of their neighbours, are able to keep in constant use machinery of the most highly specialized character, and to make it pay its expenses, though its original cost may have been high, and its rate of depreciation very rapid.

a local market for special skill

Again, in all but the earliest stages of economic development a localized industry gains a great advantage from the fact that it offers a constant market for skill. Employers are apt to resort to any place where they are likely to find a good choice of workers with the special skill which they

[1] Meanwhile attention may be called to an article on *The Migrations of Centres of Industrial Energy* by Mr Courtney in the Fortnightly Review for December 1878.

require; while men seeking employment naturally go to places where there are many employers who need such skill as theirs and where therefore it is likely to find a good market The owner of an isolated factory is often put to great shifts for want of some special skilled labour which has suddenly run short, and a skilled workman, when thrown out of employment in it, has no easy refuge. Social forces here co-operate with economic: there are often strong friendships between employers and employed, but neither side likes to feel that in case of any disagreeable incident happening between them, they must go on rubbing against one another: both sides like to be able easily to break off old associations should they become irksome. These difficulties are still a great obstacle to the success of any business in which special skill is needed, but which is not in the neighbourhood of others like it: they are however being diminished by the railway, the printing-press and the telegraph.

Sometimes however a localized industry makes too extensive demands for one kind of labour

On the other hand a localized industry has some disadvantages as a market for labour if the work done in it is chiefly of one kind, such for instance as can be done only by strong men. In those iron districts in which there are no textile or other factories to give employment to women and children, wages are high and the cost of labour dear to the employer, while the average money earnings of each family are low. But the remedy for this evil is obvious, and is found in the growth in the same neighbourhood of industries of a supplementary character Thus textile industries are constantly found congregated in the neighbourhood of mining and engineering industries, in some cases having been attracted by almost imperceptible steps, in others, as for instance at Barrow, having been started deliberately on a large scale in order to give variety of employment in a place where previously there had been but little demand for the work of women and children.

The advantages of variety of employment are combined with those of localized industries in some of our manufacturing towns, and this is a chief cause of their continued growth But on the other hand the value which the central sites of a large town have for trading purposes, enables them to command much higher ground-rents than the situations are worth for factories, even when account is taken of this combination of advantages: and there is a similar competition for dwelling space between the employés of the trading houses and the factory workers. The result is that factories now congregate in the outskirts of large towns and in manufacturing districts in their neighbourhood rather than in the towns themselves[1].

Different industries in the same neighbourhood mitigate each other's depressions.

A district which is dependent chiefly on one industry is liable to extreme depression, in case of a falling-off in the demand for its produce, or of a failure in the supply of the raw material which it uses. This evil again is in a great measure avoided by those large towns, or large industrial districts in which several distinct industries are strongly developed. If one of them fails for a time, the others are likely to support it indirectly; and they enable local shopkeepers to continue their assistance to workpeople in it.

The influence of improved means of communication on the geographical distribution of industries

§ 4. Every cheapening of the means of communication, every new facility for the free interchange of ideas between distant places alters the action of the forces which tend to localize industries. Speaking generally we may say that a lowering of tariffs, or of freights for the transport of goods, tends to make each locality buy more largely from a distance what it requires, and thus tends to concentrate particular industries in special localities: but on the other hand everything that increases people's readiness to migrate from one place to another, tends to bring skilled artisans to ply their crafts near to the consumers who will purchase their wares. These two opposing tendencies are well illustrated by the recent history of the English people.

Illustration from the recent

On the one hand the steady cheapening of freights, the opening of railways from the agricultural districts of America

[1] The movement has been specially conspicuous in the case of the textile manufactures. Manchester, Leeds and Lyons are still chief centres of the trade in cotton, woollen and silk stuffs, but they do not now themselves produce any great part of the goods to which they owe their chief fame. On the other hand London and Paris retain their positions as the two largest manufacturing towns of the world, Philadelphia coming third. The mutual influences of the localization of industry, the growth of towns and habits of town life, and the development of machinery are well discussed in Hobson's *Evolution of Capitalism*.

history of England.

and India to the sea-board, and the adoption by England of a free-trade policy, have led to a great increase in her importation of raw produce. But on the other hand the growing cheapness, rapidity and comfort of foreign travel, are inducing her trained business men and her skilled artisans to pioneer the way for new industries in other lands, and to help them to manufacture for themselves goods which they have been wont to buy from England. English mechanics have taught people in almost every part of the world how to use English machinery, and even how to make the machinery like it; and English miners have opened out mines of ore which have diminished the foreign demand for many of England's products[1].

One of the most striking movements towards the specialization of a country's industries, which history records, is the rapid increase of the non-agricultural population of England in recent times. The exact nature of this change is however liable to be misunderstood; and its interest is so great, both for its own sake, and on account of the illustrations it affords of the general principles which we have been discussing in the preceding chapter and in this, that we may with advantage pause here to consider it a little.

The diminution of her agricultural population is less than at first sight appears

In the first place, the real diminution of England's agricultural industries is not so great as at first sight appears. It is true that in the Middle Ages three-fourths of the people were reckoned as agriculturists, that only one in nine was returned to the last census as engaged in agriculture, and that perhaps not more than one in twelve will be so returned at the next census. But it must be remembered that the so-called agricultural population of the Middle Ages were not exclusively occupied with agriculture, they did for themselves a great part of the work that is now done by brewers and bakers, by spinners and weavers, by bricklayers and carpenters, by dressmakers and tailors and by many other trades.

[1] The high intelligence of the Cornish men has combined with the comparative poverty of their own mines to make them take the lead in this movement and they even send to England from distant continents part of the tin and copper which enter into many of her most valuable exports, and thus in some ways increase the specialization of her industries.

BOOK IV CH X

These self-sufficing habits died slowly, but most of them had nearly disappeared by the beginning of this century; and it is probable that the labour spent on the land at this time was not a much less part of the whole industry of the country than in the Middle Ages for, in spite of her ceasing to export wool and wheat, there was so great an increase in the produce forced from her soil, that the rapid improvement in the arts of her agriculturists scarcely availed to hold in check this action of the law of diminishing return. But gradually a great deal of labour has been diverted from the fields to making expensive machinery for agricultural purposes. This change did not exert its full influence upon the numbers of those who were reckoned as agriculturists so long as the machinery was drawn by horses: for the work of tending them and supplying them with food was regarded as agricultural But in recent years a rapid growth of the use of steam power in the fields has coincided with the increased importation of farm produce. The coal-miners who supply these steam-engines with fuel, and the mechanics who make them and manage them in the fields are not reckoned as occupied on the land, though the ultimate aim of their labour is to promote its cultivation The real diminution then of England's agriculture is not so great as at first sight appears; but there has been a change in its distribution[1].

Changes in the distribution of the agricultural population within the country

Attention has already been called to the influence which the importation of agricultural produce exerts in altering the relative values of different soils: those falling most in value which depended chiefly on their wheat crops, and which were not naturally fertile, though they were capable of being made to yield fairly good crops by expensive methods of cultivation.

[1] Dr Ogle has recently shown (*Statistical Journal*, June, 1889) that the aggregate rural population of England—i.e that living in the open country or in villages with less than 5000 inhabitants—has decreased only by 2 per cent between 1851 and 1881 but of course the decrease has been greater in certain counties "The decline was brought about by the migration of young people, mainly under twenty five years of age, from the rural to manufacturing districts, and of young men in greater proportion than women The main decrease was among those engaged in agriculture But a very considerable share of it was borne by the rural handicraftsmen There was a considerable increase among those engaged in the transport of goods, among shopkeepers, among domestic and other servants, and also, in the professional class, among those engaged in teaching."

Districts, in which such soils predominate, have contributed more than their share to the crowds of agricultural labourers who have migrated to the large towns; and thus the geographical distribution of industries within the country has been still further altered. A striking instance of the influence of the new means of transport is seen in those pastoral districts in the remoter parts of the United Kingdom, which send dairy products by special express trains to London and other large towns, meanwhile drawing their own supplies of wheat from the further shores of the Atlantic or even the Pacific Ocean.

Those set free from agriculture have gone not to manufactures

But next, the changes of recent years have not, as would at first sight appear probable, increased the proportion of the English people who are occupied in manufactures. The output of England's manufactures is certainly several times as great now as it was at the middle of the century, but those occupied in manufacture of every kind were not a larger percentage of the population in 1881 than in 1851[1]. This result is the more strange when we recollect that among the manufacturers are reckoned those who make the machinery and implements which do so great a part of the work of English agriculture.

but chiefly to industries in which there has been no great increase in the efficiency of labour.

The chief explanation of this result lies in the wonderful increase in recent years of the power of machinery. This has enabled us to produce ever increasing supplies of manufactures of almost every kind both for our own use and for exportation without requiring any considerable increase in the number of people who tend the machines And therefore we have been able to devote the labour set free from agriculture chiefly to supplying those wants in regard to which the improvements of machinery help us but little · the efficiency of machinery has prevented the industries localized in England from becoming as exclusively mechanical as they otherwise would. Prominent among the occupations which have increased since 1851 in England at the expense of

[1] Mr Booth in his admirable paper *On Occupations in the United Kingdom* 1841—1881, published in the *Statistical Journal* for 1886, separates as well as he can the dealers from the manufacturers, and finds that those engaged in manufacture were 32 7 per cent of those earning independent incomes in 1851 and only 30 7 per cent in 1881

BOOK IV. CH. X.

agriculture are education, domestic service, building, dealing and transport by road[1]. In none of these is very much direct help got from new inventions: man's labour is not much more efficient in them now than it was a century ago: and therefore if the wants for which they make provision increase in proportion to our general wealth, it is only to be expected that they should absorb a constantly growing proportion of our industry.

Transition to the subject of the next chapter

Passing away from this illustration of the action of modern forces on the geographical distribution of industries, we will resume our inquiry as to how far the full economies of division of labour can be obtained by the concentration of large numbers of small businesses of a similar kind in the same locality; and how far they are attainable only by the aggregation of a large part of the business of the country into the hands of a comparatively small number of rich and powerful firms, or, as is commonly said, by production on a large scale; or, in other words, how far the economies of production on a large scale must needs be *Internal*, and how far they can be *External*.

[1] Of course transport by railway, which is a mechanical industry, occupies more people than it did; for it is only of recent origin. But the shipping industry is of old date; and there we find that recent mechanical improvements have enabled a traffic increased fourfold to be carried without any increase in the number of those who work it. Except in the matter of tramways there has been no considerable improvement in the vehicles used on the roads, and a comparatively slight increase in traffic by road has caused those who work it to increase in numbers faster than those engaged in almost any other manual occupation.

CHAPTER XI.

INDUSTRIAL ORGANIZATION, CONTINUED. PRODUCTION ON A LARGE SCALE

The typical industries for our present purpose are those engaged in manufacture

§ 1. THE advantages of production on a large scale are best shown in manufacture; under which head we may include all businesses engaged in working up material into forms in which it will be adapted for sale in distant markets. The characteristic of manufacturing industries which makes them offer generally the best illustrations of the advantages of production on a large scale, is their power of choosing freely the locality in which they will do their work. They are thus contrasted on the one hand with agriculture and other extractive industries (mining, quarrying, fishing etc), the geographical distribution of which is determined by nature; and on the other hand with industries that make or repair things to suit the special needs of individual consumers, from whom they cannot be far removed, at all events without great loss[1].

The economy of material

The chief advantages of production on a large scale are economy of skill, economy of machinery and economy of materials: but the last of these is rapidly losing importance relatively to the other two It is true that an isolated workman often throws away a number of small things which would have been collected and turned to good account in a factory[2],

[1] "Manufacture" is a term which has long lost any connection with its original use and is now applied to those branches of production where machine and not hand work is most prominent. Roscher made the attempt to bring it back nearer to its old use by applying it to domestic as opposed to factory industries but it is too late to do this now.

[2] See Babbage's instance of the manufacture of horn *Economy of Manufactures*, ch. XXII.

BOOK IV. CH XI.

but waste of this kind can scarcely occur in a localized manufacture even if it is in the hands of small men, and there is not very much of it in any branch of industry in modern England, except agriculture and domestic cooking No doubt many of the most important advances of recent years have been due to the utilizing of what had been a waste product; but this has been generally due to a distinct invention, either chemical or mechanical, the use of which has been indeed promoted by minute subdivision of labour, but has not been directly dependent on it[1]

Again, it is true that when a hundred sets of furniture, or of clothing, have to be cut out on exactly the same pattern, it is worth while to spend great care on so planning the cutting out of the boards or the cloth, that only a few small pieces are wasted. But this is properly an economy of skill; one planning is made to suffice for many tasks, and therefore can be done well and carefully. We may pass then to the economy of machinery.

The advantages of a large factory as regards the use of specialized machinery.

§ 2. In spite of the aid which subsidiary industries can give to small manufactures, where many in the same branch of trade are collected in one neighbourhood[2], they are still placed under a great disadvantage by the growing variety and expensiveness of machinery. For in a large establishment there are often many expensive machines each made specially for one small use. Each of them requires space in a good light, and thus stands for something considerable in the rent and general expenses of the factory, and independently of interest and the expense of keeping it in repair, a heavy allowance must be made for depreciation in consequence of its being probably improved upon before long[3].

[1] Instances are the utilization of the waste from cotton, wool, silk and other textile materials, and of the hye products in the metallurgical industries and in the manufacture of soda and gas

[2] See the preceding chapter, § 3.

[3] The average time which a machine will last before being superseded is in many trades not more than fifteen years, while in some it is ten years or even less There is often a loss on the use of a machine unless it earns every year twenty per cent on its cost, and when the operation performed by such a machine costing £500 adds only a hundredth part to the value of the material that passes through it—and this is not an extreme case—there will be a loss on its use unless it can he applied in producing at least £10,000 worth of goods annually

A small manufacturer must therefore have many things done by hand or by imperfect machinery, though he knows how to have them done better and cheaper by special machinery, if only he could find constant employment for it.

Advantages with regard to the invention of improved machinery

But next, a small manufacturer may not always be acquainted with the best machinery for his purpose. It is true that if the industry in which he is engaged has been long established on a large scale, his machinery will be well up to the mark, provided he can afford to buy the best in the market In agriculture and the cotton industries for instance, improvements in machinery are devised almost exclusively by machine makers, and they are accessible to all, at any rate on the payment of a royalty for patent right. But this is not the case in industries that are as yet in an early stage of development or are rapidly changing their form, such as the chemical industries, the watchmaking industry and some branches of the jute and silk manufactures, and in a host of trades that are constantly springing up to supply some new want or to work up some new material.

The small manufacturer cannot often afford to experiment.

In all such trades new machinery and new processes are for the greater part devised by manufacturers for their own use Each new departure is an experiment which may fail, those which succeed must pay for themselves and for the failure of others; and though a small manufacturer may think he sees his way to an improvement, he must reckon on having to work it out tentatively, at considerable risk and expense and with much interruption to his other work: and even if he should be able to perfect it, he is not likely to be able to make the most of it. For instance, he may have devised a new speciality, which would get a large sale if it could be brought under general notice· but to do this would perhaps cost many thousand pounds; and, if so, he will probably have to turn his back on it. For it is almost impossible for him to discharge, what Roscher calls a characteristic task of the modern manufacturer, that of creating new wants by showing people something which they had never thought of having before, but which they want to have as soon as the notion is suggested to them in the pottery trade for example the

BOOK IV. CH XI

small manufacturer cannot afford even to make experiments with new patterns and designs except in a very tentative way His chance is better with regard to an improvement in making things for which there is already a good market. But even here he cannot get the full benefit of his invention unless he patents it, and sells the right to use it, or borrows some capital and extends his business, or lastly changes the character of his business and devotes his capital to that particular stage of the manufacture to which his improvement applies. But after all such cases are exceptional· the growth of machinery in variety and expensiveness presses hard on the small manufacturer everywhere. It has already driven him completely out of some trades and is fast driving him out of others[1].

But in some trades a factory of moderate size can have the best machinery

There are however some trades in which the advantages which a large factory derives from the economy of machinery almost vanish as soon as a moderate size has been reached. For instance in cotton spinning, and calico weaving, a comparatively small factory will hold its own and give constant employment to the best known machines for every process: so that a large factory is only several parallel smaller factories under one roof, and indeed some cotton-spinners, when enlarging their works, think it best to add a weaving department. In such cases the large business gains little or no economy in machinery, but even then it generally saves

[1] In many businesses only a small percentage of improvements are patented They consist of many small steps, which it would not be worth while to patent one at a time. Or their chief point lies in noticing that a certain thing ought to be done; and to patent one way of doing it, is only to set other people to work to find out other ways of doing it against which the patent cannot guard. If one patent is taken out, it is often necessary to "block" it, by patenting other methods of arriving at the same result; the patentee does not expect to use them himself, but he wants to prevent others from using them All this involves worry and loss of time and money· and the large manufacturer prefers to keep his improvement to himself and get what benefit he can by using it While if the small manufacturer takes out a patent, he is likely to be harassed by infringements. and even though he may win "with costs" the actions in which he tries to defend himself, he is sure to be ruined by them if they are numerous It is generally in the public interest that an improvement should be published, even though it is at the same time patented But if it is patented in England and not in other countries, as is often the case, English manufacturers may not use it, even though they were just on the point of finding it out for themselves before it was patented; while foreign manufacturers learn all about it and can use it freely.

something in building, particularly as regards chimneys, and in the economy of steam power, and in the management and repairs of engines and machinery. This last point is of rather more importance than appears at first sight; and large works even though they produce nothing but soft goods, have generally well-organized carpenters' and mechanics' shops, which not only diminish the cost of repairs, but have the important advantage of preventing delays from accidents to the plant[1].

Advantages of a large factory in buying and selling

Akin to these last, there are a great many advantages which a large factory, or indeed a large business of almost any kind, nearly always has over a small one. A large business buys in great quantities and therefore cheaply, it pays low freights and saves on carriage in many ways, particularly if it has a railway siding. It often sells in large quantities, and thus saves itself trouble, and yet at the same time it gets a good price, because it offers conveniences to the customer by having a large stock from which he can select and at once fill up a varied order, while its reputation gives him confidence It can spend large sums on advertising by commercial travellers and in other ways, its agents give it trustworthy information on trade and personal matters in distant places, and its own goods advertise one another

Alliance between large traders and small producers.

Many of these economies in the matter of buying and selling can be secured by a large trading house, which puts out its work to be done by small manufacturers or by workpeople at their own homes. So far therefore they do not tell in the direction of destroying small manufacturers, but rather of limiting the character of the work of business

[1] It is a remarkable fact that cotton and some other textile factories form an exception to the general rule that the capital required per head of the workers is generally greater in a large factory than in a small one. The reason is that in most other businesses the large factory has many things done by expensive machines which are done by hand in a small factory, so that while the wages bill is less in proportion to the output in a large factory than in a small one, the value of the machinery and the factory space occupied by the machinery is much greater. But in the simpler branches of the textile trades, small works have the same machinery as large works have; and since small steam-engines, &c are proportionately more expensive than large ones, they require a greater fixed capital in proportion to their output than larger factories do; and they are likely to require a floating capital also rather greater in proportion

BOOK IV CH XI

management done by them; as we shall see more fully in the next chapter.

Advantages of a large factory as regards specialized skill,

§ 3. Next, with regard to the economy of skill. Everything that has been said with regard to the advantages which a large establishment has in being able to afford highly specialized machinery applies equally with regard to highly specialized skill. It can contrive to keep each of its employés constantly engaged in the most difficult work of which he is capable, and yet so to narrow the range of his work that he can attain that facility and excellence which come from long-continued practice But enough has already been said on the advantage of division of labour: and we may pass to an important though indirect advantage which a manufacturer derives from having a great many men in his employment.

the selection of leading men, etc

The large manufacturer has a much better chance than a small one has, of getting hold of men with exceptional natural abilities, to do the most difficult part of his work—that on which the reputation of his establishment chiefly depends This is occasionally important as regards mere handiwork in trades which require much taste and originality, as for instance that of a house decorator, and in those which require exceptionally fine workmanship, as for instance that of a manufacturer of delicate mechanism[1]. But in most businesses its chief importance lies in the facilities which it gives to the employer for the selection of able and tried men, men whom he trusts and who trust him, to be his foremen and heads of departments. We are thus brought to the central problem of the modern organization of industry, viz. that which relates to the advantages and

[1] Thus Boulton writing in 1770 when he had 700 or 800 persons employed as metallic artists and workers in tortoiseshell, stones, glass, and enamel, says — "I have trained up many, and am training up more, plain country lads into good workmen, and wherever I find indications of skill and ability I encourage them. I have likewise established correspondence with almost every mercantile town in Europe, and am thus regularly supplied with orders for the grosser articles in common demand, by which I am enabled to employ such a number of hands as to provide me with an ample choice of artists for the finer branches of work · and I am thus encouraged to erect and employ a more extensive apparatus than it would be prudent to employ for the production of the finer articles only" Smiles' *Life of Boulton*, p 128

disadvantages of the subdivision of the work of business management.

The subdivision of the work of business management advantages of the large manufacturer;

§ 4. The head of a large business can reserve all his strength for the broadest and most fundamental problems of his trade: he must indeed assure himself that his managers, clerks and foremen are the right men for their work, and are doing their work well, but beyond this he need not trouble himself much about details. He can keep his mind fresh and clear for thinking out the most difficult and vital problems of his business, for studying the broader movements of the markets, the yet undeveloped results of current events at home and abroad; and for contriving how to improve the organization of the internal and external relations of his business.

For much of this work the small employer has not the time if he has the ability; he cannot take so broad a survey of his trade, or look so far ahead, he must often be content to follow the lead of others. And he must spend much of his time on work that is below him, for if he is to succeed at all, his mind must be in some respects of a high quality, and must have a good deal of originating and organizing force; and yet he must do much routine work

those of the small manufacturer

On the other hand the small employer has advantages of his own The master's eye is everywhere, there is no shirking by his foremen or workmen, no divided responsibility, no sending half-understood messages backwards and forwards from one department to another. He saves much of the book-keeping, and nearly all of the cumbrous system of checks that are necessary in the business of a large firm; and the gain from this source is of very great importance in trades which use the more valuable metals and other expensive materials.

And though he must always remain at a great disadvantage in getting information and in making experiments, yet in this matter the general course of progress is on his side. For External economies are constantly growing in importance relatively to Internal in all matters of Trade-knowledge: newspapers, and trade and technical publications of all kinds are perpetually scouting for him and bringing him much of the knowledge he wants—knowledge which a little while ago would have been beyond the reach of anyone who could not afford to have well-paid agents in many distant places. Again, it is to his interest also that the secrecy of business is on the whole diminishing, and that the most important improvements in method seldom remain secret for long after they have passed from the experimental stage It is to his advantage that changes in manufacture depend less on mere rules of thumb and more on broad developments of scientific principle; and that many of these are made by students in the pursuit of knowledge for its own sake, and are promptly published in the general interest. Although therefore the small manufacturer can seldom be in the front of the race of progress, he need not be far from it, if he has the time and the ability for availing himself of the modern facilities for obtaining knowledge But it is true that he must be exceptionally strong if he can do this without neglecting the minor but necessary details of the business.

Advantages of large businesses of other kinds

§ 5 The advantages which a large business has over a small one are conspicuous in manufacture, because, as we have noticed, it has special facilities for concentrating a great deal of work in a small area. But there is a strong tendency for large establishments to drive out small ones in many other industries. In particular the retail trade is being transformed, the small shopkeeper is losing ground daily

In retail trade they are on the increase

Let us look at the advantages which a large retail shop or store has in competing with its smaller neighbours. To begin with, it can obviously buy on better terms, it can get its goods carried more cheaply, and can offer a larger variety to meet the taste of customers Next, it has a great economy of skill the small shopkeeper, like the small manufacturer, must spend much of his time in routine work that requires no judgment · whereas the head of a large establishment, and even in some cases his chief assistants, spend their whole time in using their judgment Until lately these advantages have been generally outweighed by the greater facilities which the small shopkeeper has for bringing his goods to the door of his customers; for humouring their several tastes, and for knowing enough of them individually to be able safely to lend them capital, in the form of selling them goods on credit

owing to the growth of cash payments

But within recent years there have been many changes all telling on the side of large establishments The habit of buying on credit is passing away; and the personal relations between shopkeeper and customer are becoming more distant. The first change is a great step forwards: the second is on some accounts to be regretted, but not on all, for it is partly due to the fact that the increase of true self-respect among the wealthier classes is making them no longer care for the subservient personal attentions they used to require Again, the growing value of time makes people less willing than they were to spend several hours in shopping; they now often prefer to spend a few minutes in writing out a long list of orders from a varied and detailed price-list; and this they are enabled to do easily by the growing facilities for ordering and receiving parcels by post and in other ways. And when they do go shopping, tramcars and local trains are often at hand to take them easily and cheaply to the large central shops of a neighbouring town. All these changes render it more difficult than it was for the small shopkeeper to hold his own even in the provision trade, and others in which no great variety of stock is required.

and the increasing variety of the goods in common demand

But in many trades the ever-growing variety of commodities, and those rapid changes of fashion which now extend their baneful influence through almost every rank of society, weight the balance even more heavily against the small dealer, for he cannot keep a sufficient stock to offer much variety of choice, and if he tries to follow any movement of fashion closely, a larger proportion of his stock will be left stranded by the receding tide than in the case of a large shopkeeper. Again, in some branches of the clothing and furniture and other trades the increasing cheapness of machine-made goods is leading people to buy ready-made things from a large store instead of having them made to order by some small maker and dealer in their neighbourhood. Again, the large shopkeeper, not content with receiving travellers from the manufacturers, makes tours either himself or by his agent in the most important manufacturing

BOOK IV CH. XI

districts at home and abroad, and he thus dispenses almost entirely with middlemen between him and the manufacturer. On the other hand, in some branches of the textile trades, the ease with which large packets of patterns are distributed by manufacturers and warehousemen, is telling perceptibly on the side of the small shopkeeper[1].

Small shopkeepers seem likely always to retain some hold of the repairing trades: and they keep their own fairly well in the sale of perishable food, especially to the working classes, partly in consequence of their being able to sell goods on credit and to collect small debts. But on the whole they are losing ground It is not certain that they are positively decreasing in number; but they certainly do not get their share of the rapidly increasing retail business of the country[2].

The social importance of this question.

The decay of small manufacturers appeared to the economists in the first half of the century as one of the chief causes that were changing the character of England's industrial and social life · the relative decline of small shopkeepers seems to be at least as potent an influence just at the present time And it is noteworthy that those small shopkeepers who are holding their own best, are also as a rule producers on a small scale, and *vice versâ*

§ 6. We may next consider those industries whose geographical position is determined by the nature of their work.

The carrying trades

Country carriers and a few cabmen are almost the only survivals of small industry in the carrying trade: and American experience causes some doubt as to how long cabs will remain in general use. Railways and tramways are con-

[1] A tailor with moderate capital shows his customers specimens of many hundreds of the newest cloths, and perhaps orders by telegraph the selected cloth to be sent by parcels' post Again, ladies often buy their materials direct from the manufacturer, and get them made up by dressmakers who have scarcely any capital.

[2] In many trades a firm with a large capital prefers having many small shops to one large one. The buying, and what production is desirable, is concentrated under a central management, and exceptional demands can be met from a central reserve, so that each branch has large resources, without the expense of keeping a large stock The branch manager has nothing to divert his attention from his customers; and if an active man, with direct interest in the success of his branch, may prove himself a formidable rival to the small shopkeeper; as has been shown in many trades connected with clothing and food.

stantly increasing in size, and the capital required to work them is increasing at an even greater rate. The growing intricacy and variety of commerce is adding to the advantages which a large fleet of ships under one management derives from its power of delivering goods promptly, and without breach of responsibility, in many different ports; and as regards the vessels themselves time is on the side of large ships, especially in the passenger trade[1]. As a consequence the arguments in favour of the State's undertaking business are stronger in some branches of the carrying trade than in any other, except the allied undertakings of carrying away refuse, and bringing in water, gas, &c.[2]

Mines and quarries

The contest between large and small mines and quarries has not so clearly marked a tendency The history of the State management of mines is full of very dark shadows, for the business of mining depends too much on the probity of its managers and their energy and judgment in matters of detail as well as of general principle, to be well managed by State officials: and for the same reason the small mine or quarry may fairly be expected, other things being equal, to hold its own against the large one. But in some cases the cost of deep shafts, of machinery and of establishing means of communication, are too great to be borne by any but a very large business[3]

[1] A ship's carrying power varies as the cube of her dimensions, while the resistance offered by the water increases only a little faster than the square of her dimensions, so that a large ship requires less coal in proportion to its tonnage than a small one It also requires less labour, especially that of navigation while to passengers it offers greater safety and comfort, more choice of company and better professional attendance In short, the small ship has no chance of competing with the large ship between ports, which large ships can easily enter, and between which the traffic is sufficient to enable them to fill up quickly

[2] It is characteristic of the great economic change of the last half century that when the first railway bills were passed, provision was made for allowing private individuals to run their own conveyances on them, just as they do on a highway or a canal; and now we find it difficult to imagine how people could have expected, as they certainly did, that this plan would prove a practicable one

[3] While the output of coal in this country is increasing, the number of mines is diminishing but this is partly due to the closing of many of the new mines which were hastily opened some years ago when the price of coal was very high The contests between the large and small methods of production has led to interesting episodes in the African diamond mines and the American oil regions. The Sutro tunnel and the American oil ducts are good instances of the way

BOOK IV. CH XI.

The case of agriculture is deferred.

In agriculture there is not much division of labour, and there is no production on a very large scale; for a so-called "large farm" does not employ a tenth part of the labour which is collected in a factory of moderate dimensions. This is partly due to natural causes, to the changes of the seasons and to the difficulty of concentrating a great deal of labour in any one place; but it is partly also due to causes connected with varieties of land tenure And it will be best to postpone discussion of all of them till we come to study Demand and Supply in relation to Land in the sixth Book[1].

in which a provision may be made for the joint use of a number of mines, which no one of them could afford separately; but they also show how this course gives openings for the formation of powerful monopolies

[1] There is much of general interest bearing on the subjects of this and the neighbouring chapters in general economic histories, such as those of Ashley and Cunningham, and in Cooke Taylor's *Factory System*, Jevons' *Coal Question* and Hobson's *Evolution of Modern Capitalism* A further discussion of the causes which prevent a single large firm from so availing itself of the economies of production on a large scale as to drive out all its rivals, will be found below, Book v. Ch XI § 2

CHAPTER XII.

INDUSTRIAL ORGANIZATION, CONTINUED. BUSINESS MANAGEMENT.

BOOK IV. CH XII.

A problem to be solved

§ 1. We have next to study the conditions of Business Management, and in so doing we must have in view a problem that will occupy our attention as we go on. It arises from the fact that, though in manufacturing at least nearly every individual business, so long as it is well managed, tends to become stronger the larger it has grown; and though *primâ facie* we might therefore expect to see large firms driving their smaller rivals completely out of many branches of industry, yet they do not in fact do so

Business management has many forms.

Business may be taken to include all provision for the wants of others which is made in the expectation of payment direct or indirect from those who are to be benefitted. It is thus contrasted with the provision for our own wants which each of us makes for himself, and with those kindly services which are prompted by family affection and the desire to promote the well-being of others Business management or undertaking has always had many different forms, and their number and variety was never so great as in England now. Relics remain of almost every form that has ever been in use, while new forms are constantly being developed.

The primitive handicraftsman dealt directly with the consumer;

The primitive handicraftsman managed his whole business for himself; but since his customers were with few exceptions his immediate neighbours, since he required very little capital, since the plan of production was arranged for him by custom, and since he had no labour to superintend outside of his own household, these tasks did not involve any very great mental strain He was far from enjoying unbroken prosperity, war

BOOK IV. CH XII

and scarcity were constantly pressing on him and his neighbours, hindering his work and stopping their demand for his wares. But he was inclined to take good and evil fortune, like sunshine and rain, as things beyond his control: his fingers worked on, but his brain was seldom weary

and so do as a rule the learned professions now

Even in modern England we find now and then a village artisan who adheres to primitive methods, and makes things on his own account for sale to his neighbours; managing his own business and undertaking all its risks. But such cases are rare: the most striking instances of an adherence to old-fashioned methods of business are supplied by the learned professions; for a physician or a solicitor manages as a rule his own business and does all its work. This plan is not without its disadvantages· much valuable activity is wasted or turned to but slight account by some professional men of first-rate ability, who have not the special aptitude required for obtaining a business connection; they would be better paid, would lead happier lives, and would do more good service for the world if their work could be arranged for them by some sort of a middleman. But yet on the whole things are probably best as they are: there are sound reasons behind the popular instinct which distrusts the intrusion of the middleman in the supply of those services which require the highest and most delicate mental qualities, and which can have their full value only where there is complete personal confidence.

But there are exceptions even here

English solicitors however act, if not as employers or undertakers, yet as agents for hiring that branch of the legal profession which ranks highest, and whose work involves the hardest mental strain Again, many of the best instructors of youths sell their services, not directly to the consumer, but to the governing body of a college or school, or to a head master, who arranges for their purchase: the employer supplies to the teacher a market for his labour, and is supposed to give to the purchaser, who may not be a good judge himself, some sort of guarantee as to the quality of the teaching supplied

Again, artists of every kind, however eminent, often find it to their advantage to employ someone else to arrange for them with customers; while those of less established repute are sometimes dependent for their living on capitalist traders, who are not themselves artists, but who understand how to sell artistic work to the best advantage.

In most businesses the services of a special class of undertakers intervene

§ 2. But in the greater part of the business of the modern world the task of so directing production that a given effort may be most effective in supplying human wants has to be broken up and given into the hands of a specialized body of employers, or to use a more general term, of business men They "adventure" or "undertake" its risks; they bring together the capital and the labour required for the work; they arrange or "engineer" its general plan, and superintend its minor details. Looking at business men from one point of view we may regard them as a highly skilled industrial grade, from another as middlemen intervening between the manual worker and the consumer.

There are some kinds of business men who undertake great risks, and exercise a large influence over the welfare both of the producers and of the consumers of the wares in which they deal, but who are not to any considerable extent direct employers of labour The extreme type of these is the dealer on the stock exchange or the produce markets, whose daily purchases and sales are of vast dimensions, and who yet has neither factory nor warehouse, but at most an office with a few clerks in it. The good and the evil effects of the action of speculators such as these are however very complex, and we may give our attention at present to those forms of business in which administration counts for most and the subtler forms of speculation for least Let us then take some illustrations of the more common types of business, and watch the relations in which the undertaking of risks stands to the rest of the work of the business man

Illustration from house building.

§ 3 The building trade will serve our purpose well, partly because it adheres in some respects to primitive methods of business. Late in the Middle Ages it was quite common for a private person to build a house for himself without the aid of a master builder; and the habit is not even now altogether extinct. A person who undertakes his own building must hire separately all his workmen, he must

BOOK IV. CH. XII

watch them and check their demands for payment; he must buy his materials from many quarters, and he must hire, or dispense with the use of expensive machinery. He probably pays more than the current wages; but here others gain what he loses There is however great waste in the time he spends in bargaining with the men and testing and directing their work by his imperfect knowledge, and again in the time that he spends in finding out what kinds and quantities he wants of different materials, and where to get them best, and so on. This waste is avoided by that division of labour which assigns to the professional builder the task of superintending details, and to the professional architect the task of drawing plans

The chief risks of undertaking sometimes separated from detailed management in the building trades,

The division of labour is often carried still further when houses are built not at the expense of those who are to live in them, but as a building speculation When this is done on a large scale, as for instance in opening out a new suburb, the stakes at issue are so large as to offer an attractive field to powerful capitalists with a very high order of general business ability, but perhaps with not much technical knowledge of the building trade. They rely on their own judgment for the decision as to what are likely to be the coming relations of demand and supply for different kinds of houses, but they intrust to others the management of details They employ architects and surveyors to make plans in accordance with their general directions, and then enter into contracts with professional builders for carrying them out. But they themselves undertake the chief risks of the business, and control its general direction.

in the textile trades,

§ 4. We have already seen[1] how this division of responsibility prevailed in the woollen trade just before the beginning of the era of large factories · the more speculative work and the broader risks of buying and selling being taken over by the undertakers, who were not themselves employers of labour; while the detailed work of superintendence and the narrower risks of carrying out definite contracts were handed over to small masters. This plan is still extensively followed in some branches of the textile trades, especially those in which the difficulty of forecasting the future is very great.

[1] Book I Ch III § 4

Manchester warehousemen give themselves to studying the movements of fashion, the markets for raw materials, the general state of trade, of the money market and of politics, and all other causes that are likely to influence the prices of different kinds of goods during the coming season; and after employing, if necessary, skilled designers to carry out their ideas (just as the building speculator in the previous case employed architects), they give out to manufacturers in different parts of the world contracts for making the goods on which they have determined to risk their capital.

in house industries;

In the clothing trades especially we see a revival of what has been called the "house industry," which prevailed long ago in the textile industries, that is, the system in which large undertakers give out work to be done in cottages and very small workshops to persons who work alone or with the aid of some members of their family, or who perhaps employ two or three hired assistants[1]. In remote villages in almost every county of England agents of large undertakers come round to give out to the cottagers partially prepared materials for goods of all sorts, but especially clothes such as shirts and collars and gloves, and take back with them the finished goods. It is however in the great capital cities of the world, and in other large towns, especially old towns, where there is a great deal of unskilled and unorganized labour, with a somewhat low physique and morale, that the system is most fully developed, especially in the clothing trades, which employ two hundred thousand people in London alone, and in the cheap furniture trades. There is a continual contest between the factory and the domestic

[1] The German economists call this "factory like" (fabrikmassig) house industry, as distinguished from the "National" house industry, which uses the intervals of other work (especially the winter interruptions of agriculture) for subsidiary work in making textile and other goods. (See Schonberg on *Gewerbe* in his *Handbuch*.) Domestic workers of this last class were common all over Europe in the Middle Ages but are now becoming rare except in the mountains and in Eastern Europe. They are not always well advised in their choice of work, and much of what they make could be made better with far less labour in factories, so that it cannot be sold profitably in the open market: but for the most part they make for their own or their neighbours' use, and thus save the profits of a series of middlemen. Compare *Survival of domestic industries* by Gonner in the *Economic Journal*, Vol. II.

BOOK IV. CH XII

system, now one gaining ground and now the other: for instance just at present the growing use of sewing machines worked by steam power is strengthening the position of the factories in the boot trade; while factories and workshops are getting an increased hold of the tailoring trade. On the other hand the hosiery trade is being tempted back to the dwelling-house by recent improvements in hand knitting machines, and it is possible that new methods of distributing power by gas and petroleum and electric engines may exercise a like influence on many other industries.

in Sheffield trades;

Or there may be a movement towards intermediate plans, similar to those which are largely followed in the Sheffield trades Many cutlery firms for instance put out grinding and other parts of their work, at piece-work prices, to working men who rent the steam power which they require, either from the firm from whom they take their contract or from someone else: these workmen sometimes employing others to help them, sometimes working alone.

in the shipping trade,

Again, the foreign merchant very often has no ships of his own, but gives his mind to studying the course of trade, and undertakes himself its chief risks, while he gets his carrying done for him by men who require more administrative ability, but need not have the same power of forecasting the subtler movements of trade, though it is true that as purchasers of ships they have great and difficult trade risks of their own.

and in the production of books &c

Again, the broader risks of publishing a book are borne by the publisher, perhaps in company with the author, while the printer is the employer of labour and supplies the expensive types and machinery required for the business. And a somewhat similar plan is adopted in many branches of the metal trades, and of those which supply furniture, clothing, &c.

This plan has advantages,

Thus there are many ways in which those who undertake the chief risks of buying and selling may avoid the trouble of housing and superintending those who work for them. They all have their advantages, and when the workers are men of strong character, as at Sheffield, the results are on

but is liable to abuse

the whole not unsatisfactory. But unfortunately it is often the weakest class of workers, those with the least resource and the least self-control who drift into work of this kind.

The elasticity of the system which recommends it to the undertaker, is really the means of enabling him to exercise, if he chooses, an undesirable pressure on those who do his work.

For while the success of a factory depends in a great measure on its having a set of operatives who adhere steadily to it, the capitalist who gives out work to be done at home has an interest in retaining a great many persons on his books, he is tempted to give each of them a little employment occasionally and play them off one against another, and this he can easily do because they do not know one another, and cannot arrange concerted action.

Several distinct functions are combined in one hand by the ideal manufacturer

§ 5 When the profits of business are under discussion they are generally connected in people's minds with the employer of labour: "the employer" is often taken as a term practically coextensive with the receiver of business profits But the instances which we have just considered are sufficient to illustrate the truth that the superintendence of labour is but one side, and often not the most important side of business work; and that the employer who undertakes the whole risks of his business really performs two entirely distinct services on behalf of the community, and requires a twofold ability

the faculties required in him

The ideal manufacturer, for instance, if he makes goods not to meet special orders but for the general market, must, in his first rôle as merchant and organizer of production, have a thorough knowledge of *things* in his own trade He must have the power of forecasting the broad movements of production and consumption, of seeing where there is an opportunity for supplying a new commodity that will meet a real want or improving the plan of producing an old commodity He must be able to judge cautiously and undertake risks boldly; and he must of course understand the materials and machinery used in his trade.

But secondly in this rôle of employer he must be a natural leader of *men*. He must have a power of first choosing his assistants rightly and then trusting them fully; of interesting them in the business and of getting them to trust him, so as to bring out whatever enterprise and power of origination

BOOK IV. CH XII

there is in them; while he himself exercises a general control over everything, and preserves order and unity in the main plan of the business

The abilities required to make an ideal employer are so great and so numerous that very few persons can exhibit them all in a very high degree. Their relative importance however varies with the nature of the industry and the size of the business; and while one employer excels in one set of qualities, another excels in another; scarcely any two owe their success to exactly the same combination of advantages. Some men make their way by the use of none but noble qualities, while others owe their prosperity to qualities in which there is very little that is really admirable except sagacity and strength of purpose.

The supply of business ability may be discussed in connection with the forms of business management

Such then being the general nature of the work of business management, we have next to inquire what opportunities different classes of people have of developing business ability; and, when they have obtained that, what opportunities they have of getting command over the capital required to give it scope We may thus come a little closer to the problem stated at the beginning of the chapter, and examine the course of development of a business firm during several consecutive generations. And this inquiry may conveniently be combined with some examination of the different forms of business management Hitherto we have considered almost exclusively that form in which the whole responsibility and control rests in the hands of a single individual But this form is yielding ground to others in which the supreme authority is distributed among several partners or even a great number of shareholders. Private firms and joint-stock companies, co-operative societies and public corporations are taking a constantly increasing share in the management of business; and one chief reason of this is that they offer an attractive field to people who have good business abilities, but have not inherited any great business opportunities

The son of a business man has a good start

§ 6. It is obvious that the son of a man already established in business starts with very great advantages over others He has from his youth up special facilities for obtaining the knowledge and developing the faculties that are required in the management of his father's business: he learns quietly and almost unconsciously about men and manners in his father's trade and in those from which that trade buys and to which it sells, he gets to know the relative importance and the real significance of the various problems and anxieties which occupy his father's mind: and he acquires a technical knowledge of the processes and the machinery of the trade[1] Some of what he learns will be applicable only to his father's trade, but the greater part will be serviceable in any trade that is in any way allied with that; while those general faculties of judgment and resource, of enterprise and caution, of firmness and courtesy, which are trained by association with those who control the larger issues of any one trade, will go a long way towards fitting him for managing almost any other trade Further, the sons of successful business men start with more material capital than almost anyone else except those who by nurture and education are likely to be disinclined for business and unfitted for it: and if they continue their fathers' work, they have also the vantage ground of established trade connections.

But business men do not form a caste, because their abilities and tastes are not always inherited,

It would therefore at first sight seem likely that business men should constitute a sort of caste, dividing out among their sons the chief posts of command, and founding hereditary dynasties, which should rule certain branches of trade for many generations together But the actual state of things is very different For when a man has got together a great business, his descendants often fail, in spite of their great advantages, to develop the high abilities and the special turn of mind and temperament required for carrying it on with equal success He himself was probably brought up by parents of strong earnest character, and was educated by their personal influence and by struggle with difficulties in early life. But his children, at all events if they were born after he became rich, and in any case his grandchildren,

[1] We have already noticed how almost the only perfect apprenticeships of modern times are those of the sons of manufacturers, who practise almost every important operation that is carried on in the works sufficiently to be able in after years to enter into the difficulties of all their employés and form a fair judgment on their work

BOOK IV. CH. XII

are perhaps left a good deal to the care of domestic servants who are not of the same strong fibre as the parents by whose influence he was educated. And while his highest ambition was probably success in business, they are likely to be at least equally anxious for social or academic distinction[1].

For a time indeed all may go well. His sons find a firmly established trade connection, and what is perhaps even more important, a well-chosen staff of subordinates with a generous interest in the business By mere assiduity and caution, availing themselves of the traditions of the firm, they may hold together for a long time. But when a full generation has passed, when the old traditions are no longer a safe guide, and when the bonds that held together the old staff have been dissolved, then the business almost invariably falls to pieces unless it is practically handed over to the management of new men who have meanwhile risen to partnership in the firm.

and after a time new blood must be brought in by some method.

But in most cases his descendants arrive at this result by a shorter route They prefer an abundant income coming to them without effort on their part, to one which though twice as large could be earned only by incessant toil and anxiety, and they sell the business to private persons or a joint-stock company, or they become sleeping partners in it; that is sharing in its risks and in its profits, but not taking part in its management: in either case the active control over their capital falls chiefly into the hands of new men.

The method of private partnership.

§ 7. The oldest and simplest plan for renovating the energies of a business is that of taking into partnership some of its ablest employés The autocratic owner and manager of a large manufacturing or trading concern finds that, as years go on, he has to delegate more and more responsibility to his chief subordinates; partly because the work to be

[1] Until lately there has ever been in England a kind of antagonism between academic studies and business This is now being diminished by the broadening of the spirit of our great Universities, and by the growth of Colleges in our chief business centres The sons of business men when sent to the Universities do not learn to despise their fathers' trades as often as they used to do even a generation ago Many of them indeed are drawn away from business by the desire to extend the boundaries of knowledge But the higher forms of mental activity, those which are constructive and not merely critical, tend to promote a just appreciation of the nobility of business work rightly done.

done is growing heavier, and partly because his own strength is becoming less than it was. He still exercises a supreme control, but much must depend on their energy and probity: so, if his sons are not old enough, or for any other reason are not ready to take part of the burden off his shoulders, he decides to take one of his trusted assistants into partnership he thus lightens his own labours, at the same time that he secures that the task of his life will be carried on by those whose habits he has moulded, and for whom he has perhaps acquired something like a fatherly affection[1].

But there are now, and there always have been, private partnerships on more equal terms, two or more people of about equal wealth and ability combining their resources for a large and difficult undertaking In such cases there is often a distinct partition of the work of management: in manufactures for instance one partner will sometimes give himself almost exclusively to the work of buying raw material and selling the finished product, while the other is responsible for the management of the factory and in a trading establishment one partner will control the wholesale and the other the retail department. In these and other ways private partnership is capable of adapting itself to a great variety of problems: it is very strong and very elastic, it has played a great part in the past, and it is full of vitality now

The method of public joint-stock companies

§ 8. But from the end of the Middle Ages to the present time there has been in some classes of trades a movement towards the substitution of public joint-stock companies, the shares of which can be sold to anybody in the open market, for private companies, the shares in which are not transferable without the leave of all concerned. The effect of this change has been to induce people, many of whom have no special knowledge of trade, to give their capital into the hands of others employed by them and there has thus

[1] Much of the happiest romance of life, much that is most pleasant to dwell upon in the social history of England from the Middle Ages up to our own day is connected with the story of private partnerships of this class Many a youth has been stimulated to a brave career by the influence of ballads and tales which narrate the difficulties and the ultimate triumph of the faithful apprentice, who has at length married his employer's daughter and been taken into partnership by him There are no influences on national character more far-reaching than those which thus give shape to the aims of aspiring youth

BOOK IV CH XII

arisen a new distribution of the various parts of the work of business management.

The shareholders undertake the risks;

The ultimate undertakers of the risks incurred by a joint-stock company are the shareholders, but as a rule they do not take much active part in engineering the business and controlling its general policy; and they take no part in superintending its details. After the business has once got out of the hands of its original promoters, the control of it is left chiefly in the hands of Directors; who, if the company is a very large one, probably own but a very small proportion of its shares, while the greater part of them have not much technical knowledge of the work to be done. They are not generally expected to give their whole time to it, but they are supposed to bring wide general knowledge and sound judgment to bear on the broader problems of its policy, and at the same time to make sure that the "Managers" of the company are doing their work thoroughly[1]. To the Managers and their assistants is left a great part of the work of engineering the business, and the whole of the work of superintending it. but they are not required to bring any capital into it, and they are supposed to be promoted from the lower ranks to the higher according to their zeal and ability. Since the joint-stock companies in the United Kingdom have an aggregate income of £100,000,000, and do a tenth of the business of all kinds that is done in the country, they offer very large opportunities to men with natural talents for business management, who have not inherited any material capital, or any business connection.

the Directors control the Managers; who superintend the details

Those who undertake the risks cannot always

§ 9. Joint-stock companies have great elasticity and can expand themselves without limit when the work to which they have set themselves offers a wide scope; and they are

[1] Bagehot delighted to argue (see for instance *English Constitution*, Ch. VII) that a Cabinet Minister often derives some advantage from his want of technical knowledge of the business of his Department For he can get information on matters of detail from the Permanent Secretary and other officials who are under his authority; and, while he is not likely to set his judgment against theirs on matters where their knowledge gives them the advantage, his unprejudiced common sense may well overrule the traditions of officialism in broad questions of public policy and in like manner the interests of a Company may possibly sometimes be most advanced by those Directors who have the least technical knowledge of the details of its business

gaining ground in nearly all directions But they have one great source of weakness in the absence of any adequate knowledge of the business on the part of the shareholders who undertake its chief risks. It is true that the head of a large private firm undertakes the chief risks of the business, while he intrusts many of its details to others; but his position is secured by his power of forming a direct judgment as to whether his subordinates serve his interests faithfully and discreetly. If those to whom he has intrusted the buying or selling of goods for him take commissions from those with whom they deal, he is in a position to discover and punish the fraud. If they show favouritism and promote incompetent relations or friends of their own, or if they themselves become idle and shirk their work, or even if they do not fulfil the promise of exceptional ability which induced him to give them their first lift, he can discover what is going wrong and set it right.

judge whether the business is well managed

But in all these matters the great body of the shareholders of a joint-stock company are, save in a few exceptional instances, almost powerless, though a few of the larger shareholders often exert themselves to find out what is going on; and are thus able to exercise an effective and wise control over the general management of the business It is a strong proof of the marvellous growth in recent times of a spirit of honesty and uprightness in commercial matters, that the leading officers of great public companies yield as little as they do to the vast temptations to fraud which lie in their way. If they showed an eagerness to avail themselves of opportunities for wrong doing at all approaching that of which we read in the commercial history of earlier civilization, their wrong uses of the trusts imposed in them would have been on so great a scale as to prevent the development of this democratic form of business There is every reason to hope that the progress of trade morality will continue, aided in the future as it has been in the past, by a diminution of trade secrecy and by increased publicity in every form; and thus collective and democratic forms of business management may be able to extend themselves safely in many directions in which they have hitherto failed, and may

The system is rendered workable only by the modern growth of business morality

far exceed the great services they already render in opening a large career to those who have no advantages of birth.

Government undertakings

The same may be said of the undertakings of Governments imperial and local they also may have a great future before them, but up to the present time the tax-payer who undertakes the ultimate risks has not generally succeeded in exercising an efficient control over the businesses, and in securing officers who will do their work with as much energy and enterprise as is shown in private establishments. The problem of Government undertakings involves however many complex issues, into which we cannot inquire here.

Co-operative association in its ideal form

§ 10 The system of Co-operation aims at avoiding the evils of these two methods of business management. In that ideal form of Co-operative Society, for which many still fondly hope, but which as yet has been scantily realized in practice, a part or the whole of those shareholders who undertake the risks of the business are themselves employed by it. The employés, whether they contribute towards the material capital of the business or not, have a share in its profits, and some power of voting at the general meetings at which the broad lines of its policy are laid down, and the officers appointed who are to carry that policy into effect. They are thus the employers and masters of their own managers and foremen; they have fairly good means of judging whether the higher work of engineering the business is conducted honestly and efficiently, and they have the best possible opportunities for detecting any laxity or incompetence in its detailed administration. And lastly they render unnecessary some of the minor work of superintendence that is required in other establishments; for their own pecuniary interests and the pride they take in the success of their own business make each of them averse to any shirking of work either by himself or by his fellow workmen

might avoid the chief dangers of joint-stock companies.

It has difficulties in the task of business management,

But unfortunately the system has very great difficulties of its own. For human nature being what it is, the employés themselves are not always the best possible masters of their own foremen and managers, jealousies and frettings at reproof are apt to act like sand, that has got mixed with the oil in the bearings of a great and complex machinery The hardest work of business management is generally that which makes the least outward show, those who work with their hands are apt to underrate the intensity of the strain involved in the highest work of engineering the business, and to grudge its being paid for at anything like as high a rate as it could earn elsewhere. And in fact the managers of a Co-operative Society seldom have the alertness, the inventiveness and the ready versatility of the ablest of those men who have been selected by the struggle for survival, and have been trained by the perfectly free and unfettered responsibility of private business. Partly for these reasons the Co-operative system has seldom been carried out in its entirety; and its partial application has not yet attained a conspicuous success except in retailing commodities consumed by working men But within the last few years more hopeful signs have appeared of the success of *bonâ fide* productive associations, or "co-partnerships."

but it may outgrow some of these

Those working-men indeed whose tempers are strongly individualistic, and whose minds are concentrated almost wholly on their own affairs, will perhaps always find their quickest and most congenial path to material success by commencing business as small independent "undertakers," or by working their way upwards in a private firm or a public company But co-operation has a special charm for those in whose tempers the social element is stronger, and who desire not to separate themselves from their old comrades, but to work among them as their leaders. Its aspirations may in some respects be higher than its practice, but it undoubtedly does rest in a great measure on ethical motives. The true co-operator combines a keen business intellect with a spirit full of an earnest Faith, and some co-operative societies have been served excellently by men of great genius both mentally and morally—men who for the sake of the Co-operative Faith that is in them, have worked with great ability and energy, and with perfect uprightness, being all the time content with lower pay than they could have got as business managers on their own account or for a private firm. Men of this stamp are more common among the officers of co-operative societies than in other occupations; and though they are not very common even there, yet it may be hoped that the diffusion of a better knowledge of the true principles of co-operation, and the increase of general education, are every day fitting a larger number of co-operators for the complex problems of business management

Profit-Sharing

Meanwhile many partial applications of the co-operative principle are being tried under various conditions, each of which presents some new aspect of business management Thus under the scheme of Profit-Sharing, a private firm while retaining the unfettered management of its business, pays its employés the full market rate of wages, whether by Time or Piece-work, and agrees in addition to divide among them a certain share of any profits that may be made above a certain fixed minimum, it being hoped that the firm will find a material as well as a moral reward in the diminution of friction, in the increased willingness of their employés to go out of their way to do little things that may be of great benefit comparatively to the firm, and lastly in attracting to themselves workers of more than average ability and industry

Profit and Loss-Sharing

Under the scheme of Profit-and-Loss-Sharing, a small part of the market wages of the employés is held back as a contribution towards any loss that may be shown on the year's working, while they receive a more than proportionate share of the profits in a bad year

Partial Co-operation

Another partially co-operative scheme is that of some Oldham Cotton-mills. they are really joint-stock companies; but among their shareholders are many working men who have a special knowledge of the trade, though they often prefer not to be employed in the mills of which they are part owners. And another is that of the Productive establishments, owned by the main body of Co-operative Stores, through their agents, the Co-operative Wholesale Society, but in which, partly on account of technical difficulties, the workers as such have as yet no share either in the management or in the profits of the works.

At a later stage we shall have to study all those various co-operative and semi-co-operative forms of business more in detail, and to inquire into the causes of their success or failure in different classes of business, wholesale and retail, agricultural, manufacturing and trading. But we must not pursue this inquiry further now. Enough has been said to show that the world is only just beginning to be ready for the higher work of the co-operative movement, and that its many different forms may therefore be reasonably expected to attain a larger success in the future than in the past; and to offer excellent opportunities for working-men to practise themselves in the work of business management, to grow into the trust and confidence of others, and gradually rise to posts in which their business abilities will find scope

Hopes for the future

§ **11.** In speaking of the difficulty that a working-man has in rising to a post in which he can turn his business ability to full account, the chief stress is commonly laid upon his want of capital. but this is not always his chief difficulty. For instance the co-operative distributive societies have accumulated a vast capital, on which they find it difficult to get a good rate of interest, and which they would be rejoiced to lend to any set of working-men who could show that they had the capacity for dealing with difficult business problems. Co-operators who have firstly a high order of business ability and probity, and secondly the "personal capital" of a great reputation among their fellows for these qualities, will have no difficulty in getting command of enough material capital for a considerable undertaking: the real difficulty is to convince a sufficient number of those around them that they have these rare qualities. And the case is not very different when an individual endeavours to obtain from the ordinary sources the loan of the capital required to start him in business

The rise of the working-man is not hindered as much as at first sight appears, by his want of capital,

It is true that in almost every business there is a constant increase in the amount of capital required to make a fair start, but there is a much more rapid increase in the amount of capital which is owned by people who do not want to use it themselves, and are so eager to lend it out that they will accept a constantly lower and lower rate of interest for it. Much of this capital passes into the hands of bankers and others, people of keen intellect and restless energy; people who have no class prejudices and care nothing for social distinctions; and who would promptly lend it to anyone of

for the loan-fund is increasing in volume and in eagerness for employment

whose business ability and honesty they were convinced. To say nothing of the credit that can be got in many businesses from those who supply the requisite raw material or stock in trade, the opportunities for direct borrowing are now so great that an increase in the amount of capital required for a start in business is no very serious obstacle in the way of a person who has once got over the initial difficulty of earning a reputation for being likely to use it well.

He is hindered much by the growing complexity of business;

But perhaps a greater though less conspicuous hindrance to the rise of the working man is the growing complexity of business. The head of a business has now to think of many things about which he never used to trouble himself in earlier days; and these are just the kind of difficulties for which the training of the workshop affords the least preparation. Against this must be set the rapid improvement of the education of the working man not only at school, but what is more important, in after life by newspapers, and from the work of co-operative societies and trades unions, and in other ways.

but he may overcome these difficulties

About three-fourths of the whole population of England belong to the wage-earning classes; and at all events when they are well fed, properly housed and educated, they have their fair share of that nervous strength which is the raw material of business ability. Without going out of their way they are all consciously or unconsciously competitors for posts of business command The ordinary workman if he shows ability generally becomes a foreman, from that he may rise to be a manager, and to be taken into partnership with his employer. Or having saved a little of his own he may start one of those small shops which still can hold their own in a working man's quarter, stock it chiefly on credit, and let his wife attend to it by day, while he gives his evenings to it. In these or in other ways he may increase his capital till he can start a small workshop, or factory. Once having made a good beginning he will find the banks eager to give him generous credit. He must have time; and since he is not likely to start in business till after middle age he must have a long as well as a strong life; but if he has this and has also "patience, genius and good fortune" he is pretty sure to command a large capital before he dies[1] In a factory those who work with their hands have better opportunities of rising to posts of command than the book-keepers and many others to whom social tradition has assigned a higher place But in trading concerns it is otherwise, what manual work is done in them has as a rule no educating character, while the experience of the office is better adapted for preparing a man to manage a commercial than a manufacturing business

The rise may take two generations instead of one,

There is then on the whole a broad movement from below upwards. Perhaps not so many as formerly rise at once from the position of working-men to that of employers: but there are more who get on sufficiently far to give their sons a good chance of attaining to the highest posts The complete rise is not so very often accomplished in one generation; it is more often spread over two; but the total volume of the movement upwards is probably greater than it has ever been. And it may be remarked in passing that it is better for society as a whole that the rise should be distributed over two generations. The workmen who at the beginning of this century rose in such large numbers to become employers were seldom fit for posts of command· they were too often harsh and tyrannical, they lost their self-control, and were neither truly noble nor truly happy; while their children were often haughty, extravagant, and self-indulgent, squandering their wealth on low and vulgar amusements, having the worst faults of the older aristocracy without their virtues The foreman or superintendent who has still to obey as well as to

but that is not an unmixed evil.

[1] The Germans say that success in business requires "Geld, Geduld, Genie und Glück" The chances that a working-man has of rising vary somewhat with the nature of the work, being greatest in those trades in which a careful attention to details counts for most, and a wide knowledge, whether of science or of the world movements of speculation, counts for least Thus for instance "thrift and the knowledge of practical details" are the most important elements of success in the ordinary work of the pottery trade, and in consequence most of those who have done well in it "have risen from the bench like Josiah Wedgwood" (see Mr G Wedgwood's evidence before the Commission on Technical Education); and a similar statement might be made about many of the Sheffield trades But some of the working classes develop a great faculty for taking speculative risks, and if the knowledge of facts by which successful speculation must be guided, comes within their reach, they will often push their way through competitors who have started above them Some of the most successful wholesale dealers in perishable commodities such as fish and fruit have begun life as market porters

BOOK IV CH XII.

command, but who is rising and sees his children likely to rise further, is in some ways more to be envied than the small master. His success is less conspicuous, but his work is often higher and more important for the world, while his character is more gentle and refined and not less strong. His children are well-trained, and if they get wealth, they are likely to make a fairly good use of it.

An able business man speedily increases the capital at his command.

§ **12.** When a man of great ability is once at the head of an independent business, whatever be the route by which he has got there, he will with moderate good fortune, soon be able to show such evidence of his power of turning capital to good account as to enable him to borrow in one way or another almost any amount that he may need Making good profits he adds to his own capital, and this extra capital of his own is a material security for further borrowings, while the fact that he has made it himself tends to make lenders less careful to insist on a full security for their loans. Of course fortune tells for much in business: a very able man may find things going against him, the fact that he is losing money may diminish his power of borrowing If he is working partly on borrowed capital, it may even make those who have lent it refuse to renew their loans, and may thus cause him to succumb to what would have been but a passing misfortune, if he had been using no capital but his own[1]. and in fighting his way upwards he may have a chequered life full of great anxieties, and even misfortunes But he can show his ability in misfortune as well as in success: human nature is sanguine; and it is notorious that men are abundantly willing to lend to those who have passed through commercial disaster without loss to their business reputation Thus, in spite of vicissitudes, the able business man generally finds that in the long run the capital at his command grows in proportion to his ability.

1 The danger of not being able to renew his borrowings just at the time when he wants them most, puts him at a disadvantage relatively to those who use only their own capital, much greater than is represented by the mere interest on his borrowings and, when we come to that part of the doctrine of Distribution which deals with Earnings of Management, we shall find that, for this among other reasons, profits are something more than interest in addition to Net Earnings of Management, i e. those earnings which are properly to be ascribed to the abilities of business men.

Meanwhile, as we have seen, he, who with small ability is in command of a large capital, speedily loses it he may perhaps be one who could and would have managed a small business with credit, and left it stronger than he had found it. but if he has not the genius for dealing with great problems, the larger it is the more speedily will he break it up For as a rule a large business can be kept going only by transactions which, after allowing for ordinary risks, leave but a very small percentage of gain. A small profit on a large turn-over quickly made, will yield a rich income to able men· and in those businesses which are of such a nature as to give scope to very large capitals, competition generally cuts the rate of profits on the turn-over very fine. A village trader may make five per cent. less profits on his turn-over than his abler rival, and yet be able to hold his head above water But in those large manufacturing and trading businesses in which there is a quick return and a straightforward routine, the whole profits on the turn-over are often so very small that a person who falls behind his rivals by even a small percentage loses a large sum at every turn-over, while in those large businesses which are difficult and do not rely on routine, and which afford high profits on the turn-over to really able management, there are no profits at all to be got by anyone who attempts the task with only ordinary ability

A man who has not great business ability loses his capital the more rapidly the larger his business is.

These two sets of forces, the one increasing the capital at the command of able men, and the other destroying the capital that is in the hands of weaker men, bring about the result that there is a far more close correspondence between the ability of business men and the size of the businesses which they own than at first sight would appear probable And when to this fact we add all the many routes, which we have already discussed, by which a man of great natural business ability can work his way up high in some private firm or public company, we may conclude that wherever there is work on a large scale to be done in such a country as England, the ability and the capital required for it are pretty sure to be speedily forthcoming

These two forces tend to adjust the capital to the ability required to use it well.

Further, just as industrial skill and ability are getting every day to depend more and more on the broad faculties

BOOK IV CH XII

of judgment, promptness, resource, carefulness and steadfastness of purpose—faculties which are not specialized to any one trade, but which are more or less useful in all—so it is with regard to business ability. In fact business ability consists more of these general and non-specialized faculties than do industrial skill and ability in the lower grades: and the higher the grade of business ability the more various are its applications.

Business ability in command of capital has a fairly defined supply price in such a country as England

Since then business ability in command of capital moves with great ease horizontally from a trade which is overcrowded to one which offers good openings for it · and since it moves with great ease vertically, the abler men rising to the higher posts in their own trade, we see, even at this early stage of our inquiry, some good reasons for believing that in modern England the supply of business ability in command of capital accommodates itself, as a general rule, to the demand for it, and thus has a fairly defined supply price.

Finally, we may regard this supply price of business ability in command of capital as composed of three elements. The first is the supply price of capital; the second is the supply price of business ability and energy, and the third is the supply price of that organization by which the appropriate business ability and the requisite capital are brought together. We have called the price of the first of these three elements "Interest," we may call the price of the second taken by itself "*Net* Earnings of Management," and that of the second and third, taken together, "*Gross* Earnings of Management."

Net and *Gross Earnings of Management*

CHAPTER XIII

CONCLUSION. THE LAW OF INCREASING IN RELATION TO THAT OF DIMINISHING RETURN.

The relation in which the later chapters of this Book stand to the earlier.

§ 1. AT the beginning of this Book we saw how the extra Return of raw produce which Nature affords to an increased application of capital and labour, other things being equal, tends in the long run to diminish In the remainder of the Book and especially in the last four chapters we have looked at the other side of the shield, and seen how man's power of productive work increases with the volume of the work that he does Considering first the causes that determine the Supply of Labour, we saw how every increase in the physical, mental and moral vigour of a people makes them more likely, other things being equal, to rear to adult age a large number of vigorous children Turning next to the Growth of Wealth, we observed how every increase of wealth tends in many ways to make a greater increase more easy than before And lastly we saw how every increase of wealth and every increase in the numbers and intelligence of the people increased the facilities for a highly developed Industrial Organization, which in its turn adds much to the collective efficiency of capital and labour

A summary of the later chapters of this Book

Looking more closely at the economies arising from an increase in the scale of production of any kind of goods, we found that they fell into two classes—those dependent on the general development of the industry, and those dependent on the resources of the individual houses of business engaged in it and the efficiency of their management, that is, into *external* and *internal* economies

We saw how these latter economies are liable to constant fluctuations so far as any particular house is concerned. An able man, assisted perhaps by some strokes of good fortune,

BOOK IV. CH. XIII.

Summary.

gets a firm footing in the trade, he works hard and lives sparely, his own capital grows fast, and the credit that enables him to borrow more capital grows still faster; he collects around him subordinates of more than ordinary zeal and ability; as his business increases they rise with him, they trust him and he trusts them, each of them devotes himself with energy to just that work for which he is specially fitted, so that no high ability is wasted on easy work, and no difficult work is entrusted to unskilful hands. Corresponding to this steadily increasing economy of skill, the growth of his business brings with it similar economies of specialized machines and plant of all kinds, every improved process is quickly adopted and made the basis of further improvements; success brings credit and credit brings success, credit and success help to retain old customers and to bring new ones, the increase of his trade gives him great advantages in buying, his goods advertise one another, and thus diminish his difficulty in finding a vent for them. The increase in the scale of his business increases rapidly the advantages which he has over his competitors, and lowers the price at which he can afford to sell. This process may go on as long as his energy and enterprise, his inventive and organizing power retain their full strength and freshness, and so long as the risks which are inseparable from business do not cause him exceptional losses, and if it could endure for a hundred years, he and one or two others like him would divide between them the whole of that branch of industry in which he is engaged. The large scale of their production would put great economies within their reach, and provided they competed to their utmost with one another, the public would derive the chief benefit of these economies, and the price of the commodity would fall very low.

But here we may read a lesson from the young trees of the forest as they struggle upwards through the benumbing shade of their older rivals. Many succumb on the way, and a few only survive, those few become stronger with every year, they get a larger share of light and air with every increase of their height, and at last in their turn they tower above their neighbours, and seem as though they would grow on for ever,

Summary

and for ever become stronger as they grow But they do not. One tree will last longer in full vigour and attain a greater size than another; but sooner or later age tells on them all. Though the taller ones have a better access to light and air than their rivals, they gradually lose vitality, and one after another they give place to others, which, though of less material strength, have on their side the vigour of youth.

And as with the growth of trees, so is it with the growth of businesses. As each kind of tree has its normal life in which it attains its normal height, so the length of life during which a business of any kind is likely to retain full vigour is limited by the laws of nature combined with the circumstances of place and time, and the character and stage of development of the particular trade in which it lies

The laws of nature press upon it by limiting the length of the life of its original founders, and by limiting even more narrowly that part of their lives, in which their faculties retain full vigour And so after a while the guidance of the business falls into the hands of people with less energy and less creative genius, if not with less active interest in its prosperity. Perhaps it decays altogether, or it may be carried on with more or less wisdom and ability by a public company In that case, it may retain the advantages of division of labour, of specialized skill and machinery, it may even increase them by a further increase of its capital; and under favourable conditions it may secure a permanent and prominent place in the work of production But it is almost sure to have lost much of its elasticity and of its progressive force, the advantages are no longer exclusively on its side in its competition with younger and smaller rivals· and, unless it be in banking, or transport or some other of those exceptional trades, which will require a separate discussion, it can no longer obtain from every increase in its scale of production the means of reducing considerably the price at which it sells its goods or its services

The growth and the decay of the energies of a great business establishment seldom follow twice on exactly the same lines even in the same trade. they vary with the varying incidents of the life and fortune, of the personal

BOOK IV CH. XIII

Summary

friendships and the business and family connections of the individuals concerned, but they also vary much from one trade to another. Thus for instance no single very large business has appeared in agriculture, while in banking and insurance, in the supply of news, and in transport by land and sea, such small businesses as still remain find a constantly increasing difficulty in holding their own. There is no rule of universal application, but the struggle between the solid strength of steady-going firms with large capitals on the one hand, and the quick inventiveness and energy, the suppleness and power of variation of their smaller rivals on the other, seems inclined to issue in the large majority of cases in the victory of the former We may conclude that as a general rule, subject to important exceptions, an increase in the total volume of any branch of production tends to increase the average size of the businesses engaged in it

When therefore we are considering the broad results which the growth of wealth and population exert on the economies of production, the general character of our conclusions is not very much affected by the facts that many of these economies depend directly on the size of the individual establishments engaged in the production, and that in almost every trade there is a constant rise and fall of large businesses, at any one moment some firms being in the ascending phase and others in the descending. For in times of average prosperity decay in one direction is sure to be more than balanced by growth in another.

Meanwhile an increase in the aggregate scale of production of course increases those economies, which do not directly depend on the size of individual houses of business The most important of these result from the growth of correlated branches of industry which mutually assist one another, perhaps being concentrated in the same localities, but anyhow availing themselves of the modern facilities for communication offered by steam transport, by the telegraph and by the printing-press The economies arising from such sources as this, which are accessible to any branch of production, do not depend exclusively upon its own growth. but yet they are sure to grow rapidly and steadily with that growth; and they are sure to dwindle in some, though not in all respects, if it decays.

Forecast of our study of the cost of production in a *Representative firm*

§ 2. These results will be of great importance when we come to discuss the causes which govern the supply price of a commodity. We shall have to analyse carefully the normal cost of producing a commodity, relatively to a given aggregate volume of production; and for this purpose we shall have to study *the expenses of a Representative producer* for that aggregate volume On the one hand we shall not want to select some new producer just struggling into business, who works under many disadvantages, and has to be content for a time with little or no profits, but who is satisfied with the fact that he is establishing a connection and taking the first steps towards building up a successful business; nor on the other hand shall we want to take a firm which by exceptionally long-sustained ability and good fortune has got together a vast business, and huge well-ordered workshops that give it a superiority over almost all its rivals. But our representative firm must be one which has had a fairly long life, and fair success, which is managed with normal ability, and which has normal access to the economies, external and internal, which belong to that aggregate volume of production; account being taken of the class of goods produced, the conditions of marketing them and the economic environment generally.

The general argument of the present Book shows that an increase in the aggregate volume of production of anything will generally increase the size, and therefore the internal economies possessed by this representative firm; that it will always increase the external economies to which such a firm has access: and thus will enable it to manufacture at a less proportionate cost of labour and sacrifice than before

The Laws of Increasing Return.

In other words, we say broadly that while the part which Nature plays in production conforms to the law of diminishing return, the part which man plays conforms to the *Law of Increasing Return*, which may be stated thus:—An increase of capital and labour leads generally to an improved organization, and therefore in those industries which are not engaged in raising raw produce it generally gives a return increased more than in proportion; and further this improved

BOOK IV. CH XIII

organization tends to diminish or even override any increased resistance which Nature may offer to raising increased amounts of raw produce If the actions of the laws of increasing and diminishing return are balanced we have the *Law of Constant Return*, and an increased produce is obtained by labour and sacrifice increased just in proportion

and of Constant Return

The straining of the tendencies towards increasing and diminishing return against one another.

For the two tendencies towards increasing and diminishing return press constantly against one another. In the production of wheat and wool, for instance, the latter tendency has almost exclusive sway in an old country, which cannot import freely[1] In turning the wheat into flour, or the wool into blankets, an increase in the aggregate volume of production brings some new economies, but not many; for the trades of grinding wheat and making blankets are already on so great a scale that any new economies that they may attain are more likely to be the result of new inventions than of improved organization. In a country however in which the blanket trade is but slightly developed, these latter may be important; and then it may happen that an increase in the aggregate production of blankets diminishes the proportionate difficulty of manufacturing by just as much as it increases that of raising the raw material. In that case the actions of the laws of diminishing and of increasing return would just neutralize one another; and blankets would conform to the law of constant return But in most of the more delicate branches of manufacturing, where the cost of raw material counts for little, and in most of the modern transport industries the law of increasing return acts almost unopposed

We shall long be occupied with the details and the limitations of the broad truths which have just been sketched out but before closing the present Book we may stay a little to consider their bearing on the problem of the pressure of population on the means of subsistence. We are not yet in a position to deal with it thoroughly, but there is some advantage in taking a rapid survey of it at this early stage.

§ 3. Our discussion of the character and organization of industry taken as a whole tends to show that an increase in

[1] As regards the struggle of the two tendencies in agriculture, compare Book IV. Ch III § 6

the volume of labour causes in general, other things being equal, a more than proportionate increase in the total efficiency of labour. But we must not forget that other things may not be equal. The increase of numbers may be accompanied by more or less general adoption of unhealthy and enervating habits of life in overcrowded towns. Or it may have started badly, outrunning the material resources of the people, causing them with imperfect appliances to make excessive demands on the soil, and so to call forth the stern action of the law of diminishing return as regards raw produce, without having the power of minimizing its effects: having thus begun with poverty, an increase in numbers may go on to its too frequent consequences in that weakness of character which unfits a people for developing a highly organized industry

A rapid growth of population is an evil under some conditions,

All this and more may be granted, and yet it remains true that the collective efficiency of a people with a given average of individual strength and energy may increase more than in proportion to their numbers If they can for a time escape from the pressure of the law of diminishing return by importing food and other raw produce on easy terms, if their wealth is not consumed in great wars, and increases at least as fast as their numbers; and if they avoid habits of life that would enfeeble them; then every increase in their numbers is likely *for the time* to be accompanied by a more than proportionate increase in their power of obtaining material goods.

but not under others.

For it enables them to secure the many various economies of specialized skill and specialized machinery, of localized industries and production on a large scale: it enables them to have increased facilities of communication of all kinds; while the very closeness of their neighbourhood diminishes the expense of time and effort involved in every sort of traffic between them, and gives them new opportunities of getting social enjoyments and the comforts and luxuries of culture in every form. It is true that against this must be set the growing difficulty of finding solitude and quiet and even fresh air This deduction is a weighty one; but there may still remain a balance of good[1].

[1] The Englishman Mill bursts into unwonted enthusiasm when speaking

BOOK IV CH XIII

Taking account of the fact that an increasing density of population generally brings with it access to new social enjoyments we may give a rather broader scope to this statement and say:—An increase of population accompanied by an equal increase in the material sources of enjoyment and aids to production is likely to lead to a more than proportionate increase in the aggregate income of enjoyment of all kinds; provided firstly, an adequate supply of raw produce can be obtained without great difficulty, and secondly there is no such overcrowding as causes physical and moral vigour to be impaired by the want of fresh air and light and of healthy and joyous recreation for the young.

The effects of a growth of numbers must be carefully distinguished from those of the growth of wealth by which it is generally accompanied

The accumulated wealth of civilized countries is at present growing faster than the population: and though it may be true that the wealth per head would increase somewhat faster if the population did not increase quite so fast, yet as a matter of fact an increase of population is likely to continue to be accompanied by a more than proportionate increase of the material aids to production: and in England *at the present time,* with easy access to abundant foreign supplies of raw material, an increase of population is accompanied by a more than proportionate increase of the means of satisfying human wants other than the need for light, fresh air, &c. Much of this increase is however attributable not to the increase of industrial efficiency but to the increase of wealth by which it is accompanied: and therefore it does not necessarily benefit those who have no share in that wealth. And further, England's foreign supplies of raw produce may at any time be checked by changes in the trade regulations of other countries, and may be almost cut off by a great war, while the naval and military expenditure which would be necessary to make the country fairly secure against this last risk, would appreciably diminish the benefits that she derives from the action of the law of increasing return.

(*Political Economy*, Book IV Ch VI § 2) of the pleasures of wandering alone in beautiful scenery: and many American writers give fervid descriptions of the growing richness of human life as the backwoodsman finds neighbours settling around him, as the backwoods settlement developes into a village, the village into a town, and the town into a vast city. (See for instance Carey's *Principles of Social Science* and Mr Henry George's *Progress and Poverty*.)

BOOK V.

THE EQUILIBRIUM OF DEMAND AND SUPPLY.

CHAPTER I.

ON MARKETS

Most economic problems have a common kernel relating to the equilibrium of demand and supply

§ 1. In spite of a great variety in detail nearly all the chief problems of economics agree in this that they have a kernel of the same kind. This kernel is an inquiry as to the balancing of two opposed classes of motives, the one consisting of desires to acquire certain new goods, and thus satisfy wants; while the other consists of desires to avoid certain efforts or retain certain immediate enjoyments or other goods, the command over which has already been acquired, in other words it is an inquiry into the balancing of the forces of demand and supply, these terms being used in their broadest sense The purpose of the present book is to examine the general conditions of the equilibrium of demand and supply illustrations will be taken now from one class of economic problems and now from another, but the main course of the reasoning will be kept free from assumptions which specially belong to any particular class

Definition of a *Market*

§ 2 When demand and supply are spoken of in relation to one another, it is of course necessary that the markets to which they refer should be the same. As Cournot says, "Economists understand by the term *Market*, not any particular market place in which things are bought and sold, but the whole of any region in which buyers and sellers are

BOOK V. CH I

in such free intercourse with one another that the prices of the same goods tend to equality easily and quickly[1]." Or again as Jevons says —"Originally a market was a public place in a town where provisions and other objects were exposed for sale; but the word has been generalized, so as to mean any body of persons who are in intimate business relations and carry on extensive transactions in any commodity. A great city may contain as many markets as there are important branches of trade, and these markets may or may not be localized. The central point of a market is the public exchange, mart or auction rooms, where the traders agree to meet and transact business In London the Stock Market, the Corn Market, the Coal Market, the Sugar Market, and many others are distinctly localized, in Manchester the Cotton Market, the Cotton Waste Market, and others But this distinction of locality is not necessary. The traders may be spread over a whole town, or region of country, and yet make a market, if they are, by means of fairs, meetings, published price lists, the post-office or otherwise, in close communication with each other[2]."

Thus the more nearly perfect a market is, the stronger is the tendency for the same price to be paid for the same thing at the same time in all parts of the market: but of course if the market is large, allowance must be made for the expense of delivering the goods to different purchasers, each of whom must be supposed to pay in addition to the market price a special charge on account of delivery[3].

Boundaries of a market.

§ 3 In applying economic reasonings in practice it is often difficult to ascertain how far the movements of supply and demand in any one place are influenced by those in another. It is clear that the general tendency of the telegraph, the printing-press and steam traffic is to extend the area over which such influences act and to increase their force. The whole Western World may, in a sense, be re-

[1] *Recherches sur les Principes Mathématiques de la Théorie des Richesses*, Ch IV See also above Book III Ch. IV § 7.

[2] *Theory of Political Economy*, Ch. IV.

[3] Thus it is common to see the prices of bulky goods quoted as delivered "free on board" (f o. b) any vessel in a certain port, each purchaser having to make his own reckoning for bringing the goods home.

Instances of very wide markets

garded as one market for many kinds of stock exchange securities, for the more valuable metals, and to a less extent for wool and cotton and even wheat; proper allowance being made for expenses of transport, in which may be included taxes levied by any customs houses through which the goods have to pass. For in all these cases the expenses of transport, including customs duties, are not sufficient to prevent buyers from all parts of the Western World from competing with one another for the same supplies.

General conditions which affect the extent of the market for a thing Suitability for grading and sampling

There are many special causes which may widen or narrow the market of any particular commodity: but nearly all those things for which there is a very wide market are in universal demand, and capable of being easily and exactly described. Thus for instance cotton, wheat, and iron satisfy wants that are urgent and nearly universal They can be easily described, so that they can be bought and sold by persons at a distance from one another and at a distance also from the commodities. If necessary, samples can be taken of them which are truly representative. and they can even be "graded," as is the actual practice with regard to grain in America, by an independent authority, so that the purchaser may be secure that what he buys will come up to a given standard, though he has never seen a sample of the goods which he is buying and perhaps would not be able himself to form an opinion on it if he did[1].

Portability.

Commodities for which there is a very wide market must also be such as will bear a long carriage. they must be somewhat durable, and their value must be considerable in proportion to their bulk. A thing which is so bulky that its price is necessarily raised very much when it is sold far away from the place in which it is produced, must as a rule have a narrow market The market for common bricks for instance is practically confined to the near neighbourhood of the

[1] Thus the managers of a public or private "elevator," receive grain from a farmer, divide it into different grades, and return to him certificates for as many bushels of each grade as he has delivered His grain is then mixed with those of other farmers, his certificates are likely to change hands several times before they reach a purchaser who demands that the grain shall be actually delivered to him, and little or none of what that purchaser receives may have come from the farm of the original recipient of the certificate

BOOK V CH I

kilns in which they are made: they can scarcely ever bear a long carriage by land to a district which has any kilns of its own. But bricks of certain exceptional kinds have a market extending over a great part of England

The conditions of highly organized markets

§ 4. Let us then consider more closely the markets for things which satisfy in an exceptional way these conditions of being in general demand, cognizable and portable They are, as we have said, stock exchange securities and the more valuable metals.

illustrated by reference to stock exchanges

Any one share or bond of a public company, or any bond of a government is of exactly the same value as any other of the same issue it can make no difference to any purchaser which of the two he buys. Some securities, principally those of comparatively small mining, shipping, and other companies, require local knowledge, and are not very easily dealt in except on the stock exchanges of provincial towns in their immediate neighbourhood But the whole of England is one market for the shares and bonds of a large English railway. In ordinary times a dealer will sell, say, Midland Railway shares, even if he has not them himself; because he knows they are always coming into the market, and he is sure to be able to buy them.

But the strongest case of all is that of securities which are called "international," because they are in request in every part of the globe. They are the bonds of the chief governments, and of very large public companies such as those of the Suez Canal and the New York Central Railway. For bonds of this class the telegraph keeps prices at almost exactly the same level in all the stock exchanges of the world If the price of one of them rises in New York or in Paris, in London or in Berlin, the mere news of the rise tends to cause a rise in other markets, and if for any reason the rise is delayed, that particular class of bonds is likely soon to be offered for sale in the high priced market under telegraphic orders from the other markets, while dealers in the first market will be making telegraphic purchases in other markets. These sales on the one hand, and purchases on the other, strengthen the tendency which the price has to seek the same level everywhere; and unless some of the markets are in an abnormal condition, the tendency soon becomes irresistible.

On the stock exchange also a dealer can generally make sure of selling at nearly the same price as that at which he buys; and he is often willing to buy first class stocks at a half, or a quarter, or an eighth, or in some cases even a sixteenth per cent. less than he offers in the same breath to sell them at. If there are two securities equally good, but one of them belongs to a large issue of bonds, and the other to a small issue by the same government, so that the first is constantly coming on the market, and the latter but seldom, then the dealers will on this account alone require a larger margin between their selling price and their buying price in the latter case than in the former[1]. This illustrates well the great law, of which we shall have much to say when we come to consider the influence of foreign trade on economic progress, that the larger the market for a commodity the smaller generally are the fluctuations in its price, and the lower is the percentage on the turnover which dealers charge for doing business in it.

The world market for the precious metals.

Stock exchanges then are the pattern on which markets have been, and are being formed for dealing in many kinds of produce which can be easily and exactly described, are portable and in general demand. The material commodities however which possess these qualities in the highest degree are gold and silver. For that very reason they have been chosen by common consent for use as money, to represent the value of other things: the world market for them is most highly organized, and will be found to offer many subtle illustrations of the actions of the laws which we are now discussing.

§ 5. At the opposite extremity to international stock exchange securities and the more valuable metals are, firstly,

[1] In the case of shares of very small and little known companies, the difference between the price at which a dealer is willing to buy and that at which he will sell amounts to from five to twenty per cent of the selling value If he buys, he may have to carry this security a long time before he meets with any one who comes to take it from him, and meanwhile it may fall in value while if he undertakes to deliver a security which he has not himself got and which does not come on the market every day, he may be unable to complete his contract without much trouble and expense

BOOK V. CH. I

Putting aside cases of retail dealing,

things which must be made to order to suit particular individuals, such as well-fitting clothes, and, secondly, perishable and bulky goods, such as fresh vegetables, which can seldom be profitably carried long distances. The first can scarcely be said to have a wholesale market at all; the conditions by which their price is determined are those of retail buying and selling, and the study of them may be postponed[1].

we pass to a market which seems to be narrowly confined,

There are indeed wholesale markets for the second class, but they are confined within narrow boundaries; we may find our typical instance in the sale of the commoner kinds of vegetables in a country town. The market-gardeners in the neighbourhood have probably to arrange for the sale of their vegetables to the townspeople with but little external interference on either side There may be some check to extreme prices by the power on the one side of selling, and on the other of buying elsewhere, but under ordinary circumstances the check is inoperative, and it may happen that the dealers in such a case are able to combine, and thus fix an artificial monopoly price; that is, a price determined with little direct reference to cost of production, but chiefly by a consideration of what the market will bear.

though even this is subject to indirect influences from great distances

On the other hand, it may happen that some of the market-gardeners are almost equally near a second country town, and send their vegetables now to one and now to the other; and some people who occasionally buy in the first town may have equally good access to the second. The least variation in price will lead them to prefer the better market, and thus make the bargainings in the two towns to some extent mutually dependent. It may happen that this second town is in close communication with London or some other central market, so that its prices are controlled by the prices in the central market; and in that case prices in our first town also must move to a considerable extent in harmony

[1] A man may not trouble himself much about small retail purchases he may give half-a-crown for a packet of paper in one shop which he could have got for two shillings in another But it is otherwise with wholesale prices A manufacturer cannot sell a ream of paper for six shillings while his neighbour is selling it at five For those whose business it is to deal in paper know almost exactly the lowest price at which it can be bought, and will not pay more than this The manufacturer has to sell at about the market price, that is at about the price at which other manufacturers are selling at the same time

with them. As news passes from mouth to mouth till a rumour spreads far away from its forgotten source, so even the most secluded market is liable to be influenced by changes of which those in the market have no direct cognizance, changes that have had their origin far away and have spread gradually from market to market.

Thus at the one extreme are world markets in which competition acts directly from all parts of the globe; and at the other those secluded markets in which all direct competition from afar is shut out, though indirect and transmitted competition may make itself felt even in these; and about midway between these extremes lie the great majority of the markets which the economist and the business man have to study.

Limitations of market with regard to time affect the nature of the causes of which we have to take account

§ 6. Again, markets vary with regard to the period of time which is allowed to the forces of demand and supply to bring themselves into equilibrium with one another, as well as with regard to the area over which they extend And this element of Time requires more careful attention just now than does that of Space. For the nature of the equilibrium itself, and that of the causes by which it is determined, depend on the length of the period over which the market is taken to extend We shall find that if the period is short, the supply is limited to the stores which happen to be at hand· if the period is longer, the supply will be influenced by the cost of producing the commodity in question, and if the period is very long, this cost will be influenced by the cost of producing the labour and the material things required for producing the commodity This latter distinction will be seen to be one of degree only, and to be not clearly and firmly drawn and even the former is not perfectly definite, but yet it is definite enough to merit a separate discussion. Accordingly we shall consider in the next chapter those temporary equilibria of demand and supply, in which the cost of producing the commodity exerts either no influence or merely an indirect influence

At a later stage we shall have to combine the difficulties with regard to time on the side of supply with those on the side of demand, of which something has already been said[1]

[1] Book III Ch. IV §§ 5, 6.

CHAPTER II.

TEMPORARY EQUILIBRIUM OF DEMAND AND SUPPLY.

A simple instance of equilibrium between desire and effort.

§ 1. THE simplest case of balance or equilibrium between desire and effort is found when a person satisfies one of his wants by his own direct action, as for instance when he picks blackberries. At first the pleasure of eating is much more than enough to repay the trouble of picking; in fact the action of picking may itself be pleasurable for a time. But after he has eaten a good deal, the desire for more diminishes, while the task of picking begins to cause weariness. This weariness may be caused more by monotony than by fatigue. And when at last his eagerness to play and his disinclination for the work of picking counterbalance the desire for eating, equilibrium is attained. The satisfaction which he can get from picking fruit has arrived at its *maximum*: for up to that time every fresh picking has added more to his pleasure than it has taken away; and after that time any further picking would take away from his pleasure more than it would add[1].

In a casual barter there is generally no true equilibrium.

In a casual bargain that one person makes with another, as for instance when two backwoodsmen barter a rifle for a canoe, there is seldom anything that can properly be called an equilibrium of supply and demand: there is probably a margin of satisfaction on either side, for probably the one would be willing to give something besides the rifle for the canoe, if he could not get the canoe otherwise; while the other would in case of necessity give something besides the canoe for the rifle.

[1] See Book IV. Ch. I. § 2, and Mathematical Note XII.

It is indeed possible that a true equilibrium may be arrived at under a system of barter; but barter, though earlier in history than buying and selling, is in some ways more intricate; and the simplest cases of a true equilibrium value are found in the markets of a more advanced state of civilization[1].

The case of systematic barter may be deferred.

§ 2. Let us take an illustration from a corn-market in a country town. The amount which each farmer or other seller offers for sale at any price is governed by his own need for money in hand, and by his calculation of the present and future conditions of the market with which he is connected. There are some prices which no seller would accept, some which no one would refuse. There are other intermediate prices which would be accepted for larger or smaller amounts by many or all of the sellers. Let us assume for the sake of simplicity that all the corn in the market is of the same quality. An acute dealer having corn for sale may perhaps, after looking around him, come to the conclusion that if 37*s.* could be got throughout the day, the farmers between them would be willing to sell to the extent of about 1,000 quarters; and that if no more than 36*s.* could be got, several would refuse to sell, or would sell only small quantities, so that only 700 quarters would be brought forward for sale; and that a price of 35*s.* would only induce some 500 quarters to be brought forward. Suppose him further to calculate that

Illustration from a local corn-market in which a true though temporary equilibrium is attained.

[1] We may put aside also as of very little practical importance, a class of dealings which have occupied a good deal of space in economic literature. They relate to such things as pictures by the old masters, rare coins and other things, which cannot be "graded" at all; for each of them is unique, and has no direct equivalent or competitor. Anyone who offers to buy such a thing, without any thought of selling it again, has to assure himself only that the pleasure he will derive from its possession is as great as that which he could get by spending its price in any other way; the highest price to which he will go is governed by the utility or pleasure giving power to him of money on the one hand and the object of worth on the other. And therefore the price at which such a thing is sold will depend very much on whether any rich persons with a fancy for that particular thing happen to be present at its sale. If not, it will probably be bought by dealers who reckon on being able to sell it at a profit; and the variations in the price for which the same picture sells at successive auctions, great as they are, would be much greater still if it were not for the steadying influence of professional and semi-professional purchasers. The "equilibrium price" for such sales is very much a matter of accident; but the curious might reap some reward from a minute study of it.

millers and others would be willing to buy 900 quarters if they could be got at 35*s.* each, but only 700 if they could not be got for less than 36*s.*, and only 600 if they could not be got for less than 37*s*[1] He will conclude that a price of 36*s.*, if established at once, would equate supply and demand, because the amount offered for sale at that price would equal the amount which could just find purchasers at that price. He will therefore take at once any offer considerably over 36*s.*; and other sellers will do the same.

Buyers on their part will make similar calculations, and if at any time the price should rise considerably above 36*s.* they will argue that the supply will be much greater than the demand at that price, therefore even those of them who would rather pay that price than go unserved, wait, and by waiting they help to bring the price down On the other hand, when the price is much below 36*s.* even those sellers who would rather take the price than leave the market with their corn unsold, may argue that at that price the demand will be in excess of the supply: so they wait, and by waiting help to bring the price up

The price of 36*s.* has thus a claim to be called the true equilibrium price: because if it were fixed on at the beginning, and adhered to throughout, it would exactly equate demand and supply; and because every dealer who has a perfect knowledge of the circumstances of the market expects that price to be established If he sees the price differing much from 36*s.* he expects that a change will come before long, and by anticipating it he helps it to come quickly.

It is not indeed necessary for our argument that any dealers should have a thorough knowledge of the circumstances of the market. Many of the buyers may perhaps underrate the willingness of the sellers to sell, with the effect that for some time the price rules at the highest level at

[1] This result of his study of the market may be put in a tabular form thus

At the price	Sellers will be willing to sell	Buyers will be willing to buy
37*s*	1000 quarters,	600 quarters,
36*s*	700 ,,	700 ,,
35*s*	500 ,,	900 ,,

which any buyers can be found; and thus 500 quarters may be sold before the price sinks below 37*s*. But afterwards the price must begin to fall and the result will still probably be that 200 more quarters will be sold, and the market will close on a price of about 36*s*. For when 700 bushels have been sold, no seller will be anxious to dispose of any more except at a higher price than 36*s*, and no buyer will be anxious to purchase any more except at a lower price than 36*s* In the same way if the sellers had underrated the willingness of the buyers to pay a high price, some of them might begin to sell at the lowest price they would take, rather than have their corn left on their hands, and in this case much corn might be sold at a price of 35*s*, but the market would probably close on a price of 36*s*. and a total sale of 700 quarters[1]

The latent assumption, that the marginal utility of money is nearly constant to each dealer during the dealing,

§ 3 In this illustration there is a latent assumption which is in accordance with the actual conditions of most markets; but which ought to be distinctly recognized in order to prevent its creeping into those cases in which it is not justifiable We tacitly assumed that the sum which purchasers were willing to pay, and which sellers were willing to take, for the seven hundredth bushel would not be affected by the question whether the earlier bargains had been made at a high or a low rate We allowed for the diminution in the marginal utility of corn to the buyers as the amount bought increased. But we did not allow for any appreciable change in the marginal utility of money; we assumed that it would be practically the same whether the early payments had been at a high or a low rate

is generally valid as to a corn-market,

This assumption is justifiable with regard to most of the market dealings with which we are practically concerned. When a person buys anything for his own consumption, he generally spends on it a small part of his total resources; while when he buys it for the purposes of trade, he looks to re-selling it, and therefore his potential resources are not diminished In either case the marginal utility of money to him is not appreciably changed[2]

[1] A simple form of the influence which opinion exerts on the action of dealers, and therefore on market price, is indicated in this illustration we shall be much occupied with more complex developments of it later on

[2] But though this is the case as a rule, there are exceptions to the rule A

BOOK V CH II

but in a labour market the exceptions are often important

The exceptions are rare and unimportant in markets for commodities; but in markets for labour they are frequent and important When a workman is in fear of hunger, the marginal utility of money to him is very high; and if at starting he gets the worst of the bargaining, and is employed at low wages, it remains high, and he may go on selling his labour at a low rate. That is all the more probable because, while the advantage in bargaining is likely to be pretty well distributed between the two sides of a market for commodities, it is more often on the side of the buyers than on that of the sellers in a market for labour. This is one among many facts, in which we shall find, as we go on, the explanation of much of that instinctive objection which the working classes have felt to the habit of some economists, particularly those of the employer class, of treating labour simply as a commodity and regarding the labour market as like every other market; whereas in fact the differences between the two cases, though not fundamental from the point of view of theory, are yet clearly marked, and in practice often very important[1]

This difference has important results in theory and in practice,

The theory of buying and selling becomes therefore much

buyer is sometimes straitened for want of ready money, and has to let offers pass by him in no way inferior to others which he has gladly accepted. His own funds being exhausted, he could not perhaps borrow except on terms that would take away all the profit that the bargains had at first sight offered

Again, it is possible that several of those who had been counted as ready to sell corn at a price of 36s were willing to sell only because they were in urgent need of a certain amount of ready money, if they succeeded in selling some corn at a high price, there might be a perceptible diminution in the marginal utility of ready money to them, and therefore they might refuse to sell for 36s. a quarter all the corn which they would have sold if the price had been 36s throughout. In this case the sellers in consequence of getting an advantage in bargaining at the beginning of the market might retain to the end a price higher than *the* equilibrium price The price at which the market closed would be *an* equilibrium price, but not *the* equilibrium price

Conversely, if the market had opened much to the disadvantage of the sellers and they had sold some corn very cheap, so that they remained in great want of ready money, the final utility of money to them might have remained so high that they would have gone on selling considerably below 36s until the buyers had been supplied with all that they cared to take The market would then close without the true equilibrium price having ever been reached

[1] The analogy, which we are now considering, between a labour market and a market for commodities is weakened, as most others of this kind are, by the fact that each seller of labour has only one unit of labour to dispose of

more complex when we take account of the dependence of marginal utility on amount in the case of money as well as of the commodity itself. When we do this we are really reverting to the problem of barter, in which the changes in the marginal utilities of both commodities are of course prominent. As we have remarked, barter, though earlier historically than buying and selling, is really a more complex transaction and the theory of it is curious rather than important Some account of it is given in the following Note, chiefly with a view of throwing additional light on the exceptional cases which we have just been considering.

on which some light is thrown by the study of barter in the following Note

Note on Barter

Let us consider the case of two individuals engaged in barter *A* has, say a basket of apples, *B* a basket of nuts, *A* wants some nuts, *B* wants some apples. The satisfaction which *B* would get from one apple would perhaps outweigh that which he would lose by parting with 12 nuts; while the satisfaction which *A* would get from perhaps three nuts would outweigh that which he would lose by parting with one apple. The exchange will be started somewhere between these two rates but if it goes on gradually, every apple that *A* loses will increase the marginal utility of apples to him and make him more unwilling to part with any more while every additional nut that he gets will lower the marginal utility of nuts to him and diminish his eagerness for more and *vice versâ* with *B*. At last *A*'s eagerness for nuts relatively to apples will no longer exceed *B*'s, and exchange will cease because any terms that the one is willing to propose would be disadvantageous to the other Up to this point exchange has increased the satisfaction on both sides, but it can do so no further Equilibrium has been attained; but really it is not *the* equilibrium, it is *an* accidental equilibrium

The rate of barter between two individuals is governed by accident.

There is, however, one equilibrium rate of exchange which has some sort of right to be called the true equilibrium rate, because if once hit upon it would be adhered to throughout It is clear that if very many nuts were to be given throughout for an apple, *B* would be willing to do but little business, while if but very few were to be given, *A* would be willing to do but little There must be some intermediate rate at which they would be willing to do business to the same extent Suppose that this rate is six nuts for an apple, and that *A* is willing to give eight apples for 48 nuts, while *B* is willing to receive eight apples at that rate; but that *A* would not be willing to give a ninth apple for another six nuts while *B* would not be willing to give another six nuts for a ninth apple This is then the true position of equilibrium, but there is no reason to suppose that it will be reached in practice

There is a rate which may be called the true rate,

BOOK V
CH II

but it is not likely to be attained in practice

Suppose, for instance, that *A*'s basket had originally 20 apples in it and *B*'s 100 nuts, and that *A* at starting induced *B* to believe that he does not care much to have any nuts, and so manages to barter four apples for 40 nuts, and afterwards two more for 17 nuts, and afterwards one more for eight Equilibrium may now have been reached, there may be no further exchange which is advantageous to both. *A* has 65 nuts and does not care to give another apple even for eight; while *B*, having only 35 nuts, sets a high value on them, and will not give as many as eight for another apple

On the other hand, if *B* had been the more skilful in bargaining he might have perhaps induced *A* to give six apples for 15 nuts, and then two more for seven He has now given up eight apples and got 22 nuts if the terms at starting had been six nuts for an apple and he had got 48 nuts for his eight apples, he would not have given up another apple for even seven nuts, but having so few nuts he is anxious to get more and is willing to give two more apples in exchange for eight nuts, and then two more for nine nuts, and then one more for five, and then again equilibrium may be reached; for *B*, having 13 apples and 56 nuts, does not perhaps care to give more than five nuts for an apple, and *A* may be unwilling to give up one of his few remaining apples for less than six.

In both these cases the exchange would have increased the satisfaction of both as far as it went; and when it ceased, no further exchange would have been possible which would not have diminished the satisfaction of at least one of them In each case an equilibrium rate would have been reached, but it would be an arbitrary equilibrium

Nor is the case much better in barter between two groups.

Next suppose that there are a hundred people in a similar position to that of *A*, each with about 20 apples, and the same desire for nuts as *A*; and an equal number on the other side similarly situated to the original *B* Then the acutest bargainers in the market would probably be some of them on *A*'s side, some of them on *B*'s; and whether there was free communication throughout the market or not, the mean of the bargains would not be so likely to differ very widely from the rate of six nuts for an apple as in the case of barter between two people But yet there would be no such strong probability of its adhering very closely to that rate, as we saw was the case in the corn-market It would be quite possible for those on the *A* side to get in varying degrees the better of those on the *B* side in bargaining, so that after a time 6500 nuts might have been exchanged for 700 apples; and then those on the *A* side, having so many nuts, might be unwilling to do any more trade except at the rate of at least eight nuts for an apple, while those on the *B* side, having only 35 nuts apiece left on the average, might probably refuse to part with any more at that rate. On the other hand, the *B*'s might have got in various degrees the better of the *A*'s in bargaining, with the result that after a time 1300 apples had been exchanged for only 4400 nuts· the *B*'s having then 1300 apples and 5600 nuts, might be unwilling to offer more than five nuts for an apple, while the *A*'s, having only seven apples apiece left on the average, might decline that rate In the one case equilibrium would be found at a rate of eight nuts for an apple, and in the other at the rate of five nuts In each case *an* equilibrium would be attained, but not *the* equilibrium

Much of the uncertainty removed if the marginal utility of one of the two commodities is nearly constant

This uncertainty of the rate at which equilibrium is reached does not depend on the fact that one commodity is being bartered for another instead of being sold for money. It results from our being obliged to regard the marginal utilities of both commodities as varying. And indeed if we had supposed that it was a nut-growing district, and that all the traders on both sides had large stores of nuts, while only the *A*'s had apples, then the exchange of a few handfuls of nuts would not visibly affect their stores, or change appreciably the marginal utility of nuts In that case the bargaining would resemble in all fundamentals the buying and selling in an ordinary corn-market The real distinction then between the theory of buying and selling and that of barter is that in the former it generally is, and in the latter it generally is not, right to assume that the marginal utility of one of the things dealt with is practically constant.

Thus, for instance, let a single *A* with 20 apples, bargain with a single *B* Let *A* be willing to sell 5 apples for 15 nuts, a sixth for 4 nuts, a seventh for 5, an eighth for 6, a ninth for 7 and so on; the marginal utility of nuts being always constant to him, so that he is just willing to sell the eighth for 6 and so on, whether in the earlier part of the trade he has got the better of the bargaining with *B* or not Meanwhile let *B* be willing to pay 50 nuts for the first 5 apples rather than go without them, 9 for a sixth, 7 for a seventh, 6 for an eighth, and only 5 for a ninth, the marginal utility of nuts being constant to him, so that he will just give 6 nuts for the eighth apple whether he has bought the earlier apples cheaply or not. In this case the bargaining *must* issue in the transfer of eight apples, the eighth apple being given for six nuts But of course if *A* had got the better of the bargaining at first, he might have got 50 or 60 nuts for the first seven apples; while if *B* had got the better of the bargaining at first, he might have got the first seven apples for 30 or 40 nuts. This corresponds to the fact that in the corn-market discussed in the text, about 700 quarters would be sold with a final rate of 36*s*, but if the sellers had got the best of the bargaining at first, the aggregate price paid might be a good deal more than 700 times 36*s*., while if the buyers had got the better of the bargaining at first, the aggregate price would be a good deal less than 700 times 36*s*. (See Mathematical Note XII)

CHAPTER III.

EQUILIBRIUM OF NORMAL DEMAND AND SUPPLY.

BOOK V CH III

Nearly all dealings in commodities that are not very perishable, are affected by calculations of the future;

§ 1 EVEN in the corn-exchange of a country town on a market-day the equilibrium price is affected by calculations of the future relations of production and consumption; while in the leading corn-markets of America and Europe dealings for future delivery already predominate and are rapidly weaving into one web all the leading threads of trade in corn throughout the whole world Some of those dealings in "futures" are but incidents in speculative manœuvres, but in the main they are governed by calculations of the world's consumption on the one hand, and of the existing stocks and coming harvests in the Northern and Southern hemispheres on the other they take account of the areas sown with each kind of grain, of the forwardness and weight of the crops, and of the supply of things which can be used as substitutes for corn, and of the things for which corn can be used as a substitute. Thus, when buying or selling barley, they would have to take account of the supplies of such things as sugar, which can be used as substitutes for it in brewing, and again of all the various feeding stuffs, a scarcity of which might raise the value of barley for consumption on the farm If it is thought that the growers of any kind of grain in any part of the world have been losing money, and are likely to sow a less area for a future harvest, it is argued that prices are likely to rise as soon as that harvest comes into sight, anticipations of that rise will exercise an influence on present sales for future delivery, and that in its turn influences cash prices, so that these prices are indirectly affected by estimates of the expenses of producing further supplies

BOOK V CH III

But in this and the following chapters we are specially concerned with movements of price ranging over still longer periods than those for which the most far-sighted dealers in futures generally make their reckoning: we have to consider the volume of production adjusting itself to the conditions of the market, and the normal price being thus determined at the position of stable equilibrium of normal demand and normal supply.

and we are now to consider slow and gradual adjustments of supply and demand.

In this discussion we shall have to make frequent use of the terms "Cost" and "Expenses" of production; and some provisional account of them must be given before proceeding further.

§ 2 We may take up the discussion of the analogy between the supply price and the demand price of a commodity at the point at which we left it when, for the moment assuming that the efficiency of production depended solely upon the exertions of the workers, we said "the price required to call forth the exertion necessary for producing any given amount of a commodity may be called the supply price for that amount[1]." But now we have to take account of the fact that the production of a commodity generally requires many different kinds of labour and the use of capital in many forms. The exertions of all the different kinds of labour that are directly or indirectly involved in making it, together with the abstinences or rather the waitings required for saving the capital used in making it: all these efforts and sacrifices together will be called the *Real Cost of production* of the commodity. The sums of money that have to be paid for these efforts and sacrifices will be called either its *Money Cost of production*, or, for shortness, its *Expenses of production*, they are the prices which have to be paid in order to call forth an adequate supply of the efforts and waitings that are required for making it; or, in other words, they are its supply price[2].

The account of supply price carried a little further

Real and Money Cost of Production

Expenses of Production

[1] Book IV. Ch. I § 2

[2] Mill and some other economists have followed the practice of ordinary life in using the term Cost of production in two senses, sometimes to signify the difficulty of producing a thing, and sometimes to express the outlay of money that has to

BOOK V. CH. III.

The analysis of the Expenses of production of a commodity might be carried backward to any length; but it is seldom worth while to go back very far. It is for instance often sufficient to take the supply prices of the different kinds of raw material used in any manufacture as ultimate facts, without analysing these supply prices into the several elements of which they are composed, otherwise indeed the analysis would never end We may then arrange the things that are required for making a commodity into whatever groups are convenient, and call them its *Factors of production*. Its expenses of production when any given amount of it is produced are thus the supply prices of the corresponding quantities of its factors of production. And the sum of these is the supply price of that amount of the commodity.

Factors of production.

There is great variety in the relative importance of different elements of cost of production

§ 3. The typical modern market is often regarded as that in which manufacturers sell goods to wholesale dealers at prices into which but few trading expenses enter. But taking a broader view, we may consider that the supply price of a commodity is the price at which it will be delivered for sale to that group of persons whose demand for it we are considering, or, in other words, in the market which we have in view. On the character of that market will depend how many trading expenses have to be reckoned to make up the supply price[1]. For instance, the supply price of wood in the

be incurred in order to induce people to overcome this difficulty and produce it But by passing from one use of the term to the other without giving explicit warning, they have led to many misunderstandings and much barren controversy The attack on Mill's doctrine of Cost of Production in relation to Value, which is made in Cairnes' *Leading Principles*, was published just after Mill's death; and unfortunately his interpretation of Mill's words was generally accepted as authoritative, because he was regarded as a follower of Mill But in an article by the present writer on "Mill's Theory of Value" (*Fortnightly Review*, April 1876) it is argued that Cairnes had mistaken Mill's meaning, and had really seen not more but less of the truth than Mill had done

The expenses of production of any amount of a raw commodity may best be estimated with reference to the "margin of production" at which no rent is paid. But this method of speaking has great difficulties with regard to commodities that obey the law of increasing return It seemed best to note this point in passing. it will be fully discussed later on, chiefly in Ch XI

[1] We have already (Book II Ch III.) noticed that the economic use of the term "production" includes the production of new utilities by moving a thing from a place in which it is less wanted to a place in which it is more wanted, or by helping consumers to satisfy their needs

neighbourhood of Canadian forests often consists almost exclusively of the price of the labour of lumber men: but the supply price of Canadian deal in the wholesale London market consists in a large measure of freights; while the supply price of the same wood to a small retail buyer in an English country town is more than half made up of the charges of the railways and middlemen who have brought what he wants to his doors, and keep a stock of it ready for him. Again, the supply price of a certain kind of labour may for some purposes be analysed into the expenses of rearing, of general education and of special trade education. The possible combinations are numberless; and though each may have incidents of its own which will require separate treatment in the complete solution of any problem connected with it, yet at this stage of our inquiry all such incidents may be ignored, so far as the reasonings of this Book are concerned.

In calculating the expenses of production of a commodity we must take account of the fact that changes in the amounts produced are likely, even when there is no new invention, to be accompanied by changes in the relative quantities of its several factors of production. For instance, when the scale of production increases, horse or steam power is likely to be substituted for manual labour; materials are likely to be brought from a greater distance and in greater quantities, thus increasing those expenses of production which correspond to the work of carriers, middlemen and traders of all kinds.

The Law of Substitution

As far as the knowledge and business enterprise of the producers reach, they in each case choose those factors of production which are best for their purpose; the sum of the supply prices of those factors which are used is, as a rule, less than the sum of the supply prices of any other set of factors which could be substituted for them, and whenever it appears to the producers that this is not the case, they will, as a rule, set to work to substitute the less expensive method. We may call this, for convenience of reference, *The Law of Substitution*.

In the course of our future work we shall be constantly referring to this Law its applications extend over almost every field of economic inquiry, and indeed include a great part of the results that are often referred to the action of competition. From another point of view the law may be regarded as closely akin to the law of the distribution of a commodity between different uses[1].

The position from which we start.

§ 4. The position then is this: we are investigating the equilibrium of normal demand and normal supply in their most general form; we are neglecting those features which are special to particular parts of economic science, and are confining our attention to those broad relations which are common to nearly the whole of it. Thus we assume that the forces of demand and supply have free play; that there is no combination among dealers on either side; but each acts for himself, and there is *free competition;* that is, buyers compete freely with buyers, and sellers compete freely with sellers But though everyone acts for himself, his knowledge of what others are doing is supposed to be generally sufficient to prevent him from taking a lower or paying a higher price than others are doing. This is assumed provisionally to be true both of finished goods and of their factors of production, of the hire of labour and of the borrowing of capital We have already inquired to some extent, and we shall have to inquire further, how far these assumptions are in accordance with the actual facts of life But meanwhile this is the supposition on which we proceed, we assume that there is only one price in the market at one and the same time, it being understood that separate allowance is made, when necessary, for differences in the expense of delivering goods to dealers in different parts of the market, including, if it is a retail market, allowance for the special expenses of retailing.

We assume free play for demand and supply in the market

General conditions of demand

In such a market there is a demand price for each amount of the commodity, that is, a price at which each particular amount of the commodity can find purchasers in a unit of time. The circumstances which govern this price for any given amount of the commodity vary in character from one problem to another; but in every case the more of a thing is

[1] See Book III Ch. V and Book IV Ch VII § 8. This general statement of a broad principle is called a Law, not very appropriately, but for lack of a better term. Its applications are numerous, and many words would be wasted in bringing it to bear, if it had not a special name See Book I. Ch VI § 6.

offered for sale in a market the lower is the price at which it will find purchasers; or in other words, the demand price for each unit diminishes with every increase in the amount offered.

The unit of time may be chosen according to the circumstances of each particular problem. it may be a day, a month, a year, or even a generation: but in every case it must be short relatively to the whole period of the market the equilibrium of which is being investigated It is to be assumed that the general circumstances of the market remain unchanged throughout this period, that there is, for instance, no change in fashion or taste, no new substitute which might affect the demand, no new invention to disturb the supply.

The conditions of supply will vary with the length of time to which reference is made

The conditions of normal supply are less definite; and a full study of them must be reserved for later chapters. They will be found to vary in detail with the length of the period of time to which the investigation refers; chiefly because both the Material capital of machinery and other business plant, and the Immaterial capital of business skill and ability and organization, are of slow growth and slow decay.

But we may provisionally regard normal supply price as the expenses of production including gross earnings of management, of a Representative firm

Let us call to mind the Representative firm, whose economies of production, internal and external, are dependent on the aggregate volume of production of the commodity that they make[1]; and, postponing all further study of the nature of this dependence, let us assume that the normal supply price of any amount of that commodity may be taken to be its normal expenses of production (including *gross* earnings of management[2]) by that firm That is, let us assume that this is the price the expectation of which will just suffice to maintain the existing aggregate amount of production; some firms meanwhile rising and increasing their output, and others falling and diminishing theirs, but the aggregate production remaining unchanged. A price higher than this would increase the growth of the rising firms, and slacken, though it might not arrest, the decay of the falling firms, with the net result of an increase in the aggregate production. And on the other hand, a price lower than this would

[1] See Book IV. Ch XIII § 2

[2] See last paragraph of Book IV. Ch XII

BOOK V. CH. III.

hasten the decay of the falling firms, and slacken the growth of the rising firms, and on the whole diminish production.

The construction of the list of prices at which a thing can be supplied; or its supply schedule

§ 5. To give definiteness to the ideas let us suppose that a person well acquainted with the woollen trade sets himself to inquire what would be the normal supply price of a certain number of millions of yards annually of a particular kind of cloth. He would have to reckon (i) the price of the wool, coal, and other materials which would be used up in making it, (ii) wear and tear and depreciation of the buildings, machinery and other fixed capital, (iii) interest and insurance on all the capital, (iv) the wages of those who work in the factories, and (v) the gross earnings of management, (including insurance against loss) of those who undertake the risks, who engineer and superintend the working. He would of course estimate the supply prices of all these different factors of production of the cloth with reference to the amounts of each of them that would be wanted, and on the supposition that the conditions of supply would be normal

Let us suppose a list of supply prices (or a supply schedule) made on a similar plan to that of our list of demand prices (or demand schedule[1]): the supply price of the production of each amount of the commodity in a year, or any other unit of time, being written against that amount[2]. As the (annual) amount produced increases, the

[1] See Book III. Ch III § 4

Fig 18.

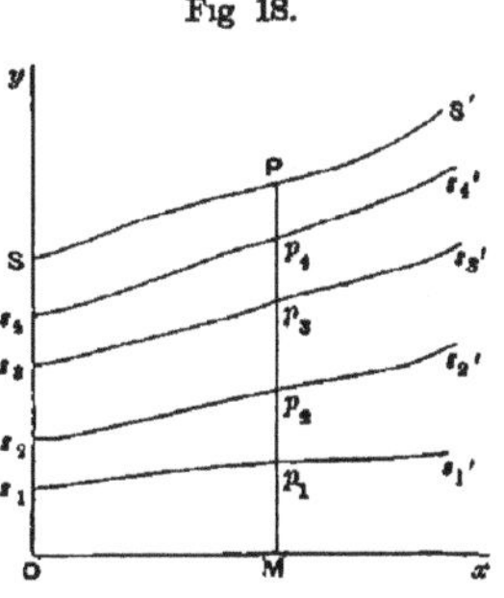

[2] Measuring, as in the case of the demand curve, amounts of the commodity along Ox and prices parallel to Oy, we get for each point M along Ox a line MP drawn at right angles to it measuring the supply price for the amount OM, the extremity of which, P, may be called a *supply point*, this price MP being made up of the supply prices of the several factors of production for the amount OM The locus of P may be called the *supply curve*.

Suppose, for instance, that we classify the expenses of production of our representative firm, when an amount OM of cloth is being produced under the heads of (i) Mp_1, the supply price of the wool and other circulating capital which would be consumed in making it, (ii) p_1p_2 the corresponding wear-and-tear and depreciation on build-

supply price may either increase or diminish, or it may even alternately increase and diminish[1]. For if nature is offering a sturdy resistance to man's efforts to wring from her a larger supply of raw material, while at that particular stage there is no great room for introducing important new economies into the manufacture, the supply price will rise; but if the volume of production were greater, it would perhaps be profitable to substitute largely machine work for hand work and steam power for muscular force; and the increase in the volume of production would have diminished the expenses of production of the commodity of our Representative firm.

We postpone cases in which the supply price diminishes as the amount produced increases

But those cases in which the supply price falls as the amount increases involve special difficulties of their own. And, in order that we may get a clear view of the broad relations between normal demand and supply, let us leave them out of account, and confine our attention in the remainder of this chapter to cases in which the normal supply price either remains constant for different amounts or increases as the amount produced increases.

What is meant by equilibrium

§ 6 When therefore the amount produced (in a unit of time) is such that the demand price is greater than the supply price, then sellers receive more than is sufficient to make it worth their while to bring goods to market to that

ings, machinery and other fixed capital, (iii) p_2p_3 the interest and insurance on all the capital, (iv) p_3p_4 the wages of those who work in the factory, and (v) p_4P the gross earnings of management, &c of those who undertake the risks and direct the work Thus as M moves from O towards the right p_1, p_2, p_3, p_4 will each trace out a curve, and the ultimate supply curve traced out by P will be thus shown as obtained by superimposing the supply curves for the several factors of production of the cloth

It must be remembered that these supply prices are the prices not of units of the several factors but of those amounts of the several factors which are required for producing a yard of the cloth Thus, for instance, p_3p_4 is the supply price not of any fixed amount of labour but of that amount of labour which is employed in making a yard where there is an aggregate production of OM yards (See above, § 3) We need not trouble ourselves to consider just here whether the ground-rent of the factory must be put into a class by itself this belongs to a group of questions which will be discussed later We are taking no notice of rates and taxes, for which he would of course have to make his account

[1] That is, a point moving along the supply curve towards the right may either rise or fall, or even it may alternately rise and fall; in other words, the supply curve may be inclined positively or negatively, or even at some parts of its course it may be inclined positively and at others negatively. (See foot-note on p. 175)

BOOK V. CH III

amount; and there is at work an active force tending to increase the amount brought forward for sale. On the other hand, when the amount produced is such that the demand price is less than the supply price, sellers receive less than is sufficient to make it worth their while to bring goods to market on that scale; so that those who were just on the margin of doubt as to whether to go on producing are decided not to do so, and there is an active force at work tending to diminish the amount brought forward for sale. When the demand price is equal to the supply price, the amount produced has no tendency either to be increased or to be diminished; it is in equilibrium.

Equilibrium-amount and *Equilibrium-price*

When demand and supply are in equilibrium, the amount of the commodity which is being produced in a unit of time may be called the *Equilibrium-amount*, and the price at which it is being sold may be called the *Equilibrium-price.*

Stable equilibria, the conditions under which they occur

Such an equilibrium is *Stable;* that is, the price, if displaced a little from it, will tend to return, as a pendulum oscillates about its lowest point; and it will be found to be a characteristic of stable equilibria that in them the demand price is greater than the supply price for amounts just less than the equilibrium amount, and *vice versâ*[1]. For when the demand price is greater than the supply price, the amount produced tends to increase, and therefore, if the demand price is greater than the supply price for amounts just less than an equilibrium amount, then if the scale of production is temporarily diminished somewhat below that equilibrium position, it will tend to return; thus the equilibrium is stable for displacements in that direction. If the demand price is greater than the supply price for amounts just less than the equilibrium amount, it is sure to be less than the supply price for amounts just greater: and therefore, if the scale of production is somewhat increased beyond the equilibrium position, it will tend to return; and the equilibrium will be stable for displacements in that direction also.

[1] When we come to discuss equilibria of demand and supply with reference to things of which the supply price diminishes as the amount produced increases, we shall find that some equilibria, which though not practically important are yet theoretically possible, are *unstable;* and that they are distinguished from stable equilibria by wanting this characteristic.

Oscillations about a position of stable equilibrium

When demand and supply are in stable equilibrium, if any accident should move the scale of production from its equilibrium position, there will be instantly brought into play forces tending to bring it back to that position; just as, if a stone hanging by a string is displaced from its equilibrium position, the force of gravity will at once tend to bring it back to its equilibrium position. The movements of the scale of production about its position of equilibrium will be of a somewhat similar kind[1].

are seldom rhythmical.

But in real life such oscillations are seldom as rhythmical as those of a stone hanging freely from a string; the comparison would be more exact if the string were supposed to hang in the troubled waters of a mill-race, whose stream was at one time allowed to flow freely, and at another partially cut off The demand and supply schedules do not in practice remain unchanged for a long time together, but are constantly being changed, and every change in them alters the equilibrium amount and the equilibrium price, and thus gives new positions to the centres about which the amount and the price tend to oscillate

Looseness of the connection between the supply price of a commodity

These considerations point to the great importance of the element of time in relation to demand and supply, to the study of which we now proceed We shall gradually discover a great many different limitations of the doctrine

[1] To represent the equilibrium of demand and supply geometrically we may draw the demand and supply curves together as in Fig 19 If then OR represents the rate at which production is being actually carried on, and Rd the demand price is greater than Rs the supply price, the production is exceptionally profitable, and will be increased R, the *amount-index*, as we may call it, will move to the right On the other hand, if Rd is less than Rs, R will move to the left If Rd is equal to Rs, that is, if R is vertically under a point of intersection of the curves, demand and supply are in equilibrium.

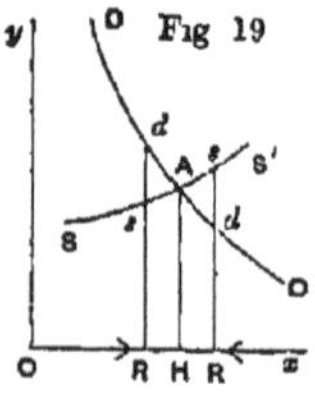

Fig 19

This may be taken as the typical diagram for stable equilibrium for a commodity that obeys the law of diminishing return But if we had made SS' a horizontal straight line, we should have represented the case of "constant return," in which the supply price is the same for all amounts of the commodity And if we had made SS' inclined negatively, but less steeply than DD' (the necessity for this condition will appear more fully later on), we should have got a case of stable equilibrium for a commodity which obeys the law of increasing return In either case the above reasoning remains unchanged without the alteration of a word or a letter; but the last case introduces difficulties which we have arranged to postpone

BOOK V CH. III

and its real cost of production.

that the price at which a thing can be produced represents its real cost of production, that is, the efforts and sacrifices which have been directly and indirectly devoted to its production. That doctrine would indeed represent facts accurately enough in a stationary society, in which people's habits of life, and the methods and volume of production remained unchanged from one generation to another; provided that people were tolerably free to choose those occupations for their capital and labour which seemed most advantageous.

The true significance of a position of normal equilibrium, and of the phrase *In the long run.*

But in an age of change such as this, the equilibrium of normal demand and supply does not thus correspond to any distinct relation of a certain aggregate of pleasures got from the consumption of the commodity and an aggregate of efforts and sacrifices involved in producing them; and it would not do so even if normal earnings and interest were exact measures of the efforts and sacrifices for which they are severally the money payments. It represents only the equilibrium of the forces working at the margins of demand and supply, tending to increase the amount demanded on the one hand, or to diminish the amount supplied at the equilibrium price.

This is the real drift of that much-quoted, and much-misunderstood doctrine of Adam Smith and other economists that the normal, or "natural," value of a commodity is that which economic forces tend to bring about *in the long run*. It is the average value which economic forces would bring about if the general conditions of life were stationary for a run of time long enough to enable them all to work out their full effect. The fact that the general conditions of life are not stationary is the source of many of the difficulties that are met with in applying economic doctrines to practical problems. And the remainder of the present volume will be chiefly occupied with interpreting and limiting this doctrine that the value of a thing tends in the long run to measure its cost of production[1].

[1] It has been objected that since "the economic world is subject to continual changes, and is becoming more complex, the longer the run the more hopeless the rectification" so that to speak of that position which value tends to reach in the long run is to treat "variables as constants" (Devas, *Political Economy*, Book IV. Ch V) The charge is so far just, that we do treat variables *provisionally* as constants For indeed that is the only method by which science has ever made

Influences of Utility and Cost of production on value.

§ 7. In the Note at the end of this Book some account will be given of the controversy whether "Cost of production" or "Utility" governs value. But it may be well to say here at once that we might as reasonably dispute whether it is the upper or the lower blade of a pair of scissors that cuts a piece of paper. It is true that when one blade is held still, and the cutting is effected by moving the other, we may say with careless brevity that the cutting is done by the second; but the statement is not strictly accurate, and is to be excused only so long as it claims to be merely a popular and not a strictly scientific account of what actually happens.

The former preponderates in market values;

In the same way, when a thing already made has to be sold, the prices which people will be willing to pay for it will be governed by their desire to have it, together with the amount they can afford to spend on it. Their desire to have it depends partly on the chance that, if they do not buy it, they will be able to get another thing like it at as low a price: this depends on the causes that govern the supply of it, and this again upon cost of production. But it may so happen that the stock to be sold is practically fixed. This for instance is the case with a fish market, in which the value of fish for the day is governed almost exclusively by the stock on the slabs in relation to the demand And if a person chooses to take the stock for granted, and say that the price is governed by demand, his brevity may perhaps be excused so long as he does not claim strict accuracy So again it may be pardonable, but it is not strictly accurate to say that the varying prices which the same rare book fetches, when sold and resold at Christie's auction room, are governed exclusively by demand.

the latter in normal values

Taking a case at the opposite extreme, we find some commodities which conform pretty closely to the law of constant return, that is to say, their average cost of production will be very nearly the same whether they are produced in small quantities or in large In such a case the normal level about which the market price fluctuates will be this definite and fixed (money) cost of production If the demand

any great progress in dealing with complex and changeful matter, whether in the physical or moral world.

happens to be great, the market price will rise for a time above the level; but as a result production will increase and the market price will fall: and conversely, if the demand falls for a time below its ordinary level.

In such a case, if a person chooses to neglect market fluctuations, and to take it for granted that there will anyhow be enough demand for the commodity to insure that some of it, more or less, will find purchasers at a price equal to this cost of production, then he may be excused for ignoring the influence of demand, and speaking of (normal) price as governed by cost of production—provided only he does not claim scientific accuracy for the wording of his doctrine, and explains the influence of demand in its right place.

Thus we may say that, *as a general rule*, the shorter the period which we are considering the greater must be the share of our attention which is given to the influence of demand on value; and the longer the period, the more important will be the influence of cost of production on value

CHAPTER IV.

INVESTMENT OF RESOURCES FOR A DISTANT RETURN. PRIME COST AND TOTAL COST

The motives determining the investment for a distant return are complex

§ 1. The true nature of the investment of resources for a distant return is disguised by the modern methods of doing business, in which the undertaker buys most of the labour required for his work; for he thinks chiefly of the expenses of production and seldom pays much attention to the efforts and sacrifices to which those payments more or less closely correspond, and which constitute the Real cost of production. It will be well therefore to begin by watching the action of a person who neither buys what he wants nor sells what he makes, but works on his own behalf; and who therefore balances the efforts and sacrifices which he makes on the one hand against the pleasures which he expects to derive from their fruit on the other, without the intervention of any money payments at all.

They may be clearly seen in the case of a man who makes a thing for his own use

Let us then take the case of a man who builds a house for himself on land, and of materials, which Nature supplies gratis, and who makes his implements as he goes, the labour of making them being counted as part of the labour of building the house. He would have to estimate the efforts required for building on any proposed plan, and to allow almost instinctively an amount increasing in geometrical proportion (a sort of compound interest) for the period that would elapse between each effort and the time when the house would be ready for his use The utility of the house to him when finished would have to compensate him not only for the efforts, but for the waitings[1].

[1] For he might have applied these efforts, or efforts equivalent to them, to producing immediate gratifications; and if he deliberately chose the deferred

BOOK V CH. IV.

If the two motives, one deterring, the other impelling, seemed equally balanced, he would be on the margin of doubt Probably the gain would be much stronger than the "real" cost with regard to some part of the house; (and from this he would derive a Producer's Surplus or Rent)[1]. But as he turned over more and more ambitious plans, there would be a point at which the advantages of any further extension would be balanced by the efforts and waitings required for making it; and that part of the building would be on the margin of profitableness of the investment of his capital[2]

There would probably be several ways of building parts of the house; some parts for instance might almost equally well be built of wood or of rough stones: the investment of capital on each plan for each part of the accommodation would be compared with the advantages offered thereby, and each would be pushed forward till the margin of profitableness had been reached. Thus there would be a great many margins of profitableness one corresponding to each kind of plan on which each kind of accommodation might be provided[3].

Transition to the investment of capital by the

§ 2 This illustration may serve to keep before us the way in which the efforts and sacrifices, which are the real cost of production of a thing, underlie the expenses which are

gratifications, it would be because, even after allowing for the disadvantages of waiting, he regarded them as outweighing the earlier gratifications which he could have substituted for them The motive force then tending to deter him from building the house would be his estimate of the aggregate of these efforts, the evil or discommodity of each being increased in geometrical proportion (a sort of compound interest) according to the corresponding interval of waiting. The motive on the other hand impelling him to build it, would be expectation of the satisfaction which he would have from the house when completed, and that again might be resolved into the aggregate of many pleasures more or less remote, and more or less certain, which he expected to derive from its use (See Book III. Ch v § 3, and Book IV. Ch VII § 8)

If he thought that this satisfaction which he would derive from the house when finished, this aggregate of discounted values of satisfactions that it would afford him, would be more than a recompense to him for all the efforts and waitings which he had undergone, he would decide to build

[1] See above, pp 314 and 217

[2] See Mathematical Note XIII

[3] On such a supposition as that made in this Section, we may look upon capital as stored-up effort, the amount of effort and the amount of sacrifice involved in the waiting for the result being measured quantitatively See Mathematical Note XIV

its Money cost. But, as has just been remarked, the modern business man commonly takes the payments which he has to make, whether for wages or raw material, as he finds them; without staying to inquire how far they are an accurate measure of the efforts and sacrifices to which they correspond. His expenditure is generally made piece-meal, and the longer he expects to wait for the fruit of any outlay, the richer must that fruit be in order to compensate him. The anticipated fruit may not be certain, and in that case he will have to allow for the risk of failure. After making that allowance, the fruit of the outlay must be expected to exceed the outlay itself by an amount which, independently of his own remuneration, increases at compound interest in proportion to the time of waiting[1].

modern undertaker of business enterprises

For brevity we may speak of any element of outlay (allowance being made for the remuneration of the undertaker himself) when increased by compound interest in this way, as *Accumulated*; just as we used the term Discounted to represent the present value of a distant pleasure. Each element of outlay has then to be accumulated for the time which will elapse between its being incurred and its bearing fruit; and the aggregate of these accumulated elements is the total outlay involved in the enterprise.

Accumulation of past and discounting of future outlays and receipts

If the enterprise were, say, to dig out a dock-basin on a contract, the payment for which would be made without fail when the work was finished; and if the plant used in the work might be taken to be worn out in the process, and valueless at the end of it, then the enterprise would be just remunerative if this aggregate of outlays accumulated up to the period of payment were just equal to that payment.

The balancing of one against the other

But in fact in nearly every business undertaking the incomings are a constant process as well as the outgoings. And to complete the case we must suppose a balance-sheet struck, looking backwards and looking forwards Looking backwards we should add together the net outlays accumu-

[1] We may, if we choose, regard the price of the business undertaker's own work as part of the original outlay, and reckon compound interest on it together with the rest Or we might substitute for compound interest a sort of "compound profit" The two courses are not strictly convertible and at a later stage we shall find that in certain cases the first is to be preferred, and in others the second

BOOK V. CH IV.

lated up to that time, deducting from each element of outlay any incomings that came in at the same time. Looking forwards we should deduct from each future incoming any outlay that would be made at the same time, together with allowance for the undertaker's own remuneration; and regarding the result as the net incoming at that time, we should discount it at compound interest for the period during which it would be deferred The aggregate of the net incomings so discounted would be balanced against the aggregate of the accumulated outlays: and if the two were just equal, the business would be just remunerative[1].

The Law of Substitution

§ 3. When at the beginning of a business an estimate is made of the profits likely to be earned in it, all the entries for outgoings and incomings alike are prospective And at that and every successive stage the mind of the undertaker is ceaselessly striving so to modify his arrangements as to obtain greater results with a given expenditure or equal results with a less expenditure. He is continually comparing the efficiency and the supply prices of different factors of production which may be used in obtaining the same result, so as to hit upon that combination which will give

[1] Almost every trade has its own difficulties and its own customs connected with the task of valuing the capital that has been invested in a business, and of allowing for the depreciation which that capital has undergone from wear-and-tear, from the influence of the elements, from new inventions, and from changes in the course of trade. These two last causes may temporarily raise the value of some kinds of fixed capital, at the same time that they are lowering that of others And people whose minds are cast in different moulds, or whose interests in the matter point in different directions, will often differ widely on the question what part of the expenditure required for adapting buildings and plant to changing conditions of trade, may be regarded as an investment of new capital, and what ought to be set down as charges incurred to balance depreciation, and treated as expenditure deducted from the current receipts, before determining the net profits or true income earned by the business These difficulties, and the consequent differences of opinion, are greatest of all with regard to the investment of capital in building up a business connection, and the proper method of appraising the goodwill of a business, or its value "as a going concern" On the whole of this subject see Matheson's *Depreciation of Factories and their Valuation.*

Another group of difficulties arises from changes in the general purchasing power of money If that has fallen, or, in other words, if there has been a rise of general prices, the value of a factory may appear to have risen when it has really remained stationary Confusions arising from this source introduce greater errors into estimates of the real profitableness of different classes of business than would at first sight appear probable But all questions of this kind must be deferred till we have discussed the theory of money

the largest incomings in proportion to any given outlay; or, in other words, he is ceaselessly occupied with the action of the law of substitution[1].

Different routes are chosen in obtaining the same end

Every locality has incidents of its own which affect in various ways the methods of arrangement of every class of business that is carried on in it But even in the same place and the same trade no two persons pursuing the same aims will adopt exactly the same routes The tendency to variation is a chief cause of progress; and the abler are the undertakers in any trade the greater will this tendency be In some trades, as for instance cotton-spinning, the possible variations are confined within narrow limits; no one can hold his own at all who does not use machinery, and very nearly the latest machinery, for every part of the work But in others, as for instance in some branches of the wood and metal trades, in farming, and in shopkeeping, there can be great variations For instance, of two manufacturers in the same trade, one will perhaps have a larger wages bill and the other heavier charges on account of machinery; of two retail dealers one will have a larger capital locked up in stock and the other will spend more on advertisements and other means of building up the immaterial capital of a profitable trade connection. And in minor details the variations are numberless. Each man's actions are influenced by his special opportunities and resources, as well as by his temperament and his associations.

The margin of profitableness is not a mere point on any one route, but a line intersecting all routes

But each man, taking account of his own means, will push the investment of capital in his business in each several direction until what appears in his judgment to be the margin of profitableness is reached, that is, until there seems to him no good reason for thinking that the gains resulting from any further investment in that particular direction would compensate him for his outlay The margin of profitableness is not to be regarded as a mere point on any one fixed line of possible investment, but as a boundary line of irregular shape cutting one after another every possible line of investment.

§ 4. When investing his capital in providing the means

[1] Book V Ch III § 3

BOOK V. CH IV.

of carrying on a business, the undertaker looks to being recouped by the price obtained for its various products, and he expects to be able under normal conditions to charge for each of them a price that will not only cover its (Money) *Special, Direct,* or *Prime cost*, but also bear its proper share of the general expenses of the business, which we may call its *Supplementary cost.* These two elements together make its (Money) *Total cost.*

Prime or Special cost. Supplementary and Total cost.

Prime cost is taken to include only the price of raw material and ordinary labour, and extra wear and tear of plant.

There are great variations in the usage of the term Prime cost in business life. But it is taken here in a narrow sense, so as to include nothing but the (Money) cost of the raw material used in making the commodity and the wages of that part of the labour spent on it which is paid by the day or the week and the extra wear and tear of plant: the salaries of the upper employees are as a rule excluded, because the charges to which the business is put on account of their salaries cannot generally be adapted quickly to changes in the amount of work there is for them to do Special costs are those incurred for a near return. Supplementary costs are those incurred for a distant return[1].

This is the special cost which a manufacturer has commonly in view when, trade being slack, he is calculating the lowest price at which it will be worth his while to accept an order, irrespectively of any effect that his action might have in spoiling the market for future orders. And in extreme cases he will even be willing to accept a lower price than this For when he has been for some time short of work, and has already dismissed all save the best of his employees, it would—to say nothing of any less selfish motive—almost answer his purpose to pay the remainder full wages to beat time, so to speak; in order that he may have them

[1] "There are many systems of Prime Cost in vogue we take Prime Cost to mean, as in fact the words imply, only the original or direct cost of production; and while in some trades it may be a matter of convenience to include in the cost of production a proportion of indirect expenses, and a charge for depreciation on plant and buildings, in no case should it comprise interest on capital or profit" (Garcke and Fells, *Factory Accounts*, Ch I) Elaborate statistics of the various elements of cost of production in certain trades have been made by the Commissioner of Labour in the United States, and his Report for 1890 contains many suggestive remarks on the subject of this chapter See also the Report of the Massachusetts Bureau of Labour for the same year

at hand when trade revives and high profits are again to be made.

Where there is much fixed capital, prices can fall far below their normal level without reaching special or prime cost

In trades which use very expensive plant, the supplementary cost of goods is a large part of their total cost; and an order at much less than their normal price may leave a large surplus above their direct and special or prime cost But if in their anxiety to prevent their plant from being idle producers accept such orders, they glut the market and tend to prevent prices from reviving. If they pursue this policy constantly and without moderation, they may keep prices so low as to drive capital out of the trade, ruining many of those employed in it, themselves perhaps among the number. During all this time the income derived from their plant and business organization will be very low; but after a while the demand for their goods will revive, and the means for meeting it will be inadequate, and the prices of the goods will then rise high above their normal level[1].

The income that in the long run covers Supplementary Costs for a normally successful business, may for a short run be regarded as a *Quasi-rent.*

§ 5 That part of the receipts of a business which is required to defray the supplementary cost of the things produced in it may in the long run be regarded as part of its normal profits, because the expectation of getting these gains in the long run was required to induce people to invest their capital and energies in the trade. But on the other hand, when once invested, the income which they yield to their owner is governed by the selling price of the products which they help to produce. We shall find reason for describing the excess of this price over the prime cost or immediate outlay required for the production as a *Quasi-rent,* because we shall find that it has some analogy to that

[1] Extreme variations of this kind are in the long run beneficial neither to producers nor to consumers, and general opinion is not altogether hostile to that code of trade morality which condemns the action of anyone who "spoils the market" by being too ready to accept a price that does little more than cover the prime cost of his goods, and allows but little on account of his general expenses The public listen with some indulgence to those who argue that a trade combination or a Trust is the only means available for securing a reasonable steadiness of price Questions of this kind are of great and growing importance, and will occupy much of our attention later on when we come to consider the causes of commercial fluctuations

BOOK V. CH IV.

Producer's Surplus, accruing from the ownership of fertile land, which is called Rent.

Provisional forecast of the long study of this principle on which we are entering

This brings us to the threshold of the main difficulty of the problem of value, and it will be well to pause a little to look at it What can be said now is not a solution of the difficulty; but a partial statement as to the general nature of the solution which will ultimately be found for it. The statement as it stands will perhaps not be completely intelligible: but it may help to prepare the way for future explanations and to fit them into their place.

Appliances for production are of many different kinds· they include land, factories, machines, business organizations (including even such as a house-letting agency, with a good connection but little or no material capital), business ability and manual skill. The owner of any one of those will not generally apply it to produce anything, unless he expects to gain in return at least enough to compensate him for the immediate and special trouble, sacrifice and outlay involved in this particular operation, and which he could escape by declining to undertake it. Any excess which he gets above this prime cost has obviously some *prima facie* resemblance to that excess value of the produce of land over the direct cost of raising it which is the basis of rent as ordinarily understood; and we are therefore justified in calling it a Quasi-rent

The question how close this resemblance is involves many subtle considerations, some of which have but little interest for the general reader, and the discussion of them is so arranged that he can omit them. Much of it will turn on the fact that while excess of the gross receipts which a producer gets for any of his commodities over their prime cost (that is, over that extra cost which he incurs in order to produce those particular things, and which he could have escaped if he had not produced them) is a temporary surplus (or quasi-rent), yet that in the long run all these temporary surpluses are needed to cover the supplementary costs of the business. They do not therefore, in the long run, yield a true surplus, corresponding to the permanent surplus which the possession of fertile land is commonly supposed to yield, and in some cases does yield, to its owner.

The element of time dominates the applications of this principle

The question how great a part of his expenses he must enter in these prime costs, and how much he must deduct from his selling price before he calculates his surplus, depends on how far he looks ahead; or in other words, on whether he is making his calculations for a long period or only for a short

If he is looking only a little way ahead, and is not afraid of spoiling his market; if he has got all his apparatus ready and standing idle, then a new order coming in will give him a surplus over its direct cost to him, consisting of the whole price which he receives after deducting the special outlay for raw material, for extra wages, and for wear and tear of plant involved in filling up the order But suppose him to be looking far ahead, and proposing to extend his factory so as to do an increased business, he does not then reckon any price as affording him a real surplus, unless, after allowing for all risks, it will yield him, in addition to prime costs, sufficient to give normal profits on all his outlay for material, plant, and for building up his business connection, together with charges for depreciation through the lapse of time, and for office and other general expenses which are not reckoned in the prime, or special and direct, costs of filling up any particular order

The conditions which govern the amount of this surplus and its relations to value depend not so much on the nature of the industry as on the period of time for which the calculation is made But a short period for one class of industry may be a long one for another, just as the age of youth for a dog is shorter than for an elephant[1]

To put the same thing in another way, when we are taking a broad view of normal value extending over a very long period of time, when we are investigating the causes which determine normal value "in the long run," when we are tracing the "ultimate" effects of economic causes, then the income that

[1] This and a few other passages are reproduced from an article *On Rent* in the *Economic Journal* for March, 1893 See also the remarks on Continuity in the Preface to the first edition of this volume

BOOK V. CH IV.

is derived from capital in these forms enters into the payments by which the expenses of production of the commodity in question have to be covered, and it directly controls the action of the producers who are on the margin of doubt as to whether to increase the means of production or not But, on the other hand, when we are considering the causes which determine normal prices for a period which is short relatively to that required for largely increasing the supply of those appliances for production, then their influence on value is chiefly indirect and more or less similar to that exerted by the free gifts of nature. The shorter the period which we are considering, and the slower the process of production of those appliances, the less part will variations in the income derived from them play in checking or increasing the supply of the commodity produced by them, and in raising or lowering its supply price; and the more nearly true will it be that, for the period under discussion, the net income to be derived from them is to be regarded as a producer's surplus or quasi-rent. And thus in passing from the free gifts of nature through the more permanent improvements in the soil to less permanent improvements, to farm and factory buildings, to steam-engines, &c., and finally to the less durable and less slowly made implements, we find a continuous series

Caution against a confusion

From this provisional and incomplete statement it will be obvious that this producer's surplus (or quasi-rent) is of a different character from that which the worker or accumulator of capital derives from the fact that much of his work or waiting involves no sacrifice, while yet the whole of it reaps a reward[1] For the basis of these surpluses is a psychological peculiarity of the individual: while the quasi-rent of an appliance for production is not generally any surplus at all in the long run; but—under the influence of changing circumstance, varying fashion, innovating invention, fluctuating credit, &c —sometimes rises above, and sometimes falls below that level which was anticipated when the appliance was brought into existence. Further light will be thrown on this question later on in the present book and in the sixth book.

[1] See pp 217—18 and 314.

CHAPTER V.

EQUILIBRIUM OF NORMAL DEMAND AND SUPPLY, CONTINUED. THE TERM NORMAL WITH REFERENCE TO LONG AND SHORT PERIODS.

This chapter discusses difficulties relating to the element of time, which are latent in ordinary discourse

§ 1. THE present chapter is chiefly occupied with differences of degree between different parts of the problem of value, and especially normal value, resulting from differences in the length of time to which the problem relates In this case, as in others, the economist merely brings to light difficulties that are latent in the common discourse of life, so that by being frankly faced they may be thoroughly overcome. For in ordinary life it is customary to use the word Normal in different senses, with reference to different periods of time, and to leave the context to explain the transition from one to another. The economist follows this practice of every-day life: but, by taking pains to indicate the transition, he sometimes seems to have created a complexity which in fact he has only revealed

Our elastic use of the term Normal is consistent with common practice

Thus, for instance, when it is said that the price of wool on a certain day was abnormally high though the average price for the year was abnormally low, that the wages of coal-miners were abnormally high in 1872 and abnormally low in 1879, that the (real) wages of labour were abnormally high at the end of the fourteenth century and abnormally low in the middle of the sixteenth; everyone understands that the scope of the term normal is not the same in these various cases. Everyone takes the context as indicating the special use of the term in each several case, and a formal interpretation clause is seldom necessary, because in ordinary conversation misunderstandings can be nipped in the bud by question and answer. Thus the difficulty arising from the elastic use of the term Normal need not be a serious one, if it is fairly faced: while on the other hand much confusion and fruitless controversy have arisen from ignoring it

Studies of the equilibrium of normal demand and supply may be divided into two classes as the periods to which they relate are long or comparatively short

§ 2. But though applications of the term Normal are thus elastic, and capable of being extended gradually from very short to very long periods, yet these periods may be divided roughly into two classes In the first class there is time for the supply of those things which are used in producing the commodity (or in other words, its factors of production) to adapt itself to the demand, in the second class there is not. The relation which this first class of normal equilibria bears to the second may be made clearer by observing that it is similar to the relation which this second class bears to the temporary equilibria discussed in Chapter II; for there the period over which we were studying the action of the forces of demand and supply was so short that cost of production could not exercise any direct influence over the supply price.

Illustration from fish-markets Temporary equilibrium Oscillations of market price about short-period normal supply price

For instance, on the day following a large catch of mackerel the price in the market may settle down after a little manœuvring to an equilibrium level at as many pence as it had been at shillings on the previous day, and this change will in no way depend on the normal cost of catching mackerel; it will be governed by the volume of the past catch, with perhaps some slight reference to the chance that a similar catch may be had on the morrow If we suppose the boat owned by a capitalist undertaker who pays the fisherman by the day, the net earnings of his boat for the day will be the excess of the price he gets for his fish over his outlay for wages and stores, together with allowance for the injury done to the boat and net by the day's work The excess on this particular day may be either more or less than the normal supply price required to make it worth his while to provide the boat and its equipment and the business organization needed for managing it and selling its catch. But if, in the long run and on the average, the excess is more than this normal supply price, capital will drift into the fishing trade; if less, it will drift out, that is to say, old boats and nets, when worn out, will seldom be replaced. And therefore, if the general conditions of the fishing trade are stationary, the earnings of the boat will oscillate about this normal supply price as a position of stable equilibrium.

Oscillations of short-period normal supply price about its equilibrium position

But next suppose there to be great increase in the general demand for fish, such for instance as might arise from the spreading of a disease through all kinds of farm stock simultaneously, by which meat was made a dear and dangerous food. The increased demand for fish could not well be met without bringing into the fishing trade some people from outside, who were not fitted by training to do its work well, and to whom many of its ordinary incidents would prove great hardships Old and unsuitable boats would be pressed into the service; the better class of boats might earn in a year enough to pay fifty per cent. or more on their total cost; and able fishermen, whether paid by shares or by the day, might for a time get twice their ordinary wages.

The (short-period) normal price of fish would be higher than before; variations in the catch of fish from day to day might make the market price oscillate at least as violently as before about this new normal level for an increased amount, but this new level would rise rapidly with every such increase of demand.

For short periods an increase in the amount produced nearly always raises normal supply price

Of course these high prices would tend to bring capital and labour into the trade. but if it were expected that the disease among live stock would not last very long, and that therefore the unusual demand for fish would die away in a few years, people would be cautious about investing capital and skill in a trade that was in danger of being glutted And therefore, though when the demand slackened off, the price would fall too, and probably below its old level; yet so long as the demand was fully maintained the price would keep up And here we see an illustration of the almost universal law that *an increase in the amount demanded raises the short-period normal supply price*

Long-period normal

§ 3 But if we turn to consider the *long-period* normal supply price, we shall find that it is determined by a different

BOOK V. CH V

demand and supply in equilibrium

set of causes, and with different results. For suppose that the disuse of meat causes a permanent distaste for it, and that an increased demand for fish continues long enough to enable the forces by which its supply is governed to work out their action fully. The source of supply in the sea might perhaps show signs of exhaustion, and the fishermen might have to resort to more distant coasts and to deeper waters, Nature giving a diminishing return to the increased application of capital and labour of a given order of efficiency. On the other hand, those might turn out to be right who think that man is responsible for but a very small part of the destruction of fish that is constantly going on; and in that case a boat starting with equally good appliances and an equally efficient crew would be likely to get nearly as good a haul after the increase in the total volume of the fishing trade as before In any case the normal real cost and therefore (the general purchasing power of money being assumed stationary) the normal money cost of equipping a good boat with an efficient crew would certainly not be higher, and probably be a little lower, after the trade had settled down to its now increased dimensions, than before For since fishermen require only trained aptitudes, and not any exceptional natural qualities, their number could be increased in less than a generation to almost any extent that was necessary to meet the demand; while the industries connected with building boats, making nets, &c., being now on a larger scale, would be organized more thoroughly and economically If therefore the waters of the sea showed no signs of depletion of fish, an increased supply could be produced at a lower price after a time sufficiently long to enable the normal action of economic causes to work itself out: and, the term Normal being taken to refer to a long period of time, the normal price of fish would decrease with an increase in the amount produced

Illustration from the cost of production of cloth

To drive this fundamental distinction well home it may be well to take an illustration from manufacture. We saw[1] that to estimate the price at which a certain quantity of cloth could be produced, a person would first calculate the

[1] Above, Ch III § 5

expenses of producing of all the different things required for the purpose with reference to the amounts of each of them that would be wanted, and on the supposition in the first instance that the conditions of supply would be normal. But now we have to notice that he would give to this term a wider or narrower range according as he was looking more or less far ahead.

Thus in estimating the wages required to call forth an adequate supply of labour to work a certain class of looms, he might take the current wages of similar work in the neighbourhood: or he might argue that there was a scarcity of that particular class of labour in the neighbourhood, that its current wages there were higher than in other parts of England, and that looking forward over several years so as to allow for immigration, he might take the normal rate of wages at a rather lower rate than that prevailing there at the time Or lastly, he might think that the wages of weavers all over the country were abnormally low relatively to others of the same grade, in consequence of a too sanguine view having been taken of the prospects of the trade half a generation ago. He might argue that this branch of work was overcrowded, that parents had already begun to choose other trades for their children which offered greater net advantages and yet were not more difficult, that in consequence a few years would see a falling-off in the supply of labour suited for his purpose; so that looking forward a long time he must take normal wages at a rate rather higher than the present average. (There are indeed not many occasions on which the calculations of a business man for practical purposes need to look forward so far, and to extend the range of the term Normal over a whole generation but in the broader applications of economic science it is sometimes necessary to extend the range even further, and to take account of the slow changes that in the course of centuries affect the supply price of the labour of each industrial grade.)

Use of the term Normal in ordinary business

Again, in estimating the normal supply price of wool, he would probably take the average of past years, making an allowance however for any probable change in the causes

BOOK V CH V

likely to affect the supply in the immediate future. He would probably reckon for the effect of such droughts as from time to time occur in Australia and elsewhere; since their occurrence is too common to be regarded as abnormal: but he would probably not allow here for the chance of our being involved in a great war, by which the Australian supplies might be cut off, he would consider that any allowance for this should come under the head of extraordinary trade risks, and not enter into his estimate of the normal supply price of wool

He would deal in the same way with the risk of civil tumult or any violent and long-continued disturbance of the labour market of an unusual character; but in his estimate of the amount of work that could be got out of the machinery, &c under normal conditions, he would probably reckon for minor interruptions from trade disputes such as are continually occurring, and are therefore to be regarded as belonging to the regular course of events, that is as not abnormal[1]

It may allow for motives that are not self-regarding

In all these calculations he would not concern himself specially to inquire how far mankind are under the exclusive influence of selfish or self-regarding motives. He might be aware that anger and vanity, jealousy and offended dignity are still almost as common causes of strikes and lockouts, as the desire for pecuniary gain. but that would not enter into his calculations all that he would want to know about them would be whether they acted with sufficient regularity for

[1] These conditions are described incidentally by Tooke (*History of Prices*, Vol. I p 104) "There are particular articles of which the demand for naval and military purposes forms so large a proportion to the total supply, that no diminution of consumption by individuals can keep pace with the immediate increase of demand by government, and consequently, the breaking out of a war tends to raise the price of such articles to a great relative height But even of such articles, if the consumption were not on a progressive scale of increase so rapid that the supply, with all the encouragement of a relatively high price, could not keep pace with the demand, the tendency is (supposing no impediment, natural or artificial, to production or importation) to occasion such an increase of quantity, as to reduce the price to nearly the same level as that from which it had advanced. And accordingly it will be observed, by reference to the table of prices, that saltpetre, hemp, iron, etc , after advancing very considerably under the influence of a greatly extended demand for military and naval purposes, tended downwards again whenever that demand was not progressively and rapidly increasing"

him to be able to make a reasonably good allowance for their influence in causing interruptions of work and increasing the normal supply price of the goods[1].

Restatement of the main result.

§ 4. To go over the ground again in another way. Market values are governed by the relation of demand to stocks actually in the market; with more or less reference to 'future' supplies, and not without some influence of trade combinations[2]. But the current supply is in itself the result of the action of producers in the past, this action has been mainly determined by their comparing the prices which they expect to get for their goods with the expenses to which they will be put in producing them. The range of expenses of which they take account will depend on whether they are merely considering the extra expenses of certain extra production with their existing plant, or are considering whether to lay down new plant for the purpose. But in any case it will be the general rule that that portion of the supply which can be most easily produced will be produced, unless the price is expected to be very low Every increase in the price expected will, as a rule, induce some people who would not otherwise have produced anything, to produce a little; while those who have produced something for the lower price, will probably produce more for the higher price

The producers who are in doubt whether to produce anything at all may be said to lie altogether on the margin of production (or, if they are agriculturists, on the margin of cultivation). Their decision exerts some influence on supply and therefore on price. But as a rule they are very few in number, there may be none in this position, and anyhow their action is far less important than that of the great body

[1] See Book I. ch v. § 9

[2] Where there is a strong combination, tacit or overt, producers may sometimes regulate the price for a considerable time together with very little reference to cost of production And if the leaders in that combination were those who had the best facilities for production, it might be said, in apparent though not in real contradiction to Ricardo's doctrines, that the price was governed by that part of the supply which was most easily produced. But as a fact, those producers whose finances are weakest, and who are bound to go on producing to escape failure, often impose their policy on the rest of the combination And it is a common saying, both in America and England, that the weakest members of a combination are frequently its rulers

BOOK V. CH. V.

of producers who will produce something whatever be the price (within certain limits), but watch the price to see how far it is worth their while to extend their production. That part of their production with regard to which such persons are on the margin of doubt as to whether it is worth while for them to produce it at the price, is to be included together with that of the persons who are in doubt whether to produce at all; the two together constitute the marginal production at that price.

The general drift of the term Normal Supply price is the same for short and long periods

Thus then the general drift of the term Normal Supply price is always the same whether the period to which it refers is short or long; but there are great differences in detail. In every case it has reference to a certain given rate of aggregate production, that is, to the production of a certain aggregate amount daily or annually. In every case it means the price the expectation of which is sufficient and only just sufficient to make it worth while for people to produce that aggregate amount: in every case it is the marginal cost of production; that is, it is the cost of production of those goods which are on the margin of not being produced at all, and which would not be produced if the price to be got for them were expected to be at all lower. But the causes which determine this margin vary with the length of the period under consideration.

But for short periods the appliances of production have to be taken for granted; and the supply price is that which is just needed to call forth those elements of supply which are on the margin of not being produced with those appliances, account

The immediate effect of the expectation of a high price is to cause people to bring into active work all their appliances of production, and to work them full time and perhaps overtime. The marginal supply price is then the money cost of production of that part of the produce which forces the undertaker to hire such inefficient labour (perhaps tired by working overtime) at so high a price, and to put himself and others to so much strain and inconvenience that he is on the margin of doubt whether it is worth his while to do it or not. The immediate effect of the expectation of a low price is to throw many appliances for production out of work, and slacken the work of others. If the producers had no fear of spoiling their markets, it would be worth their while to produce for a time for any price that covered the prime costs of production and rewarded them for their own trouble. But, as it is, they generally hold out for a higher price, each man fears to spoil his chance of getting a better price later on from his own customers, or, if he produces for a large and open market, he is more or less in fear of incurring the resentment of other producers, should he sell needlessly at a price that spoils the common market for all. The marginal production in this case is the production of those whom a little further fall of price would cause, either from a regard to their own interest or by formal or informal agreement with other producers, to suspend production for fear of further spoiling the market This then is the interpretation of marginal supply price for short periods: for which it rises with every increase in the amount that has to be produced[1].

being taken of the fear of spoiling the market.

Thus in short periods the supply of specialized skill and ability, of suitable machinery and other material capital, and of the appropriate industrial organization has not time to be fully adapted to demand; but the producers have to adjust their supply to the demand as best they can with the appliances already at their disposal On the one hand there is not time materially to increase those appliances if the supply of them is deficient; and on the other, if the supply is excessive, some of them must remain imperfectly employed, since there is not time for the supply to be much reduced by gradual decay, and by conversion to other uses. The particular income derived from them during those times does not *for the time* affect perceptibly the supply nor therefore the price of the commodities produced by them: it is a surplus of total receipts over prime (money) cost, governed by the more or less accidental relations of demand and supply for that time (i e a Quasi-rent), but unless it is sufficient to cover in the long run the supplementary costs of the business, production will gradually fall off. In this way a controlling influence over the relatively quick movements

Meanwhile the income derived from those appliances affords a surplus over prime costs

[1] We shall later study the mutual influences of fluctuations in the purchasing power of money, in credit, and in the activity of producers, and also the motives and the methods of combinations among employers to restrict their output, and of combinations among employes to restrict their work, with the double purpose of extracting better terms for themselves from their employers and of putting pressure on those of their employers who are inclined to sell nearly at prime cost and spoil the common market

of supply price during short periods is exercised by causes in the background which range over a long period; and the fear of "spoiling the market" often makes those causes act more promptly than they otherwise would

But for long periods the supply price is that which is just needed to call forth those new investments of capital, material and personal, which are required to make up a certain aggregate volume of production;

§ 5. In long periods all investments of capital and effort in providing the material plant and the organization of a business, and in acquiring trade knowledge and specialized ability, have time to be adjusted to the incomes which are expected to be earned by them: and the estimates of those incomes therefore directly govern supply and are the true long-period normal supply price of the commodities produced.

A great part of the capital invested in a business is generally spent on building up its internal organization and its external trade connections. If the business does not prosper all this capital is lost, even though its material plant may realize a considerable part of its original cost. And anyone proposing to start a new business in any trade must reckon for the chance of this loss. If himself a man of normal capacity for that class of work, he may look forward ere long to his business being a Representative one, in the sense in which we have used this term, with its fair share of those internal and external economies which the aggregate scale of production in that trade will cause to accrue to such a business. If the net receipts of such a representative business, that is, the excess of its incomings over its outgoings, seem likely to be greater than he could get by similar investments in other trades to which he has access, he will choose this trade. Thus that marginal investment of capital in a trade, on which the price of the commodity produced by it depends in the long run, is governed by estimates on the one hand of the outgoings required to build up and to work a representative firm, and on the other of the incomings, spread over a long period of time, to be got by such a price.

these economies of production, when viewed broadly increase

For we must remember that, though at any particular moment some businesses will be rising and others falling, yet when we are taking a broad view of the causes which govern normal supply price, we need not trouble ourselves with these eddies on the surface of the great tide. Such eddies will always exist, and occasionally play an important part in the history of a particular trade, the recent histories of the manufactures of silk, of watches, and of agricultural implements, and again of the shipbuilding, the sugar refining and the chemical industries afford examples of the way in which the energy or the incompetence of a few business men may exert a powerful influence on the development of a great trade in one place and its decadence in another.

generally when the aggregate production increases

Such facts are significant for some purposes, but they do not concern us just now, because looking, as we now are, at broad results only, we have no reason to believe that the eddy at any particular time will be moving in one direction rather than another. Any particular increment of production may be due to some new manufacturer who is struggling against difficulties, working with insufficient capital, and enduring great privations in the hope that he may gradually build up a good business Or it may be due to some wealthy firm which by enlarging its premises is enabled to attain new economies altogether out of proportion to the small fraction that the extension of its particular business adds to the aggregate volume of production in its trade, and reap great gains from its successful adaptation to its surroundings or from the favours of fortune But these inequalities do not prevent the steady tendency of the long-period normal supply price to diminish in many branches of industry as a direct consequence of an increase in their aggregate volumes of production

There is no sharp division between long and short periods

Of course there is no hard and sharp line of division between "long" and "short" periods Nature has drawn no such lines in the economic conditions of actual life; and in dealing with practical problems they are not wanted. Just as we contrast civilized with uncivilized races, and establish many general propositions about either group, though no hard and fast division can be drawn between the two, so we contrast long and short periods without attempting any rigid demarcation between them If it is necessary for the purposes of any particular argument to divide one case sharply from the other, it can be done by a special interpretation clause: but the occasions on which this is necessary are neither frequent nor important In those broad inquiries

BOOK V CH. V.

which will occupy the remainder of this Book, we shall be concerned almost exclusively with the true normal equilibria: but when at a later stage we come to consider the quickly moving oscillations of trade and commerce, the short-period normal, or as we may conveniently call them, the *subnormal* equilibria will claim more of our attention[1].

A new term, *subnormal*.

Relation of this Book to the next

§ 6. Such are the broad outlines of the general theory of equilibrium of normal demand and supply; but there remain many important questions to be considered. Some of these relate to the several peculiarities, and the mutual relations of the agents of production, Labour, Capital, Organization, and Land; and they will be postponed to the following Book. But there are several others which are more general in character and may be taken at once.

Scope of remaining chapters of this Book

The first group is concerned with the relations between the different factors that are required to co-operate for the production of the same goods, and with those between the

[1] Of course the periods required to adapt the several factors of production to the demand may be very different; the number of skilled compositors for instance, cannot be increased nearly as fast as the supply of type and printing-presses. And this cause alone would prevent any rigid division being made between long and short periods. But in fact a theoretically perfect long period must give time enough to enable not only the factors of production of the commodity to be adjusted to the demand, but also the factors of production of those factors of production to be adjusted and so on; and this, when carried to its logical consequences, will be found to involve the supposition of a stationary state of industry, in which the requirements of a future age can be anticipated an indefinite time beforehand. Some such assumption is indeed unconsciously implied in many popular renderings of Ricardo's theory of value, if not in his own versions of it; and it is to this cause more than any other that we must attribute that simplicity and sharpness of outline, from which the economic doctrines in fashion in the first half of this century derived some of their seductive charm as well as most of whatever tendency they may have to lead to false practical conclusions.

The periods for which prices are reckoned may be divided into any number of classes according to their length. But four classes stand out. In each, price is governed by the relations between demand and supply. But as regards *market* prices, "supply" is taken to mean the *stock of the commodity* in question which is on hand, or at all events "in sight." As regards *short-normal* or *sub-normal* prices, "supply" means broadly what can be produced for the price in question with the existing *stock of plant*, personal and impersonal, in the given time. As regards (full) *normal* prices, supply means what can be produced by plant, which itself can be remuneratively produced and applied within the given time. While lastly there are *secular* movements of normal price, caused by the gradual growth of knowledge, of population and of capital, and the changing conditions of demand and supply from one generation to another.

joint products of the same branch of production, &c. Some interruption of the natural course of the argument is involved by taking these next but though they do not directly continue the train of thought pursued in this chapter, they throw on it an important side-light of which it seemed best to avail ourselves before proceeding further.

Chapters VI, VII. Chapters VIII, IX, X.

The argument of the present chapter, with regard to the influence of time on value, is continued in the second group, which deals with the various relations in which the incomes derived from the free gifts of nature, and possessions of all kinds, personal and impersonal, stand to value. In this group several difficulties, that have been slightly touched on as yet, will be examined at length, with the purpose among others of bringing out the complete continuity between the theory of the income derived from land and from other things which are commonly said to be made by man, but really are only turned to account by him; since man can create only utilities, whether he is working on land or on a movable commodity.

This further study of these incomes from possessions (or quasi-rents) will lead the way to a rather technical discussion of the relations between marginal and average supply price expenses of production, and of problems in which two or more positions of stable equilibrium between normal demand and normal supply may, theoretically at least, be possible

Chapter XI

The last group relates to the bearings of the theories of demand and supply, and of monopolies on the famous doctrine that free competition tends to make the aggregate satisfaction a maximum

Chapters XII, XIII.

All of these discussions are integral parts of a complete understanding of the theory of value: but at all events the last two groups are not essential to the discussion of the broad problem of Distribution and Exchange, which will occupy our attention in the following Book. And the summary of their chief results given in the concluding chapters of this Book may suffice for the present purpose of those readers who desire to get as soon as possible to the application of the theory of value to social questions

Some of these chapters may be passed over for the present

CHAPTER VI.

JOINT AND COMPOSITE DEMAND: JOINT AND COMPOSITE SUPPLY.

BOOK V CH VI

Derived demand and *joint demand*

§ 1. THE demand for the things used for making other things, and their factors of production, is indirect; it is *derived* from the demand for the things towards the production of which they contribute, or, in other words, the demands for all the various factors of production of a finished commodity are joined together in the *joint demand* for it[1]. Thus the demand for beer is direct, and is a joint demand for hops, malt, brewers' labour, and the other factors of production of beer: and the demand for any one of them is an indirect demand derived from that for beer. Again, there is a direct demand for new houses; and from this there arises a joint demand for the labour of all the various building trades, and for bricks, stone, wood, etc., which are factors of production of building work of all kinds, or as we may say for shortness, of new houses But the demand for any one of these, as for instance the labour of plasterers, is only an indirect, or *Derived*, demand.

Illustration taken from a labour dispute in the building trade.

Let us take an illustration from a class of events that are of frequent occurrence in the labour market; the period over which the disturbance extends being short, and the causes of which we have to take account as readjusting demand and

[1] Compare Book III Ch III § 6 It will be recollected that the things in a form ready for immediate use have been called *goods of the first Order*, or *Consumers' goods*, and that things used as Factors of production of other goods have been called *Producers' goods*, or *goods of the second and higher Orders* or *Intermediate* goods also that it is rather difficult to say when goods are really finished, and that many things are commonly treated as finished Consumers' goods before they are really ready for consumption, e g flour (Book II Ch. III § 1)

supply being only such as are able to operate within that short period.

This case has important practical bearings, which give it a special claim on our attention, but we should notice that, referring as it does to short periods, it is an exception to our general rule of selecting illustrations in this and the neighbouring chapters from cases in which there is time enough for the full long-period action of the forces of supply to be developed.

Let us then suppose that the supply and demand for building being in equilibrium, there is a strike on the part of one group of workers, say the plasterers, or that there is some other disturbance to the supply of plasterers' labour. In order to isolate and make a separate study of the demand for that factor, we suppose firstly that the general conditions of the demand for new houses remain unchanged (that is, that the demand schedule for new houses remains valid); and secondly we assume that there is no change in the general conditions of supply of the other factors, two of which are of course the business faculties and the business organizations of the master builders, (that is, we assume that their lists of supply prices also remain valid). Then a temporary check to the supply of plasterers' labour will cause a proportionate check to the amount of building: the demand price for the diminished number of houses will be a little higher than before, and the supply prices for the other factors of production will not be greater than before[1] Thus new houses can now be sold at prices which exceed by a good margin the sum of the prices at which these other requisites for the production of houses can be bought; and that margin gives the limit to the possible rise of the price that will be offered for plasterers' labour, on the supposition that plasterers' labour is indispensable. The different amounts of this margin, corresponding to different checks to the supply of plasterers' labour, are governed by the general rule that.—

[1] This is at any rate true under all ordinary conditions: there will be less extra charges for overtime; and the price of the labour of carpenters, bricklayers and others is likely rather to go down than to go up, and the same is true of bricks and other building materials

BOOK V. CH. VI.

Law of Derived Demand

The price that will be offered for any thing used in producing a commodity is, for each separate amount of the commodity, limited by the excess of the price at which that amount of the commodity can find purchasers, over the sum of the prices at which the corresponding supplies of the other things needed for making it will be forthcoming. Or, to use technical terms, the demand schedule for any factor of production of a commodity can be *Derived* from that for the commodity by subtracting from the demand price of each separate amount of the commodity the sum of the supply prices for corresponding amounts of the other factors.

It must always be remembered that this Derived schedule has no validity except on the supposition that we are isolating this one factor for separate study, that its own conditions of supply are disturbed, that there is at the time no independent disturbance affecting any other element in the problem; and that therefore in the case of each of the other factors of production the selling price may be taken to coincide always with the supply price[1]

[1] In illustrating this by a diagram it will be well, for the sake of shortness of wording, to divide the expenses of production of a commodity into the supply prices of two things of which it is made; let us then regard the supply price of a knife as the sum of the supply prices of its blade and handle, and neglect the expense of putting the two together. Let ss' be the supply curve for handles and SS' that for knives; so that M being any point on Ox, and MqQ being drawn vertically to cut ss' in q and SS' in Q, Mq is the supply price for OM handles, qQ is the supply price for OM blades and MQ the supply price for OM knives. Let DD' the demand curve for knives cut SS' in A, and AaB be drawn vertically as in the figure Then in equilibrium OB knives are sold at a price BA of which Ba goes for the handle and aA for the blade.

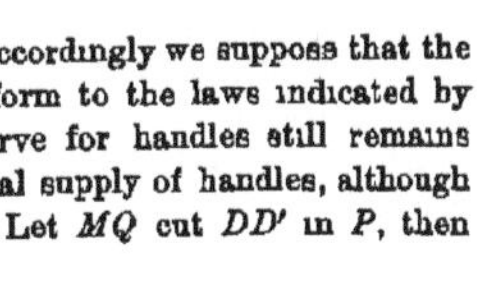

Fig 20

(In this illustration we may suppose that sufficient time is allowed to enable the forces which govern supply price to work themselves out fully, and we are at liberty therefore to make our supply curves inclined negatively This change will not affect the argument, but on the whole it is best to take our typical instance with the supply curve inclined positively)

Now let us suppose that we want to isolate for separate study the demand for knife handles Accordingly we suppose that the demand for knives and the supply of blades conform to the laws indicated by their respective curves also that the supply curve for handles still remains in force and represents the circumstances of normal supply of handles, although the supply of handles is temporarily disturbed Let MQ cut DD' in P, then

§ 2. When however we come to apply this theory to the actual conditions of life, it will be important to remember that if the supply of one factor is disturbed, the supply of others is likely to be disturbed also In particular, when the factor by which the supply is disturbed in one class of labour, as that of the plasterers, the employers' earnings generally act as a buffer. That is to say, the loss falls in the first instance on them, but by discharging some of their workmen and lowering the wages of others, they ultimately distribute a great part of it among the other factors of production. The details of the process by which this is effected are various, and depend on the action of trade combinations, on the higgling and bargaining of the market, and on other causes with which we are not just at present concerned.

Cautions as to the practical applications of the theory

We may note the general conditions, under which a check to the supply of a thing that is wanted not for direct use, but as a factor of production, may cause a very great rise in its price The first condition is that the factor itself should

Conditions under which a check to supply may raise much

MP is the demand price for OM knives and Qq is the supply price for OM blades. Take a point p in MP such that Pp is equal to Qq, and therefore Mp is the excess of MP over Qq; then Mp is the demand price for OM handles Let dd' be the locus of p obtained by giving M successive positions along Ox and finding the corresponding positions of p; then dd' is the derived demand curve for handles Of course it passes through a We may now neglect all the rest of the figure except the curves dd', ss', and regard them as representing the relations of demand for and supply of handles, other things being equal, that is to say, in the absence of any disturbing cause which affects the law of supply of blades and the law of demand for knives Ba is then the equilibrium price of handles, about which the market price oscillates, in the manner investigated in the preceding chapter, under the influence of demand and supply, of which the schedules are represented by dd' and ss' It has already been remarked that the ordinary demand and supply curves have no practical value except in the immediate neighbourhood of the point of equilibrium. And the same remark applies with even greater force to the equation of derived demand

Since $Mp - Mq = MP - MQ$, therefore A being a point of stable equilibrium, the equilibrium at a also is stable, whether the supply curves are positively or negatively inclined

In the illustration that has just been worked out the unit of each of the factors remains unchanged whatever be the amount of the commodity produced; for one blade and one handle are always required for each knife; but when a change in the amount of the commodity produced occasions a change in the amount of each factor that is required for the production of a unit of the commodity, the demand and supply curves for the factor got by the above process are not expressed in terms of fixed units of the factor They must be translated back into fixed units before they are available for general use. (See Mathematical Note XIV *bis*)

BOOK V. CH. VI.

the price of a requisite of production

be essential, or nearly essential to the production of the commodity, no good substitute being available at a moderate price.

The second condition is that the commodity in the production of which it is a necessary factor, should be one for which the demand is stiff and inelastic, so that a check to its supply will cause consumers to offer a much increased price for it rather than go without it, and this of course includes the condition that no good substitutes for the commodity are available at a price but little higher than its equilibrium price. If the check to house building raises the price of houses very much, builders, anxious to secure the exceptional profits, will bid against one another for such plasterers' labour as there is in the market[1]

The third condition is that only a small part of the expenses of production of the commodity should consist of the price of this factor. Since the plasterer's wages are but a small part of the total expenses of building a house, a rise of even 50 per cent. in them would add but a very small percentage to the expenses of production of a house and would check demand but little[2].

The fourth condition is that even a small check to the amount demanded should cause a considerable fall in the supply prices of other factors of production, for that will increase the margin available for paying a high price for this one[3] If, for instance, bricklayers and other classes of workmen, or the employers themselves cannot easily find other things to do, and cannot afford to remain idle, they may be willing to work for much lower earnings than before, and this will increase the margin available for paying higher wages to

[1] We have to inquire under what conditions the ratio pM to aB will be the greatest, pM being the demand price for the factor in question corresponding to a supply reduced from OB to OM, that is reduced by the given amount BM The second condition is that PM should be large, and since the elasticity of demand is measured by the ratio which BM bears to the excess of PM over AB, the greater PM is, the smaller, other things being equal, is the elasticity of demand

[2] The third condition is that when PM exceeds AB in a given ratio, pM shall be caused to exceed Ba in a large ratio and other things being equal, that requires Ba to be but a small part of BA

[3] That is, if Qq had been smaller than it is, Pp would have been smaller and Mp would have been larger See also Mathematical Note xv

plasterers. These four conditions are independent, and the effects of the last three are cumulative.

The moderating influence of the law of substitution,

The rise in plasterers' wages would be checked if it were possible either to avoid the use of plaster, or to get the work done tolerably well and at a moderate price by people outside the plasterers' trade. The law of substitution here as elsewhere exercises a subduing influence on forces which might otherwise lead to startling results The tyranny which one factor of production of a commodity might in some cases exercise over the other factors through the law of derived demand is tempered by the law of substitution[1].

and of the power of modifying the proportions which the several factors of production of a commodity bear to one another

Again, an increased difficulty in obtaining one of the factors of a finished commodity can often be met by modifying the character of the finished product Some plasterers' labour may be indispensable, but people are often in doubt how much plaster work it is worth while to have in their houses, and if there is a rise in its price they will have less of it The intensity of the satisfaction of which they would be deprived if they had a little less of it, is its marginal utility, the price which they are just willing to pay in order to have it, is the true demand price for plasterers' work up to the amount which is being used So again there is a joint demand for malt and hops in ale: but their proportions can be varied, the difference in the price which can be got for two kinds of ale similar in other respects, but of which one has more hops than the other, is a representative of the causes which govern the demand price for hops[2].

The relations between plasterers, bricklayers, &c, are representative of much that is both instructive and romantic in the history of alliances and conflicts between trades unions in allied trades But the most numerous instances of Joint demand are those of the demand for a raw material and the

[1] Dr Böhm Bawerk in his excellent *Grundzuge der Theorie des wirtschaftlichen Guterwerts* (*Jahrbuch fur Nationalokonomie und Statistik*, vol XIII p. 59) shows that if all but one of the factors of production of a commodity have available substitutes in unlimited supply, by which their own price is rigidly fixed, the derived demand price for the remaining factor will be the excess of the demand price for the finished product over the sum of the supply prices thus fixed for the remaining factors This is an interesting special case of the law given in the text

[2] See Mathematical Note XVI

BOOK V. CH. VI.

operatives who work it up, as for instance cotton or jute or iron or copper, and those who work up these several materials. Again, the relative prices of different articles of food vary a good deal with the supply of skilled cooks' labour thus for instance many kinds of meat and many parts of vegetables which are almost valueless in America, where skilled cooks are rare and expensive, have a good value in France, where the art of cooking is widely diffused.

Composite Demand

§ 3. We have already[1] discussed the way in which the demand for any commodity is made up or compounded of the demands of the different groups of people, who may need it. But we now may extend this notion of *Composite Demand* to requisites of production, which are needed by several groups of producers Nearly every raw material and nearly every kind of labour is applied in many different branches of industry, and contributes to the production of a great variety of commodities. Each of these commodities has its own direct demand from which the derived demand for any of the factors made in using it can be found The total demand for the factor is the sum of the derived demands for it, in each of its several uses, and these may be added together, in just the same way as the partial demands of several classes of society for a finished commodity are added together, and thus make up the total demand for it[2].

[1] See Book III Ch IV. § 2.

[2] Thus, let a factor of production have three uses Let d_1d_1' be the demand curve for it in its first use From N any point on Oy draw Np_1 horizontally to cut d_1d_1' in p_1, then Np_1 is the amount that is demanded for the first use at price ON Produce Np_1 to p_2, and further on to P making p_1p_2 and p_2P of such lengths as to represent the amounts of the factor demanded at price ON for the second and third uses respectively As N moves along Oy let p_2 trace out the curve d_2d_2' and let P trace out the curve DD' Thus d_2d_2' would be the demand curve for the factor if it had only its first and second uses DD' is its demand curve for all three uses. It is immaterial in what order we take the several uses In the case represented, the demand for the second use begins at a lower price and that for the third use begins at a higher price than does the demand for the first use (See Mathematical Note XVII.)

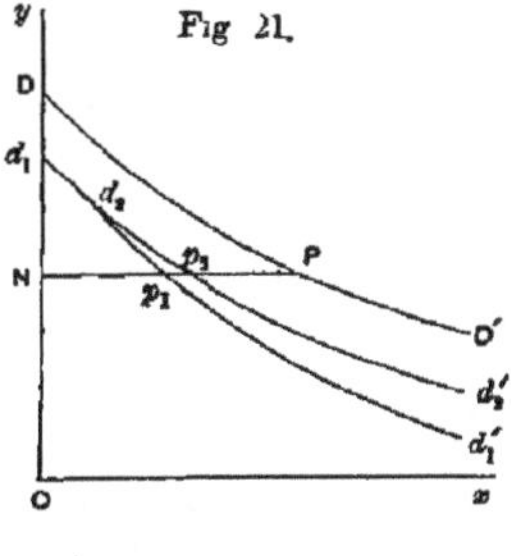

Fig 21.

Joint Supply

§ 4. We may now pass to consider the case of things which cannot be produced separately, and have therefore a *Joint Supply* such as beef and hides, or wheat and straw. It corresponds to that of things which have a joint demand, and it may be discussed almost in the same words, by merely substituting "demand" for "supply," and *vice versâ* When two or more things are produced by one and the same process; so that the expenses of producing them all together are not greater than the expenses of producing one of them alone would be, then these things are called *Joint Products.* Thus wheat and straw are joint products; beef and hides are joint products[1]

In manufacture and agriculture, in the carrying and distributing trades, it is often a matter of the greatest difficulty to decide what are the real expenses of any one of the many operations that are being done at the same time. The difficulty is greatest with regard to those fixed charges which would run on if little or nothing were being done in

[1] If it is desired to isolate the relations of demand and supply for a joint product, the derived supply price is found in just the same way as the derived demand price for a factor of production was found in the parallel case of demand Other things must be assumed to be equal (that is, the supply schedule for the whole process of production must be assumed to remain in force and so must the demand schedule for each of the joint products except that to be isolated). The derived supply price is then found by the rule that it must equal the excess of the supply price for the whole process of production over the sum of the demand prices of all the other joint products, the prices being taken throughout with reference to corresponding amounts

We may again illustrate by a simple example Let SS' be the supply curve for bullocks, dd' the demand curve for their carcases, that is, for the meat derived from them M being any point on Ox draw Mp vertically to cut dd' in p, and produce it to P so that pP represents the demand price for OM hides. Then MP is the demand price for OM bullocks, and DD' the locus of P is the demand curve for bullocks it may be called the total demand curve Let DD' cut SS' in A; and draw AaB as in the figure Then in equilibrium OB bullocks are produced and sold at the price BA of which Ba goes for the carcase and aA for the hide

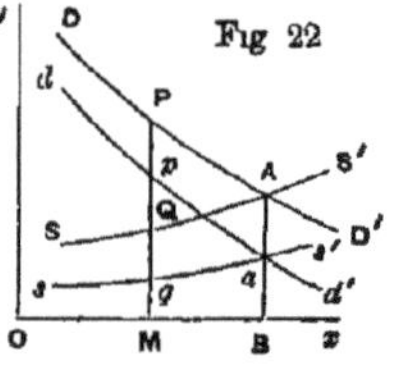

Let MP cut SS' in Q. From QM cut off Qq equal to Pp, then q is a point on the derived supply curve for carcases For if we assume that the selling price of OM hides is always equal to the corresponding demand price Pp, it follows that since it costs QM to produce each of OM bullocks there remains a price $QM-Pp$, that is qM, to be borne by each of the OM hides. Then ss' the locus of q, and dd are the supply and demand curves for hides (See Mathematical Note XVIII)

BOOK V CH. VI.

the establishment; and we shall be much occupied hereafter with the troubles that arise from this source.

But, where the relative proportions of joint products can be modified,

There are however very few cases of joint products the cost of production of both of which together is exactly the same as that of one of them alone So long as any product of a business has a market value, it is almost sure to have devoted to it some special care and expense, which would be diminished, or dispensed with if the demand for that product were to fall very much Thus, for instance, if straw were valueless, farmers would exert themselves more than they do to make the ear bear as large a proportion as possible to the stalk. Again, the importation of foreign wool has caused English sheep to be selected almost exclusively for their tendency to develop early heavy weights of good meat It is only when one of two things produced by the same process is valueless, unsaleable, and yet does not involve any expense for its removal, that there is no inducement to attempt to modify their relative proportions

we can often isolate the marginal expenses of production of any of them

And it is only in these exceptional cases that there is, as a rule, any great difficulty in ascertaining the separate supply price of each of the joint products For when it is possible to modify the proportions of these products, it can always be ascertained what part of the whole expense of the process of production would be saved, by so modifying these proportions as slightly to diminish the amount of one of the joint products, without affecting the amounts of the others. That part of the expense is the expense of production of the marginal element of that product, it is the supply price of which we are in search[1].

Composite Supply

§ 5. We may pass to the problem of *Composite Supply* which is analogous to that of composite demand. It is closely connected with the law of substitution which has been noticed already We may consider that two things are *Rivals* or competing commodities[2], when they are capable of satisfying the same demand If the causes which govern

Rival commodities

[1] See Mathematical Note XIX

[2] This latter phrase is used by Prof Fisher in his brilliant *Mathematical Investigations in the theory of value and prices*, which throw much light on the subjects discussed in the present chapter

their production are nearly the same, they may for many purposes be treated as one commodity[1]. For instance, beef and mutton may be treated as varieties of one commodity for many purposes, but they must be treated as separate for others, as for instance for those in which the question of the supply of wool enters. Rival things are however often not finished commodities, but factors of production. For instance, there are many rival fibres which are used in making ordinary printing paper[2].

cannot generally remain in the field together, if any of them obeys the Law of Increasing Return

Continued rivalry is as a rule possible only when none of the rivals has its supply governed by the law of increasing return The equilibrium is stable only when none of them is able to drive the others out, and this is the case when all of them conform to the law of diminishing return; because then if one did obtain a temporary advantage and its use increased, its supply price would rise, and then the others would begin to undersell it But if one of them conformed to the law of increasing return, the rivalry would soon cease, for whenever it happened to gain a temporary advantage over its rivals its increased use would lower its supply price and therefore increase its sale—its supply price would then be further lowered, and so on· thus its advantage over its rivals would be continually increased until it had

[1] Comp Jevons, *l.c* pp 145, 6

[2] The want which all the rivals tend to satisfy is met by a composite supply, the total supply at any price being the sum of the partial supplies at that price.

Thus, for instance, N being any point on Oy draw Nq_1q_2Q parallel to Ox such that Nq_1, q_1q_2 and q_2Q are respectively the amounts of the first, second and third of those rivals which can be supplied at the price ON Then NQ is the total composite supply at that price, and the locus of Q is the total supply curve of the means of satisfying the want in question Of course the units of the several things which are rivals must be so taken that each of them satisfies the same amount of the want In the case represented in the figure small quantities of the first rival can be put on the market at a price too low to call forth any supply of the other two, and small quantities of the second at a price too low to call forth any of the third. (See Mathematical Note xx)

Fig. 23.

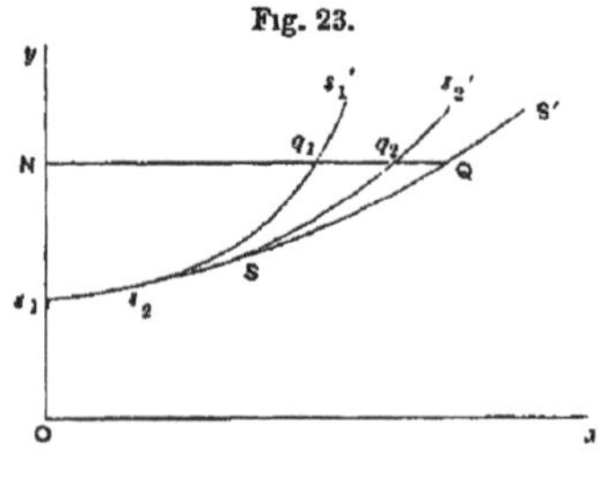

BOOK V CH. VI

driven them out of the field. It is true that there are apparent exceptions to this rule, and things which conform to the law of increasing return do sometimes seem to remain for a long time in the field as rivals: such is the case perhaps with different kinds of sewing machines and of electric lights But in these cases the things do not really satisfy the same wants, they appeal to slightly different needs or tastes; there is still some difference of opinion as to their relative merits; or else perhaps some of them are patented or in some other way have become the monopoly of particular firms In such cases custom and the force of advertising may keep many rivals in the field for a long time; particularly if the producers of those things which are really the best in proportion to their expenses of production are not able effectively to advertise and push their wares by travellers and other agencies.

The connections between the causes governing the values of different things are often intricate Illustrations

§ 6 All the four chief problems which have been discussed in this chapter have some bearing on the causes that govern the value of almost every commodity: and many of the most important cross connections between the values of different commodities are not obvious at first sight.

Thus when charcoal was generally used in making iron, the price of leather depended in some measure on that of iron; and the tanners petitioned for the exclusion of foreign iron in order that the demand on the part of English iron smelters for oak charcoal might cause the production of English oak to be kept up, and thus prevent oak bark from becoming dear[1]. Again, the development of railways and other means of communication for the benefit of one trade, as for instance wheat growing in some parts of America and

[1] Toynbee (*Industrial Revolution*, p 80) This instance may serve to remind us of the way in which an excessive demand for a thing may cause its sources of supply to be destroyed, and thus render scarce any joint products that it may have for the demand for wood on the part of the ironmakers led to a relentless destruction of many forests in England. Again, an excessive demand for lamb was assigned as a cause of the prevailing scarcity of sheep a few years ago, while some argued on the contrary that the better the price to be got for spring lamb sold to the rich, the more profitable would be the production of sheep, and the cheaper would mutton be for the people. The fact is that an increase of demand may have opposite effects according as it does or does not act so suddenly as to prevent producers from adapting their action to it

silver mining in others, greatly lowers some of the chief expenses of production of nearly every other product of those districts. Again, the prices of soda, and bleaching materials and other products of industries, the chief raw material of which is salt, move up and down relatively to one another with almost every improvement in the various processes which are used in those industries; and every change in those prices affects the prices of many other goods; for the various products of the salt industries are more or less important factors in many branches of manufacture

Again, cotton and cotton-seed oil are joint products, and the recent fall in the price of cotton is largely due to the improved manufacture and uses of cotton-seed oil Now, as the history of the cotton famine shows, the price of cotton largely affects that of wool, linen and other things of its own class, while cotton-seed oil is ever opening up new rivalries with things of its own class Again, many new uses have been found for straw in manufacture, and these inventions, together with the growth of an urban population in the West, are giving a high value to straw that used to be burnt, and are therefore lowering the value of wheat[1]

[1] See Mathematical Note XXI It may be observed that the Austrian doctrine of Imputed value has something in common with that of Derived value given in this chapter Whichever phrase be used, it is important that we should recognize the continuity between the old doctrine of value and the new, and that we should treat Imputed or Derived values merely as elements which take their place with many others in the broad problem of Distribution and Exchange The new phrases merely give the means of applying to the ordinary affairs of life, some of that precision of expression which is the special property of mathematical language Producers have always to consider how the demand for any raw material in which they are interested is dependent on the demand for the things in making which it is used, and how it is influenced by every change that affects them, and this is really a special case of the problem of ascertaining the efficient value of any one of the forces, which contribute to a common result In mathematical language this common result is called a *function* of the various forces and the (marginal) contribution, which any of them is making to it, is represented by the (small) change in the result which would result from a (small) change in that force, that is by the *differential coefficient* of the result with regard to that force In other words the Imputed value, or the Derived value of a factor of production, if used for only one product, is the differential coefficient of that product with regard to that factor, and so on in successive complications, as indicated in the Mathematical Notes XIV—XXI (Some objections to parts of Prof Wieser's doctrine of Imputed values are well urged by Prof Edgeworth, *Economic Journal*, Vol v pp 279—85)

CHAPTER VII.

PRIME AND TOTAL COST IN RELATION TO JOINT PRODUCTS. COST OF MARKETING INSURANCE AGAINST RISK. COST OF REPRODUCTION

Supplementary costs of Joint products

§ 1. We may now return to the consideration of Prime and Supplementary costs, with special reference to the proper distribution of the latter between the Joint products of a business.

Difficulty arising when one branch of a business supplies a raw material to another

It often happens that a thing made in one branch of a business is used as a raw material in another, and then the question of the relative profitableness of the two branches can be accurately ascertained only by an elaborate system of book-keeping by double entry, though in practice it is more common to rely on rough estimates made by an almost instinctive guess. Some of the best illustrations of this difficulty are found in agriculture, especially when the same farm combines permanent pasture and arable land worked on long rotation[1].

Difficulties as to the joint products of the same business,

Another difficult case is that of the shipowner who has to apportion the expenses of his ship between heavy goods and goods that are bulky but not heavy. He tries, as far as may be, to get a mixed cargo of both kinds; and an important element in the struggle for existence of rival ports is the disadvantage under which those ports lie which are able to offer a cargo only of bulky or only of heavy goods. while a port whose chief exports are weighty but not bulky, attracts to its neighbourhood industries which make for

[1] There is scope for applications of mathematical or semi mathematical analyses such as are indicated in the last chapter, to some of the chief practical difficulties of book-keeping by double entry in different trades.

export goods that can be shipped from it at low freights. The Staffordshire Potteries, for example, owe part of their success to the low freights at which their goods are carried by ships sailing from the Mersey with iron and other heavy cargoes.

are often overcome through the power of varying the details of the plan of production.

But there is free competition in the shipowning trade, and it has great powers of variation as regards the size and shape of ships, the routes which they take, and the whole method of trading, and thus in many ways the general principle can be applied, that the relative proportions of the joint products of a business should be so modified that the marginal expenses of production of either product should be equal to its marginal demand price[1]. Or, in other words, the amount of carrying power for each kind of cargo has a constant tendency to move towards equilibrium at a point at which the demand price for that amount in a normal state of trade is just sufficient to cover the expenses of providing it; these expenses being reckoned so as to include not only its (money) prime cost, but also all those general expenses of the business which are in the long run incurred on its account, whether directly or indirectly[2]

A first approximation is sometimes got by treating Supplementary as proportional to Prime cost.

In some branches of manufacture it is customary to make a first approximation to the total cost of producing any class of goods, by assuming that their share of the general expenses of the business is proportionate either to their prime cost, or to the special labour bill that is incurred in making them. Corrections can then be made to meet such cases as those of goods which require either more or less than an average share of space or light, or of the use of expensive machinery; and so on.

All such questions are of considerable interest, but we must not pursue them in detail. There are however two

[1] Compare Ch VI § 4.

[2] Of course this does not apply to railway rates For a railway company having little elasticity as to its methods of working, and often not much competition from outside, has no inducement to endeavour to adjust the charges which it makes for different kinds of traffic to their cost to itself In fact though it may ascertain the prime cost in each case easily enough, it cannot determine accurately what are the relative total costs of fast and slow traffic, of short and long distance traffic, of light and heavy traffic; nor again of extra traffic when its lines and its trains are crowded and when they are nearly empty.

BOOK V CH VII.

elements of the general expenses of a business, the sharing of which between the different branches requires some special attention. They are the expense of marketing and that of insurance against risk.

The difficulty of assigning to each branch of a business its share of the expenses of marketing

§ 2 Some kinds of goods are easily marketed, there is a steady demand for them, and it is always safe to make them for stock. But for that very reason competition cuts their price "very fine," and does not allow a large margin above the direct cost of making them. Sometimes the tasks of making and selling them can be rendered almost automatic, so as to require very little to be charged on their account under the heads of the expenses of management and marketing. But in practice it is not uncommon to charge such goods with even less than the small share that would properly fall to them, and to use them as a means of obtaining and maintaining a business connection, that will facilitate the marketing of other classes of goods, the production of which cannot so well be reduced to routine, for as to these there is not so close a competition. Manufacturers, especially in trades connected with furniture and dress, and retailers in almost all trades, frequently find it best to use certain of their goods as a means of advertising others, and to charge the first with less and the second with more than their proportionate share of Supplementary expenses In the former class they put those goods which are so uniform in character and so largely consumed that nearly all purchasers know their value well, in the second those with regard to which purchasers think more of consulting their fancy than of buying at the lowest possible price.

becomes very great when the Law of Increasing Return acts strongly;

All difficulties of this kind are much increased by that instability of supply price which results from the action of the law of increasing return, whenever that action is very powerful We have seen that in seeking the normal supply price in such cases we must select as representative a business which is managed with normal ability and so as to get its fair share of the economies both Internal and External resulting from industrial organization; and that these economies, though they fluctuate with the fortunes of particular businesses, yet increase generally when the aggregate production increases Now it is obvious that if a manufacturer makes a commodity the increased production of which would put largely increased Internal economies within his reach, it is worth his while to sacrifice a great deal in order to push its sales in a new market. If he has a large capital, and the commodity is one in much demand, his expenditure for this purpose may be very great, even exceeding that which he devotes directly to the manufacture: and if, as is likely, he is pushing at the same time several other commodities, nothing more than a very rough guess can be made as to what share of this expenditure should be charged to the sales of each of them in the current year, and what share should be charged to the connection which he is endeavouring to build up for them in the future.

especially when the production falls into the hands of a few large firms.

In fact when the production of a commodity conforms to the law of increasing return in such a way as to give a very great advantage to large producers, it is apt to fall almost entirely into the hands of a few large firms, and then the normal marginal supply price cannot be isolated on the plan just referred to, because that plan assumes the existence of a great many competitors with businesses of all sizes, some of them being young and some old, some in the ascending and some in the descending phase. The production of such a commodity really partakes in a great measure of the nature of a monopoly, and its price is likely to be so much influenced by the incidents of the campaign between rival producers, each struggling for an extension of territory, that no free play is allowed to the normal action of economic forces, and it can scarcely be said to have a normal supply price

Economies in production are often balanced by local facilities for marketing

Economic progress is constantly offering new facilities for marketing goods at a distance it not only lowers cost of carriage, but what is often more important, it enables producers and consumers in distant places to get in touch with one another. In spite of this, the advantages of the producer who lives on the spot are very great in many trades; they often enable him to hold his own against competitors at a distance whose methods of production are more economical. He can sell in his own neighbourhood as cheaply as they can, because though the prime cost is greater for his goods

BOOK V CH VII.

than for theirs, he escapes much of the supplementary cost which they incur for marketing. But time is on the side of the more economic methods of production; his distant competitors will gradually get a stronger footing in the place, unless he or some new man adopts their improved methods.

A great part of these expenses of marketing results from the risk that a thing preparing for a certain market will not find the expected sale there. But it still remains to make a closer study of the relation in which insurance against the risks of a business stands to the supply price of any particular commodity produced in it.

An insurance cannot be effected at moderate rates against all business risks

§ 3. The manufacturer and the trader commonly insure against injury by fire and loss at sea; and the premiums which they pay are among the general expenses, a share of which has to be added to the prime cost in order to determine the total cost of their goods But no insurance can be effected against the great majority of business risks.

Even as regards losses by fire and sea, insurance companies have to allow for possible carelessness and fraud; and must therefore, independently of all allowances for their own expenses and profits, charge premiums considerably higher than the true equivalent of the risks run by the buildings or the ships of those who manage their affairs well. The injury done by fire or sea however is likely, if it occurs at all, to be so very great that it is generally worth while to pay this extra charge, partly for special trade reasons, but chiefly because the total utility of wealth increases less than in proportion to its amount. But the greater part of business risks are so inseparably connected with the general management of the business that an insurance company which undertook them would really make itself responsible for the business and in consequence every firm has to act as its own insurance office with regard to them. The charges to which it is put under this head are part of its general expenses, and a share of them has to be added to the prime cost of each of its products

Caution against overlooking certain

But here there are two difficulties. In some cases insurance against risk is apt to be left out of account altogether, in others it is apt to be counted twice over

Thus a large shipowner sometimes declines to insure his ships with the underwriters: and sets aside part at least of the premiums that he might have paid to them, to build up an insurance fund of his own But he must still, when calculating the Total cost of working a ship, add to its prime cost a charge on account of insurance And he must do the same thing, in some form or other, with regard to those risks against which he could not buy an insurance policy on reasonable terms even if he wanted to. At times, for instance, some of his ships will be idle in port, or will earn only nominal freights. and to make his business remunerative in the long run he must, in some form or other, charge his successful voyages with an insurance premium to make up for his losses on those which are unsuccessful.

insurance expenses,

In general, however, he does this, not by making a formal entry in his accounts under a separate head, but by the simple plan of taking the average of successful and unsuccessful voyages together; and when that has once been done, insurance against these risks cannot be entered as a separate item in cost of production, without counting the same thing twice over. Having decided to run these risks himself, he is likely to spend a little more than the average of his competitors, in providing against their occurrence, and this extra expense enters in the ordinary way into his balance-sheet It is really an insurance premium in another form, and therefore he must not count insurance against this part of the risk separately, for then he would be counting it twice over[1].

and against counting others twice over

When a manufacturer has taken the average of his sales of dress materials over a long time, and bases his future action on the results of his past experience, he has already allowed for the risks that the machinery will be depreciated

[1] Again, certain insurance companies in America take risks against fire in factories at very much less than the ordinary rates, on condition that some prescribed precautions are taken, such as providing automatic sprinklers and making the walls and floors solid The expense incurred in these arrangements is really an insurance premium, and care must be taken not to count it twice over A factory which undertakes its own risks against fire will have to add to the prime cost of its goods an allowance for insurance at a lower rate, if it is arranged on this plan, than if built in the ordinary way

BOOK V CH VII

by new inventions that will render it nearly obsolete and that his goods will be depreciated by changes in fashion. If he were to allow separately for insurance against these risks, he would be counting the same thing twice over[1].

But uncertainty is an evil in itself,

§ 4. But though when we have counted up the average receipts of a risky trade, there is no separate allowance to be made for insurance against risk; there may be, and often is, something to be allowed as a charge on account of uncertainty. It is true that an adventurous occupation, such as gold mining, has special attractions for some people: the deterrent force of risks of loss in it is less than the attractive force of chances of great gain, even when the value of the latter estimated on the actuarial principle is much less than that of the former, and as Adam Smith has pointed out[2], a risky trade, in which there is an element of romance, often becomes so overcrowded that the average earnings in it are lower than if there were no risks to be run. But in the large majority of cases the influence of risk is in the opposite direction, a railway stock that is certain to pay four per cent. will sell for a higher price than one which is equally likely to pay one or seven per cent. or any intermediate amount.

and an average gain generally counts for less, the more uncertain the elements of which it is made up

Every trade then has its own peculiarities, but in most cases the evils of uncertainty count for something, though not very much in some cases a slightly higher average price is required to induce a given outlay, if that average is the mean of widely divergent and uncertain results, than if the adventurer may reckon confidently on a return that differs but little from that average To the average price therefore we must add a recompense for uncertainty, if that is unusually great, though if we added insurance against risk we should be counting the greater part of that twice over[3]

[1] Again, when a farmer has calculated the expenses of raising any particular crop with reference to an average year, he must not count in addition insurance against the risk that the season may be bad, and the crop a failure for in taking an average year, he has already set off the chances of exceptionally good and bad seasons against one another. When the earnings of a ferryman have been calculated on the average of a year, allowance has already been made for the risk that he may sometimes have to cross the stream with an empty boat

[2] *Wealth of Nations*, Book I Ch X

[3] The evils resulting from the uncertainty involved in great business risks are well shown by Von Thunen (*Isolirter Staat*, II I. p 82)

To substitute cost of reproduction for cost of production in the theory of normal values is to make no real change;

§ 5. This discussion of the risks of trade has again brought before us the fact that the value of a thing, though it tends to equal its normal (money) cost of production, does not coincide with it at any particular time, save by accident Carey, observing this, suggested that we should speak of value in relation to (money) cost of Reproduction instead of in relation to cost of production.

The suggestion has, however, no significance so far as normal values are concerned. For normal cost of production and normal cost of reproduction are convertible terms, and no real change is made by saying that the normal value of a thing tends to equal its normal (money) cost of reproduction instead of its normal cost of production. The former phrase is less simple than the latter, but means the same thing.

and though the market value of a thing is sometimes nearer cost of reproduction than cost of production, it is not governed by cost of reproduction

And no valid argument for the change can be founded on the fact, which may be readily admitted, that there are some few cases in which the market value of a thing is nearer its cost of reproduction than the cost that was actually incurred in producing that particular thing. The present price of an iron ship for instance, made before the great recent improvements in the manufacture of iron, might diverge less from the cost of reproducing it, that is of producing another just like it by modern methods, than from that which was actually incurred in producing it But the price would probably be less than the cost of reproduction of the ship, because the art of designing ships has improved as fast as that of manufacturing iron. It may still be urged that the price of the ship is equal to that of producing a ship, which would be equally serviceable, on a modern plan and by modern methods, but even if that were true, it would not be the same thing as saying that the value of the ship is equal to its cost of reproduction; and, as a matter of fact, when, as often happens, an unexpected scarcity of ships causes freights to increase very rapidly, those who are anxious to reap the harvest of profitable trade, will pay for a ship in sailing order a price much above that for which a shipbuilding firm would contract to produce another equally good and deliver it some time hence. Cost of reproduction exerts little direct influence on value, save when purchasers can conveniently wait for the production of new supplies.

Again, there is no connection between cost of reproduction and price in the cases of food in a beleaguered city, of quinine the supply of which has run short in a fever-stricken island, of a picture by Raphael, of a book that nobody cares to read, of an armour-clad ship of obsolete pattern, of fish when the market is glutted, of fish when the market is nearly empty, of a cracked bell, of a dress material that has gone out of fashion, or of a house in a deserted mining village

CHAPTER VIII.

ON THE VALUE OF AN APPLIANCE FOR PRODUCTION IN RELATION TO THAT OF THE THINGS PRODUCED BY IT

§ 1. We have now to return to the study of the influence of the element of time on the causes which govern value, and mode of operation, taking up the study where it was left in Chapters IV. and V, with special reference to the (Derived) value of an appliance for production which we partially considered in Chapter VI

Our argument is applicable to personal as well as to material goods but will be kept for the present in its most general form.

Nearly the whole of our inquiry will apply to markets for labour as well as to markets for commodities; to the supply of skill as well as to that of business organization, to the investment of capital in education and industrial training as well as to its investment in the improvement of land or the making of machinery, to the income derived from that genius which is, so far as we know, the free and almost arbitrary gift of nature, as well as to that derived from a vineyard of unique natural fertility But the human elements of production have important incidents that are peculiar to themselves, and to introduce them here would add needless complexity to problems which are necessarily intricate. It will be best therefore to keep our argument for the present in its most general form, and to defer to the next Book our application of it to the price of human abilities, although a great part of its interest lies in this application

We shall find that much that appears at first sight to be true only of the rent of land is true of many other kinds of income, subject to suitable modifications with regard to the element of Time, and that on the other hand the Rent of land in a newly settled country has at first strong points of resemblance to the gains got by "making," that is adapting

BOOK V CH VIII.

to human use, other material things. It has indeed been shown by a long series of writers, among whom Senior and Mill, Hermann and Mangoldt are conspicuous, that much of what is commonly called profits ought rather to be regarded as belonging to a special class of income derived from "a differential advantage in producing a commodity," that is, the possession by one or more persons of facilities for production that are not accessible to all. Since the leading and representative member of this class is the rent of land, the name of Rent is sometimes applied to the whole class: though this course is not without danger[1]

The allied doctrines that marginal expenses of production control value, and that rent does not enter into cost of production.

The principle which we have to study, is that speaking broadly, the price of anything and the amount of it that is produced are together governed by the general relations of demand and supply. that the price just covers the expenses of production of that part of this amount which is raised at the greatest disadvantage, that every other part yields a surplus above its direct cost, and that this surplus is a result and not a cause of the selling price. For the price is governed by the relations of supply and demand, and while, of course, the surplus does not affect the demand, so neither does it affect the supply, since it is yielded only by a part of the produce which would be produced even at a lower price

In other words, there is a part of the produce which is on

[1] Thus Mill says, *Political Economy*, Book III Ch V § 4, "Any difference in favour of certain producers or in favour of production in certain circumstances is the source of a gain, which though not called rent unless paid periodically by one person to another is governed by laws entirely the same with it The price paid for a differential advantage in producing a commodity cannot enter into the cost of production of the commodity" Again Senior pointing, though not very clearly, towards the element of time as holding the key of the division between rent and profits, says (*Political Economy*, p 129), "for all useful purposes the distinction of profits from rent ceases as soon as the capital from which a given revenue arises has become, whether by gift or by inheritance, the property of a person to whose abstinence and exertions it did not owe its creation" And within the last few years this subject has been pursued with great zeal and ability by many writers, especially in Austria and America.

It may be mentioned that rent is compared with profits rather than with interest, because it commonly includes an element of earnings of management and undertaking but this is a question of degree, and there are a few exceptional cases in which a net rent emerges that may more fitly be compared with interest This point will require further discussion at a later stage

the margin of doubt as to whether it will be supplied or not, and the expenses of production of this part of the produce are often said to *determine* the price of the whole. But, more strictly, we should say that they take direct part in governing it that is, that the price of the whole will, other things being equal, be raised or lowered, according as it is decided to produce or not to produce these marginal elements For those parts which do yield a surplus, will generally be produced whatever the price is, provided only it is not so low as wholly to destroy that surplus, and that surplus is therefore governed by the price and does not govern it: while there is no surplus yielded by that part of the produce the expenses of production of which do take direct part in governing the price. No surplus therefore enters into *that* (money) cost of production which gives the level at which the whole supply is held fixed This then is what we mean by the phrase "Producer's surplus does not enter into cost of production"; or in Ricardo's words, "Rent does not enter into cost of production." It is one of those short phrases which do not explain themselves, and are easily misunderstood, but it has an important meaning, and it is applicable to many different kinds of income

are true only in a rather forced sense.

The point of the doctrine is to be sought in the fact that the cost of production of the marginal produce can be ascertained (theoretically at least) from the circumstances of the margin, without reasoning in a circle, and that the cost of production of other parts of the produce cannot. For other parts yield a rent or a quasi-rent, or both, which are governed not by the circumstances of production of the parts in question, but by the price of the whole produce. The costs of production of these parts cannot be reckoned up without counting in the corresponding rents and quasi-rents, and therefore the price of the commodity cannot be deduced from them without reasoning in a circle.

Another aspect of the same truth is that the income earned by machinery and other plant already in existence is not any given percentage on their cost of production, but is a quasi-rent determined by the value of what they produce If they are of obsolete fashion, this quasi-rent is small. But whether it is large or small, this value is found by capitalising their quasi-rent; and if we were to turn round, and say that their quasi-rent would return a certain rate of interest on their value, then we should be reasoning in a circle.

The question is of academic rather than general interest.

This then is the principle which we have to study in detail. So large a part of the economic controversy of this century, and even of this generation, appears to proceed from a misunderstanding of its general bearings and in particular of the place which the element of time holds in it, that some fulness of illustration and some persistency of repetition may be advisable; in spite of the fact that it is largely of an academic character, and that the general reader has little interest in some of its intricacies.

§ 2. We may take our first illustration from a class of incomes which is not commonly classed as Rent, but to which that term may be safely applied. For the eminent claim to be called a true producer's surplus or rent is not confined to the income derived from land or other (Real) property, but extends to that derived from all things the supply of which cannot be increased.

An illustration. The income from meteoric stones may be a true Rent, if their number cannot be increased;

For instance, suppose that a meteoric shower of a few thousand stones as hard as diamonds, but very large, fell all in one place, so that they were all picked up at once, and no amount of search could find any more. These stones, able to cut the hardest material, would revolutionize many branches of industry; and the owners of them would have a differential advantage in production that would afford a large Producer's Surplus: this would be a true economic rent, whether they used the stones themselves or loaned them out to manufacturers, though only in the latter case would it be called Rent. Its amount would be governed by the value of services the stones rendered in production; and this would in the main be governed by the cost of equivalent services of chilled steel and other cutting tools, which are made by man and have therefore a normal supply price

Again, if the stones were of exceptional splendour, and useful for ornament rather than for manufacturing purposes, they might be worn by their owners, or let out to be worn by others; and the money value of the satisfactions they rendered would be a true rent, corresponding to the money value of the satisfactions derived from a building site of exceptional beauty, whether its owner lives on it or lets it to others[1].

and a tax on it falls on the owners

The influence of taxes on value affords excellent illustration of many of the subtlest points in the theory of value. Let us take advantage of this. A special tax on these stones would fall entirely on their owners (a lessee being regarded as a part-owner), for it would not diminish their supply and therefore would not alter the gross value of the utilities and gratifications which they can be made to afford[2]

But if the supply can be increased slowly, the income is for long periods, profits, and for short periods a quasi rent

But next let us suppose that the stones were not all found at once, but were scattered over the surface of the earth on public ground, and that a long and laborious search might expect to be rewarded by finding one here and there. Then people would hunt for the stones only up to that point, or margin, at which the probable gain of so doing would in the long run just reward the outlay of labour and capital required for finding them; and the long-period normal value of the stones would be kept in equilibrium between demand and supply, the number of the stones gathered annually being in the long run just that for which the normal demand price was equal to the normal supply price A special tax on these stones would ultimately fall upon the consumers of the utilities produced by them. But, for some time, it would fall chiefly on the owners, for it could not for some time materially diminish the supply of the stones, nor therefore of their services, and accordingly it could not greatly raise the value of their services. This shows that the income derived

[1] Similar remarks apply to pictures by a deceased artist If these are let out for show, the gratifications which they produce are the source of a money income, which, after deductions for the immediate outlays, is a net producer's surplus or rent. If retained by the owners for their own pleasure, they yield equally a true rent of real satisfaction, for it is always understood that the "rental value" of a country includes rents which the owners of land who keep it in their own occupation are supposed to pay to themselves

[2] It should perhaps be noticed in passing, though it is not relevant to the main issue, that in so far as the pictures or the stones, retained for private use, were valued not for their beauty but for the show of wealth which they made, a tax on them would increase their value for display, and therefore would give more to the State than it took from those who paid it

BOOK V CH. VIII

from the stones may be regarded as a quasi-rent for short periods.

If it can be increased quickly the income is an ordinary profit except for very short periods.

Next let us suppose that the stones were brittle, and were soon broken and destroyed, but that new supplies could be found quickly In that case a tax on them would almost at once diminish the supply and raise the price of the services rendered by them, and therefore would be transferred to the consumers.

The truths indicated by this illustration may be presented in a more general form thus:—

General proposition as to the incidence of taxes on rents, quasi-rents and profits

A tax on any set of things that are already produced, falls exclusively on the owners of those things, if it is not accompanied by a tax, or the expectation of a tax, on the production, or bringing into use, of similar or rival things. If it falls also on all rival things, and the supply of them is not absolutely fixed, its incidence will be gradually transferred to the consumers For any period, for which a tax would fall mainly on the consumers, the income derived from the things may be regarded as of the nature of profits entering directly into supply price. For a shorter period, in which the tax falls mainly on the owners (lessees being regarded as part-owners), the income may be regarded as more or less of the nature of rent.

Illustration from the rent of land

§ 3. Our next illustration may be from the rent of land in an old country such as England But, at starting, three cautions may be entered In the first place, Rent is here taken as another name for the *Surplus produce* which is in excess of what is required to remunerate the cultivator for his capital and labour, and if the cultivator owns the land himself, he of course retains this surplus

Next, the "Marginal" application of capital and labour by the return to which we estimate the amount required to remunerate the farmer, is not necessarily applied to land on the margin of cultivation: it is on the *margin of profitable expenditure* on land of any quality.

Lastly, the doctrine does not mean that a tenant farmer need not take his rent into account when making up his year's balance-sheet when he is doing that, he must count his rent just in the same way as he does any other expense.

What it does mean is that when the farmer is calculating whether it is worth his while to apply more capital and labour to the land, *then* he need not think of his rent, for he will have to pay this same rent whether he applies this extra marginal capital and labour or not: and therefore if the marginal produce due to this "dose" seems likely to give him normal profits, he applies it, and his rent does not *then* enter into his calculations.

Thus the doctrine is, that the price of the produce, in so far as it depends on supply, is governed by the action of the farmers with regard to their marginal produce; and that since this action is not affected by the rent they have to pay, therefore rent does not enter into the price of the marginal produce, and therefore does not enter into the price of any part[1].

The doctrine, that rent does not enter into cost of production, is not misleading with regard to agricultural produce as a whole

If, following Ricardo, we suppose that all kinds of agricultural produce can be regarded as converted into certain quantities of corn, and then take it for granted that all the land will be used for agricultural purposes of some kind or other, with the exception of building sites which are a small and nearly fixed part of the whole; it is then true that the price of agricultural produce taken as a whole cannot in the long run be greater, and cannot in the long run be less, than its marginal expenses of production (or, to use the ordinary metaphor, than the expenses on the margin of cultivation) More simply, other things being equal, it is *governed* in the long run by these expenses, these expenses are not in any way affected, directly or indirectly, by the true rent (exclusive of the quasi-rent of improvements) paid for the land; and therefore this rent does not enter into

[1] Adam Smith is attacked by Ricardo for putting rent on the same footing with wages and profits as parts of (money) cost of production, and no doubt he does this sometimes But yet he says elsewhere, "Rent it is to be observed enters into the composition of the price of commodities in a different way from wages and profit High or low wages and profit are the causes of high or low price high or low rent is the effect of it It is because high or low wages and profit must be paid in order to bring a particular commodity to market that its price is high or low But it is because its price is high or low a great deal more, or very little more, or no more than what is sufficient to pay those wages and profits, that it affords a high rent, or a low rent, or no rent at all" (*Wealth of Nations*, Book I Chapter XI) In this, as in many other instances, he anticipated in one part of his writings truths which in other parts he has seemed to deny We shall recur to his and Ricardo's doctrines as to the rent of mines later on

BOOK V. CH VIII

the expenses of production of agricultural produce taken as a whole.

But when the doctrine is applied to any one kind of produce taken separately, it is misleading

§ 4. But when applied to the case of one kind of agricultural produce considered separately, the doctrine is liable to be understood in a sense in which it is not true For instance the production of those oats which only just pay their way is often said to "determine" the price of all other oats; rent, it is argued, does not enter into their cost of production, and therefore rent does not enter into the supply price of oats. But this, though true in a sense, is misleading.

It is true that when we know what are the most unfavourable conditions under which oats are grown, we can calculate the supply price of oats by reckoning up their expenses of production, just as we can discover the temperature by looking at the thermometer But as it would be misleading to say that the height of the thermometer determines the temperature, so a great deal of confusion has arisen from saying simply that the normal value of oats is determined by their production under the most unfavourable circumstances under which they are grown This statement needs to be completed by adding that those circumstances are, no less than the normal value itself, governed by the general conditions of demand and supply, and that one of the chief of these conditions is the amount of land which is capable of growing oats, but for which there is so great a demand for other purposes that it affords a higher rent, when used for them, than when used for growing oats. For the expenses of production of those oats which only just pay their way, are greater than they would be, were it not that much of the land which would return the largest crops of oats to the smallest outlay is diverted to growing other crops that will enable it to pay a higher rent than oats would afford, and therefore the rent that land on which oats could be grown, can be made to pay for other purposes, though it does not "enter into" the expenses of production and the normal value of oats, yet does indirectly affect them[1]

[1] As Mill points out when discussing "some peculiar cases of value," all questions relating to the competition of crops for the possession of particular soils are complicated by the rotation of crops and similar causes (*Principles*, Book III

We conclude then that the doctrine that rent does not enter into money-cost of production applies to agriculture only when carefully limited, and if Ricardo had studied its limitations more carefully he would probably have seen that there remained no reason for confining its scope to agriculture. It may be taken in a sense in which it is not true of agricultural rent; when properly interpreted, it is equally true of all kinds of rent[1].

Ch xvi. § 2) He does not however appear to have noticed the bearing of these remarks on the general problem of "Rent in its relation to Value"

[1] This method of treating the rent of land may be supplemented by another, proceeding rather on Cournot's plan of starting with value as determined by a monopoly, and then introducing the competition of many rivals so as to work towards the circumstances of a free market

We will take the case of perennial springs of natural mineral water. If there were only one spring of the kind, its owner would have a pure Monopoly, which he may be supposed to let out on lease The lessee would fix the price of the water so that the aggregate (yearly) receipts from the sales would exceed the aggregate (yearly) expenses of working the business by as large a sum as possible. and this excess (his own Earnings of Management being included in the expenses of working) would be the rent which the owner of the spring could compel him to pay (We shall soon discuss the question of Monopoly in some detail, and shall observe more closely the fact that Monopoly rent is rent determined, other things being equal, by the price of the water, and does not enter into that price This fact is in harmony with the doctrine we are discussing, but is not an illustration of it)

Next suppose that there are several such springs, owned by different persons, not acting in combination, and that the supply drawn from each of them can be increased by expensive pumping appliances, which yield a constantly diminishing return The equilibrium price will be such as just to remunerate each producer for his marginal production, that is, for the last gallon of water which his expenditure enables him to raise, when the amounts raised from the several springs are such that they are together equal to the amount which purchasers are willing to buy at that price The rental value of each spring will be the excess which this price affords over the expenses of working it Thus the price will be determined by the relations of demand and supply, it will take part directly in determining the rent and will not be determined by the rent rent will not enter into its expenses of production

If however one of the smaller springs happened to be so situated that it could not be worked without injury to a valuable site, it would probably not be worked at all, the fact that the site had a high rental value for other purposes would cut off part of the supply of mineral water that otherwise would have been forthcoming, and this would cause more water to be obtained from the other springs at expenses increased more than in proportion. The expenses of production of that part which is raised at the greatest disadvantage, would be greater than before, and producers would at once raise their prices if the price did not rise enough to cover these expenses, the supply would be curtailed, and the scarcity of supply would compel the price to rise The price therefore would be raised in consequence of the high rent that could be got by using for other purposes one of the sites on which machinery for pumping mineral water might have been

BOOK V CH VIII

Those limitations and conditions which are necessary to make the doctrine true of agricultural rents are sufficient to make it true of urban rents.

§ 5. We have seen[1] that the law of diminishing return applies to the use of land for the purposes of living and working on it in all trades Of course in the trade of building, as in agriculture, it is possible to apply capital too thinly. Just as a squatter may find that he can raise more produce by cultivating only a half of the 160 acres allotted to him than by spreading his labour over the whole, so even when ground has scarcely any value, a very low house may be dear in proportion to its accommodation But, as in agriculture, there is a certain application of capital and labour to the acre which gives the highest return, and further applications after this give a less return, so it is in building. The amount of capital per acre which gives the maximum return varies in agriculture with the nature of the crops, with the state of the arts of production, and with the character of the markets to be supplied, and similarly in building, the capital per square foot which would give the maximum return, if the site had no scarcity value, varies with the purpose for which the building is wanted But when the site has a scarcity value, it is worth while to go on applying capital beyond this maximum rather than pay the extra ground-rent required for extending the site In places where ground-rent is high, each square foot is made to yield perhaps twice the accommodation, at more than twice the cost, that it would be made to give, if used for similar purposes where ground-rent is low We may apply the phrase *the Margin of Building* to that accommodation which it would not be worth while to obtain from a given site if its ground-rent were a little lower, and, to fix the ideas, we may suppose this accommodation to be given by the top floor of the building[2].

The Margin of Building.

erected Thus again we see that the proposition that rent does not enter into expenses of production, when rightly understood, is not inconsistent with the fact that if some of the possible sources of supply of the commodity in question have been diverted to purposes that will enable them to render a higher rent, this diminution of supply will raise prices

[1] Book IV Ch III.

[2] Houses built in flats are often provided with a lift which is run at the expense of the owner of the house, and in such cases, at all events in America, his top floor sometimes lets for a higher rent than any other If the site is very valuable and the law does not limit the height of his house in the interest of his neighbours, he

Additional rooms on the margin of building pay no ground-rent.

By erecting this floor, instead of spreading the building over more ground, a saving of ground-rent is effected, which just compensates for the extra expense and inconvenience of the plan. The accommodation given by this floor, when allowance has been made for its incidental disadvantages, is only just enough to be worth what it costs without allowing anything for ground-rent, and the expenses of production of the things raised on this floor, if it is part of a factory, are just covered by their price, there is no surplus for ground-rent. The expenses of production of manufactures may then be reckoned as those of the goods which are made on the margin of building, so as to pay no ground-rent On the understanding that we do so reckon them, it is true that ground-rent does not enter into the expenses of manufacture; and this understanding is exactly parallel to that which has to be supplied in order to make Ricardo's doctrine true, when applied to agriculture. For, the expenses of production of oats are increased by the fact that land which could yield good crops of oats is in great demand for growing other crops, which enable it to yield a higher rent; while the printing-presses which may be seen at work in London some sixty feet above the ground could afford to do their work a little cheaper if the ground were not so much in demand for other uses, and pressure of ground-rent did not push the margin of building up so high[1].

may build very high but at last he will reach the margin of building At last he will find that the extra expenses for foundations and thick walls, and for his lift, together with some resulting depreciation of the lower floors, makes him stand to lose more than he gains by adding one more floor; the extra accommodation which it only just answers his purpose to supply is then to be regarded as at the margin of building, even though the gross rent be greater for the higher floors than for the lower

[1] Jevons in the Preface to the Second Edition of his *Theory of Political Economy* argues in the direction of treating agricultural rent on the same footing as ground-rent. But he goes on —"If land which has been yielding £2 per acre rent, as pasture, be ploughed up and used for raising wheat, must not the £2 per acre be debited against the expenses of production of wheat?" It is true that Mill was inconsistent in answering this question in the negative, while he maintained that when land capable of yielding rent in agriculture is applied to some other purpose, the rent which it would have yielded is an element in the cost of production of the commodity which it is employed to produce But still the proper answer to Jevons' question is in the negative For there is no connection between this particular sum of £2 and the expenses of production of that

BOOK V. CH VIII

The indirect effect of rent on Expenses of production must not be overlooked either in manufacture or in agriculture

Reverting to a caution given at the beginning of this chapter against misunderstanding the general bearing of Ricardo's doctrine, we may notice that this argument does not imply that a manufacturer when making up the profit and loss account of his business would not count his rent among his expenses. If the ground-rent in, say, Leeds rises, a manufacturer finding his expenses of production increased may move to another town or into the country, and leave the land on which he used to work to be built over with shops and warehouses, for which a town situation is more valuable than it is for factories[1]. For he may think that the saving in ground-rent that he will make by moving into the country, together with other advantages of the change, will more than counterbalance its disadvantages In a discussion as to whether it was worth his while to do so, the ground-rent of his factory would be reckoned among the expenses of production of his cloth.

This is true But it is no less true that in making up the profit and loss account of the cultivation of land, the farmer's rent must be reckoned among his expenses A hop-grower, for instance, may find that on account of the high rent which he pays for his land, the price of his hops will not cover their expenses of production where he is, and he may abandon hop-growing, or seek other land for it; while the land that he leaves may perhaps be let to a market-gardener. After a while the demand for land in the neighbourhood may again become so great that the aggregate price which

wheat which only just pays its way The amount of capital applied in cultivation is elastic, and is stretched until the return to it only just repays the outlay this limit is determined by the general circumstances of supply and demand, and is independent of the particular sum of £2 which the land will afford as rent Mill ought to have said, "When land capable of being used for producing one commodity (whether agricultural produce or not) is used for producing another, the price of the first is raised by the consequent limitation of its field of production The price of the second will be the expenses of production (wages and profits) of that part of it which only just pays its way, that which is produced on the margin of cultivation or building. And if for the purposes of any particular argument we take together the whole expenses of the production on that site, and divide these among the whole of the commodity produced, then, the rent which we ought to count in is not that which the site would pay if used for producing the first commodity, but that which it does pay when used for producing the second"

[1] Compare the latter part of Book IV. Ch III § 7

the market-gardener obtains for his produce will not pay its expenses of production, including rent; and so he in his turn makes room for, say, a building company

Mining Royalties enter into the cost of production of minerals.

§ 6. Mines, quarries, &c. form a class by themselves, as has already been indicated[1]. For, except when they are practically inexhaustible, the excess of their income over their direct outgoings has to be regarded, in part at least, as the price got by the sale of stored-up goods—stored up by Nature indeed, but now treated as private property; and therefore the marginal supply price of minerals includes a royalty in addition to the marginal expenses of working the mine This royalty on a ton of coal, when accurately adjusted, represents that diminution in the value of the mine, regarded as a source of wealth in the future, which is caused by taking the ton out of Nature's storehouse Ricardo was technically right when he said that rent does not enter into the marginal expenses of production of mineral produce. But he ought to have added that the incomes derived from mines, which are not practically inexhaustible, are in fact partly rent and partly royalty; and that though the rent does not, the minimum royalty does enter directly into the expenses paid for any part of the produce, whether it is marginal or not.

[1] Book IV. Ch III. § 7.

CHAPTER IX.

ON THE VALUE OF AN APPLIANCE FOR PRODUCTION IN RELATION TO THAT OF THE THINGS PRODUCED BY IT, CONTINUED.

Scope of the Chapter

§ 1 THE illustrations in the last chapter related generally to fixed and stable conditions. Those in the present chapter will bear on the application to less permanent incomes of the rule that Rent does not enter into cost of production We have to inquire what modifications are needed to adapt it to incomes derived from factors of production, the supply of which, though not permanently limited, cannot be increased quickly enough to affect appreciably the production of the commodity in question *during the period which we have in view when speaking of its normal supply price.* In order to emphasize this continuity the better we will study the incomes derived from land in a newly settled country we shall find that for some purposes they are to be classed as profits, or at most as quasi-rents, rather than rents

When a new country is first settled land is to be regarded as yielding profits rather than rent

A settler who takes up land in a new country exercises no exclusive privilege, for he only does what anyone else is at liberty to do He undergoes many hardships, if not personal dangers, and perhaps runs some risk that the land may turn out badly, and that he may have to abandon his improvements. On the other hand, his venture may turn out well, the flow of population may trend his way, and the value of his land may soon give as large a surplus over the normal remuneration of his outlay on it as the fishermen's haul does when they come home with their boat full. But in this there is nothing which presents itself to him as rent. He has engaged in a risky business which was open to all, and his energy and good fortune have given him an exceptionally high reward others might have taken the same chance as he did, and from a business point of view they ought to have done so, if they thought that, after discounting all the hardships and risks of the venture, it would yield a surplus which could fairly be called the rent of a special privilege or monopoly.

Thus the income which he expects the land to afford in the future enters into the calculations of the settler, and adds to the motives which determine his action when on the margin of doubt as to how far to carry his enterprise. He regards its "discounted value"[1] as profits on his capital, and as earnings of his own labour, in so far as his improvements are made with his own hands.

A settler often takes up land with the expectation that the produce which it affords while in his possession will fall short of an adequate reward for his hardships, his labour and his expenditure He looks for part of his reward to the value of the land itself, which he proposes after a while to sell to some new-comer who has no turn for the life of a pioneer. Sometimes even, as the British farmer learns to his cost, the new settler regards his wheat almost as a by-product, the main product for which he works is a farm, the title-deeds to which he will earn by improving the land, and the value of which will steadily rise[2].

[1] Compare Book III Ch v § 3

[2] It has even been maintained that any new country which should refuse to settlers the power of acquiring an absolute right of property in the soil, and should grant long leases only, would see the stream of immigrants into it speedily run away. But there does not seem to be any strong reason for thinking that this effect would be more than temporary for the more far-seeing class of immigrants might think that what was kept from them as "individual wealth" was more than returned to them as shareholders in the "collective wealth" And even if not, it may be doubtful whether the few people who first arrive on a new shore are justified in assuming that they have the right to dispose of its vast resources in perpetuity Warned by the experiences of the past our own generation might well pause before entering into new engagements that purport to bind its successors for all time The gain which the world as a whole can get from turning the stream of migration in this direction rather than that, is not very great distant generations may think that the fee-simple of the soil was too high a price to pay for such a purpose, and that, since a hundred years, though nothing in the life of the race, is long relatively to individual lives, a free lease for a hundred years would have been a sufficient price to pay But this takes us out beyond

BOOK V. CH IX.

When there are no more title-deeds to be earned in equally favoured situations, rent emerges,

§ 2. But when the land is all taken up, the desire to obtain its title-deeds no longer acts as a motive to further improvement and to further production. Henceforth that net income which the land affords to its owner in excess of normal profits on his fresh application of capital is a producer's surplus standing outside of those gains which are required to cover the marginal expenses of production. As population and wealth increase in the neighbourhood this net income also will increase; but except in so far as the improvement may be due to the direct action of individual owners, the whole of it may be regarded as a rent coming under the general argument of the preceding chapter.

and the shorter the period under consideration, the wider are the classes of improvements, the income of which is classed as rent

Its amount therefore will be governed, other things being equal, by the supply price of produce at the margin of cultivation and it will play very little direct part in governing that price For that price will be governed chiefly by the results which landowners and farmers can get from applying capital and labour in the further development of the resources of the soil, and in cultivating it by more intensive methods than those of the early settler The results of all kinds of improvements, both those which bear fruit slowly and those which bear fruit quickly, will be watched, and their success or failure will influence those who are thinking of investing more capital in the soil. Local variations of land tenure and custom will affect the issue, but in every case it will be true that the marginal supply price of produce in the near future will not be affected by improvements that bear fruit slowly, in the same way that it is by those which act quickly.

An illustrative instance

Suppose, for instance, that a war, which was not expected to last long, were to cut off part of our food supplies People would set themselves to raise heavier crops by such extra application of capital or labour as was likely to yield a speedy return; they would consider the results of artificial manures, of the use of clod-crushing machines, and so on,

the range of our present inquiries the point with which we are concerned just here is that anything that affects the hopes of distant gain on the part of the settler exerts a clearly marked, though perhaps slowly acting influence on the amount of produce which will be forthcoming in the country at any given time

and the more favourable these results were, the lower would be the price of produce in the coming year which they regarded as necessary to make it worth their while to incur additional outlay in these directions. But the war would have very little effect on their action as to improvements that would not bear fruit till it was over.

In any inquiry then as to the causes that will determine the prices of corn during a short period, that fertility which the soil derives from slowly made improvements has to be taken for granted as it then exists, almost in the same way as if it had been made by Nature. But in the long run the net returns to the investment of capital in the land, taking successful and unsuccessful returns together, do not afford more than an adequate motive to such investment. If poorer returns had been expected than those on which people actually based their calculations, fewer improvements would have been made, and in any case the improvements would depend partly on the conditions of land tenure, and the enterprise and ability and command over capital on the part of landlords and tenants which existed at the time and place in question. In this connection we shall find, when we come to study land tenure, that there are large allowances to be made for the special conditions of different places

But meanwhile we may conclude that, when the enterprise of landowners is most active, the extra income derived from improvements that have been made in the land by its individual owner—this income being so reckoned as not to include any benefit which would have been conferred on the land by the general progress of society independently of his efforts and sacrifices—does not as a rule give a surplus beyond what is required to remunerate him for those efforts and sacrifices. He may have under-estimated the gains which will result from them, but he is about equally likely to have made an over-estimate. If he has estimated them rightly, his interest would lead him to make the investment as soon as it showed signs of being profitable: and in the absence of any special reason to the contrary we may suppose him to have done this.

On these suppositions then, when we are considering

BOOK V CH IX

General results as to agriculture for long periods and for short

periods which are long in comparison with the time required to make improvements of any kind, and bring them into full operation, the net incomes derived from them are to be regarded as the price required to be paid for the efforts and sacrifices of those who make them. The expenses of making them thus directly enter into marginal expenses of production, and directly govern long-period supply price. But in short periods, that is, in periods short relatively to the time required to make and bring into full bearing improvements of the class in question, the incomes derived from them exercise no such direct influence on supply price, and when we are dealing with such periods these incomes may be regarded as a quasi-rent which takes little direct part in determining, but is rather dependent on the price of the produce. It may be noted, however, that rent proper is estimated on the understanding that the original properties of the soil are unimpaired And when the income derived from improvements is regarded as a quasi-rent, it is to be understood that they are kept up in full efficiency: if they are being deteriorated, the equivalent of the injury done to them must be deducted from the income they are made to yield before we can arrive at that *Net* income which is to be regarded as their quasi-rent

are applicable to all branches of industry;

§ **3** These results do not depend upon the special qualities of land, or on the special conditions of agriculture, they are generally applicable to all branches of industry This is perhaps already obvious enough for the main substance of the argument has already been given in Chapter v. But the subject is one of so much difficulty that the space given in this section to repeating, in another form, what has been said there, may not be wasted.

as is further shown by an illustration relating to manufacture

Let us suppose then that an exceptional demand for a certain kind of textile fabrics is caused by, say, a sudden movement of the fashions The special machinery required for making that fabric will yield for the time an income, which bears no direct relation to the expenses of making the machinery; but is rather a high quasi-rent governed by the price that can be got for the produce and consisting of the excess of the aggregate price of that produce, over the direct outlay (including wear-and-tear) incurred in its production.

Next, suppose that the tide has turned, and that the demand for a certain class of goods is much less than had been expected. The factories with the most imperfect appliances and the worst machinery in other factories will be thrown out of work: those machines which it is just worth while to keep in work will just pay the actual expenses of working them, but will yield no surplus. Their produce will be on the margin of production, and the excess of the price got for the goods made by the better appliances over wear-and-tear, together with the actual expenses of working them, will be the income which these appliances yield during the short period of depression. In this case the income will be not more but less than normal profits on the original investment.

Arguments relating to rents extended to quasi-rents

The argument of the last section but one of the preceding chapter applies, so far as short periods are concerned, to quasi-rents very nearly in the same way as to true Rents. When existing factories or machinery which could be applied to producing one commodity are diverted to producing another because the demand for that is such as to enable them to earn a higher income by producing it, then *for the time* the supply of the first will be less, and its price higher than if the machinery had not been able to earn a higher income by another use. But as in the case of rent, there will be no direct or numerical relation between the increase in the price of the first commodity and the income that the machinery can earn by producing the second.

The analogy between quasi-rent and rent relates only to short periods.

§ 4. Similar illustrations might be taken from any other branch of business. Each branch has special features of its own, but with proper modifications in detail, the same general principle applies to all. In every case the net income derived from the investment of capital, when once that investment has been made, is a quasi-rent. That is to say, when the causes which determine short-period fluctuations of production are under discussion, this quasi-rent may be classed with rent proper, on the ground that it stands outside of the payments which influence producers to take such action as would increase the available supply within a short period But this resemblance to rent is only partial and in a sense superficial.

and has no bearing on the broader problems of economic progress

For when land or other free gifts of nature have once become private property, their rent proper does not act as a direct incentive to make and save the means of production: though of course a violent appropriation of it might destroy that security on which all such motives depend. It is a true surplus. But the quasi-rent of capital is, speaking generally, no true surplus If it had been expected to be less than it actually is, the motives to work and to save the product of work would have been less. And if this quasi-rent were to be diminished now, in such a way as to diminish the expectations of the future gain likely to result from the effort and sacrifice involved in working and saving the product of work, the growth of individual capital would at once be checked. The existing plant might indeed be sufficient to prevent the change from considerably affecting the supply of finished commodities, for a few years: but the broad course of economic development would be changed; and, so far as it depends on the supply of individual capital, it would be arrested

It is true that what was lost in this direction might be counterbalanced by a corresponding growth of Collective capital. Whether there would be any considerable chance of this is a matter on which opinions differ. But when we come to discuss the schemes of modern socialists it will be important to remember that, though there is some real analogy between the quasi-rent of capital and rent proper, yet the analogy does not reach far. It has no validity at all except when short periods only are under discussion. it has no bearing on those broad and slow movements on which the general progress and the ultimate well-being of mankind depend.

CHAPTER X.

ON THE VALUE OF AN APPLIANCE FOR PRODUCTION IN RELATION TO THAT OF THE THINGS PRODUCED BY IT, CONTINUED. SITUATION RENT. COMPOSITE RENT.

BOOK V CH X

Relation in which this Chapter stands to the two preceding

§ 1. We have now considered the relation in which cost of production stands to the income derived from the ownership of the "original powers" of land and other free gifts of Nature, and also to that which is directly due to the investment of private capital But there is a third class, holding an intermediate position between these two, of which something should be said here It consists of those incomes, or rather those parts of incomes which are the indirect result of the general progress of society, rather than the direct result of the investment of capital and labour by individuals for the sake of securing certain gains to themselves

Influence of situation on the value of agricultural land

We have already seen how Nature nearly always gives a less than proportionate return, when measured by the *amount* of the produce raised, to increasing applications of capital and labour in the cultivation of land; but that, on the other hand, if the more intensive cultivation is the result of the growth of a non-agricultural population in the neighbourhood, this very concourse of people is likely to raise the real price which the cultivator can get for every part of his produce. We saw how this influence opposes, and usually outweighs the action of the law of diminishing return when the produce is measured according to its value and not according to its amount; the cultivator gets good markets in which to supply his wants, as well as good markets in which to sell, he buys more cheaply while he sells more dearly, and the conveniences and enjoyments of social life are ever being brought more within his reach[1].

In all trades access to External economies depends partly on Situation

Again, we saw how the economies which result from a high industrial organization[2] often depend only to a small extent on the resources of individual firms. Those *internal* economies which each establishment has to arrange for itself are frequently very small as compared with those *external* economies which result from the general progress of the industrial environment, the Situation of a business nearly always plays a great part in determining the extent to which it can avail itself of external economies

It is true that situation often counts for little with regard to those economies that result from the gradual growth of knowledge, or from the gradual development of world markets for commodities the value of which is great in proportion to their bulk. Cost of carriage is not a very large element in the budget of a watch-factory wherever it is placed· though near access to markets where specialized skill can be easily got may be very important to it But in the great majority of industries the success of a business depends chiefly upon the resources and the markets of its own immediate neighbourhood; and the Situation value which a site derives from the growth of a rich and active population close to it, or from the opening up of railways and other good means of communication with existing markets, is the most striking of all the influences which changes in the industrial environment exert on cost of production.

Situation Rent

§ 2 If in any industry, whether agricultural or not, two producers have equal facilities in all respects, except that one has a more convenient situation than the other, and can buy or sell in the same markets with less cost of carriage, the differential advantage which his situation gives him is the aggregate of the excess charges for cost of carriage to which his rival is put. And we may suppose that other advantages of situation, such for instance as the near access to a labour market specially adapted to his trade, can be translated in like manner into money values. When this

[1] Book IV Ch III § 6 [2] *Ib* Ch X—XIII

is done for, say, a year, and all are added together we have the annual money value of the advantages of situation which the first business has over the second, and the corresponding difference in the incomes derived from the two businesses is commonly regarded as a difference of *Situation Rent* If we suppose the second of the two sites to have less advantages of situation than any other, we may regard it as having no special situation rent; and then the income derived from the differential advantage of the former site constitutes the whole of its situation rent[1].

Exceptional cases in which the income derived from advantageous situation is to be regarded as profits rather than rent

§ 3 There are however some exceptional cases in which this income derived from an advantageous situation is not properly to be regarded as rent but rather as profits Sometimes, for instance, the settlement of a whole town, or even district is planned on business principles, and carried out as an investment at the expense and risk of a single person or company. The movement may be partly due to philanthropic or religious motives, but its financial basis will in any case be found in the fact that the concourse of numbers is itself a cause of increased economic efficiency. Under ordinary circumstances the chief gains arising from this efficiency would accrue to those who are already in possession of the place: but the chief hopes of commercial success, by those who undertake to colonise a new district or build a new town, are usually founded on securing these gains for themselves

[1] If we suppose that two farms, which sell in the same market, return severally to equal applications of capital and labour amounts of produce, the first of which exceeds the second by the extra cost of carrying its produce to market, then the rent of the two farms will be the same (The capital and labour applied to the two farms are here supposed to be reduced to the same money measure, or which comes to the same thing, the two farms are supposed to have equally good access to markets in which to buy) Again, if we suppose that two mineral springs A and B supplying exactly the same water are capable of being worked each to an unlimited extent at a constant money cost of production, this cost being, say two pence a bottle at A whatever the amount produced by it, and two pence halfpenny at B, then those places to which the cost of carriage per bottle from B is a half penny less than from A, will be the neutral zone for their competition (If the cost of carriage be proportional to the distance, this neutral zone is a hyperbola of which A and B are foci) A can undersell B for all places on A's side of it, and *vice versa*, and each of them will be able to derive a Monopoly Rent from the sale of its produce within its own area This is a type of a great many fanciful, but not uninstructive, problems which readily suggest themselves Compare Von Thunen's brilliant researches in *Der isolirte Staat*

BOOK V CH. X

Illustrations from Saltaire and Pullman City

When, for instance, Mr Salt and Mr Pullman determined to take their factories into the country and to found Saltaire and Pullman city, they foresaw that the land, which they could purchase at its value for agricultural purposes, would obtain the special situation value which town property derives from the immediate neighbourhood of a dense population. And similar considerations have influenced those, who, having fixed upon a site adapted by nature to become a favourite watering-place, have bought the land and spent large sums in developing its resources: they have been willing to wait long for any net income from their investment in the hope that ultimately their land would derive a high situation value from the concourse of people attracted to it[1].

In all such cases the yearly income derived from the land (or at all events that part of it which is in excess of the agricultural rent) is for many purposes to be regarded as profits rather than rent. And this is equally true, whether the land is that on which the factory itself at Saltaire or Pullman city is built, or that which affords a high "ground-rent" as the site of a shop or store, whose situation will enable it to do a brisk trade with those who work in the factory For in such cases great risks have to be run; and in all undertakings in which there are risks of great losses, there must also be hopes of great gains The normal expenses of production of a commodity must include payment for the ventures required for producing it, sufficient to cause those who are on the margin of doubt whether to venture or not, to regard the probable net amount of their gains—net, that is, after deducting the probable amount of their losses—as compensating them for their trouble and their outlay. And that the gains resulting from such ventures are not much more than sufficient for this purpose is shown by the fact that they are not as yet very common They are however likely to be more frequent in those industries which are in the hands of very powerful corporations. A large railway company, for instance, can found a Crewe or a New Swindon

[1] Cases of this kind are of course most frequent in new countries But they are not very rare in old countries. Saltburn is a conspicuous instance.

for manufacturing railway plant without running any great risk[1].

Improvements effected at the joint expense of the landowners concerned

Somewhat similar instances are those of a group of landowners who combine to make a railway, the net traffic receipts of which are not expected to pay any considerable interest on the capital invested in making it; but which will greatly raise the value of their land In such cases part of the increase of their incomes as landowners ought to be regarded as profits on capital which they have invested in the improvement of their land: though the capital has gone towards making a railway instead of being applied directly to their own property.

Other cases of like nature are main drainage schemes, and other plans for improving the general condition of agricultural or town property, in so far as they are carried out by the landowners at their own expense, whether by private agreement or by the levying of special rates on themselves. Similar cases again are found in the investment of capital by a nation in building up its own social and political organization as well as in promoting the education of the people and in developing its sources of material wealth.

Thus that improvement of the environment, which adds to the value of land and of other free gifts of nature, is in a good many cases partly due to the deliberate investment of capital by the owners of the land for the purpose of raising its value; and therefore a portion of the consequent increase of income may be regarded as profits when we are considering long periods But in many cases it is not so, and any increase

[1] Governments have great facilities for carrying out schemes of this kind, especially in the matter of choosing new sites for garrison towns, arsenals, and establishments for the manufacture of the materials of war In comparisons of the expenses of production by Government and by private firms, the sites of the Government works are often reckoned only at their agricultural value But such a plan is misleading A private firm has either to pay heavy annual charges on account of its site, or to run very heavy risks if it tries to make a town for itself And therefore in order to prove that Government management is for general purposes as efficient and economical as private management, a full charge ought to be made in the balance-sheets of Government factories for the town-value of their sites In those exceptional branches of production for which a Government can found a manufacturing town without incurring the risks that a private firm would incur in a similar case, that point of advantage may fairly be reckoned as an argument for Governments undertaking those particular businesses

BOOK V CH X

in the net income derived from the free gifts of nature which was not brought about by, and did not supply the direct motive to, any special outlay on the part of the landowners, is to be regarded as rent for all purposes

Composite rent

§ 4. The so-called rent of a building is generally composed of two elements, one the quasi-rent of the building itself, and the other the rent—often chiefly a situation rent—of the ground on which it is built The task of distinguishing between these two elements may be taken here as a special case of a more general problem of composite rents

Its component elements can be distinguished in some but not in all cases

At starting there may appear to be some contradiction in the statement that a thing is yielding at the same time two rents: for a rent is in some sense a residual income after deducting the expenses of working it and it may seem that there cannot be two residues But really we often find a true producer's surplus or rent, which itself includes two or more minor rents.

For instance, the rent of a flour-mill worked by water includes the rent of the site on which it is built, and the rent of the water power which it uses. Suppose that it is contemplated to build a mill in a place where there is a limited water power which could be applied equally well on any one of many sites; then the rent of the water power together with the site selected for it is the sum of two rents, which are respectively the equivalent of the differential advantages which possession of the site gives for production of any kind, and which the ownership of the water power gives for working a mill on any of the sites And these two rents, whether they happen to be owned by the same person or not, can be clearly distinguished and separately estimated both in theory and in practice

But this cannot be done if there are no other sites on which a mill can be built · and in that case, should the water power and the site belong to different persons, there is nothing but "higgling and bargaining" to settle how much of the excess of the value of the two together over that which the site has for other purposes shall go to the owner of the latter And even if there were other sites at which the water power could be applied, but not with equal efficiency, there would still be no means of deciding how the owners of the site and the water power should share the excess of the producer's surplus which they got by acting together, over the sum of that which the site would yield for some other purpose, and of that which the water power would yield if applied elsewhere The mill would probably not be put up till an agreement had been made for the supply of water power for a term of years: but at the end of that term similar difficulties would arise as to the division of the aggregate producer's surplus afforded by the water power and the site with the mill on it.

Difficulties of this kind are continually arising with regard to attempts by partial monopolists, such as railway, gas, water and electrical companies, to raise their charges on the consumer who has adapted his business arrangements to make use of their services, and perhaps laid down at his own expense a costly plant for the purpose. For instance, at Pittsburgh when manufacturers had just put up furnaces to be worked by natural gas instead of coal, the price of the gas was suddenly doubled And the whole history of mines is full of difficulties of this kind, with neighbouring landowners as to rights of way, &c, and with the owners of neighbouring cottages, railways and docks

CHAPTER XI.

THE EQUILIBRIUM OF NORMAL DEMAND AND SUPPLY CONCLUDED. MULTIPLE POSITIONS OF EQUILIBRIUM

Plan of the chapter

§ 1. In the present chapter we have, firstly, to examine the relation in which average expenses of production stand to normal supply price; secondly, to consider further the conditions of production and marketing in industries which obey the law of increasing return, to look again at the causes which limit the production of individual firms in those industries and hinder any one of them from driving its rivals out of the field as soon as it has once got a start over them, thirdly, to take up that study of normal equilibrium with regard to commodities obeying the law of increasing return which we avoided in Chapter V. and postponed to this place, and lastly, to discuss some points of a rather technical character relating to the interpretation of normal supply price and the normal demand and supply schedules and multiple positions of equilibrium The second of these tasks is of general interest, the rest are of rather an academic character

The terms *average* and *aggregate* expenses of production have only a conventional meaning in a world of rapid change

Firstly, then, as to the relations between average expenses of production and normal supply price. The last few chapters have thrown some light on the relations in which the normal supply price of a commodity stands to its so-called "average" expenses of production at any time. In this use the term is somewhat misleading. For in the world in which we live, most of the appliances of production, material and personal, by which a commodity was made, came into existence long before. Their values are therefore not likely to be just what the producers expected them to be originally; but some of their values will be greater, and others less. The present incomes earned by them will be governed by the general relations between the demand for, and the supply of their products; and their values will be arrived at by capitalizing these incomes (which will be of the nature of quasi-rents).

It is obvious therefore that when making out a list of normal supply prices, which, in conjunction with the list of normal demand prices, is to determine the equilibrium position of normal value, we cannot take for granted the values of these appliances for production without reasoning in a circle. In a world of change, such as ours is, the terms "aggregate" or "average" expenses of production have in general no exact and definite meaning, though of course they may be legitimately used, with an artificial interpretation clause, for the special purposes of a particular problem

But let us suppose a perfectly stationary state, in which the same things are done in the same way and to the same extent for many generations.

One such use is found when we suppose a world in which everything is, and has long been, in a stationary state, in which the same amounts of the same things have been produced in the same ways by the same classes of people for many generations together; and in which therefore this supply of the appliances for production has had full time to be adjusted to the steady demand.

Of course we might assume that in our stationary state every business remained always of the same size, and with the same trade connection. But we need not go so far as that, it will suffice to suppose that firms rise and fall with the same regular monotony as the trees of a forest; and that, though some firms may turn the economies of production on a large scale to better account than others, yet they will not obtain a preponderating influence in, and change the character of, their own branch of industry. The "representative" firm would therefore be of a constant size, as the representative tree of a virgin forest is, its internal economies would be constant, and its external also, because the aggregate volume of production would be constant. The marginal price, the expectation of which just induced persons to enter the trade, would be sufficient to cover in the long run the cost of building up a trade connection which was afterwards to decay; these would be the normal expenses governing the normal supply price for long periods.

And in such a state there would be no distinction between long-period and short-period normal value, or between true normal price and sub-normal price, at all events if we supposed that in that monotonous world the harvests themselves were uniform: for the representative firm being always of the same size, and always doing the same class of business to the same extent and in the same way with no slack times, and no specially busy times, its normal expenses by which the normal supply price is governed would be always the same. The demand and the supply lists of prices would always be the same, and normal price would never vary.

In such a state there would be no quasi-rents; but true rents would remain

There would be no such things as quasi-rents. for the income earned by every appliance of production being truly anticipated beforehand, would represent the normal measure of the efforts and appliances required to call it into existence. But true rents would remain. For that which cannot be increased by man's effort in time however long, would still have no supply price; and its value would still be found by capitalizing the income derived from the differential advantages which it offered for production; and that income would be determined by the expenses of production of that part of the supply which had not the benefit of any permanent differential advantages; i.e. by the marginal expenses of production.

Aggregate expenses of production would then be definite and, rents being counted in, average expenses would then be equal to marginal and to normal expenses.

The aggregate expenses of production might then be found either by multiplying these marginal expenses by the number of units of the commodity, or by adding together all the actual expenses of production of its several parts, and adding in all the rents earned by differential advantages for production The aggregate expenses of production being determined by either of these routes, the average expenses could be deduced by dividing out by the amount of the commodity; and would be the normal supply price, whether for long periods or for short.

In this stationary state we have supposed every particular

thing to bear its proper share of supplementary costs, and have supposed that it would not ever be worth while for a producer to accept a particular order at a price other than the total cost, in which is to be reckoned a charge for the task of building up the trade connection and external organization of a representative firm[1].

[1] This case may be illustrated by the adjoining diagram, in which SS' is not a true supply curve, but has properties, which are often erroneously attributed to the supply curve; and some study of it may be useful, if for no other purpose, yet as a means of guarding the true supply curve against misunderstandings. We will call it the *Particular Expenses Curve*. As usual the amount of a commodity is measured along Ox, and its price along Oy OH is the amount of the commodity produced annually, AH is the equilibrium price of a unit of it. The producer of the OHth unit is supposed to have no differential advantages; but the producer of the OMth unit has differential advantages which enable him to produce with an outlay PM, a unit which it would have cost him an outlay AH to produce without those advantages The locus of P is our particular expenses curve; and it is such that any point P being taken on it, and PM being drawn perpendicular to Ox, PM represents the particular expenses of production incurred for the production of the OMth unit The excess of AH over $PM = QP$, and is a producer's surplus or rent. For convenience the owners of differential advantages may be arranged in descending order from left to right; and thus SS' becomes a curve sloping upwards to the right

Proceeding as in the case of consumer's surplus or rent (Bk. III Ch VI. § 1), we may regard MQ as a thin parallelogram or as a thick straight line And as M takes consecutive positions along OH, we get a number of thick straight lines cut in two by the curve SA, the lower part of each representing the expenses of production of a unit of the commodity, and the upper the contribution which that unit affords towards rent The lower set of thick lines taken together fill up the whole space $SOHA$, which therefore represents the aggregate of the expenses of production of an amount OH The upper set of thick lines taken together fill up the space FSA, which therefore represents producer's surplus or rent in the ordinary sense of the term Subject to the corrections mentioned in Bk. III Ch VI § 2, DFA represents the surplus satisfaction which consumers get from an amount OH over that, the value of which is represented to them by a sum of money equal to $OH \times HA$, and the diagram shows how the name "consumer's rent" was suggested for this surplus

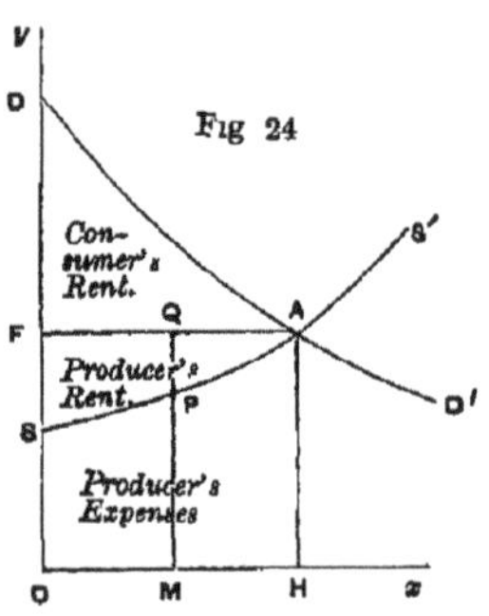

Now the difference between the particular expenses curve and a normal supply curve lies in this, that in the former we do, and in the latter we do not, take the general economies of production as fixed and uniform throughout The particular expenses curve is based throughout on the assumption that the aggregate production is OH, and that all the producers have access to the internal and external economies which belong to this scale of production, and, these assumptions being carefully borne in mind, the curve may be used to represent a particu-

BOOK V CH. XI

We now pass from this hypotheme

§ 2 The hypothesis of a stationary state is useful to illustrate many points in economics; but it is the nature of such hypotheses to be treacherous guides if pursued far away from their starting point they soon lead us into a region of unreal abstractions, and, in particular, this one is not suitable

lar phase of any industry, whether agricultural or manufacturing, but cannot be taken to represent its general conditions of production.

That can be done only by the normal supply curve, in which *PM* represents the normal expenses of production of the *OM*th unit on the supposition that *OM* units (not any other amount, as *OH*) are being produced; and that the available economies of production external and internal are those which belong to a representative firm where the aggregate volume of production is *OM* These economies will generally be less than if the aggregate volume of production were the larger quantity *OH*, and therefore, *M* being to the left of *H*, the ordinate at *M* for the supply curve will be greater than for a particular expenses curve drawn for an aggregate production *OH*.

It follows that the area *SAF* which represents aggregate rent in our present diagram would have represented something less than the aggregate rent, if *SS'* had been a normal supply curve even for agricultural produce (*DD'* being the normal demand curve). For even in agriculture the general economies of production increase with an increase in the aggregate scale of production

If however we choose to ignore this fact for the sake of any particular argument; that is, if we choose to assume that *MP* being the expenses of production of that part of the produce which was raised under the most difficult circumstances (so as to pay no rent) when *OM* units were produced, it remains also the expenses of production (other than rent) of the *OM*th unit even when *OH* is produced; or in other words, if we assume that the increase in production from the amount *OM* to the amount *OH* did not alter the expenses of production of the *OM*th unit, then we may regard *SAF* as representing the aggregate rent even when *SS'* is the normal supply curve It may be occasionally convenient to do this, attention being of course called every time to the nature of the special assumption made

But no assumption of the kind can be made with regard to the supply curve of a commodity that obeys the laws of increasing return. To do so would be a contradiction in terms The fact that the production of the commodity obeys that law, implies that the general economies available when the aggregate volume of production is large, are so much greater than when it is small, as to override the increasing resistance that Nature offers to an increased production of the raw materials of which the industry makes use In the case of a particular expenses curve, *MP* will always be less than *AH* (*M* being to the left of *H*) whether the commodity obeys the law of increasing or diminishing returns; but on the other hand in the case of a Supply curve, for a commodity that obeys the law of increasing returns, *MP* would generally be greater than *AH*

It remains to say that if we are dealing with a problem in which some even of those appliances for production which were made by man, have to be taken as a given quantity for the time, so that their earnings will be of the nature of a quasi rent; we may then draw a particular expenses curve, in which *MP* stands for the expenses of production in the narrower sense in which such quasi-rents are excluded, and the area *SAF* would thus represent the aggregate of rents proper and of these quasi-rents This method of treating short-period normal value problems has attractions, and may perhaps ultimately be of service but it requires careful handling, for the assumptions on which it rests are very slippery.

for that part of the pure theory of equilibrium of normal demand and supply which remains for us to discuss; and which relates to industries that obey the law of increasing return, a law that belongs essentially to an age of change and progress.

and proceed to study further the causes that govern normal supply price in an industry that obeys the law of increasing return

It will be recollected that the general view of that theory, given in Chapter III. of this Book, left out of account all cases in which the supply price falls as the amount produced increases; because they present special difficulties which would have obscured those main outlines of the theory of which we were then seeking to obtain a general view. These difficulties arise chiefly from the facts, firstly, that the law of increasing return seldom shows its true character in a *short* period of time, and, secondly, that in the *long* period of time required for its full operation, the general conditions of equilibrium are likely to be modified by external changes[1].

Let us begin with the first of these two difficulties, and consider further the conditions of production and marketing with regard to short periods in industries that obey the law of increasing return, and inquire what are the reasons which induce any particular producer of a commodity, which obeys the law of increasing return, to produce as much as he does and no more The fact that the economies of production on a large scale act differently in different trades, makes it difficult to adapt a general theory of equilibrium to the conditions of these industries; and we are compelled to go back a little, and work, partly over old ground, from details to general results.

[1] These difficulties lie rather below the surface and are often concealed in popular discussions of the equilibrium conditions of trade; but they have made themselves felt with great force in the attempts made, from the time of Cournot and von Thunen downwards, to express those conditions by mathematical formulæ. Some, among whom Cournot himself is to be counted, have before them what is in effect the supply schedule of an individual firm, representing that an increase in its output gives it command over so great internal economies as much to diminish its expenses of production, and they follow their mathematics boldly, but apparently without noticing that it leads inevitably to the ultimate monopoly of the whole business of its trade in its district by whatever firm first got a good start. While others avoiding this horn of the dilemma, maintain that there is no true equilibrium at all for commodities which obey the law of increasing return; and some would appear even to have called in question the validity of any supply schedule which represents prices diminishing as the amount produced increases.

BOOK V. CH. XI.

It may seem that it is the interest of each producer not to limit, but to increase its production

The question is more difficult to answer with regard to commodities that obey the law of increasing than those that obey the law of diminishing return. With regard to the latter, the producer whose normal marginal expenses of production are just equal to the normal demand price in the market, would generally have no inducement to raise additional produce, even though he could market it on the same terms as the rest. But in the case of a commodity that obeys the law of increasing return, the point at which the producer should stop is not so clearly marked out. It may seem at first sight that by doubling his production, he will increase very much his internal economies, and, marketing his output on nearly the same terms as before, he will more than double his profits. It may be argued that so long as this course is open to him, his production can never be in equilibrium.

It must be admitted that individual businesses whose products obey the law of increasing return are seldom in a state of equilibrium,

Now it must be admitted fully that in a trade in which there are large Internal economies of production still available, an individual firm is seldom in a position of true equilibrium. For a new man working his way with small capital and small trade connection, in a trade in which the economies of production on a large scale tell powerfully on the side of large firms, would probably be able to continue for a time to increase his normal output, to lower his normal expenses per unit, and the price at which he is able to sell. If, as his business increased, his faculties adapted themselves to his larger sphere, as they had done to his smaller, if he retained his originality, and versatility and power of initiation, his perseverance, his tact and his good luck for a hundred years together; he might have absorbed into his own hands the whole volume of production in his branch of trade for his district: and if his goods were not very difficult of transport, he might have extended this district very wide. During all this time there would have been no equilibrium, but only movement; and at the end his price would not be a normal expenses of production price, but that of a limited monopoly, that is, of a monopoly limited by the consideration that a very high price would bring rival producers into the field

But all that this shows is, that we must be careful not to

regard the conditions of supply by an individual producer as typical of those which govern the general supply in a market, without taking account of the fact that very few firms have a long-continued life of active progress; and that while some are growing, others are sure to be decaying, like the older trees of the forest, so that their normal productive power remains nearly constant, though the yield of each one of them is generally either on the rise or on the decline. This argument has been dwelt on so long in this and the preceding Book, that we may take its broad outlines for granted, and consider an objection to applying it to the particular question before us.

but their movements tend to compensate one another,

The objection is that the decay of human energies is after all a slow process, and that, if a large output would cost much less in proportion than a small one, an able and energetic man could often find the means of increasing his output tenfold or more within a period very short in comparison with the length of his own life. This also must be admitted. It is true that a man who is prospering can often borrow capital so fast and therefore can increase his material appliances so fast, that the expansion of his business might be very rapid, if he could both market his new output easily, and at the same time obtain very important internal economies by every increase of his output. It must be admitted further that there are a few industries, in which these two conditions do coexist; and that such industries are, for that very reason, in so transitional a state that for the time there is nothing to be gained by trying to apply the statical theory of equilibrium of normal demand and supply to them They must be thought of as in motion, rather than at rest. But, on the other hand, these industries are very few in number For, though there are many industries in which an individual producer could secure much increased Internal economies by a great increase of his output; and there are many in which he could market that output easily, yet there are few in which he could do both. And this is not an accidental but almost a necessary result

save in certain exceptional industries

There are not very many industries obeying the law of increasing return in which a producer has equally good

For in general each producer's market is more or less limited

access to the whole of a large market. No doubt he may in the case of goods which can be *graded*[1], and which can be sold in a public market. But, most goods that can be graded are raw produce, and of the rest nearly all are simple commodities, such as steel rails or calico, the production of which can be reduced to routine, for the same reasons that enable them to be graded. In the industries which produce them no firm can hold its own at all unless equipped with expensive appliances of nearly the latest type; and there remains no very great difference between the economies available by a large and by a very large firm[2]. In these industries, in short, the tendency of large firms to drive out small ones has already gone so far as to exhaust most of the strength of those forces by which it was originally promoted.

And even in these industries, to produce for an open market, means generally to produce for sale to middlemen who will sell to others those producers, who can miss out one in the link of middlemen, will often gain by so doing a good deal more than the additional economies to be got by increasing an already large and well-found stock of machinery; and when this is so, a large part of the value of any business will consist of its particular trade connections and external organization, in spite of the fact that the commodities which it produces resemble those made by many other firms.

An individual producer can seldom extend his special market quickly

But the majority of commodities with regard to which the law of increasing return acts strongly are, more or less, specialities many of them aim at creating a new want, or at meeting an old want in a new way. Many of them are adapted to special tastes; some can never have a very large market, and some have merits that are not easily tested, and must win their way to general favour slowly. In all such cases the sales of each business are limited, more or less according to circumstances, to the particular market which it has slowly acquired There are firms whose business connections have been built up by a gradual investment of capital, and are worth nearly as much as, or possibly even more than, the whole of their material capital. When a business is thus confined more or less to its own particular market, a

[1] See Book v Chapter II

[2] See above, p. 362

hasty increase in its production is likely to lower the demand price in that market out of all proportion to the increased Internal economies that it will gain, even though its production is but small relatively to the broad market for which in a more general sense it may be said to produce[1]. So generally is this recognized that, when trade is slack, a producer will often try to sell his surplus goods outside of his own particular market at prices that do little more than cover their prime costs, while within that market he still tries to sell at prices that nearly cover supplementary costs, a great part of which are the returns expected on capital invested in building up the external organization of his business.

The conditions of equilibrium for short periods are similar for the laws of increasing and diminishing return

To conclude, then, the supplementary costs are generally, though not always, large relatively to prime costs for commodities that obey the law of increasing return; because their production needs the investment of a large capital in material appliances and in building up trade connections Each firm has often to acquire a market of its own, partly because of the difficulties of grading, and when this is the case, it seldom sells much at short notice outside this market except at less than total cost price. This does not alter the character, but does increase the intensity of those fears of spoiling his own peculiar market, or incurring odium from other producers for spoiling the common market, which we have already learnt to regard as controlling the short-period supply price of goods when the appliances of production are not fully employed[2].

[1] This may be expressed by saying that when we are considering an individual producer, we must couple his supply curve—not with the general demand curve for his commodity in a wide market—but with the particular demand curve of his own special market. And this particular demand curve will generally be very steep, steeper than his own supply curve is likely to be even when an increased output will give him an important increase of Internal economies The whole of this argument lends itself easily to expression in mathematical language

[2] Of course this rule is not universal It may be noted, for instance, that the net loss of an omnibus, that is not full and loses a fourpenny fare, is nearer fourpence than threepence, though the omnibus trade conforms perhaps to the law of constant return, and if it were not for the fear of spoiling his market, the Regent Street shoemaker, whose goods are made by hand, but whose expenses of marketing are very heavy, would be tempted to go further below his normal price in order to avoid losing a special order, than a shoe manufacturer who uses much expensive machinery and avails himself generally of the economies of production on a large scale

But when they are fully employed, a temporary increase in demand is likely to raise the short-period supply price quite as much for commodities that obey the law of increasing return as for others For the very fact that their production generally requires much specialized skill and specialized machinery will make a quick increase in the output possible only by working much overtime under great disadvantages; and perhaps calling into use some imperfect skill and some old-fashioned machinery. And therefore the supply schedule for short periods must generally show a price increasing and not diminishing with an increase in the amount produced. There are exceptions to this rule; but their conditions are so peculiar, that each must be treated by itself, there is nothing to be gained by forcibly moulding our general supply schedules, so as to fit their special conditions.

But for long periods the conditions are wholly different

§ 3 It is then only as regards the long-period normal supply price that the true nature of the law of increasing return is shown. If there is a prospect of a permanent large demand for a thing, it will be worth while to invest capital in building up the material appliances, and the external and internal organization of large businesses, which will be able to sell profitably at a low price. The long-period supply price for large amounts will be low, because it is in effect the supply price not of particular things, but of the whole processes of production of those things The law of increasing return is in truth a law that the supply price of the *processes of production* (and marketing) of large quantities of certain goods falls, when the scale of those processes increases

The long-period supply price is really the price of a process.

An illustration in the case of manufactured commodities.

It is true for instance that if a sudden fashion were to set in for wearing watch-shaped aneroid barometers, highly paid labour, that had no special training for the work, would have to be drawn in from other trades, there would be a good deal of wasted effort and for a time the real and the money cost of production would be increased. But it is also true that if the fashion lasted a considerable time, then independently of any new invention in the cost of making aneroids the process of production on a large scale would be economical. For specialized skill in abundance would shortly be forthcoming, and properly graduated to the various work to be done: with a large use of the method of interchangeable parts, specialized machinery would do better and more cheaply much of the work that is now done by hand. and a steady increase in the annual output of watch-shaped aneroids will lower very much their long-period supply price, as a result of that development of industrial organization which normally belongs to a large scale of production.

The relative position of the long-period demand and supply regulates the stability of the adjustment of demand and supply.

Now their long-period supply price when it has been thus lowered, might be either greater or less than the normal demand price for the corresponding scale of production, when at last the force of fashion died away, and the demand for aneroids was again based solely on their real utility In the former case capital and labour would avoid that trade. Of the firms already started some might pursue their course though with less net gains (lower quasi-rents) than they had hoped, but others would try to edge their way into some nearly related branch of production that was more prosperous: and as old firms dwindled, there would be few new ones to take their place. The scale of production would dwindle again; and the old position of equilibrium would have shown itself stable against assaults

But now let us turn to the other case, in which the long-period supply price for the increased output fell so far that the demand price remained above it In that case undertakers, looking forward to the life of a firm started in that trade, considering its chances of prosperity and decay, discounting its future outlays and its future incomings, would conclude that the latter showed a good balance over the former: capital and labour would stream rapidly into the trade, and the production might perhaps be increased tenfold before the fall in the demand price became as great as the fall in the long-period supply price, and a position of stable equilibrium had been found.

Two or more positions of stable equilibrium can theoretically result from

For indeed, though in that account of the oscillations of demand and supply about a position of stable equilibrium, which was given at the end of the third Chapter, we tacitly implied, as is commonly done, that there could be only one position of stable equilibrium in a market: yet in fact under

BOOK V CH. XI

the same set of conditions; and such cases sometimes, though rarely, occur in practice

certain conceivable, though rare, conditions there can be two, or more positions of real equilibrium of demand and supply, any one of which is equally consistent with the general circumstances of the market, and any one of which if once reached would be stable, until some great disturbance occurred[1].

[1] Besides positions of stable equilibrium, there are theoretically at least positions of unstable equilibrium they are the dividing boundaries between two positions of stable equilibria, the watersheds, so to speak, dividing two river basins, and the price tends to flow away from them in either direction

When demand and supply are in unstable equilibrium, then, if the scale of production be disturbed ever so little from its equilibrium position, it will move rapidly away to one of its positions of stable equilibrium; as an egg if balanced on one of its ends would at the smallest shake fall down, and lie lengthways. Just as it is theoretically possible, but practically impossible, that an egg should stand balanced on its end, so it is theoretically possible, but practically impossible, that the scale of production should stay balanced in unstable equilibrium

Thus in Fig 25, the curves intersect several times and the arrow-heads on Ox show the directions in which, according to its situation, R tends to move along Ox This shows that if R is at H or at L and is displaced slightly in either direction, it will, as soon as the disturbing cause is over, return to the equilibrium position from which it was displaced, but that if it is at K and is displaced towards the right, it will continue even after the cessation of the disturbing cause, to move to the right till it reaches L, and if displaced towards the left it will continue to move to the left till it reaches H That is to say, H and L are points of stable equilibrium and K is a point of unstable equilibrium We are thus brought to the result that —

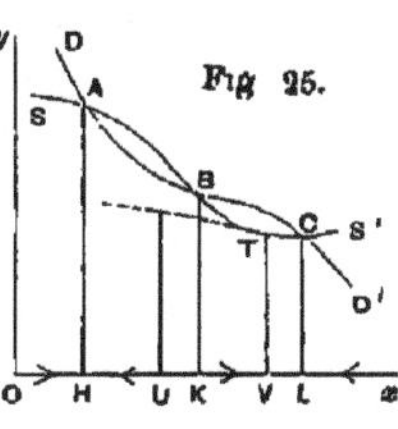

The equilibrium of demand and supply corresponding to a point of intersection of the demand and supply curves is stable or unstable according as the demand curve lies above or below the supply curve just to the left of that point, or, which is the same thing, according as it lies below or above the supply curve just to the right of that point (If the curves touch one another at any point, the equilibrium corresponding to it will be stable for displacements in one direction, and unstable for displacements in the other No practical interest attaches to the investigation of this barely possible case)

We have seen that the demand curve is inclined throughout negatively. From this it follows that if just to the right of any point of intersection the supply curve lies above the demand curve, then if we move along the supply curve to the right we must necessarily keep above the demand curve till the next point of intersection is reached that is to say, the point of equilibrium next on the right-hand side of a point of stable equilibrium, must be a point of unstable equilibrium, and, it may be proved in like manner, that so must the adjacent point of intersection on the left-hand side In other words, in cases in which the curves cut each other more than once points of stable and unstable equilibrium alternate.

Also the last point of intersection reached as we move to the right must be a point of stable equilibrium For if the amount produced were increased indefinitely the price at which it could be sold would necessarily fall almost to zero;

The pure theory in its earlier stages diverges but little from actual facts, but if pushed far its practical value rapidly diminishes.

§ 4. It must be admitted however that the theory of stable equilibrium of normal demand and supply in its most abstract form assumes a certain rigidity in the conditions of demand and supply, which does not really exist. It helps indeed to give definiteness to our ideas, and in its elementary stages it does not diverge from the actual facts of life so far as to prevent its giving a fairly trustworthy picture of the chief methods of action of the strongest and most persistent group of economic forces But when pushed to its more remote and intricate logical consequences, especially those connected with multiple positions of equilibrium, it slips away from the conditions of real life, and soon ceases to be of much service in dealing with practical problems. One cause of this divergence is the fact that, if the normal production of a commodity increases and afterwards again diminishes to its old amount, the demand price and the supply price are not likely to return, as the pure theory assumes that they will, to their old positions for that amount

The assumption that the list of demand prices is rigid.

We have already noticed[1] that the increase in consumption arising from a fall in price is of gradual, and sometimes even of slow growth. and now we have to lay stress on the fact that habits which have once grown up around the use of a commodity while its price is low, are not quickly abandoned when its price rises again. If therefore after the supply has gradually increased, some of the sources from which it is derived should be closed, or any other cause should occur to make the commodity scarce, many consumers will be reluctant to depart from their wonted ways For instance, the prices of cotton during the American war showed that the

but the price required to cover the expense of producing it would not so fall. Therefore, if the supply curve be produced sufficiently far towards the right, it must at last lie above the demand curve

The first point of intersection arrived at as we proceed from left to right may be a point either of stable or of unstable equilibrium If it be a point of unstable equilibrium, this fact will indicate that the production of the commodity in question on a small scale will not remunerate the producers, so that its production cannot be commenced at all unless some passing accident has caused temporarily an urgent demand for the commodity, or has temporarily lowered the expenses of producing it, or unless some enterprising firm is prepared to sink a large capital in overcoming the initial difficulties of the production, and bringing out the commodity at a price which will ensure large sales

[1] Book III Ch IV. § 6

BOOK V. CH XI

consumers were bidding for the reduced supply a price higher than that for which an equal amount could have been sold, if its previous low price had not brought it into common use to meet a great variety of wants, many of which indeed it had itself created Thus then the list of demand prices which holds for the forward movement of the production of a commodity will seldom hold for the return movement, but will in general require to be raised[1].

The assumption that the list of supply prices is rigid

Again, the list of supply prices may have fairly represented the actual fall in the supply price of the thing which takes place when the supply is being increased; but if the demand should fall off, or if for any other reason, the supply should have to be diminished, the supply price would not move back by the course by which it had come, but would take a lower course. The list of supply prices which had held for the forward movement would not hold for the backward movement, but would have to be replaced by a lower schedule. This is true whether the production of the commodity obeys the law of diminishing or increasing return; but it is of special importance in the latter case, because the fact that the production does obey this law, proves that its increase leads to great improvements in organization.

For, when any casual disturbance has caused a great increase in the production of any commodity, and thereby has led to the introduction of extensive economies, these economies are not readily lost. Developments of mechanical appliances, of division of labour and of the means of transport, and improved organization of all kinds, when they have been once obtained are not readily abandoned. Capital and labour, when they have once been devoted to any particular industry, may indeed become depreciated in value, if there is a falling off in the demand for the wares which they produce. but they cannot quickly be converted to other occupations, and their competition will for a time prevent a diminished demand from causing an increased price of the wares[2].

[1] That is, for any backward movement of the amount offered for sale, the left end of the demand curve would probably need to be raised in order to make it represent the new conditions of demand.

[2] For instance, the shape of the supply-curve in Fig 25, implies that if the ware in question were produced on the scale OV annually, the economies intro-

BOOK V CH. XI

A small change in demand or supply often changes much the equilibrium price

Partly for this reason there are not very many cases in which two positions of stable equilibrium would stand out as possible alternatives at one and the same moment, even if all the facts of the market could be ascertained with perfect accuracy. But when the conditions of a branch of manufacture are such that the supply price would fall very rapidly, if there should be any great increase in the scale of production, then a passing disturbance by which the demand for the commodity was increased might cause a very great fall in the stable equilibrium price, a very much larger amount than before being henceforward produced for sale at a very much lower price. This is always possible when, if we could trace the lists of demand and supply prices far ahead, we should find them keeping close together[1]. For if the supply prices for largely increased amounts are but very little above the corresponding demand prices, a moderate increase in demand, or a comparatively slight new invention or other cheapening of production may bring supply and demand prices together and make a new equilibrium Such a change resembles in some respects a movement from one alternative position of stable equilibrium to another, but differs from the latter in that it cannot occur except when there is some change in the conditions of normal demand or normal supply.

The imperfections of a statical treatment of social problems

§ 5. The difficulties that have just been discussed have very deep roots They really arise from the fact that in economics, as in other sciences, we are unable to discuss at once the effects of all the causes at work. We speak of the prices at which certain amounts of a commodity will be normally demanded or supplied, and leave provisionally out of calculation the facts that large changes in the amounts produced or supplied can as a rule only be effected gradually, and that during the time in which they are being effected

duced into its production would be so extensive as to enable it to be sold at a price TV If these economies were once effected the shape of the curve SS' would probably cease to represent accurately the circumstances of supply The expenses of production, for instance, of an amount OU would no longer be much greater proportionately than those of an amount OV Thus in order that the curve might again represent the circumstances of supply it would be necessary to draw it lower down, as the dotted curve in the figure.

[1] That is, when at a good distance to the right of the equilibrium point, the supply curve is but little above the demand curve

BOOK V. CH. XI.

many other changes are sure to take place, by which the general social and economic conditions of the problem will be altered.

are partly inevitable,

This brings us to the second of the difficulties of which mention was made at the beginning of the second Section. And indeed we find here a special application of the broad truth that economic problems are imperfectly presented when they are treated as problems of statical equilibrium, and not of organic growth. For though the former treatment alone can give us definiteness and precision of thought, and is therefore a necessary introduction to a more philosophic treatment of society as an organism; it is yet only an introduction[1].

partly such as the progress of science may diminish

But not all this imperfection lies in the nature of the case, part of it results from the imperfections of our analytical methods, and may conceivably be much diminished in a later age by the gradual improvement of our scientific machinery. We should have made a great advance if we could represent roughly, as a function of time itself, the chief of the changes in those elements which we are not specially considering; that is, in the particular case of lists of demand and supply prices, if we could represent the normal demand price and supply price as functions both of the amount normally produced and of the time at which that amount became normal[2].

A plan for evading some of them is given in the next Chapter

Meanwhile we have to make special provision for all events external to the special changes which we are considering. So long as there is no substantive alteration in the conditions of demand or supply, so long as the only important changes in the price at which purchasers can be found for the commodity, and the price at which producers can afford

[1] See above, Book I Ch VI. § 2

[2] That is to say, instead of normal demand and supply curves we should use demand and supply surfaces, price being measured along the axis of z, time along that of y, and amount along that of x. Even now there might be some interest in working out, analytically or geometrically, the curves of intersection of such surfaces drawn on various assumptions as to the influence of time. And though for many years to come work of this kind must be rather a mathematical diversion, than a solid contribution to economics, yet it may show the way towards such methods of study of social and economic history and statistics, as may enable future generations to impart to such demand and supply surfaces a reality that is altogether beyond our present range

to supply it, are those changes which are due to an increase or diminution in the volume of the amount of the commodity produced and sold, so long we may regard the demand schedule and the supply schedule as representing the broad outlines of normal demand and normal supply. But any great and lasting change in fashion, any substantive new invention, any diminution of population by war or pestilence, or the development or dwindling away of a source of supply of the commodity in question, or of a raw material used in it, or of another commodity which is a rival and possible substitute for it:—any such change as these may cause the prices set against any given annual (or daily) consumption and production of the commodity to cease to be its normal demand and supply prices for that volume of consumption and production, or, in other words, they may render it necessary to make out a new demand schedule or a new supply schedule, or both of them. We proceed to study the problems thus suggested.

CHAPTER XII.

THEORY OF CHANGES OF NORMAL DEMAND AND SUPPLY IN RELATION TO THE DOCTRINE OF MAXIMUM SATISFACTION

BOOK V CH XII

What is meant by an increase of normal demand,

§ 1. WE have seen that an increase of normal demand involves generally an increase in the price at which each several amount can find purchasers: or which is the same thing, at each several price a greater quantity than before can find purchasers, (and this we have called a rising of the list of demand prices, or demand schedule) This increase of normal demand may be caused by the commodity's coming more into fashion, by the opening out of a new use for it or of new markets for it, by the permanent falling off in the supply of some commodity for which it can be used as a substitute, by a permanent increase in the wealth and general purchasing power of the community, and so on. Changes in the opposite direction will cause a falling off in demand and a sinking of the list of demand prices.

or of normal supply.

An increase of normal supply means an increase of the amounts that can be supplied at each several price, and a diminution of the price at which each separate amount can be supplied, (thus an increase of normal supply involves a lowering of the list of supply prices, or supply schedule)[1].

[1] A rise or fall of the demand or supply schedule involves of course a rise or fall of the demand or supply curve

[If the change is gradual, the supply curve will assume in succession a series of positions, each of which is a little below the preceding one, and in this way we might have represented the effects of that gradual improvement of industrial organization which arises from an increase in the scale of production, and which we have represented by assigning to it an influence upon the supply price for long-period curves In an ingenious paper privately printed by Mr H Cunynghame, a suggestion is made, which seems to come in effect to proposing that a long-period supply curve should be regarded as in some manner representing a series of short-period curves, each of these curves would assume throughout its

This change may be caused by the opening up of a new source of supply, whether by improved means of transport or in any other way, by an advance in the arts of production, such as the invention of a new process or of new machinery, or again, by the granting of a bounty on production. Conversely, a diminution of normal supply (or a raising of the supply schedule) may be caused by the closing up of a new source of supply or by the imposition of a tax[1].

The typical case of rapid oscillation is that of the current or market price about its normal (or rather its subnormal) position of equilibrium. But, as has already been explained, the subnormal (or short-period normal) level moves in a similar manner, though more slowly and less conspicuously about a long-period normal level. The longer the periods to which our reasonings apply, and for which our normal lists of demand and supply prices are taken, the fewer will be the disturbing causes which are so great and lasting, as to amount to a distinct change in the general conditions of demand and supply, and to necessitate the making out of a new list of demand prices, or of supply prices, or both. And therefore in the great majority of cases to which the reasonings of this chapter are applicable, the supply price will increase with the amount produced. But the exceptions to this rule, though not numerous, are important.

Effects of an increase of normal demand

§ 2. We have, then, to regard the effects of an increase of normal demand from three points of view, according as the commodity in question obeys the law of constant or of diminishing or of increasing return: that is, its supply price is practically constant for all amounts, or increases or diminishes with an increase in the amount produced

whole length that development of industrial organization which properly belongs to the scale of production represented by the distance from Oy of the point in which that curve cuts the long-period supply curve (compare the end of the note on p 503) and similarly with regard to demand]

[1] The theory of the incidence of taxation has been generally treated as a branch of the application of economic science to the practical Art of Government But really it is an integral part of the general theory of value; and there is a gain of scientific completeness in regarding in the first instance a tax on a thing simply as one of many causes which may raise its normal supply price It will be best not to trace in detail the incidence of particular taxes until we come to discuss taxation as a whole but meanwhile a tax may be taken as a representative instance of the changes which may affect supply price.

BOOK V CH XII.

In the first case an increase of demand simply increases the amount produced without altering its price; for the normal price of a commodity which obeys the law of constant return is determined absolutely by its expenses of production: demand has no influence in the matter beyond this, that the thing will not be produced at all unless there is some demand for it at this fixed price

If the commodity obeys the law of diminishing return an increase of demand for it raises its price and causes more of it to be produced, but not so much more as it would, if it obeyed the law of constant return

On the other hand, if the commodity obeys the law of increasing return an increase of demand causes much more of it to be produced,—more than if the commodity obeyed the law of constant return,—and at the same time lowers its price. If, for instance, a thousand things of a certain kind have been produced and sold weekly at a price of 10*s*, while the supply price for two thousand weekly would be only 9*s*, a very small increase in normal demand may cause this to become the normal price, since we are considering periods long enough for the full normal action of the causes that determine supply to work itself out[1] The converse

[1] Diagrams are of especial aid in enabling us to comprehend clearly the problems of this chapter.

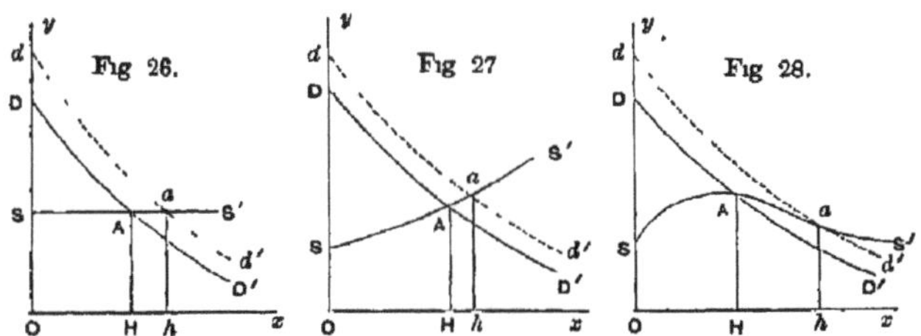

The three figures 26, 27, 28 represent the three cases of constant, diminishing and increasing return respectively. The return in the last case is a diminishing one in the earlier stages of the increase of production, but an increasing one in those subsequent to the attainment of the original position of equilibrium, i e for amounts of the commodity greater than OH. In each case SS' is the supply curve, DD' the old position of the demand curve, and dd' its position after there has been increase of normal demand In each case A and a are the old and new positions of equilibrium respectively, AH and ah are the old and new normal or equilibrium prices, and OH and Oh the old and new equilibrium amounts Oh is in every case

holds in each case should normal demand fall off instead of increasing

Effects of increased facilities of supply

§ 3. We have seen that an increase in normal demand, while leading in every case to an increased production, will in some cases raise and in others lower prices. But now we are to see that increased facilities for supply (causing the supply schedule to be lowered) will always lower the normal price at the same time that it leads to an increase in the amount produced. For so long as the normal demand remains unchanged an increased supply can be sold only at a diminished price, but the fall of price consequent on a given cheapening of supply will be much greater in some cases than in others. It will be small if the commodity obeys the law of diminishing return; because then the difficulties attendant on an increased production will tend to counteract the new facilities of supply. On the other hand, if the commodity obeys the law of increasing return, the

greater than OH, but in fig 27 it is only a little greater, while in fig 28 it is much greater (This analysis may be carried further on the plan adopted later on in discussing the similar but more important problem of the effects of changes in the conditions of normal supply) In fig 26 ah is equal to AH, in fig 27 it is greater, in fig. 28 it is less

The effect of a falling-off of normal demand can be traced with the same diagrams, dd' being now regarded as the old and DD' as the new position of this demand curve, ah being the old equilibrium price, and AH the new one

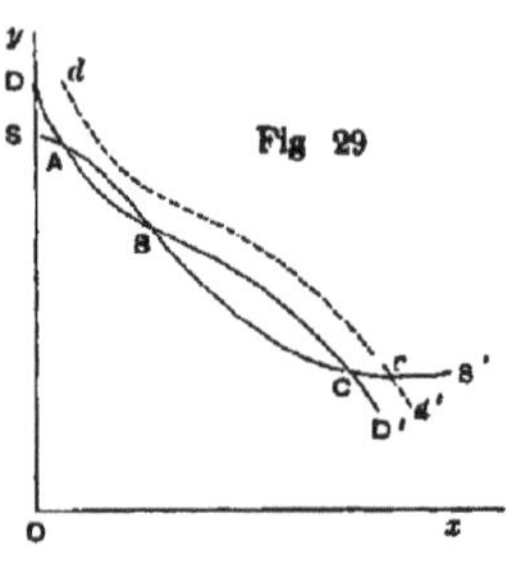

[It is interesting to trace the effect of changes of this kind when the curves cut one another several times, as in A, B and C in fig 29 Suppose the demand curve to rise gradually, then the points of intersection corresponding to A and B will approach one another, until they coalesce. Thus whether price when in equilibrium was actually at A or at C originally (it could not have been at B, because the equilibrium there is unstable) it will by a sufficient rise of demand move away to c

If the supply curve to the right of A had kept above the original demand curve, but only a little above it, so as to have only one point of intersection with it, its point of intersection with the new, and slightly raised demand curve might have been a long way to the right of A; thus representing a simpler instance of the way in which a small increase in the normal demand for a commodity that obeys the law of increasing return may cause a very great fall in its price and a very great increase of its consumption.]

BOOK V. CH. XII.

increased production will bring with it increased facilities, which will co-operate with those arising from the change in the general conditions of supply; and the two together will enable a great increase in production and consequent fall in price to be attained before the fall of the supply price overtakes the fall of the demand price. If it happens that the demand is very elastic, then a small increase in the facilities of normal supply, such as a new invention, a new application of machinery, the opening up of new and cheaper sources of supply, the taking off a tax or granting a bounty, may cause an enormous increase of production and fall of price[1].

[1] All this can be most clearly seen by the aid of diagrams, and indeed there are some parts of the problem which cannot be satisfactorily treated without their aid. The three figures 30, 31, 32 represent the three cases of constant and diminishing and increasing returns, respectively In each case DD' is the demand curve, SS' the old position, and ss' the new position of the supply curve A is the old, and a the new position of stable equilibrium Oh is greater than OH, and ah is less than AH in every case but the changes are small in fig 31 and great in fig 32 Of course the demand curve must be below the old supply curve to the right of A, otherwise A would be a point not of stable, but of unstable equilibrium

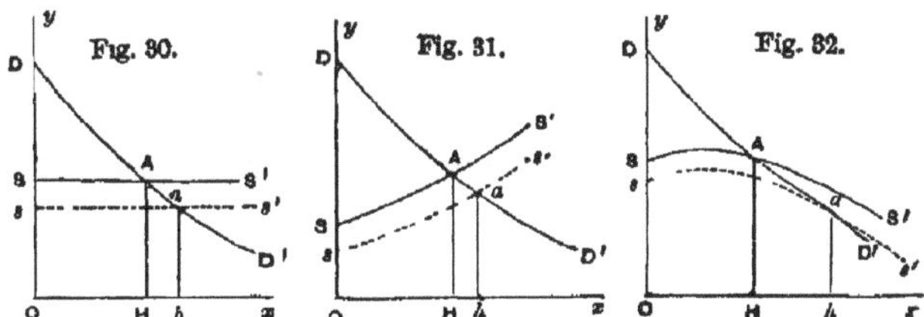

But subject to this condition the more elastic the demand is, that is, the more nearly horizontal the demand curve is at A the further off will a be from A, and the greater therefore will be the increase of production and the fall of price.

The whole result is rather complex. But it may be stated thus Firstly, given the elasticity of demand at A, the increase in the quantity produced and the fall in price will both be the greater, the greater be the return got from additional capital and labour applied to the production That is, they will be the greater, the more nearly horizontal the supply curve is at A in fig 31, and the more steeply inclined it is in fig 32 (subject to the condition mentioned above, that it does not lie below the demand curve to the right of A, and thus turn A into a position of unstable equilibrium). Secondly, given the position of the supply curve at A, the greater the elasticity of demand the greater will be the increase of production in every case, but the smaller will be the fall of price in fig. 31, and the greater the fall of price in fig 32 Fig 30 may be regarded as a limiting case of either fig 31 or 32

All this reasoning assumes that the commodity either obeys the law of diminishing return or obeys the law of increasing return throughout If it

If we take account of the circumstances of composite and joint supply and demand discussed in Chapter VI., we have suggested to us an almost endless variety of problems which can be worked out by the methods adopted in these two chapters.

Changes that raise or lower the supply schedule may be represented by a tax or bounty

§ 4. We may now consider the effects which a change in the conditions of supply may exert on consumers' surplus or rent. For brevity of language a tax may be taken as representative of those changes which may cause a general increase, and a bounty as representative of those which may cause a general diminution in the normal supply price for each several amount of the commodity.

The case of constant return

Firstly, if the commodity is one, the production of which obeys the law of constant return, so that the supply price is the same for all amounts of the commodity, consumers' rent will be diminished by more than the increased payments to the producer; and therefore, in the special case of a tax, by more than the gross receipts of the State. For in so far as the consumption of the commodity is maintained, the consumer loses what the State receives: and on that part of the consumption which is destroyed by the rise in price, the consumers' rent is destroyed; and of course there is no payment for it to the producer or to the State[1].

obeys first one, and then the other, so that the supply curve is at one part inclined positively and at another negatively, no general rule can be laid down as to the effect on price of increased facilities of supply, though in every case this must lead to an increased volume of production A great variety of curious results may be got by giving the supply curve different shapes, and in particular such as cut the demand curve more than once

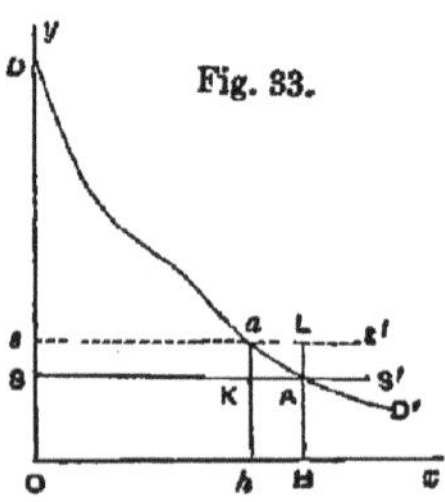

[1] This is most clearly seen by aid of a diagram SS', the old constant return supply curve cuts DD' the demand curve in A DSA is the consumers' rent Afterwards a tax Ss being imposed the new equilibrium is found at a, and consumers' rent is Dsa The gross tax is only the rectangle $sSKa$, that is, a tax at the rate of Ss on an amount sa of the commodity And this falls short of the loss of consumers' rent by the area aKA The net loss aKA is small or great, other things being equal, as aA is or is not inclined steeply Thus it is smallest for those commodities the demand for which is most inelastic, that is, for necessaries If therefore a given aggregate taxation has to be levied ruthlessly from any class it will cause less loss of consumers' rent if levied on necessaries than if levied on comforts.

BOOK V. CH. XII.

Conversely, the gain of consumers' rent caused by a bounty on a commodity that obeys the law of constant return, is less than the bounty itself. For on that part of the consumption which existed before the bounty, consumers' rent is increased by just the amount of the bounty, while on the new consumption that is caused by the bounty, the gain of the consumers' rent is less than the bounty[1]

The case of diminishing return

If however the commodity obey the law of diminishing return, a tax by raising its price, and diminishing its consumption, will lower its expenses of production other than the tax: and the result will be to raise the supply price by something less than the full amount of the tax. In this case the gross receipts from the tax *may* be greater than the resulting loss of consumers' rent, and they *will* be greater if the law of diminishing return acts so sharply that a small diminution of consumption causes a great falling-off in the expenses of production other than the tax[2].

On the other hand, a bounty on a commodity which obeys the law of diminishing return will lead to increased production, and will extend the margin of cultivation to places and conditions in which the expenses of production, exclusive of the bounty, are greater than before. Thus it will lower the price to the consumer and increase

[1] If we now regard ss' as the old supply curve which is lowered to the position SS' by the granting of a bounty, we find the gain of consumers' rent to be $sSAa$. But the bounty paid is Ss on an amount SA, which is represented by the rectangle $sSAL$ and this exceeds the gain of consumers' rent by the area aLA

[2] Let the old supply curve be SS' fig 34, and let the imposition of a tax raise it to ss', let A and a be the old and new positions of equilibrium, and let straight lines be drawn through them parallel to Ox and Oy, as in the figure. Then the tax being levied, as shown by the figure, at the rate of aE on each unit, and Oh, that is, CK units, being produced in the new position of equilibrium, the gross receipts of the tax will be $cFEa$, and the loss of consumers' rent will be $cCAa$; that is, the gross receipts from the tax will be greater or less than the loss of consumers' rent as $CFEK$ is greater or less than aKA, and in the figure as it stands it is much greater If however we had drawn SS' to indicate only very slight action of the law of diminishing return, that is, if it had been nearly horizontal in the neighbourhood of A, then EK would have been very small; and $CFEK$ would have become less than aKA.

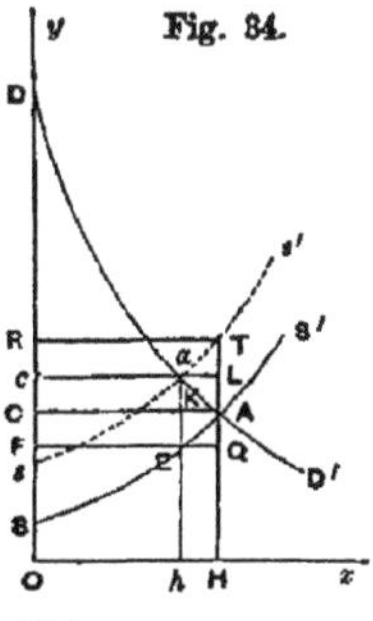

consumers' rent less than if it were given for the production of a commodity which obeyed the law of constant return In that case the increase of consumers' rent was seen to be less than the direct cost of the bounty to the State, and therefore in this case it is much less[1].

The case of increasing return.

By similar reasoning it may be shown that a tax on a commodity which obeys the law of increasing return is more injurious to the consumer than if levied on one which obeys the law of constant return; because it diminishes consumers' rent by much more than the total payments which it brings in[2] On the other hand, a bounty on such a commodity causes so great a fall in its price to the consumer, that the consequent increase of consumers' rent may exceed the total payments made by the State to the producers; and certainly will do so in case the law of increasing return acts at all sharply[3]

[1] To illustrate this case we may take ss' in fig 34 to be the position of the supply curve before the granting of the bounty, and SS' to be its position afterwards Thus a was the old equilibrium point, and A is the point to which the equilibrium moves when the bounty is awarded The increase of consumers' rent is only $cCAa$, while the payments made by the State under the bounty are, as shown by the figure, at the rate of AT on each unit of the commodity, and as in the new position of equilibrium there are produced OH, that is, CA units, they amount altogether to $RCAT$ which includes and is necessarily greater than the increase of consumers' rent

[2] Thus taking SS' in fig. 35 to be the old position of the supply curve, and ss' its position after the tax, A to be the old and a the new positions of equilibrium, we have, as in the case of fig 34, the total tax represented by $cFEa$, and the loss of consumers' rent by $cCAa$; the former being always less than the latter

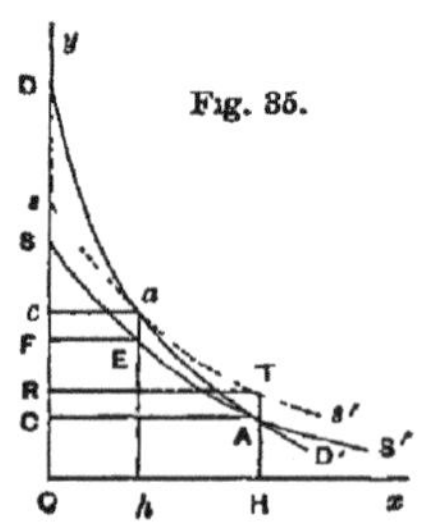

Fig. 35.

[3] To illustrate this case we may take ss' in fig 35 to be the position of the supply curve before the granting of the bounty, and SS' to be its position afterwards Then, as in the case of fig 34, the increase of consumers' rent is represented by $cCAa$, while the direct payments made by the State under the bounty are represented by $RCAT$ As the figure is drawn, the former is much larger than the latter But it is true that if we had drawn ss' so as to indicate a very slight action of the law of increasing return, that is, if it had been very nearly horizontal in the neighbourhood of a, the bounty would have increased relatively to the gain of consumers' rent, and the case would have differed but little from that of a bounty on a commodity which obeys the law of constant return, represented in fig 33

These results throw light on the doctrine of *Maximum Satisfaction*

These results are suggestive of some principles of taxation which will require our careful study hereafter; when we shall take account of the expenses of collecting a tax and of administering a bounty, and of the many indirect effects, some economic and some moral, which a tax or a bounty is likely to produce. But the present form of these results is well adapted for our immediate purpose of examining a little more closely than we have done hitherto the general doctrine that a position of (stable) equilibrium of demand and supply is a position also of *Maximum Satisfaction*. That is a doctrine which needs to be interpreted carefully.

There is a limited sense in which the doctrine is generally true

§ 5. There is indeed one interpretation of the doctrine according to which every position of equilibrium of demand and supply may fairly be regarded as a position of maximum satisfaction[1]. For it is true that so long as the demand price is in excess of the supply price, exchanges can be effected at prices which give a surplus of satisfaction to buyer or to seller or to both. The marginal utility of what he receives is greater than that of what he gives up, to at least one of the two parties; while the other, if he does not gain by the exchange, yet does not lose by it. So far then every step in the exchange increases the aggregate satisfaction of the two parties. But when equilibrium has been reached, demand price being now equal to supply price, there is no room for any such surplus: the marginal utility of what each receives no longer exceeds that of what he gives up in exchange: and when the production increases beyond the equilibrium amount, the demand price being now less than the supply price, no terms can be arranged which will be acceptable to the buyer, and will not involve a loss to the seller.

It is true then that a position of equilibrium of demand and supply is a position of maximum satisfaction in this limited sense, that the aggregate satisfaction of the two parties concerned increases until that position is reached, and that any production beyond the equilibrium amount could not be permanently maintained so long as buyers and sellers acted freely as individuals, each in his own interest.

[1] Unstable equilibrium may now be left out of account.

But when not taken in this limited sense, the doctrine is open to great exceptions

But occasionally it is stated, and very often it is implied, that a position of equilibrium of demand and supply is one of maximum aggregate satisfaction in the full sense of the term that is, that an increase of production beyond the equilibrium level would directly (*i e.* independently of the difficulties of arranging for it, and of any indirect evils it might cause) diminish the aggregate satisfaction of both parties. The doctrine so interpreted is not universally true

It assumes that equal sums of money measure equal utilities to all concerned,

In the first place it assumes that all differences in wealth between the different parties concerned may be neglected, and that the satisfaction which is rated at a shilling by any one of them, may be taken as equal to one that is rated at a shilling by any other Now it is obvious that, if the producers were as a class very much poorer than the consumers, the aggregate satisfaction might be increased by a stinting of supply when it would cause a great rise in demand price (*i e* when the demand is inelastic); and that if the consumers were as a class much poorer than the producers, the aggregate satisfaction might be increased by extending the production beyond the equilibrium amount and selling the commodity at a loss. This point however may well be left for future consideration. It is in fact only a special case of the broad proposition that the aggregate satisfaction can *primâ facie* be increased by the distribution, whether voluntarily or compulsorily, of some of the property of the rich among the poor; and it is reasonable that the bearings of this proposition should be set aside during the first stages of an inquiry into existing economic conditions This assumption therefore may be properly made, provided only it is not allowed to slip out of sight.

and it ignores the fact that a fall in price due to improvements benefits consumers without injuring producers

But in the second place the doctrine of maximum satisfaction assumes that every fall in the price which producers receive for the commodity, involves a corresponding loss to them, and this is not true of a fall in price which results from improvements in industrial organization. When a commodity obeys the law of increasing return, an increase in its production beyond equilibrium point may cause the supply price to fall much; and though the demand price for the

BOOK V. CH. XII.

increased amount may be reduced even more, so that the production would result in some loss to the producers, yet this loss may be very much less than that money value of the gain to purchasers which is represented by the increase of consumers' rent.

Aggregate satisfaction can therefore *primâ facie* be increased beyond the level attained by the free play of demand and supply

In the case then of commodities with regard to which the law of increasing return acts at all sharply, or in other words, for which the normal supply price diminishes rapidly as the amount produced increases, the direct expense of a bounty sufficient to call forth a greatly increased supply at a much lower price, would be much less than the consequent increase of consumers' rent. And if a general agreement could be obtained among consumers, terms might be arranged which would make such action amply remunerative to the producers, at the same time that they left a large balance of advantage to the consumers[1].

We are not here concerned with the indirect evils of artificial arrangements for this purpose

§ 6. One simple plan would be the levying of a tax by the community on their own incomes, or on the production of goods which obey the law of diminishing return, and devoting the tax to a bounty on the production of those goods with regard to which the law of increasing return acts sharply. But before deciding on such a course they would have to take account of considerations, which are not within the scope of the general theory now before us, but are yet of great practical importance. They would have to reckon up the direct and indirect costs of collecting a tax and administering a bounty; the difficulty of securing that the burdens of the tax and the benefits of the bounty were equitably distributed; the openings for fraud and corruption; and the danger that in the trade which had got a bounty and in other trades which hoped to get one, people would divert their

[1] Though not of great practical importance, the case of multiple positions of (stable) equilibrium offers a good illustration of the error involved in the doctrine of maximum satisfaction when stated as a universal truth For the position in which a small amount is produced and is sold at a high price would be the first to be reached, and when reached would be regarded according to that doctrine as that which gave the absolute maximum of aggregate satisfaction. But another position of equilibrium corresponding to a larger production and a lower price would be equally satisfactory to the producers, and would be much more satisfactory to the consumers, the excess of consumers' rent in the second case over the first would represent the increase in aggregate satisfaction.

energies from managing their own businesses to managing those persons who control the bounties.

BOOK V. CH XII.

Besides these semi-ethical questions there will arise others of a strictly economic nature, relating to the effects which any particular tax or bounty may exert on the interests of landlords, urban or agricultural, who own land adapted for the production of the commodity in question. These are questions which must not be overlooked, but they differ so much in their detail that they cannot fitly be discussed here[1].

[1] The incidence of a tax on agricultural produce will be discussed later on by the aid of diagrams similar to those used to represent the fertility of land (Book IV Ch III). Landlords' rent absorbs a share of the aggregate selling price of almost all commodities: but it is most prominent in the case of those which obey the law of diminishing return, and an assumption of no extreme violence will enable fig 34 on p 524 to represent roughly the leading features of the problem

We have already seen (Note on p 503) that we are not properly at liberty to assume that the expenses of raising the produce from the richer lands and under the more favourable circumstances are independent of the extent to which the production is carried, since an increased production is likely to lead to an improved organization, if not of farming industries themselves, yet of those subsidiary to them, and especially of the carrying trade We may however permit ourselves to make this assumption provisionally, so as to get a clear view of the broad outlines of the problem, though we must not forget that in any applications of the general reasonings based on it account must be taken of the facts which we here ignore On this assumption then SS' being the supply curve before the imposition of a tax, landlords' rent is represented by CSA After the tax has been imposed and the supply curve raised to ss' the landlords' rent becomes the amount by which $cOha$, the total price got for Oh produce sold at the rate ha, exceeds the total tax $cFEa$, together with $OhES$ the total expenses of production, exclusive of rent, for Oh produce that is, it becomes FSE (In the figure the curve ss' has the same shape as SS', thereby implying that the tax is *specific*, that is, is a uniform charge on each unit of the commodity whatever be its value. The argument so far does not depend on this assumption, but if it is made we can by a shorter route get the new landlords' rent at csa, which then is equal to FSE) Thus the loss of landlords' rent is $CFEA$, and this added to $cCAa$ the loss of consumers' rent, makes up $cFEAa$, which exceeds the gross tax by aAE

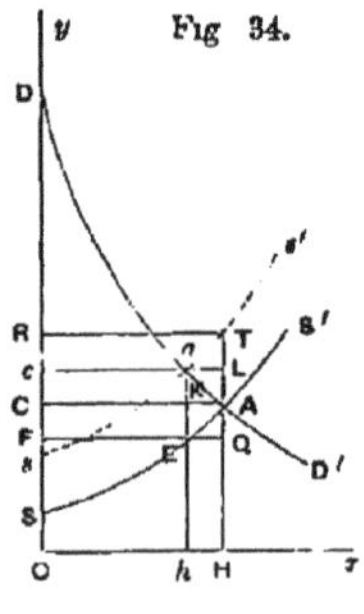

On the other hand, the direct payments under a bounty would exceed the increase of consumers' rent, and of landlords' rent calculated on the above assumptions For taking ss' to be the original position of the supply curve, and SS' to be its position after the bounty, the new landlords' rent on these assumptions is CSA, or which is the same thing RsT, and this exceeds the old landlords' rent csa by $RcaT$ The increase of consumers' rent is $cCAa$; and therefore the

BOOK V CH XII

Restatement of *primâ facie* exceptions to the doctrine of *Economic Harmony* that it is best for all that each should spend his income as he pleases

§ 7. Enough has been said to indicate the character of the second great limitation which has to be introduced into the doctrine of *Economic Harmony*, which asserts truly that the Maximum Satisfaction is *generally* to be attained by encouraging each individual to spend his own resources in that way which suits him best We have already noticed that if he spends his income in such a way as to increase the demand for the services of the poor and to increase their incomes, he adds something more to the total happiness than if he adds an equal amount to the incomes of the rich, because the happiness which an additional shilling brings to a poor man is much greater than that which it brings to a rich one; and that he does good by buying things the production of which raises, in preference to things the production of which lowers the character of those who make them. But further, even if we assume that a shilling's worth of happiness is of equal importance to whomsoever it comes, and that every shilling's worth of consumer's rent is of equal importance from whatever commodity it is derived, we have to admit that the manner in which a person spends his income is a matter of direct economic concern to the community. For in so far as he spends it on things which obey the law of diminishing return, he makes those things more difficult to be obtained by his neighbours, and thus lowers the real purchasing power of their incomes; while in so far as he spends it on things which obey the law of increasing return, he makes those things more easy of attainment to others, and thus increases the real purchasing power of their incomes

Again, it is commonly argued that an equal *ad valorem* tax levied on all economic commodities (material and immaterial), or which is the same thing a tax on expenditure, is *primâ facie* the best tax; because it does not divert the expenditure of individuals out of its natural channels: we have now seen that this argument is invalid. But ignoring

total bounty, which is $RCAT$, exceeds the gain of consumers' rent and landlords' rent together by TaA

For reasons stated in the Note on pp. 503—4, the assumption on which this reasoning proceeds is inapplicable to cases in which the supply curve is inclined negatively

for the time the fact that the direct economic effect of a tax or a bounty never constitutes the whole, and very often not even the chief part of the considerations which have to be weighed before deciding to adopt it, we have found:—firstly, that a tax on expenditure generally causes a greater destruction of consumers' rent than one levied exclusively on commodities as to which there is but little room for the economies of production on a large scale, and which obey the law of diminishing return, and secondly, that it might even be for the advantage of the community that the Government should levy taxes on commodities which obey the law of diminishing return, and devote part of the proceeds to bounties on commodities which obey the law of increasing return.

These conclusions, it will be observed, do not by themselves afford a valid ground for Government interference, for the indirect evils of that are likely to outweigh any direct good that it may do. But they show that much remains to be done, by a careful collection of the statistics of demand and supply, and a scientific interpretation of their results, in order to discover what are the limits of the work that society can with advantage do towards turning the economic actions of individuals into those channels in which they will add the most to the sum total of happiness[1].

[1] It is remarkable that Malthus, *Political Economy*, Ch. III § 9, argued that, though the difficulties thrown in the way of importing foreign corn during the great war turned capital from the more profitable employment of manufacture to the less profitable employment of agriculture, yet if we take account of the consequent increase of agricultural rent, we may conclude that the new channel may have been one of "higher national, though not higher individual profits." In this no doubt he was right, but he overlooked the far more important injury inflicted on the public by the consequent rise in the price of corn, and the consequent destruction of consumers' rent. Senior takes account of the interests of the consumer in his study of the different effects of increased demand on the one hand and of taxation on the other in the case of agricultural and manufactured produce (*Political Economy*, pp 118—123) Advocates of Protection in countries which export raw produce have made use of arguments tending in the same direction as those given in this Chapter; and similar arguments are now used, especially in America (as for instance by Mr H C. Adams), in support of the active participation of the State in industries which conform to the law of increasing return The graphic method has been applied, in a manner somewhat similar to that adopted in the present Chapter, by Dupuit in 1844, and, independently, by Fleeming Jenkin (*Edinburgh Philosophical Transactions*) in 1871

CHAPTER XIII.

THE THEORY OF MONOPOLIES.

BOOK V CH XIII

We are now to compare the monopolist's gains from a high price with the benefits to the public of a low price

§ 1. THE doctrine of Maximum Satisfaction has never been applied to the demand for a supply of monopolized commodities. It has never been supposed that the monopolist in seeking his own advantage is naturally guided in that course which is most conducive to the wellbeing of society regarded as a whole, he himself being reckoned as of no more importance than any other member of it. But there is much to be learnt from a study of the relations in which his interests stand to those of the rest of society, and of the general conditions under which it might be possible to make arrangements more beneficial to society as a whole than those which he would adopt if he consulted only his own interests and with this end in view we are now to seek for a scheme for comparing the relative quantities of the benefits which may accrue to the public and to the monopolist from the adoption of different courses of action by him.

At a later stage we shall have to study the Protean shapes of modern trade combinations and monopolies, some of the most important of which, as for example "Trusts," are of very recent growth At present we have to consider only those general causes determining monopoly values, that can be traced with more or less distinctness in every case in which a single person or association of persons has the power of fixing either the amount of a commodity that is offered for sale or the price at which it is offered.

Net *Monopoly Revenue*

§ 2. The *primâ facie* interest of the owner of a monopoly is clearly to adjust the supply to the demand, not in such a way that the price at which he can sell his commodity shall just cover its expenses of production, but in such a way as to afford him the greatest possible total net revenue.

But here we meet with a difficulty as to the meaning of the term Net revenue. For the supply price of a freely-produced commodity includes normal profits, the whole of which, or at all events what remains of them after deducting interest on the capital employed and insurance against loss, is often classed indiscriminately as net revenue. And when a man manages his own business, he often does not distinguish carefully that portion of his profits, which really is his own earnings of management, from any exceptional gains arising from the fact that the business is to some extent of the nature of a monopoly

This difficulty however is in a great measure avoided in the case of a public company, where all, or nearly all, the expenses of management are entered in the ledger as definite sums, and are subtracted from the total receipts of the company before its net income is declared.

The net income divided among the shareholders includes interest on the capital invested and insurance against risk of failure, but little or no earnings of management, so that the amount by which the dividends are in excess of what may fairly be allowed as interest and insurance, is the *Monopoly Revenue* which we are seeking.

Since then it is much easier to specify exactly the amount of this net revenue when a monopoly is owned by a public company than when it is owned by an individual or private firm, let us take as a typical instance the case of a gas company that has the monopoly of the supply of gas to a town. For the sake of simplicity the company may be supposed to have already invested the whole of its own capital in fixed plant, and to borrow any more capital, that it may want to extend its business, on debentures at a fixed rate of interest.

The demand schedule is as usual,

§ 3. The demand schedule for gas remains the same as it would be if gas were a freely-produced commodity, it specifies the price per thousand feet at which consumers in the town will among them use any given number of

BOOK V CH. XIII

but the supply schedule must be drawn on a special plan

feet But the supply schedule must represent the normal expenses of production of each several amount supplied, and these include interest on all its capital, whether belonging to its shareholders or borrowed on debentures, at a fixed normal rate; they include also the salaries of its directors, and permanent officials adjusted (more or less accurately) to the work required of them, and therefore increasing with an increase in the output of gas A *Monopoly Revenue Schedule* may then be constructed thus:—Having set against each several amount of the commodity its demand price, and its supply price estimated on the plan just described, subtract each supply price from the corresponding demand price and set the residue in the monopoly revenue column against the corresponding amount of the commodity.

The *Monopoly Revenue Schedule*

Thus for instance if a thousand million feet could be sold annually at a price of 3*s*. per thousand feet, and the supply price for this amount were 2*s* 9*d*. per thousand feet, the monopoly revenue schedule would show 3*d*. against this amount indicating an aggregate net revenue when this amount was sold, of three million pence, or £12,500. The aim of the company having regard only to their own immediate dividends will be to fix the price of their gas at such a level as to make this aggregate net revenue the largest possible[1].

[1] Thus DD' being the demand curve, and SS' the curve corresponding to the supply schedule described in the text, let MP_2P_1 be drawn vertically from any point M in Ox, cutting SS' in P_2 and DD' in P_1, and from it cut off $MP_3 = P_2P_1$, then the locus of P_3 will be our third curve, QQ', which we may call the *monopoly revenue curve* The supply price for a small quantity of gas will of course be very high; and in the neighbourhood of Oy the supply curve will be above the demand curve, and therefore the net revenue curve will be below Ox It will cut Ox in K and again in H, points which are vertically under B and A, the two points of intersection of the demand and supply curves The maximum monopoly revenue will then be obtained by finding a point q_3 on QQ' such that Lq_3 being drawn perpendicular to Ox, $OL \times Lq_3$ is a maximum Lq_3 being produced to cut SS' in q_2 and DD' in q_1, the company, if desiring to obtain the greatest immediate monopoly revenue, will fix the price per thousand feet at Lq_1, and consequently will sell OL thousand feet, the expenses of production will be Lq_2 per thousand feet, and the aggregate net revenue will be $OL \times q_2q_1$, or which is the same thing $OL \times Lq_3$

The dotted lines in the diagram are known to mathematicians as rectangular hyperbolas; but we may call them *constant revenue curves* for they are such that if from a point on any one of them lines be drawn perpendicular to Ox

§ 4. Now suppose that a change takes place in the conditions of supply; some new expense has to be incurred, or some old expense can be avoided, or perhaps a new tax is imposed on the undertaking or a bounty is awarded to it

A tax, fixed in total amount, on a monopoly, will not diminish

First let this increase or diminution of the expenses be a fixed sum, bearing on the undertaking as one undivided whole and not varying with the amount of the commodity produced. Then, whatever be the price charged and the

and Oy respectively (the one representing revenue per thousand feet and the other representing the number of thousand feet sold), then the product of these

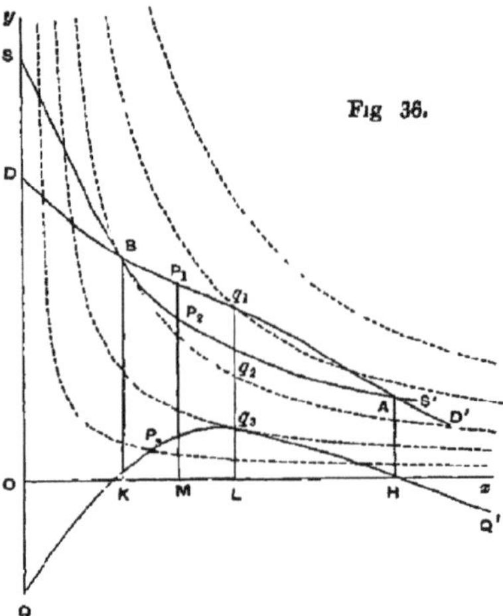

Fig 36.

will be a constant quantity for every point on one and the same curve This product is of course a smaller quantity for the inner curves, those nearer Ox and Oy, than it is for the outer curves And consequently since P_3 is on a smaller constant revenue curve than q_3 is, $OM \times MP_3$ is less than $OL \times Lq_3$. It will be noticed that q_3 is the point in which QQ' touches one of these curves That is, q_3 is on a larger constant revenue curve than is any other point on QQ', and therefore $OL \times Lq_3$ is greater than $OM \times MP_3$, not only in the position given to M in the figure, but also in any position that M can take along Ox That is to say, q_3 has been correctly determined as the point on QQ' corresponding to the maximum total monopoly revenue And thus we get the rule — If through that point in which QQ' touches one of a series of constant revenue curves, a line be drawn vertically to cut the demand curve, then the distance of that point of intersection from Ox will be the price at which the commodity should be offered for sale in order that it may afford the maximum monopoly revenue (See Mathematical Note XXII)

BOOK V CH. XIII

production,

amount of the commodity sold, the monopoly revenue will be increased or diminished, as the case may be, by this sum, and therefore that selling price which afforded the maximum monopoly revenue before the change will afford it afterwards; the change therefore will not offer to the monopolist any inducement to alter his course of action. Suppose for instance that the maximum monopoly revenue is got when twelve hundred million cubic feet are sold annually, and that this is done when the price is fixed at 30*d.* per thousand feet: suppose that the expenses of production for this amount are at the rate of 26*d.*, leaving a monopoly revenue at the rate of four pence per thousand feet, that is £20,000 in all. This is its maximum value: if the company fixed the price higher at, say, 31*d.* and sold only eleven hundred million feet, they would perhaps get a monopoly revenue at the rate of 4·2 pence per thousand feet, that is £19,250 in all, while in order to sell thirteen hundred millions they would have to lower their price to, say, 28*d.* and would get a monopoly revenue at the rate of perhaps 3·6*d.* per thousand feet, that is £19,500 in all Thus by fixing the price at 30*d* they get £750 more than by fixing it at 31*d.*, and £500 more than by fixing it at 28*d.* Now let a tax of £10,000 a year be levied on the gas company as a fixed sum independent of the amount they sell. Their monopoly revenue will become £10,000 if they charge 30*d*, £9,250 if they charge 31*d.*, and £9,500 if they charge 28*d.* They will therefore continue to charge 30*d*

nor will one proportioned to monopoly revenue,

The same is true of a tax or a bounty proportioned not to the gross receipts of the undertaking, but to its monopoly revenue. For suppose next that a tax is levied, not of one fixed sum, but a certain percentage, say 50 per cent of the monopoly revenue The company will then retain a monopoly revenue of £10,000 if they charge 30*d*, of £9,625 if they charge 31*d.*, and of £9,750 if they charge 28*d* They will therefore still charge 30*d*[1]

[1] If to the expenses of working a monopoly there be added (by a tax or otherwise) a lump sum independent of the amount produced, the result will be to cause every point on the monopoly revenue curve to move downwards to a point on a constant revenue curve representing a constant revenue smaller

It should however be noticed that if a tax or other new additional expense exceeds the maximum monopoly revenue, it will prevent the monopoly from being worked at all, it will convert the price which had afforded the maximum monopoly revenue into the price which would reduce to a minimum the loss that would result from continuing to work the monopoly: and conversely with regard to a fixed bounty or other fixed diminution of aggregate working expenses.

But it will have that effect if it is proportional to the quantity produced

But a change in the total expenses of working a monopoly, whether due to a tax, a bounty, or any other cause, is more likely than not to vary in the same direction as the amount of the commodity produced: and then it will affect the monopolist's action. A tax proportional to the amount produced causes a greater total loss of monopoly revenue when the amount produced is large than when it is small, and we shall find that it causes the sales which afford the maximum revenue to be somewhat smaller than before, and offers an inducement to the monopolist to raise his price and contract his sales. If before the imposition of the tax, the net revenue was only a little greater than that which would have been afforded by much smaller sales, then the monopolist would gain by reducing his production very greatly, and hence in such cases as this, the change is likely to cause a very great diminution of production and rise of price. The opposite effects will be caused by a change which diminishes the expense of working the monopoly by a sum that varies directly with the amount produced under it.

In the last example, for instance, a tax of 2*d* on each thousand feet sold would have reduced the monopoly revenue to £10,083 if the company charged 31*d* per thousand feet and therefore sold eleven hundred millions; to £10,000 if they charged 30*d*. and therefore sold twelve hundred millions, and to £8,666 if they charged 28*d*. and therefore sold thirteen hundred million feet. Therefore the tax would induce the

by a *fixed amount* than that on which it lies. Therefore the maximum revenue point on the new monopoly revenue curve lies vertically below that on the old: that is, the selling price and the amount produced remain unchanged. As to the effects of a tax proportional to monopoly revenue, see Mathematical Note XXIII.

BOOK V CH XIII.

company to raise the price to something higher than 30*d.*; they would perhaps go to 31*d.*, perhaps somewhat higher; for the figures before us do not show exactly how far it would be their interest to go

On the other hand, if there were a bounty of 2*d.* on the sale of each thousand feet, the monopoly revenue would rise to £28,416 if they charged 31*d*, to £30,000 if they charged 30*d.*, and to £30,333 if they charged 28*d.*: it would therefore cause them to lower the price[1].

[1] In the text it is supposed that the tax or bounty is directly proportional to the sales· but the argument, when closely examined, will be found to involve no further assumption than that the aggregate tax or bounty increases with every increase in that amount the argument does not really require that it should increase in exact proportion to that amount

Much instruction is to be got by drawing diagrams to represent various conditions of demand and of (monopoly) supply, with the resultant shapes of the monopoly revenue curve A careful study of the shapes thus obtained will give more assistance than any elaborate course of reasoning in the endeavour to realize the multiform action of economic forces in relation to monopolies. A tracing may be made on thin paper of the constant revenue curves in one of the diagrams, and this, when laid over a monopoly revenue curve, will indicate at once the point, or points, of maximum revenue For it will be found, not only when the demand and supply curves cut one another more than once, but also when

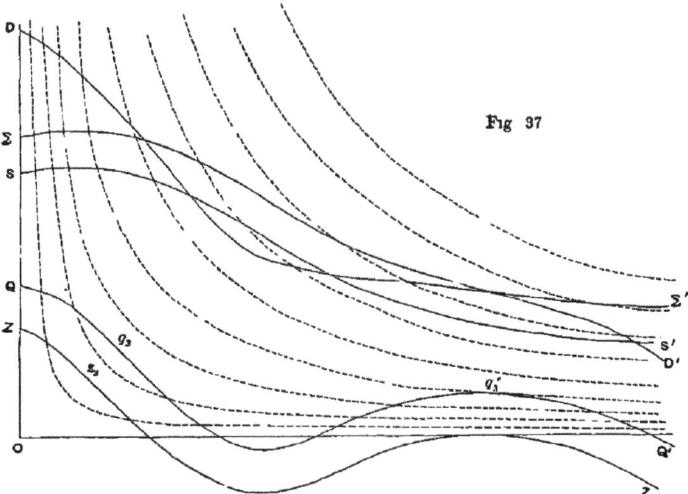

they do not, there will often be, as in fig 37, several points on a monopoly revenue curve at which it touches a constant revenue curve Each of these

In comparing monopoly price with competition price,

§ 5. The monopolist would lose all his monopoly revenue if he produced for sale an amount so great that its supply price, as here defined, was equal to its demand price: the amount which gives the maximum monopoly revenue is always considerably less than that. It may therefore appear as though the amount produced under a monopoly is always less and its price to the consumer always higher than if there were no monopoly. But this is not the case

it must be remembered that a monopoly can generally be worked economically

For when the production is all in the hands of one person or company, the total expenses involved are generally less than would have to be incurred if the same aggregate production were distributed among a multitude of comparatively small rival producers. They would have to struggle with one another for the attention of consumers, and would necessarily spend in the aggregate a great deal more on advertising in all its various forms than a single firm would, and they would be less able to avail themselves of the many various economics which result from production on a large scale In particular they could not afford to spend as much on improving methods of production and the machinery used in it, as a single large firm which knew

points will show a true maximum monopoly revenue; but one of them will generally stand out pre-eminent as being on a larger constant revenue curve than any of the others and therefore indicating a larger monopoly revenue than they

If it happens, as in fig 37, that this chief maximum q'_3 lies a long way to the right of a smaller maximum q_3, then the imposition of a tax on the commodity, or any other change that raised its supply curve throughout, would lower by an equal amount the monopoly revenue curve Let the supply curve be raised from SS' to the position $\Sigma\Sigma'$, and in consequence let the monopoly revenue curve fall from its old position QQ' to ZZ'; then the chief point of maximum revenue will move from q'_3 to z_3, representing a great diminution of production, a great rise of price and a great injury to the consumers The converse effects of any change, such as a bounty on the commodity, which lowers its supply price throughout and raises the monopoly revenue curve, may be seen by regarding ZZ' as the old and QQ' as the new position of that curve It will be obvious on a little consideration (but the fact may with advantage be illustrated by drawing suitable diagrams), that the more nearly the monopoly revenue curve approximates to the shape of a constant revenue curve, the greater will be the change in the position of the maximum revenue point which results from any given alteration in the expenses of production of the commodity generally. This change is great in fig 37 not because DD' and SS' intersect more than once, but because two parts of QQ', one a long way to the right of the other, lie in the neighbourhood of the same constant revenue curve

BOOK V. CH XIII.

that it was certain itself to reap the whole benefit of any advance it made.

This argument does indeed assume the single firm to be managed with ability and enterprise, and to have an unlimited command of capital—an assumption which cannot always be fairly made. But where it can be made, we may generally conclude that the supply schedule for the commodity if not monopolized would show higher supply prices than those of our monopoly supply schedule; and therefore the equilibrium amount of the commodity produced under free competition would be less than that for which the demand price is equal to the monopoly supply price[1].

And the monopolist may lower his price with a view to the future development of his business,

§ 6. So far we have supposed the owner of a monopoly to fix the price of his commodity with exclusive reference to the immediate net revenue which he can derive from it. But, in fact, even if he does not concern himself with the interests of the consumers, he is likely to reflect that the demand for a thing depends in a great measure on people's familiarity with it; and that if he can increase his sales by taking a price a little below that which would afford him the maximum net revenue, the increased use of his commodity will before long recoup him for his present loss The lower the price of gas, the more likely people are to have it laid on to their houses; and when once it is there, they are likely to go on making some use of it, even though a rival, such as mineral oil, may be competing closely with it. The case is stronger when a railway company has a practical monopoly of the transport of persons and goods to a sea-port, or to a suburban district which is as yet but partly built over, the railway company may then find it worth while, as

[1] In other words, though L lies necessarily a good deal to the left of H, according to the notation in fig 36; yet the supply curve for the commodity, if there were no monopoly, might lie so much above the present position of SS' that its point of intersection with DD' would lie much to the left of A in the figure, and might not improbably lie to the left of L Something has already been said (Book IV. Ch XI and XII), as to the advantages which a single powerful firm has over its smaller rivals in those industries in which the law of increasing return acts strongly, and as to the chance which it might have of obtaining a practical monopoly of its own branch of production, if it were managed for many generations together by people whose genius, enterprise and energy equalled those of the original founders of the business

a matter of business, to levy charges much below those which would afford the maximum net revenue, in order to get merchants into the habit of using the port, to encourage the inhabitants of the port to develop their docks and warehouses, or to assist speculative builders in the new suburb to build houses cheaply and to fill them quickly with tenants, thus giving to the suburb an air of early prosperity which goes far towards insuring its permanent success.

In such cases as these a railway company though not pretending to any philanthropic motives, yet finds its own interests so closely connected with those of the purchasers of its services, that it gains by making some temporary sacrifice of net revenue with the purpose of increasing consumers' rent And an even closer connection between the interests of the producers and the consumers is found when the land-owners of any district combine to make a branch railway through it, without much hope that the traffic will afford the market rate of interest on the capital which they invest—that is, without much hope that the monopoly revenue of the railway, as we have defined it, will be other than a negative quantity—but expecting that the railway will add so much to the value of their property as to make their venture on the whole a profitable one And when a municipality undertakes the supply of gas or water, or facilities for transport by improved roads, by new bridges, or by tramways, the question always arises whether the scale of charges should be high, so as to afford a good net revenue and relieve the pressure on the rates; or should be low, so as to increase consumers' rent.

or from a direct interest in the welfare of consumers.

§ 7. It is clear then that some study is wanted of calculations by which a monopolist should govern his actions, should he regard an increase of consumers' rent as equally desirable to him, if not with an equal increase of his own monopoly revenue, yet with an increase, say, one-half or one-quarter as great

If the consumers' rent which arises from the sale of the commodity at any price, is added to the monopoly revenue derived from it, the sum of the two is the money measure of the net benefits accruing from the sale of the commodity to

The *Total Benefit* of a monopoly is the sum of the

BOOK V CH XIII

monopoly revenue and consumers' rent

producers and consumers together, or as we may say the *Total Benefit* of its sale. And if the monopolist regards a gain to the consumers as of equal importance with an equal gain to himself, his aim will be to produce just that amount of the commodity which will make this total benefit a maximum[1].

[1] In fig 38 DD', SS', and QQ' represent the demand, supply, and monopoly revenue curves drawn on the same plan as in fig 36 From P_1 draw P_1F perpendicular to Oy; then DFP_1 is the consumers' rent derived from the sale of OM thousand feet of gas at the price MP_1 In MP_1 take a point P_4 such that $OM \times MP_4 =$ the area DFP_1 then as M moves from O along Ox, P_4 will trace out our fourth curve, OR, which we may call the *Consumers' Rent Curve* (Of course it passes through O, because when the sale of the commodity is reduced to nothing, the consumers' rent also vanishes)

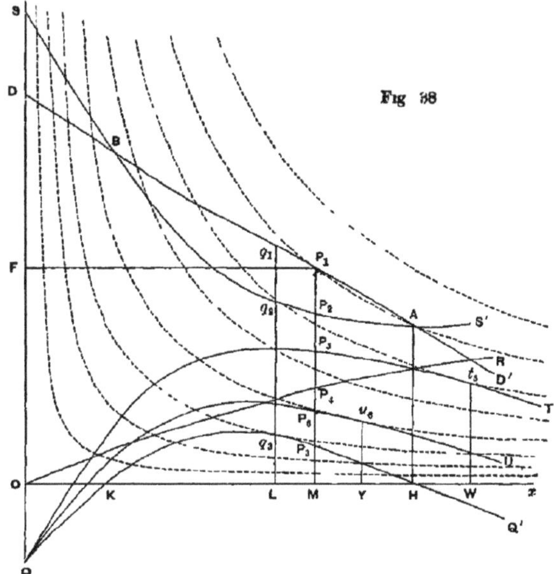

Next from P_3P_1 cut off P_3P_5 equal to MP_4, so that $MP_5 = MP_3 + MP_4$ Then $OM \times MP_5 = OM \times MP_3 + OM \times MP_4$: but $OM \times MP_3$ is the total monopoly revenue when an amount OM is being sold at a price MP_1, and $OM \times MP_4$ is the corresponding consumers' rent Therefore $OM \times MP_5$ is the sum of the monopoly revenue and the consumers' rent, that is the (money measure of the) total benefit which the community will derive from the commodity when an amount OM is produced. The locus of P_5 is our fifth curve, QT, which we may call the *Total Benefit Curve* It touches one of the constant revenue curves at t_5, and this shows

But if the consumers' rent be counted at only a fraction of its actual value, the sum of the two may be called *Compromise Benefit*

But it will seldom happen that the monopolist can and will treat £1 of consumers' rent as equally desirable with £1 of monopoly revenue. Even a Government which considers its own interests coincident with those of the people has to take account of the fact that, if it abandons one source of revenue, it must in general fall back on others which have their own disadvantages. For they will necessarily involve friction and expense in collection, together with some injury to the public, of the kind which we have described as a loss of consumers' rent: and they can never be adjusted with perfect fairness, especially when account is taken of the unequal shares that different members of the community will get of the benefits for the sake of which it is proposed that the Government should forego some of its revenue.

Suppose then that the monopolist makes a compromise, and reckons £1 of consumers' rent as equivalent to say 10*s* of monopoly revenue. Let him calculate the monopoly revenue to be got from selling his commodity at any given price, and to it let him add one half the corresponding consumers' rent: the sum of the two may be called the *Compromise Benefit*, and his aim will be to fix on that price which will make the compromise benefit as large as possible[1].

General results

The following general results are capable of exact proof; but on a little consideration they will appear so manifestly true as hardly to require proof. Firstly, the amount which the monopolist will offer for sale will be greater (and the price at which he will sell it will be less) if he is to any

that the (money measure of the) total benefit is a maximum when the amount offered for sale is OW; or, which is the same thing, when the price of sale is fixed at the demand price for OW.

[1] If he compromises on the basis that £1 of consumers' rent is equally desirable with £n of monopoly revenue, n being a proper fraction, let us take a point P_6 in P_3P_5 such that $P_3P_6 = n\ P_3P_5$, or, which is the same thing, nMP_4. Then $OM \times MP_6 = OM \times MP_3, + nOM \times MP_4$, that is, it is equal to the monopoly revenue derived from selling an amount OM_1 of the commodity at the price $MP_1, + n$ times the consumers' rent derived from this sale: and is therefore the compromise benefit derived from that sale. The locus of P_6 is our sixth curve, QU, which we may call the *compromise benefit curve*. It touches one of the constant revenue curves in u_6; which shows that the compromise benefit attains its maximum when amount OY is sold, or which is the same thing, when the selling price is fixed at the demand price for the amount OY.

BOOK V CH XIII

extent desirous to promote the interests of consumers than if his sole aim is to obtain the greatest possible monopoly revenue, and secondly, the amount produced will be greater (and the selling price will be less) the greater be the desire of the monopolist to promote the interests of consumers; *i e.*, the larger be the percentage of its actual value at which he counts in consumers' rent with his own revenue[1].

The importance of the interests of consumers has been under-estimated,

§ 8. Not many years ago there were many who contended that:—"An English ruler, who looks upon himself as the minister of the race he rules, is bound to take care that he impresses their energies in no work that is not worth the labour that is spent upon it, or—to translate the sentiment into plainer language—that he engages in nothing that will not produce an income sufficient to defray the interest on its cost[2]." Such phrases as this may sometimes have meant little more than that a benefit which consumers were not willing to purchase at a high price and on a large scale, was likely to exist for the greater part only in the specious counsels of those who had some personal interest in the proposed undertakings, but probably they more often indicated a tendency to under-estimate the magnitude of that interest which consumers have in a low price, and which we call consumers' rent[3].

because direct personal

One of the chief elements of success in private business is the faculty of weighing the advantages and disadvantages

[1] That is to say, firstly, OY fig 38 is always greater than OL, and secondly, the greater n is, the greater OY is (See Mathematical Note xxiii)

[2] The words are quoted from a leading article in *The Times* for July 30, 1874 they fairly represent a great body of public opinion

[3] Fig 39 may be taken to represent the case of a proposed Government undertaking in India The supply curve is above the demand curve during its whole length, showing that the enterprise to which it refers is unremunerative, in the sense that whatever price the producers fix, they will lose money, their monopoly revenue will be a negative quantity. But QT the total benefit curve rises above Ox, and touches a constant revenue curve in t_5 If then they offer for sale an amount OW (or, which is the same thing, fix the price at the demand price for OW), the resultant consumers' rent, if taken at its full value, will outweigh the loss on working by an amount represented by $OW \times Wt_5$ But suppose that, in order to make up the deficiency, Government must levy taxes, and that taking account of all indirect expenses and other evils, these cost the public twice what they bring in to the Government, it will then be necessary to count two rupees of the consumers' rent as compensating for a Government outlay of only one rupee; and the net gain of the

of any proposed course, and of assigning to them their true relative importance. He who by practice and genius has acquired the power of attributing to each factor its right quantity, is already well on the way to fortune; and the increase in the efficiency of our productive forces is in a great measure due to the large number of able minds who are devoting themselves ceaselessly to acquiring these business instincts. But unfortunately the advantages thus weighed against one another are nearly all regarded from one point of view, that of the producer, and there are not many who concern themselves to weigh against one another the relative quantities of the interests which the consumers and the producers have in different courses of action. For indeed the requisite facts come within the direct experience of only a very few persons, and even in the case of those few, only to a very

experience seldom helps much towards forming correct estimates of them,

undertaking will then be represented by the compromise benefit curve QU, drawn midway between the monopoly revenue (negative) curve QQ' and the total benefit curve QT. This touches a constant revenue curve in u_6, showing

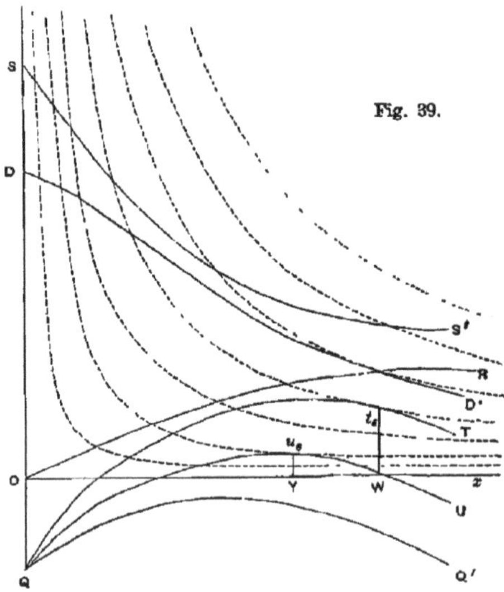

Fig. 39.

that if the amount OY is offered for sale, or, which is the same thing, if the price is fixed at the demand price for OY, there will result a net gain to India represented by $OY \times Yu_6$

BOOK V CH XIII

limited extent and in a very imperfect way. Moreover when a great administrator has acquired those instincts with regard to public interests which able business men have with regard to their own affairs, he is not very likely to be able to carry his plans with a free hand At all events in a democratic country no great public undertaking is secure of being sustained on consistent lines of policy, unless its advantages can be made clear, not only to the few who have direct experience of high public affairs, but also to the many who have no such experience and have to form their judgment on the materials set before them by others.

and our public statistics are not yet properly organized.

Judgments of this kind must always be inferior to those which an able business man forms, by the aid of instincts based on long experience with regard to his own business. But they may be made much more trustworthy than they are at present, if they can be based on statistical measures of the relative quantities of the benefits and the injuries which different courses of public action are likely to cause to the several classes of the community Much of the failure and much of the injustice, in which the economic policies of Governments have resulted, have been due to the want of statistical measurement. A few people who have been strongly interested on one side have raised their voices loudly, persistently and all together, while little has been heard from the great mass of people whose interests have lain in the opposite direction, for, even if their attention has been fairly called to the matter, few have cared to exert themselves much for a cause in which no one of them has more than a small stake. The few therefore get their way, although if statistical measures of the interests involved were available, it might prove that the aggregate of the interests of the few was only a tenth or a hundredth part of the aggregate of the interests of the silent many

Statistical arguments are often misleading at first; but free discussion clears away

No doubt statistics can be easily misinterpreted, and are often very misleading when first applied to new problems. But many of the worst fallacies involved in the misapplications of statistics are definite and can be definitely exposed, till at last no one ventures to repeat them even when addressing an uninstructed audience. and on the whole argu-

BOOK V CH. XIII.

Statistical fallacies.

ments which can be reduced to statistical forms, though still in a backward condition, are making more sure and more rapid advances than any others towards obtaining the general acceptance of all who have studied the subjects to which they refer. The rapid growth of collective interests, and the growing tendency towards collective action in economic affairs, make it every day more important that we should know what quantitative measures of public interests are most needed and what statistics are required for them, and that we should set ourselves to obtain these statistics

Hopes for the future from the statistical study of demand and consumers' rent

It is perhaps not unreasonable to hope that as time goes on, the statistics of consumption will be so organized as to afford demand schedules sufficiently trustworthy, to show in diagrams that will appeal to the eye, the quantities of consumers' rent that will result from different courses of public and private action. By the study of these pictures the mind may be gradually trained to get juster notions of the relative magnitudes of the interests which the community has in various schemes of public and private enterprise; and sounder doctrines may replace those traditions of an earlier generation, which had perhaps a wholesome influence in their time, but which damped social enthusiasm by throwing suspicion on all projects for undertakings by the public on its own behalf which would not show a balance of direct pecuniary profit.

The practical bearings of many of the abstract reasonings in which we have recently been engaged will not be fully apparent till we approach the end of this treatise. But there seemed to be advantages in introducing them thus early, partly because of their close connection with the main theory of equilibrium of demand and supply, and partly because they throw side lights on the character and the purposes of that investigation of the causes which determine Distribution and Exchange on which we are about to enter.

CHAPTER XIV.

SUMMARY OF THE GENERAL THEORY OF EQUILIBRIUM OF DEMAND AND SUPPLY.

§ 1. In the present Book we have studied the theory of the mutual relations of demand and supply in their most general form; taking as little account as possible of the special incidents of particular applications of the theory, and leaving over for the following Book the study of the bearings of the general theory on the special features of the several agents of production, Labour, Capital, and Land.

Ch. I On markets

The difficulties of the problem depend chiefly on variations in the area of space, and the period of time over which the market in question extends; the influence of time being more fundamental than that of space

Ch II Temporary equilibrium of demand and supply

Even in a market of very short period, such as that of a provincial corn-exchange on market-day, the "higgling and bargaining" might probably oscillate about a mean position, which would have some sort of a right to be called the equilibrium price but the action of dealers in offering one price or refusing another would depend little, if at all, on calculations with regard to cost of production. They would look chiefly at present demand on the one hand, and on the other at the stocks of the commodity already available It is true that they would pay some attention to such movements of production in the near future as might throw their shadow before; but in the case of perishable goods they would look only a very little way beyond the immediate present. Cost of production has for instance no perceptible influence on the day's bargaining in a fish-market.

Chs III IV. V Equilibrium of normal demand and supply The element of time.

Passing from these temporary equilibria to the stable equilibria of normal demand and normal supply, we find that in the language both of professed writers on economics and of men of business, there is much elasticity in the use of the term Normal when applied to the causes that determine value; but there is one division which, though it has no sharp outlines, is yet fairly well marked.

Long period or true normal price

On the one side of this division are long periods, in which the normal action of economic forces has time to work itself out more fully; in which therefore a temporary scarcity of skilled labour, or of any other of the agents of production, can be remedied, and in which those economies that normally result from an increase in the scale of production—normally, that is without the aid of any substantive new invention—have time to develop themselves The expenses of a representative firm, managed with normal ability and having normal access to the internal and external economies of production on a large scale, may be taken as a standard for estimating normal expenses of production: and when the period under survey is long enough to enable the investment of capital in building up a new business to complete itself and to bear full fruits, then the marginal supply price is that, the expectation of which in the long run just suffices to induce capitalists to invest their material capital, and workers of all grades to invest their personal capital in the trade.

Short period normal price or sub-normal price.

On the other side of the line of division are periods of time long enough to enable producers to adapt their production to changes in demand, in so far as that can be done with the existing provision of specialized skill, specialized capital, and industrial organization; but not long enough to enable them to make any important changes in the supplies of these factors of production For such periods the stock of material and personal appliances of production has to be taken in a great measure for granted, and the marginal increment of supply is determined by estimates of producers as to the amount of production it is worth their while to get out of those appliances If trade is brisk all energies are strained to their utmost, overtime is worked, and then the limit to

BOOK V. CH. XIV. production is given by want of power rather than by want of will to go further or faster. But if trade is slack every producer has to make up his mind how near to prime cost it is worth his while to take fresh orders. And here there is no definite law, the chief operative force is the fear of spoiling the market; and that acts in different ways and with different strengths on different individuals and different industrial groups. For the chief motive of all open combinations and of all informal silent and "customary" understandings whether among employers or employed is the need for preventing individuals from spoiling the common market by action that may bring them immediate gains, but at the cost of a greater aggregate loss to the trade. No doubt this aggregate loss to the trade may be compensated by a much greater aggregate gain to consumers as a body, and one of the most urgent economic problems of the present day is to inquire in what classes of cases it is desirable that a trade should continue to produce boldly with but little reference to the danger of spoiling the market Some side lights are thrown on this question by the investigations of consumers' rent in the last two chapters of this Book; but a full study of it is deferred to a later stage.

Ch. VI. Joint and composite demand and supply

§ 2. We next turned aside to consider the relations of demand and supply with reference to things that need to be combined together for the purposes of satisfying a joint demand, of which the most important instance is that of the specialized material capital, and the specialized personal skill that must work together in any trade. For there is no direct demand on the part of consumers for either alone, but only for the two conjointly; the demand for either separately is a derived demand, which rises, other things being equal, with every increase in the demand for the common products, and with every diminution in the supply price of the joint factors of production. In like manner commodities of which there is a joint supply, such as gas and coke, or beef and hides, can each of them have only a derived supply price, governed by the expenses of the whole process of production on the one hand, and on the other by the demand for the remaining joint products.

The composite demand for a thing, resulting from its being used for several different purposes, and the composite supply of a thing, that has several sources of production, present no great difficulty; for the several amounts demanded for the different purposes, or supplied from different sources, can be added together, on the same plan as was adopted in Book III, for combining the demands of the rich, the middle classes and the poor for the same commodity

Ch VII. Distribution of the supplementary costs

Next we made some study of the division of the supplementary costs of a business,—and especially those connected with building up a trade connection, with marketing, and with insurance—among the various products of that business

Chs. VIII. IX. X. The value of an appliance for production in relation to that of the things produced by it

§ 3. Returning to those central difficulties of the equilibrium of normal demand and supply which are connected with the element of time, we investigated more fully the relation between the value of an appliance for production and that of the things produced by it

The possession of any rare natural advantages affords to the producers a *surplus* or *rent*

When different producers have different advantages for producing a thing, its price must be sufficient to cover the expenses of production of those producers who have no special and exceptional facilities; for if not they will withhold or diminish their production, and the scarcity of the amount supplied, relatively to the demand, will raise the price. When the market is in equilibrium, and the thing is being sold at a price which covers these expenses, there remains a surplus beyond their expenses for those who have the assistance of any exceptional advantages If these advantages arise from the command over free gifts of nature, the surplus is called a producer's surplus or producer's rent: there is a surplus in any case, and if the owner of a free gift of nature lends it out to another, he can generally get for its use a rent equivalent to this surplus.

Ricardo's doctrine that rent does not enter into cost of production is badly expressed, but when rightly inter-

Ricardo argued that rent does not enter into cost of production, having in view on the one hand the rent of farming land in general, and on the other the cost of production of agricultural produce in general and in this connection the doctrine cannot easily be misunderstood. But when applied to the cost of production of one particular crop, though still literally true as it stands, experience shows that it is liable to

BOOK V. CH. XIV.

preted is applicable to all classes of rents

be interpreted in senses in which it is not true For if land which had been used for growing hops, is found capable of yielding a higher rent as market-garden land, the area under hops will undoubtedly be diminished; and this will raise their marginal cost of production and therefore their price. The rent which land will yield for one kind of produce, though it does not directly enter into those expenses, yet does act as the channel through which a demand for the land for that kind of produce increases the difficulties of supply of other kinds; and thus does indirectly affect their expenses of production. A mining royalty is not a rent, and enters into expenses of production. Ricardo's doctrine requires to be carefully interpreted even with regard to farm rents; but, when so interpreted, it is applicable to other classes of rents, and, subject to some further conditions, to the income yielded by appliances for production which man has made, and especially such of them as are durable, and the supply of which cannot be rapidly increased.

The income derived from appliances for production which have already been made, bears for the time a resemblance to rent, which is the closer the more durable they are

Thus when we are taking a broad view of normal value, when we are investigating the causes which determine normal value "in the long run," when we are tracing the "ultimate" effects of economic causes, then the income that is derived from capital in these forms enters into the payments by which the expenses of production of the commodity in question have to be covered, and it directly controls the action of the producers who are on the margin of doubt as to whether to increase the means of production or not. But, on the other hand, when we are considering the causes which determine normal prices for a period which is short relatively to that required for largely increasing the supply of those appliances for production, then their influence on value is chiefly indirect and more or less similar to that exerted by the free gifts of nature. The shorter the period which we are considering, and the slower the process of production of those appliances, the less part will variations in the income derived from them play in checking or increasing the supply of the commodity produced by them, and in raising or lowering its supply price, and the more nearly true will it be that, for the period under discussion, the net income to be derived from them is to be regarded as a producer's surplus or quasi-rent.

Situation rent is the type of a large class of incomes

In passing from the free gifts of nature through the more permanent improvements in the soil, to less permanent improvements, to farm and factory buildings, to steam-engines, &c, and finally to the less durable and less slowly made implements, we find a continuous series. And even that part of the rental value of land which is derived from advantages of situation—situation rent as it may be called—passes by imperceptible gradations from the character of a pure rent, in cases in which the owners of the land have had no direct part in improving its environment, to that of a quasi-rent or even profits when the conditions of the environment, to which the land owes its situation value, were deliberately brought about by, and at the expense of, the owners of that land in order to raise its value Thus the situation rent of land presents close analogies to many different classes of income derived from advantages of the environment, or conjuncture. Later on we shall find that many of the most interesting applications of the principle which we have just discussed are to human agents of production; but in the present Book we confine our attention to the material agents of production.

The supply of durable requisites of production is not quickly adapted to demand

The supply of durable appliances for production, or goods of the second order, is governed by estimates that generally reach forward over a longer time, and are therefore more liable to error than those which govern the immediate adaptation of supply to demand with regard to goods ready for immediate consumption. But further, the supply of these appliances depends partly on the supply of appliances for making them, that is, of things removed by two stages from the commodity with which we started. The demand for these appliances for making appliances is derived ultimately from the demand for the finished commodity; and the adjustment of supply to demand in their case is a still more difficult process, it ranges over a still longer period of time, and is still more liable to error· and so on, backwards, without limit.

§ 4. The terms "aggregate" and "average" cost of Ch. XI.

BOOK V. CH XIV

The relations between average and normal expenses of production.

production can have no precise meaning in a world of rapid change such as that in which we live; since the quasi-rents of the appliances of production, both material and personal, are governed for short periods more by the value of the things they produce, than by their own cost of production. For instance, machinery of a pattern on which improvements have been made, has its value determined by capitalizing the quasi-rents it can earn; and to count profits on this value as part of the aggregate expenses of production of the commodities it produces, is to reason in a circle. In a rigidly stationary state however in which supply could be perfectly adjusted to demand in every particular, the normal expenses of production, the marginal expenses, and the average expenses (rent being counted in) would be one and the same thing. This point is dwelt on in order to show clearly what the normal supply schedule does mean, and what it does not mean.

The influence of the law of increasing return on the relations between amount produced and supply price does not show its true character in short periods

This brings us to consider some difficulties of a rather technical character connected with the marginal expenses of production of a commodity that obeys the law of increasing return. The difficulties arise from the attempt to represent supply price as dependent on the amount produced, without allowing for the length of time that is necessarily occupied by each individual business in extending its internal, and still more its external organization, and in consequence they have been most conspicuous in mathematical and semi-mathematical discussions of the theory of value. For when changes of supply price and amount produced are regarded as dependent exclusively on one another without any reference to gradual growth, it appears reasonable to argue that the marginal supply price for each individual producer is the addition to his aggregate expenses of production made by producing his last element; that this marginal price is likely in many cases to be diminished by an increase in his output much more than the demand price in the general market would be by the same cause; and that therefore the statical theory of equilibrium is inapplicable to commodities which obey the law of increasing return.

To this argument it may be replied that in many industries

each producer has a special market in which he is well known, and which he cannot extend quickly; and that therefore, though it might be physically possible for him to increase his output rapidly, he would run the risk of forcing down very much the demand price in his special market, or else of being forced to sell his surplus production outside on less favourable terms. And though there are industries in which each producer has access to the whole of a large market, yet in these there remain but few internal economies to be got by an increase of output, when the existing plant is already well occupied No doubt there are industries as to which neither of these statements is true: they are in a transitional state, and it must be conceded that the statical theory of equilibrium of normal demand and supply cannot be profitably applied to them But such cases are not numerous, and with regard to the great bulk of manufacturing industries, the connection between supply price and amount showed a fundamentally different character for short periods and for long.

For short periods, the difficulties of adjusting the internal and external organization of a business to rapid changes in output are so great that the supply price must generally be taken to rise with an increase and to fall with a diminution in the amount produced.

Its operation in long periods.

But in long periods both the internal and the external economies of production on a large scale have time to develop themselves, the marginal supply price is not the expenses of production of any particular bale of goods, but it is the whole expenses (including insurance, and gross earnings of management) of a marginal increment in the aggregate process of production and marketing This supply price falls generally with an increase in the amount normally produced, if it falls more rapidly than the demand price in the neighbourhood of the position of equilibrium, the equilibrium is unstable, in the opposite case it is stable.

The pure theory of multiple points of equilibrium

Under certain possible, though rather improbable, conditions there may be two or more positions of equilibrium alternately stable and unstable But this portion of the theory, though necessary for logical completeness, rests on

BOOK V. CH. XIV.

rigid and artificial assumptions, and has but little practical importance.

Ch XII. Changes in normal demand and supply, with some reference to the doctrine of Maximum Satisfaction

§ 5. Some study of the effects of a tax; regarded as a special case of a change in the general conditions of demand and supply suggests that, when proper allowance is made for the interests of consumers, in the form of consumers' surplus or rent, there is less *primâ facie* cause than the earlier economists supposed, for the general doctrine of so-called "Maximum Satisfaction", *i.e.* for the doctrine that the free pursuit by each individual of his own immediate interest, will lead producers to turn their capital and labour, and consumers to turn their expenditure into such courses as are most conducive to the general interests. We have nothing to do at this stage of our inquiry, limited as it is to analysis of the most general character, with the important question how far, human nature being constituted as it is at present, collective action is likely to be inferior to individualistic action in energy and elasticity, in inventiveness and directness of purpose, and whether it is not therefore likely to waste through practical inefficiency more than it could save by taking account of all the interests affected by any course of action. But even without taking account of the evils arising from the unequal distribution of wealth, there is *primâ facie* reason for believing that the aggregate satisfaction, so far from being already a maximum, could be much increased by collective action in promoting the production and consumption of things in regard to which the law of increasing return acts with especial force.

Ch XIII. Theory of monopolies

This position is confirmed by the study of the theory of monopolies It is the immediate interest of the monopolist so to adjust the production and sale of his wares as to obtain for himself the maximum net revenue, and the course which he thus adopts, is unlikely to be that which affords the aggregate maximum satisfaction. The divergence between individual and collective interests is *primâ facie* less important with regard to those things which obey the law of diminishing return, than with regard to those which obey the law of increasing return · but, in the case of the latter, there is strong *primâ facie* reason for believing that it might often be to the interest of the community directly or indirectly to intervene, because a largely increased production would add much more to consumers' rent than to the aggregate expenses of production of the goods. More exact notions on the relations of demand and supply, particularly when expressed in the form of diagrams, may help us to see what statistics should be collected, and how they should be applied in the attempt to estimate the relative magnitudes of various conflicting economic interests, public and private.

Note on Ricardo's Theory of Value.

General drift of this note.

Ricardo's theory of cost of production in relation to value occupies so important a place in the history of economics that any misunderstanding as to its real character must necessarily be very mischievous; and unfortunately it is so expressed as almost to invite misunderstanding. In consequence there is a widely spread belief that it has needed to be reconstructed by the present generation of economists. The purpose of the present Note is to show cause for not accepting this opinion, and for holding on the contrary that the foundations of the theory as they were left by Ricardo remain intact, that much has been added to them, and that very much has been built upon them, but that little has been taken from them.

Ricardo had practical experience, but was abstract and unsystematic as a writer

When Ricardo was addressing a general audience, he drew largely upon his wide and intimate knowledge of the facts of life, using them "for illustration, verification, or the premises of argument" But in his *Principles of Political Economy* "the same questions are treated with a singular exclusion of all reference to the actual world around him" (see an admirable article on *Ricardo's Use of Facts* in the first volume of the Harvard *Quarterly Journal of Economics*, edited by Prof Dunbar) And he wrote to Malthus in May, 1820 (the same year in which Malthus published his *Principles of Political Economy considered with a view to their practical application*), "Our differences may in some respects, I think, be ascribed to your considering my book as more practical than I intended it to be My object was to elucidate principles, and to do this I imagined strong cases, that I might show the operation of those principles." His book makes no pretence to be systematic. He was with difficulty induced to publish it; and if in writing it he had in view any readers at all, they were chiefly those statesmen and business men with whom he associated. So he purposely omitted many things which were necessary for the logical completeness of his argument, but which they would regard as obvious And further, as he told Malthus in the following October, he was "but a poor master of language" His exposition is as confused as his thought is profound, he uses words in artificial senses which he does not explain, and to which he does not adhere, and he changes from one hypothesis to another without giving notice

If then we seek to understand him rightly, we must interpret him generously, more generously than he himself interpreted Adam Smith. When his words are ambiguous, we must give them that interpretation which other passages in his writings indicate that he would have wished us to give them If we do this with the desire to ascertain what he really meant, his doctrines, though very far from complete, are free from many of the errors that are commonly attributed to them

He took utility for granted, because its influence was relatively simple,

He considers, for instance (*Principles*, Ch I § 1), that utility is "absolutely essential" to (normal) value though not its measure, while the value of things "of which there is a very limited quantity. .varies with the wealth and inclinations of those who are desirous to possess them" And elsewhere (*Ib* Ch. IV.) he insists on the way in which the market fluctuations of prices are determined by the amount available for sale on the one hand, and "the wants and wishes of mankind" on the other

Again, in a profound, though very incomplete, discussion of the difference between "Value and Riches" he seems to be feeling his way towards the distinction between marginal and total utility For by Riches he means total utility, and he seems to be always on the point of stating that value corresponds to the increment of Riches which results from that part of the commodity which it is only just worth the while of purchasers to buy; and that when the supply runs short, whether temporarily in consequence of a passing accident, or permanently in consequence of an increase in cost of production, there is a rise in that marginal increment of Riches which is measured by value, at the same time that there is a diminution in the aggregate Riches, the total utility, derived from the commodity Throughout the whole discussion he is trying to say, though (being ignorant of the terse language of the differential calculus) he did not get hold of the right words in which to say it neatly, that marginal utility is raised and total utility is lessened by any check to supply

and he analysed cost of production because its influence is less obvious.

But while not thinking that he had much to say that was of great importance on the subject of utility, he believed that the connection between cost of production and value was imperfectly understood; and that erroneous views on this subject were likely to lead the country astray in practical problems of taxation and finance, and so he addressed himself specially to this subject But here also he made short cuts

For, though he was aware that commodities fall into three classes according as they obey the law of diminishing, of constant, or of increasing return; yet he thought it best to ignore this distinction in a theory of value applicable to all kinds of commodities. A commodity chosen at random was just as likely to obey one as the other of the two laws of diminishing and of increasing return; and therefore he thought himself justified in assuming provisionally that they all obeyed the law of constant return. In this perhaps he was justified, but he made a mistake in not stating explicitly what he was doing.

1. Cost of production dependent on quantity of labour used directly,

He argued in the first Section of his first Chapter that "in the early stages of society" where there is scarcely any use of capital, and where any one man's labour has nearly the same price as any other man's, it is, broadly speaking, true that "the value of a commodity, or the quantity of a commodity for which it will exchange, depends on the relative quantity of labour which is necessary for its production." That is, if two things are made by four and twelve men's labour for a year all the men being of the same grade, the normal value of the former will be three times that of the latter. For if ten per cent. has to be added for profits on the capital invested in the one case, ten per cent. will need to be added in the other also. [If w be a year's wages of a worker of this class, the costs of production will be $4w \times \frac{110}{100}$, and $12w \times \frac{110}{100}$ and the ratio of these is 4 : 12, or 1 : 3.]

2, also on quality of that labour,

But he went on to show that these assumptions cannot be properly made in later stages of civilization, and that the relation of value to cost of production is more complex than that with which he started; and his next step was to introduce in Section II the consideration that "labour of different qualities is differently rewarded." If the wages of a jeweller are twice as great as those of a working labourer, an hour's work of the one must count for two hours' work of the other. Should there be a change in their relative wages, there will of course be a corresponding change in the relative values of things made by them. But instead of analysing, as economists of this generation do, the causes which make (say) jewellers' wages change from one generation to another relatively to those of ordinary labourers, he contented himself with stating that such variations cannot be great.

3, on labour spent previously on implements,

Next in Section III he urged that in reckoning the cost of production of a commodity, account must be taken not only of the labour applied immediately to it, but also of that which is bestowed on the implements, tools and buildings with which such labour is assisted; and here the element of time which he had carefully kept in the background at starting, was necessarily introduced.

4, on the length of time which must elapse before the goods can

Accordingly in Section IV he discusses more fully the different influences exerted on the value of "a set of commodities" [he uses this simple method sometimes to evade the difficulties of the distinctions between prime cost and total cost] and especially he takes account of the different effects of the application of circulating capital which is

be brought to market,

consumed in a single use, and fixed as durable capital, and again of the time for which labour must be invested in making machinery to make commodities If that be long, they will have a greater cost of production and be "more valuable to compensate for the greater length of time, which must elapse before they can be brought to market"

5, on the consequent influence of the rate of profits on relative value

And lastly in Section v. he sums up the influence which different lengths of investment, whether direct or indirect, will have upon relative values; arguing correctly that if wages all rise and fall together the change will have no permanent effect on the relative values of different commodities But he argues if the rate of profits falls it will lower the relative values of those commodities the production of which requires capital to be invested a long while before they can be brought to market. For if in one case the average investment is for a year and requires ten per cent to be added to the wages bill for profits, and in another is for two years and requires twenty per cent to be added; then a fall of profits by one-fifth will reduce the addition in the latter case from 20 to 16, and in the former only from 10 to 8 [If their direct labour cost is equal the ratio of their values before the change will be $\frac{120}{110}$ or 1 091; and after the change $\frac{116}{108}$ or 1 074; a fall of nearly two per cent] His argument is avowedly only provisional; in later chapters he takes account of other causes of differences in profits in different industries, besides the period of investment. But it seems difficult to imagine how he could more strongly have emphasized the fact that Time or Waiting as well as Labour is an element of cost of production than by occupying his first chapter with this discussion. Unfortunately however he delighted in short phrases, and he thought that his readers would always supply for themselves the explanations of which he had given them a hint

He corrects Malthus' anticipation of Marx's misunderstanding

Once indeed, in a note at the end of the sixth Section of his first Chapter, he says —"Mr Malthus appears to think that it is a part of my doctrine that the cost and value of a thing should be the same; it is, if he means by cost, 'cost of production' including profits. In the above passage, this is what he does not mean, and therefore he has not clearly understood me" And yet Rodbertus and Karl Marx claim Ricardo's authority for the statement that the natural value of things consists solely of the labour spent on them; and even those German economists who most strenuously combat the conclusions of these writers, are often found to admit that they have interpreted Ricardo rightly, and that their conclusions follow logically from his

But he was too spare of words.

This and other facts of a similar kind show that Ricardo's reticence was an error of judgment It would have been better if he had occasionally repeated the statement that the values of two commodities are to be regarded as in the long run proportionate to the amount of labour required for making them, only on the condition that other things are equal: *i e*, that the labour employed in the two cases is equally skilled, and therefore equally highly paid; that it is assisted by proportionate amounts of capital, account being taken of the period of its investment; and that the rates of profits are equal He does not state clearly, and in some cases he perhaps did not fully and clearly perceive how, in the problem of normal value, the various elements govern one another *mutually*, and not *successively* in a long chain of causation And he was more guilty than almost anyone else of the bad habit of endeavouring to express great economic doctrines in short sentences.

[Prof Ashley in a suggestive criticism of this Note, as part of an attempted "Rehabilitation of Ricardo" (*Economic Journal*, Vol. I.) insists that it has been commonly believed that Ricardo did in fact habitually think of mere quantities of labour as constituting cost of production, and governing value, subject only to "slight modifications"; and that this interpretation of him is the most consistent with his writings as a whole It is not disputed that this interpretation has been accepted by many able writers: otherwise there would have been little need for rehabilitating, *i e* clothing more fully his somewhat too naked doctrines But the question whether Ricardo is to be supposed to have meant nothing by the first chapter of his book, merely because he did not constantly repeat the interpretation clauses contained in it, is one which each reader must decide for himself according to his temperament. it does not lend itself to be solved by argument It is claimed not that his doctrines contained a complete theory of value. but only that they were in the main true as far as they went Rodbertus and Marx interpreted Ricardo's doctrine, to mean that interest does not enter into that cost of production which governs (or takes part in governing) value and as regards this Prof. Ashley appears to concede all that is claimed here when (p. 480) he takes it as beyond question that Ricardo "regarded the payment of interest, that is, of something more than the mere replacement of capital, as a matter of course."]

The brilliant one-sidedness of Jevons.

There are few writers of modern times who have approached as near to the brilliant originality of Ricardo as Jevons has done. But he appears to have judged both Ricardo and Mill harshly, and to have attributed to them doctrines narrower and less scientific than those which they really held. And his desire to emphasize an aspect of value to which they had given insufficient prominence, was probably in some measure accountable for his saying, "Repeated reflection and inquiry have led me to the somewhat novel opinion that *value depends entirely upon utility*" (*Theory*, p. 1). This statement seems to be no less one-sided and fragmentary, and much more misleading, than that into which Ricardo often glided with careless brevity, as to the dependence of value on cost of production, but which he never regarded as more than a part of a larger doctrine, the rest of which he had tried to explain.

Jevons continues:—"We have only to trace out carefully the natural laws of variation of utility as depending upon the quantity of commodity in our possession, in order to arrive at a satisfactory theory of exchange, of which the ordinary laws of supply and demand are a necessary consequence... Labour is found often to determine value, but only in an indirect manner by varying the degree of utility of the commodity through an increase or limitation of the supply." As we shall presently see, the latter of these two statements had been made before in almost the same form, loose and inaccurate as it is, by Ricardo and Mill; but they would not have accepted the former statement For while they regarded the natural laws of variation of utility as too obvious to require detailed explanation, and while they admitted that cost of production could have no effect upon exchange value if it could have none upon the amount which producers brought forward for sale, their doctrines imply that what is true of supply, is true *mutatis mutandis* of demand, and that the utility of a commodity could have no effect upon its exchange value if it could have none on the amount which purchasers took off the market. Let us then turn to examine the chain of causation in which Jevons' central position is formulated in his Second Edition, and compare it with the position taken up by Ricardo and Mill. He says (p 179) —

Jevons' central position.

"Cost of production determines supply.
Supply determines final degree of utility.
Final degree of utility determines value"

Now if this series of causations really existed, there could be no great harm in omitting the intermediate stages and saying that cost of production determines value. For if A is the cause of B, which is the cause of C, which is the cause of D, then A is the cause of D. But in fact there is no such series.

Jevons implies that the things balanced against one another in a market are utilities, really they are indirect measures of utility

A preliminary objection might be taken to the ambiguity of the terms "cost of production" and "supply"; which Jevons ought to have avoided, by the aid of that technical apparatus of semi-mathematical phrases, which was at his disposal, but not at Ricardo's. A graver objection lies against his third statement For the price which the various purchasers in a market will pay for a thing, is determined not solely by the final degrees of its utility to them, but by these in conjunction with the amounts of purchasing power severally at their disposal. The exchange value of a thing is the same all over a market, but the final degrees of utility to which it corresponds are not equal at any two parts. Jevons supposed himself to be getting nearer the foundations of exchange value when in his account of the causes which determine it, he substituted the phrase "final degree of utility," for "the price which consumers are only just willing to pay,"—the phrase which in the present treatise is condensed into "marginal demand price." When for instance describing (Second Edition, p. 105) the settlement of exchange between "one trading body possessing only corn, and another possessing only beef," he makes his diagram represent "a person" as gaining a "utility" represented by one line and losing a "utility" represented by another. But that is not what really happens, a trading body is not "a person," it gives up things which represent equal purchasing power to all of its members, but very different utilities. It is true that Jevons was himself aware of this; and that his account can be made consistent with the facts of life by a series of interpretations, which in effect substitute "demand-price" and "supply-price" for "utility" and "disutility". but when, so amended, they lose much of their aggressive force against the older doctrines and if both are to be held severely to a strictly literal interpretation, then the older method of speaking, though not perfectly accurate, appears to be nearer the truth than that which Jevons and some of his followers have endeavoured to substitute for it.

He substitutes a catena of causes for mutual causation

But the greatest objection of all to his formal statement of his central doctrine is that it does not represent supply price, demand price and amount produced as mutually determining one another (subject to certain other conditions), but as determined one by another in a series It is as though when three balls A, B, and C rest against one another in a bowl, instead of saying that the position of the three mutually determines one another under the action of gravity, he had said that A determines B, and B determines C Some one else however with equal justice might say that C determines B and B determines A. And in reply to Jevons a catena rather less untrue than his can be made by inverting his order and saying —

Utility determines the amount that has to be supplied,

The amount that has to be supplied determines cost of production,

Cost of production determines value,

because it determines the supply price which is required to make the producers keep to their work.

Ricardo's correct though inadequate treatment of utility, took some account of the element of time

Let us then turn to Ricardo's doctrine which, though unsystematic and open to many objections, seems to be more philosophic in principle and closer to the actual facts of life. He says, in the letter to Malthus already quoted.—"M. Say has not a correct notion of what is meant by value when he contends that a commodity is valuable in proportion to its utility. This would be true if buyers only regulated the value of commodities; then indeed we might expect that all men would be willing to give a price for things in proportion to the estimation in which they held them; but the fact appears to me to be that the buyers have the least in the world to do in regulating price, it is all done by the competition of the sellers, and, however really willing the buyers might be to give more for iron than for gold, they could not, because the supply would be regulated by cost of production . You say demand and supply regulates value [*sic*], this I think is saying nothing, and for the reason I have given in the beginning of this letter: it is supply which regulates value, and supply is itself controlled by comparative cost of production Cost of production, in money, means the value of labour as well as of profits." (See pp. 173—6 of Dr Bonar's excellent edition of these letters.) And again in his next letter, "I do not dispute either the influence of demand on the price of corn or on the price of all other things: but supply follows close at its heels and soon takes the power of regulating price in his [sic] own hands, and in regulating it he is determined by cost of production."

These letters were not indeed published when Jevons wrote, but there are very similar statements in Ricardo's *Principles*. Mill also, when discussing the value of money (Book III Ch IX § 3), speaks of "the law of demand and supply which is acknowledged to be applicable to all commodities, and which in the case of money as of most other things, is controlled but not set aside by the law of cost of production, since cost of production would have no effect on value if it could have none on supply" And again, when summing up his theory of value (Book III. Ch XVI. § 1), he says. "From this it appears that demand and supply govern the fluctuations of prices in all cases, and the permanent values of all things of which the supply is determined by any agency other than that of free competition. but that, under the régime of free competition, things are, on the average, exchanged for each other at such values and sold for such prices as afford equal expectation of advantage to all classes of producers; which can only be when things exchange for one another in the ratio of their cost of production" And, on the next page, speaking of commodities which have a joint cost of production, he says, "since cost of production here fails us we must resort to a law of value anterior to cost of production and more fundamental, the law of demand and supply."

Jevons' position less different than it appears,

Jevons (p 215), referring to this last passage, speaks of "the fallacy involved in Mill's idea that he is reverting to *an anterior law of value*, the law of supply and demand, the fact being that in introducing the cost of production principle, he has never quitted the law of supply and demand at all. The cost of production is only one circumstance which governs supply and thus indirectly influences values."

This criticism seems to contain an important truth; though the wording of the last part is open to objection. If it had been made in Mill's time he would probably have accepted it, and would have withdrawn the word "anterior" as not expressing his real meaning. The "cost of production principle" and the "final utility" principle are undoubtedly component parts of the one all-ruling law of supply and demand; each may be compared to one blade of a pair of scissors. When one blade is held still, and the cutting is effected by moving the other, we may say with careless brevity that the cutting is done by the second; but the statement is not one to be made formally, and defended deliberately. [See above, Ch. III. § 7]

and he underrated

Perhaps Jevons' antagonism to Ricardo and Mill would have been less if he had not himself fallen into the habit of speaking of relations which really exist only between demand price and value as though they held between utility and value; and if he had emphasized as Cournot had done, and as the use of mathematical forms might have been expected to lead him to do, that fundamental symmetry of the general relations in which demand and supply stand to value, which coexists with striking differences in the details of those relations We must not indeed forget that, at the time at which he wrote, the demand side of the theory of value had been much neglected; and that he did excellent service by calling attention to it and developing it. There are few thinkers whose claims on our gratitude are as high and as various as those of Jevons but that must not lead us to accept hastily his criticisms on his great predecessors (See an article on Jevons' *Theory* by the present writer in the *Academy* for April 1, 1872.)

the broad symmetry of demand and supply

It seemed right to select Jevons' attack for reply, because, in England at all events, it has attracted more attention than any other. But somewhat similar attacks on Ricardo's theory of value had been made by many other writers Among them may specially be mentioned Mr Macleod, whose writings before 1870 anticipated much both of the form and substance of recent criticisms on the classical doctrines of value in relation to cost, by Profs Walras and Carl Menger, who were contemporary with Jevons, and Profs v. Böhm-Bawerk and Wieser, who were later

Other critics

The carelessness of Ricardo with regard to the element of Time has been imitated by his critics, and has thus been the twofold source of misunderstanding. It has done, and is doing, much to hinder, and hide from view, the continuity of the development of economic science For they attempt to disprove doctrines as to the ultimate tendencies, the causes of causes, the *causæ causantes*, of the relations between cost of production and value, by means of arguments based on the causes of temporary changes, and short-period fluctuations of value. Doubtless nearly everything they say when expressing their own opinions is true in the sense in which they mean it; some of it is new and much of it is improved in form. But they do not appear to make any progress towards establishing their claim to have discovered a new doctrine of value which is in sharp contrast to the old; or which calls for any considerable demolition, as distinguished from development and extension, of the old doctrine.

have imitated Ricardo's carelessness in exposition as to the element of time, and have failed to subvert his central doctrine

BOOK VI.

VALUE,

OR

DISTRIBUTION AND EXCHANGE.

CHAPTER I.

PRELIMINARY SURVEY OF DISTRIBUTION AND EXCHANGE.

The Physiocrats assumed, in accordance with the peculiar circumstances of their time and country, that wages were at their lowest possible level,

§ 1. THE simplest account of the causes which determine the distribution of the national income is that given by the French economists who just preceded Adam Smith, and it is based upon the peculiar circumstances of France in the latter half of last century. The taxes, and other exactions levied from the French peasant, were then limited only by his ability to pay; and few of the labouring classes were far from starvation. So the Economists or Physiocrats, as they were called, assumed for the sake of simplicity, that there was a natural law of population according to which the wages of labour were kept at starvation limit[1]. They did not suppose

[1] Thus Turgot, who for this purpose may be reckoned with the Physiocrats, says (*Sur la Formation et Distribution des Richesses*, § VI.) "In every sort of occupation it must come to pass, and in fact it does come to pass, that the wages of the artisan are limited to that which is necessary to procure him a subsistence. He earns no more than his living (Il ne gagne que sa vie)" When however Hume wrote, pointing out that this statement led to the conclusion that a tax on wages must raise wages; and that it was therefore inconsistent with the observed fact that wages are often low where taxes are high and *vice versâ*, Turgot replied (March, 1767) to the effect that his iron law was not supposed to be fully operative in short periods, but only in long See Say's Turgot, English Ed. pp 53, &c

that this was true of the whole working population, but the exceptions were so few, that they thought that the general impression given by their assumption was true: somewhat in the same way as it is well to begin an account of the shape of the earth, by saying that it is an oblate spheroid, although a few mountains do project as much as a thousandth part of its radius beyond the general level.

and that much the same was true of the interest on Capital

Again, they knew that the rate of interest in Europe had fallen during the five preceding centuries, in consequence of the fact that "economy had in general prevailed over luxury." But they were impressed very much by the sensitiveness of capital, and the quickness with which it evaded the oppressions of the tax-gatherer by retiring from his grasp; and they therefore concluded that there was no great violence in the supposition that if its profits were reduced below what they then were, capital would speedily be consumed or migrate. Accordingly they assumed, again for the sake of simplicity, that there was something like a natural, or necessary rate of profit, corresponding in some measure to the natural rate of wages, that if the current rate exceeded this necessary level, capital would grow rapidly, till it forced down the rate of profit to that level; and that, if the current rate went below that level, capital would shrink quickly, and the rate would be forced upwards again. They thought that, wages and profits being thus fixed by natural laws, the natural value of everything was governed simply as the sum of wages and profits required to remunerate the producers[1]

Adam Smith worked out this conclusion more fully than

[1] From these premisses the Physiocrats logically deduced the conclusion that the only net produce of the country disposable for the purposes of taxation is the rent of land, that when taxes are placed on capital or labour, they make it shrink till its net price rises to the natural level The landowners have, they argued, to pay a gross price which exceeds this net price by the taxes together with all the expenses of collecting them in detail, and an equivalent for all the impediments which the tax-gatherer puts in the way of the free course of industry, and therefore the landowners would lose less in the long run if, being the owners of the only true surplus that exists, they would undertake to pay direct whatever taxes the King required; especially if the King would consent to "laisser faire, laisser passer," that is, to let every one make whatever he chose, and take his labour and send his goods to whatever market he liked

These rigid assumptions were partially relaxed by Adam Smith,

the Physiocrats did; though it was left for Ricardo to make clear that the labour and capital needed for production must be estimated at the margin of cultivation, so as to avoid the element of rent. But Adam Smith saw also that labour and capital were not at the verge of starvation in England, as they were in France. In England the wages of a great part of the working classes were sufficient to allow much more than the mere necessaries of existence; and capital had too rich and safe a field of employment there to be likely to go out of existence, or to emigrate. So when he is carefully weighing his words, his use of the terms "the natural rate of wages," and "the natural rate of profit," has not that sharp definition and fixedness which it had in the mouths of the Physiocrats, and he goes a good way towards explaining how they are determined by the ever-fluctuating conditions of demand and supply He even insists that the liberal reward of labour "increases the industry of the common people"; that "a plentiful subsistence increases the bodily strength of the labourer; and the comfortable hope of bettering his condition, and of ending his days perhaps in ease and plenty, animates him to exert that strength to the utmost. Where wages are high, accordingly, we shall always find the workman more active, diligent and expeditious, than where they are low, in England, for example, than in Scotland; in the neighbourhood of great towns than in remote country places[1]" And yet he sometimes fell back into the old way of speaking, and thus caused careless readers to suppose that he believed the mean level of the wages of labour to be fixed by an iron law at the bare necessaries of life

and by Malthus

Malthus again, in his admirable survey of the course of wages in England from the thirteenth to the eighteenth centuries, showed how their mean level oscillated from century to century, falling sometimes down to about half a peck of corn a day, and rising sometimes up to a peck and a half or even, in the fifteenth century, to about two pecks: a height beyond which they have never passed except in our own day. But although he observed that "an inferior mode of living may be a cause as well as a consequence of poverty," he traced

[1] *Wealth of Nations*, Bk I. Ch. VIII

this effect almost exclusively to the consequent increase of numbers; he did not anticipate the stress which economists of our own generation lay on the influence which habits of living exercise on the efficiency, and therefore on the earning power of the labourer[1].

Ricardo was more unguarded in his language,

Ricardo's language was even more unguarded than that of Adam Smith and Malthus. It is true, indeed, that he said distinctly[2]:—"It is not to be understood that the natural price of labour estimated in food and necessaries is absolutely fixed and constant...It essentially depends on the habits and customs of the people." But, having said this once, he did not take the trouble to repeat it constantly; and most of his readers forgot that he ever said it. In the course of his argument he frequently adopted a mode of speaking similar to that of the Physiocrats; and seemed to imply that the tendency of population to increase rapidly as soon as wages rise above the bare necessaries of life, causes wages to be fixed by "a natural law" to the level of these bare necessaries. This law has been called, especially in Germany, Ricardo's "iron" or "brazen" law many German socialists believe that this law is in operation now, and will continue to be so, as long as the plan on which production is organized remains "capitalistic" or "individualistic"; and they claim Ricardo as an authority on their side[3]

but there is no good cause for attributing to him a belief in the so called "iron law of wages"

In fact, however, Ricardo was not only aware that the necessary or natural limit of wages was fixed by no iron law, but is determined by the local conditions and habits of each place and time: he was further keenly sensitive to the importance of a higher "standard of living," and called on the friends of humanity to exert themselves to encourage the growth of a resolve among the working classes not to allow their wages to fall anywhere near the bare necessaries of life[4].

[1] *Political Economy*, Ch IV § 2. [2] *Principles*, Ch V.

[3] Some German economists, who are not socialists, and who believe that no such law exists, yet maintain that the doctrines of Ricardo and his followers stand or fall with the truth of this law, while others (*e g* Roscher, *Gesch der Nat Oek in Deutschland*, p 1022) protest against the socialist misunderstandings of Ricardo

[4] It may be well to quote his words. "The friends of humanity cannot but wish that in all countries the labouring classes should have a taste for comforts and enjoyments, and that they should be stimulated by all legal means in their

BOOK VI CH. I

The persistency with which many writers continue to attribute to him a belief in the "iron law" can be accounted for only by his delight "in imagining strong cases," and his habit of not repeating a hint, which he had once given, that he was omitting for the sake of simplicity the conditions and limitations that were needed to make his results applicable to real life[1].

Mill also insisted on the progressive deterioration caused by unduly low wages

Mill did not make any great advance in the theory of wages beyond his predecessors, in spite of the care with which he set himself to emphasize the distinctly human element in economics He, however, followed Malthus in dwelling on those lessons of history which show that, if a fall of wages caused the labouring classes to lower their standard of comfort "the injury done to them will be permanent, and their deteriorated condition will become a new minimum

exertions to procure them There cannot be a better security against a superabundant population In those countries, where the labouring classes have the fewest wants, and are contented with the cheapest food, the people are exposed to the greatest vicissitudes and miseries They have no place of refuge from calamity, they cannot seek safety in a lower station; they are already so low, that they can fall no lower. On any deficiency of the chief article of their subsistence, there are few substitutes of which they can avail themselves, and dearth to them is attended with almost all the evils of famine" (*Principles*, Ch v)

It is noteworthy that McCulloch, who has been charged, not altogether unjustly, with having adopted the extremest tenets of Ricardo, and applied them harshly and rigidly, yet chooses for the heading of the fourth Chapter of his Treatise *On Wages* —"Disadvantage of Low Wages, and of having the Labourers habitually fed on the cheapest species of food Advantage of High Wages."

[1] This habit of Ricardo's has already been discussed in the Note at the end of the last Chapter Prof Brentano, in his inaugural address at Vienna, gives as a reason for believing that the English classical economists really held the iron law of wages, the fact that they frequently speak of the minimum of wages as depending on the price of corn But the term "corn" was used by them, as it was by Petty, when (*Taxes and Contributions*, Ch. xiv) he speaks of "the Husbandry of Corn, which we will suppose to contain all necessaries of life, as in the Lord's Prayer we suppose the word Bread doth; and let the production of a bushel of this Corn be supposed of equal labour to that of producing an ounce of silver." Of course Ricardo took a less hopeful view of the prospects of the working classes than we do now Even the agricultural labourer can now feed his family well and have something to spare while even the artisan would then have required the whole of his wages, at all events after a poor harvest, to buy abundant and good food for his family. Prof Ashley (in the article referred to above, p. 561) insists on the narrowness of Ricardo's hopes as compared with those of our own age, he describes instructively the history of the passage quoted in the text; and shows that even Lassalle did not attribute absolute rigidity to his brazen law

tending to perpetuate itself as the more ample minimum did before[1]."

But it is only in our own generation that a careful study has begun to be made of the effects that high wages have in increasing the efficiency not only of those who receive them, but also of their children and grand-children In this matter the lead has been taken by General Walker and other American economists; and the application of the comparative method of study to the industrial problems of different countries of the Old and New Worlds is forcing constantly more and more attention to the fact that highly paid labour is generally efficient and therefore not dear labour; a fact which, though it is more full of hope for the future of the human race than any other that is known to us, will be found to exercise a very complicating influence on the theory of Distribution

But our own generation is the first to study carefully the influence of wages on efficiency

§ 2 Since Mill's time much progress has been made More careful analysis has shown that no simple solution of the problem of Distribution can be valid; and that attempts to make a short cut to the solution must necessarily cause confusion, if they are put forward as anything more than illustrations based on fancied hypotheses, and designed to throw light not on the problem as a whole, but on some particular difficulty in it. This and the following three sections will accordingly be given to a series of illustrations of the influence of demand on the earnings of labour, drawn from an imaginary world in which everyone owns the capital that aids him in his labour, so that the problem of the relations of capital and labour does not arise in it.

The problem of distribution may be illustrated by simple cases

There is a sense in which the agents of production may be regarded as two, Nature and man. In return to the labour of men, Nature yields resources varying with his diligence and with the advance made by the arts of production, and these resources are divided out among mankind in a manner that is very complex when the problem is

Commencement of a series of hypothetical illustrations drawn from a society

[1] Book II Ch XI § 2 He had just complained that Ricardo supposed the standard of comfort to be invariable, having apparently overlooked passages such as that quoted in the last note but one He was however well aware that Ricardo's "minimum rate of wages" depended on the prevalent Standard of Comfort, and had no connection with the bare necessaries of life.

BOOK VI. CH. I.

in which the problem of the relations between capital and labour do not exist. First case, in which population is stationary, and all men are industrially equal and interchangeable

Demand is still the main regulator of distribution,

obscured by difference in industrial rank and ability, by subdivision into trades, and above all by the ownership of private capital.

To make the central notion stand out clearly, let us then start not with the actual conditions of modern life, but with an imaginary society, in which but little capital is used, and everyone owns that which he uses, and in which the gifts of nature are so abundant that they are free and unappropriated. Let us suppose that everyone is not only of equal capacity, but of equal willingness to work, and does in fact work equally hard. also that all work is unskilled,—or rather unspecialized in this sense, that if any two people were to change occupations, each would do as much and as good work as the other had done. We may suppose also that everyone produces things ready for sale without the aid of others, and that he himself disposes of them to their ultimate consumers: so that the demand for everything is direct. In this case the problem of value is very simple. Things exchange for one another in proportion to the labour spent in producing them. If the supply of any one thing runs short, it may for a little time sell for more than its normal price: it may exchange for things the production of which had required more labour than it had. But people will at once leave other work to produce it, and in a very short time its value will fall to the normal level. There may be slight temporary disturbances, but as a rule anyone's earnings will be equal to those of anyone else In other words, each will have an equal share in the net sum total of things and services produced; or, as we may say, the *National Dividend* This will constitute the demand for labour; and might be called the common Wages-Fund, or Earnings-Fund; or better still Earnings-stream, since a Fund fails to suggest the constant flow of new goods into the world through supply, which flow out again through demand and consumption.

If now a new invention doubles the efficiency of work in any trade, so that a man can make twice as many things of a certain kind in a year without requiring additional appliances, then those things will fall to half their old exchange value. The effective demand for everyone's labour will be a little increased, and the share which he can draw from the common earnings-stream will be a little larger than before. He may if he chooses take twice as many things of this particular kind, together with his old allowance of other things: or he may take somewhat more than before of everything. If there be an increase in the efficiency of production in many trades the common earnings-stream or dividend will be considerably larger; the commodities produced by those trades will constitute a considerably larger demand for those produced by others, and increase the purchasing power of everyone's earnings.

also in the next case, in which population is stationary, and all are industrially equal but not interchangeable,

§ 3 Nor will the position be greatly changed if we suppose that some specialised skill is required in each trade, provided other things remain as before · that is, provided the workers are still supposed to be all of equal capacity and industry; and all trades to be equally agreeable and equally easy to be learnt. The normal rate of earnings will still be the same in all trades; for if a day's labour in one trade produces things that sell for more than a day's labour in others, and this inequality shows any signs of lasting, people will bring up their children by preference to the favoured trade. It is true that there may be some slight irregularities The drifting from one trade to another must occupy time; and some trades may for a while get more than their normal share of the earnings-stream, while others get less, or even lack work But in spite of these disturbances, the current value of everything will fluctuate about its normal value; which will in this case, as in the preceding, depend simply on the amount of labour spent on the thing: for the normal value of all kinds of labour will still be equal. The productive power of the community will have been increased by the division of labour, the common national dividend or earnings-stream will be larger, and as all will, putting aside passing disturbances, share alike in it, each will be able to buy with the fruits of his own labour things more serviceable to him than he could have produced for himself.

In this stage, as in those considered before, it is still

true that the value of each thing corresponds closely to the amount of labour spent upon it; and that the earnings of everyone vary with the demand for man's work offered by Nature, in the then existing state of the arts of production

§ 4. We have seen how, in some extreme doctrines as to population, it was supposed that the real cost of rearing a family was a fixed quantity; that, if earnings rose above this sum population increased rapidly, pressed against Nature's steady diminishing demand for man, and forced wages down. On this supposition the cost of rearing a family was the absolute governor of wages, subject only to slight disturbances, under an iron or brazen law It will be of service to balance against this an equally extreme supposition, in which the cost of rearing and training workers exercises no influence on their numbers. This case is one step nearer to reality than the supposition that the numbers of the people are rigidly fixed.

and again if population increases, but not under the influence of economic causes,

Let us conceive then that the growth of population proceeds at a rate, which is either fixed, or governed wholly by other than economic causes Thus it may be influenced by changes in custom, in moral opinion and in medical knowledge. But we are to suppose that the earnings of parents are always sufficient for the immediate needs of themselves and their children, that no change in their earnings affects either way birth-rate or death-rate; and, a more violent supposition still, that it does not affect either their own willingness to work, or the physical, mental, and moral strength of the rising generation. We are still supposing all labour to be of the same grade, and the national dividend to be divided out equally to each family, save for some slight passing inequalities In this case every improvement in the arts of production or transport, every new discovery, every new victory over Nature will increase equally the comforts and luxuries at the command of each family.

even though the law of diminishing return asserts itself.

But on the other hand, the growth of population, if even a very slow rate of increase is maintained long enough, must ultimately outgrow the improvements in the arts of production, and cause the law of diminishing return to assert itself; and the value of any kind of produce must equal

BOOK VI CH. I.

that of the labour, aided on our supposition by a uniform quantity of capital throughout, which is required to produce it on the margin of cultivation. (The marginal application of labour may be on land that will barely repay any labour at all, or it may be that cultivation of fertile land which is only just remunerative.) The surplus which is returned by Nature to the labour applied under advantageous circumstances, may conceivably be appropriated to public uses: or conceivably everyone may have an equal share of land; and in either case there will be a true surplus But the problem of Distribution and Exchange will present the simple form of Nature's offering for man's labour a demand, which, at all events after some considerable applications of labour have been made, will be at a diminishing rate The aggregate produce is the national dividend, in which each gets an equal share, each standing to gain equally by any improvement in the arts of production whether in his own trade or any other[1].

The same is true if men are of many grades, but the numbers in each grade are still supposed not to be governed by economic causes.

§ 5. Next suppose that labour is not all of one industrial grade, but of several[2]. Suppose also that parents always bring up their children to an occupation in their own grade, having a free choice within that grade, but not outside it. Further, suppose that the increase of population in each grade is governed by other than economic causes, as before it may be fixed, or it may be influenced by changes in custom, in moral opinion &c. In this case also the aggregate national dividend will still be governed by the abundance of Nature's return to man's work in the existing state of the arts of production, but the distribution of that dividend between the different grades will be unequal, and governed by demand.

For instance if artists form a grade or caste by themselves; then, their number being fixed, or at least controlled by causes independent of their earnings, their earnings will be governed by the resources which the population have available for spending on such gratifications as artists can

[1] This illustrative case will perhaps help to bring out more clearly the parallelism between a man's demand for anything, and nature's demand for man's work, which are represented in outline by the laws of *diminishing utility*, and *diminishing return* respectively see footnotes on pp. 169, 235

[2] Either four as Mill suggested, or any other number (see above, p 301).

supply for them, and their desire for such gratifications. Given the abundance of the national dividend, the earnings of artists will be governed simply by the demand for their efforts; under some conditions of demand these earnings might rise very high; under others they might fall very low.

It may so happen that the progress of invention is always finding new openings for one particular grade of labour, and making a little of its work go further relatively to other grades than before. It will then be paid at an ever increasing rate, and as, by hypothesis, this will exercise no influence on the number of people in the grade, their earnings will rise without ceasing. This however is likely to be held in check by the competition of some other grade of labour, which may be made available in substitution for it, the earnings of each being proportional to their (marginal) efficiency. But we must not pursue this further just now.

Return to the real conditions of life, which are however considered only on the side of demand.

§ 6 We may now leave the imaginary world, in which everyone owns the capital that aids him in his work; and return to our own, where the relations of labour and capital play a great part in the problem of distribution. But let us still, for the sake of simplicity, confine our attention to the manner in which the national dividend is distributed among the various agents of production, in accordance with the quantity of each several agent, and the services which it renders. The other side of the problem, viz. the reflex influence which the remuneration of each agent exerts on the supply of that agent, is as important as that which we are discussing, though we leave it on one side for the present, to be taken up in the next chapter.

The distribution of resources between different uses

In the world to which we thus return, the action of economic forces is largely directed by a set of men who specialize themselves in the organization of business, and through whose agency the principle to which we have given the name of the law of *Substitution* becomes effective.

That fundamental principle is most clearly seen when we consider the distribution of the resources of an individual between their various uses[1], or to take one step further, the investment of his resources for a distant return[2].

[1] Book III. Ch v [2] Book v. Ch v.

BOOK VI. CH. I

The conclusion we reached in the latter case was that each man, taking account of his own means, will push the investment of his resources in each several direction until what appears in his judgment to be the margin of profitableness is reached; that is, until there seems to him no good reason for thinking that the gains resulting from any further investment in that particular direction would compensate him for his outlay. The margin of profitableness is not to be regarded as a mere point on any one fixed line of possible investment; but as a boundary line of irregular shape cutting one after another every possible line of investment[1].

The principle of substitution worked through the agency of business men.

In modern life however the distribution of people's resources among the various agents of production is practically effected through the co-operation of the managers of business enterprises, and the general action of the principle of substitution may be thus described.—So far as the knowledge and business enterprise of the producers reach, they will in each case choose those factors of production which are best for their purpose the sum of the prices which they pay for those factors which are used is, as a rule, less than the sum of the prices which they would have to pay for any other set of factors which could be substituted for them: whenever it appears to the producers that this is not the case, they will, as a rule, set to work to substitute the less expensive method[2]. The principle thus expressed in technical language is in close harmony with such common sayings of every-day life, as that "everything tends to find its own level," that "most men earn just about what they are worth," that "if one man can earn twice as much as another, that shows that his work is worth twice as much," that "machinery will displace manual labour whenever it can do the work cheaper" This tendency does not indeed act without hindrance It may be restricted by custom or law, by professional etiquette or trade-union regulation it may be weakened by want of enterprise, or it may be softened by a generous unwillingness to part with old associates. But it

[1] See p 433 But only by mathematical language can all the many sides of this problem be expressed at once with precision and brevity, as *e g* in Note XIV

[2] See p 419

BOOK VI CH. I.

never ceases to act and it permeates all the economic adjustments of the modern world.

Illustrations

Thus in building there are some purposes for which bricks would be used, even if they were much dearer relatively to wood than they are; and others for which wood would be used, even if it were much dearer relatively to bricks than it is: but the applications of each material will be carried just so far that it would no longer be cheaper than the other relatively to the advantages gained by using it. Again, there are some kinds of field work for which horse-power is clearly more suitable than steam-power, and *vice versa:* but we may now suppose that there have been no great recent improvements in horse or steam machinery, and that therefore the experience of the past has enabled farmers gradually to apply the law of substitution; and on this supposition the application of steam-power will have been pushed just so far that any further use of it in the place of horse-power would bring no net advantage. There will however remain a margin on which they could be *indifferently* applied (as Jevons would have said), and on that margin the net efficiency of either will be proportionate to the net cost of applying it[1].

Similarly, if there are two methods of obtaining the same result, one by skilled and the other by unskilled labour, that one will be adopted which is the more efficient in proportion to its cost. There will be a margin on which either will be indifferently applied[2]. On that line the efficiency of each will be in proportion to the price paid for it, account being taken of the special circumstances of different districts and of different workshops in the same district. In other words,

[1] This margin will vary with local circumstances, as well as with the habits, inclinations, and resources of individual farmers The difficulty of applying steam machinery in small fields and on rugged ground would be overcome more generally in those districts in which labour is scarce than in those in which it is plentiful; especially if, as is probable, coal be cheaper, and the feed of horses dearer in the former than the latter.

[2] Skilled manual labour being generally used for special orders and for things of which not many are required of the same pattern, and unskilled labour aided by specialized machinery being used for others. The two methods are to be seen side by side on similar work in every large workshop but the position of the line between them will vary a little from one workshop to another

the wages of skilled and unskilled labour will bear to one another the same ratio that their efficiencies do at the margin of indifference.

Again, there will be a rivalry between hand-power and machine-power similar to that between two different kinds of hand-power or two different kinds of machine-power. Thus hand-power has the advantage for some operations, as, for instance, for weeding out valuable crops that have an irregular growth; horse-power in its turn has a clear advantage for weeding an ordinary turnip field; and the application of each of them will be pushed in each district till any further use of it would bring no net advantage there. On the margin of indifference between hand-power and horse-power their prices must be proportionate to their efficiency, and thus the law of substitution will have established directly a relation between the wages of labour and the price that has to be paid for horse-power.

Explicit applications of this law to distribution were first made by von Thunen

If we neglected differences between the grades of labour, and regarded all labour as of one kind, or at least as all expressed in terms of a certain kind of labour of standard efficiency, we might look for the margin of indifference between the direct application of labour and that of material capital, and we might say shortly, to quote von Thünen's words, that "the efficiency of capital must be the measure of its earnings, since if the labour of capital were cheaper than that of men, the undertaker would dismiss some of his workmen, and in the opposite case he would increase their number[1]."

[1] *Der Isolirte Staat*, II. I. p. 123 He argues (*ib.* p 124) that therefore "the rate of interest is the element by which the relation of the efficiency of capital to that of human labour is expressed", and finally, in words which have recently become famous, though he himself has gained but little credit for them, he says (p. 162). "Die Nutzung des zulezt angelegten Kapitaltheilchens bestimmt die Hohe des Zinsfusses." He had already (p 96) enunciated a general law of diminishing return for successive doses of capital in any branch of production; and what he says on this subject has much historic interest, though it does not show how to reconcile the fact that an increase in the capital employed in an industry may increase the output more than in proportion, with the fact that a continued influx of capital into an industry must ultimately lower the rate of profits earned in it. His treatment of these and other great economic principles, though primitive in many respects, yet stands on a different footing from his fanciful and unreal assumptions as to the causes that determine the accumulation of

But, of course, the increased competition of capital in general for employment is of a different character from the competition of machinery for employment in any single trade. The latter may push a particular kind of labour out of employment altogether; the former cannot displace labour in general, for it must cause an increased employment of the makers of those things which are used as capital. And in fact, the substitution of capital for labour is really the substitution of labour, combined with much waiting, in the place of other forms of labour combined with little waiting[1]. We shall return to this subject at the end of next chapter.

Marginal uses do not govern value, but are governed together with value by the general conditions of demand and supply.

§ 7. Thus the margins of the applications of each agent of production, including land, are determined, in the sense of being governed, by the general conditions of demand and supply: that is, on the one hand by the urgency of all the uses to which the agent can be put, taken together with the means at the command of those who need it; and, on the other hand, by the available supplies of it, whether these are fixed, as in the case of land, or capable of increase, as in the case of labour. In the very act of governing the marginal uses of each agent, these general conditions govern also its marginal net efficiency in each use; and therefore its exchange value in each use while equality is maintained between its values for each use by the constant tendency of the law of substitution to shift it from uses in which its services are of less value to others in which they are of greater[2].

capital, and as to the relations in which wages stand to the stock of capital From these he deduces the quaint result that the natural rate of wages of labour is the geometric mean between the labourer's necessaries, and that share of the product which is due to his labour when aided by capital. By the natural rate he means the highest that can be sustained; if the labourer were to get more than this for a time, the supply of capital would, von Thunen argues, be so checked as to cause him in the long run to lose more than he gained

[1] As von Thunen was well aware *Ib.* p 127

[2] An objection raised by some critics that the part played by the marginal use of an agent of production is represented, in modern economics, as governing the whole, is thus seen to rest on a misapprehension The withdrawal of iron from any of its necessary uses would have just the same influence on its value as its withdrawal from its marginal uses, in the same way as in the case of a boiler for cooking under high pressure, the pressure in the boiler would be affected by the escape of any other steam just as it would by the escape of the steam in one of

As a rule many kinds of labour, of raw material, of machinery and other plant, and of business organization both internal and external, go to the production of a commodity: and the advantages of economic freedom are never more strikingly manifest than when a business man endowed with genius is trying experiments, at his own risk, to see whether some new method, or combination of old methods will not be more efficient than the old. Every business man indeed according to his energy and ability is constantly endeavouring to obtain a notion of the relative efficiency of every agent of production that he employs, as well as of others that might possibly be substituted for some of them He works generally by trained instinct rather than formal calculation, but his processes are substantially similar to those indicated in our study of derived demand. That is, he estimates as best he can how much *net* addition to the value of his total product will be caused by a certain extra use of any one agent; *net* that is after deducting for any extra expenses that may be indirectly caused by the change, and adding for any incidental savings. The result is the net product of that agent, and he endeavours to employ each up to that margin at which its net product would no longer exceed the price he would have to pay for it[1].

Illustrations of the way in which the net

§ 8. We have already followed some simple estimates of this sort. We have noticed, for instance, how the propor-

the safety valves but in fact the steam does not escape except through the safety valves; and iron, or any other agent of production, is not thrown out of use except at points on its marginal use See above, p. 475, and compare the illustration taken from the derived demand for plasterers' labour, in Book V Ch. VI.

[1] The change might be such as could only be made on a large scale, as for instance the substitution of steam power for hand power in a certain factory; and in that case there would be a certain element of uncertainty and risk in the change Such breaches of continuity are however inevitable both in production and consumption if we regard the action of single individuals But as there is a continuous demand in a large market for hats and watches and wedding cakes, though no individual buys many of them (see Book III Ch. III § 5), so there will always be trades in which small businesses are most economically conducted without steam power, and larger businesses with, while businesses of intermediate size are on the margin Again there will always be some things done by hand power even in large establishments in which steam is already in use, which are done by steam power elsewhere (see above, § 6).

product of an agent of production may be estimated

tion of hops and malt in ale can be varied, how the extra price which can be got for ale by increasing the quantity of hops in it is a representative of the causes which govern the demand price for hops. Assuming that no further trouble or expense of any kind is involved by this additional use of hops, and that the expediency of using this extra amount is doubtful, the extra value thus given to the ale is the marginal net product of the hops of which we are in search[1]. In this case, as in most others, the net product is an improvement in quality or a general contribution to the value of the product; it is not a definite part of the produce which can be separated from the rest. But in exceptional cases that can be done.

Thus suppose an employer in doubt whether he has enough labour to turn his stock, machinery and other trade appliances to good account, and whether he could not, by hiring one more man, increase the production by more than the equivalent of his wages, without having to supply additional capital in any other way. A sheep farmer, for instance, may be in doubt whether his staff of shepherds is sufficient. He may find that if he hired an additional man, without making any other change, and without incurring any extra expenditure for implements, buildings &c., then so many more lambs will be kept alive, and the flocks generally so much better cared for, that he may expect to send to market twenty more sheep every year. This man will require no extra plant on which interest has to be charged; and he may be supposed to save the farmer himself just as much trouble in some ways as he gives in others, so that nothing has to be allowed for earnings of management (even when these are interpreted broadly so as to include insurance against risk &c.). Then the net produce of that shepherd's labour will be twenty sheep: if the farmer can hire him for ever so little less than the price of twenty sheep, he will decide to do so, otherwise not. The shepherd who is on the margin of not being employed—the *marginal* shepherd,

[1] See p. 457, and Mathematical Note XVI. See also other illustrations in Book V. Ch. VI. and VII.

as we may call him—adds to the total produce a net value just equal to his own wages[1].

It must however be remembered that the price which it is just worth while for the farmer to pay for this labour, merely gauges the outcome of multitudinous causes which between them govern the wages of shepherds; as the movements of a safety valve may gauge the outcome of the multitudinous causes that govern the pressure in a boiler[2].

This illustration has been chosen from a simple industry; but, though the form may be different, the substance of the problem is the same in every industry. Subject to conditions

[1] Theoretically a deduction from this has to be made for the fact that by throwing twenty extra sheep on the market, the farmer will lower the price of sheep generally, and therefore lose a little on his other sheep This correction may be of appreciable importance in special cases But in general discussions such as this, in which we are dealing with a very small addition to the supply thrown by one of many producers on a large market, it becomes very small (mathematically a small quantity of the second order), and may be neglected In the case of a monopolist who supplied the whole of a market, we had to take account of it; and also when discussing the considerations that induce any producer, or association of producers to abstain from "spoiling" that particular branch of a large market with which they are directly connected, especially in times of depression. This point is discussed at some length in Mathematical Note XIV, the whole of which has a close bearing on this section, and the reader may be asked to reckon it in as part of the present discussion.

[2] The fact that this marginal shepherd added twenty to the sheep whom the farmer could send to market rested no doubt on physical laws, given the conditions under which he worked. But those conditions include the amount of land at the farmer's disposal which is influenced by the demand for land for raising timber, oats, deer etc. Again the conditions include the number of shepherds that the farmer already has, and that is governed by the general conditions of the broad problem of distribution and exchange, and in particular by the number of those from whom the ranks of shepherds could have been recruited during the current generation, by the demand for mutton and wool and by the area from which supplies of them can be obtained, and by the effectiveness of the shepherds on all other farms.

Further the net product of the shepherd in the exceptional case which we have chosen, plays no greater part in governing the wages of shepherds, than does that of any of the last (marginal) shepherds on farms where they cannot be profitably employed without considerable extra outlay in other directions, as for land, buildings, implements, labour of management, &c Thus the net product of such shepherds cannot be ascertained simply, but it is a case of derived demand (see Book V Ch VI), and requires us to take account of the prices which have to be paid for the aid of all these other agents of production It will be noticed that this holds with regard to all agents of production, however they may differ from one another on the side of supply. It is as true of "land," which is of fixed aggregate quantity, and of which the value is uninfluenced even in the long run by cost of production, as it is of labour and capital, of which the ultimate values are determined by laws of demand and supply co-ordinately.

BOOK VI CH. I

which are indicated in the foot-note, but are not important for our main purpose, the wages of every class of labour tend to be equal to the net produce due to the additional labour of the marginal labourer of that class[1].

The scientific use of partial and incomplete statements

It may be objected that the doctrine that the earnings of a worker tend to be equal to the net produce of his work, has by itself no real meaning; since in order to estimate "net produce," we have to take for granted all the expenses of production of the commodity on which he works, other than his own wages. The objection is valid against a claim that it contains a theory of wages; but not against a claim that the doctrine throws into clear light the action of one of the causes that govern wages. For indeed it is always a difficult task to hold in mind at one and the same time all the actions and reactions of a great number of causes which mutually determine one another; and although the able business man

[1] This method of illustrating the net produce of a man's labour is not easily applicable to industries in which a great deal of capital and effort has to be invested in gradually building up a trade connection; and especially if they are such as obey the law of increasing return. In both cases there is a difficulty of accounts, making it almost impossible to decide what part of the gains of the business would have been lost for want of the services of any individual worker. (See Book v. ch. vii. §§ 1, 2 and ch. xi. § 2.) But in the latter case there is a second and more fundamental difficulty. For the employer, in taking on an additional worker, may estimate only for the direct good that that man's work will do to his business; whereas to find the total net product of the man's work, even from the employer's point of view, account should also be taken of the part which it plays in enabling the business to avail itself of the economies of production on a large scale. The employer, if of an enterprising temperament, may take account of these also: but there is still something omitted. The increase in the size of that business will tend to increase the demand for subsidiary industries, and in other ways to increase the (external) economies available for other businesses in the same trade; and, since this additional gain to the community will not accrue to the employer himself, it cannot be expected that he should hand it on to the workman. The question why this extra gain, accruing to the undertaker in such an industry from an increase in his business, does not ultimately cause the whole industry to fall into the hands of one large firm, has been discussed in Book IV. Ch. XII. On the whole subject see Book V. Ch. XI. and the summary of that chapter on pp. 554–6.

This is indeed a special application of that general failure of the so-called doctrine of *Maximum Satisfaction* which we have already noticed (Book V. Ch. XII.). For independently of such considerations as that a great benefit to a poor man will be outweighed in the balance of market exchange by a small benefit to a rich man, that doctrine fails in the case of industries which obey the law of increasing return, because the payment which any particular worker or employer receives in those industries is less than the true equivalent of the net product of his services to the community.

acquires a sort of instinct that enables him to do it as regards his own affairs, and much of the higher training of science is devoted to acquiring a more general power of the kind; yet everyone finds his task lightened, when he breaks up a difficult problem, and takes one part of it at a time The strain necessarily involved by the problem of Distribution and Exchange, is so great that we should avail ourselves of every aid.

Remarks generally similar apply to the demand for capital

§ 9. In later chapters we shall need to take other illustrations for special purposes of the principle illustrated in the last section from the case of manual labour, and in particular to show how the value of some parts of the work of business management can be measured, when it is found that the effective output of a business is increased as much by some additional superintendence, as it would be by the hire of an additional ordinary worker. Again, the earnings of a machine can sometimes be estimated by the addition to the output of a factory which it might effect in certain cases without involving any incidental extra expense

Generalizing from the work of a particular machine to that of machinery of a given aggregate value, it may be said that in a certain factory an extra £100 worth of machinery can be applied so as not to involve any other extra expense, and so as to add annually £3 worth to the net output of the factory, after allowing for its own wear and tear. If the investors of capital push it into every occupation in which it seems likely to gain a high reward; and if, after this has been done and equilibrium has been found, it still pays and only just pays to employ this machinery, we can infer from this fact that the yearly rate of interest is three per cent But illustrations of this kind merely indicate part of the action of the great causes which govern value. They cannot be made into a theory of interest, any more than into a theory of wages, without reasoning in a circle.

It may however be well to push a little further our illustration of the nature of the demand for capital for any use; and to observe the way in which the aggregate demand for it is made up of the demands for many different uses.

Illustration of the de-

To fix the ideas, let us take some particular trade, say that of hat-making, and inquire what determines the amount

mand for capital in a particular trade

of capital which it absorbs. Suppose that the rate of interest is 3 per cent.[1] per annum on perfectly good security; and that the hat-making trade absorbs a capital of one million pounds. This implies that the hat-making trade can turn the whole million pounds' worth of capital to so good account that they would pay 3 per cent. per annum *net* for the use of it rather than go without any of it.

Some things are necessary to them; they must have not only some food, clothing, and house room, but also some Circulating capital, such as raw material, and some Fixed capital, such as tools and perhaps a little machinery. And though competition prevents anything more than the ordinary trade profit being got by the use of this necessary capital; yet the loss of it would be so injurious that those in the trade would have been willing to pay 50 per cent on it, if they could not have got the use of it on easier terms There may be other machinery which the trade would have refused to dispense with if the rate of interest had been 20 per cent per annum, but not if it had been higher. If the rate had been 10 per cent., still more would have been used, if it had been 6 per cent, still more, if 4 per cent, still more; and finally the rate being 3 per cent. they use more still. When they have this amount, the marginal utility of the machinery, *i.e* the utility of that machinery which it is only just worth their while to employ, is measured by 3 per cent.

A rise in the rate of interest would diminish their use of machinery; for they would avoid the use of all that did not give a net annual surplus of more than 3 per cent. on its value And a fall in the rate of interest would lead them to demand the aid of more capital, and to introduce machinery which gave a net annual surplus of something less than 3 per cent on its value. Again, the lower the rate of interest, the more substantial will be the style of building used for the hat-making factories and the homes of the hat-makers; and a fall in the rate of interest will lead to the employment of more capital in the hat-making trade in the form of larger

[1] The charge made to traders for loans is generally much more than 3 per cent per annum, but as we shall see in Chapter VI. it includes other things besides true Net interest.

stocks of raw material, and of the finished commodity in the hands of retail dealers[1].

BOOK VI CH. I

The aggregate demand for capital.

The methods in which capital will be applied may vary much even within the same trade Each undertaker having regard to his own means, will push the investment of capital in his business in each several direction until what appears in his judgment to be the margin of profitableness is reached; and that margin is, as we have said, a boundary line cutting one after another every possible line of investment, and moving irregularly outwards in all directions whenever there is a fall in the rate of interest at which extra capital can be obtained. Thus the demand for the loan of capital is the aggregate of the demands of all individuals in all trades, and it obeys a law similar to that which holds for the sale of commodities just as there is a certain amount of a commodity which can find purchasers at any given price. When the price rises the amount that can be sold diminishes, and so it is with regard to the use of capital.

And as with borrowings for productive purposes, so with those of spendthrifts or Governments who mortgage their

[1] Compare Book v Ch iv, and Jevons's *Theory*, Chapter vii on the "Advantage of Capital to Industry" Jevons however, like some later writers, appears to have regarded this doctrine as reaching further than it does towards a complete theory of the causes which govern interest; and in view of recent discussions it may be permissible to reproduce from the *Academy* for April 1, 1872, a criticism of his "General expression for the rate of interest" in the same chapter. "To put part of [Jevons'] argument in another way Suppose that *A* and *B* employ the same capital in producing hats by different processes If *A*'s process occupies a week longer than *B*'s, the number of hats he obtains, in excess of the number obtained by *B*, must be the interest for a week on the latter number. Thus the rate of interest is expressed as the ratio of two numbers without the aid of any theory of value expressed but not determined" [in the sense of governed] "The relative productiveness of slow and rapid processes of manufacture is but one of the determining causes of the rate of interest if any other cause made this fall, *B*'s process would be abandoned The rate of interest affects the duration of the remunerative processes of manufacture, no less than it is affected by it Just as the motion of every body in the solar system affects and is affected by the motion of every other, so it is with the elements of the problem of political economy It is right and necessary to break up the problem, to neglect for the time the influence of some elements, to investigate the variations of any one element which must, *cæteris paribus*, accompany certain assumed variations in one or more others Such investigations give results which, even as they stand, are roughly applicable to certain special cases But this does not justify us in speaking, in general, of one element as determined by another; as for instance, of value as determined by cost of production, or of wages as determined by value."

future resources in order to obtain the means of immediate expenditure. It is true that their actions are often but little governed by cool calculation, and that they frequently decide how much they want to borrow with but little reference to the price they will have to pay for the loan; but still the rate of interest exercises a perceptible influence on borrowings even of this kind.

Further study of the general notion of the national dividend

§ 10. There is one more difficulty connected with the demand for the various agents of production, which we must consider before we end this chapter and enter on the study of the mutual relations of demand and supply for those agents. The difficulty relates to the mode of estimating the national dividend

When we speak of the national dividend, or distributable net income of the whole nation, as divided into the shares of land, labour and capital, we must be clear as to what things we are including, and what things we are excluding. It will seldom make very much difference to our argument whether we use all the terms broadly, or all the terms narrowly. But it is essential that our usage should be consistent throughout any one argument; and that whatever is included on one side of the account of the demand for, and supply of, capital should be included also on the other.

The labour and capital of the country, acting on its natural resources, produce annually a certain net aggregate of commodities, material and immaterial, including services of all kinds This is the true net annual income, or revenue, of the country, or, the national dividend. We may, of course, estimate it for a year or for any other period, the important point is, as already hinted, that it is a continuous stream always flowing, and not a reservoir or store, or in the narrower sense of the word a "Fund[1]." The terms National Income and National Dividend are convertible; only the latter is the more convenient when we are looking at the national income in the character of the sum of the new sources of enjoyments that are available for distribution.

[1] See above, p 572 In Prof Newcomb's words it is a *Flow* and not a Fund (See his *Political Economy*, Book IV Ch I)

Common usage is followed in delimiting income, whether that which goes into or that which comes out from the national dividend

We have already noticed that many of the services which a person renders to himself are not in practice counted as part of his income; though if they were performed for him by a valet or hairdresser they would be reckoned among the commodities (or economic goods) on which he spent his means: that is, they would be reckoned as part of his real income We have noticed also that though the benefits which a man derives from living in his own house are commonly reckoned as part of his real income, and estimated at the net rental value of his house, the same plan is not followed with regard to the benefits which he derives from the use of his furniture and clothes. It is best here to follow the common practice, and not count as part of the national income or dividend anything that is not commonly counted as part of the income of the individual. Thus, unless anything is said to the contrary, the services which a person renders to himself, and those which he renders gratuitously to members of his family or friends; the benefits which he derives from using his own personal goods, or public property such as toll-free bridges, are not reckoned as parts of the national dividend, but are left to be accounted for separately[1].

[1] It would be possible, and, for some theoretical purposes, it would be best to include them but if they are included in the national dividend, the efforts and the material wealth which are their sources must be counted as part of the labour and capital which are agents of production; and the services and the benefits themselves must be counted as earnings of labour or interest on capital as the case may be It will be recollected that in Book II Ch IV, the standard delimitations of Capital and Income were chosen specially with reference to this their most important use

It is to be understood that the excess of profits over interest is here provisionally reckoned among earnings, subject to a stricter analysis at a later stage Speaking broadly, taxes may be regarded as those parts of the national dividend which the community elects to devote to the expenses of Government, the share of taxes which the merchant pays may be regarded as coming out of his profits, those which the working-man pays as coming out of his wages; and so on There are, however, some cases in which it is convenient to regard taxes as a distinct share of the Dividend; and to regard the other shares as modified accordingly

CHAPTER II.

PRELIMINARY SURVEY OF DISTRIBUTION AND EXCHANGE, CONTINUED

Ricardo and his followers were familiar with the action of the law of substitution, but they laid insufficient stress on the side of demand; and in the reaction too exclusive importance has been assigned to it

§ 1 Ricardo and the able business men who followed in his wake were familiar with such facts as those which we have been considering But they took the operation of demand too much for granted as a thing which did not need to be explained: they did not emphasize it, nor did they make clear the important position which it really holds in their doctrine of value, and did not even trouble themselves to work out its more remote results And they seem to have been rightly guided by their intuitions, when they silently determined that the forces of supply were those, the study of which was the more urgent and involved the greater difficulty. But it must be confessed that their partial neglect of the forces of demand has given occasion to much confusion, and has obscured important truths And in the reaction, as we have just seen, too much insistence has been laid on the fact that the earnings of every agent of production come from, and are for the time mainly governed by the value of the product which it takes part in producing; its earnings being so far governed on the same principle as the rent of land. And some have even thought it possible to constitute a complete theory of Distribution out of multifold applications of the law of rent But they will not reach to that end.

When we inquire what it is that determines the marginal efficiency of a factor of production, whether it be any kind of labour or material capital, we find that the immediate solution requires a knowledge of the available supply of that factor; and that the ultimate solution requires a knowledge also of the causes that determine that supply. The nominal value of everything, whether it be a particular kind of labour or capital or anything else, rests, like the keystone of an arch, balanced in equilibrium between the contending pressures of its two opposing sides, the forces of demand press on the one side, and those of supply on the other.

The amounts and prices of the several agents of production mutually determine one another.

The production of everything, whether an agent of production or a commodity ready for immediate consumption, is carried forward up to that limit or margin at which there is equilibrium between the forces of demand and supply. The amount of the thing and its price, the amounts of the several factors or agents of production used in making it, and their prices—all these elements mutually determine one another, and if an external cause should alter any one of them the effect of the disturbance extends to all the others.

Parallel instances from physics

In the same way, when several balls are lying in a bowl, they mutually determine one another's positions, and again when a heavy weight is suspended by several elastic strings of different strengths and lengths attached to different points in the ceiling, the equilibrium positions of all the strings and of the weight mutually determine one another If any one of the strings that is already stretched is shortened, everything else will change its position, and the length and the tension of every other string will be altered also.

And though (if we neglect certain elements of prime cost) the earnings of each agent are for the time of the nature of a rent yet those earnings react on the supply of the agent; and therefore on the amount and therefore on the value of the produce raised by it; and therefore on the demand for the agent itself, and therefore on its earnings, and thus the chain of reciprocal influences is complete. But the doctrine of rent, properly so called, relates to those agents of production of which the supply cannot be increased, and is unaffected by the earnings to be gained by increasing the supply. And those earnings of agents of production which we have called quasi-rents, because they are mainly governed for short periods by the value of the products, are governed ultimately by the laws of supply at least as much as by the

BOOK VI. CH. II.

laws of demand. To make this clear, it will be well to turn back and recall the substance of our studies of the supply of the agents of production in Books IV. and V.

Influence of his remuneration on the individual's willingness to work

§ 2. We have seen that the effective supply of any agent of production at any time depends firstly on the stock of it in existence, and secondly on the willingness of those, in whose charge it is, to apply it in production. This willingness is not decided simply by the immediate return which is expected; though there may be a lower limit, which in some cases may be described as a prime cost, below which no work will be done at all. A manufacturer for instance has no hesitation in declining to put his machinery in motion for an order that will not cover the extra direct money outlay caused by the work, together with the actual wear and tear of the machinery; while there are somewhat similar considerations with regard to the wear and tear of the worker's own strength and to the fatigue and other discommodities of his work. And, though for the present we are concerned with cost and remuneration under normal conditions rather than with the direct cost to the individual of any particular piece of work that he does; yet it may be well to make a short statement about them here in order to avoid misconceptions[1].

Sometimes any remuneration is almost superfluous,

It has already been noticed[2] that when a man is fresh and eager, and doing work of his own choice, it really costs him nothing. For as some socialists have urged with pardonable exaggeration, few people know how much they enjoy moderate work, till something occurs to prevent them from working altogether. But rightly or wrongly, most persons believe that the greater part of the work which they do, when earning their living, yields them no surplus of pleasure, but on the contrary costs them something. They are glad when the hour for stopping arrives: perhaps they forget that the earlier hours of their work have not cost them as much as the last: they are rather apt to think of nine hours' work as costing them nine times as much as the last hour, and it seldom occurs to them to think of themselves as reaping

[1] Especially in view of some recent discussions in Austria and America.

[2] See Book I. Ch. V. § 6, Book II. Ch. III. § 2, and Book IV. Ch. I. § 2, and Ch. XI. § 1.

BOOK VI CH II

a producer's surplus or rent, through being paid for every hour at a rate sufficient to compensate them for the last, and most distressing hour[1].

but generally, though not always, increased remuneration stimulates to increased exertions

The longer a man works, or even is on duty, the greater is his desire for a respite, unless indeed he has become numbed by his work; while every hour's additional work gives him more pay, and brings him nearer to the stage at which his most urgent wants are satisfied; and the higher the pay, the sooner this stage is reached. It depends then on the individual, whether with growing pay new wants arise, and new desires to provide comforts for others or for himself in after years; or he is soon satiated with those enjoyments that can be gained only by work, and then craves more rest, and

[1] Recent discussions on the eight hours day have often turned very little on the fatigue of labour; for indeed there is much work in which there is so little exertion, either physical or mental, that what exertion there is counts rather as a relief from ennui than as fatigue A man is on duty, bound to be ready when wanted, but perhaps not doing an hour's actual work in the day; and yet he will object to very long hours of duty because they deprive his life of variety, of opportunities for domestic and social pleasures, and perhaps of comfortable meals and rest

If a man is free to cease his work when he likes, he does so when the advantages to be reaped by continuing seem no longer to over-balance the disadvantages If he has to work with others, the length of his day's work is often fixed for him; and in some trades the number of days' work which he does in the year is practically fixed for him But there are scarcely any trades, in which the amount of exertion which he puts into his work is rigidly fixed If he be not able or willing to work up to the minimum standard that prevails where he is, he can generally find employment in another locality where the standard is lower, while the standard in each place is set by the general balancing of the advantages and disadvantages of various intensities of work by the industrial populations settled there The cases therefore in which a man's individual volition has no part in determining the amount of work he does in a year, are as exceptional as the cases in which a man has to live in a house of a size widely different from that which he prefers, because there is none other available It is true that a man who would rather work eight hours a day than nine at the same rate of tenpence an hour, but is compelled to work nine hours or none, suffers a loss from the ninth hour, or reaps a negative rent from it, and that in such cases one must take the day as the unit But the general law of costs is not disturbed by this fact, any more than the general law of utility is disturbed by the fact that a concert or a cup of tea has to be taken as a unit: and that a person who would rather pay five shillings for half a concert than ten for a whole, or twopence for half a cup of tea than fourpence for a whole cup, incurs a loss on the second half. There seems therefore to be no good foundation for the suggestion made by Prof v Bohm-Bawerk (*The Ultimate Standard of Value*, § IV published in the *Zeitschrift fur Volkswirtschaft*, vol II and again in the *Annals of American Academy*, vol V), that value must be determined generally by demand, without direct reference to cost, because the effective supply of labour is a fixed quantity.

BOOK VI. CH. II.

more opportunities for activities that are themselves pleasurable. No universal rule can be laid down, but experience seems to show that the more ignorant and phlegmatic of races and of individuals, especially if they live in a southern clime, will stay at their work a shorter time, and will exert themselves less while at it, if the rate of pay rises so as to give them their accustomed enjoyments in return for less work than before. But those whose mental horizon is wider, and who have more firmness and elasticity of character, will work the harder and the longer the higher the rate of pay which is open to them; unless indeed they prefer to divert their activities to higher aims than work for material gain. But this point will need to be discussed more fully under the head of the influence of progress on value[1]

The dependence in the long run of the supply of efficient labour on the rate of earnings and the manner in which they are spent

§ 3. When however we turn from the immediate influence exerted by a rise in wages on the work done by an individual to its ultimate effect after a generation or two, the result is less uncertain. It is indeed true that a permanent increase of prosperity is quite as likely to raise as to lower the birth-rate; though a temporary improvement will give a good many young people the opportunity to marry and set up house, for which they have been waiting. But on the other hand, an increase of wages is almost certain to diminish the death-rate, unless it has been obtained at the price of the neglect by mothers of their duties to their children. And the case is much stronger when we look at the influence of high wages on the physical and mental vigour of the coming generation

For each grade of work there is a certain consumption

[1] See Ch XII. Bad harvests, war prices, and convulsions of credit have at various times compelled some workers, men, women and children, to over-work themselves And cases of ever-increasing exertion in return for a constantly sinking wage, though not as numerous now as is often alleged, have not been very rare in past times They may be compared with the exertions of a failing firm to secure some return for their outlay by taking contracts at little more than enough to recompense them for their prime, or special and direct cost. And on the other hand almost every age, our own perhaps less than most others, has stories of people who in a sudden burst of prosperity, have contented themselves with the wages to be earned by very little work, and have thus contributed to bring the prosperity to a close. But such matters must be deferred till after a study of commercial fluctuations In ordinary times the artisan, the professional man or the capitalist undertaker decides, as an individual or as a member of a trade association, what is the lowest price against which he will not strike.

which is strictly speaking necessary in this sense, that if any of it is curtailed the work cannot be done efficiently: the adults might indeed take good care of themselves at the expense of their children, but that would only defer the decay of efficiency for one generation. Further there are conventional necessaries, which are so strictly demanded by custom and habit, that in fact people generally would give up much of their necessaries strictly so called rather than go without the greater part of these. Thirdly there are habitual comforts, which some, though not all, would not entirely relinquish even when hardly pressed. Many of these conventional necessaries and customary comforts are the embodiment of material and moral progress. Their extent varies from age to age and place to place; and with its variations there is a corresponding but inverse variation in the extent to which man, himself always the sole end of all production, is also an economical agent of production.

The supply of labour corresponds quickly to the demand for it when there is no great expenditure on things that are not necessary for efficient work.

Any increase in consumption that is strictly necessary to efficiency pays its own way and adds to, as much as it draws from, the national dividend. But an increase of consumption, that is not thus necessary, can be afforded only through an increase in man's command over nature: and that can come about through advance in knowledge and the arts of production, through improved organization and access to larger and richer sources of raw material, and lastly through the growth of capital and the material means of attaining desired ends in any form.

Thus the question how closely the supply of labour responds to the demand for it, is in a great measure resolved into the question how great a part of the present consumption of the people at large consists of necessaries, strictly so called, for the life and efficiency of young and old, how much consists of conventional necessaries which theoretically could be dispensed with, but practically would be preferred by the majority of the people to some of those things that were really necessary for efficiency, and how much is really superfluous regarded as a means towards production, though of course part of it may be of supreme importance regarded as an end in itself.

The earlier French and English economists, as we noted

Most expenditure of the working classes conduces to efficiency in backward countries,

at the beginning of this chapter, classed nearly all consumption under the first head They did so, partly for simplicity, and partly because the working classes were then poor in England and very poor in France, and they inferred that the supply of labour would correspond to changes in the effective demand for it in the same way, though of course not quite as fast as that of machinery would. And an answer not very different from theirs must be given to the question with regard to the less advanced countries even now for throughout the greater part of the world the working classes can afford but few luxuries and not even many conventional necessaries, and any increase in the demand for them made by the other agents of production would result in so great an increase of their numbers as to bring down their earnings quickly to nearly the old level at their mere expenses of rearing Over a great part of the world wages are governed, nearly after the so-called iron or brazen law, which ties them close to cost of rearing, and sustaining a rather inefficient class of labourers

and even in the rich western world

As regards the modern western world the answer is materially different, so great has been the recent advance in knowledge and freedom, in vigour and wealth, and in the easy access to rich distant fields for the supply of wealth and raw material. But it is still true even in England to-day that much the greater part of the consumption of the main body of the population conduces to sustain life and vigour, not perhaps in the most economical manner, but yet without any great waste Doubtless some indulgences are positively harmful, but these are diminishing relatively to the rest[1] Most of that expenditure which is not strictly economical as a means towards efficiency, yet helps to form habits of ready resourceful enterprise, and gives that variety to life without which men become dull and stagnant, and achieve little though they may plod much, and it is well recognized that even in western countries skilled labour is generally the cheapest where wages are the highest It may be admitted that the industrial development of Japan is tending to show that some of the more expensive conventional necessaries

[1] The chief exception perhaps being that of gambling

might conceivably be given up without a corresponding diminution of efficiency but, though this experience may be fruitful of far-reaching results in the future, yet it has little bearing on the past and the present. It remains true that, taking man as he is, and has been hitherto, in the western world the earnings that are got by efficient labour are not much above the lowest that are needed to cover the expenses of rearing and training efficient workers, and of sustaining and bringing into activity their full energies[1].

General conclusion.

We conclude then that an increase of wages, unless earned under unwholesome conditions, almost always increases the strength, physical, mental and even moral of the coming generation; and that, other things being equal, an increase in the earnings that are to be got by labour increases its rate of growth, or, in other words, a rise in its demand price increases the supply of it If the state of knowledge, and of social and domestic habits be given; then the vigour of the people as a whole if not their numbers, and both the numbers and vigour of any trade in particular, may be said to have a supply price in this sense, that there is a certain level of the demand price which will keep them stationary, that a higher price would cause them to increase, and that a lower price would cause them to decrease[2].

The influences of demand and supply on wages are co-ordinate.

Thus demand and supply exert co-ordinate influences on wages, neither has a claim to predominance; any more than has, to use an old simile once more, either blade of a pair of scissors, or either pier of an arch. Wages tend to equal the

[1] On all locomotives there is some brass or copper work designed partly for ornament, and which could be omitted or displaced without any loss to the efficiency of the steam engine Its amount does in fact vary with the taste of the officials who select the patterns for the engines of different railways But it might happen that custom required a great deal of such expenditure of a definite character that the custom would not yield to argument, and that the railway companies could not venture to offend against it In that case, when dealing with periods during which the custom ruled, we should have to include the cost of that ornamental metal work in the cost of producing a certain amount of locomotive horse-power, on the same level with the cost of the piston itself And there are many practical problems, especially such as relate to periods of but moderate length, in which conventional and real necessaries may be placed on nearly the same footing

[2] This sentence is repeated with the requisite corrections (see the *Corrigenda*) from p 301

net product, or to correspond to the marginal productivity which rules their demand price; and wages tend to retain a close though indirect and intricate relation with the cost of rearing, training and sustaining the energy of efficient labour The various elements of the problem mutually determine (in the sense of governing) one another, and incidentally this secures that supply-price and demand-price tend to equality: wages are not governed by demand-price nor by supply-price, but by the whole set of causes which govern demand and supply[1]

The phrase general rate of wages presents difficulties

§ 4. In the last section we spoke frequently of the general rate of wages, or of the wages of labour in general. Such phrases are convenient in a broad view of distribution, and especially when we are considering the general relations of capital and labour. But in fact there is no such thing in modern civilization as a general rate of wages Each of a hundred or more groups of workers has its own wage problem, its own set of special causes, natural and artificial, controlling the supply price, and limiting the number of its members; each has its own demand price governed by the need that other agents of production have of its services

There are similar but less difficulties in the phrase a general rate of interest

The case is rather different with regard to capital in general It is true that some forms of capital are more narrowly specialized than any forms of labour, and that they are even more liable to violent variations of value in consequence of economic changes. But those individuals, who are most affected by such changes, are those whose special rôle it is to bear the brunt of economic vicissitudes and risks and to gain in the long run by doing so; and important as they are for subsequent stages of our inquiry, they may be

[1] The reiteration in this section has seemed to be unavoidable in consequence of the misunderstandings of the main argument of the present Book by various critics, among whom must be included even the acute Prof v Bohm-Bawerk For in the article recently quoted (see especially Section v), he seems to hold that a self-contradiction is necessarily involved in the belief that wages correspond both to the net product of labour and also to the cost of rearing and training labour and sustaining its efficiency (or, more shortly, though less appropriately, the cost of production of labour) On the other hand the mutual interactions of the chief economic forces are set forth in an able article by Prof Carver on *The theory of wages adjusted to recent theories of value* in the *Quarterly Journal of Economics* for July 1894

neglected just now. No social or economic issue, that is vital for our immediate purpose, is confused by ignoring the influence of economic change on the relative values of different kinds of machinery and so on.

The flow of investment of resources for future needs consists of two streams. The smaller consists of new additions to the accumulated stock: the larger merely replaces that which is destroyed; whether by immediate consumption, as in the case of raw material, fuel, etc., by wear and tear, as in that of railway irons, by the lapse of time, as in that of a thatched roof or a trade directory; or by all these combined. The annual flow of this second stream is probably not less than a quarter of the total stock of capital, even in a country in which the prevailing forms of capital are as durable as in England It is therefore not unreasonable to assume for the present that the owners of capital in general have been able in the main to adapt its forms to the normal conditions of the time, so as to derive as good a *net* income from their investments in one way as another. On that supposition we may speak of capital in general as being accumulated under the expectation of a certain net interest which is the same for all its forms[1].

The rate of interest applies strictly to new investments only the value of old investments is governed by their earnings

But we must recollect that we can properly speak of the rate of interest on any save new investments of capital only in a very limited sense For instance, we may perhaps estimate that a trade capital of some seven thousand millions is invested in the different trades of this country at about three per cent net interest. But such a method of speaking, though convenient and justifiable for many purposes,

[1] As Prof Clark says, the second stream may be regarded from two points of view First there is something permanent, a body of "pure capital" to use his phrase, like the permanent body of a waterfall; and secondly there are the particular machines, raw material &c., which are ever coming, passing away and being replaced, like the particular drops of water that pass through the permanent fall

Among the questions which are here left on one side for future study are the way in which the *net* interest of capital is to be distinguished not only from gross profits but from much that is frequently reckoned under the head of interest, though it really contains elements of earnings of management and insurance against risk and again how changes in the general purchasing power of money cause the net interest that is really being earned by capital to be sometimes higher than it appears and sometimes lower.

BOOK VI. CH. II.

is not accurate. What ought to be said is that, taking the rate of net interest on the marginal investments, or on the investments of new capital in each of those trades, to be about three per cent, then the aggregate net income rendered by the whole of the trade-capital invested in the various trades is such that, if capitalized at 33 years' purchase (that is on the basis of interest at three per cent.), it would amount to some seven thousand million pounds. For the capital already invested in improving land and erecting buildings, and in making railways and machinery, has its value determined by the net income (or quasi-rent) which it will produce and if its prospective income-yielding power should diminish, its value would fall accordingly and would be the capitalized value of that smaller income after allowing for depreciation[1].

Summary of earlier conclusions

We have seen[2] how the accumulation of wealth is governed by a great variety of causes: by custom, by habits of self-control and of realizing the future, and above all by the power of family affection. security is a necessary condition for it, and the progress of knowledge and intelligence furthers it in many ways. But though affected by many causes other than the rate of interest, and though the rate of saving of many people is but little affected by the rate of interest, while a few who have determined to secure an income of a certain fixed amount for themselves or their family will save less with a high rate than with a low rate of interest, yet a strong balance of evidence seems to rest with the opinion that a rise in the rate of interest, or demand price for saving, tends to increase the volume of saving.

The rate of interest is determined in the long run by the two sets of forces of supply and demand respectively.

Thus then interest, being the price paid for the use of capital in any market, tends towards an equilibrium level such that the aggregate demand for capital in that market, at that rate of interest, is equal to the aggregate stock forthcoming there at that rate. If the market, which we are considering, is a small one—say a single town, or a single trade in a progressive country—an increased demand for capital in

[1] The same result is of course got by aggregating the discounted values of all its probable future net incomes on the plan discussed in Bk v. Ch. IV. § 2

[2] Book IV Ch. VII., summarized in § 10.

it will be promptly met by an increased supply drawn from surrounding districts or trades. But if we are considering the whole world, or even the whole of a large country as one market for capital, we cannot regard the aggregate supply of it as altered quickly and to a considerable extent by a change in the rate of interest. For the general fund of capital is the product of labour and waiting; and the extra work, and the extra waiting, to which a rise in the rate of interest would act as an incentive, would not quickly amount to much as compared with the work and waiting, of which the total existing stock of capital is the result. An extensive increase in the demand for capital in general will therefore be met for a time not so much by an increase of supply, as by a rise in the rate of interest; which will cause capital to withdraw itself partially from those uses in which its marginal utility is lowest. It is only slowly and gradually that the rise in the rate of interest will increase the total stock of capital.

Land is on a different footing from other agents of production for the purposes of this chapter

§ 5. Land, by which is here meant all those agents of production which are supplied freely by nature in quantities less than man needs, is on a different footing from man himself and those agents of production which are made by man, among which are included improvements made by him on the land itself[1]. For while the supplies of all other agents of production respond in various degrees and various ways to the demand for their services, land makes no such response. Thus if the earnings of any class of labour rise, a compensatory action tends to increase its numbers, or efficiency, or both, and, if not to lower again its rate of earnings per head, yet at least to enable them to be paid from an increased national dividend, and not at the expense of other agents of production. And the same is true as regards capital: but it is not true as regards land. While

[1] It is not necessary to repeat here the discussion of the difficulties which surround any attempt to separate practically the "inherent" properties of the land in an old country from those which it has derived from man's action (see Book IV. Ch. II. § 1) nor to dwell on the special circumstances of land in a new country, in which the cultivator may obtain land not from another cultivator, but direct from nature herself, and in which therefore the rent of land has not yet acquired its special features (see Book V. Ch. IX. § 1).

BOOK VI. CH II

therefore the value of land, in common with the values of other agents of production, is subject to those influences which were discussed towards the end of the preceding chapter, it is not subject to those which have been brought into the reckoning in the present discussion

It shares with other agents those influences which were discussed in the last chapter.

Land shares the influences of the laws of demand and of substitution which were discussed in the last chapter, because the existing stock of it, like the existing stock of capital or of labour of any kind, tends to be shifted from one use to another till nothing could be gained for production by any further shifting. For indeed, as we have seen, a manufacturer or a cultivator, owning both land and buildings (or any other plant), regards the two as bearing similar relations to his business Either will afford him aid and accommodation at first liberally and afterwards with diminishing return as he endeavours to force more and more from them; till at last he will doubt whether the overcrowding of his workshops or his storerooms is not so great a source of trouble that it would answer his purpose to save by obtaining more space. And when he comes to decide whether to obtain that space by taking in an extra piece of land or by building his factory a floor higher, he weighs the net product of more capital applied in building against the net product of more land, just as he might weigh it against the net product of any other agent of production Land is in short but a particular form of capital from the point of view of the individual manufacturer[1].

And the same is substantially true of the individual cultivator The question whether he has carried his cultivation of a particular piece of land as far as he profitably can, and whether he should try to force more from it or to take in another piece of land, is of the same kind as the question whether he should buy a new plough or try to get a little more work out of his present stock of ploughs, using them sometimes when the soil is not in a very favourable condition, and feeding his horses a little more lavishly. He, like the manufacturer, weighs the net product of a little more land against the other uses to which he could put the capital sum that he would have to expend in order to obtain it. Thus

[1] Book V Ch VIII § 5 See also Book VI Ch IX § 5.

the income that is derived from a factory, a warehouse, or a plough (allowance being made for wear and tear, etc.) is governed, so far as the stage which we considered in the last chapter is concerned, in the same way as is the income from land. In each case the income tends to equal the value of the marginal net product of the agent: in each case this is governed for the time by the total stock of the agent and the need that other agents have of its aid.

But its special features are vital for the broad problem of distribution as a whole.

That is one side of the question. The other is that land (in an old country) does not share the reflex influences, discussed in this chapter, which a high rate of earnings exerts on the supply of other agents of production, and consequently on their contributions to the national dividend, and consequently on the real cost at which their services are purchased by other agents of production. We have seen that this difference is not important in connection with the quickly passing changes of the market, for relatively to them the stocks of nearly all agents of production are approximately fixed, and their earnings are therefore in part at least of the nature of a quasi-rent. But the stock of land (in an old country) at any time is the stock for *all* time: and when a manufacturer or cultivator decides to take in a little more land to his business, he decides in effect to take it away from someone else's business: though he adds a little more land to his business, yet the nation adds no land to its business. In contrast with this, the building an additional floor on one factory or putting an extra plough on one farm does not generally take a floor from another factory or a plough from another farm: the nation adds a factory floor or a plough to its business as the individual does to his: there is an increase of the national dividend which is to be shared out, and in the long run the increased earnings of the manufacturer or farmer are not as a rule at the cost of other producers. We conclude then that the peculiarity in the earnings from land and other gifts of nature which arises from the fact that their stock cannot be increased by man, is seldom of much importance as regards the affairs of any individual trader, nor even as regards market fluctuations of wages and prices; but that it is of vital

BOOK VI. CH. II.

importance relatively to the broad central problem of normal distribution[1].

The earnings of the several agents of production, according to their marginal services, exhaust the national dividend.

§ 6. This part of the argument may be seen from another side in a study of the relations in which the different kinds of surpluses that we have considered at various stages of our inquiry stand to the national dividend and to one another. The argument of this section is however difficult, and almost exclusively of academic interest; and it should be omitted by the general reader

The net aggregate of all the commodities produced is itself the true source from which flow the demand prices for all these commodities, and therefore for the agents of produc-

[1] As has been intimated in Book V Ch VIII—X., part of the argument of which has been reproduced in this section, the difference between rent and the earnings of other agents of production is nowhere more conspicuous nor more important than in the applications of the theory of value to the incidence of taxation: (see especially p. 478); a point to which we shall need frequently to recur in the second volume of this treatise Some parts of the general argument of this section will be further developed in Book VI Ch IX The position that rent of land stands on a similar footing to the hire of a pony for a particular day, but not to the hire of ponies in general, when account is taken of the possibilities of increasing or diminishing their number, is maintained, in opposition to a part of the argument of the Duke of Argyll's *Unseen Foundations of Society*, in an article by the present writer in the *Economic Journal*, Vol. III

The tendency of Austrian economists to minimise the influence which cost of production exerts on value naturally leads them to give little prominence to the differences between land and other agents of production And a similar position in this respect has been taken by some of those who have applied mathematical expressions to the theory of value. They have laid stress on the fact that the land turned to account by the individual undertaker appears on the same footing with the other agents of production in the general function which expresses his output, (the differential coefficient of this function with regard to that or any other agent corresponding equally to the net product or earnings for him of a unit of that agent, see the foot-note on p. 464), and they have apparently inferred that land and its earnings figure in the general doctrine of distribution on a like footing with other agents of production and their earnings They have applied a proposition, which is true and important in one class of problems, to a problem which would appear to belong to a different class; (see the review by Mr Flux of Mr Wicksteed's interesting *Co-ordination of the Laws of Distribution* in the *Economic Journal*, Vol IV, especially p 312).

Mr H M Thompson (*Theory of Wages*, Chapter IV.) also inclines against a distinctive treatment of the share which land receives of the National Dividend, and he lays stress on the elasticity of man's resources in subjugating to his use new and distant lands and developing old lands. But where we are contrasting the fixity of the supply of land in an old country with the elasticity of the supplies of labour and capital, it would seem that we must not class with the former the results of improvements in agriculture and transport: for they belong to the latter

tion used in making them. Or, to put the same thing in another way, this national dividend is at once the aggregate net product of, and the sole source of payment for, all the agents of production within the country: it is divided up into earnings of labour, interest of capital, and lastly the producer's surplus, or rent, of land and of other differential advantages for production. It constitutes the whole of them and the whole of it is distributed among them; and the larger it is, the larger, other things being equal, will be the share of each of them. Further it is distributed among them, speaking generally, in proportion to the need which people have for their several services—*i e* not the *total* need, but the *marginal* need. By this is meant the need at that point, at which people are indifferent whether they purchase a little more of the services (or the fruits of the services) of one agent, or devote their further resources to purchasing the services (or the fruits of the services) of other agents[1].

But yet everyone as consumer gets a surplus of satisfaction over his payments at these rates

While the national dividend is thus completely absorbed in remunerating the owner of each agent of production at its marginal rate, it yet generally yields him a surplus which has two distinct, though not independent sides. It yields to him, as consumer, a surplus consisting of the excess of the total utility to him of the commodity over the real value to him of what he paid for it. For his marginal purchases, those which he is only just induced to buy, the two are equal. but those parts of his purchases for which he would gladly have paid a higher price than go without them, yield him a surplus of satisfaction: a true net benefit which he, as consumer, derives from the facilities offered to him by his surroundings or conjuncture. He would lose this surplus, if his surroundings were so altered as to prevent him from obtaining any supplies of that commodity, and to compel him to divert the means which he spends on that to other commodities (one of which might be increased leisure) of which at present he does not care to have further supplies at their respective prices.

Another side of the surplus which a man derives from his

[1] Compare Mr Wicksteed's *Co ordination of the Laws of Distribution*, p 46

and a surplus of satisfaction accrues from payment at these rates to most workers, and to most savers

surroundings is better seen when he is regarded as producer, whether by direct labour, or by the accumulated, that is acquired and saved, material resources in his possession. As a worker, he derives a *worker's surplus*, through being remunerated for all his work at the same rate as for that last part, which he is only just willing to render for its reward, though much of the work may have given him positive pleasure As capitalist (or generally as owner of accumulated wealth in any form) he derives a *saver's surplus* through being remunerated for all his saving, that is waiting, at the same rate as for that part which he is only just induced to undergo by the reward to be got for it. And he generally is remunerated at that rate even though he would still have made some savings if he had been compelled to pay for their safe keeping, and had reaped a negative interest from them[1].

These surpluses must be distinguished from the

A great part of a worker's earnings are of the nature of a deferred return to the trouble and expense of preparing him for his work; and there is therefore a great difficulty in estimating his surplus Nearly all his work may be pleasur-

[1] This point was emphasized by Gossen and Jevons; and among the many interesting American and Austrian writings on it, special reference may be made to Prof. Clark's *Surplus Gains of Labour*. See also above, Book IV. Ch. I

These two sets of surpluses are not independent and it would be easy to reckon them up so as to count the same thing twice For when we have reckoned the producer's surplus at the value of the general purchasing power which he derives from his labour or saving, we have reckoned implicitly his consumer's surplus too, provided his character and the circumstances of his environment are given. This difficulty might be avoided analytically; but in no case would it be practically possible to estimate and add up the two series. The consumer's surplus, the worker's surplus, and the waiter's surplus, which any one is capable of deriving from his surroundings, depend on his individual character. They depend in part on his general sensibility to the satisfactions and dissatisfactions of consumption and of working and waiting severally; and in part also on the elasticity of his sensibilities, that is on the rates at which they change with an increase of consumption, of work and of waiting respectively. Consumer's surplus has relation in the first instance to individual commodities, and each part of it responds directly to changes in the conjuncture affecting the terms on which that commodity is to be had while the two kinds of producer's surplus appear always in terms of the general return that the conjuncture gives to a certain amount of purchasing power. The two kinds of producer's surplus are independent and cumulative, and they stand out distinct from one another in the case of a man working and saving things for his own use While the intimate connection between both of them and consumer's surplus is shown by the fact that, in estimating the weal and woe in the life of a Robinson Crusoe, it would be simplest to reckon his producer's surpluses on such a plan as to include the whole of his consumer's surplus.

able, and he may be earning a good wage for the whole of it: but in reckoning up the balance of human weal and endurance we must set off against this much effort and sacrifice endured by his parents and by himself in past time: but we cannot say clearly how much. In a few lives there may be a balance of evil: but there is reason to think that there is a balance of good in most lives, and a large balance in some. The problem is as much philosophical as economic; it is complicated by the fact that man's activities are ends in themselves as well as means of production, and also by the difficulty of dividing clearly the immediate and direct (or prime) cost of human effort from its total cost; and it must be left imperfectly solved[1].

excess of earnings of an appliance of production over the prime cost of its work. The line is not easily drawn for human agents.

The case is in some respects simpler when we pass to consider the earnings of material appliances for production. The work and the waiting by which they have been provided, yield their own worker's and waiter's surplus just mentioned, and in addition a surplus (or quasi-rent) of the excess of total money returns over direct outlay; provided we confine our attention to short periods only. But for long periods, that is, in all the more important problems of economic science, and especially in the problems discussed in this chapter, there is no distinction between immediate outlay and total outlay. And in the long run the earnings of each agent are, as a rule, sufficient only to recompense at their marginal rates the sum total of the efforts and sacrifices required to produce them. If less than these marginal rates had been forthcoming the supplies would have been diminished, and on the whole therefore there is in general no extra surplus in this direction.

But as regards material agents such additional surplus vanishes when all outlays are reckoned in,

This last statement applies in a sense to land which has been but recently taken up, and possibly it might apply to much land in old countries, if we could trace its records back to their earliest origins. But the attempt would raise controversial questions in history and ethics, as well as in economics; and the aims of our present inquiry are prospective rather than retrospective. Looking forward rather than backwards, and not concerning ourselves with the equity and

with a partial exception in the case of land.

[1] But see below, Ch. v

the proper limits of the present private property in land, it is important for us to note that that part of the national dividend which goes as earnings of land is a surplus in a sense in which the earnings from other agents are not a surplus[1].

This concludes the main body of our preliminary discussion of distribution and exchange. But there are some points on which a little more should be said here The first relates to the mutual interactions of various groups of the agents of production, with special reference to the fact that the bond between the earnings of workers in the same grade is generally stronger than that between the earnings of workers in different grades. The second relates to the nature of the influences which the supply of capital exerts on wages in general and will bring us near to the so-called Wages-Fund theory

[1] The argument again is given at some length above, Book v Ch VIII—X, and in the article *On Rent* in reply to the Duke of Argyll already referred to; and some parts of it will be further developed below in Ch IX, X. moreover its substance has much in common with that near the end of the last chapter But yet it relates to a matter on which misunderstandings are so frequent, that it should perhaps be set out clearly here

All appliances of production, whether machinery, or factories with the land on which they are built, or farms, are alike in yielding large surpluses over the prime costs of particular acts of production to a man who owns and works them also in yielding him normally no special surplus in the long run above what is required to remunerate him for his trouble and sacrifice and outlay in purchasing and working them (no special surplus, as contrasted with his general worker's and waiter's surplus) But there is this difference between land and other agents of production, that if a tax, or combination to raise wages, or his own preference for an easy life with a small income over a hard life with a large income, had deterred the manufacturer from building or buying the factory, there might probably have been one factory the less in the world, or at best an inferior one in place of his in the long run there is no disposable surplus on factory buildings. But if he had not bought the land on which the factory was built, the land with its permanent convenience of space, its permanent income of sunlight and air, and (though that may be of much less importance) those properties of its soil which are indestructible, would have remained for others to use From a social point of view land yields a permanent surplus, which perishable things made by man do not The more nearly it is true that the earnings of any agent of production are required to keep up the supply of it, the more closely will its supply so vary that the share which it is able to draw from the national dividend conform to the cost of maintaining the supply and in an old country land stands in an exceptional position, because its earnings are not affected by this cause The difference between land and other durable agents is however mainly one of degree and a great part of the interest of the study of the rent of land arises from the illustrations which it affords of a great principle that permeates every part of economics

BOOK VI. CH II

Mutual relations between the work and earnings of different groups of workers. An increase in the supply of any agent will benefit most other agents, but not necessarily of all.

§ 7. In studying the influence which increased efficiency and increased earnings in one trade exert on the condition of others we may start from the general fact that, other things being equal, the larger the supply of any agent of production, the further will it have to push its way into uses for which it is not specially fitted; the lower will be the demand price with which it will have to be contented in those uses in which its employment is on the verge or margin of not being found profitable, and, in so far as competition equalizes the price which it gets in all uses, this price will be its price for all uses. The extra production resulting from the increase in that agent of production will go to swell the national dividend, and other agents of production will benefit thereby: but that agent itself will have to submit to a lower rate of pay.

For instance, if without any other change, capital increases fast, the rate of interest must fall, if without any other change, the number of those ready to do any particular kind of labour increases, their wages must fall. In either case there will result an increased production, and an increased national dividend in either case the loss of one agent of production must result in a gain to others, but not necessarily to all others. Thus the opening up of rich quarries of slate or the increase in numbers or efficiency of quarrymen, would tend to improve the houses of all classes; and it would tend to increase the demand for bricklayers' and carpenters' labour, and raise their demand-price. But it would injure the makers of roofing tiles as producers of building materials, more than it benefited them as consumers. The increase in the supply of this one agent increases the demand for many others by a little, and for some others by much, but for some it lessens the demand.

Wages of a worker expressed provisionally in terms of the Net products of workers in the same grade,

Now we know that the wages of any worker, say for instance a shoemaker, tend to be equal to the net product of his labour and that since the wages of all workers in the same grade tend to be equal to one another, therefore in a state of equilibrium every worker will be able with the earnings of a hundred days' labour to buy the net products of a hundred days' labour of other workers in the same grade with himself he may select them in whatever way he chooses, so as to make up that aggregate sum[1].

or of other grades

If the normal earnings of workers in another grade are half as high again as his own, the shoemaker must spend three days' wages in order to get the net product of two days' labour of a worker in that grade; and so in proportion.

The dependence of wages on the efficiency of labour

Thus, other things being equal, every increase in the net efficiency of labour in any trade, including his own, will raise in the same proportion the real value of that part of his wages which the shoemaker spends on the products of that trade; and other things being equal, the equilibrium level of the real wages of the shoemaker depends directly on, and varies directly with, the average increase in the efficiency of the trades, including his own, which produce those things on which he spends his wages. Conversely, if any trade rejects an improvement by which its efficiency could be increased ten per cent., it inflicts on the shoemaker an injury measured by ten per cent. of that part of his wages which he spends on the products of that trade. But an increased efficiency on the part of workers, whose products compete with his own, may injure him temporarily at least, especially if he is not himself a consumer of those products.

The relations between grades. An increased supply of business ability raises the wages of manual labour

Again, the shoemaker will gain by anything that changes the relative positions of different grades in such a way as to raise his grade relatively to others. He will gain by an increase of medical men whose aid he occasionally needs And he will gain more if those grades which are occupied chiefly with the tasks of managing business, whether manufacturing, trading or any other, receive a great influx from other grades. for then the earnings of management will be lowered permanently relatively to the earnings of manual work, there will be a rise in the net product of every kind of manual labour, and, other things being equal, the shoemaker will get more of every commodity on which he spends those wages that represent his own net product

[1] It will be recollected that the net product of an individual agent of production cannot as a rule be separated mechanically from that of other agents which co-operate with it see p. 482

§ 8. The process of Substitution, of which we have been discussing the tendencies, is one form of Competition; and it may be well to insist again that we do not assume that competition is perfect. Perfect competition requires a perfect knowledge of the state of the market; and though no great departure from the actual facts of life is involved in assuming this knowledge on the part of dealers when we are considering the course of business in Lombard Street, the Stock Exchange, or in a wholesale Produce Market; it would be an altogether unreasonable assumption to make when we are examining the causes that govern the supply of labour in any of the lower grades of industry. For if a man had sufficient ability to know everything about the market for his labour, he would have too much to remain long in a low grade. The older economists, in constant contact as they were with the actual facts of business life, must have known this well enough, but partly for brevity and simplicity, partly because the term "free competition" had become almost a catchword, partly because they had not sufficiently classified and conditioned their doctrines, they often seemed to imply that they did assume this perfect knowledge.

We do not assume perfect knowledge and freedom of competition,

It is therefore specially important to insist that we do not assume the members of any industrial group to be endowed with more ability and forethought, or to be governed by motives other than those which are in fact normal to, and would be attributed by every well-informed person to, the members of that group; account being taken of the general conditions of time and place. There may be a good deal of wayward and impulsive action, sordid and noble motives may mingle their threads together; but there is a constant tendency for each man to select such occupations for himself and his children as seem to him on the whole the most advantageous of those which are within the range of his resources, and of the efforts which he is able and willing to make in order to reach them.

but only the enterprise and business habits which are in fact normal to each several rank of industry.

§ 9. The last group of questions, which still remain to be discussed, is concerned with the relation of capital in general to wages in general[1]. It is obvious that though

We pass to the relations of capital and labour

[1] In Section 4 we noticed that the study of Distribution is much more

BOOK VI. CH II.

in general. There is a real if restricted competition for the field of employment between capital and labour.

capital in general is constantly competing with labour for the field of employment in particular trades; yet since capital itself is the embodiment of labour as well as of waiting, the competition is really between some kinds of labour aided by a good deal of waiting, and other kinds of labour aided by less waiting. On the one side, for instance, are many who make shoes by hand, and a very few who make awls and other simple implements, aided by a little waiting, on the other are a relatively small number who work powerful sewing-machines which were made by engineers, aided by a good deal of waiting. There is a real and effective competition between labour in general and waiting in general. But it covers a small part of the whole field; and is of small importance relatively to the benefits which labour derives from obtaining cheaply the aid of capital, and therefore of efficient methods in the production of things that it needs[1].

For speaking generally, an increase in the power and the willingness to save, will cause the services of waiting to be pushed constantly further, so as to obtain employment at a rate of interest, which will constantly fall unless invention opens new advantageous uses of roundabout methods of production. In either case, but especially in the latter, the growth of capital increases the national dividend; and thus opens out new and rich fields for the employment of labour in other directions, which more than compensate for the partial displacement of the services of labour by those of waiting in particular trades.

An increase of capital

The increase of the national dividend owing to the growth of capital and invention is certain to affect all classes

concerned with the causes that govern the earnings of each of many different groups of labour, than with causes that affect them all in approximately the same manner But yet these latter have some interest even for the modern economist And the fact that the earlier economists, partly in consequence of the special industrial conditions of their time, gave great prominence to discussions of general wages, makes it important to lay considerable stress on them in the interest of the continuity of the science

[1] We are leaving on one side here the competition for employment between labour in the narrower sense of the term and the work of the undertaker himself and his assistant managers and foremen A great part of Ch VII and VIII is given to this difficult and important problem.

of commodities; and to enable the shoemaker, for instance, to purchase with his earnings more food and clothes, more and better supplies of water, artificial light and heat, travel, and so on It may be admitted that a few improvements affect only commodities consumed by the rich, in the first instance at least, that no part of the corresponding increase of the national dividend goes directly to the labouring classes, and that they do not at once gain anything to compensate for the probable disturbance of some of their members in particular trades. But such cases are rare, and generally on a small scale and even in them there is nearly always some indirect compensation For improvements, designed for the luxuries of the rich, soon spread themselves to the comforts of other classes. And, though it is not a necessary consequence, yet in fact a cheapening of luxuries does generally lead in various ways to increased desires on the part of the rich for things made by hand and for personal services, and increases also the means at their disposal for gratifying those desires. This points to another aspect of the relation between capital in general and wages in general

lowers the marginal charge for its use and raises real wages

§ 10 It is commonly said that, though those workers who have little or no accumulated wealth of their own, have much to gain by an increase of the capital in that narrower sense of the term in which it is nearly convertible with trade capital that supports and aids them in their work, yet they have little to gain from an increase of other forms of wealth not in their own hands No doubt there are a few kinds of wealth the existence of which scarcely affects the working classes; while they are directly affected by every increase of (trade) capital, the greater part of which is constantly passing through their hands as implements or materials of their work, while part of the rest is directly used or even consumed by them[1]. And from this it seems natural to conclude

The benefits which wage-earners derive from the increase of wealth not owned by them and not in the form of trade capital.

[1] At all events according to most definitions There are some indeed who confine capital to "intermediate goods," and must therefore exclude hotels, and lodging-houses and workmen's cottages, at all events as soon as they are used But grave objections to the adoption of this definition have already been indicated (Book II Ch IV § 8).

that the working classes must gain when other forms of wealth become trade capital and *vice versâ*. But if private people generally gave up keeping carriages and yachts, and hired them out from capitalist undertakers, there would result a smaller demand for hired labour. For part of what would have been paid as wages would go as profits to a middleman[1].

It may be objected that if other forms of wealth take the place of trade capital on a large scale, there may be a scarcity of the things needed to aid labour in its work and even of those needed to support it. This may be a real danger in some oriental countries. But in the western world, and especially in England, the total stock of capital is equal in value to the aggregate of the commodities consumed by the working classes during many years: and a very small increase in the demand for those forms of capital, that minister directly to labour's needs, relatively to other forms, would quickly bring forward an increased supply of them, either imported from some other part of the world, or specially produced to meet the new demand. There is therefore no necessity to trouble ourselves much on this score. If the marginal efficiency of labour is kept high, its net product will be high; and so will therefore its earnings: and the constantly flowing stream of the national dividend will divide itself up in corresponding proportions, giving always an adequate supply of commodities for immediate consumption by the workers, and assigning to the production of those commodities an adequate stock of implements. When the general conditions of demand and supply have decided what part of the national dividend the other classes of society are free to spend as they will, and when the inclinations of those classes have decided the mode in which they will distribute their expenditure between present and deferred

[1] See above, p. 145. Again, an increased use of brass furniture that needs much cleaning, and generally of modes of living that require the assistance of many indoor and outdoor servants, operates on the demand for labour in the same way as the use of hand-made goods in place of goods made by expensive machinery and other fixed capital. It may be true that the employment of a great number of domestic servants is an ignoble and wasteful use of a large income: but there is no other equally selfish method of spending it which tends so directly to increase the share of the national dividend which goes to the working classes.

gratifications, etc., it matters not to the working classes whether orchids come from private conservatories, or from the glass houses which belong to professional florists, and which are therefore trade capital.

Further explanations

§ 11. It is to be understood that the share of the national dividend, which any particular industrial class receives during the year, consists either of things that were made during the year, or of the equivalents of those things For many of the things made, or partly made, during the year are likely to remain in the possession of capitalists and undertakers of industry and to be added to the stock of capital; while in return they, directly or indirectly, hand over to the working classes some things that had been made in previous years.

The sense in which it is true that the earnings of labour depend on advances made by capital.

The ordinary bargain between labour and capital is that the wage-receiver gets command over commodities in a form ready for immediate consumption, and in exchange carries his employer's goods a stage further towards being ready for immediate consumption But while this is true of most employees, it is not true of those who finish the processes of production. For instance, those who put together and finish watches, give to their employers far more commodities in a form ready for immediate consumption, than they obtain as wages. And if we take one season of the year with another, so as to allow for seed and harvest time, we find that workmen as a whole hand over to their employers more finished commodities than they receive as wages. But—to say nothing of machinery and factories, of ships and railroads—the houses loaned to workmen, and even the raw materials in various stages which will be worked up into commodities consumed by them, represent a far greater provision of capital for their use than the equivalent of the advances which they make to the capitalist, even when they work for a month for him before getting any wages. And in this sense we are justified in saying that the earnings of labour depend upon advances made to labour by capital[1].

[1] The details of this doctrine, and the exaggerated importance attached to it by English economists early in this century, are described in the Note at the end of this Chapter.

BOOK VI CH. II.

The resources of individual employers are returned to them through sales to customers

Some German economists have argued that the resources with which the employer pays wages come from consumers. But this appears to involve a misapprehension It might be true of an individual employer if the consumer paid him in advance for what he produced. but in fact the rule goes the other way; the consumer's payments are more often in arrear, and merely give deferred command over ready commodities in return for ready commodities. It may be admitted that if the producer could not sell his goods, he might not be able for the time to hire labour; but that would only mean that the organization of production was partially out of gear: a machine may stop if one of its connecting rods gets out of order, but that does not mean that the driving force of the machine is to be found in the rod

But in a broad view all are consumers, and to say that the resources of producers come from consumers, is but to say that they come from the national dividend.

Nor again is the amount which the employer pays as wages at any time governed by the price which consumers *do* pay him for his wares; though it generally is largely influenced by his expectations of the price they *will* pay him. It is indeed true that in the long run and under normal conditions, the prices which consumers do pay him and those which they will pay him are practically the same. But when we pass from the particular payments of an individual employer to the normal payments of employers generally—and it is really only with these latter that we are now concerned—consumers cease to form a separate class, for every one is a consumer The national dividend goes exclusively to consumers, and these consumers are also the producers, that is the owners of the agents of production, labour, capital and land. Children and others who are supported by them, and the government which levies taxes on them, do but expend part of their income for them[1] To say therefore that the resources of employers generally are ultimately drawn from those of consumers generally, is undoubtedly true But it is only another way of saying that all resources have been parts of the national dividend, which have been directed into forms suitable for deferred, instead of immediate use; and if

1 Unless indeed we reckon as separate items of the national income the security and other benefits which government provides

any of them are now applied to any other purpose than immediate consumption, it is in the expectation that their place will be taken (with increment or profit) from the incoming flow of the national dividend[1].

The older theories of wages were working their way towards modern doctrine

In all this then there is nothing to make the relations between capital in general and labour in general differ widely from those between any other two agents of production, in the general scheme of distribution already explained The modern doctrine is the outcome to which all the earlier theories of the relations between labour or capital were working their way, and differs only in its greater exactness, completeness and homogeneity, from that given by Mill in the third chapter of his fourth book; the only place in which he collects together all the various elements of the problem.

The broad theory of distribution already given covers the general relations of capital and labour,

Capital in general and labour in general are agents co-operating in the production of the national dividend, and drawing from it their earnings in the measure of their respective (marginal) efficiencies in production No doubt their mutual dependence is of the closest; capital without labour is dead: the labourer without the aid of his own or someone else's capital would not long be alive. Where labour is energetic, capital reaps a high reward and grows apace, and, thanks to capital and knowledge, the ordinary labourer in the western world is in many respects better fed, clothed and even housed than were princes in earlier times. The co-operation of capital and labour is as essential as that of the spinner of yarn and the weaver of cloth: there is a little priority on the part of the spinner; but that gives him no pre-eminence. The prosperity of each is bound up with the strength and activity of the other; though each may gain temporarily, if not permanently, a somewhat larger share of the national dividend at the expense of the other.

In the modern world, the employer or undertaker, who

[1] In an interesting article in the *Quarterly Journal of Economics* for January 1895, Prof Taussig explains how Hermann and some other German economists have endeavoured to modify the old English Wages-fund doctrine that wages are dependent on the resources of the employer, by tracing the dependence of these on the resources of consumers: and he indicates how, when account is taken of the fact that there is no general class of consumers, the old doctrine is thus made imperceptibly to merge into its modern form

though the rôle of the undertaker is of growing importance

may have but little capital as his own, acts as the boss of the great industrial wheel. The interests of owners of capital and of workers radiate towards him and from him. and he holds them all together in a firm grip. He will therefore take a predominant place in those discussions of fluctuations of employment and of wages, which are deferred to the second volume of this treatise; and a prominent, though not predominant, place in those discussions of the secondary features in the mode of action of demand and supply peculiar to labour, capital and land respectively, which will occupy the next eight chapters.

Note on the Doctrine of the Wages-Fund.

Early in this century special causes emphasized the dependence of labour on the aid of capital,

At the beginning of this century, great as was the poverty of the English people, foreign countries were poorer still. In most of them population was sparse, and therefore food was cheap; but for all that they were underfed, and could not provide themselves with the sinews of war. France, after her first victories, helped herself along by the forced contributions of others. But the countries of Central Europe could not support their own armies without England's aid. Even America with all her energy and national resources, was not rich, she could not have subsidised Continental armies. The economists looked for the explanation, and found it chiefly in England's accumulated capital, which, though small when judged by our present standard, was very much greater than that of any other country Other nations were envious of England, and wanted to follow in her steps, but they were unable to do so, partly indeed for other reasons, but chiefly because they had not capital enough. Their annual income was required for immediate consumption. There was not in them a large class of people who had a good store of wealth set by, which they did not need to consume at once, and which they could devote to making machines and other things that would aid labour and enable it to produce a larger store of things for future consumption A special tone was given to their arguments by the facts that capital was scarce everywhere, even in England; that the efficiency of labour was becoming more and more dependent on the machinery by which it was aided, and lastly, that some foolish followers of Rousseau were telling the working classes that they would be better off without any capital at all

In consequence, the economists gave extreme prominence to the statements; first, that labour requires the support of capital, *i.e.* of good clothes, &c., that have been already produced, and secondly, that labour requires the aid of capital in the form of factories, stores of raw material, &c. Of course the workman might have supplied his own capital, but in fact he seldom had more than a little store of clothes and furniture, and perhaps a few simple tools of his own—he was dependent for everything else on the savings of others. The labourer received clothes ready to wear, bread ready to eat, or the money with which he could purchase them. The capitalist received a spinning of wool into yarn, a weaving of yarn into cloth, or a ploughing of land, and only in a few cases commodities ready for use, coats ready to be worn, or bread ready to be eaten There are, no doubt, important exceptions, but the ordinary bargain between employers and employed is that the latter receives things ready for immediate use and the former receives help towards making things that will be of use hereafter. These facts the economists expressed by saying that all labour requires the support of capital, whether owned by the labourer or by someone else, and that when anyone works for hire, his wages are, as a rule, advanced to him out of his employer's capital—advanced, that is, without waiting till the things which he is engaged in making are ready for use These simple statements have been a good deal criticised, but they have never been denied by anyone who has taken them in the sense in which they were meant

but this dependence was exaggerated by some careless expressions

The older economists, however, went on to say that the amount of wages was limited by the amount of capital; and this statement cannot be defended; at best it is but a slovenly way of talking It has suggested to some people the notion that the total amount of wages that could be paid in a country in the course of, say a year, was a fixed sum If by the threat of a strike, or in any other way, one body of workmen got an increase of wages, they would be told that in consequence other bodies of workmen must lose an amount exactly equal in the aggregate to what they had gained. Those who have said this, have perhaps thought of agricultural produce, which has but one harvest in the year. If all the wheat raised at one harvest is sure to be eaten before the next, and if none can be imported, then it is true that if anyone's share of the wheat is increased, there will be just so much less for others to have. But this does not justify the statement that the amount of wages payable in a country is fixed by the capital in it, a doctrine which has been called 'the vulgar form of the wages-fund theory[1].'

Mill attempted to discuss wages be-

It has already been noticed (Book I. Ch. IV. § 7) that Mill in his later years under the combined influence of Comte, of the Socialists, and of the general tendencies of public sentiment, set himself to bring

[1] These three paragraphs are reproduced from a paper written in the *Co-operative Annual*, and reprinted in the *Report of the Industrial Remuneration Conference*, 1885, which contained the outlines of the central argument of this and the previous chapter

fore he had reached the theory of value

into prominence the human, as opposed to the mechanical, element in economics. He desired to call attention to the influences which are exerted on human conduct by custom and usage, by the ever-shifting arrangements of society, and by the constant changes in human nature; the pliability of which he agreed with Comte in thinking that the earlier economists had underrated. It was this desire which gave the chief impulse to his economic work in the latter half of his life, as distinguished from that in which he wrote his *Essays on Unsettled Questions*; and which induced him to separate Distribution from Exchange, and to argue that the laws of Distribution are dependent on "particular human institutions," and liable to be perpetually modified as man's habits of feeling, and thought, and action pass from one phase to another. He thus contrasted the laws of Distribution with those of Production, which he regarded as resting on the immutable basis of physical Nature; and again with the laws of Exchange, to which he attributed something very much like the universality of Mathematics. It is true that he sometimes spoke as though Political Economy consisted chiefly of discussions of the Production and Distribution of Wealth, and thus seemed to imply that he regarded the theory of Exchange as a part of the theory of Distribution. But yet he kept the two separate from one another; he treated of Distribution in his second and fourth Books, and gave his third Book to the "Machinery of Exchange" (compare his *Principles of Political Economy*, Book II Ch I § 1, and Ch. XVI § 6)

He was thus drawn on to an incomplete statement, and the correction of it in his fourth Book has not been generally noticed;

In doing this he allowed his zeal for giving a more human tone to economics to get the better of his judgment, and to hurry him on to work with an incomplete analysis. For, by putting his main theory of wages before his account of supply and demand, he cut himself off from all chance of treating that theory in a satisfactory way, and in fact he was led on to say (*Principles*, Book II. Ch XI. § 1), that "Wages depend mainly upon .the proportion between population and capital;" or rather, as he explains later on, between "the number of the labouring class who work for hire," and "the aggregate of what may be called the Wages-Fund which consists of that part of circulating capital...which is expended in the direct hire of labour."

The fact is that the theories of Distribution and Exchange are so intimately connected as to be little more than two sides of the same problem, that in each of them there is an element of "mechanical" precision and universality, and that in each of them there is an element, dependent on "particular human institutions," which has varied, and which probably will vary, from place to place and from age to age And if Mill had recognised this great truth, he would not have been drawn on to appear to substitute, as he did in his second Book, the statement of the problem of wages for its solution: but would have combined the description and analysis in his second Book, with the short but profound study of the causes that govern the distribution of the national dividend, given in his fourth Book; and the progress of economics would have been much hastened

As it was, when his friend Thornton, following in the wake of Longe, Cliffe Leslie, Jevons and others, convinced him that the phrases in his second Book were untenable, he yielded too much; and overstated the extent of his own past error and of the concessions which he was bound to make to his assailants. He said (*Dissertations*, Vol. IV. p 46). "There is no law of nature making it inherently impossible for wages to rise to the point of absorbing not only the funds which he (the employer) had intended to devote to carrying on his business, but the whole of what he allows for his private expenses beyond the necessaries of life. The real limit to the rise is the practical consideration how much would ruin him, or drive him to abandon the business, not the inexorable limits of the Wages Fund." He did not make it clear whether this statement refers to immediate or ultimate effects, to short periods or long: but in either case it appears untenable

partly because he took a less scientific position in his answers to Thornton

As regards long periods it does not go far enough for wages could not rise permanently so as to absorb nearly as large a share of the national dividend as is here indicated. And for short periods, it goes too far: for a well-organized strike at a critical juncture may force from the employer for a short time more than the whole value of his output, after paying for raw material during that time, and thus make his gross profits for the time a negative quantity. And indeed the theory of wages whether in its older or newer form, has no direct bearing on the issue of any particular struggle in the labour market that depends on the relative strength of the competing parties But it has much bearing on the general policy of the relation of capital to labour, for it indicates what policies do, and what do not, carry in themselves the seeds of their own ultimate defeat; what policies can be maintained, aided by suitable organization, and what policies will ultimately render either side weak, however well organized.

The bearing of the theory of wages on the issue of particular trade conflicts is indirect and remote

After a while Cairnes, in his *Leading Principles*, endeavoured to resuscitate the Wages-fund Theory by expounding it in a form, which he thought would evade the attacks that had been made on it But, though in the greater part of his exposition, he succeeded in avoiding the old pitfalls, he did so only by explaining away so much which is characteristic of the doctrine, that there is very little left in it to justify its title. He states however (p. 203) that "the rate of wages, other things being equal varies inversely with the supply of labour;" and this seems to point in a wrong direction. For an increase of labour must increase the national dividend, which is one of the causes that govern wages, and therefore if the supply of labour increases, other things *cannot* be equal. He goes on to derive an "unexpected consequence," that an increase in the supply of labour, when it is of a kind to be used in conjunction with fixed capital and raw material, would cause the Wages-fund to undergo "diminution as the number

Cairnes explained away the crudities of the wages-fund doctrine in its extreme forms,

but his position is not clear.

BOOK VI CH. II

who are to share it is increased." But that result would follow only if the aggregate of wages were not influenced by the aggregate of production; and in fact this last cause is the most powerful of all those which influence wages.

The wages-fund doctrine relates only to the demand side of the question.

It may be noticed that the extreme forms of the Wages-fund theory represent wages as governed entirely by demand; though the demand is represented crudely as dependent on the stock of capital But some popular expositors of economics appear to have held at the same time both this doctrine and the iron law of wages, which represent wages as governed rigidly by the cost of rearing human beings. They might of course have softened each of them and then worked the two into a more or less harmonious whole, as Cairnes did later. But it does not appear that they did so

It was applied in support of some important truths,

The proposition that *industry is limited by capital*, was often interpreted so as to make it practically convertible with the Wages-fund theory It can be explained so as to be true. but a similar explanation would make the statement that "capital is limited by industry" equally true. It was however used by Mill chiefly in connection with the argument that the aggregate employment of labour cannot generally be increased by the simple plan of cutting people off, by Protective duties or in other ways, from opportunities of satisfying their wants in that manner which they would prefer The effects of protective duties are very complex and cannot be discussed here; but Mill is clearly right in saying that in general the capital, that is applied to support and aid labour in any new industry created by such duties, "must have been withdrawn or withheld from some other, in which it gave, or would have given, employment to probably about the same quantity of labour which it employs in its new occupation" Or to put the argument in a more modern form, such legislation does not *primâ facie* increase either the national dividend or the share of that dividend which goes to labour For it does not increase the supply of capital; nor does it, in any other way, cause the marginal efficiency of labour to rise relatively to that of capital. The rate that has to be paid for the use of capital is therefore not lowered, the national dividend is not increased (in fact it is almost sure to be diminished); and as neither labour nor capital gets any new advantage over the other in bargaining for the distribution of the dividend, neither can benefit by such legislation

but they can be defended without it.

Symmetry of some of the relations between capital and labour.

This doctrine of Mill's might indeed logically be inverted; so as to assert that the labour required to give effect to capital in a new industry created by protective duties must have been withdrawn or withheld from some other, in which it gave, or would have given effect to probably about the same quantity of capital as in its new occupation. But this statement though equally true would not appeal with equal force to the minds of ordinary people. For as the buyer of goods is commonly regarded as conferring a special benefit on the seller, though in fact the services which buyers and sellers render to one another are in the long run co-ordinate, so the employer is commonly regarded as conferring a special benefit on the worker, whose labour he buys, though in the long run the services which the employers and employees render to one another are co-ordinate. The causes and consequences of this pair of facts will occupy us much at later stages of our inquiry

Some interesting contributions to the history of the Wages-fund theory are to be found in the article by Prof. Taussig in the *Quarterly Journal of Economics* already referred to, and in Mr Cannan's *Production and Distribution*, 1776–1848. General Walker's writings have thrown much light on the whole subject. The instances of employees rendering their labour in advance of payment, which he has collected, are instructive in many ways, and, though they do not perhaps much affect the main issue, they bear effectively on some turns of the controversy.

CHAPTER III.

DEMAND AND SUPPLY IN RELATION TO LABOUR REAL AND NOMINAL EARNINGS.

The scope of the present and the following seven Chapters

§ 1. WHEN discussing the general theory of equilibrium of demand and supply in the last Book, and the main outlines of the central problem of distribution and exchange in the first two chapters of this Book, we left on one side, as far as might be, all considerations turning on the special qualities and incidents of the agents of production. We did not inquire in detail how far the general theories of the relations between the value of an appliance for production and that of the product, which it helps to make, are applicable to the incomes earned by natural abilities, or by skill and knowledge acquired long ago, whether in the ranks of the employers, the employed, or the professional classes. We avoided difficulties connected with the analysis of Profits, paying no attention to the many different scopes which the usage of the market-place assigns to this term, and even the more elementary term Interest; and we took no account of the influence of varieties of tenure on the form of demand for land. These and some other deficiencies will be made good by more detailed analysis in the following three groups of chapters on demand and supply in relation to labour, to capital and business power, and to land, respectively.

The present chapter is devoted to methods of estimating and reckoning earnings It is mainly a mere formal question of arithmetic or bookkeeping: but much error has arisen from treating it carelessly.

Competition tends to make weekly wages in similar employments not equal, but proportionate to the efficiency of the workers

§ 2. When watching the action of demand and supply with regard to a material commodity, we are constantly met by the difficulty that two things which are being sold under the same name in the same market, are really not of the same quality and not of the same value to the purchasers. Or, if the things are really alike, they may be sold even in the face of the keenest competition at prices which are nominally different, because the conditions of sale are not the same: for instance, a part of the expense or risk of delivery which is borne in the one case by the seller may in the other be transferred to the buyer. But difficulties of this kind are much greater in the case of labour than of material commodities: the true price that is paid for labour often differs widely, and in ways that are not easily traced, from that which is nominally paid.

It is commonly said that the tendency of competition is to equalize the earnings of people engaged in the same trade or in trades of equal difficulty; but this statement requires to be interpreted carefully. For competition tends to make the earnings got by two individuals of unequal efficiency in any given time, say, a day or a year, not equal, but unequal; and, in like manner, it tends not to equalize, but to render unequal the average weekly wages in two districts in which the average standards of efficiency are unequal. Given that the average strength and energy of the working-classes are higher in the North of England than in the South, it then follows that the more completely "competition makes things find their own level," the more certain is it that average weekly wages will be higher in the North than in the South. Cliffe Leslie and some other writers have naively laid stress on local variations of wages as tending to prove that there is very little mobility among the working-classes, and that the competition among them for employment is ineffective. But most of the facts which they quote relate only to wages reckoned by the day or week: they are only half-facts, and when the missing halves are supplied, they generally support the opposite inference to that on behalf of which they are quoted. For it is found that local variations of weekly wages and of efficiency generally correspond: and thus the facts

BOOK VI CH III.

tend to prove the effectiveness of competition, so far as they bear on the question at all. We shall however presently find that the full interpretation of such facts as these is a task of great difficulty and complexity.

Time-earnings

The earnings, or wages, which a person gets in any given time, such as a day, a week, or a year, may be called his *Time-earnings*, or *Time-wages*: and we may then regard competition, or to speak more exactly, economic freedom and enterprise, as tending to make time-earnings in occupations of equal difficulty and in neighbouring places not equal, but proportionate to the efficiency of the workers.

Payment by *Piece-work.*

But this phrase, "the efficiency of the workers," has some ambiguity. When the payment for work of any kind is apportioned to the quantity and quality of the work turned out, it is said that uniform rates of *Piece-work* wages are being paid; and if two persons work under the same conditions and with equally good appliances, they are paid in proportion to their efficiencies when they receive piece-work wages calculated by the same lists of prices for each several kind of work. If however the appliances are not equally good, a uniform rate of piece-work wages gives results disproportionate to the efficiency of the workers. If, for instance, the same lists of piece-work wages were used in Lancashire cotton mills supplied with old-fashioned machinery, as in those which have the latest improvements, the apparent equality would represent a real inequality. The more effective competition is, and the more perfectly economic freedom and enterprise are developed, the more surely will the lists be higher in the mills that have old-fashioned machinery than in the others

In order therefore to give its right meaning to the statement that economic freedom and enterprise tend to equalize wages in occupations of the same difficulty and in the same neighbourhood, we require the use of a new term. We may find it in *Efficiency-wages*, or more broadly *Efficiency-earnings*; that is, earnings measured, not as time-earnings are with reference to the time spent in earning them; and not as piece-work earnings are with reference to the amount of output resulting from the work by which they are earned,

Efficiency-earnings

but with reference to the exertion of ability and *efficiency* required of the worker[1].

The law of the tendency towards equality of efficiency-earnings.

The tendency then of economic freedom and enterprise (or, in more common phrase, of competition), to cause every one's earnings to find their own level, is a tendency to equality of efficiency-earnings in the same district. This tendency will be the stronger, the greater is the mobility of labour, the less strictly specialized it is, the more keenly parents are on the look-out for the most advantageous occupations for their children, the more rapidly they are able to adapt themselves to changes in economic conditions, and lastly the slower and the less violent these changes are

Low-waged labour is generally dear, if working with expensive machinery

This statement of the law is, however, still subject to a slight correction. For we have hitherto supposed that it is a matter of indifference to the employer whether he employs few or many people to do a piece of work, provided his total wages-bill for the work is the same. But that is not the case. Those workers who earn most in a week when paid at a given rate for their work, are those who are cheapest to their employers (and ultimately to the community, unless indeed they overstrain themselves, and work themselves out prematurely) For they use only the same amount of fixed capital as their slower fellow workers; and, since they turn out more work, each part of it has to bear a less charge on this account The prime costs are equal in the two cases; but the total cost of that done by those who are more efficient, and get the higher time-wages, is lower than that

[1] In earlier editions the term *Task-wages* was given as an alternative to *Efficiency-wages*, but that term is in some trades applied to wages paid by the day on condition that a certain definite *task* be accomplished in it. If as generally is the case the workman is at liberty to exceed the *minimum* task, and to be paid in proportion, the system is really one of piece-work; formal expression being given to the condition latent in all piece-work in which expensive plant is used, that the plant shall be turned to fairly good account The variations in the conditions of hiring in different trades and places are numerous, but they bear more intimately on labour politics than on normal wages, and what has to be said about them may conveniently be deferred to a later stage. Meanwhile reference may be made to a full discussion of them in Mr Schloss' *Methods of Industrial Remuneration;* and an article by him in the *Economic Journal*, Vol II Many interesting facts bearing on the matter are to be found in the *Report of the Labour Commission*, and in Mr Charles Booth's *Life and Labour in London*

BOOK VI CH. III.

done by those who get the lower time-wages at the same rate of piece-work payment[1].

This point is seldom of much importance in out-of-door work, where there is abundance of room, and comparatively little use of expensive machinery; for then, except in the matter of superintendence, it makes very little difference to the employer, whose wages-bill for a certain piece of work is £100, whether that sum is divided between twenty efficient or thirty inefficient workers. But when expensive machinery is used which has to be proportioned to the number of workers, the employer would often find the total cost of his goods lowered if he could get twenty men to turn out for a wages-bill of £50 as much work as he had previously got done by thirty men for a wages-bill of £40. In all matters of this kind the leadership of the world lies with America, and it is not an uncommon saying there, that he is the best business man who contrives to pay the highest wages.

The corrected law then stands that the tendency of economic freedom and enterprise is generally to equalize efficiency-earnings in the same district: but where much expensive fixed capital is used, it would be to the advantage of the employer to raise the time-earnings of the more efficient workers more than in proportion to their efficiency.

Of course this tendency is liable to be opposed by special customs and institutions, and, in some cases, by trades-union regulations[2].

[1] This argument would be subject to corrections in cases in which the trade admitted of the employment of more than one shift of workpeople. It would often be worth an employer's while to pay to each of two shifts as much for an eight hours' day as he now pays to one shift for a ten hours' day For though each worker would produce less, each machine would produce more on the former than on the latter plan. But to this point we shall return.

[2] Ricardo did not overlook the importance of the distinction between variations in the amount of commodities paid to the labourer as wages, and variations in the profitableness of the labourer to his employer He saw that the real interest of the employer lay not in the amount of wages that he paid to the labourer, but in the ratio which those wages bore to the value of the produce resulting from the labourer's work and he decided to regard the rate of wages as measured by this ratio and to say that wages rose when this ratio increased, and that they fell when it diminished. It is to be regretted that he did not invent some new term for this purpose; for his artificial use of a familiar term has seldom been understood by others, and was in some cases even forgotten by himself (Compare

§ 3. Thus much with regard to estimates of the work for which the earnings are given: but next we have to consider more carefully the facts, that in estimating the real earnings of an occupation account must be taken of many things besides its money receipts, and that on the other side of the account we must reckon for many incidental disadvantages besides those indirectly involved in the strain and stress of the work

Real wages and Nominal wages.

As Adam Smith says, "the *real wages* of labour may be said to consist in the quantity of the necessaries and conveniences of life that are given for it; its *Nominal wages* in the quautity of money...... The labourer is rich or poor, is well or ill rewarded, in proportion to the real, not to the nominal, wages of his labour[1]." But the words "that are given for it" must not be taken to apply only to the necessaries and conveniences that are directly provided by the purchaser of the labour or its products; for account must be taken also of the advantages which are attached to the occupation, and require no special outlay on his part.

Allowance must be made for variations in the purchasing power of money, with special reference to the consumption of the grade of labour concerned.

In endeavouring to ascertain the real wages of an occupation at any place or time, the first step is to allow for variations in the purchasing power of the money in which nominal wages are returned. This point cannot be thoroughly dealt with till we come to treat of the theory of money as a whole. But it may be remarked in passing that this allowance would not be a simple arithmetical reckoning, even if we had perfectly accurate statistics of the history of the prices of all commodities. For if we compare distant places or distant times, we find people with different wants, and different means of supplying those wants: and even when we confine our attention to the same time and place

Senior's *Political Economy*, pp 142—8) The variations in the productiveness of labour which he had chiefly in view were those which result from improvements in the arts of production on the one hand, and on the other from the action of the law of diminishing return, when an increase of population required larger crops to be forced from a limited soil. Had he paid careful attention to the increase in the productiveness of labour that results directly from an improvement in the labourer's condition, the position of economic science, and the real well-being of the country, would in all probability be now much further advanced than they are. As it is, his treatment of wages is less instructive than that of Malthus

[1] *Wealth of Nations*, Book I Ch v

we find people of different classes spending their incomes in very different ways. For instance, the prices of velvet, of operatic entertainments and scientific books are not very important to the lower ranks of industry; but a fall in the price of bread or of shoe leather affects them much more than it does the higher ranks Differences of this kind must always be borne in mind, and it is generally possible to make some sort of rough allowance for them[1].

§ 4. We have already noticed[2] that a person's total real income is found by deducting from his gross income the outgoings that belong to its production; and that this gross income includes many things which do not appear in the form of money payments and are in danger of being overlooked

Allowance must be made for trade expenses

Firstly, then, with regard to the outgoings. We do not here reckon the expenses of education, general and special, involved in the preparation for any trade: nor do we take account of the exhaustion of a person's health and strength in his work. Allowance for them may be best made in other ways. But we must deduct all trade expenses, whether they are incurred by professional men or artisans. Thus from the barrister's gross income we must deduct the rent of his office and the salary of his clerk: from the carpenter's gross income we must deduct the expenses which he incurs for

[1] *The Report of the Poor Law Commissioners on the Employment of Women and Children in Agriculture*, 1843, p. 297, contains some interesting specimens of yearly wages paid in Northumberland in which very little money appeared. Here is one —10 bushels of wheat, 30 of oats, 10 of barley, 10 of rye, 10 of peas; a cow's keep for a year; 800 yards of potatoes, cottage and garden; coal-shed; £3 10*s* in cash, and 2 bushels of barley in lieu of hens.

Many plans have been suggested for making a special estimate of the purchasing power of money with regard to those things that are chiefly consumed by the working classes, the importance of each thing being taken in such estimate as proportionate to the amount spent on it in an average working class budget Mr Edward Atkinson has suggested that this measure of purchasing power should be called "a standard ration" But at best it could only be approximate, partly because the working classes contain within themselves several different grades, with corresponding variations in the percentages of their incomes which they devote to purchasing different things (See the latter half of the Note at the end of Book III. Ch IV) General Walker's Treatise *On Wages* and Roscher's *Political Economy*, contain many suggestive remarks and facts bearing on the subjects of this section, and indeed of the whole chapter

[2] Book II Ch. V

tools; and when estimating the earnings of quarrymen in any district we must find out whether local custom assigns the expenses of tools and blasting powder to them or their employers. Such cases are comparatively simple; but it is more difficult to decide how large a part of the expenses, which a medical man incurs for house and carriage and social entertainments, are to be regarded as trade expenses, or how much of the charges to which a postman is put for boots, or a domestic servant or an attendant in a fashionable shop for clothes, should be deducted under this head[1]

Where wages are partly paid in kind, the allowances must be taken at their value to those who receive them, not at their cost to those who give them

§ 5. Next let us take account of the different modes of payment which are adopted in different occupations. We may select for study the case of domestic servants. We have already noticed that when they have to supply themselves at their own cost with expensive clothes, which they would not buy if free to do as they liked, the value of their wages to them is somewhat lowered by this compulsion. And when the employer provides expensive liveries, houseroom and food for his servants, these are generally worth much less to them than they cost to him. It is therefore an error to reckon the real wages of domestic servants, as some statisticians have done, by adding to their money wages the equivalent of the cost to their employer of everything that he provides for them[2].

On the whole, when the Truck system prevails in any

[1] This class of questions is closely allied to those raised when discussing the definitions of Capital and Income in Book II; where a caution has already been entered against overlooking elements of income that do not take the form of money. Earnings of many even of the professional and wage receiving classes are in a considerable measure dependent on their being in command of some material capital

[2] Again, when a farmer hauls coals free for his men, choosing, of course, times when his horses have little to do, the real addition to their earnings is much greater than the cost to him. The same applies to many perquisites and allowances, as for instance, when the employer allows his men to have without payment commodities which though useful to them, are almost valueless to him on account of the great expenses involved in marketing them, or, again, when he allows them to buy for their own use at the wholesale price commodities which they have helped to produce When however this permission to purchase is changed into an obligation to purchase, the door is opened to grave abuses The farmer who compels his men to take from him spoilt wheat at the wholesale price of good wheat, is really paying them lower wages than he appears to be

trade in an old country, we may fairly assume that the real rate of wages is lower than the nominal. The most virulent forms of the system have always been those which have lain beneath the surface, and in our own day they still flourish in those industries which retain a semi-mediæval character, while they seldom exist in those in which the modern factory system prevails. The influence of the system for evil in the past has been so great, that it may rank with the old poor law and the unhealthy conditions of juvenile labour early in the century as a chief cause of the degradation of large numbers of the working classes: but its influence is not now great save in a few trades[1].

[1] In a new country in which large agricultural, mining, and other businesses often spring up at a great distance from any considerable town, the employers are compelled to supply their workpeople with everything they want, either by paying part of their wages in the form of allowances of food, clothing &c, or by opening stores for them. Stores of this kind are generally managed on a straightforward business-like principle, and wholesome customs and traditions thus started are apt to survive even when the employers' shops have ceased to be necessary in consequence of the growth of fairly good independent shops in the neighbourhood. The shops remain an almost unmixed benefit to all concerned so long as dealing at them is voluntary, and, even when it becomes compulsory, they may be on the whole a benefit to the workpeople, provided they are managed with ability and honesty For, since the employers ensure themselves prompt sales and certain payments by contracting that a certain part of the wages paid by them shall be taken out in purchases at the stores, they are able to work these stores more cheaply than ordinary retail shops, and thus to pay, with an equal profit to themselves, higher real wages than would otherwise be possible

But employers, whose main business is in a healthy condition, are generally too busy to be willing to manage such shops unless there is some strong reason for doing so, and consequently in old countries those who have adopted the Truck system have more often than not done so with the object of getting back by underhand ways part of the wages which they nominally paid away They have compelled those who work at home to hire machinery and implements at exorbitant rents, they have compelled all their workpeople to buy adulterated goods at short weights and high prices, and in some cases even to spend a very large part of their wages on goods on which it was easiest to make the highest rate of profits, and especially on spirituous liquors Mr Lecky, for instance, records an amusing case of employers who could not resist the temptation to buy theatre tickets cheap, and compel their workpeople to buy them at full price (*History of the Eighteenth Century*, VI p 158) The evil is however at its worst when the shop is kept not by the employer, but by the foreman or by persons acting in concert with him; and when he, without openly saying so, gives it to be understood that those who do not deal largely at the shop will find it difficult to get his good word For an employer suffers more or less from anything that injures his work people, while the exactions of an unjust foreman are but little held in check by regard for his own ultimate interest.

The story of the abuses of the Truck system in modern England is told in a

Uncertainty of success may be allowed for by striking an average, as a first approximation;

§ 6. Next we have to take account of the influences exerted on the real rate of earnings in an occupation by the uncertainty of success and the inconstancy of employment in it.

We should obviously start by taking the earnings of an occupation as the average between those of the successful and unsuccessful members of it; but care is required to get the true average. For if the average earnings of those who are successful are £2000 a year, and of those who are unsuccessful are £400 a year, the average of the whole will be £1200 a year if the former group is as large as the latter, but if, as is perhaps the case with barristers, the unsuccessful are ten times as numerous as the successful, the true average is but £550. And further, many of those who have failed most completely, are likely to have left the occupation altogether, and thus to escape being counted.

but separate allowance must be made for the evils of uncertainty and anxiety.

And again, though, by taking this average, we obviate the necessity of making any separate allowance for insurance against risk, account generally remains to be taken of the evil of uncertainty. For there are many people of a sober steady-going temper, who like to know what is before them, and who would far rather have an appointment which offered a certain income of say £400 a year than one which was not unlikely to yield £600, but had an equal chance of affording only £200. Uncertainty, therefore, which does not appeal to great ambitions and lofty aspirations, has special attractions for very few, while it acts as a deterrent to many of those who are making their choice of a career. And as a rule the certainty of moderate success attracts more than an expectation of an uncertain success that has an equal actuarial value.

Though a few extremely

But on the other hand, if an occupation offers a few extremely high prizes, its attractiveness is increased out of

long series of Parliamentary Reports, which come down to the present time and while the evil itself has been steadily diminishing, the intensity of the light thrown on what remains has been increasing as steadily. An excellent account of the payments in kind by which the agricultural labourer's wages are supplemented is given by Mr Kebbel (*The Agricultural Labourer*, 2nd Ed., Ch. II.). A table to be found in Vol. XX. of the United States Census for 1880 shows that of 778 manufacturing firms which answer questions as to the mode of payment adopted by them, 681, or 88 per cent., pay in cash but in some of the States which are thinly populated the proportion is not much more than one-half.

BOOK VI CH III.

high prizes have a disproportionately great attractive force.

all proportion to their aggregate value. For this there are two reasons. The first is that young men of an adventurous disposition are more attracted by the prospects of a great success than they are deterred by the fear of failure; and the second is that the social rank of an occupation depends more on the highest dignity and the best position which can be attained through it than on the average good fortune of those engaged in it. It is an old maxim of statecraft that a Government should offer a few good prizes in every department of its service: and in aristocratic countries the chief officials receive very high salaries, while those of the lower grades are comforted in the receipt of salaries below the market level for similar services by their hopes of ultimately rising to a coveted post, and by the social consideration which in such countries always attends on public officers. This arrangement has the incidental effect of favouring those who are already rich and powerful; and partly for that reason it is not adopted in democratic countries. They often go to the opposite extreme, and pay more than the market rates for their services to the lower ranks, and less to the upper ranks. But that plan, whatever be its merits on other grounds, is certainly an expensive one.

Irregularity of employment can be allowed for by a simple average in some cases;

We may next consider the influence which inconstancy of employment exerts on wages. It is obvious that in those occupations, in which employment is irregular, the pay must be high in proportion to the work done: the medical man and the shoeblack must each receive when at work a pay which covers a sort of retaining fee for the time when he has nothing to do. If the advantages of their occupations are in other respects equal, and their work equally difficult, the bricklayer when at work must be paid a higher rate than the joiner, and the joiner than the railway guard. For work on the railways is nearly constant all the year round, while the joiner and the bricklayer are always in danger of being made idle by slackness of trade, and the bricklayer's work is further interrupted by frost and rain. The ordinary method of allowing for such interruptions is to add up the earnings for a long period of time and to take the average of them; but this is not quite satisfactory unless we assume that the rest and leisure, which a man gets when out of employment, are of no service to him directly or indirectly[1].

This assumption may be fairly made in some cases; for waiting for work often involves so much anxiety and worry that it causes more strain than the work itself would do[2]. But that is not always so. Interruptions of work that occur in the ordinary course of business, and raise no fears about the future, give opportunity for the system to recruit itself and lay in stores of energy for future exertions. The successful barrister, for instance, is subject to a severe strain during some parts of the year; and that is itself an evil: but when allowance has been made for it, he may be regarded as losing very little in the long run by being prevented from earning any fees during the legal vacations[3].

but not in all; each case must be treated on its own merits

§ 7. Next we must take account of the opportunities which a man's surroundings may afford of supplementing the earnings which he gets in his chief occupation, by doing work of other kinds. And account may need to be taken also of the opportunities which these surroundings offer for the work of other members of his family.

Supplementary earnings

Many economists have even proposed to take as their unit the earnings of a family: and there is much to be said for this plan with reference to agriculture and those old-fashioned domestic trades in which the whole family works together, provided that allowance is made for the loss resulting from any consequent neglect by the wife of her household duties. But in modern England trades of this kind are exceptional, the occupation of the head of a family seldom exerts much direct influence on those of its other members, though of course when the place in which he works is fixed, the employments, to which his family can get easy access, are limited by the resources of the neighbourhood.

Family earnings

[1] These considerations are specially important with regard to piece-work; the rate of earnings being in some cases much reduced by short supplies of material to work on, or by other interruptions, avoidable or unavoidable.

[2] The evils of irregularity of employment are well stated in a lecture on that subject given by Prof. Foxwell in 1886.

[3] Workers in the higher grades are generally allowed holidays with pay; but those in the lower grades generally forfeit their pay when they take holidays. The causes of this distinction are obvious; but it naturally raises a feeling of grievance of a kind, to which the inquiries by the Labour Commission gave vent. See e.g. Group B 24, 431—6.

BOOK VI. CH. III.

The attractiveness of a trade depends not on its money-earnings, but its *Net Advantages*,

§ 8. Thus then the attractiveness of a trade depends on many other causes besides the difficulty and strain of the work to be done in it on the one hand, and the money-earnings to be got in it on the other. And when the earnings in any occupation are regarded as acting on the supply of labour in it, or when they are spoken of as being its supply price, we must always understand that the term is only used as a short expression for its *Net Advantages*[1]. We must take account of the facts that one trade is healthier or cleanlier than another, that it is carried on in a more wholesome or pleasant locality, or that it involves a better social position; as is instanced by Adam Smith's well-known remark that the aversion which many people have for the work of a butcher, and to some extent for the butcher himself, raises the earnings of butchers above those of bakers.

subject to differences between individuals,

Of course individual character will always assert itself in estimating particular advantages at a high or a low rate Some persons, for instance, are so fond of having a cottage to themselves that they prefer living on very low wages in the country to getting much higher wages in the town; while others are indifferent as to the amount of houseroom they get, and are willing to go without the comforts of life provided they can procure what they regard as its luxuries. This was the case, for example, with a family of whom the Royal Commission on the Housing of the Working Classes in 1884 were told· their joint earnings were £7 a week, but they chose to live in one room, so as to be able to spend money freely on excursions and amusements.

Personal peculiarities, such as these, prevent us from predicting with certainty the conduct of particular individuals But if each advantage and disadvantage is reckoned at the average of the money values it has for the class of people who would be likely to enter an occupation, or to bring up their children to it, we shall have the means of estimating roughly the relative strengths of the forces that tend to increase or diminish the supply of labour in that occupation *at the time and place* which we are considering. For it cannot be too often repeated that grave errors are likely to result from taking over an estimate of this kind based on the

[1] See Book II Ch V. § 2.

circumstances of one time and place, and applying it without proper precaution to those of another time or another place.

between races,

In this connection it is interesting to observe the influence of differences of national temperament in our own time. Thus in America we see Swedes and Norwegians drift to agriculture in the North-west, while the Irish, if they go on the land at all, choose farms in the older Eastern States. The preponderance of Germans in the furniture and the brewing industries, and of Irish and French Canadians in the textile industries of the United States, and the preference of the Jewish immigrants in London for the boot-making industries and for retail trade—all these are due partly to differences in national aptitudes, but partly also to differences in the estimates that people of different races form of the incidental advantages and disadvantages of different trades.

and between industrial grades

Lastly, the disagreeableness of work seems to have very little effect in raising wages, if it is of such a kind that it can be done by those whose industrial abilities are of a very low order. For the progress of sanitary science has kept alive many people who are unfit for any but the lowest grade of work. They compete eagerly for the comparatively small quantity of work for which they are fitted, and in their urgent need they think almost exclusively of the wages they can earn: they cannot afford to pay much attention to incidental discomforts, and indeed the influence of their surroundings has prepared many of them to regard the dirtiness of an occupation as an evil of but minor importance.

An evil paradox

And from this arises the strange and paradoxical result that the dirtiness of some occupations is a cause of the lowness of the wages earned in them. For employers find that this dirtiness adds much to the wages they would have to pay to get the work done by skilled men of high character working with improved appliances, and so they often adhere to old methods which require only unskilled workers of but indifferent character, and who can be hired for low (Time-) wages, because they are not worth much to any employer. There is no more urgent social need than that labour of this kind should be made scarce and dear.

CHAPTER IV.

DEMAND AND SUPPLY IN RELATION TO LABOUR, CONTINUED.

BOOK VI CH. IV

The importance of many peculiarities in the action of demand and supply with regard to labour depends much on the cumulativeness of their effects;

§ 1. THE action of demand and supply with regard to labour was discussed in the last chapter with reference to the difficulties of ascertaining the real as opposed to the nominal price of labour. But some peculiarities in this action remain to be studied which are of a more vital character: because they affect not merely the form, but also the substance of the action of the forces of demand and supply; and to some extent they limit and hamper the free action of those forces We shall find that the influence of many of them is not at all to be measured by their first and most obvious effects: and that those effects which are cumulative are generally far more important in the long run than those which are not, however prominent the latter may appear.

thus resembling the influence of custom

The problem has thus much in common with that of tracing the economic influence of custom. For it has already[1] been noticed, and it will become more clear as we go on, that the direct effects of custom in causing a thing to be sold for a price sometimes a little higher and sometimes a little lower than it would otherwise fetch, are not really of very great importance, because any such divergence does not, as a rule, tend to perpetuate and increase itself; but on the contrary, if it becomes considerable, it tends itself to call into action forces that counteract it. Sometimes these forces break down the custom altogether, but more often they evade it

[1] Book I. Ch II § 2.

by gradual and imperceptible changes in the character of the thing sold, so that the purchaser really gets a new thing at the old price under the old name. These direct effects then are obvious, but they are not cumulative. On the other hand, the indirect effects of custom in hindering the methods of production and the character of producers from developing themselves freely are not obvious; but they generally are cumulative, and therefore exert a deep and controlling influence over the history of the world If custom checks the progress of one generation, then the next generation starts from a lower level than it otherwise would have done; and any retardation which it suffers itself is accumulated and added to that of its predecessor, and so on from generation to generation[1].

And so it is with regard to the action of demand and supply on the earnings of labour. If at any time it presses hardly on any individuals or class, the direct effects of the evils are obvious. But the sufferings that result are of different kinds: those, the effects of which end with the evil by which they were caused, are not generally to be compared in importance with those that have the indirect effect of lowering the character of the workers or of hindering it from becoming stronger. For these last cause further weakness and further suffering, which again in their turn cause yet further weakness and further suffering, and so on cumulatively On the other hand, high earnings, and a strong character, lead to greater strength and higher earnings, which again lead to still greater strength and still higher earnings, and so on cumulatively.

First peculiarity the worker sells his work, but retains property in himself

§ 2. The first point to which we have to direct our attention is the fact that human agents of production are not bought and sold as machinery and other material agents of production are. The worker sells his work, but he himself remains his own property: those who bear the expenses

[1] It ought, however, to be remarked that some of the beneficial effects of custom are cumulative. For among the many different things that are included under the wide term "custom" are crystallized forms of high ethical principles, rules of honourable and courteous behaviour, and of the avoidance of troublesome strife about paltry gains; and much of the good influence which these exert on race character is cumulative.

BOOK VI CH. IV.

of rearing and educating him receive but very little of the price that is paid for his services in later years[1].

Consequently the investment of capital in him is limited by the means, the forethought, and the unselfishness of his parents.

Whatever deficiencies the modern methods of business may have, they have at least this virtue, that he who bears the expenses of production of material goods, receives the price that is paid for them. He who builds factories or steam-engines or houses, or rears slaves, reaps the benefit of all net services which they render so long as he keeps them for himself, and when he sells them he gets a price which is the estimated net value of their future services. The stronger and the more efficient he makes them, the better his reward; and therefore he extends his outlay until there seems to him no good reason for thinking that the gains resulting from any further investment would compensate him. He must do this prudently and boldly, under the penalty of finding himself worsted in competition with others who follow a broader and more far-sighted policy, and of ultimately disappearing from the ranks of those who direct the course of the world's business. The action of competition, and the survival in the struggle for existence of those who know best how to extract the greatest benefits for themselves from the environment, tend in the long run to put the building of factories and steam-engines into the hands of those who will be ready and able to incur every expense which will add more than it costs to their value as productive agents. But the investment of capital in the rearing and early training of the workers of England is limited by the resources of parents in the various grades of society, by their power of forecasting the future, and by their willingness to sacrifice themselves for the sake of their children

This evil is comparatively small in the higher ranks of society,

This evil is indeed of comparatively small importance with regard to the higher industrial grades. For in those grades most people distinctly realize the future, and "discount it at a low rate of interest." They exert themselves much to

[1] This is consistent with the well-known fact that slave labour is not economical, as Adam Smith remarked long ago that "The fund destined for replacing or repairing, if I may say so, the wear-and-tear of the slave is commonly managed by a negligent master or careless overseer. That destined for performing the same office for the free man is managed by the free man himself.. with strict frugality and parsimonious attention"

select the best careers for their sons, and the best trainings for those careers; and they are generally willing and able to incur a considerable expense for the purpose. The professional classes especially, while generally eager to save some capital *for* their children, are even more on the alert for opportunities of investing it *in* them. And whenever there occurs in the upper grades of industry a new opening for which an extra and special education is required, the future gains need not be very high relatively to the present outlay, in order to secure a keen competition for the post.

but very great in the lower ranks,

But in the lower ranks of society the evil is great For the slender means and education of the parents, and the comparative weakness of their power of distinctly realizing the future, prevent them from investing capital in the education and training of their children with the same free and bold enterprise with which capital is applied to improving the machinery of any well-managed factory. Many of the children of the working-classes are imperfectly fed and clothed; they are housed in a way that promotes neither physical nor moral health, they receive a school education which, though in modern England it may not be very bad so far as it goes, yet goes only a little way; they have few opportunities of getting a broader view of life or an insight into the nature of the higher work of business, of science or of art, they meet hard and exhaustive toil early on the way, and for the greater part keep to it all their lives. At last they go to the grave carrying with them undeveloped abilities and faculties; which, if they could have borne full fruit, would have added to the material wealth of the country—to say nothing of higher considerations—many times as much as would have covered the expense of providing adequate opportunities for their development.

and the evil is cumulative

But the point on which we have specially to insist now is that this evil is cumulative. The worse fed are the children of one generation, the less will they earn when they grow up, and the less will be their power of providing adequately for the material wants of their children; and so on. and again, the less fully their own faculties are developed, the less will they realize the importance of developing the

BOOK VI. CH. IV.

best faculties of their children, and the less will be their power of doing so. And conversely any change that awards to the workers of one generation better earnings, together with better opportunities of developing their best qualities, will increase the material and moral advantages which they have the power to offer to their children: while by increasing their own intelligence, wisdom and forethought, it will also to some extent increase their willingness to sacrifice their own pleasures for the well-being of their children; though there is much of that willingness now even among the poorest classes, so far as their means and the limits of their knowledge will allow.

The son of the artisan has a better start in life than the son of the unskilled labourer;

§ 3 The advantages which those born in one of the higher grades of society have over those born in a lower, consist in a great measure of the better introductions and the better start in life which they receive from their parents; and the importance of this good start in life is nowhere seen more clearly than in a comparison of the fortunes of the sons of artisans and of unskilled labourers. There are not many skilled trades to which the son of an unskilled labourer can get easy access; and in the large majority of cases the son follows the father's calling. In the old-fashioned domestic industries this was almost a universal rule, and, even under modern conditions, the father has often great facilities for introducing his son to his own trade. Employers and their foremen generally give to a lad whose father they already know and trust, a preference over one for whom they would have to incur the entire responsibility. And in many trades a lad, even after he has got entrance to the works, is not very likely to make good progress and obtain a secure footing, unless he is able to work by the side of his father, or some friend of his father's, who will take the trouble to teach him and to let him do work that requires careful supervision, but has an educational value.

he is brought up in a more refined home and with more of a mother's care.

And the son of the artisan has further advantages. He generally lives in a better and cleaner house, and under material surroundings that are more consistent with refinement than those with which the ordinary labourer is familiar. His parents are likely to be better educated, and to have a higher notion of their duties to their children; and, last but not least, his mother is likely to be able to give more of her time to the care of her family.

The great importance of this last element

If we compare one country of the civilized world with another, or one part of England with another, or one trade in England with another, we find that the degradation of the working-classes varies almost uniformly with the amount of rough work done by women. The most valuable of all capital is that invested in human beings; and of that capital the most precious part is the result of the care and influence of the mother, so long as she retains her tender and unselfish instincts, and has not been hardened by the strain and stress of unfeminine work.

This draws our attention to another aspect of the principle already noticed, that in estimating the cost of production of efficient labour, we must often take as our unit the family. At all events we cannot treat the cost of production of efficient men as an isolated problem; it must be taken as part of the broader problem of the cost of production of efficient men together with the women who are fitted to make their homes happy, and to bring up their children vigorous in body and mind, truthful and cleanly, gentle and brave[1].

[1] Sir William Petty discussed "The Value of the People" with much ingenuity; and the relation in which the cost of rearing an adult male stands to the cost of rearing a family unit was examined in a thoroughly scientific manner by Cantillon, *Essai*, Part I. Chap. XI, and again by Adam Smith, *Wealth of Nations*, Book I Ch VIII and in more recent times by Dr Engel, in his brilliant Essay *Der Preis der Arbeit*, and by Dr Farr and others Many estimates have been made of the addition to the wealth of a country caused by the arrival of an immigrant whose cost of rearing in his early years was defrayed elsewhere, and who is likely to produce more than he consumes in the country of his adoption. The estimates have been made on many plans, all of them rough, and some apparently faulty in principle but most of them find the average value of an immigrant to be about £200. It would seem that, if we might neglect provisionally the difference between the sexes, we should calculate the value of the immigrant on the lines of the argument of Book V Ch. IV. § 2. That is, we should "discount" the probable value of all the future services that he might render, add them together, and deduct from them the sum of the "discounted" values of all the wealth and direct services of other persons that he would consume and it may be noted that in thus calculating each element of production and consumption at its probable value, we have incidentally allowed for the chances of his premature death and sickness, as well as of his failure or success in life Or again we might estimate his value at the money cost of production

BOOK VI CH IV

§ 4. As the youth grows up, the influence of his parents

which his native country had incurred for him; which would in like manner be found by adding together the "accumulated" values of all the several elements of his past consumption and deducting from them the sum of the "accumulated" values of all the several elements of his past production

So far we have taken no account of the difference between the sexes. But it is clear that the above plans put the value of the male immigrants too high and that of the female too low unless allowance is made for the service which women render as mothers, as wives and as sisters, and the male immigrants are charged with having consumed these services, while the female immigrants are credited with having supplied them. (See Mathematical Note XXIV)

Many writers assume, implicitly at least, that the net production of an average individual and the consumption during the whole of his life are equal; or, in other words, that he would neither add to nor take from the material well-being of a country, in which he stayed all his life On this assumption the above two plans of estimating his value would be convertible; and then of course we should make our calculations work by the latter and easier method We may, for instance, guess that the total amount spent on bringing up an average child of the lower half of the labouring classes, say two-fifths of the population, is £100, for the next fifth we may put the sum at £175, for the next fifth at £300, for the next tenth at £500, and the remaining tenth at £1200, or an average of £300. But of course some of the population are very young and have had but little spent on them, others have got nearly to their life's end, and therefore, on these assumptions, the average value of an individual is perhaps £200

These estimates include large allowances for parental and other services, that are not actually paid for by money But it may be noted that, on the alternative plan of capitalizing net productive power, we ought properly to count in all production of real benefits, even though no money passes in exchange for them But, as Prof R Mayo Smith has well pointed out (*Emigration and Immigration*, Chapter VI), both of the suggested methods of valuation are open to great objections when used as the basis of a public policy with regard to immigration. For immigrants coming from a country in which the standard of life is low, to one in which it is high, may injure it materially as well as morally even though they carry in their own persons a good deal of invested capital, and produce in the country of their adoption, more than they consume, before they die But both of these methods are much less misleading when applied to estimate the injury done to a country, such as Ireland, by the loss through emigration of a great many young people, whose bringing up has cost the country much, and who if they had stayed would have produced more than they consumed, while the old and the infirm stay behind to consume more than they produce

Professor Nicholson (in the first number of the *Economic Journal*) estimates the living capital of the United Kingdom at £47,000 millions, i e about £1,300 a head; or, say, 33 years' purchase (equal to the value of a permanent annuity) of the gross money income of the country exclusive of rent proper and interest on capital (about £900 millions), together with half as much again added in on account of the real income, consisting of private services and family offices for which no money payment is made (His own method of arriving at this result is different) But it seems doubtful whether an estimate of the capital value of the population as a whole can serve any useful purpose; and, if any is made at all, it should perhaps be based on net, rather than on gross earning power. For the outgoings of life, its pains and its efforts, have as good a right to enter into our account as its incomings, its pleasures and enjoyments

and his schoolmaster declines. and thenceforward to the end of his life his character is moulded chiefly by the nature of his work and the influence of those with whom he associates for business, for pleasure and for religious worship.

The technical training of the workshop depends in a great measure on the unselfishness of the employer.

A good deal has already been said of the technical training of adults, of the decadence of the old apprenticeship system, and of the difficulty of finding anything to take its place. Here again we meet the difficulty that whoever may incur the expense of investing capital in developing the abilities of the workman, those abilities will be the property of the workman himself: and thus the virtue of those who have aided him must remain for the greater part its own reward.

It is true that high-paid labour is really cheap to those employers who are aiming at leading the race, and whose ambition it is to turn out the best work by the most advanced methods They are likely to give their men high wages and to train them carefully, partly because it pays them to do so, and partly because the character that fits them to take the lead in the arts of production is likely also to make them take a generous interest in the well-being of those who work for them. But though the number of such employers is increasing, they are still comparatively few And even they cannot always afford to carry the investment of capital in the training of their men as far as they would have done, if the results of the investment accrued to them in the same way as the results of any improvements they might make in their machinery. Even they are sometimes checked by the reflection that they are in a similar position to that of a farmer who, with an uncertain tenure and no security of compensation for his improvements, is sinking capital in raising the value of his landlord's property.

Its benefits are cumulative, but accrue only in part to him or his heirs

Again, in paying his workpeople high wages and in caring for their happiness and culture, the liberal employer confers benefits which do not end with his own generation. For the children of his workpeople share in them, and grow up stronger in body and in character than otherwise they would have done The price which he has paid for labour will have borne the expenses of production of an increased supply of high industrial faculties in the next generation: but these faculties will be the property of others, who will have the right to hire them out for the best price they will fetch: neither he nor even his heirs can reckon on reaping much material reward for this part of the good that he has done.

Second peculiarity.

§ 5. The next of those characteristics of the action of demand and supply peculiar to labour, which we have to study, lies in the fact that when a person sells his services, he has to present himself where they are delivered. It matters nothing to the seller of bricks whether they are to be used in building a palace or a sewer: but it matters a great deal to the seller of labour, who undertakes to perform a task of given difficulty, whether or not the place in which it is to be done is a wholesome and a pleasant one, and whether or not his associates will be such as he cares to have. In those yearly hirings which still remain in some parts of England, the labourer inquires what sort of a temper his new employer has, quite as carefully as what rate of wages he pays

The seller of labour must deliver it himself

The effects of this are not generally cumulative, and their real importance is seldom very great.

This peculiarity of labour is of great importance in many individual cases, but it does not often exert a broad and deep influence of the same nature as that last discussed The more disagreeable the incidents of an occupation, the higher of course are the wages required to attract people into it: but whether these incidents do lasting and wide-spreading harm depends on whether they are such as to undermine men's physical health and strength or to lower their character. When they are not of this sort, they are indeed evils in themselves, but they do not generally cause other evils beyond themselves; their effects are seldom cumulative.

Since however no one can deliver his labour in a market in which he is not himself present, it follows that the mobility of labour and the mobility of the labourer are convertible terms: and the unwillingness to quit home, and to leave old associations, including perhaps some loved cottage and burial-ground, will often turn the scale against a proposal to seek better wages in a new place. And when the different members of a family are engaged in different trades, and a migration, which would be advantageous to one member, would be injurious to others, the inseparability of the worker from his work considerably hinders the adjustment of the supply of labour to the demand for it. But of this more hereafter.

Third and fourth peculiarities. Labour is perishable,

§ 6. Again, labour is often sold under special disadvantages, arising from the closely connected group of facts that labour power is "perishable," that the sellers of it are commonly poor and have no reserve fund, and that they cannot easily withhold it from the market.

and the sellers of it are often at a disadvantage in bargaining. But many material commodities are perishable

Perishableness is an attribute common to the labour of all grades: the time lost when a worker is thrown out of employment cannot be recovered, though in some cases his energies may be refreshed by rest[1]. It must however be remembered that much of the working power of material agents of production is perishable in the same sense; for a great part of the income, which they also are prevented from earning by being thrown out of work, is completely lost. There is indeed some saving of wear-and-tear on a factory, or a steam-ship, when it is lying idle: but this is often small compared with the income which its owners have to forego: they get no compensation for their loss of interest on the capital invested, or for the depreciation which it undergoes from the action of the elements or from its tendency to be rendered obsolete by new inventions.

Again, many vendible commodities are perishable. In the strike of dock labourers in London in 1889, the perishableness of the fruit, meat, &c. on many of the ships told strongly on the side of the strikers.

Disadvantages in bargaining are greatest generally among the lowest grades of labour

The want of reserve funds and of the power of long withholding their labour from the market is common to nearly all grades of those whose work is chiefly with their hands. But it is especially true of unskilled labourers, partly because their wages leave very little margin for saving, partly because when any group of them suspends work, there are large numbers who are capable of filling their places. And, as we shall see presently when we come to discuss trade combinations, it is more difficult for them than for skilled artisans to form themselves into strong and lasting combinations; and so to put themselves on something like terms of equality in

[1] See above, Ch III § 6

bargaining with their employers. For it must be remembered that a man who employs a thousand others, is in himself an absolutely rigid combination to the extent of one thousand units among buyers in the labour market.

They do not attach to domestic servants,

But these statements do not apply to all kinds of labour Domestic servants though they have not large reserve funds, and seldom any formal trades-union, are sometimes better able than their employers to act in concert. The total real wages of domestic servants of fashionable London are very high in comparison with other skilled trades in which equal skill and ability are required. But on the other hand those domestic servants who have no specialized skill, and who hire themselves to persons with very narrow means, have not been able to make even tolerably good terms for themselves they work very hard for very low wages.

nor to professional men

Turning next to the highest grades of industry, we find that as a rule they have the advantage in bargaining over the purchaser of their labour. Many of the professional classes are richer, have larger reserve funds, more knowledge and resolution, and much greater power of concerted action, with regard to the terms on which they sell their services, than the greater number of their clients and customers.

Those sellers of commodities who are poor and numerous relatively to the purchasers are at a disadvantage in bargaining, in the same way as are the sellers of labour.

If further evidence were wanted that the disadvantages of bargaining under which the vendor of labour commonly suffers, depend on his own circumstances and qualities, and not on the fact that the particular thing which he has to sell is labour; such evidence could be found by comparing the successful barrister or solicitor or physician, or opera singer or jockey with the poorer independent producers of vendible goods. Those, for instance, who in remote places collect shell-fish to be sold in the large central markets, have little reserve funds or knowledge of the world, and of what other producers are doing in other parts of the country: while those to whom they sell, are a small and compact body of wholesale dealers with wide knowledge and large reserve funds; and in consequence the sellers are at a great disadvantage in bargaining. And much the same is true of the women and children who sell hand-made lace, and of the garret masters of East London who sell furniture to large and powerful dealers.

The disadvantage is cumulative in two ways

It is however certain that manual labourers as a class are at a disadvantage in bargaining; and that the disadvantage wherever it exists is likely to be cumulative in its effects. For though, so long as there is any competition among employers at all, they are likely to bid for labour something not very much less than its real value to them, that is, something not very much less than the highest price they would pay rather than go on without it; yet anything that lowers wages tends to lower the efficiency of the labourer's work, and therefore to lower the price which the employer would rather pay than go without that work. The effects of the labourer's disadvantage in bargaining are therefore cumulative in two ways. It lowers his wages; and as we have seen, this lowers his efficiency as a worker, and thereby lowers the normal value of his labour. And in addition it diminishes his efficiency as a bargainer, and thus increases the chance that he will sell his labour for less than its normal value[1].

[1] On the subject of this Section compare Book v Ch. II § 3, and the subsequent Note on Barter Prof Brentano was the first to call attention to several of the points discussed in this chapter See also Howell's *Conflicts of Capital and Labour*.

CHAPTER V.

DEMAND AND SUPPLY IN RELATION TO LABOUR, CONCLUDED.

The fifth peculiarity of labour consists in the great length of time required for providing additional supplies of specialized ability.

§ 1. THE next peculiarity in the action of demand and supply with regard to labour, which we have to consider, is closely connected with some of those we have already discussed It consists in the length of time that is required to prepare and train labour for its work, and in the slowness of the returns which result from this training.

We find the clearest signs of the deliberate adjustment of supply of expensively trained labour to the demand for it, in the choice made by parents of occupations for their children, and in their efforts to raise their children into a higher grade than their own.

Adam Smith's comparison of the incomes earned by machinery and by a skilled worker

It was these chiefly that Adam Smith had in view when he said.—"When any expensive machine is erected, the extraordinary work to be performed by it before it is worn out, it must be expected, will replace the capital laid out upon it, with at least the ordinary profits. A man educated at the expense of much labour and time to any of those employments which require extraordinary dexterity and skill, may be compared to one of those expensive machines. The work which he learns to perform, it must be expected, over and above the usual wages of common labour, will replace to him the whole expense of his education, with at least the ordinary profits of an equally valuable capital. It must do this too in a reasonable time, regard being had to the very uncertain duration of human life, in the same manner as to the more certain duration of the machine."

But this statement is to be received only as a broad indication of general tendencies. For independently of the fact that in rearing and educating their children, parents are governed by motives different from those which induce a capitalist undertaker to erect a new machine, the period over which the earning power extends is generally greater in the case of a man than of a machine; and therefore the circumstances by which the earnings are determined are less capable of being foreseen, and the adjustment of supply to demand is both slower and more imperfect. For though factories and houses, the main shafts of a mine and the embankments of a railway may have much longer lives than those of the men who made them; yet these are exceptions to the general rule.

must be modified on account of the shortness of the lives of most machines, though there are important exceptions

§ 2. Not much less than a generation elapses between the choice by parents of a skilled trade for one of their children, and his reaping the full results of their choice. And meanwhile the character of the trade may have been almost revolutionized by changes, of which some probably threw long shadows before them, but others were such as could not have been foreseen even by the shrewdest persons and those best acquainted with the circumstances of the trade.

Parents in choosing trades for their children must look forward a whole generation, and their forecasts are very liable to error

The working classes in nearly all parts of England are constantly on the look-out for advantageous openings for the labour of themselves and their children; and they question friends and relations, who have settled in other districts, as to the wages that are to be got in various trades, and as to their incidental advantages and disadvantages. But it is very difficult to ascertain the causes that are likely to determine the distant future of the trades which they are selecting for their children; and there are not many who enter on this abstruse inquiry. The majority assume without a further thought that the condition of each trade in their own time sufficiently indicates what it will be in the future; and, so far as the influence of this habit extends, the supply of labour in a trade in any one generation tends to conform to its earnings not in that but in the preceding generation.

Again, some parents, observing that the earnings in one

trade have been for some years rising relatively to others in the same grade, assume that the course of change is likely to continue in the same direction. But it often happens that the previous rise was due to temporary causes, and that, even if there had been no exceptional influx of labour into the trade, the rise would have been followed by a fall instead of a further rise and, if there is such an exceptional influx, the consequence may be a supply of labour so excessive, that its earnings remain below their normal level for many years.

In this connection we must often take as our unit not a particular trade, but a whole grade of labour

Next we have to recall the fact that, although there are some trades which are difficult of access except to the sons of those already in them, yet the majority draw recruits from the sons of those in other trades in the same grade: and therefore when we consider the dependence of the supply of labour on the resources of those who bear the expenses of its education and training, we must often regard the whole grade, rather than any one trade, as our unit; and say that, in so far as the supply of labour is limited by the funds available for defraying its cost of production, the supply of labour in any grade is determined by the earnings of that grade in the last rather than in the present generation.

It must, however, be remembered that the birth-rate in every grade of society is determined by many causes, among which deliberate calculations of the future hold but a secondary place· though, even in a country in which tradition counts for as little as it does in modern England, a great influence is exerted by custom and public opinion which are themselves the outcome of the experience of past generations

Allowance must however be made for the movements of adult labour,

§ 3 But we must not omit to notice those adjustments of the supply of labour to the demand for it, which are effected by movements of adults from one trade to another, one grade to another, and one place to another. The movements from one grade to another can seldom be on a very large scale; although it is true that exceptional opportunities may sometimes develop rapidly a great deal of latent ability among the lower grades Thus, for instance, the sudden opening out of a new country, or such an event as the

American War, will raise from the lower ranks of labour many men who bear themselves well in difficult and responsible posts

BOOK VI. CH V

But the movements of adult labour from trade to trade and from place to place can in some cases be so large and so rapid as to reduce within a very short compass the period which is required to enable the supply of labour to adjust itself to the demand. That general ability which is easily transferable from one trade to another, is every year rising in importance relatively to that manual skill and technical knowledge which are specialized to one branch of industry[1] And thus economic progress brings with it on the one hand a constantly increasing changefulness in the methods of industry, and therefore a constantly increasing difficulty in predicting the demand for labour of any kind a generation ahead; but on the other hand it brings also an increasing power of remedying such errors of adjustment as have been made.

which are of increasing importance in consequence of the increasing demand for general ability

§ 4. Let us now revert to the principle that the income derived from the appliances for the production of a commodity exerts a controlling influence in the long run over their own supply and price, and therefore over the supply and the price of the commodity itself, but that within short periods there is not time for the exercise of any considerable influence of this kind. And let us inquire how this principle needs to be modified when it is applied not to the material agents of production, which are only a means towards an end, and which may be the private property of the capitalist, but to human beings who are ends as well as means of production and who remain their own property

The remainder of this Chapter is occupied with the differences between the adjustments of demand and supply in relation to labour for long and for short periods

To begin with we must notice that, since labour is slowly produced and slowly worn out, we must take the term "long period" more strictly, and regard it as generally implying a greater duration, when we are considering the relations of normal demand and supply for labour, than when we are con-

A "long period" with regard to the supply of labour must generally be very long

[1] On the subject of this section compare Book IV Ch VI, Mr Charles Booth's *Life and Labour in London* and Mr H Ll Smith's paper on *Modern Changes in the mobility of labour*

sidering them for ordinary commodities There are many problems, the period of which is long enough to enable the supply of ordinary commodities, and even of most of the material appliances required for making them, to be adjusted to the demand; and long enough therefore to justify us in regarding the average prices of those commodities during the period as "normal," and as equal to their normal expenses of production in a fairly broad use of the term; while yet the period would not be long enough to allow the supply of labour to be adjusted at all well to the demand for it. The average earnings of labour during this period therefore would not be at all certain to give about a normal return to those who provided the labour; but they would rather have to be regarded as determined by the available stock of labour on the one hand, and the demand for it on the other. Let us consider this point more closely.

The case of independent handicraftsmen;

§ 5. Market variations in the price of a commodity are governed by the temporary relations between demand and the stock that is in the market or within easy access of it When the market price so determined is above its normal level, those who are able to bring new supplies into the market in time to take advantage of the high price receive an abnormally high reward; and if they are small handicraftsmen working on their own account, the whole of this rise in price goes to increase their earnings.

but it can also be traced under the modern system of industry

In the modern industrial world, however, those who undertake the risks of production and to whom the benefits of any rise in price, and the evils of any fall, come in the first instance, are capitalist undertakers of industry. Their net receipts in excess of the immediate outlay involved for making the commodity, that is, its prime (money) cost, are a return derived for the time being from the capital invested in their business in various forms, including their own faculties and abilities (and are of the nature of a quasi-rent). But, when trade is good, the force of competition among the employers themselves, each desiring to extend his business, and to get for himself as much as possible of this high return, makes them consent to pay higher wages to their employees in order to obtain their services; and even if they act in concert, and refuse for a time any concession, a combination among their employees may force it from them under penalty of foregoing the harvest, which the favourable turn of the market is offering. The result generally is that before long a great part of the gains are being distributed among the employees; and that their earnings remain above the normal level so long as the prosperity lasts.

Illustration from the history of the coal trade.

Thus the high wages of miners during the inflation, which culminated in 1873, were governed for the time by the relation in which the demand for their services stood to the amount of skilled mining labour available, the unskilled labour imported into the trade being counted as equivalent to an amount of skilled labour of equal efficiency. Had it been impossible to import any such labour at all, the earnings of miners would have been limited only by the elasticity of the demand for coal on the one hand, and the gradual coming to age of the rising generation of miners on the other. As it was, men were drawn from other occupations which they were not eager to leave; for they could have got high wages by staying where they were, since the prosperity of the coal and iron trades was but the highest crest of a swelling tide of credit. These new men were unaccustomed to underground work; its discomforts told heavily on them, while its dangers were increased by their want of technical knowledge, and their want of skill caused them to waste much of their strength. The limits therefore which their competition imposed on the rise of the special earnings of miners' skill were not narrow: (its quasi-rent could become very high).

When the tide turned those of the new-comers who were least adapted for the work left the mines; but even then the miners who remained were too many for the work to be done, and their wage fell, till it reached that limit at which they could get more by selling their labour in other trades. And that limit was a low one; for the swollen tide of credit, which culminated in 1873, had undermined solid business, impaired the true foundations of prosperity, and left nearly every trade in a more or less unhealthy and depressed condition. The

BOOK VI. CH. V.

miners had therefore to sell their skilled labour in markets which were already over full, and in which their special skill counted for nothing.

In estimating the return for the labourer's skill, account must be taken not only of his wear-and-tear,

§ 6. We have already remarked that only part of the returns derived from an improvement which is being exhausted can be regarded as being its special net earnings (or quasi-rent) of it; for a sum equivalent to the exhaustion of the capital value of the improvement must be deducted from these returns, before they can be counted as net income of any kind. And similarly allowance must be made for the wear-and-tear of a machine, as well as for the cost of working it, before we can arrive at the quasi-rent earned by it. But it is clear that the miner is liable to wear-and-tear as much as machinery is, and in his case also a deduction must be made from his earnings on account of wear-and-tear when the return of his special skill is being estimated.

but also of his fatigue, and other inconveniences of his work.

But in his case there is a further difficulty. For while the owner of machinery does not suffer from its being kept long at work when the expenses of working it, including wear-and-tear, have once been allowed for; the owner of skilled faculties does suffer when they are kept long at work, and he suffers incidental inconveniences, such as loss of recreation and of freedom of movement, &c. If the miner has only four days' work in one week and earns £1, and in the next week he has six days' work and earns £1. 10*s.*, only part of this extra 10*s.* can be regarded as return for his skill, for the remainder must be reckoned as the recompense of his additional fatigue as well as wear-and-tear[1].

Conclusion, and re-statement of the argument with regard to the dependence of fluctuations of earnings on

To conclude this part of our argument. The market price of everything, *i.e.* its price for short periods, is determined mainly by the relations in which the demand for it stands to the available stocks of it, and in the case of any agent of production, whether it be a human or a material agent, this demand is "derived" from the demand for those things which it is used in making. In these relatively short periods

[1] Compare above, Ch II. § 2 If they have any considerable stock of trade implements, they are to that extent capitalists; and part of their income is quasi-rent on this capital

fluctuations in wages follow, and do not precede, fluctuations in the selling prices of the goods produced.

the state of the market

But the incomes which are being earned by all agents of production, human as well as material, and those which appear likely to be earned by them in the future, exercise a ceaseless influence on those persons by whose action the future supplies of these agents are determined. There is a constant tendency towards a position of normal equilibrium, in which the supply of each of these agents shall stand in such a relation to the demand for its services, as to give to those who have provided the supply a sufficient reward for their efforts and sacrifices If the economic conditions of the country remained stationary sufficiently long, this tendency would realize itself in such an adjustment of supply to demand, that both machines and human beings would earn generally an amount that corresponded fairly with their cost of rearing and training, conventional necessaries as well as those things which are strictly necessary being reckoned for. But conventional necessaries might change under the influence of non-economic causes, even while economic conditions themselves were stationary: and this change would affect the supply of labour, and would lessen the national dividend and slightly alter its distribution. As it is, the economic conditions of the country are constantly changing, and the point of adjustment of normal demand and supply in relation to labour is constantly being shifted.

The extra income earned by some natural abilities may be regarded as a rent,

§ 7. We may now discuss the question under what head to class those high incomes which are earned by extraordinary natural abilities. Since they are not the result of the investment of human effort in an agent of production for the purpose of increasing its efficiency, there is a strong *primâ facie* cause for regarding them as of the nature of a rent, or producer's surplus, resulting from the possession of a differential advantage for production, freely given by nature. This analogy has been noticed by a long series of writers[1]: it is instructive and suggestive; but we must be on our guard against the temptation to extend it beyond its proper scope,

[1] See the references given in Book v Ch VIII § 1.

BOOK VI. CH. V.

and to apply it without those conditions which are required to make it true.

so long as we are merely analysing the source of the incomes of individuals,

The analogy is valid and useful so long as we are merely analysing the component parts of the income earned by an individual And there is some interest in the inquiry how much of the income of successful men is due to chance, to opportunity, to the conjuncture, how much to the good start that they have had in life; how much is profits on the capital invested in their special training, how much is the reward of exceptionally hard work; and how much remains as a producer's surplus or rent resulting from the possession of rare natural gifts.

But when we are considering the whole body of those engaged in any occupation, we are not at liberty to treat the exceptionally high earnings of successful men as rent, without making allowance for the low earnings of those who fail.

but not when we are considering the normal earnings of a trade,

For the supply of labour in any occupation is governed, other things being equal, by the earnings of which it holds out the prospect. The future of those who enter the occupation cannot be predicted with certainty: some, who start with the least promise, turn out to have great latent ability, and, aided perhaps by good luck, they earn large fortunes; while others, who made a brilliant promise at starting, come to nothing. For the chances of success and failure are to be taken together, much as are the chances of good and bad hauls by a fisherman or of good and bad harvests by a farmer, and a youth when selecting an occupation, or his parents when selecting one for him, are very far from leaving out of account the fortunes of successful men. These fortunes are therefore part of the price that is paid in the long run for the supply of labour and ability that seeks the occupation: they enter into the true or "long period" normal supply price of labour in it. They are not, as some writers have urged, a rent which does not enter into that price, and which is rather determined by that price.

or considering fluctuations of earnings,

It is true that, if we confined our attention to short periods, we might fairly say that the incomes earned by the natural genius already existing among those who had specialized themselves in a certain trade, do not enter directly into the marginal expenses of production of the goods made in it, nor therefore into their price: they are governed by that price (and therefore are rather to be regarded as a quasi-rent) But the same is true, as we have just seen, of the earnings of all who have acquired skill and aptitudes specialized to the trade, even though they have no great natural talents.

save in the extreme case of a class of persons born with rare abilities specialized to particular branches of production.

It may be conceded, again, that, if a certain class of people were marked out from their birth as having special gifts for some particular occupation, and for no other, so that they would be sure to seek that occupation in any case, then the earnings which such men would get might be left out of account as exceptional, when we were considering the chances of success or failure for ordinary persons. But as a matter of fact that is not the case, for a great part of a person's success in any occupation depends on the development of talents and tastes, the strength of which cannot be clearly predicted until he has already committed himself to a choice of occupation. Such predictions are at least as fallible as those which a new settler can make as to the future fertility and advantages of situation of the various plots of land that are offered for his selection[1]. And partly for this reason the income derived from rare natural qualities bears a closer analogy to the surplus produce from the holding of a settler who has made an exceptionally lucky selection, than to the rent of land in an old country. But land and human beings differ in so many respects, that even that analogy, if pursued very far, is apt to mislead· and the greatest caution is required in the application of the term Rent to the earnings of extraordinary ability.

Finally, it may be observed that the argument of Book v. Chapters VIII. and IX., with regard to the special earnings (whether of the nature of rents or quasi-rents) of appliances capable of being used in several branches of production, is applicable to the special earnings of natural abilities, and of skill. When land capable of being used for producing

[1] Comp. Book v Ch. IX. § 1.

one commodity is used for another, the supply price of the first is raised, though not by an amount dependent on the rent which the land would yield in this second use So when trained skill or natural abilities which could have been applied to produce one commodity, are applied for another, the supply price of the first is raised through the narrowing of its sources of supply.

CHAPTER VI.

DEMAND AND SUPPLY IN RELATION TO CAPITAL. A FURTHER STUDY OF INTEREST.

§ 1 THE relations between demand and supply cannot be studied by themselves in the case of capital any more than they could in the case of labour. All the elements of the great central problem of distribution and exchange mutually govern one another: and the first two chapters of this Book, and more especially the parts that relate directly to capital, may be taken without rehearsal as an introduction to this and the next two chapters. But before entering on the detailed analysis with which they will be mainly occupied, something may be said as to the position which the modern study of capital and interest holds in relation to earlier work.

Chapters I and II. discuss the main principles of the action of demand and supply in relation to capital; we now go to details

The aid which economic science has given towards understanding the part played by capital in our industrial system is solid and substantial; but it has made no startling discoveries. Everything of importance which is now known to economists has long been acted upon by able business men, though they may not have been able to express their knowledge clearly, or even accurately.

The individual doctrines of economics as to capital are not new, but are the basis of action in ordinary life.

Everyone is aware that no payment would be offered for the use of capital unless some gain were expected from that use, and further that these gains are of many kinds. Some borrow to meet a pressing need, real or imaginary, and pay others to sacrifice the present to the future in order that they themselves may sacrifice the future to the present. Some borrow to obtain machinery, and other "intermediate" goods, with which they may make things to be sold at a

BOOK VI. CH. VI

profit; some to obtain hotels, theatres and other things which yield their services directly, but are yet a source of profit to those who control them. Some borrow houses for themselves to live in, or else the means wherewith to buy or build their own houses; and the absorption of the resources of the country in such things as houses increases, other things being equal, with every increase in those resources and every consequent fall in the rate of interest, just as does the absorption of those resources in machinery or docks or other intermediate goods[1].

Everyone knows that people, who have the means of lending, will not lend gratis as a rule; because even if they have not themselves some good use to which to turn the capital or its equivalent, they are sure to be able to find others to whom its use would be of benefit, and who would pay for the loan of it: and they stand out for the best market[2].

Everyone knows that few, even among the Anglo-Saxon and other steadfast and self-disciplined races, care to save a large part of their incomes, and that many openings have been made for the use of capital in recent times by the progress of discovery and the opening up of new countries: and thus everyone understands generally the causes which have kept the supply of accumulated wealth so small relatively to the demand for its use, that that use is on the balance a source of gain, and can therefore require a payment when loaned. Everyone is aware that the accumulation of wealth is held in check, and the rate of interest so far sustained, by the preference which the great mass of humanity have for present over deferred gratifications. And indeed the true work of economic analysis in this respect is, not to emphasize this familiar truth, but to point out how much more numer-

[1] The demand for durable stone houses in place of wood houses which give nearly equal accommodation for the time is a sure sign that a country is growing in wealth and that capital is to be had at a lower rate of interest; and it acts on the market for capital and on the rate of interest in the same way as would a demand for new factories or railways

[2] That the supply of capital is held back by the *prospectiveness* of its uses, and men's unreadiness to look forward, while the demand for it comes from its *productiveness*, in the broadest sense of the term, is indicated in Book II. Ch. IV.

ous are the exceptions to this general preference than would appear at first sight[1].

But economics has important and difficult work to do in connecting individual truths to make an organic whole,

These truths are familiar; and they are the basis of the theory of capital and interest. But in the affairs of ordinary life truths are apt to present themselves in fragments The presentation may be vivid, but it is seldom complete. Particular relations are seen clearly one at a time; but the interactions of mutually self-determining causes are seldom grouped as a whole. The chief task of economics then as regards capital is to set out in order and in their mutual relations, all the forces which operate in the production and accumulation of wealth and the distribution of income; so that as regards both capital and other agents of production they may be seen *mutually determining* one another

and in analysis,

Next it has to analyse the influences which sway men in their choice between present and deferred gratifications, including leisure and opportunities for forms of activity that are their own reward. But here the post of honour lies with mental science; the received doctrines of which economics applies, in combination with other material, to its special problems[2].

especially of the constituents of profits and their mutual relations

Its work is therefore heavier in that analysis, on which we are to be engaged in this and the next two chapters, of the gains that are derived from the aid of accumulated wealth in the attainment of desirable ends, especially when that wealth takes the form of trade capital For these gains or profits contain many elements, some of which belong to interest for the use of capital in a broad sense of the term; while others constitute *net* interest, or interest properly so called Some constitute the reward of managing ability and of

[1] See Book III Ch v. §§ 3, 4; and Book IV. Ch. VII § 8 It is a good corrective of this error to note how small a modification of the conditions of our own world would be required to bring us to another in which the mass of the people are so anxious to provide for old age and for their families after them, and in which the new openings for the advantageous use of accumulated wealth in any form are so small, that the amount of wealth for the safe custody of which people are willing to pay exceeds that which others desire to borrow; and where in consequence even those who saw their way to make a gain out of the use of capital, would be able to exact a payment for taking charge of it; and interest would be negative all along the line

[2] Compare Book I. Ch v, Book III. Ch v, Book IV Ch VII

BOOK VI. CH. VI

enterprise, including the bearing of risks; and others again belong not so much to any one of these agents of production but to their combination.

The economic doctrine of capital has progressed continuously and without abrupt change.

The scientific doctrine of capital has had a long history of continuous growth and improvement in these three directions during the last three centuries. Adam Smith appears to have seen indistinctly, and Ricardo to have seen distinctly, almost everything of primary importance in the theory, very much as it is known now: and though one writer has preferred to emphasize one of its many sides, and another another, there seems no good reason for believing that any great economist since the time of Adam Smith has ever completely overlooked any side; and especially is it certain that nothing which would be familiar to men of business was overlooked by the practical financial genius of Ricardo. But there has been progress, almost everyone has improved some part, and given it a sharper and clearer outline; or else has helped to explain the complex relations of its different parts. Scarcely anything done by any great thinker has had to be undone, but something new has constantly been added[1].

[1] The question has already been raised (p 152) whether Prof v Böhm-Bawerk has not slightly underrated the acumen of his predecessors in their writings on capital and interest, and whether what he regards as mere naïve fragments of theories were not rather the utterances of men well acquainted with the practical workings of business, and who partly for some special purpose, and partly through want of system in exposition, gave such disproportionate stress to some elements of the problem as to throw the others into the background. And perhaps part of the air of paradox with which he invests his own theory of capital may be the result of a similar disproportionate emphasis, and an unwillingness to recognize that the various elements of the problem *mutually* govern one another. Attention has already been called to the fact that, though he excludes houses and hotels, and indeed everything that is not strictly speaking an intermediate good, from his definition of capital, yet the demand for the use of goods, that are not intermediate, acts as directly on the rate of interest, as does that for capital as defined by him. Connected with this use of the term capital is a doctrine on which he lays great stress, viz. that "methods of production which take time are more productive" (*Positive Capital*, Book v Ch IV. p 261), or again that "every lengthening of a roundabout process is accompanied by a further increase in the technical result" (*Ib* Book II Ch II. p 84). But is not this to treat as the cause what is really an effect as much as a cause? Are there not innumerable processes which take a long time and are roundabout; but are not productive and therefore are not used? Is it not the fact that because interest has to be paid for, and can be gained by the use of capital, therefore those long and roundabout

BOOK VI CH. VI.

But they were not known in the Middle Ages.

§ 2. But if we go back to mediæval and ancient history we certainly do seem to find an absence of clear ideas as to the nature of the services which capital renders in production, and for which interest is the payment; and since this early history is exercising an indirect influence on the problems of our own age, something should be said of it here.

In early stages of civilization the abuses of loans at interest may exceed their uses;

In primitive communities there were but few openings for the employment of fresh capital in enterprise, and anyone who had property that he did not need for his own immediate use, would seldom forego much by lending it on good security to others without charging any interest for the loan. Those who borrowed were generally the poor and the weak, people whose needs were urgent and whose powers of bargaining were very small. Those who lent were as a rule either people who spared freely of their superfluity to help their distressed neighbours, or else professional money-lenders. To these last the poor man had resort in his need; and they frequently made a cruel use of their power, entangling him in meshes from which he could not escape without great suffering, and perhaps the loss of the personal freedom of himself or his children. Not only uneducated people, but the sages of early times, the fathers of the mediæval church, and the English rulers of India in our own time, have been inclined to say, that money-lenders "traffic in other people's misfortunes, seeking gain through their adversity: under the pretence of compassion they dig a pit for the oppressed[1]."

methods which involve much locking up of capital are avoided unless they are more productive than others? Should we not rather say that the fact that many roundabout methods are in various degrees productive is one of the causes that affect the rate of interest; and that the rate of interest and the extent to which roundabout methods are employed are two of the elements of the central problem of distribution and exchange that mutually determine one another? See above, p 587 n

[1] From St Chrysostom's Fifth Homily, see above Book I. Ch II § 8 Compare also Ashley's *Economic History*, Book VI Ch VI; and Bentham *On Usury*, Lecky's *Rationalism in Europe*, the economic histories of Kautz, Ingram and Cunningham, the economic treatises of Knies, Roscher and Nicholson, Thorburn's *Musalmans and Money-lenders in the Punjab* and several recent articles in the *Economic Review*. The sentiment against usury had its origin in tribal relationships, in many other cases besides that of the Israelites, perhaps in all cases, and, as Cliffe-Leslie remarks (*Essays*, 2nd Edition, p 244) —It was "inherited from pre-historic times, when the members of each community still regarded themselves as kinsmen, when communism in property existed at least in practice, and no one

In such a state of society it may be a question for discussion, whether it is to the public advantage that people should be encouraged to borrow wealth under a contract to return it with increase after a time: whether such contracts, taken one with another, do not on the whole diminish rather than increase the sum total of human happiness.

and this fact retarded the growth of clear notions as to the nature of the services rendered by capital.

But unfortunately attempts were made to solve this difficult and important practical question by a philosophical distinction between the interest for the loan of money and the rental of material wealth. Aristotle had said that money was barren, and that to derive interest from lending it out was to put it to an unnatural use. And following his lead Scholastic writers argued with much labour and ingenuity that he who lent out a house or a horse might charge for its use, because he gave up the enjoyment of a thing that was directly productive of benefit. But they found no similar excuse for the interest on money: that, they said, was wrong, because it was a charge for a service which did not cost the lender anything[1].

Mediæval confusion of thought on this subject.

If the loan really cost him nothing, if he could have made no use of the money himself, if he was rich and the borrower poor and needy, then it might no doubt be argued that he was morally bound to lend his money gratis: but on the same grounds he would have been bound to lend without charge to a poor neighbour a house which he would not himself inhabit, or a horse for a day's work of which he had himself no need. The doctrine of these writers therefore really implied, and in fact it did convey to people's minds the mischievous fallacy that—independently of the special circumstances of the borrower and the lender—the loan of money, *i.e.* of command over things in general, is not a sacrifice on the part of the lender and a benefit to the borrower, of the same kind as the loan of a particular commodity: they obscured the fact that he who borrows money can buy,

who had more than he needed could refuse to share his superfluous wealth with a fellow-tribesman in want."

[1] They also made a distinction between *hiring* things which were themselves to be returned, and *borrowing* things the equivalent of which only had to be returned This distinction, however, though interesting from an analytical point of view, has very little practical importance

for instance, a young horse, whose services he can use, and whom he can sell, when the loan has to be returned, at as good a price as he paid for him. The lender gives up the power of doing this, the borrower acquires it: there is no substantial difference between the loan of the purchase price of a horse and the loan of a horse[1].

In the modern world similar causes have promoted the spread of erroneous analysis

§ 3. History has in part repeated itself: and in the modern Western World a new reforming impulse has derived strength from, and given strength to, another erroneous analysis of the nature of interest. As civilization has progressed, the loans of wealth to needy people have become steadily more rare, and a less important part of the whole; while the loans of capital for productive use in business have grown at an ever-increasing rate. And in consequence, though the borrowers are not now regarded as the subjects of oppression, a grievance has been found in the fact that all producers, whether working with borrowed capital or not, reckon interest on the capital used by them as among the expenses which they require to have returned to them in the long run in the price of their wares as a condition of their continuing business. On this account, and on account of the openings which the present industrial system offers of amassing great wealth by sustained good fortune in speculation, it has been argued that the payment of interest in modern times oppresses the working classes indirectly, though not directly; and that it deprives them of their fair share of the benefits resulting from the growth of knowledge. And hence is derived the practical conclusion that it would be for the general happiness, and therefore right, that no private person should be allowed to own any of the means of production, nor any direct means of enjoyment, save such as he needs for his own use.

Connection between

This practical conclusion has been supported by other arguments which will claim our attention; but at present

[1] Prof. Cunningham has described well the subtleties by which the mediæval church explained away her prohibition of loans at interest, in most of those cases in which the prohibition would have been seriously injurious to the body politic. These subtleties resemble the legal fictions by which the judges have gradually explained away the wording of laws, the natural interpretation of which seemed likely to be mischievous. In both cases some practical evil has been avoided at the expense of fostering habits of confused and insincere thought.

BOOK VI. CH. VI

The practical proposals of Rodbertus and Karl Marx and their doctrine of value. Their main conclusion was assumed in an untrue premiss

we are only concerned with the doctrine that has been used by William Thompson[1], Rodbertus, Karl Marx, and others in support of it. They argued that labour always produces a "Surplus"[2] above its wages and the wear-and-tear of capital used in aiding it: and that the wrong done to labour lies in the exploitation of this surplus by others. But this assumption that the whole of this Surplus is the product of labour, already takes for granted what they ultimately profess to prove by it; they make no attempt to prove it; and it is not true. It is not true that the spinning of yarn in a factory, after allowance has been made for the wear-and-tear of the machinery, is the product of the labour of the operatives. It is the product of their labour, together with that of the employer and subordinate managers, and of the capital employed; and that capital itself is the product of labour and waiting: and therefore the spinning is the product of labour of many kinds, and of waiting. If we admit that it is the product of labour alone, and not of labour and waiting, we can no doubt be compelled by inexorable logic to admit that there is no justification for Interest, the reward of waiting, for the conclusion is implied in the premiss. Rodbertus and Marx do indeed boldly claim the authority of Ricardo for their premiss; but we have already seen (in the Note on Ricardo's theory of value at the end of last Book), that it is really as opposed to his explicit statement and the general tenor of his theory of value, as it is to common sense.

To put the same thing in other words; if it be true that the postponement of gratifications involves *in general* a sacrifice on the part of him who postpones, just as additional effort does on the part of him who labours; and if it be true that this postponement enables man to use methods of production of which the first cost is great, but by which the aggregate of enjoyment is increased, as certainly as it would

[1] Dr Anton Menger, in *Das Recht auf den vollen Arbeitsertrag*, has shown well how both the practical conclusions as to the nationalization of the means of production and the theoretical basis of the arguments of Rodbertus and Karl Marx had been in a great measure anticipated in earlier works, and especially William Thompson's *Principles of the Distribution of Wealth most conducive to Human Happiness*, 1824.

[2] This is Marx's phrase. Rodbertus had called it a "Plus"

be by an increase of labour; then it cannot be true that the value of a thing depends simply on the amount of labour spent on it. Every attempt to establish this premiss has necessarily assumed implicitly that the service performed by capital is a "free" good, rendered without sacrifice, and therefore needing no interest as a reward to induce its continuance; and this is the very conclusion which the premiss is wanted to prove. The strength of Rodbertus' and Marx's sympathies with suffering must always claim our respect: but what they regarded as the scientific foundation of their practical proposals appears to be little more than a series of arguments in a circle to the effect that there is no economic justification for interest, while that result has been all along latent in their premisses; though, in the case of Marx, it was shrouded by mysterious Hegelian phrases, with which he "coquetted," as he tells us in his Preface.

Net and *Gross* interest.

§ 4. We may now proceed with our analysis. The interest of which we speak when we say that interest is the earnings of capital simply, or the reward of waiting simply, is *Net* interest, but what commonly passes by the name of Interest, includes other elements besides this, and may be called *Gross* interest

Gross interest includes some Insurance against risk,

These additional elements are the more important, the lower and more rudimentary the state of commercial security and of the organization of credit. Thus, for instance, in mediæval times, when a prince wanted to forestall some of his future revenues, he borrowed perhaps a thousand ounces of silver, and undertook to pay back fifteen hundred at the end of a year There was however no perfect security that he would fulfil the promise; and perhaps the lender would have been willing to exchange that promise for an absolute certainty of receiving thirteen hundred at the end of the year. In that case, while the nominal rate at which the loan was made was fifty per cent., the real rate was thirty

and also Earnings of Management,

The necessity for making this allowance for insurance against risk is so obvious, that it is not often overlooked. But it is less obvious that every loan causes some trouble to the lender; that when, from the nature of the case, the loan involves considerable risk, a great deal of trouble has

BOOK VI CH VI

often to be taken to keep these risks as small as possible; and that then a great part of what appears to the borrower as interest, is, from the point of view of the lender, earnings of management of a troublesome business.

and therefore varies with the circumstances of each loan.

At the present time the net interest on capital in England is a little under three per cent. per annum; for no more than that can be obtained by investing in such first-rate stock-exchange securities as yield to the owner a secure income without appreciable trouble or expense on his part. And when we find capable business men borrowing on perfectly secure mortgages, at (say) four per cent., we may regard that gross interest of four per cent. as consisting of net interest, or interest proper, to the extent of a little under three per cent, and of earnings of management by the lenders to the extent of rather more than one per cent [1]

Cases in which gross interest is very high

Again, a pawnbroker's business involves next to no risk; but his loans are generally made at the rate of 25 per cent. per annum, or more, the greater part of which is really earnings of management of a troublesome business. Or to take a more extreme case, there are men in London and Paris and probably elsewhere who make a living by lending money to costermongers: the money is often lent at the beginning of the day for the purchase of fruit, &c., and returned at the end of the day, when the sales are over, at a profit of ten per cent.; there is little risk in the trade, and the money is seldom lost[2]. Now a farthing invested at ten per cent. a day would amount to a billion pounds at the

[1] Mortgages for long periods are sometimes more sought after by lenders than those for short periods, and sometimes less The former save the trouble of frequent renewal, but they deprive the lender of command over his money for a long time, and thus limit his freedom. First-class stock-exchange securities combine the advantages of very long and very short mortgages For their holder can hold them as long as he likes, and can convert them into money when he will; though, if at the time credit is shaken and other people want ready money, he will have to sell at a loss If they could always be realized without a loss, and if there were no brokers' commissions to be paid on buying and selling, they would not yield a higher income than money lent "on call" at the lender's choice of time; and that will always be less than the interest on loans for any fixed period, short or long

[2] Again, Dr Jessop (*Arcady*, p. 214) tells us "there are hosts of small money-lenders in the purlieus of the cattle markets who make advances to speculators *with an eye*," lending sums, amounting in exceptional cases up to £200, at a Gross interest of ten per cent for the twenty-four hours.

end of a year. But no one can become rich by lending to costermongers; because no one can lend much in this way. The so-called interest on the loans really consists almost entirely of earnings of a kind of work for which few capitalists have a taste.

Further analysis of gross interest

§ 5. It is then necessary to analyse a little more carefully the extra risks which are introduced into business when much of the capital used in it has been borrowed. Let us suppose that two men are carrying on similar businesses, the one working with his own, the other chiefly with borrowed capital.

Trade Risks

There is one set of risks which is common to both; which may be described as the *Trade Risks* of the particular business in which they are engaged. They arise from fluctuations in the markets for their raw materials and finished goods, from unforeseen changes of fashion, from new inventions, from the incursion of new and powerful rivals into their respective neighbourhoods, and so on. But there is another set of risks, the burden of which has to be borne by the man working with borrowed capital, and not by the other; and we may call them *Personal Risks*. For he who lends capital to be used by another for trade purposes, has to charge a high interest as insurance against the chances of some flaw or deficiency in the borrower's personal character or ability[1].

Personal Risks.

Analysis of Personal risks.

The borrower may be less able than he appears, less energetic, or less honest. He has not the same inducements, as a man working with his own capital has, to look failure straight in the face, and withdraw from a speculative enterprise as soon as it shows signs of going against him. On the contrary, should his standard of honour not be high, he may be not very keen of sight as to his losses For if he withdraws at once, he will have lost all he has of his own, and if he allows the speculation to run on, any additional loss will fall on his creditors; and any gain will come to himself. Many creditors lose through semifraudulent inertness of this kind on the part of their debtors, and a few lose through deliberate fraud: the debtor for instance may conceal

[1] See also below, Ch VIII § 2.

BOOK VI. CH. VI.

in subtle ways the property that is really his creditors', until, his bankruptcy being over, and he having entered on a new business career, he can bring gradually into play his secret reserve funds without exciting over-much suspicion

Gross interest does not tend to equality.

The price then that the borrower has to pay for the loan of capital, and which he regards as interest, is from the point of view of the lender more properly to be regarded as profits: for it includes insurance against risks which are often very heavy, and earnings of management for the task, which is often very arduous, of keeping those risks as small as possible. Variations in the nature of these risks and of the task of management will of course occasion corresponding variations in the gross interest, so called, that is paid for the use of money. The tendency of competition is therefore not towards equalizing this gross interest: on the contrary, the more thoroughly lenders and borrowers understand their business, the more certainly will some classes of borrowers obtain loans at a lower rate than others

But the agencies of the modern money market tend to equalize rapidly the rates of net interest on different uses of capital.

We must defer to a later stage our study of the marvellously efficient organization of the modern money market by which capital is transferred from one place where it is superabundant to another where it is wanted; or from one trade that is in the process of contraction to another which is being expanded: and at present we must be contented to take it for granted that a very small difference between the rates of net interest to be got on the loan of capital in two different modes of investment in the same Western country will cause capital to flow, though perhaps by indirect channels, from the one to the other.

It is true that if either of the investments is on a small scale, and few people know much about it, the flow of capital may be slow. One person, for instance may be paying five per cent on a small mortgage, while his neighbour is paying four per cent on a mortgage which offers no better security. But in all large affairs the rate of net interest (so far as it can be disentangled from the other elements of profits) is nearly the same all over England. And further the divergencies between the average rates of net interest in different countries of the Western World are rapidly diminishing, as a result of the general growth of intercourse, and especially of the fact that the leading capitalists of all these countries hold large quantities of stock-exchange securities, which yield the same revenue and are sold practically at the same price on the same day all over the world[1].

NOTE ON CHANGES IN THE PURCHASING POWER OF MONEY IN RELATION TO THE REAL RATE OF INTEREST.

In reckoning true, as contrasted with nominal, interest we make assumptions as to the purchasing power of money

Throughout the present volume we are supposing, in the absence of any special statement to the contrary, that all values are expressed in terms of money of fixed purchasing power, just as astronomers have taught us to determine the beginning or the ending of the day with reference not to the actual sun but to a *mean sun* which is supposed to move uniformly through the heavens. (See Book I Ch. I. § 5.) Further, the influences which changes in the purchasing power of money do actually exert on the terms on which loans are arranged, are most conspicuous in the market for short loans—a market which differs in many of its incidents from any other, and a full discussion of their influences must be deferred. Nevertheless it seems right to notice them here in passing, at all events as a point of abstract theory For the rate of interest which the borrower is willing to pay measures the benefits that he expects to derive from the use of the capital only on the assumption that the money has the same purchasing power when it is borrowed and when it is returned.

[1] When we come to discuss the Money Market we shall have to study the causes which render the supply of capital for immediate use much larger at some times than at others; and which at certain times make bankers and others contented with an extremely low rate of interest, provided the security be good and they can get their money back into their own hands quickly in case of need At such times they are willing to lend for short periods even to borrowers, whose security is not first rate, at a rate of interest that is not very high. For their risks of loss are much reduced by their power of refusing to renew the loan, if they notice any indication of weakness on the part of the borrower, and since short loans on good security are fetching only a nominal price, nearly the whole of what interest they get from him is insurance against risk, and remuneration of their own trouble But on the other hand such loans are not really very cheap to the borrower they surround him by risks, to avoid which he would often be willing to pay a much higher rate of interest. For if any misfortune should injure his credit, or if a disturbance of the money market should cause a temporary scarcity of loanable capital, he may be quickly brought into great straits He may not be able to obtain a renewal of the loan on moderate, or even on any terms, and may thus be cut short in his most hopeful enterprises One of the chief symptoms of an impending commercial crisis is a rapid succession of forced sales at a loss by those who have been trading with capital borrowed for short periods. Loans to traders at nominally low rates of interest, if for short periods only, do not therefore really form exceptions to the general rule discussed in the text

BOOK VI. CH VI.

For short periods this may be best measured in commodities. A rise in the value of money makes the true rate of interest higher than the nominal.

Let us suppose, for instance, that a man borrows £100 under contract to pay back £105 at the end of the year. If meanwhile the purchasing power of money has risen 10 per cent. (or which is the same thing, general prices have fallen in the ratio of 10 to 11), he cannot get the £105 which he has to pay back without selling one-tenth more commodities than would have been sufficient for the purpose at the beginning of the year. Assuming, that is, that the things which he handles have not changed in value relatively to things in general, he must sell at the end of the year commodities which would have cost him £115. 10*s.* at the beginning, in order to pay back with interest his loan of £100; and therefore he has lost ground unless the commodities have increased under his hands 15½ per cent. While nominally paying 5 per cent. for the use of his money, he has really been paying 15½ per cent.

On the other hand, if prices had risen so much that the purchasing power of money had fallen 10 per cent. during the year, and he could get £100 for things which cost him £90 at the beginning of the year; then, instead of paying 5 per cent. for the loan, he would really be paid 5½ per cent. for taking charge of the money.

When we come to discuss the causes of alternating periods of inflation and depression of commercial activity, we shall find that they are intimately connected with those variations in the real rate of interest which are caused by changes in the purchasing power of money. For when prices are likely to rise, people rush to borrow money and buy goods, and thus help prices to rise; business is inflated, and is managed recklessly and wastefully, those working on borrowed capital pay back less real value than they borrowed, and enrich themselves at the expense of the community. When afterwards credit is shaken and prices begin to fall, everyone wants to get rid of commodities and get hold of money which is rapidly rising in value; this makes prices fall all the faster, and the further fall makes credit shrink even more, and thus for a long time prices fall because prices have fallen.

Fluctuations would not be much lessened by basing our currency on two metals instead of one. Slow changes are on a different footing.

We shall find that fluctuations in prices are caused only to a very slight extent by fluctuations in the supply of the precious metals; and that they would not be much diminished by the adoption of gold and silver instead of gold as the basis of our currency. But the evils which they cause are so great, that it is worth while to do much in order to diminish them a little. These evils however are not necessarily inherent in those slow changes in the purchasing power of money which follow the course of man's changing command over nature. During the last fifty years improvements in the arts of production and in the access to rich sources of supply of raw material, have doubled the efficiency of man's labour in procuring the things which he wants: and an injustice would have been done to those members of the working classes whose money wages are much influenced by custom if the purchasing power of a sovereign in terms of commodities had remained stationary, instead of following, as it has, the increasing command by man over Nature.

CHAPTER VII.

DEMAND AND SUPPLY IN RELATION TO CAPITAL, BUSINESS POWER AND INDUSTRIAL ORGANIZATION.

This chapter and the following continue the analyses of Book IV. Ch. XII XIII

§ 1 IN the concluding chapters of Book IV. we made some study of the various forms of business management, and the faculties required for them, and we saw how the supply of business power in command of capital may be regarded as consisting of three elements, the supply of capital, the supply of the business power to manage it, and the supply of the organization by which the two are brought together and made effective for production. In the last chapter we were concerned mainly with interest, the earnings of the first of these elements. In this chapter we are mainly occupied with the earnings of the second and third taken together, which we have called *Gross* earnings of management, and with the relation in which this stands to the earnings of the second taken by itself which we have called *Net* earnings of management[1]. We are to carry this study further; and to inquire more closely into the nature of the services which the business undertaker renders to society, and the rewards of this work; and we shall find that the causes by which these are governed are less arbitrary, and present closer analogies to those which govern other kinds of earnings, than is commonly supposed.

The success of any form of business manage-

We must however make a distinction at starting. We must call to mind[2] the fact that the struggle for survival tends to make those methods of organization prevail, which are best fitted to *thrive in* their environment, but not neces-

[1] See p. 392 [2] See Book IV. Ch. VIII

BOOK VI. CH. VII

ment in the struggle for survival depends more on its immediate efficiency than on the remote benefits which it may confer by pioneering new methods.

sarily those best fitted to *benefit* their environment, unless it happens that they are duly rewarded for all the benefits which they confer, whether direct or indirect. And in fact this is not so. For as a general rule the law of substitution—which is nothing more than a special and limited application of the law of survival of the fittest—tends to make one method of industrial organization supplant another when it offers a direct and immediate service at a lower price. The indirect and ultimate services which either will render have, as a general rule, little or no weight in the balance; and as a result many businesses languish and die, which might in the long run have done good work for society if only they could have obtained a fair start. This is especially true of some forms of co-operative associations.

In this connection we may divide employers and other undertakers into two classes, those who open out new and improved methods of business, and those who follow beaten tracks The services which the latter perform for society are chiefly direct and seldom miss their full reward: but it is otherwise with the former class.

For instance, economies have lately been introduced into some branches of iron manufacture by diminishing the number of times which the metal is heated in passing from pig iron to its final form, and some of these new inventions have been of such a nature that they could neither be patented nor kept secret. Let us suppose then that a manufacturer with a capital of £50,000 is getting in normal times a net profit of £4,000 a year, £1,500 of which we may regard as his earnings of management, leaving £2,500 for the other two elements of profits. We assume that he has been working so far in the same way as his neighbours, and showing an amount of ability which, though great, is no more than the normal or average ability of the people who fill such exceptionally difficult posts, that is, we assume that £1,500 a year is the normal earnings for the kind of work he has been doing. But as time goes on, he thinks out a way of dispensing with one of the heatings that have hitherto been customary; and in consequence, without increasing his expenses, he is able to increase his annual output by things which can be sold for £2,000 net. So long, therefore, as he can sell his wares at the old price, his earnings of management will be £2,000 a year above the average, and he will earn the full reward of his services to society. His neighbours however will copy his plan, and probably make more than average profits for a time. But soon competition will increase the supply, and lower the price of their wares, until their profits fall to about their old level; for no one could get extra high wages for making eggs stand on their ends after Columbus's plan had become public property

Many business men whose inventions have in the long run been of almost priceless value to the world, have earned even less by their discoveries than Milton by his *Paradise Lost* or Millet by his *Angelus*, and while many men have amassed great wealth by good fortune, rather than by exceptional ability in the performance of public services of high importance, it is probable that those business men who have pioneered new paths have often conferred on society benefits out of all proportion to their own gains, even though they have died millionaires. Although then we shall find that the rewards of every business undertaker tend to be proportionate to the *direct* services he renders to the community, this will by itself go but a small way towards proving that the existing industrial organization of society is the best conceivable, or even the best attainable; and it must not be forgotten that the scope of our present inquiry is limited to a study of the action of causes that determine the earnings of business undertaking and management *under existing social institutions.*

We will begin by tracing the action of the law of substitution in adjusting the rewards of the services rendered to society by ordinary workmen, by foremen, and by employers of different grades.

The law of substitution adjusts the demand for the services of foremen

§ 2. We have already noticed that a great part of the work done by the head of a small business himself, is relegated in a large business to salaried heads of departments, managers, foremen and others. And this thread will guide us to much that is useful for our present inquiry. The simplest case is that of the earnings of the ordinary foreman; with which we may begin.

BOOK VI CH. VII.

as compared with those of ordinary workmen.

Let us suppose, for instance, that a railway contractor or a dockyard manager finds that it answers best to have one foreman to every twenty labourers, and to pay him twice the wages of one of them. This means that, if he found himself with 500 labourers and 24 foremen, he would expect to get just a little more work done at the same expense by adding one more foreman, than by adding two more ordinary labourers: while if he had had 490 labourers and 25 foremen, he would have found it better to add two more labourers. If he could have got his foreman for one and a half times the wages of a labourer, perhaps he would have employed one foreman to every fifteen labourers. But, as it is, the number of foremen employed is determined at one-twentieth of that of the labourers, and their demand price at twice the labourers' wages[1].

In exceptional cases the foremen may earn their wages by overdriving those whose work they superintend. But we may now suppose them to contribute to the success of the undertaking in a legitimate way, by securing a better organization of its details, so that fewer things are done amiss and need to be undone; so that everyone finds the help that he wants in moving heavy weights, &c., ready for him just when he wants it, so that all machinery and implements are kept in good working order, and no one has to waste his time and strength by working with inadequate appliances, and so on. The wages of foremen who do work of this kind may be taken as typical of a great part of the earnings of management: society, acting through the individual employer, offers an effective demand for their services until that margin is reached at which the aggregate efficiency of industry would be increased by adding workers of some other grade more than by adding the foremen whose wages would add an equal amount to the expenses of production.

So far the employer has been regarded as the agent through whom the law of substitution acts in contriving and arranging the factors of production so that the maximum of direct services (estimated by their money measure) should be performed at a minimum money cost. But now we have

[1] With this argument may be compared that of Book VI. Ch. I. § 8.

to look at the work of the employers themselves being contrived and arranged for them, though of course in a more haphazard fashion, by the immediate action of their own competition.

The law of substitution adjusts the earnings of the head of a business and those of foremen and managers. Illustration from the gradual rise of a working carpenter

§ 3 Let us then look next at the way in which the work of foremen and salaried managers is constantly being weighed against that of the heads of businesses. It will be interesting to watch the course of a small business as it gradually expands. A house carpenter, for instance, steadily increases his stock of tools, till he can hire a small workshop, and undertake odd jobs for private persons, who have to agree with him as to what is to be done. The work of management and of undertaking what little risks there are, is shared between them and him, and, as this gives them a great deal of trouble, they are not willing to pay him at a high rate for what work of management he does[1].

His work as a small master-builder

So his next step is to undertake all the different sides of small repairs. He has now entered on the career of a master-builder; and if his business grows, he gradually withdraws himself from manual labour, and to some extent even from the superintendence of its details. Substituting for his own work that of hired men, he has now to deduct their wages from his receipts, before he can begin to reckon his profits· and unless he proves himself to have a business ability up to the normal level of that grade of industry which he has now entered, he will probably soon lose all the little capital which he has gained, and after a short struggle return to that humbler rank of life in which he has prospered. Should his ability be just about that level, he will, with average good fortune, retain his position and perhaps gain a little ground: and the excess of his receipts over his outgoings will be representative of the normal earnings of management in his grade

Changes in the character of his work as the scale of his business increases

If his ability be greater than that which is normal in his grade, he will be able to obtain as good a result with a given outlay for wages and other expenses, as most of his rivals can with a larger outlay: he will have substituted his extra ability in organization for some of their outlay;

[1] Comp. Book IV Ch. XII § 3

BOOK VI. CH. VII

and his earnings of management will include the value of that outlay with which he has dispensed. He will thus increase his capital and his credit: and be able to borrow more, and at a lower rate of interest. He will obtain a wider business acquaintanceship and connection; and he will get an increased knowledge of materials and processes, and opportunities for bold but wise and profitable adventure; until at last he has delegated to others nearly all those duties which occupied his whole time even after he had ceased to do manual work himself[1].

The adjustment between the earnings of undertakers on a large and on a small scale

§ 4. Having watched the law of substitution adjusting the earnings of foremen and of ordinary workmen, and again of employers and foremen, we may now look at its action in adjusting the earnings of employers on a small scale and those on a large scale.

Our carpenter having become a master-builder on a very large scale, his undertakings will be so many and so great as to have occupied the time and energies of some scores of employers who superintended all the details of their several businesses. Throughout this struggle between large businesses and small, we see the law of substitution constantly in operation; the large employer substituting a little of his own work and a good deal of that of salaried managers and foremen for that of a small employer. When, for instance, tenders are invited for erecting a building, a builder with a

[1] The employer of a large number of workmen has to economize his energies on the same plan that is followed by the leading officers of a modern army. For as Mr Wilkinson says (*The Brain of an Army*, pp. 42—6) —"Organization implies that every man's work is defined, that he knows exactly what he must answer for, and that his authority is coextensive with his responsibility [In the German army] every commander above the rank of a captain deals with a body composed of units, with the interior affairs of none of which he meddles, except in the case of failure on the part of the officer directly responsible .. The general commanding an army corps has to deal directly with only a few subordinates He inspects and tests the condition of all the various units, but...he is as far as possible unhampered by the worry of detail. He can make up his mind coolly." Bagehot in characteristic fashion had remarked (*Lombard Street*, Ch VIII) that if the head of a large business "is very busy, it is a sign of something wrong," and had compared (Essay on the *Transferability of Capital*) the primitive employer with a Hector or Achilles mingling in the fray, and the typical modern employer with "a man at the far end of a telegraph wire—a Count Moltke with his head over some papers—who sees that the proper persons are slain, and who secures the victory"

large capital often finds it worth his while to enter the lists, even though he lives at a distance. The local builders secure great economies in having workshops and men whom they can trust already near the spot; while he gains something through buying his materials on a large scale, through his command of machinery, especially for woodwork, and perhaps through being able to borrow what capital he wants on easier terms. These two sets of advantages frequently about balance one another; and the contest for the field of employment often turns on the relative efficiencies of the undivided energies of the small builder, and of that slight supervision, which is all that the abler but busier large builder can afford to give himself, though he supplements it by the work of his local manager and of the clerks in his central office[1].

An undertaker working with borrowed capital is at a disadvantage in some trades

§ 5 We may next watch the action of the law of substitution in pushing forward undertakers working chiefly with their own capital in some trades, and in others those working chiefly with borrowed capital. The personal risks, against which the lender of capital to be used in business requires to be indemnified, vary to some extent with the nature of that business, as well as with the circumstances of the individual borrower. They are very high in some cases, as for instance when a man is starting in a new branch of the electrical trades, in which there is very little past experience to go by, and the lender cannot easily form any independent judgment as to the progress which is being made by the borrower; and in all such cases the man working with borrowed capital is at a great disadvantage, the rate of profit is determined chiefly by the competition of those who apply their own capital. It may happen that not many such men have access to the trade, and in that case the competition may not be keen, and the rate of profit may be high; that is, it may exceed considerably net interest on the capital together with earnings of management on a scale commensurate with the difficulty of the business done, though that difficulty will probably be above the average.

And again, the new man with but little capital of his own is at a disadvantage in trades which move slowly

[1] Comp Book IV. Ch. XI § 4.

BOOK VI. CH VII.

and in which it is necessary to sow a long time before one reaps.

But in others he plays a leading part;

But in all those industries in which bold and tireless enterprise can reap a quick harvest; and in particular wherever high profits are to be made for a time by cheaper reproductions of costly wares, there the new man is in his element: it is he who by his quick resolutions and dexterous contrivances, and perhaps also a little by his natural recklessness, "forces the pace."

for he will work hard for a small reward.

And he often holds his own with great tenacity even under considerable disadvantages; for the freedom and dignity of his position are very attractive to him. Thus the peasant proprietor whose little plot is heavily mortgaged, the small so-called "sweater" or "garret master" who takes out a sub-contract at a low price, will often work harder than the ordinary workman, and for a lower net income. And the manufacturer who is doing a large business with comparatively little capital of his own will reckon his labour and anxiety almost as nothing, for he knows that he must anyhow work for his living, and he is unwilling to go into service to another: he will therefore work feverishly for a gain that would not count much in the balance with a wealthier rival, who, being able to retire and live in comfort on the interest of his capital, may be doubting whether it is worth while to endure any longer the wear-and-tear of business life.

The inflation of prices which culminated in 1873, enriched borrowers in general, and in particular business undertakers, at the expense of other members of society. New men therefore found their way into business made very smooth; and those who had already made or inherited business fortunes, found their way made smooth for retiring from active work. Thus Bagehot, writing about that time[1], argued that the growth of new men was making English business increasingly democratic: and, though admitting that "the propensity to variation in the social as in the animal kingdom is the principle of progress," he pointed out regretfully how much the country might have gained by the long duration of families of merchant princes. But in recent years there has been some

[1] *Lombard Street*, Introductory chapter.

reaction, due partly to social causes, and partly to the influence of a continued fall in prices. The sons of business men are rather more inclined than they were a generation ago to take pride in their fathers' callings; and they find it harder to satisfy the demands of an ever-increasing luxury on the income which would be theirs if they withdrew from business.

The managing officials of joint-stock companies earn their salaries by labour simply.

§ 6. But the weighing in the balance of the services and therefore the earnings of employees against the earnings of management of business men is in some ways best illustrated by reference to Joint-stock companies. For in them most of the work of management is divided between salaried directors (who indeed hold a few shares themselves) and salaried managers and other subordinate officials, most of whom have little or no capital of any kind, and their earnings, being almost the pure earnings of labour, are governed in the long run by those general causes which rule the earnings of labour of equal difficulty and disagreeableness in ordinary occupations.

Disadvantages of public companies,

Joint-stock companies are hampered by internal frictions, and conflicts of interest between shareholders and debenture holders, between ordinary and preferred shareholders, and between all these and the directors; and by the need for an elaborate system of checks and counterchecks. They seldom have the enterprise, the energy, the unity of purpose and the quickness of action of a private business.

and their advantages.

But these disadvantages are of relatively small importance in some trades. That publicity, which is one of the chief drawbacks of public companies in many branches of manufacture and of speculative commerce, is a positive advantage in ordinary banking and insurance and kindred businesses; while in these, as well as in most of the transport industries (railways, tramways, canals, and the supply of gas, water, and electricity), their unbounded command over capital gives them almost undisputed sway.

The largest public companies are often found in trades in which prices are

A peculiar feature of this latter class of industries is that their fixed capital is large relatively to their circulating, and the prime cost of the goods produced or the services rendered by them is small relatively to the total (or true normal) cost which must be defrayed in the long run in order to make their

BOOK VI CH. VII.

naturally unstable. But on the whole they exert a steadying influence on employment

business remunerative. When several companies whose business is of this kind are in keen competition, they are under a great temptation to attract custom by selling at much less than normal cost; but probably they do not yield to this temptation more than, or even as much as, private capitalists would under similar circumstances. And on the whole those powerful joint-stock companies, which have great traditions and look forward to a distant future, pursue a far-seeing if a sluggish policy. They are seldom willing to sacrifice their reputation for the sake of a temporary gain; they are not inclined to drive such hard bargains with their employees as will make their service unpopular; and they exercise generally a steadying influence on the demand for capital, and on the demand for labour of all kinds, and especially for the services of those who, having business ability but no capital of their own, desire to reap some earnings of management as salaried officials of a great undertaking. And as has already been observed, co-operation promises, more than any other form of business association, to turn to good account the capabilities of the working man for the higher posts of business management[1]

Co-operation.

Modern methods of business exercise in the aggregate a powerful tendency to adjust earnings of management to the difficulty of the work done

§ 7. Thus then each of the many modern methods of business has its own advantages and disadvantages: and its application is extended under the action of the law of substitution in every direction until that limit or margin is reached, at which its special advantages for that use no longer exceed its disadvantages. Or, to put the same thing in another way, the margin of profitableness of different methods of business organization for any particular purpose, is to be regarded not as a point on any one line, but a boundary line of irregular shape cutting one after another every possible line of business organization; and these modern methods, partly on account of their great variety, but partly also on account of the scope which many of them offer to men of business ability who have no capital, render possible a much closer correspondence between the earnings

[1] Some aspects of joint-stock companies and of co-operative associations have been indicated in Book IV. Ch XII. §§ 9, 10, and others will be discussed later on.

of undertaking and management and the services by which those earnings are got than could be generally attained under the primitive system in which capital was scarcely ever applied to production by any save its owners. For then it could only be by a fortunate accident that those who had the capital and the opportunity for carrying on any trade or performing any service, of which the public was in need, had the aptitudes and the abilities required for the task. But, as it is, that share of the normal expenses of production of any commodity which is commonly classed as profits, is so controlled on every side by the action of the law of substitution, that it cannot long diverge from the normal supply price of the capital needed, added to the normal supply price of the ability and energy required for managing the business, and lastly the normal supply price of that organization by which the appropriate business ability and the requisite capital are brought together.

The supply of business ability is drawn from a wide area,

The supply of business power is large and elastic, since the area from which it is drawn is wide. Everyone has the business of his own life to conduct, and in this he can gain some training for business management, if he has the natural aptitudes for it. There is therefore no other kind of useful rare and therefore highly-paid ability which depends so little on labour and expense applied specially to obtaining it, and so much on "natural qualities." And, further, business power is highly non-specialized, because in the large majority of trades, technical knowledge and skill become every day less important relatively to the broad and non-specialized faculties of judgment, promptness, resource, carefulness and steadfastness of purpose[1]

and is non-specialized

It is true that in small businesses, in which the master is little more than the head workman, specialized skill is very important. And it is true that "each sort of trade has a tradition of its own, which is never written, probably could

[1] Book IV. Ch XII. § 12 As General Walker has well said (*Wages Question*, ch XIV). When the forms of productions cease to be few and simple, it becomes "no longer true that a man becomes an employer because he is a capitalist. Men command capital because they have the qualifications to profitably employ labour. To these captains of industry capital and labour resort for opportunity to perform their several functions."

BOOK VI. CH. VII

not be written, which can only be learnt in fragments, and which is best taken in early life, before the mind is shaped and the ideas fixed. But each trade in modern commerce is surrounded by subsidiary and kindred trades, which familiarize the imagination with it, and make its state known[1]" Moreover those general faculties, which are characteristic of the modern business man, increase in importance as the scale of business increases. It is they which mark him out as a leader of men, and which enable him to go straight to the kernel of the practical problems with which he has to deal, to see almost instinctively the relative proportions of things, to conceive wise and far-reaching policies, and to carry them out calmly and resolutely[2].

Difficulties of obtaining accurate knowledge as to the true earnings of management in different trades.

It must be admitted indeed that the adjustment of supply to demand in the case of business ability is somewhat hindered by the difficulty of ascertaining exactly what is the price that is being paid for it in any trade. It is comparatively easy to find out the wages of bricklayers or puddlers by striking an average between the wages that are earned by men of various degrees of efficiency, and allowing for the inconstancy of their employment. But the gross earnings of management which a man is getting, can only be found after making up a careful account of the true profits of his business, and deducting interest on his capital. The exact state of his affairs is often not known by himself; and it can seldom be guessed at all accurately even by those who are in the same trade with himself. It is not true even in a little village at the present day that everyone knows all his neighbour's affairs. As Cliffe Leslie said, "The village inn-

[1] Bagehot, *Postulates*, p. 75.

[2] Bagehot (l. c pp. 94—5) says that the great modern commerce has "certain general principles which are common to all kinds of it, and a person can be of considerable use in more than one kind if he understands these principles and has the proper sort of mind. But the appearance of this common element is in commerce, as in politics, a sign of magnitude, and primitive commerce is all petty. In early tribes there is nothing but the special man—the clothier, the mason, the weapon-maker Each craft tried to be, and very much was, a mystery except to those who carried it on The knowledge required for each was possessed by few, kept secret by these few, and nothing else was of use but this monopolised and often inherited acquirement, there was no 'general' business knowledge The idea of a general art of money making is very modern, almost everything ancient about it is individual and particular."

keeper, publican or shopkeeper, who is making a small fortune does not invite competition by telling his neighbours of his profits, and the man who is not doing well does not alarm his creditors by exposing the state of his affairs[1]."

They do not reach far,

But though it may be difficult to read the lessons of an individual trader's experience, those of a whole trade can never be completely hidden, and can not be hidden at all for long. Although one cannot tell whether the tide is rising or falling by merely watching half-a-dozen waves breaking on the seashore, yet a very little patience settles the question; and there is a general agreement among business men that the average rate of profits in a trade cannot rise or fall much without general attention being attracted to the change before long And though it may sometimes be a more difficult task for a business man than for a skilled labourer, to find out whether he could improve his prospects by changing his trade, yet the business man has great opportunities for discovering whatever can be found out about the present and future of other trades; and if he should wish to change his trade, he will generally be able to do so more easily than the skilled workman could.

and on the whole the adjustment of those earnings to the difficulty and importance of the work done is fairly accurate

On the whole then we may conclude that the rarity of the natural abilities and the expensiveness of the special training required for the work affect normal earnings of management in much the same way as they do the normal wages of skilled labour. In either case, a rise in the income to be earned sets in operation forces tending to increase the supply of those capable of earning it; and in either case, the extent to which the supply will be increased by a given rise of income, depends upon the social and economic condition of those from whom the supply is drawn. For though it is true that an able business man who starts in life with a great deal of capital and a good business connection is likely to obtain higher earnings of management than an equally able man who starts without these advantages; yet there are similar, though smaller, inequalities between the earnings of

[1] *Fortnightly Review*, June 1879, reprinted in his *Essays*.

professional men of equal abilities who start with unequal social advantages; and the wages even of a working man depend on the start he has had in life almost as much as on the expense which his father has been able to afford for his education[1].

[1] See Book VI. Ch IV. § 3.

CHAPTER VIII.

DEMAND AND SUPPLY IN RELATION TO CAPITAL AND BUSINESS POWER, CONCLUDED.

§ 1. THE causes that govern earnings of management have not been studied with any great care till within the last fifty years. The earlier economists did not do much good work in this direction because they did not adequately distinguish the component elements of profits, but searched for a simple general law governing the average rate of profits —a law which, from the nature of the case, cannot exist

On the supposed general tendency of the rate of profits to equality

In analysing the causes that govern profits the first difficulty which we meet is in some measure verbal. It arises from the fact that the head of a small business does himself much of the work which in a large business is done by salaried managers and foremen, whose earnings are deducted from the net receipts of the large business before its profits are reckoned, while the earnings of the whole of his labour are reckoned among his profits. This difficulty has long been recognized. Adam Smith himself pointed out that:—"The whole drugs which the best employed apothecary in a large market-town will sell in a year may not perhaps cost him above thirty or forty pounds. Though he should sell them, therefore, for three or four hundred or a thousand per cent. profit this may frequently be no more than the reasonable wages of his labour in the only way in which he can charge them, upon the price of the drugs. The greater part of the apparent profit is real wages disguised in the garb of profit In a small seaport town a little grocer will make forty or fifty per cent. upon a stock of a single

In a large business some earnings of management are classed as salaries; and in a small business much wages of labour is classed as profits

hundred pounds, while a considerable wholesale merchant in the same place will scarce make eight or ten per cent. upon a stock of ten thousand[1]."

Profits *per annum* and *on the turnover*

It is here important to distinguish between the *annual* rate of profits on the capital invested in a business, and the rate of profits that are made every time the capital of the business is turned over; that is, every time sales are made equal to that capital, or the rate of profits *on the turnover*. At present we are concerned with profits *per annum*.

A correction of this anomaly of language removes the chief source of the opinion that profits are high in a small business

The greater part of the nominal inequality between the normal rates of profit per annum in small businesses and in large would disappear, if the scope of the term profits were narrowed in the former case or widened in the latter, so that it included in both cases the remuneration of the same classes of services. There are indeed some trades in which the rate of profit, rightly estimated, on large capitals tends to be higher than on small, though if reckoned in the ordinary way it would appear lower. For of two businesses competing in the same trade, that with the larger capital can nearly always buy at the cheaper rate, and can avail itself of many economies in the specialization of skill and machinery and in other ways, which are out of the reach of the smaller business: while the only important special advantage, which the latter is likely to have, consists of its greater facilities for getting near its customers and consulting their individual wants

In some trades they are really lower in small businesses than in large;

In trades in which this last advantage is not important, and especially in some manufacturing trades in which the large firm can sell at a better price than the small one, the outgoings of the former are proportionately less and the incomings larger, and therefore, if profits are so reckoned as to include the same elements in both cases, the rate of profit in the former case must be higher than in the latter.

[1] *Wealth of Nations*, Book I. Ch. x Senior, *Outlines*, p. 203, puts the normal rate of profits on a capital of £100,000 at less than 10 per cent, on one of £10,000 or £20,000 at about 15 per cent, on one of £5,000 or £6,000 at 20 per cent., and "a much larger per-centage" on smaller capitals Compare also § 4 of the preceding Chapter of the present Book It should be noted that the nominal rate of profits of a private firm is increased when a manager, who brings no capital with him, is taken into partnership and rewarded by a share of the profits instead of a salary.

But these are the very businesses in which it most frequently happens that large firms after first crushing out small ones, either combine with one another and thus secure for themselves the gains of a limited monopoly, or by keen competition among themselves reduce the rate of profit very low. There are many branches of the textile, the metal, and the transport trades in which no business can be started at all except with a large capital; while those that are begun on a moderate scale struggle through great difficulties, in the hope that, after a time, it may be possible to find employment for a large capital, which will yield earnings of management high in the aggregate though low in proportion to the capital.

but in these trades there are few small businesses left,

There are some trades which require a very high order of ability, but in which it is nearly as easy to manage a very large business as one of moderate size. In rolling mills, for instance, there is little detail which cannot be reduced to routine, and a capital of £1,000,000 invested in them can be controlled by one able man. A rate of profits of 20 per cent., which is not a very high average rate for some parts of the iron trade, would give the owner of such works earnings of management amounting to more than £150,000 a year. And since iron-masters can with so little additional effort get the earnings of management on an increased capital, wealthy men remain in business longer than in most others; and the competition of the great iron-masters with one another is said to have reduced the average rate of profits in their trade below the ordinary level.

and in some of these trades the normal rate of profits is very low.

The rate of profits is low in nearly all those trades which require very little ability of the highest order, and in which a public or private firm with a good connection and a large capital can hold its own against new-comers, so long as it is managed by men of industrious habits with sound common sense and a moderate share of enterprise And men of this kind are seldom wanting either to a well-established public company or to a private firm which is ready to take the ablest of its servants into partnership

On the whole, then, we may conclude firstly that the true rate of profits in large businesses is higher than at first sight

General result of the com-

BOOK VI. CH. VIII.

parison between large businesses and small

appears, because much that is commonly counted as profits in the small business ought to be classed under another head, before the rate of profits in it is compared with that in a large business: and secondly that, even when this correction has been made, the rate of profit reckoned in the ordinary way declines generally as the size of the business increases.

Profits per annum are generally high in trades in which the work of management is difficult and risky;

§ 2. The normal earnings of management are of course high in proportion to the capital, and therefore the rate of profits per annum on the capital is high, when the work of management is heavy in proportion to the capital. The work of management may be heavy because it involves great mental strain in organizing and devising new methods, or because it involves great anxiety and risk: and these two things frequently go together. Individual trades have indeed peculiarities of their own, and all rules on the subject are liable to great exceptions. But the following general propositions will be found to be valid, other things being equal, and to explain many inequalities in the normal rates of profit in different trades.

where the circulating capital is large relatively to the fixed,

Firstly, the extent of the work of management needed in a business depends more on the amount of the circulating capital used than on that of the fixed. The rate of profit tends therefore to be low in trades in which there is a disproportionately large amount of durable plant, that requires but little trouble and attention when once it has been laid down As we have seen, these trades are likely to get into the hands of joint-stock companies: and the aggregate salaries of the directors and higher officials bear a very small proportion to the capital employed in the case of railway and water companies, and, even in a more marked degree, of companies that own canals and docks and bridges[1].

and especially where the

Next, given the proportion between the fixed and circulating capital of a business, the work of management will

[1] A manufacturer, who owns the factory he uses, has generally to be contented with a lower rate of profit per annum on his capital, than another who works in a hired factory, for the profits on capital invested in buildings are low, because no great trouble is involved by owning them and letting them out More generally, if a man has borrowed much of the capital he uses in business, his profits even after he has paid a rather high interest on his borrowings, will as a rule be large in proportion to his own capital

generally be the heavier, and the rate of profits the higher, the more important the wages-bill is relatively to the cost of material and the value of the stock in trade. In trades that handle costly materials, success depends very much upon good fortune and ability in buying and selling, and the order of mind required for interpreting rightly and reducing to their proper proportions the causes that are likely to affect price is rare, and can command high earnings. The allowance to be made for this is so important in certain trades as to have induced some American writers to regard profits as remuneration of risk simply; and as consisting of what remains after deducting interest and earnings of management from gross profits. But this use of the term seems on the whole not advantageous, because it tends to class the work of management with mere routine superintendence It is of course true that as a rule a person will not enter on a risky business, unless, other things being equal, he expects to gain from it more than he would in other trades open to him, after his probable losses had been deducted from his probable gains on a fair actuarial estimate If there were not a positive evil in such risk, people would not pay premia to insurance companies, which they know are calculated on a scale sufficiently above the true actuarial value of the risk to pay the companies' great expenses of advertising and working and yet to yield a surplus of net profits. And where the risks are not insured for, they must be compensated in the long run on a scale about as high as would be required for the premia of an insurance company, if the practical difficulties of insurance against business risks could be overcome. But further many of those who would be most competent to manage difficult businesses with wisdom and enterprise, are repelled from great risks, because their own capital is not large enough to bear great losses. Thus a risky trade is apt to get into the hands of rather reckless people; or perhaps into the hands of a few powerful capitalists, who work it ably, but arrange among themselves that the market shall not be forced so as to prevent them from having a high rate of profit on the average[1].

Wages-bill is very large relatively to the capital

Risk as an element of profits and of cost.

[1] On risk as an element of cost see Book v. Ch vii § 4. There would be an

BOOK VI. CH. VIII.

In ordinary trades, profits often vary nearly with the wages-bill.

In trades in which the speculative element is not very important, so that the work of management consists chiefly of superintendence, the earnings of management will follow pretty closely on the amount of work done in the business; and a very rough but convenient measure of this is found in the wages-bill. And perhaps the least inaccurate of all the broad statements that can be made with regard to a general tendency of profits to equality in different trades, is that where equal capitals are employed, profits tend to be a certain percentage per annum on the total capital, together with a certain percentage on the wages-bill[1].

advantage in a careful analytical and inductive study of the attractive or repellent force which various kinds of risks exert on persons of various temperaments, and as a consequence on earnings and profits in risky occupations; it might start from Adam Smith's remarks on the subject. The influence of joint-stock companies on the investment of capital in risky trades will be discussed in the second volume.

[1] There is a great difficulty in ascertaining even approximately the amounts of capital of different kinds invested in different classes of business; for much of it is always shifting from one use to another; much of it is constantly changing in value, as the result of new improvements and many other causes, a good deal of it is apt to be overlooked, and a good deal more to be counted twice over (this applies especially to buildings and other capital that are owned by one person and used by another); and finally business men are seldom willing to publish the best guess they can make as to the amount of their capital. But guided mainly by the valuable statistics of American Bureaux, inexact as they avowedly are in this particular matter, we may conclude that the annual output is less than the capital in industries where the industry is very expensive, and the processes through which the raw material has to go are very long, as watch and cotton factories· but that it is more than four times the capital in businesses in which the raw material is expensive and the process of production rapid, as *e g.* boot factories; as well as in some industries, which make only a slight change in the form of their material, such as sugar-refining, and slaughtering and meat-packing.

Next, analysing the turnover of circulating capital and comparing the cost of raw material to the wages-bill, we find that the former is much less than the latter in watch-factories, where the bulk of the material is small, and in stone, brick and tile works, where it is of a common sort but in the large majority of industries the cost of material is much greater than the wages-bill, and on the average of all the industries it is three and a-half times as great. And in the Slight change industries it is generally from twenty-five to fifty times as great.

Many of these inequalities disappear if the value of the raw material, coal, etc used in a business is deducted before reckoning its output This plan is commonly followed by careful statisticians in estimating the manufacturing output of a country, so as to avoid counting say yarn and cloth, twice over, and similar reasons should make us avoid both cattle and fodder crops in the agricultural product of a country. This plan is however not quite satisfactory. For logically one ought to deduct the looms which a weaving factory buys as well as its yarn Again, if the factory itself was reckoned as a product of the building trades, its value should be deducted from the output (over a term of years) of the weaving trade. Similarly with regard to farm buildings. Farm horses ought certainly

§ 3. We may now pass from profit per annum and examine the causes that govern profit on the turnover. It is obvious that while the normal rate of profit per annum varies within narrow limits, the profit on the turnover may vary very widely from one branch of trade to another, because they depend on the length of time and the amount of work required for the turnover. Thus wholesale dealers, who buy and sell large quantities of produce in single transactions, and who are able to turn over their capital very rapidly, may make large fortunes though their average profit on the turnover is less than one per cent.; and, in the extreme case of large stock-exchange dealings, even when it is only a small fraction of one per cent. But a shipbuilder who has to put labour and material into the ship, and to provide a berth for it, a long while before it is ready for sale, and who has to take care for every detail connected with it, must add a very high percentage to his direct and indirect outlay in order to remunerate him for his labour, and the locking up of his capital[1].

The rate of profits on the turn-over varies much more widely than the annual rate of profits on capital.

Illustrative instances

Again, in the textile industries some firms buy raw material and turn out finished goods, while others confine themselves to spinning, to weaving, or to finishing· and it is obvious that the rate of profit on the turnover of one of the first class must be equal to the sum of the rates of profit of one of each of the three other classes[2]. Again, the retail

not to be counted, nor for some purposes any horses used in trade. But the plan of deducting simply raw material has its uses, if its inaccuracy is clearly recognized.

[1] He would however not need to charge a high rate of profits per annum on that part of his capital which he had sunk in the earlier stages of building the ship; for that capital, when once invested, would no longer require any special exercise of his ability and industry, and it would be sufficient for him to reckon his outlay "accumulated" at a high rate of compound interest; but in that case he must count the value of his own labour as part of his early outlay On the other hand, if there be any trade in which a continuous and nearly uniform expenditure of trouble is called for on all the capital invested, then it would be reasonable in that trade to find the "accumulated" value of the earlier investments by the addition of a "compound" rate of profit (i.e a rate of profit increasing geometrically as compound interest does). And this plan is frequently adopted in practice for the sake of simplicity even where it is not theoretically quite correct (Compare foot-note on p. 431.)

[2] Strictly speaking it will be a little greater than the sum of these three, because it will include compound interest over a longer period.

dealer's profit on the turnover is often only five or ten per cent. for commodities which are in general demand, and which are not subject to changes of fashion; so that while the sales are large, the necessary stocks are small, and the capital invested in them can be turned over very rapidly, with very little trouble and no risk. But a profit on the turnover of nearly a hundred per cent. is required to remunerate the retailer of some kinds of fancy goods which can be sold but slowly, of which varied stocks must be kept, which require a large space for their display, and which a change of fashion may render unsaleable except at a loss; and even this high rate is often exceeded in the case of fish, fruit, flowers and vegetables[1].

But each branch of trade has its customary or fair rate of profit on the turnover.

§ 4. We see then that there is no general tendency of profits on the turnover to equality; but there may be, and as a matter of fact there is in each trade and in every branch of each trade, a more or less definite rate of profits on the turnover which is regarded as a "fair" or normal rate. Of course these rates are always changing in consequence of changes in the methods of trade; which are generally begun by individuals who desire to do a larger trade at a lower rate of profit on the turnover than has been customary, but at a larger rate of profit per annum on their capital. If however there happens to be no great change of this kind going on, the traditions of the trade that a certain rate of profit on the turnover should be charged for a particular class of work are of great practical service to those in the trade. Such traditions are the outcome of much experience tending to show that, if that rate is charged, a proper allowance will be made for all the costs[2] incurred for that particular purpose, and in

The practical advantages of this customary rate, and how it is ultimately determined.

[1] The fishmongers and greengrocers in working-class quarters especially lay themselves out to do a small business at a high rate of profits; because each individual purchase is so small that the customer would rather buy from a dear shop near at hand than go some way to a cheaper one The retailer therefore may not be getting a very good living though he charges a penny for what he bought for less than a halfpenny That same thing was however perhaps sold by the fisherman or the farmer for a farthing or even less and the direct cost of carriage and insurance against loss will not account for any great part of this last difference. Thus there seems to be some justification for the popular opinion that the middlemen in these trades have special facilities for obtaining abnormally high profits by combination among themselves.

[2] That is for the Total cost, Supplementary as well as Prime. See Book V. Ch. IV.

addition the normal rate of profits per annum in that class of business will be afforded. If they charge a price which gives much less than this rate of profit on the turnover they can hardly prosper; and if they charge much more they are in danger of losing their custom, since others can afford to undersell them. This is the "fair" rate of profit on the turnover which an honest man is expected to charge for making goods to order, when no price has been agreed on beforehand, and it is the rate which a court of law will allow, in case a dispute should arise between buyer and seller[1].

Profits are a constituent element of normal supply-price

§ 5. DURING all this inquiry we have had in view chiefly the ultimate, or long-period or true normal results of economic forces; we have considered the way in which the supply of business ability in command of capital tends in the long run to adjust itself to the demand; we have seen how under the

[1] The expert evidence that is given in such cases is full of instruction to the economist in many ways, and in particular because of the use of mediæval phrases as to the customs of the trade, with a more or less conscious recognition of the causes which have produced those customs, and to which appeal must be made in support of their continued maintenance And it almost always comes out finally that if the "customary" rate of profit on the turnover is higher for one class of job than another, the reason is that the former does (or did a little while ago) require a longer locking-up of capital; or a greater use of expensive appliances (especially such as are liable to rapid depreciation, or cannot be kept always employed, and therefore must pay their way on a comparatively small number of jobs); or that it requires more difficult or disagreeable work, or a greater amount of attention on the part of the undertaker; or that it has some special element of risk for which insurance has to be made And the unreadiness of experts to bring to light these justifications of custom, which are lying almost hidden from themselves in the recesses of their own minds, gives ground for the belief that if we could call to life and cross-examine mediæval business men, we should find much more half conscious adjustment of the rate of profit to the exigencies of particular cases than has been suggested by historians. Many of them fail sometimes to make it clear whether the customary rate of profits of which they are speaking is a certain rate on the turnover, or such a rate on the turnover as will afford in the long run a certain rate of profits per annum on the capital Of course the greater uniformity of the methods of business in mediæval times, would enable a tolerably uniform rate of profits on the capital per annum to exist without causing so great variations in the rate on the turnover as are inevitable in modern business But still it is clear that if one kind of rate of profits were nearly uniform, the other would not be, and the value of much that has been written on mediæval economic history seems to be somewhat impaired by the absence of a distinct recognition of the differences between the two kinds, and between the ultimate sanctions on which customs relating severally to them must depend.

BOOK VI. CH. VIII.

action of the law of substitution it seeks constantly every business and every method of conducting every business in which it can render services that are so highly valued by persons who are able to pay good prices for the satisfaction of their wants, that those services will in the long run earn a high reward. The motive force is the competition of undertakers: each one tries every opening, forecasting probable future events, reducing them to their true relative proportions, and considering what surplus is likely to be afforded by the receipts of any undertaking over the outlay required for it. All his prospective gains enter into the profits which draw him towards the undertaking; all the investments of his capital and energies in making the appliances for future production, and in building up the "immaterial" capital of a business connection, have to show themselves to him as likely to be profitable, before he will enter on them: the whole of the profits which he expects from them enter into the reward, which he expects in the long run for his venture And if he is a man of normal ability (normal that is for that class of work), and is on the margin of doubt whether to make the venture or not, they may be taken as true representatives of the (marginal) normal expenses of production of the services in question. Thus the whole of the normal profits enter into true or long-period supply price.

But the income derived from capital already invested is generally determined by the price of the product

But so soon as his skill, his material capital, and his business connection are to any extent specialized to any one branch of business; then to that extent incomes earned by these factors of production cease to exert a direct influence on the value of the products due to them: and on the other hand the value of those products (in conjunction with the other circumstances of the case) determines the income which can be derived from these factors; (*i.e.* it determines what we have called their quasi-rents).

The reader is referred to the application of this doctrine to the earnings of industrial skill, which is given in the fifth chapter of this Book; for the argument of that chapter is valid generally with regard to the earnings of business power. There are, however, some differences between the two cases, which call for our study.

The causes which govern the normal levels of wages and the various elements of profits, resemble one another

§ 6. The motives which induce a man and his father to invest capital and labour in preparing him for his work as an artisan, as a professional man, or as a business man, are similar to those which lead to the investment of capital and labour in building up the material plant and the organization of a business. In each case the investment (so far as man's action is governed by deliberate motive at all) is carried up to that margin at which any further investment appears to offer no balance of gain, no excess or surplus of utility over "dis-utility;" and the price, that is expected as a reward for all this investment, is therefore a part of the normal expenses of production of the services rendered by it.

A long period of time is however needed in order to get the full operation of all these causes, so that exceptional success may be balanced against exceptional failure. On the one hand are those who succeed abundantly because they turn out to have rare ability or rare good fortune either in the particular incidents of their speculative enterprises, or in meeting with a favourable opportunity for the general development of their business. And on the other are those who are mentally or morally incapable of making good use of their training and their favourable start in life, who have no special aptitude for their calling, whose speculations are unfortunate, or whose businesses are cramped by the encroachment of rivals, or left stranded by the tide of demand receding from them and flowing in some other direction

more nearly than those which govern fluctuations in their values

But though these disturbing causes may thus be neglected in problems relating to normal earnings and normal value, they assume the first rank; and exert a predominating influence, with regard to the incomes earned by particular individuals at particular times. And, since these disturbing causes affect profits and the earnings of management in very different ways from those in which they affect ordinary earnings, there is a scientific necessity for treating differently profits and ordinary earnings when we are discussing temporary fluctuations and individual incidents. Questions relating to market fluctuations cannot indeed be properly handled till the theories of money, credit and foreign trade have been discussed but even at this stage we may note the

BOOK VI CH. VIII.

following contrasts between the ways in which disturbing causes such as we have just described affect profits and ordinary earnings.

First difference Profits fluctuate with prices and in even greater ratio

§ 7. In the first place the undertaker's profits bear the first brunt of any change in the price of those things which are the product of his capital (including his business organization), of his labour and of the labour of his employees, and as a result fluctuations of his profits generally precede fluctuations of their wages, and are much more extensive. For, other things being equal, a comparatively small rise in the price for which he can sell his product is not unlikely to increase his profit manyfold, or perhaps to substitute a profit for a loss That rise will make him eager to reap the harvest of good prices while he can; and he will be in fear that his employees will leave him or refuse to work He will therefore be more able and more willing to pay the high wages, and wages will tend upwards But experience shows that (whether they are governed by sliding scales or not) they seldom rise as much in proportion as prices; and therefore they do not rise nearly as much in proportion as profits.

but the wages of employees lag behind, and their fluctuations are less

Another aspect of the same fact is that when trade is bad, the employee at worst is earning nothing towards the support of himself and his family, but the employer's outgoings are likely to exceed his incomings, particularly if he is using much borrowed capital. In that case even his gross earnings of management are a negative quantity; that is, he is losing his capital[1] In very bad times this happens to a great number, perhaps the majority of undertakers, and it happens almost constantly to those who are less fortunate, or less able, or less well fitted for their special trade than others.

Second difference The profits of individuals differ more widely than ordinary earnings do, and their average value is over-

§ 8. To pass to another point, the number of those who succeed in business is but a small per-centage of the whole; and in their hands are concentrated the fortunes of others several times as numerous as themselves, who have made savings of their own, or who have inherited the savings of others and lost them all, together with the fruits of their own efforts, in unsuccessful business. In order therefore to find the average profits of a trade we must not divide the

[1] In this connection compare the Note at the end of the Chapter before last

aggregate profits made in it by the number of those who are reaping them, nor even by that number added to the number who have failed: but from the aggregate profits of the successful we must subtract the aggregate losses of those who have failed, and perhaps disappeared from the trade; and we must then divide the remainder by the sum of the numbers of those who have succeeded and those who have failed. It is probable that the true gross earnings of management, that is, the excess of profits over interest, is not on the average more than a half, and in some risky trades not more than a tenth part, of what it appears to be to persons who form their estimate of the profitableness of a trade by observation only of those who have secured its prizes There are however, as we shall presently see, reasons for thinking that the risks of trade are on the whole diminishing rather than increasing[1].

estimated, because those who lose all their capital disappear from sight.

[1] A century ago many Englishmen returned from the Indies with large fortunes, and the belief spread that the average rate of profits to be made there was enormous But, as Sir W Hunter points out (*Annals of Rural Bengal*, Ch. VI), the failures were numerous, but only "those who drew prizes in the great lottery returned to tell the tale." And at the very time when this was happening, it used commonly to be said in England that the families of a rich man and his coachman would probably change places within three generations It is true that this was partly due to the wild extravagance common among young heirs at that time, and partly to the difficulty of finding secure investments for their capital The stability of the wealthy classes of England has been promoted almost as much by the spread of sobriety and education as by the growth of methods of investment, which enable the heirs of a rich man to draw a secure and lasting income from his wealth though they do not inherit the business ability by which he acquired it There are however even now districts in England, in which the majority of manufacturers are workmen or the sons of workmen And in America, though foolish prodigality is perhaps less common than in England, yet the greater changefulness of conditions, and the greater difficulty of keeping a business abreast of the age, have caused it commonly to be said that a family passes "from shirt sleeves to shirt sleeves" in three generations Mr Wells says (*Recent Economic Changes*, p 351), "There has long been a substantial agreement among those competent to form an opinion, that ninety per cent of all the men who try to do business on their own account fail of success" And Mr J H. Walker gives (*Quarterly Journal of Economics*, Vol II. p. 448) some detailed statistics with regard to the origin and careers of the manufacturers in the leading industries of Worcester in Massachusetts between 1840 and 1888 More than nine-tenths of them began life as journeymen; and less than ten per cent. of the sons of those who were on the list of manufacturers in 1840, 1850 and 1860, had any property in 1888, or had died leaving any. And as to France, M Leroy Beaulieu says (*Repartition des Richesses*, Ch XI) that out of every hundred new businesses that are started twenty disappear almost at once, fifty or sixty vegetate neither rising nor falling, and only ten or fifteen are successful

BOOK VI. CH. VIII.

Third difference. The true earnings of effort are nearly always a considerable part of the income of the artisan and professional man, but not of the business undertaker.

§ 9. We may pass to another difference between the fluctuations of profits and ordinary earnings. We have seen that, when the artisan or professional man has once obtained the skill required for his work, a part of his earnings are for the future really a quasi-rent of the capital and labour invested in fitting him for his work, in obtaining his start in life, his business connections, and generally his opportunity for turning his faculties to good account; and only the remainder of his income is true earnings of effort. But this remainder is generally a large part of the whole. And here lies the contrast. For when a similar analysis is made of the profits of the undertaker of business, the proportions are found to be different in his case nearly all is quasi-rent.

For fluctuations in the activity of his business do not cause proportionate fluctuations of his own exertions.

The quasi-rent which the undertaker of business on a large scale gets from the capital, material and immaterial, invested in his business is so great, and liable to such violent fluctuations from a considerable negative to a large positive quantity, that he often thinks very little of his own labour in the matter. If profitable business opens out to him, he regards the harvest accruing from it as almost pure gain; there is so little difference between the trouble of having his business on his hands only partially active, and that of working it to its full capacity, that as a rule it scarcely occurs to him to set off his own extra labour as a deduction from those gains they do not present themselves to his mind as to any considerable extent earnings purchased by extra fatigue, in the same way as the extra earnings got by working overtime do to the artisan. This fact is the chief cause, and to some extent the justification, of the imperfect recognition by the general public, and even by some economists, of the fundamental unity underlying the causes that determine normal profits and normal wages.

Fourth difference. Although rare abilities in any occupation command an income which is of the nature

§ 10. Closely allied to the preceding difference is another When an artisan or a professional man has exceptional natural abilities, which are not made by human effort, and are not the result of sacrifices undergone for a future gain, they enable him to obtain a surplus income over what ordinary persons could expect from similar exertions following on similar investments of capital and labour in their education and start in life, a surplus which is of the nature of rent.

of rent, at least so long as we consider the individual only, yet this element is specially prominent in profits.

But, to revert to a point mentioned at the end of last chapter, the class of business undertakers contains a disproportionately large number of persons with high natural ability, since, in addition to the able men born within its ranks it includes also a large share of the best natural abilities born in the lower ranks of industry. And thus while profits on capital invested in education is a specially important element in the incomes of professional men taken as a class, the rent of rare natural abilities may be regarded as a specially important element in the incomes of business men, so long as we consider them as individuals. (In relation to normal value the earnings even of rare abilities are, as we have seen, to be regarded rather as a quasi-rent than as a rent proper.)

Exceptions to this rule.

But there are exceptions to this rule The humdrum business man, who has inherited a good business and has just sufficient force to keep it together, may reap an income of many thousands a year, which contains very little rent of rare natural qualities. And, on the other hand, the greater part of incomes earned by exceptionally successful barristers, and writers, and painters, and singers, and jockeys may be classed as the rent of rare natural abilities—so long at least as we regard them as individuals, and are not considering the dependence of the normal supply of labour in their several occupations on the prospects of brilliant success which they hold out to aspiring youth.

Changes in the industrial environment affect the profits of individual businesses more than they do ordinary earnings

The quasi-rent of a particular business is often very much affected by changes in its industrial environment and opportunity or conjuncture But similar influences affect the quasi-rent of the skill of many classes of workers. The discovery of rich copper-mines in America and Australia lowered the quasi-rent of the skill of Cornish miners, so long as they stayed at home: and every new discovery of rich mines in the new districts raised the quasi-rent of the skill of those miners who had already gone there. And again, the growth of a taste for theatrical amusements while raising the normal earnings of actors, and inducing an increased

BOOK VI. CH. VIII. supply of their skill, raises the quasi-rent of the skill of those already in the profession, a great part of which is, from the point of view of the individual, a rent of rare natural qualities. Not nearly all these changes in the industrial environment are local in their action: but the chief of them are. And this brings us to consider again situation rent in connection with the general problem of demand and supply in relation to land[1].

[1] General Walker's excellent services with regard to the causes that determine wages on the one hand and earnings of management on the other, make it all the more to be regretted that instead of developing the old tradition that all earnings of rare natural abilities have in them, from the point of view of the individual, something of the nature of rent, he has worked out only that side of the tradition which relates to earnings of management And his treatment of that side does not appear altogether satisfactory. He maintains (*Political Economy*, § 311) that profits do not form a part of the price of manufactured products, and he does not limit that doctrine to short periods, for which, as we have seen, the income derived from all skill whether exceptional or not, whether that of an employer or a workman, may be regarded as a quasi-rent And he uses the word "profits" in an artificial sense, for, having excluded interest altogether from profits, he assumes that the "No-profits employer" earns "on the whole or in the long run the amount which he could have expected to receive as wages if employed by others" (*First Lessons*, 1889, § 190) that is to say, the "No-profits employer" obtains, in addition to interest on his capital, what we have called the normal net earnings of management, not indeed of men of extraordinary ability, but of men of such ability as his is Thus profits in General Walker's sense probably exclude at least four-fifths of what are ordinarily classed as profits in England (the proportion would be rather less in America, and rather more on the Continent than in England) So that his doctrine would appear to mean only that that part of the employer's income, which is due to exceptional abilities or good fortune, does not enter into price But, as we have seen, the prizes as well as the blanks of every occupation, whether it be that of an employer or not, take their part in determining the number of persons who seek that occupation and the energy with which they give themselves to their work and therefore do enter into normal supply price General Walker appears to rest his argument mainly on the important fact, which he has done much to make prominent, that the ablest employers, who in the long run get the highest profits, are as a rule those who pay the highest wages to the workman and sell at the lowest price to the consumer. But it is an equally true and an even more important fact that those workmen who get the highest wages are as a rule those who turn their employers' plant and material to best account (see Book VI. Ch III § 2), and thus enable him both to get high profits for himself and to charge low prices to the consumer And therefore the argument, in so far as it is valid at all, applies to the "rare ability" part of the earnings of all kinds of labour, as much as of earnings of management. But for the reasons given in the last paragraph of the fifth Chapter of this Book, the analogy between the rent of land and the earnings of rare natural abilities cannot safely be pressed far

CHAPTER IX.

DEMAND AND SUPPLY IN RELATION TO LAND. PRODUCER'S SURPLUS.

The rent of land is a species of a large genus. We suppose land to be cultivated by its owners, to avoid questions affecting its tenure.

§ 1. We have seen that the rent of land is no unique fact, but simply the chief species of a large genus of economic phenomena; and that the theory of the rent of land is no isolated economic doctrine, but merely one of the chief applications of a particular corollary from the general theory of demand and supply; and that there is a continuous gradation from the true Rent of those free gifts which have been appropriated by man, through the income derived from permanent improvements of the soil, to those yielded by farm and factory buildings, steam-engines and less durable goods[1]. In the present Chapter we have to study those incidents of the rent of land which differentiate it from other species belonging to the same genus: but many of them are connected with special forms of land tenure, and in order that our reasoning at this stage may apply to all forms of tenure, we will suppose that the cultivation of the land is undertaken by its owner.

The income attributed to the inherent properties of land

We may call to mind that the land has an "inherent" income of heat and light and air and rain, which man cannot appreciably affect; and advantages of situation, many of which are beyond man's control, while but few of the remainder are the direct result of the investment of capital and effort in the land by its individual owners These are the chief of its properties, the supply of which is not dependent on human effort, and which would therefore not

[1] See Book V. especially Ch. VIII.—X.

BOOK VI. CH IX

be increased by extra rewards to that effort: and a tax on which would always fall exclusively on the owners[1].

The income derived from permanent improvements.

On the other hand those chemical or mechanical properties of the soil, on which its fertility largely depends, can be modified, and in extreme cases entirely changed by man's action. But a tax on the income derived from improvements which, though capable of general application are yet slowly made and slowly exhausted, would not appreciably affect the supply of them during a short period, nor therefore the supply of produce due to them. It would consequently fall in the main on the owner; a leaseholder being regarded for the time as owner, subject to a mortgage. In a long period, however, it would diminish the supply of them, would raise the normal supply price of produce and fall on the consumer[2].

Résumé and application of the discussion in Book IV. as to the action of the Law of Diminishing Return.

§ 2. Now let us revert to our study of the Law of Diminishing Return in agriculture in the fourth Book; *still supposing that the owner of the land undertakes its cultivation*, so that our reasoning may be general, and independent of the incidents of particular forms of land tenure.

We saw how the return to successive doses of capital and labour, though it may increase for the first few doses, will begin to diminish, when the land is already well cultivated. The cultivator continues to apply additional capital and labour, till he reaches a point at which the return is only just sufficient to repay his outlay and reward him for his own work. That will be the dose on the margin of cultivation, whether it happens to be applied to rich or to poor land; an amount equal to the return to it will be required, and will be sufficient to repay him for each of his previous doses The excess of the gross produce over this amount is his producer's surplus[3].

[1] This is a special case of the general principles discussed in Book V Ch VIII. § 2 But compare Book V Ch X., especially § 3, for exceptions to the rule as to Situation Rent

[2] This argument is equally applicable to urban land, buildings being of the character of improvements which are slowly made and slowly exhausted.

[3] As Mr Hollander says (*Quarterly Journal of Economics*, Jan 1895), "marginal expenditure occurs both in extensive and intensive cultivation, and the marginal product is derived in part from no-rent land and in part from no-rent usee of land."

He looks forward as far as he can: but it is seldom possible to look forward very far. And at any given time he takes for granted all that richness of the soil which results from permanent improvements; and the income (or quasi-rent) derived from those improvements, together with that due to the original qualities of the soil, constitutes his producer's surplus or rent. Henceforth it is only the income derived from new investments that appears as earnings and profits: he carries these new investments up to the margin of profitableness; and his producer's surplus or rent is the excess of the gross income from the improved land over what is required to remunerate him for the fresh doses of capital and labour he annually applies.

This surplus depends on, firstly, the richness of the land, and secondly, the relative values of those things which he has to sell and of those things which he needs to buy The richness or fertility of the land, we have seen, cannot be measured absolutely, for it varies with the nature of the crops raised, and with the methods and intensity of cultivation. Two pieces of land cultivated always by the same man with equal expenditures of capital and labour, are likely, if they yield equal crops of barley, to give unequal crops of wheat; if they return equal crops of wheat when cultivated slightly or in a primitive fashion, they are likely to yield unequal crops when cultivated intensively, or on modern methods. Further, the prices at which the various requisites of the farm can be bought, and its various products sold, depend on the industrial environment; and changes in that are continually changing the relative values of different crops and therefore the relative values of land in different situations.

The cultivators must be supposed to be of normal ability and enterprise.

Lastly, we suppose the cultivator to be of normal ability relatively to the task he has undertaken, and the circumstances of time and place. If he is of less ability his actual gross produce will be less than that which normally should come from the land: it will be yielding to him less than its true producer's surplus. If, on the contrary, he is of more than normal ability, he will be getting in addition to the producer's surplus due to the land, some producer's surplus due to rare ability.

BOOK VI. CH IX

A rise in the real value of produce generally raises the produce value of the surplus,

§ 3. We have already traced in some detail the way in which a rise in the value of agricultural produce increases the producer's surplus measured in terms of produce from all lands, but especially from those where the law of diminishing return acts but feebly[1]; and we saw that generally speaking it raises the value of poor lands relatively to rich: or in other words, that if a person anticipates a rise in the value of produce, he may expect a larger future income from investing a given sum of money in poor land at present prices than from investing it in rich land[2].

and its real value even more

Next, the producer's surplus, that is, measured in terms of general purchasing power, will rise relatively to its produce value, in the same ratio as the value of produce measured in the same way has risen. that is to say, a rise in the value of produce causes a double rise in the value of producer's surplus.

Necessity for distinguishing between changes in the labour value of produce, and in its general purchasing power

The term the "real value" of produce is indeed ambiguous Historically it has most often been used to mean the real value from the point of view of the consumer. This use is rather dangerous: for there are some purposes for which to consider real value from the point of view of the producer. But with this caution we may use the term "labour-value" to express the amount of labour of a given kind that the produce will purchase; and "real value" to mean the amount of necessaries, comforts, and luxuries of life that a given amount of produce will purchase. A rise in the labour-value of raw produce may imply an increasing pressure of population on the means of subsistence; and a rise of the producer's surplus from land due to that cause goes together

[1] Book IV. Ch. III § 3. Thus we see that if the value of produce rises from OH' to OH (figs. 12, 13, 14), so that while an amount of produce OH was required to remunerate a dose of capital and labour before the rise, an amount OH' would suffice after the rise, then the producer's surplus will be increased a little in the case of lands of the class represented in fig. 12, with regard to which the law of diminishing return acts quickly, much more with regard to the second class of lands (fig 13), and most of all with regard to the third class (fig 14).

[2] Ib. § 4. Comparing two pieces of land (figs 16 and 17) with regard to which the law of diminishing return acts in a similar way, but of which the first is rich and the second poor, we found that the rise of producer's surplus from AHC to $AH'C'$, caused by a rise in the price of produce in the ratio OH to OH', was much larger in proportion in the second case

with, and is a sort of measure of, the degradation of the people. But if, on the other hand, the rise in the real value of raw produce has been caused by an improvement of the arts of production, other than agricultural, it will probably be accompanied by a rise in the purchasing power of wages.

Ricardo's doctrine with regard to the effects of improvements on Producer's Surplus, though often stated carelessly, was thought out carefully.

§ 4. In all this it has been clear that the producer's surplus from land is an evidence not of the greatness of the bounty of nature, as was held by the Physiocrats and in a more modified form by Adam Smith, but of the inequality of that bounty. But it must be remembered that inequalities of situation relatively to the best markets are just as powerful causes of (Real) producer's surplus, as are inequalities of absolute productiveness[1].

This truth and its chief consequences, many of which seem now so obvious, were first made manifest by Ricardo. He delighted to argue that no surplus can be reaped from the ownership of those of nature's gifts the supply of which is everywhere practically unlimited: and in particular that there would be no surplus from land if there were an unlimited supply of it all equally fertile and all equally accessible. He carried this argument further, and showed that an improvement in the arts of cultivation, equally applicable to

[1] England is so small and so thickly peopled, that even milk and vegetables which require to be marketed quickly, and even hay in spite of its bulk, can be sent across the country at no inordinate expense: while for the staple products, corn and live stock, the cultivator can get nearly the same net price in whatever part of England he is. For this reason English economists have ascribed to fertility the first rank among the causes which determine the value of agricultural land; and have treated situation as of secondary importance. They have often regarded the producer's surplus of land as the excess of the produce which it yields, over what is returned to equal capital and labour (applied with equal skill) to land that is so barren as to be on the margin of cultivation, without taking the trouble to state explicitly either that the two pieces of land must be in the same neighbourhood, or that separate allowance must be made for differences in the expense of marketing. But this method of speaking does not come naturally to economists in new countries, where the richest land may lie uncultivated, because it has not good access to markets. To them situation appears at least coordinate with fertility as a cause determining the value of land. They think of land on the margin of cultivation, as land far from markets; and the producer's surplus presents itself as the excess value of the produce from well-situated land over that which equal labour, capital (and skill), would get on the worst situated land; allowance being made for differences of fertility, if necessary.

all soils (which is equivalent to a general increase in the natural fertility of land), will be nearly sure to lower the aggregate corn-surplus and quite sure to lower the aggregate real surplus derived from the land that supplies a given population with raw produce. He also pointed out that, if the improvements affected chiefly those lands that were already the richest, it might raise the aggregate surplus; but that, if it affected chiefly the poorer class of lands, it would lower that aggregate very much.

It is quite consistent with this proposition to admit that an improvement in the arts of cultivation of the land of England now would raise the aggregate surplus from her land, unless it were accompanied by an equal improvement in the arts of production in those countries from which she imports raw produce; or, which comes to the same thing for this purpose, by an improvement in the means of communication with them. And as Ricardo himself says, improvements that apply equally to all the land supplying the same market, "as they give a great stimulus to population, and at the same time enable us to cultivate poorer lands with less labour, are ultimately of immense advantage to the landlords[1]."

The argument so far applicable to nearly all systems of land tenure.

§ 5. The argument of this chapter so far is applicable to all systems of land tenure, which recognize private ownership of land in any form; for it is concerned with that producer's surplus, which accrues to the owner if he cultivates his land himself; or, if he does not, then accrues to him and his tenants, regarded as a firm engaged in the business of cultivation. Thus it holds true, whatever be the division which custom or law or contract may have arranged between them with regard to their several shares of the cost of cultivation on the one hand, and the fruits of the cultivation on the other. The greater part of it is also independent of the stage of economic development which has been reached; and it is valid if little or no produce is sent to market, if dues are levied in kind and so on[2].

1 Foot-note to his third Chapter.

2 Petty's memorable statement of the law of rent (*Taxes and Contributions*, IV. 13) is so worded as to apply to all forms of tenure and to all stages of

But the broad line of division between the landlord's and the farmer's share in the modern English system is also that which is most important for science.

At the present day, in those parts of England where custom and sentiment count for least, and free competition and enterprise for most in the bargaining for the use of land, it is commonly understood that the landlord supplies, and in some measure maintains, those improvements which are slowly made and slowly worn out. That being done, he requires of his tenant the whole producer's surplus which the land thus equipped is estimated to afford in a year of normal harvests and normal prices, after deducting enough to replace the farmer's capital with normal profits, the farmer standing to lose in bad years and gain in good years. In this estimate it is implicitly assumed that the farmer is a man of normal ability and enterprise for that class of holding; and therefore, if he rises above that standard, he will himself reap the benefit, and, if he falls below it, will himself bear the loss, and perhaps ultimately leave the farm In other words, the landlord obtains that part of the income derived from the land which has to be regarded as a rent or a quasi-rent; that is, as governed, for all periods of moderate length, mainly by the market for the produce, and with little reference to the cost of providing the various agents employed in raising it; while the tenant retains that part which is to be regarded, even for short periods, as profits entering directly into the normal price of the produce, because the produce would not be produced unless it were expected to yield those profits.

The more fully therefore the distinctively English features of land tenure are developed, the more nearly is it true that the line of division between the tenant's and the landlord's share coincides with the deepest and most important line of cleavage in economic theory; viz., that between the quasi-rents which do not, and the profits which do, directly enter

civilization —"Suppose a man could with his own hands plant a certain scope of Land with Corn, that is, could Digg, or Plough; Harrow, Weed, Reap, Carry home, Thresh, and Winnow so much as the Husbandry of this Land requires; and had withal Seed wherewith to sow the same I say, that when this man hath subducted his seed out of the proceed of his Harvest, and also what himself hath both eaten and given to others in exchange for Clothes, and other Natural necessaries; that the Remainder of Corn, is the natural and true Rent of the Land for that year, and the *medium* of seven years, or rather of so many years as make up the Cycle, within which Dearths and Plenties make their revolution, doth give the ordinary Rent of the Land in Corn"

into the normal supply prices of produce for periods of moderate length. This fact perhaps more than any other was the cause of the ascendancy of English economic theory early in this century; it helped English economists to pioneer the way so far ahead, that even in our own generation, when as much intellectual activity has been devoted to economic studies in other countries as in England, nearly all the new constructive ideas are found to be but developments of others which were latent in the older English work.

The fact itself appears accidental but perhaps it was not. For this particular line of cleavage involves less friction, less waste of time and trouble in checks and counter-checks than any other. It may be doubted whether the so-called English system will endure. It has great disadvantages, and it may not be found the best in a future stage of civilization. But when we come to compare it with other systems, we shall see that it afforded great advantages to a country, which pioneered the way for the world in the development of free enterprise; and which therefore was impelled early to adopt all such changes as give freedom and vigour, elasticity and strength.

§ 6. It may be well to refer once again to the relations between land, whether agricultural or urban, and other forms of wealth regarded from the point of view of the individual investor.

The distinction between land and other forms of wealth is slight, even in an old country, when we are not looking far ahead

Even from the point of view of normal value, the distinction, though a real one, is slighter than is often supposed; and, even in an old country, the distinction between land and other forms of wealth has very little bearing on the detailed transactions of ordinary life. Suppose a cultivator with spare capital to be in doubt whether to buy more land, or to get better buildings and plant for what he already has: he may expect that in either case he would obtain the same increase of net produce (after allowing for depreciation of his perishable plant) by the same total outlay; and, for him as an individual, the question whether to cultivate a large piece of land lightly or a smaller piece intensively, is to be decided by business calculations of just the same character as those that govern other applications of his capital and energy.

On the other hand even in a new country a far-seeing statesman will feel a greater responsibility to future generations when legislating as to land than as to other forms of wealth. Thus from the economic and from the ethical point of view, land must everywhere and always be classed as a thing by itself. And in an old country this distinction is vital for a broad survey of the causes that govern normal value. For the net income derived from the inherent properties of land is a true surplus; which does not directly enter even in the long run into the normal expenses of production, and which are required as rewards for the work and inventive energy of labourers and undertakers. It thus differs from the incomes derived from buildings, machinery, &c., which are in the long run needed (in the present state of human character and social institutions), to sustain the full force of production, invention, and accumulation. The sudden appropriation by the State either of rents, or of these incomes which we have called quasi-rents would indeed destroy security and shake the foundations of society: but if from the first the State had retained true rents in its own hands, the vigour of industry and accumulation need not have been impaired, and nothing at all like this can be said of quasi-rents. The same is true of urban ground rent, which, as we have seen, is governed on the same principle as that of agricultural rent[1].

[1] This matter has been argued very fully in Book V Ch VIII—X, and again in Book VI Ch. II §§ 4, 5 But a numerical illustration may be added here, which without going over exactly the same ground as those arguments will help to bring some of them clearly to mind Suppose a person planning a hotel or a factory; and considering how much land to take for the purpose If land is cheap he will take much of it, if it is dear he will take less and build high. Suppose him to calculate the expenses of building and working his establishment with frontages of 100 and 110 feet respectively, in ways equally convenient on the whole to himself, his customers and employée, and therefore equally profitable to himself Let him find that the difference between the two plans, after capitalizing future expenditure, shows an advantage of £500 in favour of the larger area; he will then be inclined to take the larger if the land is to be got at less than £50 per foot of frontage, but not otherwise; and £50 will be the marginal value of land to him. He might have reached this result by calculating the increased value of the business that could be done with the same outlay in other respects on the larger site as compared with the smaller, or again by building on less expensive ground instead of in a less favourable situation. But, by whatever route he makes his

BOOK VI. CH. IX

The highest ground-rents are generally paid by trading establishments. Their demand for space is elastic, and does not bear a fixed relation to the volume of their business.

§ 7. The demand for exceptionally valuable urban land comes from traders of various kinds, wholesale and retail, more than from manufacturers: and it may be worth while to say something here as to the features of demand that are special to their case.

If two factories in the same branch of trade have equal outputs they are sure to have nearly equal floor space. But there is no close relation between the size of trading establishments and their turn-overs. Plenty of space is for them a matter of convenience and a source of extra profit, but it is not physically indispensable The larger their space, the greater the stock which they can keep on hand, and the greater the advantage to which they can display specimens of it; and especially is this the case in trades that are subject to changes of taste and fashion. In such trades the dealers exert themselves to collect within a comparatively small space representatives of all the best ideas that are in vogue, and still more of those that are likely soon to be so; and the higher their ground-rent the more prompt they must be in getting rid, even at a loss, of such things as are a little behind the time and do not improve the general character of their stocks. If the locality is one in which customers are more likely to be tempted by a well-chosen stock than by low prices, the traders will charge prices that give a high rate of profit on a comparatively small turn-over; but if not, they will choose low prices and try to force a large business in proportion to their capital and the size of their premises, just as in some neighbourhoods the market-gardener finds it best to gather his peas young when they are full of flavour, and in others to let them grow till they weigh heavily in the scales. Whichever plan the traders follow, there will be some conveniences which they are in doubt whether it is worth while to offer to

calculation, its character is similar to that by which he decides whether it is worth his while to buy business plant of any other kind and he regards the net income (allowance being made for depreciation) which he expects to get from either investment as standing in the same general relation to his business, and if the advantages of the situation are such, that all the land available can find employments for which its marginal use is represented by a capital value of £50 per foot of frontage, then that will be the current value of the land

the public, since they calculate that the extra sales gained by such conveniences are only just remunerative, and do not contribute any surplus towards rent. The goods which they sell in consequence of these conveniences are marginal goods into whose expenses of marketing rent does not enter any more than it does into those of the peas which the market-gardener only just finds it worth his while to produce.

Rent does not enter into the marginal price of the trader's services

Prices are low in some very highly-rented shops, because their doors are passed by great numbers of people who cannot afford to pay high prices for the gratification of their fancy; and the shopkeeper knows that he must sell cheaply, or not sell at all. He has to be content with a low rate of profit each time he turns over his capital; but, as he can turn over his capital many times a year, his annual net profits are very great, and he is willing to pay a very high rent for the situation in which they can be earned. On the other hand, prices are very high in some of the quiet streets in the fashionable parts of London and in many villages; because in the one case customers must be attracted by a very choice stock, which can only be sold slowly, and in the other the aggregate turn-over is very small indeed. In neither place can the trader make profits that will enable him to pay as high a rent as those of some cheap but bustling shops in the East end of London It appears then that rent does not enter into retail price any more than it enters into the price charged by the trader or the manufacturer; intensive demands for land may come from the opportunities it offers either for moderate sales at high prices or for very large sales at lower prices.

But a rise of ground-rents may be an indication of a scarcity of space that will tend to raise traders' prices

It is however true that, if without any increase in traffic such as brings extra custom, a situation becomes more valuable for purposes other than shopkeeping; then only those shopkeepers will be able to pay their way who can manage to secure a large custom relatively to the prices which they charge and the class of business which they do. There will therefore be a smaller supply of shopkeepers in all trades for which the demand has not increased: and those who remain, will be able to charge a higher price than before, while offering equal conveniences and attractions to their customers. The

BOOK VI. CH. IX.

rise of ground-rents in the district will thus be an indication of a scarcity of space which, other things being equal, will raise the prices of retail goods, just in the same way as the rise of agricultural rents in any district will indicate a scarcity of land which will raise the marginal expenses of production, and therefore the price of any particular crop.

The capital value of land

§ 8. In conclusion it may be noticed that the capitalized value of land is the actuarial "discounted" value of all the net incomes which it is likely to afford, allowance being made on the one hand for all incidental expenses, including those of collecting the rents, and on the other for its mineral wealth, its capabilities of development for any kind of business, and its advantages, material, social and æsthetic, for the purposes of residence. The money equivalent of those direct gratifications which the ownership of land affords, does not appear in the returns of the money income derived from it, but does enter into its capital money value[1]

Note on Ricardo's Doctrine as to the Incidence of Taxes and the Influence of Improvements in Agriculture.

Malthus justly complains of Ricardo's inconsistency in paying

Much has already been said about the excellence of Ricardo's thought and the imperfections of his expression of it, and in particular notice has been taken of the causes which led him to lay down the Law of Diminishing Return without proper qualifications. Similar remarks apply to his treatment of the influence of improvements and

[1] The value of land is commonly expressed as a certain number of times the current money rental, or in other words a certain "number of years' purchase" of that rental and other things being equal it will be the higher, the more important these direct gratifications are, as well as the greater the chance that they and the money income afforded by the land will rise. The number of years' purchase would be increased also by an expected fall either in the future normal rate of interest or in the purchasing power of money.

It may be mentioned that the discounted value of a very distant rise in the value of land is much less than is commonly supposed For instance, if we take interest only at five per cent (and of course a much higher rate prevailed during the Middle Ages), £1 invested at compound interest would amount to about £130 in 100 years, £17,000 in 200 years, and £40,000,000,000 in 500 years and therefore an expenditure by the State of £1 in securing to itself the reversion of a rise in the value of land which came into operation now for the first time would have been a bad investment, unless the value of that rise now exceeded £130, if the payment was made 100 years ago; if 200 years ago the gain ought now to amount to £17,000, if 500 years ago to £40,000,000,000

the incidence of taxes in agriculture. He was especially careless in his criticisms of Adam Smith; and as Malthus justly said (Summary of Section x of his *Political Economy*), "Mr Ricardo, who generally looks to permanent and final results, has always pursued an opposite policy in reference to the rents of land. It is only by looking to temporary results, that he could object to Adam Smith's statement, that the cultivation of rice or of potatoes would yield higher rent than corn" And Malthus was perhaps not far wrong when he added —"Practically, there is reason to believe that, as a change from corn to rice must be gradual, not even a temporary fall of rent would take place."

more attention to proximate than ultimate results as regards rent and improvements in agriculture.

Nevertheless, in Ricardo's time it was of great practical importance to insist, and it is of much scientific interest even now to know, that in a country which cannot import much corn, it is very easy so to adjust taxes on cultivation and so to hinder improvements as to enrich the landlords for a time and to impoverish the rest of the people. No doubt when the people had been thinned by want, the landlords would suffer in pocket: but that fact took little of the force from Ricardo's contention that the enormous rise of agricultural prices and rents which occurred during his life was an indication of an injury to the nation beyond all comparison greater than the benefits received by the landlords. But let us now pass in review some of those arguments in which Ricardo delighted to start from sharply defined assumptions, so as to get clear net results, which would strike the attention, and which the reader might combine for himself so as to make them applicable to the actual facts of life.

Let us first suppose that the "corn" raised in a country is absolutely necessary; *i.e* that the demand for it has no elasticity, and that any change in its marginal cost of production would affect only the price that people paid for it, and not the amount of it consumed. And let us suppose that no Corn is imported. Then the effect of a tax of one-tenth on Corn would be to cause its real value to rise till nine-tenths as much as before would suffice to remunerate the marginal dose, and therefore every dose. The gross Corn surplus on every piece of land would therefore remain the same as before, but one-tenth being taken away as a tax, the remainder would be nine-tenths of the old Corn surplus. Since, however, each part of it would have risen in real value in the ratio of ten to nine, the Real Surplus would remain unchanged

But let us follow Ricardo and assume the demand for Corn to be fixed; then a tax on it would not affect rents

But the assumption that the demand for produce is absolutely inelastic is a very violent one. The rise in price would in fact be sure to cause an immediate falling-off in the demand for some kinds of produce, if not for the staple cereals · and therefore the value of Corn, *i e.* produce in general, would never rise in full proportion to the tax, and less capital and labour would be applied in the cultivation of all lands. There would thus be a diminution in the Corn surplus from all lands,

But this assumption is unreal

BOOK VI CH. IX

but not in the same proportion from all, and since a tenth of the Corn surplus would be taken by the tax, while the value of each part of it would have risen in less than the ratio of ten to nine, there would be a double fall in the Real surplus. (The diagrams in Book IV. to which we have just referred suggest at once translations of those reasonings into the language of geometry.)

The immediate fall would be very great under modern conditions in which free importation of Corn prevents its real value from being much raised by the tax; and the same result would follow gradually, even in the absence of importation, if the rise in its real value diminished the numbers of the people; or, what is at least as probable, if it had the effect of lowering the standard of living, and the efficiency of the working population. These two effects would operate very much in the same way on the producer's surplus; both would make labour dear to the employer, while the latter would also make real time wages low to the worker.

Ricardo's reasonings on all these questions are rather difficult to follow because he often gives no hint when he passes from results which are "immediate" and relate to a "short period" relatively to the growth of population, and those which are "ultimate," and relate to a "long period" in which the labour value of raw produce would have time materially to affect the numbers of the people and therefore the demand for raw produce. When such interpreting clauses are supplied, very few of his reasonings will be found invalid.

On the same assumption improvements which increase the return to each dose of capital by equal amounts will cause a double fall of real rents.

We may now pass to his argument with regard to the influence of improvements in the arts of agriculture, which he divides into two classes A special scientific interest attaches to his treatment of the first, which consists of those improvements that "I can obtain the same produce with less capital, and without disturbing the difference between the productive powers of the successive portions of capital[1];" of course neglecting for the purpose of his general argument the fact that any given improvement may be of greater service to one particular piece of land than another (See above, Book IV. Ch. III. § 4.) Assuming as before that the demand for Corn has no elasticity, he proved that capital would be withdrawn from the poorer lands (and from the more intensive cultivation of the richer lands), and therefore the surplus measured in Corn, the Corn surplus—as we may say—obtained by applications of capital under the most favourable circumstances, will be a surplus relatively to lands not so poor as those which were on the margin of cultivation before, and the differential productiveness of any two applications of capital remaining, by hypothesis, unchanged, the

[1] Ch. II. *Collected Works*, p 42 Comp. Cannan's ***Production and Distribution*** 1776—1848, pp. 325–6 Ricardo's distinction between his two classes of improvements is not altogether happy, and need not be considered here

Corn surplus must necessarily fall, and of course the real value and the labour value of the surplus will fall much more than in proportion.

This may be made clear by the adjoining figure; in which curve AC represents the return which the land of the whole country, regarded as one farm, makes to doses of capital and labour applied to it, these doses being arranged not in the order of their application, but in that of their productiveness In equilibrium OD doses are applied, the price of the Corn being such that a return DC is just sufficient to remunerate a dose; the whole amount of Corn raised being represented by the area $AODC$, of which AHC represents the aggregate Corn surplus. [We may pause to notice that the only change in the interpretation of this diagram which is required by our making it refer to the whole country instead of a single farm, arises from our not being able now, as we could then, to suppose that all the several doses of capital are applied in the same neighbourhood, and that therefore the values of equal portions (of the same kind) of produce are equal We may however get over this difficulty by reckoning the expenses of transporting the produce to a common market as part of its expenses of production; a certain part of every dose of capital and labour being assigned to the expenses of transport.]

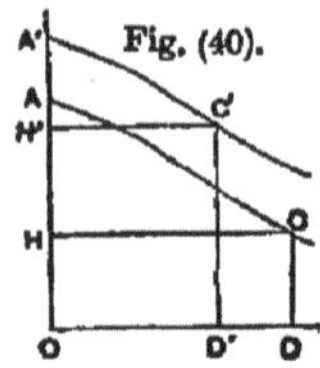

Now an improvement of Ricardo's first class will increase the return to the dose applied under the most favourable conditions from OA to OA', and the returns to other doses, not in like *proportion*, but by equal *amounts*. The result is that the new produce curve $A'C'$ will be a repetition of the old produce curve AC, but raised higher than it by the distance AA'. If, therefore, there were an unlimited demand for corn, so that the old number of doses, OD, could be profitably applied, the aggregate Corn surplus would remain the same as before the change. But in fact such an immediate increase of production could not be profitable; and therefore an improvement of this kind must necessarily lessen the aggregate Corn surplus And on the assumption made here by Ricardo that the aggregate produce is not increased at all, only OD' doses will be applied, OD' being determined by the condition that $A'OD'C'$ is equal to $AODC$, and the aggregate Corn surplus will shrink down to $A'H'C'$. This result is independent of the shape of AC; and, which is the same thing, of the particular figures selected for the numerical illustration which Ricardo used in proof of his argument

Mill substituted equal proportions for equal amounts, and then

And here we may take the occasion to remark that numerical instances can as a rule be safely used only as illustrations and not as proofs for it is generally more difficult to know whether the result has been implicitly assumed in the numbers shown for the special case than it is to determine independently whether the result is true or

BOOK VI CH. IX.

tried to establish the same result, but incorrectly.

not. Ricardo himself had no mathematical training But his instincts were unique, and very few trained mathematicians could tread as safely as he over the most perilous courses of reasoning. Even the acute logical mind of Mill was unequal to the task.

Mill characteristically observed that it is much more probable that an improvement would increase the returns to capital applied to different classes of land in equal proportions than by equal amounts. (See his second case, *Political Economy*, Book IV. Ch. III. § 4.) He did not notice that by so doing he cut away the basis of Ricardo's sharply defined argument, which was that the change did not alter the differential advantages of different applications of capital. And though he arrived at the same result as Ricardo, it was only because his result was implicitly contained in the figures he chose for his numerical illustration

The adjoining figure tends to show that there is a class of economic problems which cannot be safely treated by any one of less genius than Ricardo without the aid of some apparatus, either of mathematics or of diagrams, that present as a continuous whole the schedules of economic forces, whether with regard to the Law of Diminishing Return or to those of Demand and Supply. The curve AC has the same interpretation in this figure as in the last; but the improvement has the effect of increasing the return to each dose of capital and labour by one-third, i.e. in an equal proportion and not by an equal amount. and the new produce curve $A'C'$ stands much higher above AC at its left end than at its right. Cultivation is restricted to OD' doses, where the area $A'OD'C'$, representing the new aggregate product, is as before equal to $AODC$; and $A'H'C'$ is as before the new aggregate Corn surplus. Now it can be easily proved that $A'H'C'$ is four-thirds of AKE, and whether this is greater or less than AHC depends upon the particular shape assigned to AC. If AC be a straight line or nearly a straight line (both Mill's and Ricardo's numbers represented points on a straight Produce line) $A'H'C'$ would be less than AHC; but with the shape assigned to AC in our figure $A'H'C'$ is greater than AHC. And thus Mill's argument is, while Ricardo's is not, dependent for its conclusion on the particular shape assumed by them for the gross produce curve.

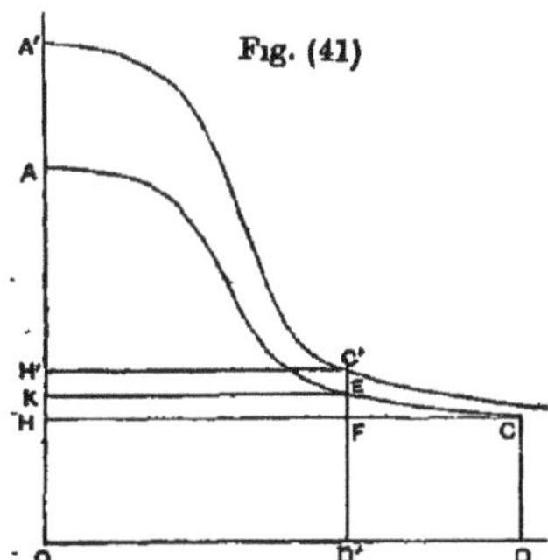

Fig. (41)

(Mill assumes that the cultivated part of a country consists of three quantities of land, yielding at an equal expense 60, 80, and 100 bushels; and he then shows that an improvement which increased the return to each dose of capital by one-third, would lower corn rents in the ratio of 60 to $26\frac{2}{3}$ But if he had taken the distribution of fertility in a country to be such that the land consisted of three qualities yielding at an equal expense 60, 65, and 115 bushels, as is done roughly in our figure, he would have found in that case the improvement would raise corn rents in the ratio 60 to $66\frac{2}{3}$)

Ricardo's paradox applies to urban land also

Finally it may be noticed that Ricardo's paradox as to the possible effects of improvements on the rent of land is applicable to urban as well as agricultural land For instance, the American plan of building stores sixteen stories high with steel frames, and served with elevators, may be supposed suddenly to become very efficient, economical and convenient in consequence of improvements in the arts of building, lighting, ventilation and the making of elevators. In that case the trading part of each town would occupy a less area than now; a good deal of land would have to revert to less remunerative uses; and the net result might possibly be a fall in the aggregate ground-rent of the town.

CHAPTER X.

DEMAND AND SUPPLY IN RELATION TO LAND, CONTINUED. LAND TENURE.

Early forms of Land-tenure have generally been based on partnerships, controlled by tradition rather than by conscious contract

§ 1. IN early times, and in some backward countries even in our own age, all rights to property depend on general understandings rather than on precise laws and documents. In so far as these understandings can be reduced to definite terms and expressed in the language of modern business, they are generally to the following effect:—The ownership of land is vested, not in an individual, but in a firm of which one member or group of members is the sleeping partner, while another member or group of members (it may be a whole family) is the working partner[1].

The so-called landlord is generally the sleeping partner,

The sleeping partner is sometimes the ruler of the State, sometimes he is an individual who inherits what was once the duty of collecting the payments due to this ruler from the cultivators of a certain part of the soil, but what, in the course of silent time, has become a right of ownership, more or less definite, more or less absolute. If, as is generally the case, he retains the duty to make certain payments to the ruler of the State, the partnership may be regarded

[1] The sleeping partner may be a village community; but recent investigations, especially those of Mr Seebohm, have given cause for believing that the communities were not often "free" and ultimate owners of the land. For a good summary of the controversy as to the part which the village community has played in the history of England the reader is referred to the first chapter of Prof. Ashley's *Economic History*. Mention has already been made of the ways in which primitive forms of divided ownership of the land hindered progress (Book I. Ch. II. § 2).

as containing three members, of whom two are sleeping partners[1].

and his share of the produce is not a true rent

The sleeping partner, or one of them, is generally called the proprietor, or landholder or landlord, or even the land-owner But this is an incorrect way of speaking, when he is restrained by law, or by custom which has the force of law, from turning the cultivator out of his holding either by an arbitrary increase of the payments exacted from him or by any other means. In that case the property in the land vests not in him alone, but in the whole of the firm of which he is only the sleeping partner; the payment made by the working partner is not a rent at all, but is that fixed sum, or that part of the gross proceeds, as the case may be, which the constitution of the firm binds him to pay; and, in so far as the custom or law which regulates these payments is fixed and unalterable, the theory of rent has but little direct application

But custom is much more plastic than at first appears,

§ 2 But in fact the payments and dues, which custom is supposed to stereotype, nearly always contain elements which are incapable of precise definition; while the accounts of them handed down by tradition are embodied in loose and vague impressions, or at best are expressed in words that make no attempt at scientific exactness[2]

as is shown even by recent English history.

We can watch the influence of this vagueness in the agreements between landlord and tenant even in modern England, for they have always been interpreted by the aid

[1] The firm may be further enlarged by the introduction of an intermediary who collects payments from a number of cultivators, and after deducting a certain share, hands them over to the head of the firm He is not a middleman in the sense in which the word is used ordinarily in England, that is, he is not a sub-contractor, liable to be dismissed at the end of a definite period for which he has contracted to collect the payments He is a partner in the firm, having rights in the land as real as those of the head partner, though, it may be, of inferior value The case may be even more complex than this There may be many intermediate holders between the actual cultivators and the person who holds direct from the State The actual cultivators also vary greatly in the character of their interests, some having a right to sit at fixed rents and to be altogether exempt from enhancement, some to sit at rents which are enhanceable only under certain prescribed conditions, some being mere tenants from year to year

[2] Prof Maitland in the article on *Court Rolls* in the *Dictionary of Political Economy* observes that "we shall never know how far the tenure of the mediæval tenant was precarious until these documents have been examined."

BOOK VI CH X

of customs, which have ever been imperceptibly growing and dwindling again, to meet the changing exigencies of successive generations. We change our customs more quickly than our forefathers did, and we are more conscious of our changes and more willing to convert our customs into legal enactments, and to make them uniform[1].

Even now the adjustment of rents to the changes in the letting value of the land is partly tacit and almost unconscious.

At the present day, in spite of minute legislation and carefully drawn agreements, there remains a wide margin of uncertainty as to the amount of capital which the landlord will from time to time invest in maintaining and extending the farm buildings and other improvements It is in these matters, quite as much as in his direct money relations with the tenant, that the generous and liberal landlord shows himself, and, what is specially important for the general argument of this chapter, alterations in the real net rent required of the tenant are as often made by a quiet readjustment of the shares of the expenses of working the farm that are borne by the landlord and the tenant as by a change in the money rent. Thus corporate bodies and many large private landowners often let their tenants go on from year to year, without any attempt to make the money rents follow the changes in the real letting value of the land; and there are many farms which are not let on lease and yet the rent of which has nominally remained unchanged during the agricultural inflation which culminated in 1874, and during the depression which followed. But in the earlier period the farmer, who knew he was under-rented, could not put pressure on his landlord to lay out capital in drainage or new buildings or even in repairs, and had to humour him as

[1] Thus Mr Pusey's Committee of the House of Commons in 1848 reported, "That different usages have long prevailed in different counties and districts of the country, conferring a claim on an outgoing tenant for various operations of husbandry.. That these local usages are imported into leases or agreements, unless the terms of the agreement expressly, or by implication, negative such a presumption. That in certain parts of the country a modern usage has sprung up, which confers a right on the outgoing tenant to be reimbursed certain expenses . other than those above referred to . That this usage appears to have grown out of improved and spirited systems of farming, involving a large outlay of capital . That these [new] usages have gradually grown into general acceptance in certain districts, until they have ultimately become recognized there as the custom of the country." Many of them are now enforced by law. See below, § 10

regards the game and in other matters; while just now the landlord, who has a steady tenant, will do many things, that are not stipulated for in the agreement, in order to retain him. Thus, while the money rent has remained stationary, the real rent has changed.

Thus caution is needed when applying the Ricardian analysis to modern English land problems;

This fact is an important illustration of the general proposition, that the economic theory of rent, the Ricardian theory as it is sometimes called, does not apply to modern English land tenure without many corrections and limitations both as regards substance and form; and that a further extension of these corrections and limitations will make the theory applicable to all forms of Mediæval and Oriental land tenure, in which any sort of private ownership is recognized. The difference is only one of degree.

as well as to earlier systems.

§ 3. But the difference of degree is very great. This is partly because in primitive times and backward countries the sway of custom is more undisputed, partly because, in the absence of scientific history, shortlived man has little better means of ascertaining whether custom is quietly changing, than the fly, born to-day and dead to-morrow, has of watching the growth of the plant on which it rests. But the chief reason is that the conditions of partnership were expressed in terms which were seldom capable of exact definition and measurement.

For the terms of partnership in them were vague, elastic, and capable of unconscious modification in many ways.

For the share of the senior partner in the firm, or the landlord as we may for shortness call him, generally included (either with or without a right to a certain share of the produce) the right to claim certain labour services and dues, tolls and presents; and the amount which he obtained under each of those heads varied from time to time, from place to place, and from one landlord to another. Whenever payments of all kinds made by the cultivator left him a margin beyond the necessaries of life for him and his family, together with those comforts and luxuries which were established by custom, the landlord was likely to use his superior strength to raise the payments in some form or other. If the chief payments were a certain share of the produce, he might increase that share: but, as that could seldom be done without an appearance of violence, he would

BOOK VI. CH X

be more likely to increase the number and weight of his minor imposts, or to insist that the land be more intensively cultivated, and a larger part of it be given to crops that cost much labour and are of great value. Thus changes went on, smoothly for the most part, silently and almost imperceptibly, like the hour-hand of a clock; but in the long run they were very thorough[1].

The protective force of custom

The protection which custom afforded to the tenant was not indeed unimportant even as regards these dues. For he always knew pretty well what demands he would have to meet at any particular time. The moral sense of all around him, high and low, protested against any attempt on the part of his landlord to make a sudden and violent increase in the payments and dues, the tolls and fines which were recognized as usual; and thus custom rounded off the edges of change.

It is moreover true that these vague and variable elements of rent were generally but a small part of the whole, and that in those not very rare cases in which the money rent remained fixed for very long periods together, the tenant had a kind of partnership in the soil, which he owed partly to the forbearance of his landlord if it happened that the true net value of the land had risen, but partly also to the constraining force of custom and public opinion This force in some measure resembled the force which holds rain-

[1] Thus the value of a service of a certain number of days' work would depend partly on the promptness with which the labourer left his own hayfield when called to that of his landlord, and on the energy he put into his work His own rights, such as that of cutting wood or turf, were elastic; and so were those of his landlord which bound him to allow flocks of pigeons to devour his crops unmolested, to grind his corn in the lord's mill, and to pay tolls levied on the lord's bridges and in his markets Next, the fines or presents, or "abwabs" as they are called in India, which the tenant might be called on to pay, were more or less elastic, not only in their amounts but in the occasions on which they were levied. Under the Moguls the tenants in chief had often to pay a vast number of such imposts in addition to their nominally fixed share of the produce: and they passed these on, increased in weight and with additions of their own, to the inferior tenants. The British Government has not levied them itself; but it has not been able, in spite of many efforts, to protect the inferior tenants from them For instance, in some parts of Orissa, Sir W W Hunter found that the tenants had to pay, besides their customary rent, 33 different cesses They paid whenever one of their children married, they paid for leave to erect embankments, to grow sugar-cane, to attend the festival of Juggernaut, &c. (*Orissa*, I 55—9.)

drops on the lower edge of a window frame: the repose is complete till the window is violently shaken, and then they fall altogether, and in like way the legal rights of the landlord which had long lain latent were sometimes brought suddenly into action in a period of great economic change[1].

[1] In India at the present time we see very various forms of tenure existing side by side, sometimes under the same name and sometimes under different names. There are places in which the raiyats and the superior holders own between them the property in the land subject to definite dues to Government, and where the raiyat is safe not only from being ejected, but also from being compelled by fear of violence to pay over to his superior holder more than that share of the Producer's Surplus which custom strictly prescribes. In that case the payment which he makes is, as has already been said, simply the handing over to the other partner in the firm of that share of the receipts of the firm which under the unwritten deed of partnership belongs to him. It is not a rent at all. This form of tenure, however, exists only in those parts of Bengal in which there have been no great recent dislocations of the people, and in which the police are sufficiently active and upright to prevent the superior holders from tyrannizing over the inferior.

In the greater part of India the cultivator holds directly from the Government under a lease the terms of which can be revised at intervals. And the principle on which those leases are arranged, especially in the North-West and North-East, where new land is being settled, is to adjust the annual payments due for it to the probable Surplus Produce of the land, after deducting the cultivator's necessaries and his little luxuries, according to the customary standard of the place, and on the supposition that he cultivates with the energy and skill that are normal in that place. Thus as between man and man in the same place the charge is of the nature of economic rent. But, since unequal charges will be levied in two districts of equal fertility, of which one is cultivated by a vigorous and the other by a feeble population, its method of adjustment as between different districts is rather that of a tax, than a rent. For taxes are supposed to be apportioned to the net income which actually is earned, and rents to that which would be earned by an individual of normal ability: a successful trader will pay on ten times as large an actual income ten times as large a tax as his neighbour who lives in equally advantageous premises and pays equal rents.

The whole history of India records little of that quiet stability which has come over the rural parts of England since war, famine, and plague have ceased to visit us. Extensive movements seem to have been nearly always in progress, partly in consequence of the recurrence of famines (for, as the Statistical Atlas of India shows, there are very few districts which have not been visited at least once by a severe famine during this century), partly of the devastating wars which one set of conquerors after another has inflicted on the patient people, and partly of the rapidity with which the richest land reverts to a thick jungle. The land which has supported the largest population is that which, when deprived of its human inhabitants, most quickly provides shady harbours for wild beasts, for venomous snakes, and for malaria; these prevent the return of the refugees to their old homes, and cause them often to wander far before they settle. When land has been depopulated, those who have the control over it, whether the Government or private persons, offer very favourable terms in order to attract cultivators from elsewhere; this competition for tenants very much influences the relations of

BOOK VI. CH. X.

Metayage or rental by shares

§ 4. The question whether the payments made by the cultivator for the use of his land should be reckoned in money or in produce is of growing interest with reference to both India and England. But we may pass it by for the present and consider the more fundamental distinction between the "English" system of rental and that of holding land on "shares," as it is called in the New World, or the "Metayer[1]" system as it is called in the Old.

has many forms in Europe and America

In a great part of Latin Europe the land is divided into holdings, which the tenant cultivates by the labour of himself and his family, and sometimes, though rarely, that of a few hired labourers, and for which the landlord supplies buildings, cattle and, sometimes even, farm implements. In America there are few agricultural tenancies of any kind, but

cultivators and superior holders for a long distance around them; and therefore, in addition to the changes of customary tenure, which, though impalpable at any time, have been always going on, there have been in almost every place many epochs in which the continuity even of the former custom has been broken and keen competition has reigned supreme

These disturbing forces of war, famine, and plague were frequent in mediæval England, but their violence was less And further, the rate of movement of nearly all changes in India has been greater than it would have been if the average period of a generation were as long as in the colder climate of England. Peace and prosperity therefore enable Indian populations to recover from their calamities more quickly, and the traditions which each generation holds of the doings of its fathers and grandfathers run back for a shorter time, so that usages of comparatively recent growth are more easily believed to have the sanction of antiquity. Change can move faster without being recognized as change

Modern analysis may be applied to the contemporary conditions of land tenure in India and other Oriental countries, the evidence as to which we can examine and cross-examine, in such a way as to throw light on the obscure and fragmentary records of mediæval land tenures, which may indeed be examined, but cannot be cross-examined There is of course great danger in applying modern methods to primitive conditions · it is easier to misapply them than to apply them rightly But the assertion, which has been sometimes made, that they cannot be usefully applied at all appears to be based on a conception of the aims, methods and results of analysis, which has little in common with that presented in this, and other modern treatises See *A Reply* in the *Economic Journal*, Sep 1892

[1] The term Metayer applies properly only to cases in which the landlord's share of the produce is one-half, but it is usually applied to all arrangements of this kind whatever the landlord's share be. It must be distinguished from the Stock lease system in which the landlord provided part at least of the stock, but the tenant managed the farm entirely at his own risk subject to a fixed annual payment to the landlord for land and stock. In mediæval England this system was much used, and the Metayer system appears not to have been unknown (See Professor Rogers, *Six Centuries of Work and Wages*, Ch x)

two-thirds of those few are small holdings let out to white men of the poorer class, or to freed negroes, on some plan by which labour and capital share in the produce[1].

BOOK VI. CH. X.

It offers to the man without capital some of the advantages of co-operative production. But it involves much friction

This plan enables a man who has next to no capital of his own to obtain the use of it at a lower charge than he could in any other way, and to have more freedom and responsibility than he would as a hired labourer; and thus the plan has many of the advantages of the three modern systems of co-operation, profit sharing, and payment by piece-work[2]. But though the metayer has more freedom than the hired labourer he has less than the English farmer. His landlord has to spend much time and trouble, either of his own or of a paid agent, in keeping the tenant to his work, and he must charge for these a large sum, which, though going by another name, is really earnings of management.

If the control of the landlord is slight the cultivation is poor;

For, when the cultivator has to give to his landlord half of the returns to each dose of capital and labour that he applies to the land, it will not be to his interest to apply any doses the total return to which is less than twice enough to reward him. If, then, he is free to cultivate as he chooses, he will cultivate far less intensively than on the English plan, he will apply only so much capital and labour as will give him returns more than twice enough to repay himself: so that his landlord will get a smaller share even of those returns than he would have on the plan of a fixed payment[3].

[1] In 1880 74 per cent. of the farms of the United States were cultivated by their owners, 18 per cent, or more than two-thirds of the remainder, were rented for a share of the produce, and only 8 per cent were held on the English system. The largest proportion of farms that were cultivated by persons other than their owners were in the Southern States. In some cases the landowner—the farmer as he is called there—supplies not only horses and mules, but their feed, and in that case the cultivator—who in France would be called not a Metayer but a Maître Valet—is almost in the position of a hired labourer paid by a share of what he gets, as is for instance a hired fisherman whose pay is the value of a part of the catch The tenant's share varies from one-third, where the land is rich and the crops such as to require little labour, to four-fifths, where there is much labour and the landlord supplies little capital. There is much to be gained from a study of the many various plans on which the share contract is based.

[2] The relations between publisher and author on the "half-profits" system resemble in many ways those between landlord and metayer

[3] This can be most clearly seen by aid of diagrams of the same kind as those used in Book IV Ch. III A *tenant's-share curve* would be drawn standing

BOOK VI. CH. X

This is the case in many parts of Europe, in which the tenant has practical fixity of tenure; and then it is only by constant interference that the landlord can keep up the amount of labour he puts on his farm, and keep down the use he makes of the farm cattle for outside work, the fruits of which he does not share with his landlord

but if it is effective the results may not be very different from those on the English plan.

But even in the most stationary districts the amount and quality of the stock which custom requires the landlord to provide are being constantly, though imperceptibly, modified to suit the changing relations of demand and supply. And if the tenant has no fixity of tenure, the landlord can deliberately and freely arrange the amount of capital and labour supplied by the tenant and the amount of capital supplied by himself to suit the exigencies of each special case[1].

one-half (or one-third or two-thirds) as high above OD as AC does, the area below that curve would represent the tenant's share, that above the landlord's. OH being, as before, the return required to remunerate the tenant for one dose, he will, if left to his own devices, not carry cultivation beyond the point at which the tenant's-share curve cuts HC and the landlord's will therefore be a less proportion of the returns to a slighter cultivation than under the English plan Diagrams of this kind may be used to illustrate the way in which Ricardo's analysis of the causes that govern the Producer's Surplus from land, apply to systems of tenure other than the English A little further change will adapt them to such customs as those found in Persia, where land itself is of small value; and "the harvest is divided into five parts, which are apportioned as follows, one part to each 1, land; 2, water for irrigation, &c; 3, seed; 4, labour, 5, bullocks The landlord generally owns two, so he gets two fifths of the harvest"

[1] This is already done in America, and in many parts of France; and some good judges think that the practice may be extended largely, and infuse new life into what a little while ago was regarded as the decaying system of Metayage If worked out thoroughly, it will result in the cultivation being carried just about as far and affording the landlord the same income as he would have on the English plan for equally fertile and well-situated land equipped with the same capital, and in a place in which the normal ability and enterprise of candidates for farms is the same

On the elasticity of Metayage in France see an interesting article by Mr Higgs in the *Economic Journal*, Jan. 1894 See also an article on *Rural France* in the *Edinburgh Review* for Oct 1887, and M. Leroy-Beaulieu, *Répartition des Richesses*, Ch. IV, especially p 151

Starting as in the last note, let the Circulating capital supplied by the landlord be represented by a distance OK marked off along OD. Then, if the landlord controls the amount OK freely and in his own interest, and can bargain with his tenant as to the amount of labour he applies, it can be proved geometrically that he will so adjust it as to force the tenant to cultivate the land just as intensively as he would under the English tenure; and his share will then be the same as under it. If he cannot modify the

It is obvious then that the advantages of the metayer system are considerable when the holdings are very small, the tenants poor, and the landlords not averse to taking much trouble about small things: but that it is not suitable for holdings large enough to give scope to the enterprise of an able and responsible tenant. It is commonly associated with the system of peasant proprietorship; and we may consider that next

The peasant proprietor has many virtues and many sources of happiness;

§ 5. The position of a peasant proprietor has great attractions. He is free to do what he likes, he is not worried by the interference of a landlord, and the anxiety lest another should reap the fruits of his work and self-denial. His feeling of ownership gives him self-respect, and stability of character, and makes him provident and temperate in his habits. He is scarcely ever idle, and seldom regards his work as mere drudgery; it is all for the land that he loves so well.

but he is wastefully penurious, and is an industrious but inefficient worker.

"The magic of property turns sand into gold," said Arthur Young It undoubtedly has done so in many cases in which the proprietors have been men of exceptional energy. But such men might perhaps have done as well or better if their horizon had not been limited to the narrow hopes of a peasant proprietor. For indeed there is another side to the picture. "Land," we are told, "is the best savings-bank for the working man." Sometimes it is the second best. But the very best is the energy of himself and his children; and the peasant proprietors' thoughts are so full of the one that they often starve the other Many even of the richest of them stint the food of themselves and their families. they pride themselves on the respectability of their houses and furniture, but they live in their kitchens for economy, and are practically worse housed and far worse fed than the better class of English cottagers. And the poorest of them work hard during very long hours, but do not really get through much work, because they feed themselves worse

amount *OK*, but can still control the amount of the tenant's labour, then with certain shapes of the produce curve, the cultivation will be more intensive than it would be on the English plan; but the landlord's share will be somewhat less. This paradoxical result has some scientific interest, but little practical importance.

than the poorest English labourers They do not understand that wealth is useful only as the means towards a real income of happiness; they sacrifice the end to the means[1].

There are some well-to-do French and German peasants, but against them must be set the many rich men in the Old World and the New who are descended from English labourers

And it must be recollected that the English labourers represent the failure rather than the success of the English system They are the descendants of those who for many successive generations have not availed themselves of the opportunities by which their abler and more adventurous neighbours were rising to leading posts at home, and, what is far more important, were acquiring the fee simple of a great part of the surface of the globe Of the causes which have contributed to make the English race the chief owners of the New World, the most important is that bold enterprise which has made a man, who is rich enough to be a peasant proprietor, generally refuse to be content with the humdrum life and the narrow income of a peasant. And among the causes which have fostered this enterprise, none is more important than the absence of the temptations to wait about for a petty inheritance, and to marry for the sake of property rather than in the free exercise of individual choice—temptations which have often dulled the energy of youth in places in which peasant properties have predominated.

The American farmer.

It is partly in consequence of the absence of these temptations that the "farmers" of America, though they are men of the working class cultivating their own land with their own hands, do not resemble "peasant proprietors." They invest their income freely and wisely in developing the energies of themselves and their children, and these energies constitute the chief part of their capital, for their land generally is as yet of but little value Their minds are always active, and though many of them have little technical know-

[1] The term "peasant proprietor" is a very vague one it includes many who by thrifty marriages have collected into one hand the results of several generations of hard work and patient saving; and in France some of these were able to lend freely to the Government after the great war with Germany. But the savings of the ordinary peasant are on a very small scale; and in three cases out of four his land is starved for want of capital: he may have a little money hoarded or invested, but no good grounds have been shown for believing that he often has much.

On the wastefulness of consuming less than the necessaries for efficiency compare Book II. Ch. III. § 5, and Book VI. Ch. IV § 2.

ledge of agriculture, their acuteness and versatility enable them to find out almost unerringly the best solution of the problem immediately before them.

American methods of cultivation.

That problem is generally to obtain a produce large in proportion to the labour spent on it, though small in proportion to the abundant land at their disposal. In some parts of America however, in which land is beginning to get a scarcity value, and in which the immediate neighbourhood of good markets is making an intensive cultivation profitable, the methods of farming and of tenure are rearranging themselves on the English model. And within the last few years there have been signs of a tendency on the part of native Americans to hand over to persons of recent European origin the farms of the West, as they have already done the farms of the East, and as they did long ago the textile industries.

The English system though somewhat harsh gives great power.

§ 6. Let us then turn to that English system of tenure. It is faulty and harsh in many respects; but it stimulated and economized the enterprise and energy, which, aided by England's geographical advantages and freedom from devastating wars, gave her the leadership of the world in the arts of manufacture and colonization and, though in a less marked degree, in agriculture. England has learnt lessons in agriculture from many countries and especially the Netherlands; but on the whole she has taught far more than she has learnt. And there is now no country except the Netherlands, which can compare with her in the amount of produce per acre of fertile land; and no country in Europe which obtains nearly so high returns in proportion to the labour expended in getting them[1]

[1] It would seem that England gets more produce per acre of fertile land than even the Netherlands, though there is some doubt about it The Netherlands have led the way for England in more paths of industrial enterprise than any other country has, and this enterprise has diffused itself from their thickly scattered towns over the whole land. But there is error in the common opinion that they support as dense a population as England does, and yet export on the balance a great deal of agricultural produce For Belgium imports a great part of her food; and even Holland imports as much food as she exports, though her non-agricultural population is small In France, farm crops and even potatoes are on the average only about half as heavy as in England proper, and France has only about half the weight of cattle and sheep in proportion to her area. On the other hand, the small cultivators of France excel in poultry and

BOOK VI. CH. X

For it enables the landlord to supply that part of the capital for which he can be easily and effectively responsible;

The chief merit of the system is that it enables the landlord to keep in his own hands the responsibility for that part and only that part of the property which he can look after with but little trouble to himself, and little vexation to his tenant; and the investment of which, though requiring both enterprise and judgment, does not demand constant supervision of minor details His part consists of land, buildings and permanent improvements, and averages in England five times that which the farmer has to supply himself, and he is willing to supply his part in the enterprise with this great capital at a net rent which seldom gives interest at as much as three per cent. on its cost. There is no other business in which a man can borrow what capital he wants at so low a rate, or can often borrow so large a part of his capital at any rate at all The metayer indeed may be said to borrow an even larger share, but at a much higher rate[1]

and it gives considerable freedom to the forces of selection.

The second merit of the English system, which partly follows from the first, is that it gives the landlord considerable freedom in the selection of an able and responsible tenant. So far as the management of land, as opposed to its ownership, goes, the accident of birth counts for less in England than in any other country of Europe But we have already seen that even in modern England the accident of birth counts for a good deal in the access to posts of command in all kinds of business, to the learned professions and even to skilled manual trades. And it counts for somewhat more in English agriculture. For the good and bad qualities of landlords combine to prevent their selecting tenants on strictly commercial principles. They seldom go far afield for a new tenant. and until quite recently, they have seldom given facilities for an able working man, similar in character to the American farmer, to make a start on a small farm which he can cultivate with his own hands and those of his family and a few hired men.

fruit and other light branches of production for which her superb climate is well suited.

[1] For long periods the landlord may be regarded as an active partner and the predominant partner in the business for short periods his place is rather that of the sleeping partner On the part played by his enterprise compare the Duke of Argyle's *Unseen Foundations of Society*, especially p 374

Improvements in agriculture come slowly

§ 7. The number of people who have the opportunity of making a step forward in the arts of agriculture is very great. And since the different branches of agriculture differ from one another in general character less than do those of manufacture, it might have been expected that new ideas in it would have followed one another quickly and have been speedily diffused. But on the contrary progress has been slow. For the most enterprising agriculturists drift towards the town, those who stay behind live more or less isolated lives; and, as a result of natural selection and education, their minds have always been more staid than those of townsmen, and less ready to suggest or even to follow new paths And further, though a manufacturer is nearly always safe in copying a plan that has worked well with his neighbour in the same trade, a farmer is not: for every farm has slight peculiarities of its own, so that the blind adoption of a plan, that has worked well close by, is likely to fail, and its failure encourages others in the belief that old and tried ways are the best.

The difficulty of keeping exact farming accounts

Again, the variety in agricultural detail makes the proper keeping of farming accounts very difficult. There are so many joint products and so many bye products, so many complex and shifting relations of debtor and creditor between the several crops and methods of feeding, that an ordinary farmer, even if he were as fond of accounts as he is in fact averse to them, would have great difficulty in ascertaining, otherwise than by a semi-instinctive guess, what is the price that will just pay him to raise a certain amount of extra produce. He may know its prime cost with fair certainty, but he seldom knows its true total cost; and this increases the difficulty of reading quickly the teachings of experience and making progress by their aid[1].

[1] The difficulty is even greater in small holdings For the capitalist farmer does at all events measure the prime cost in terms of money. But the cultivator working with his own hands often puts into his land as much work as he feels able to do, without estimating carefully its money value in relation to its product.

Although peasant proprietors resemble the heads of other small businesses in their willingness to work harder than those whom they hire and for less reward; yet they differ from the small masters in manufacture in this, that they often do not hire extra labour even when it would pay them well to do so. If all that they and their family can do for their land is less than enough for it, it is generally

Want of ability on the part of one undertaker is not compensated by great ability on the part of others, as it is in manufactures.

And there is another difference between the mode of action of competition in agriculture and in manufacture. If one manufacturer is unenterprising, others may be able to step into the opening which he leaves vacant: but when one landowner does not develop the resources of his land in the best way, others cannot make up for the deficiency without calling into play the law of diminishing return; so that his want of wisdom and enterprise makes the marginal supply price a little higher than it otherwise would be It is however true that the difference between the two cases is only one of degree, since the growth of any branch of manufactures may be retarded perceptibly by any falling-off in the ability and enterprise of the leading firms engaged in it. The chief agricultural improvements have been made by landlords who have themselves been townsmen or at least have associated a good deal with townsmen, and by manufacturers in trades subsidiary to agriculture[1].

Man's part in agriculture conforms to the law of increasing return

§ 8. Though nature yields generally a less than proportionate return to an increased amount of labour of a given efficiency; man's part conforms generally to the law of increasing return, (i.e., it increases in aggregate efficiency more than in proportion to the number of workers), in agriculture as well as in manufacture[2]. But yet the economies of production on a large scale are not quite similar in the two cases.

Agriculture cannot be a localized nor a highly specialized industry,

Firstly, agriculture must be spread over the broad land: raw material can be brought to the manufacturer for him to work on; but the agriculturist must seek his work. Again, the workers on the land must adapt their work to

under-cultivated. if more, it is often cultivated beyond the remunerative limit. It is a common rule that those who give the time which is free from their main occupation to some other industry, often regard their earnings in this last, however low, as an extra gain; and they sometimes even work below what would be a starvation wage to those who depend on that industry for support This is especially true when the side-industry is that of cultivating, partly for the pleasure of doing it, a small plot of land with imperfect appliances

[1] Mr R. Prothero (*English Farming*, Ch. VI) gives some instances of prolonged resistance to changes, and adds that an Act had to be passed in England as late as 1634 "agaynst plowynge by the taile."

[2] See Book IV. Ch. XIII especially p. 397; also Book IV Ch III. §§ 5, 6; also the last paragraph of the note on p. 604

the seasons, and can seldom confine themselves entirely to one class of work; and in consequence agriculture, even under the English system, cannot move fast in the direction of the methods of manufacture.

but there are forces tending to move it towards the methods of manufacture

But yet there are considerable forces tending to push it in that direction. The progress of invention is constantly increasing the number of serviceable, but expensive machines, for most of which a small farmer can find employment during only a very short time. He may hire some of them; but there are many the use of which he can get only by co-operation with his neighbours, and the uncertainties of the weather prevent this plan from working very smoothly in practice[1].

It requires a constantly increasing knowledge, and this increases the economies to be got by highly organized methods of management

Again, the farmer must go beyond the results of his own and his father's experience in order to keep abreast of the changes of the day. He should be able to follow the movements of agricultural science and practice closely enough to see their chief practical applications to his own farm. To do all this properly requires a trained and versatile mind; and a farmer who has these qualities could find time to direct the general course of the management of several hundred, or even of several thousand acres, and the mere superintendence of his men's work in matters of detail is not a task fitting for him. The work which he ought to do is as difficult as that of a large manufacturer, and he would never dream of spending his own strength on minute supervision which he can easily hire subordinates to do. A farmer who can do this higher work, must be wasting his strength on work that is beneath him, unless he employs many gangs of workmen each of them under a responsible foreman. But there are not many farms which give scope for this, and there is therefore very little inducement for really able men to enter the business of farming; the best enterprise and ability of the country generally avoid agriculture and go to trades in which there is

[1] Horse-power is dearer relatively to both steam-power and hand-power in England than in most other countries England has taken the lead in the improvement of field steam machinery, and America in that of horse machinery and hand implements The cheapness of horse-power tells generally on the side of moderate sized farms *versus* very small ones, but the cheapness of steam-power tells on the side of very large farms, except in so far as the use of field steam machinery can be hired economically and at convenient times

BOOK VI. CH. X.

room for a man of first-rate ability to do nothing but high class work, to do a great deal of it, and therefore to get high earnings of management[1].

Another economic plan is that of rather small farms in the work of which the farmer and his wife take some share

If it be assumed, as is the modern fashion, that the farmer is not to work habitually with his men and to encourage them by his presence, it seems best for the economy of production that farms should be as large as is practicable under the existing condition of land tenure; so as to give room for the use of highly specialized machines and for the exercise of great ability on the part of the farmer. But if a farm is not very large, and if, as is often the case, the farmer has no greater ability and activity of mind than is commonly to be found among the better class of working foremen in manufactures, then it would be best for others, and in the long run for himself, that he should return to the old plan of working among his men. Perhaps also his wife might return to some of those lighter tasks in and near the farmhouse which tradition ascribes to her. They require discretion and judgment, they are not inconsistent with education and culture; and combined with it they would raise and not lower the tone of her life, and her real claims to a good social position. There is some reason for thinking that the stern action of the principle of natural selection is now displacing those farmers, who have not the faculty to do difficult head-work, and yet decline to do hand-work. Their places are being taken by men of more

[1] The experiment of working farms on a very large scale is difficult and expensive, because it requires farm buildings and means of communication specially adapted to it; and it may have to overcome a good deal of resistance from custom and sentiment not altogether of an unhealthy kind The risk also would be great; for in such cases those who pioneer often fail, though their route when well trodden may be found to be the easiest and best

Our knowledge on many disputed points would be much increased and valuable guidance gained for the future if some private persons, or joint-stock companies, or co-operative associations, would make a few careful experiments of what have been called "Factory farms." On this plan there would be a central set of buildings (there might be more than one) from which roads and even light tramways extended in all directions In these buildings the recognized principles of factory management would be applied, machinery would be specialized and economized, waste of material would be avoided, bye products would be utilized, and above all the best skill and managing power would be employed, but only for its proper work.

than average natural ability who, with the help of modern education, are rising from the ranks of labourers; who are quite able to manage the ordinary routine work of a model farm; and who are giving to it a new life and spirit by calling their men to come and work, instead of telling them to go and work. Very large farms being left out of view, it is with rather small farms worked on these principles that the immediate future of English agriculture seems to lie. Very small holdings however have great advantages wherever so much care has to be given to individual plants, that machinery is out of place; and there is reason for hoping that they will continue to hold their own in raising vegetables, flowers and fruit.

Very small holdings

The gross rent of small holdings must be high relatively to their acreage.

§ 9. We may next consider how far landlords will in their own interest adjust the size of holdings to the real needs of the people. Small holdings often require more expensive buildings, roads and fences, and involve greater trouble and incidental expenses of management to the landlord in proportion to their acreage than do large holdings, and while a large farmer who has some rich land can turn poor soils to good account, small holdings will not flourish generally except on good soil[1]. Their gross rental per acre must therefore always be at a higher rate than that of large farms. But it is contended that, especially when land is heavily burdened by settlements, landlords are unwilling to incur the expense of subdividing farms, unless they see their way to rents for small holdings that will give them, in addition to high profits on their outlay, a heavy insurance fund against the chance of having to throw the holdings together again, and that the rental for small holdings, and especially for those of only a few acres, is extravagantly high in many parts of the country. Sometimes the prejudices of the landlord and his desire for undisputed

But it is sometimes at a scarcity value;

[1] The interpretation of this term varies with local conditions and individual wants. On permanent pasture land near a town or an industrial district the advantages of small holdings are perhaps at their maximum, and the disadvantages at their minimum. If the land is arable, it must not be light, but strong, and the richer the better, and this is especially the case with holdings so small as to make much use of the spade If the land is hilly and broken the small cultivator loses but little from his want of command of machinery.

BOOK VI. CH X

authority make him positively refuse to sell or let land to persons who are not in harmony with him on social, political or religious questions; but it seems certain that evils of this kind have always been confined to a few districts, and that they are rapidly diminishing.

and that is contrary to the public interest

But they rightly attract much attention For there is a public need in every district for small holdings, as well as large, for allotments and large gardens, and generally for holdings so small that they can be worked by people who have some other occupation[1].

There should be no artificial hindrances to peasants' properties.

And lastly though peasant proprietorship, as a system, is unsuited to the economic conditions of England, to her soil, her climate, and the temper of her people, yet there are a few peasant proprietors in England who are perfectly happy in this condition; and there are a few others who would buy small plots of land and would live happily on them, if they could get just what they wanted where they wanted it. Their temper is such that they do not mind working hard and living sparely, provided they need call no one master; they love quiet and dislike excitement; and they have a great capacity for growing fond of land. Reasonable opportunity should be given to such people to invest their savings in small plots of land, on which they may raise suitable crops with their own hands; and at the very least the present grievous legal charges on the transfer of small plots should be diminished[2].

Co-operation has

Co-operation might seem likely to flourish in agriculture

[1] They increase the number of people who are working in the open air with their heads and their hands: they give to the agricultural labourer a stepping-stone upwards, prevent him from being compelled to leave agriculture to find some scope for his ambition, and thus check the great evil of the continued flow of the ablest and bravest farm lads to the towns They break the monotony of existence, they give a healthy change from indoor life, they offer scope for variety of character and for the play of fancy and imagination in the arrangement of individual life, they afford a counter attraction to the grosser and baser pleasures; they often enable a family to hold together that would otherwise have to separate; under favourable conditions they improve considerably the material condition of the worker; and they diminish the fretting as well as the positive loss caused by the inevitable interruptions of their ordinary work.

[2] In 1885 the number of the holdings between one and five acres in England was a quarter of the whole number of holdings and since then they have rapidly increased.

and to combine the economies of production on a large scale with many of the joys and the social gains of small properties But it requires habits of mutual trust and confidence; and unfortunately the bravest and the boldest, and therefore the most trustful, of the countrymen have always moved to the towns, and agriculturists are a suspicious race. Co-operative movements in agriculture therefore must needs be very cautious, until the way has been well prepared for them by the less ambitious but safer system of profit-sharing.

great opportunities but also great difficulties in agriculture

As co-operation might combine more of the advantages of all systems of tenure, so the cottier system of Ireland often combined the disadvantages of all; but its worst evils and their causes are rapidly disappearing, and the economic elements of the problem are just now overshadowed by the political. We must therefore pass it by[1].

§ 10. The failures of the English system of land tenure in Ireland have brought into clear relief difficulties which are inherent in it, but which have been kept in the background in England by the conformity of the system to the business habits and the character of the people. The chief of these difficulties arise from the fact that while the system is competitive in its essence, the conditions of agriculture even in England offer a strong resistance to the full action of free competition. To begin with, there are special difficulties in ascertaining the facts on which that action must be based. We have just noticed the difficulty of keeping exact farming accounts: to this must be added that a

The English system of tenure is competitive, but competition does not act easily in agriculture

Difficulty of deciding what are

[1] The Ricardian theory of rent ought not to bear the greater part of the blame that has been commonly thrown on it, for those mistakes which English legislators made during the first half of this century in trying to force the English system of land tenure on India and Ireland. The theory concerns itself with the causes that determine the amount of the Producer's surplus from land at any time; and no great harm was done when this surplus was regarded as the landlord's share, in a treatise written for the use of Englishmen in England. It was an error in jurisprudence and not in economics that caused our legislators to offer to the Bengal tax-collector and Irish landlord facilities for taking to themselves the whole property of a cultivating firm, which consisted of tenant and landlord in the case of Ireland, and in the case of Bengal, of the Government and tenants of various grades; for the tax-collector was in most cases not a true member of the firm, but only one of its servants. But wiser and juster notions are prevailing now in the Government of India as well as of Ireland

BOOK VI. CH X

farmer's calculations as to the rent which it is worth his while to undertake to pay, are further hampered by the difficulty of deciding what is a normal harvest and a normal level of prices For good and bad seasons come so much in cycles that many years are required to afford a trustworthy average of them[1]: and in those many years the industrial environment is likely to have changed much; the local demand, the facilities for selling his own produce in distant markets and those which assist competitors from a distance to sell their produce in his local markets may all have changed

normal prices and harvests.

Difficulty arising from local variations in the standard of normal farming skill and enterprise

The landlord in determining what rent to accept is met by this difficulty and also by another, arising out of variations in the standards of ability among farmers in different parts of the country. The Producer's Surplus, or English rent, of a farm is that excess which its produce yields over its expenses of cultivation, including normal profits to the farmer; it being assumed that that farmer's ability and enterprise are such as are normal for farms of that class *in that place.* The difficulty in view is to decide whether these last words are to be interpreted broadly or narrowly.

Ethical and economic elements are here closely intermingled.

It is clear that if a farmer falls below the standard of ability of his own district, if his only forte is in driving hard bargains, if his gross produce is small and his net produce even smaller in proportion, in such a case the landlord acts in the interest of all when he hands over the farm to a more competent tenant, who will pay better wages, obtain a much higher net produce and pay a somewhat higher rent. On the other hand, when the local standard of normal ability and enterprise is low, it is not clearly right from an ethical point of view, nor is it clearly in the business interests of the landlord in the long run, that he should endeavour to take to himself a greater rent than can be paid by a farmer who reaches that standard; even though it could be obtained by importing a farmer from another district in which the standard is higher[2].

[1] Compare Tooke and Newmarch, *History of Prices*, Vol. VI. App. III.

[2] Difficulties of this kind are practically solved by compromises which experience has justified, and which are in accordance with the scientific interpretation of the term "normal" If a local tenant showed extraordinary ability, the

The tenant's freedom to make and reap the fruits of improvements.

Closely related to this question is one as to the freedom the tenant should have to develop the natural capabilities of his land at his own risk, with the understanding that if he is successful he is to retain something more than mere normal profits on his enterprise. So far as minor improvements go, this difficulty is in a great measure met by long leases These have done much for Scotland. but they have disadvantages of their own[1].

Custom, and, within recent years, legislation, have given the English tenant claims for compensation for improvements made by him which do not alter the character of his holding, and the fruits of which come in quickly. But he cannot claim the compensation till he quits his tenancy: and it is theoretically possible for a hard landlord to exact more than a fair rent from an improving farmer who has an affection for his ancestral home. Such cases are however rare[2].

landlord would be thought grasping who, by threatening to import a stranger, tried to extort a higher rent than the normal local farmer could make the land pay. On the other hand, a farm being once vacant, the landlord would be thought to act reasonably if he imported a stranger who would set a good model to the district, and who shared about equally with the landlord the extra net surplus due to his ability and skill, which, though not strictly speaking exceptional, were yet above the local standard. Compare the action of Settlement Officers in India with regard to equally good land cultivated by energetic and unenergetic races, noticed in the foot-note on p 727.

[1] The chief of these is that a great change in the Industrial Environment in its broader sense, if favourable to the land, may enrich the leaseholder without any merit of his own, and if unfavourable, may break him in spite of his best efforts The opening up of the wheat fields of the North West of America struck some Scotch farmers with long leases almost as heavily as it did many peasant proprietors in the West of Europe. As Sir James Caird points out (*Landed Interest*, Ch XI) the Earl of Leicester's plan of allowing the tenant proper freedom of cropping, till the last four years of his lease, would remove many other evils that have attached to, but are not inherent in the system

[2] The Agricultural Holdings Act of 1881 enforces customs which Mr Pusey's committee eulogized, but did not propose to enforce Many improvements are made partly at the expense of the landlord and partly at that of the tenant, the former supplying the materials, and the latter the labour In other cases it is best that the landlord should be the real undertaker of the improvements, bearing the whole expense and risk, and realizing the whole gain. Partly for the sake of simplicity in working, the law provides that compensation for permanent improvements can be claimed only if they have been made with the consent of the landlord. But Prof Nicholson argues with great force (*Tenant's Gain not Landlord's Loss*, Ch X) that the tenant should be allowed to claim for all improvements necessary for good husbandry, after giving the landlord notice and time to make them himself, provided only they do not alter the character of the holding. New light on all these questions is to be expected from the Report of the Royal Commission on Agriculture

BOOK VI. CH. X.

Conflict between public and private interests in the matter of building on open spaces,

§ 11. Finally a word may be said as to private and public interests with regard to open spaces in towns. Wakefield and the American economists have taught us how a sparsely inhabited new district is enriched by the advent of every new settler. The converse truth is that a closely peopled district is impoverished by every one who adds a new building or raises an old one higher. The want of air and light, of peaceful repose out-of-doors for all ages and of healthy play for children, exhausts the energies of the best blood of England which is constantly flowing towards our large towns. By allowing vacant spaces to be built on recklessly we are committing a great blunder from a business point of view, since for the sake of a little material wealth we are wasting those energies which are the factors of production of all wealth; and we are sacrificing those ends towards which material wealth is only a means. It is a difficult question to decide how far the expense of clearing open spaces in land already built on should fall on the neighbouring owners, but it seems right that for the future every new building erected, save in the open country, should be required to contribute in money or in kind towards the expenses of open places in its neighbourhood[1].

and in other matters.

We are however trenching on those general relations between collective and private interests, which we shall have to study carefully at a later stage. We shall then have to face several ethico-economic problems as to the limits of perpetual private rights in land "from the centre of the earth to the sky above it;" we shall have to enter on such questions as whether the interests of the mine-owner make him sufficiently careful of Nature's stored-up treasures, especially when they occur in poor seams; and again whether there is a balance of public advantage in allowing the shopkeeper in a town who has given a special value to his premises by the ability with which he has done business in them, a similar claim to compensation for disturbance to that which has been recognized in the case of the improving agricultural tenant.

[1] It must be borne in mind that a special tax on new building land would however tend to give something of a monopoly value to the land already built on, and thus raise ground-rents of existing buildings.

CHAPTER XI.

GENERAL VIEW OF DISTRIBUTION.

The Summary given in Book V. Ch XIV is continued in the present Chapter by one which traces a thread of continuity transverse to the earlier one.

§ 1. In the Summary at the end of Book V. we traced a continuous thread running through and connecting the applications of the general theory of equilibrium of demand and supply to different periods of time; from those so short that cost of production could exercise no direct influence on value, to those so long that the supply of the appliances of production could be fairly well adjusted to the indirect demand for them, which is "derived" from the direct demand for the commodities which they produce.

In the present Book we have been concerned with another thread of continuity; which lies transversely to the thread connecting different periods of time, and connects the various agents and appliances for production, material and human. It thus establishes a fundamental unity between them, in spite of their important differences of outward feature.

The causes that determine the normal supply prices of material and per-

There is a general correspondence between the causes that govern the supply prices of material and of personal capital: the motives which induce a man to accumulate personal capital *in* his son's education, are similar to those which control his accumulation of material capital *for* his son. There is a continuous transition from the father who works and waits in order that he may bequeath to his son a rich and firmly-established manufacturing or trading business, to one who works and waits in order to support his son while he is slowly acquiring a thorough medical education, and

sonal capital are very similar in general character,

ultimately to buy for him a lucrative practice. Again there is the same continuous transition from him to one who works and waits in order that his son may stay long at school, and may afterwards work for some time almost without pay while learning a skilled trade, instead of being forced to support himself early in an unskilled occupation, such as that of an errand-boy. For such occupations, because they lead the way to no future advance, sometimes offer comparatively high wages to young lads.

in spite of important differences

It is indeed true that the only persons, who, as society is now constituted, are very likely to invest much in developing the personal capital of a youth's abilities are his parents: and that many first-rate abilities go for ever uncultivated because no one, who can develop them, has had any special interest in doing so. This fact is very important practically, for its effects are cumulative. But it does not give rise to a fundamental difference between material and human agents of production for it is analogous to the fact that much good land is poorly cultivated because those who would cultivate it well have not access to it.

Again, since human beings grow up slowly and are slowly worn out, and parents in choosing an occupation for their children must as a rule look forward a whole generation, changes in demand take a longer time to work out their full effects on supply in the case of human agents than of most kinds of material appliances for production, and a specially "long" period is required in the case of labour to give full play to the economic forces which tend to bring about a normal adjustment between demand and supply[1].

The income

§ 2. That part of a man's income which he owes to the

[1] Comp Book IV Ch. V VI VII and XII; and Book VI. Ch IV. V. and VII To repeat another statement of nearly the same thing when we are considering periods of moderate length—say of a few years—the average earnings of skill or ability of any kind, have to be regarded more as a quasi-rent determined by the demand for their services, and less as normal profits on the labour and waiting needed for the acquirement of that skill or ability, than is the case with regard to such material appliances for production as are quickly made and quickly worn out. But, on the other hand, a great part of the earnings of a worker are the payment required to induce him to undergo a certain strain or fatigue And this may be regarded as the prime cost of his labour, while the remainder is the supplementary cost required to make up in the long run its total supply price

possession of extraordinary natural abilities may be regarded by him as analogous to the rent of other free gifts of nature, such as the "inherent" properties of land. But in reference to normal prices, it is to be classed rather with the profits derived by free settlers from the cultivation of new land, or again with the find of the pearl-fisher. The plot of one settler turns out better and that of another worse than was expected; the good find of one dive of the pearl-fisher compensates for many others that are fruitless: and the high income which one barrister, or engineer, or trader earns by his natural genius has to be counted with the comparative failures of many others, they perhaps appeared of no less promise when young, and they received as costly an education and start in life, but their services to production were less than his in proportion to their cost

derived from rare natural abilities is a rent from the point of view of the individual, but not for the purposes of the theory of normal value

The ablest business men are generally those who get the highest profits, and at the same time do their work most cheaply, and it would be as wasteful if society were to give their work to inferior people who would undertake to do it more cheaply, as it would be to give a valuable diamond to be cut by a low waged but unskilled cutter. And, just as the wages of skilled cutters enter into the normal supply price of cut diamonds, so the earnings of management of able business men enter into the normal supply price of the goods which they provide[1]

§ 3. The marginal efficiency of human agents of production on the one hand, and that of material agents on the other, are weighed against one another and compared with their marginal costs, and each tends to be applied as far as it is more efficient than the other in proportion to its cost. A chief function of business undertakers is to facilitate the free action of this great law of substitution. Generally to the public benefit, but sometimes in opposition to it, they are constantly comparing the services of machinery, and of labour, and again of unskilled and skilled labour, and of extra foremen and managers; they are constantly devising and experimenting with new arrangements which involve

Business undertakers are the agents by whose means the law of substitution weighs against one another the services of the different industrial classes

[1] Compare Book v. Ch. IX. §§ 2, 3, Book VI Ch. v. § 7, and Ch VIII § 9

BOOK VI CH. XI.

the use of different factors of production, and selecting those most profitable to themselves[1].

The efficiency as compared with the cost of almost every class of labour, is thus continually being weighed in the balance in one or more branches of production against some other classes of labour: and each of these in its turn against others. This competition is primarily "vertical:" it is a struggle for the field of employment between groups of labour belonging to different grades, but engaged in the same branch of production, and inclosed, as it were, between the same vertical walls. But meanwhile "horizontal" competition is always at work, and by simpler methods. for, firstly, there is great freedom of movement of adults from one business to another within each trade; and secondly, parents can generally introduce their children into almost any other trade of the same grade with their own in their neighbourhood. By means of this combined vertical and horizontal competition there is an effective and closely adjusted balance of payments to services as between labour in different grades; in spite of the fact that the labour in any one grade is mostly recruited even now from the children of those in the same grade[2].

The action of this law though chiefly round-about is very thorough in the long run

The working of the law of substitution is thus chiefly indirect. When two tanks containing fluid are joined by a pipe, the fluid, which is near the pipe in the tank with the higher level, will flow into the other, even though it be rather viscous, and thus the general levels of the tanks will tend to be brought together, though no fluid may flow from the further end of the one to the further end of the other; and if several tanks are connected by pipes, the fluid in all will tend to the same level, though some tanks have no direct connection with others. And similarly the law of substitution is constantly tending by indirect routes to apportion earnings to efficiency between trades, and even between grades, which are not directly in contact with one another, and which appear at first sight to have no way of competing with one another.

[1] Compare Book v. Ch III § 3, and Book VI Ch. I. § 2, and Ch. VII. § 2.

[2] Compare Book IV Ch VI § 7, Book VI. Ch. V. § 2.

§ 4. There is no breach of continuity as we ascend from the unskilled labourer to the skilled, thence to the foreman, to the head of a department, to the general manager of a large business paid partly by a share of the profits, to the junior partner, and lastly to the head partner of a large private business: and in a joint-stock company there is even somewhat of an anti-climax when we pass from the directors to the ordinary shareholders, who undertake the chief ultimate risks of the business Nevertheless business undertakers are to a certain extent a class apart.

The position of business undertakers

For while it is through their conscious agency that the law of substitution chiefly works in balancing one factor of production against another, with regard to them it has no other agency than the indirect influence of their own competition. So it works blindly, or rather wastefully, it forces many to succumb who might have done excellent work if they had been favoured at first and, in conjunction with the law of increasing return, it strengthens those who are strong, and hands over the businesses of the weak to those who have already obtained a partial monopoly.

makes the action of the law of substitution with regard to them indiscriminating and wasteful;

But on the other hand there is also a constant increase in the forces which tend to break up old monopolies, and to offer to men, who have but little capital of their own, openings both for starting new businesses and for rising into posts of command in large public and private concerns, and these forces tend to put business ability in command of the capital required to give it scope.

On the whole the work of business management is done cheaply—not indeed as cheaply as it may be in the future when men's collective instincts, their sense of duty and their public spirit are more fully developed; when society exerts itself more to develop the latent faculties of those who are born in a humble station of life, to diminish the secrecy of business, and when the more wasteful forms of speculation and of competition are held in check. But yet it is done so cheaply as to contribute to production more than the equivalent of its pay. For the business undertaker, like the skilled artisan, renders services which society needs, and

their work may be done more cheaply hereafter, but it is worth to society even now more than it costs

BOOK VI CH XI.

which it would probably have to get done at a higher cost if he were not there to do them[1].

Contrasts between fluctuations of current profits and wages

The similarity between the causes that determine the normal rewards of ordinary ability on the one hand, and of business power in command of capital on the other, does not extend to the fluctuations of their current earnings For the undertaker stands as a buffer between the buyer of goods and all the various classes of labour by which they are made He receives the whole price of the one and pays the whole price of the others. The fluctuations of his profits go with fluctuations of the prices of the things he sells, and are more extensive: while those of the wages of his employees come later and are less extensive. The earnings at any particular time (or the quasi-rent) of his capital and ability are sometimes large, but sometimes also a negative quantity: whereas those of the ability of his employees are never very large, and are never a negative quantity The wage-receiver is likely to suffer much when out of work, but that is because he has no reserve, not because he is a wage-receiver[2].

The various agents of production are the sole source of employment for one another

§ 5 Returning to the point of view of the second chapter of this Book, we may call to mind the double relation in which the various agents of production stand to one another. On the one hand they are often rivals for employment, any one that is more efficient than another in proportion to its cost tending to be substituted for it, and thus limiting the demand price for the other. And on the other hand they all constitute the field of employment for each other: there is no field of employment for any one, except in so far as it is provided by the others: the national dividend which is the joint product of all, and which increases with the supply of each of them, is also the sole source of demand for each of them

[1] We postpone a criticism of the contention of the socialists that it would be better for the State to take the work into its own hands and hire business managers to conduct it · and we postpone a study of those forms of speculation and commercial competition which are not beneficial to society, and perhaps are even harmful

[2] Compare Book v Ch II § 8 and Book vi Ch iv § 6 and Ch. viii §§ 7—9

How an increase of capital enriches the field for the employment of labour

Thus an increase of material capital causes it to push its way into new uses; and though in so doing it may occasionally diminish the field of employment for manual labour in a few trades, yet on the whole it will very much increase the demand for manual labour and all other agents of production. For it will much increase the national dividend, which is the common source of the demand for all; and since by its increased competition for employment it will have forced down the rate of interest, therefore the joint product of a dose of capital and labour will now be divided more in favour of labour than before.

This new demand for labour will partly take the form of the opening-out of new undertakings which hitherto could not have paid their way. It will, for instance, lead to the making of railways and waterworks in districts which are not very rich, and which would have continued to drag their goods along rough roads, and draw up their water from wells, if people had not been able and willing to support labour while making railway embankments and water conduits, and to wait for the fruits of their investment long and for a relatively low reward

Another part of this new demand for labour will come from the makers of new and more expensive machinery in all branches of production. For when it is said that machinery is substituted for labour, this means that one class of labour combined with much waiting is substituted for another combined with less waiting: and for this reason alone, it would be impossible to substitute capital for labour in general, except indeed locally by the importation of capital from other places.

It remains true however that the chief benefit which capital confers upon labour is not by opening out to it new employments, but by increasing the joint product of land, labour and capital (or of land, labour and waiting), and by reducing the share of that product which any given amount of capital (or of waiting) can claim as its reward.

An increase in number or efficiency of any

§ 6 In discussing the influence which a change in the supply of work of any one industrial group exerts on the field of employment for other kinds of labour, there was no

group of workers has similar results on other workers,

need to raise the question whether the increase of work came from an increase in the numbers or in the efficiency of those in the group: for that question is of no direct concern to the others. In either case there is the same addition to the national dividend: in either case competition will compel them to force themselves to the same extent into uses in which their marginal utility is lower; and will thus lessen to the same extent the share of the joint product which they are able to claim in return for a given amount of work of a given kind.

but very different results on themselves

But the question is of vital importance to the members of that group. For, if the change is an increase of one-tenth in their average efficiency, then each ten of them will have as high an aggregate income as each eleven of them would have if their numbers had increased by one-tenth, their efficiency remaining unchanged[1].

We shall have to look at some other aspects of this question in the next chapter while discussing the relative merits of increased leisure and increased material production as aims of progress.

Relations between the interests of different classes of workers in the same trade

§ 7. But meanwhile we must stay to consider in relation to one another the interests of different industrial classes engaged in the same trade.

This solidarity is a special case of the general fact that the demand for the several factors of production of any commodity is a joint demand, and we may refer back to the illustration of this general fact which is given in Book v. Ch. VI We there saw how a change in the supply of (say) plasterers' labour would affect the interests of all other branches of the building trades in the same way, but much more intensely than it would the general public. The fact is that the incomes derived from the specialized capital and the specialized skill belonging to all the various industrial

[1] Suppose, for instance, that an increase in the supply of work of the group by one-tenth forced them into work in which their marginal uses were lower, and thus lowered by a thirtieth their wages for any given amount of work, then, if the change came from an increase in their numbers, their average wages would fall by a thirtieth. But if it came from an increase in their efficiency, their wages would rise by about a fifteenth. (More exactly they would be $\frac{11}{10} \times \frac{29}{30} = 1\frac{19}{300}$ of what they were before)

classes engaged in producing houses, or calico, or anything else, depend very much on the general prosperity of the trade. And in so far as this is the case they may be regarded for short periods as shares of a composite or joint income of the whole trade The share of each class tends to rise when this aggregate income is increased by an increase in their own efficiency or by any external cause. But when the aggregate income is stationary, and any one class gets a better share than before, it must be at the expense of the others. This is true of the whole body of those engaged in any trade, and will be found to be true in a special sense of those who have spent a great part of their lives in working together in the same business establishment.

The gains of a business even as seen by the employer arise from several different sources.

§ 8 The earnings of a successful business, looked at from the point of view of the undertaker himself, are the aggregate of the earnings, firstly, of his own ability, secondly, of his plant and other material capital, and thirdly, of his business organization and connection. But really it is more than the sum of these. For his efficiency depends partly on his being in that particular business; and if he were to sell it at a fair price, and then engage himself in another business, his income would probably be much diminished

But there is often a part of it which attaches to the employees, and would be lost if they sought other employment.

The point of view of the undertaker however does not include the whole gains (or quasi-rents) of the business: for there is another part which attaches to his employees. Indeed, in some cases and for some purposes, nearly the whole income of a business may be regarded as a quasi-rent, that is an income determined for the time by the state of the market for its wares, with but little reference to the cost of preparing for their work the various things and persons engaged in it. In other words it is a *composite quasi-rent*[1] divisible among the different persons in the business by bargaining, supplemented by custom and by notions of fairness—results which are brought about by causes, that bear some analogy to those that, in early forms of civilization, have put the producer's surplus from the land almost permanently into the hands not of single individuals, but of cultivating firms.

[1] Compare Book v Ch. x. § 4.

BOOK VI. CH. XI.

Thus the head clerk in a business often has an acquaintance with men and things, the use of which he could sell at a high price to rival firms: but on the other hand it may be of a kind to be of no value save to the business in which he already is; and then his departure would perhaps injure it by several times the value of his salary, while probably he could not get half that salary elsewhere. And when a firm has a speciality of its own, many of its ordinary workmen would lose a great part of their wages by going away, and at the same time injure the firm seriously. The chief clerk may be taken into partnership, and the whole of the employees may be paid partly by a share in the profits of the concern; but whether this is done or not, their earnings are determined, not so much by competition and the direct action of the law of substitution, as by a bargain between them and their employers, the terms of which are theoretically arbitrary. In practice however they will probably be governed by a desire to "do what is right," that is, to agree on payments that represent the normal earnings of such ability, industry and special training as the employees severally possess, with something added if the fortunes of the firm are good, and something subtracted if they are bad.

When there would be no such loss, the quasi-rent of the employees' skill depends on the prosperity of the trade in general

It is important to see how the position of such employees differs from that of others, whose services would be of almost equal value to any business in a large trade. The income of one of those in any week consists, as we have seen, partly of a recompense for the fatigue incurred by the work of that week, and partly of a quasi-rent of his specialized skill and ability: and, assuming competition to be perfectly efficient, this quasi-rent is determined by the price which either his present employers, or any other, would be willing to pay for his services in the state in which the market for their wares is during that week. The prices that have to be paid for given work of a given kind being thus determined by the general conditions of the trade, these prices enter into the direct outgoings which have to be deducted from its gross earnings in order to ascertain the quasi-rent of this particular firm at the time. But in the rise or fall of that quasi-rent the employees would have no share.

But in fact competition is not thus perfectly efficient. Even where the same price is paid all over the market for the same work with the same machinery, the prosperity of a firm increases the chance of advancement for each of its employees, and also his chance of continuous employment when trade is slack, and much-coveted overtime when trade is good.

Profit-sharing.

Thus there is *de facto* some sort of profit-and-loss sharing between almost every business and its employees, and perhaps this is in its very highest form when, without being embodied in a definite contract, the solidarity of interests between those who work together in the same business is recognized with cordial generosity as the result of true brotherly feeling. But such cases are not very common; and as a rule the relations between employers and employed are raised to a higher plane both economically and morally by the adoption of the system of profit-sharing, especially when it is regarded as but a step towards the still higher but much more difficult level of true co-operation.

When employers and employed are in combination the division of the whole income of the trade is in some measure arbitrary.

§ 9. If the employers in any trade act together and so do the employed, the solution of the problem of wages becomes indeterminate. The trade as a whole may be regarded as receiving a quasi-rent consisting of the excess of the aggregate price which it can get for such wares as it produces over what it has to pay to other trades for the raw materials &c. it buys[1]; and there is nothing but bargaining to decide the exact shares in which this should go to employers and employed. No lowering of wages will be permanently in the interest of employers, which is unnecessary and drives many skilled workers to other markets, or even to other industries in which they abandon the quasi-rent of their special skill; and wages must be high enough in an average year to attract young people to the trade. This sets lower limits to wages, and upper limits are set by corresponding necessities as to the supply of capital and business power. But what point between these limits should be taken at any time can be decided only by higgling and bargaining; which

[1] Regarding the whole trade as a "nation," this becomes the national dividend: and this analogy is of service when the pure theory of international commerce is applied to the relations between different trades in the same country.

BOOK VI. CH. XI. are however likely to be tempered somewhat by ethico-prudential considerations, especially if there be a good Court of conciliation in the trade.

The case is in practice even more complex, because each group of employees is likely to have its own union, and to fight for its own hand. The employers act as buffers: but a strike for higher wages on the part of one group may, in effect, strike the wages of some other group almost as hard as the employers' profits.

We must postpone the consideration of the causes and effects of trade combinations and of alliances and counter-alliances among employers and employed, as well as among traders and manufacturers. They present a succession of picturesque incidents and romantic transformations, which arrest public attention and seem to indicate a coming change of our social arrangements now in one direction and now in another; and their importance is certainly great and grows rapidly. But it is apt to be exaggerated, for indeed many of them are little more than eddies, such as have always fluttered over the surface of progress. And though they are on a larger and more imposing scale in this modern age than before; yet now, as ever, the main body of movement depends on the deep silent strong stream of the tendencies of normal distribution and exchange; which "are not seen," but which control the course of those episodes which "are seen." For even in conciliation and arbitration, the central scientific difficulty is to discover what is that normal level from which the decisions of the Court must not depart far under penalty of destroying their own authority[1].

[1] See Mr L. L. Price's *Industrial Peace* and a Preface to it by the present writer.

CHAPTER XII.

THE INFLUENCE OF PROGRESS ON VALUE.

The field of employment for capital and labour

§ 1. THE field of employment which any place offers for labour and capital depends, firstly, on its natural resources; secondly, on the power of turning them to good account, derived from its progress of knowledge and of social and industrial organization; and thirdly, on the access that it has to markets in which it can sell those things of which it has a superfluity. The importance of this last condition is often underrated; but it stands out prominently when we look at the history of new countries.

is not always rich in new countries which have no good access to the markets of the Old World.

It is commonly said that wherever there is abundance of good land to be had free of rent, and the climate is not unhealthy, the real earnings of labour and the interest on capital must both be high. But this is only partially true. The early colonists of America lived very hardly. Nature gave them wood and meat almost free: but they had very few of the comforts and luxuries of life. And even now there are, especially in South America and Africa, many places to which Nature has been abundantly generous, which are nevertheless shunned by labour and capital, because they have no ready communications with the rest of the world. On the other hand high rewards may be offered to capital and labour by a mining district in the midst of an alkaline desert, when once communications have been opened up with the outer world, or again by a trading centre on a barren sea-coast; though, if limited to their own resources, they could support but a scanty population, and that in abject poverty. And the splendid markets which the Old World has offered to the

BOOK VI. CH. XII

products of the New, since the growth of steam communication, have rendered North America and Australia the richest large fields for the employment of capital and labour that there have ever been.

Old countries offer a market for mortgages of the future incomes of a new country,

But after all the chief cause of the modern prosperity of new countries lies in the markets that the old world offers, not for goods delivered on the spot, but for promises to deliver goods at a distant date. A handful of colonists having assumed rights of perpetual property in vast tracts of rich land, are anxious to reap in their own generation its future fruits, and as they cannot do this directly, they do it indirectly, by selling in return for the ready goods of the old world promises to pay much larger quantities of the goods that their own soil will produce in a future generation. In one form or another they mortgage their new property to the old world at a very high rate of interest. Englishmen and others, who have accumulated the means of present enjoyment, hasten to barter them for larger promises in the future than they can get at home a vast stream of capital flows to the new country, and its arrival there raises the rate of wages very high. The new capital filters but slowly towards the outlying districts: it is so scarce there, and there are so many persons eager to have it, that it often commands for a long time two per cent. a month, from which it falls by gradual stages down to six, or perhaps even five per cent., a year. For the settlers being full of enterprise, and seeing their way to acquiring private title-deeds to property that will shortly be of great value, are eager to become independent undertakers, and if possible employers of others; so wage-earners have to be attracted by high wages, which are paid in a great measure out of the commodities borrowed from the old world on mortgages, or in other ways.

and the consequent influx of capital into the latter

raises daily wages very high,

but labour is not dear because it is efficient

It is, however, difficult to estimate exactly the real rate of wages in outlying parts of new countries. The workers are picked men with a natural bias towards adventure; hardy, resolute, and enterprising; men in the prime of life, who do not know what illness is, and the strain of one kind and another which they go through, is more than the average English, and much more than the average European labourer could sustain. There are no poor among them, because there are none who are weak: if anyone becomes ailing, he is forced to retire to some more thickly-peopled place where there is less to be earned, but where also a quieter and less straining life is possible. Their earnings are very high if reckoned in money; but they have to buy at very high prices, or altogether dispense with, many of the comforts and luxuries which they would have obtained freely, or at low prices, if they had lived in more settled places. But it is true that many of these things are of but little real utility, and can be easily foregone, where no one has them and no one expects them

As time goes on though the law of diminishing return may not be acting very strongly,

As population increases, the best situations being already occupied, nature gives generally less return of raw produce to the marginal effort of the cultivators, and this tends a little to lower wages. But even in agriculture the law of increasing return is constantly contending with that of diminishing return, and many of the lands which were neglected at first, give a generous response to careful cultivation[1]; and meanwhile the development of roads and railroads, and the growth of varied markets and varied industries, render possible innumerable economies in production. Thus the actions of the laws of increasing and diminishing return appear pretty well balanced, sometimes the one, sometimes the other being the stronger.

There is no reason so far why there should be any fall in the rate of real wages for labour of a given efficiency. For if, taking one thing with another, the law of production is that of constant return, there will be no change in the reward to be divided between a dose of capital and labour, that is, between capital and labour working together in the same proportions as before And, since the rate of interest has fallen, the share which capital takes of this stationary joint reward is less than before; and therefore the amount of it remaining for labour is greater.

Of course the aggregate share of capital may have increased For instance, while labour has doubled capital may have quadrupled, and the rate of interest may be two-thirds

[1] Comp. Book IV. Ch. III. §§ 5, 6.

BOOK VI. CH. XII.

of what it was; and then, though each dose of capital gets a lower reward by one-third, and leaves for labour a larger share of the joint product of a dose of capital and labour, the aggregate share of capital will have risen in the ratio of eight to three[1].

the influx of capital becomes relatively slower and wages tend to fall.

But whether the law of production of commodities be one of constant return or not, that of the production of new title-deeds to land is one of rapidly diminishing return. The influx of foreign capital, though perhaps as great as ever, becomes less in proportion to the population; wages are no longer paid largely with commodities borrowed from the old world: and this is the chief reason of the subsequent fall in the necessaries, comforts and luxuries of life which can be earned by work of a given efficiency. But there are two other causes tending to lower average daily wages measured in money The first is, that as the comforts and luxuries of civilization increase, the average efficiency of labour is lowered by the influx of immigrants of a less sturdy character than the earlier settlers And the second is, that many of these new comforts and luxuries do not enter directly into money wage, but are an addition to it. We took account of them when arriving at the conclusion that the action of the law of increasing return would on the whole countervail that of diminishing return and we ought to count them in at their full value when tracing the changes in real wages Many historians have compared wages at different epochs with exclusive reference to those things which have always been in common consumption. But from the nature of the case, it is just these things to which the law of diminishing return applies, and which tend to become scarce as population increases. The view thus got is one-sided and misleading in its general effect.

And time wages measured in money fall faster than real efficiency wages

England's present industrial problems are a development of those of the last century

§ 2. The influence which access to distant markets exerts on the growth of the national dividend has been conspicuous in the history of England also. Her present economic condition is the direct result of those tendencies to production on a large scale, and to wholesale dealings in labour as well

[1] Much of the argument of Mr Henry George's *Progress and Poverty* is vitiated by his having overlooked this distinction.

as in goods which had long been slowly growing; but which in the eighteenth century received a twofold impetus from mechanical inventions, and the growth of consumers beyond the seas, who imported large quantities of goods of the same pattern[1]. Then were the first beginnings of that system of interchangeable parts, and the application of special machinery to make the special machinery by which nearly everything in common use is made. Then first was seen the full force which the law of increasing return gives in a manufacturing country with localized industries and large capitals, particularly when many of the large stocks of capital are combined together either into Joint-stock or Regulated companies, or into modern Trusts. And then began that careful "grading" of goods for sale in distant markets, which has already led to national and even international speculative combinations in produce markets and stock-exchanges; and the future of which no less than that of more lasting combinations among producers, whether undertakers of industry or working men, is the source of some of the gravest practical problems with which the coming generation will have to deal

The key-notes of the modern movement

The key-notes of the modern movement are the reduction of a great number of tasks to one pattern; the diminution of friction of every kind which might hinder powerful agencies from combining their action and spreading their influence over vast areas, and the development of transport by new methods and new forces. The macadamized roads and the improved shipping of the eighteenth century broke up local combinations and monopolies, and offered facilities for the growth of others extending over a wider area: and in our own age the same double tendency is resulting from every new extension and cheapening of communication by land and sea, by printing-press and telegraph.

In the eighteenth century foreign trade affected chiefly that part of the national dividend

§ 3 But though in the eighteenth century, as now, the real national dividend of England depended much on the action of the law of increasing return with regard to her exports, the mode of dependence has very much changed Then England had something approaching to a monopoly of the new methods of manufacture, and each bale of her goods

[1] Comp. Book I Ch. III § 4.

BOOK VI CH. XII.

which consisted of comforts and luxuries.

would be sold—at all events when their supply was artificially limited—in return for a vast amount of the produce of foreign countries. But, partly because the time was not yet ripe for carrying bulky goods great distances, her imports from the far-east and the far-west consisted chiefly of comforts and luxuries for the well-to-do; they had but little direct effect in lowering the labour-cost of necessaries to the English workman. Indirectly indeed her new trade lowered the cost of hardware, clothing and such other English manufactures as he consumed; because the production on a large scale of these things for consumers beyond the sea cheapened them for him. But it had very little effect on the cost of his food, and that was left to rise under the law of diminishing return, which was called into action by the rapid increase of population, caused by the growth of new manufacturing centres where there were not the customary restraints of a narrow village life. And a little later the great French war, and a series of bad harvests, raised that cost to much the highest point it has ever reached in Europe.

But now it gives England an immense command over necessaries.

But gradually the influence of foreign trade began to tell on the cost of production of our staple food. As the population of America spread westward from the Atlantic, richer and still richer wheat soils have come under cultivation; and the economies of transport have increased so much, especially in recent years, that the total cost of importing a quarter of wheat from the farms on the outskirts of cultivation has diminished rapidly, though the distance of that margin has been increasing. And thus England has been saved from the need of more and more intensive cultivation. The bleak hill-sides, up which the wheat fields were laboriously climbing in Ricardo's time, have returned to pasture; and the ploughman works now only where land will yield plentiful returns to his labour: whereas if England had been limited to her own resources, he must have plodded over ever poorer and poorer soils, and must have gone on continually re-ploughing land that had already been well ploughed, in the hope of adding by this heavy toil an extra bushel or two to the produce of each acre. Perhaps in an average year now, the ploughing which only just pays its expenses, the ploughing "on the margin of cultivation" gives twice as much produce as it gave in Ricardo's time, and five times as much or more, as it would have given now if with her present population England had been compelled to raise all her own food.

England has gained less than at first appears from the recent improvements in manufactures

§ 4. Every improvement in the manufacturing arts increases England's power of meeting the various wants of backward countries; so that it answers their purpose to divert their energies from making things by hand for their own use, to growing raw material with which to buy manufactures from her. In this way the progress of invention opens a wider field for the sale of her special products, and enables her more and more to confine her own production of food to conditions under which the law of diminishing return does not make itself much felt. But the same is not true of our trade with America, who quickly follows if she does not anticipate, England's improvements. The Bessemer, and other new processes, have enabled England to make steel that will push its way further than it could before in India and China, but not in America The amount of food and other raw material which can be bought in Illinois with a ton of steel cannot be more than the produce of as much capital and labour as would make a ton of steel in Illinois by the new processes, and therefore it has fallen as the efficiency of English and American labour in making steel has increased It is for this reason, as well as because of the heavy tariffs levied on her goods by many countries, that in spite of England's large trade, the progress of invention in the manufacturing arts has added less than might have been otherwise expected to her real national dividend.

It is no slight gain that she can make cheaply clothes and furniture and other commodities for her own use: but those improvements in the arts of manufacture which she has shared with other nations, have not directly increased the amount of raw produce which she can obtain from other countries with the product of a given quantity of her own capital and labour. Probably more than three-fourths of the whole benefit she has derived from the progress of manu-

BOOK VI. CH. XII.

Her highest gains have come from the cheapening of transport of various kinds.

factures during the present century has been through its indirect influences in lowering the cost of transport of men and goods, of water and light, of electricity and news; for the dominant economic fact of our own age is the development not of the manufacturing, but of the transport industries. It is these that are growing most rapidly in aggregate volume and in individual power, and which are giving rise to the most anxious questions as to the tendencies of large capitals to turn the forces of economic freedom to the destruction of that freedom: but, on the other hand, it is they also which have done by far the most towards increasing England's wealth.

Some of the influences of progress on the normal labour-values: firstly, of the chief requisites of a civilized life, viz corn,

§ 5. Thus the new economic age has brought with it great changes in the relative values of labour and the chief requisites of life; and many of these changes are of a character which could not have been anticipated at the beginning of this century. The America then known was ill-suited for growing wheat; and the cost of carrying it great distances by land was prohibitive. The labour value of wheat—that is the amount of labour which will purchase a peck of wheat—was then at its highest point, and now is at its lowest. It would appear that agricultural wages have been generally below a peck of wheat a day, but that in the first half of the eighteenth century they were about a peck, in the fifteenth a peck and a-half or perhaps a little more, while now they are two or three pecks. Prof Rogers's estimates for the middle ages are higher: but he seems to have taken the wages of the more favoured part of the population as representative of the whole. In the middle ages, even after a fairly good harvest, the wheat was of a lower quality than the ordinary wheat of to-day, while after a bad harvest much of it was so musty that now-a-days it would not be eaten at all, and the wheat seldom became bread without paying a high monopoly charge to the mill belonging to the lord of the manor.

meat,

It is true that, where population is very sparse, nature supplies grass and therefore animal food almost *gratis;* and in South America beggars pursue their calling on horseback. During the middle ages however the population of England was always dense enough to give a considerable labour value to meat, though it was of poor quality. For cattle, though only about a fifth as heavy as now, had very large frames: their flesh was chiefly in those parts from which the coarsest joints come; and since they were nearly starved in the winter and fed up quickly on the summer grass, the meat contained a large percentage of water, and lost a great part of its weight in cooking. At the end of the summer they were slaughtered and salted: and salt was dear. Even the well-to-do scarcely tasted fresh meat during the winter[1] A century ago very little meat was eaten by the working classes; while now, though its price is a little higher than it was then, they probably consume more of it, on the average, than at any other time in English history.

house room.

Turning next to the rent of house room, we find that ground-rents in towns have risen, both extensively and intensively. For an increasing part of the population is living in houses on which ground-rents at an urban scale have to be paid, and that scale is rising. But house rent proper, that is what remains of the total rent after deducting the full rental value of the ground, is probably little, if at all, higher than at any previous time for similar accommodation, for the rate of profits on the turnover which is earned by capital engaged in building is now low, and the labour cost of building materials has not much altered. And it must be remembered that those who pay the high town rents get in return the amusements and other advantages of modern town life, which many of them would not be willing to forego for the sake of a much greater gain than their total rent.

The labour value of wood, though lower than at the beginning of the century, is higher than in the middle ages: but that of mud, brick or stone walls has not much changed; while that of iron—to say nothing of glass—has fallen much.

And indeed the popular belief that house rent proper has risen, appears to be due to an imperfect acquaintance with the way in which our forefathers were really housed. The

[1] It is a significant fact that rabbits, which were probably neither better nor worse than in our own time, were then ten times as dear relatively to an ox as now. Their furs were highly prized, but only counted for a quarter of their whole value. (Rogers's *History*, Vol. I p. 588)

modern suburban artisan's cottage contains sleeping accommodation far superior to that of the gentry in the middle ages; and the working classes had then no other beds than loose straw, reeking with vermin, and resting on damp mud floors. But even these were probably less unwholesome, when bare and shared between human beings and live stock, than when an attempt at respectability covered them with rushes, which were nearly always vile with long accumulated refuse. It is undeniable that the housing of the very poorest classes in our towns now is destructive both of body and soul: and that with our present knowledge and resources we have neither cause nor excuse for allowing it to continue. And it is true that in earlier times bad housing was in so far a less evil than now, as those who were badly housed by night had abundant fresh air by day. But a long series of records, ending with the evidence of Lord Shaftesbury and others before the recent Commission on the housing of the poor, establishes the fact that all the horrors of the worst dens of modern London had their counterpart in worse horrors of the lairs of the lowest stratum of society in every previous age.

fuel, Fuel, like grass, is often a free gift of nature to a sparse population; and during the middle ages the cottagers could generally, though not always, get the little brushwood fire needed to keep them warm as they huddled together round it in huts which had no chimney through which the heat could go to waste. But as population increased the scarcity of fuel pressed heavily on the working classes, and would have arrested England's progress altogether, had not coal been ready to take the place of wood as fuel for domestic purposes, as well as for smelting iron. It is now so cheap that even the comparatively poor can keep themselves warm indoors without living in an unwholesome and stupefying atmosphere.

clothing, This is one of the great services that coal has wrought for modern civilization. Another is to provide cheap underclothing, without which cleanliness is impossible for the masses of the people in a cold climate: and that is perhaps the chief of the benefits that England has gained from the direct application of machinery to making commodities for her own use. Another, and not less important service, is to provide abundant water, even in large towns[1]; and another to supply, with the aid of mineral oil, that cheap and artificial light which is needed not only for some of man's work, but, what is of higher moment, for the good use of his evening leisure. To this group of requisites for a civilized life, derived from coal on the one hand, and modern means of transport on the other, we must add, as has just been noticed, the cheap and thorough means of communication of news and thought by steam-presses, by steam-carried letters and steam-made facilities for travel. We have already referred to these agencies, aided by electricity, as rendering possible the civilization of the masses in countries the climate of which is not so warm as to be enervating, and as preparing the way for true self-government and united action by the whole people, not merely of a town such as Athens, Florence or Bruges, but of a broad country, and even in some respects of the whole civilized world[2].

water, light, news and travel.

§ 6. We have seen that the national dividend is at once the aggregate net product of, and the sole source of payment for, all the agents of production within the country, that the larger it is, the larger, other things being equal, will be the share of each agent of production, and that an increase in the supply of any agent will generally lower its price, to the benefit of other agents.

The influence of progress on the values of the chief agents of production:

This general principle is specially applicable to the case of land. An increase in the amount of productiveness of the land that supplies any market redounds in the first instance to the benefit of those capitalists and workers who are in possession of other agents of production for the same market. And the influence on values which has been exerted in the modern age by the new means of transport is nowhere so conspicuous as in the history of land; its value rises with every improvement in its communications with

it has sometimes lowered the value of English agricultural land,

[1] Primitive appliances will bring water from high ground to a few public fountains but the omnipresent water supply which both in its coming and its going performs essential services for cleanliness and sanitation, would be impossible without coal-driven steam-pumps and coal-made iron pipes.

[2] Book I. Ch. II §§ 6, 7

BOOK VI. CH. XII.

markets in which its produce can be sold, and its value falls with every new access to its own markets of produce from more distant places. It is not very long ago that the home counties were full of fears that the making of good roads would enable the more distant parts of England to compete with them in supplying London with food; and now the differential advantages of English farms are in some respects being lowered by the importation of food that has travelled on Indian and American railroads, and being carried in ships made of Bessemer steel and driven by triple expansion engines[1].

but not of agricultural and urban land taken together

But as Malthus contended, and Ricardo admitted, anything that promotes the prosperity of the people promotes also in the long run that of the landlords of the soil It is true that English rents rose very fast when, at the beginning of this century, a series of bad harvests struck down a people that could not import their food; but a rise so caused could not from the nature of the case have gone very much further. And the adoption of free trade in corn in the middle of the century, followed by the expansion of American wheat-fields, is rapidly raising the real value of the land urban and rural taken together, that is, it is raising the amount of the necessaries, comforts and luxuries of life which can be purchased by the aggregate rental of all the landowners urban and rural taken together[2].

[1] A somewhat similar case is that of many quiet summer resorts. Their humble attractions absorbed the attention of neighbouring residents fifty years ago, but now they are impoverished by those modern facilities of travel which induce people to take longer journeys in search of change of scene, and enrich more fashionable and more distant resorts As steam carriage favours those soils which are exceptionally fertile but distant from good markets, so it favours those pleasure resorts which have exceptionally beautiful scenery, even though they are far away.

[2] Mr W Sturge (in an instructive paper read before the Institute of Surveyors, Dec 1872) estimates that the agricultural (money) rent of England doubled between 1795 and 1815, and then fell by a third till 1822; after that time it has been alternately rising and falling; and it is now about 45 or 50 millions as against 50 or 55 millions about the year 1873, when it was at its highest It was about 30 millions in 1810, 16 millions in 1770, and 6 millions in 1600 (Compare Mr Giffen's *Growth of Capital*, Ch v, and Porter's *Progress of the Nation*, Sect II Ch I) But the rental of urban land in England is now rather greater than the rent of agricultural land and in order to estimate the full gain of the landlords from the expansion of population and general progress, we must reckon in the values of the land on which there are now railroads, mines, docks, &c. Taken

Progress may lower the value of the appliances of production where this can be separated from that of their sites;

§ 7. But though the development of the industrial environment tends on the whole to raise the value of land, it more often than not lessens the value of machinery and other kinds of fixed capital, in so far as their value can be separated from that of the sites on which they rest. A sudden burst of prosperity may indeed enable the existing stock of appliances in any trade to earn for a time a very high income. But things which can be multiplied without limit cannot retain for long a scarcity value, and if they are fairly durable, as for instance ships and blast furnaces and textile machinery, they are likely to suffer great depreciation from the rapid progress of improvement.

but not if the value of their sites is reckoned in.

The value of such things as railways and docks however depends in the long run chiefly on their situation. If that is good, the progress of their industrial environment will raise their net value even after allowance has been made for the charges to which they may be put in keeping their appliances abreast of the age[1].

It has greatly increased the supply of capital

§ 8. Political Arithmetic may be said to have begun in England in the seventeenth century; and from that time onwards we find a constant and nearly steady increase in the amount of accumulated wealth per head of the population[2].

The growth of wealth is promoted by man's increased willingness to sacrifice the present for the future,

Man, though still somewhat impatient of delay, has gradually become more willing to sacrifice ease or other enjoyment in order to obtain them in the future He has acquired a greater "telescopic" faculty; that is, he has acquired an increased power of realizing the future and bringing it clearly before his mind's eye: he is more prudent, and has more self-control, and is therefore more inclined to estimate at a high rate future ills and benefits—these terms being used broadly to include the highest and lowest affections of the human mind. He is more unselfish, and

all together, the money rental of England's soil is probably twice as high, and its Real rental three or four times as high, as it was when the corn laws were repealed.

[1] Of course there are exceptions Economic progress may take the form of building new railways that will draw off much of the traffic of some of those already existing, or of increasing the size of ships till they can no longer enter docks the entrance to which is through shallow waters.

[2] See Book IV Ch. VII and especially the Note on the Statistics of the Growth of Wealth

BOOK VI. CH. XII.

therefore more inclined to work and save in order to secure a future provision for his family; and there are already faint signs of a brighter time to come, in which there will be a general willingness to work and save in order to increase the stores of public wealth and of public opportunities for leading a higher life.

in spite of a slackening in his willingness to work very long hours

But though he is more willing than in earlier ages to incur present ills for the sake of future benefits, it is doubtful whether we can now trace a continued increase in the amount of exertion which he is willing to undergo for the sake of obtaining positive pleasures, whether present or future. During many generations the industry of the Western World has steadily become more sedulous: holidays have diminished, the hours of work have increased, and people have from choice or necessity contented themselves with less and less search for pleasure outside their work. But it would seem that this movement has reached its maximum, and is now declining. In all grades of work except the very highest, people are getting to prize relaxation more highly than before, and are becoming more impatient of the fatigue that results from excessive strain, and they are perhaps on the whole less willing than they used to be to undergo the constantly increasing "discommodity" of very long hours of work, for the sake of obtaining present luxuries. These causes would make them less willing than before to work hard in order to provide against distant needs, were it not that there is an even more rapid increase in their power of realizing the future, and perhaps—though this is more doubtful—in their desire for that social distinction which comes from the possession of some small store of accumulated wealth[1].

The increase of capital has lowered its proportionate though not its total income

This increase of capital per head tended to diminish its marginal utility, and therefore the rate of interest on new investments; but not uniformly, because there were meanwhile great variations in the demand for capital, both for political and military and for industrial purposes. Thus the rate of interest which was vaguely reported to be 10 per cent.

[1] Compare two suggestive articles by Prof. Giddings in the *Harvard Journal of Economics* for Jan 1890 and Jan 1891.

during a great part of the middle ages, had sunk to 3 per cent. in the earlier half of the eighteenth century; but the immense industrial and political demand for capital raised it again, and it was relatively high during the great war. It fell as soon as the political drain had ceased; but it rose again in the middle of this century, when railways and the development of new countries made a great new demand for capital. These new demands have not slackened, but the rate of interest is again falling fast, in consequence of the great recent accumulations of wealth in England, on the Continent, and above all in America.

There is a relative fall in the earnings of trained ability

§ 9. The growth of general enlightenment and of a sense of responsibility towards the young has turned a great deal of the increasing wealth of the nation from investment as material capital to investment as personal capital. There has resulted a largely increased supply of trained abilities, which has much increased the national dividend, and raised the average income of the whole people. but it has taken away from these trained abilities much of that scarcity value which they used to possess, and has lowered their earnings not indeed absolutely, but relatively to the general advance; and it has caused many occupations, which not long ago were accounted skilled, and which are still spoken of as skilled, to rank with unskilled labour as regards wages.

A striking instance is that of writing It is true that many kinds of office work require a rare combination of high mental and moral qualities, but almost any one can be easily taught to do the work of a copying clerk, and probably there will soon be few men or women in England who cannot write fairly well. When all can write, the work of copying, which used to earn higher wages than almost any kind of manual labour, will rank among unskilled trades[1]

[1] In fact the better kinds of artisan work educate a man more, and will be better paid than those kinds of clerk's work which call for neither judgment nor responsibility. And, as a rule, the best thing that an artisan can do for his son is to bring him up to do thoroughly the work that lies at his hand, so that he may understand the mechanical, chemical or other scientific principles that bear upon it, and may enter into the spirit of any new improvement that may be made in it. If his son should prove to have good natural abilities, he is far more likely to rise to a high position in the world from the bench of an artisan than from the desk of a clerk.

BOOK VI. CH. XII.

Earnings in old and familiar skilled occupations tend to fall relatively to those in new

Again a new branch of industry is often difficult simply because it is unfamiliar; and men of great force and skill are required to do work, which can be done by men of ordinary capacity or even by women and children, when the track has once been well beaten: its wages are high at first, but they fall as it becomes familiar. And this has caused the rise of average wages to be underrated, because it so happens that many of the statistics, which seem typical of general movements of wages, are taken from trades which were comparatively new a generation or two ago, and are now within the grasp of men of much less real ability than those who pioneered the way for them[1].

The consequence of such changes as these is to increase the number of those employed in occupations which are called skilled, whether the term is now properly applied or not: and this constant increase in the numbers of workers in the higher classes of trades has caused the average of all labour to rise much faster than the average of representative wages in each trade[2].

Artisans' wages

In the middle ages, though some men of great ability remained artisans all their lives, and became artists, yet as a class the artisans ranked more nearly with the unskilled

[1] Comp Book IV Ch VI §§ 1, 2, and Ch. IX, especially § 6 As the trade progresses, improvements in machinery are sure to lighten the strain of accomplishing any given task, and therefore to lower task wages rapidly But meanwhile the pace of the machinery, and the quantity of it put under the charge of each worker, may be increased so much that the total strain involved in the day's work is greater than before. On this subject employers and employed frequently differ It is for instance certain that time wages have risen in the textile trades; but the employees aver, in contradiction to the employers, that the strain imposed on them has increased more than in proportion In this controversy wages have been estimated in money, but when account is taken of the increase in the purchasing power of money, there is no doubt that real efficiency wages have risen; that is, the exertion of a given amount of strength, skill and energy is rewarded by a greater command over commodities than formerly

[2] This may be made clearer by an example. If there are 500 men in grade A earning 12*s*. a week, 400 in grade B earning 25*s* and 100 in grade C earning 40*s*, the average wages of the 1000 men are 20*s* If after a time 300 from grade A have passed on to grade B, and 300 from grade B to grade C, the wages in each grade remaining stationary, then the average wages of the whole thousand men will be about 28*s*. 6*d*. And even if the rate of wages in each grade had meanwhile fallen 10 per cent, the average wages of all would still be about 25*s* 6*d*, that is, would have risen more than 25 per cent Neglect of such facts as these, as Mr Giffen has pointed out, is apt to cause great errors

labourers than they do now. At the beginning of the new industrial era a hundred years ago the artisans had lost much of their old artistic traditions and had not yet acquired that technical command over their instruments, that certainty and facility in the exact performance of difficult tasks which belong to the modern skilled artisan, and observers early in this century were struck by the social gulf that was opening out between the artisan and the unskilled labourer. This change was a consequence partly of the increase of the wages of the artisan, which rose to about double those of the unskilled labourer; and partly of the same cause that secured him his high wages, that is the great increase in the demand for highly skilled labour, especially in the metal trades, and the consequent rapid absorption of the strongest characters among the labourers and their children into the ranks of the artisans, for the breaking down, just at that time, of the old exclusiveness of the artisans, had made them less than before an aristocracy by birth and more than before an aristocracy by worth. But about a generation ago, as has just been explained, some of the simpler forms of skilled trades began to lose their scarcity value, as their novelty wore off; and at the same time continually increasing demands began to be made on the ability of those in some trades, that are traditionally ranked as unskilled. The navvy for instance, and even the agricultural labourer, have often to be trusted with expensive and complicated machinery, which a little while ago were thought to belong only to the skilled trades, and the real wages of these two representative occupations are rising fast[1].

rose relatively to those of unskilled labour at the beginning of the century

but now that tendency is reversed.

Again there are some skilled and responsible occupations, such as those of the head heaters and rollers in iron works, which require great physical strength, and involve much discomfort: and in them wages are very high. For the

[1] The rise of wages of agricultural labourers would be more striking than it is, did not the spread of modern notions to agricultural districts cause many of the ablest children born there to leave the fields for the railway or the workshop, to become policemen, or to act as carters or porters in towns. Perhaps there is no stronger evidence of the benefits of modern education and economic progress than the fact that those who are left behind in the fields, though having less than an average share of natural abilities, are yet able to earn much higher Real wages than their fathers.

BOOK VI. CH. XII.

temper of the age makes those who can do high class work, and can earn good wages easily, refuse to undergo hardship, except for a very high reward.

There is a relative fall in the wages of elderly men;

§ 10 We may next consider the changes in the relative wages of old and young men, of women and children.

The conditions of industry change so fast that long experience is in some trades almost a disadvantage, and in many it is of far less value than a quickness in taking hold of new ideas and adapting one's habits to new conditions. In these trades an elderly man finds it difficult to get employment except when trade is brisk, at all events if he is a member of a union which will not allow him to work for less than the full wages of the district In any case he is likely to earn less after he is fifty years old than before he is thirty; and the knowledge of this is tempting artisans to follow the example of unskilled labourers, whose natural inclination to marry early has always been encouraged by the desire that their family expenses may begin to fall off before their own wages begin to shrink. Trades-unions are afraid that abuses might creep in if they allowed men "with grey hairs" to compete for employment at less than full wages; but many of them are coming to see that it is to their own interest, as it certainly is to that of the community, that such men should not be forced to be idle.

and a rise in the wages of boys and girls,

A second and even more injurious tendency of the same kind is that of the wages of children to rise relatively to those of their parents. Machinery has displaced many men, but not many boys; the customary restrictions which excluded them from some trades are giving way; and these changes, together with the spread of education, while doing good in almost every other direction, are doing harm in this that they are enabling boys, and even girls, to set their parents at defiance and start in life on their own account.

and of women

The wages of women are for similar reasons rising fast relatively to those of men. And this is a great gain in so far as it tends to develop their faculties, but an injury in so far as it tempts them to neglect their duty of building up a true home, and of investing their efforts in the personal capital of their children's character and abilities.

§ 11. The relative fall in the incomes to be earned by moderate ability, however carefully trained, is accentuated by the rise in those that are obtained by many men of extraordinary ability. There never was a time at which moderately good oil paintings sold more cheaply than now, and there never was a time at which first-rate paintings sold so dearly. A business man of average ability and average good fortune gets now a lower rate of profits on his capital than at any previous time; while yet the operations, in which a man exceptionally favoured by genius and good luck can take part, are so extensive as to enable him to amass a huge fortune with a rapidity hitherto unknown.

The earnings of exceptional genius are rising,

The causes of this change are chiefly two, firstly, the general growth of wealth; and secondly, the development of new facilities for communication, by which men, who have once attained a commanding position, are enabled to apply their constructive or speculative genius to undertakings vaster, and extending over a wider area, than ever before.

as a result of two causes

It is the first cause, almost alone, that enables some barristers to command very high fees, for a rich client whose reputation, or fortune, or both, are at stake will scarcely count any price too high to secure the services of the best man he can get. and it is this again that enables jockeys and painters and musicians of exceptional ability to get very high prices. In all these occupations the highest incomes earned in our own generation are the highest that the world has yet seen. But so long as the number of persons who can be reached by a human voice is strictly limited, it is not very likely that any singer will make an advance on the £10,000 said to have been earned in a season by Mrs Billington at the beginning of this century nearly as great as that which the business leaders of the present generation have made on those of the last.

of which one acts almost alone on professional incomes,

For the two causes have co-operated to put enormous power and wealth in the hands of those business men of our own generation who have had first-rate genius, and have been favoured by fortune. This is most conspicuous in America, where several men who began life poor, have amassed more than £10,000,000 each It is true that a great part of these

while both act fully with regard to business incomes

BOOK VI. CH. XII.

gains have come, in some cases, from the wrecks of the rival speculators who had been worsted in the race. But in others, as for instance, that of the late Mr Vanderbilt, they were earned mainly by the supreme economizing force of a great constructive genius working at a new and large problem with a free hand, and Mr Vanderbilt probably saved to the people of the United States more than he accumulated himself[1].

Progress is fast improving the condition of the great body of the working classes.

§ 12. But these fortunes are exceptional. The diffusion of knowledge, the improvement of education, the growth of prudent habits among the masses of the people, and the opportunities which the new methods of business offer for the safe investment of small capitals,—all these forces are telling on the side of the poorer classes as a whole relatively to the richer. The returns of the income tax and the house tax, the statistics of consumption of commodities, the records of salaries paid to the higher and the lower ranks of servants of Government and public companies, tend in the same direction, and indicate that middle class incomes are increasing faster than those of the rich, that the earnings of artisans are increasing faster than those of the professional classes, and that the wages of healthy and vigorous unskilled labourers are increasing faster even than those of the average artisan[2].

[1] It should be noticed however that some of these gains may be traced to those opportunities for the formation of trade combinations engineered by a few able, wealthy and daring men to exploit for their own benefit a great body of manufactures, or the trade and traffic of a large district. That part of this power, which depends on political conditions, and especially on the Protective tariff, may pass away. But the area of America is so large, and its condition so changeful, that the slow and steady-going management of a great joint-stock company on the English plan is at a disadvantage in competition with the vigorous and original scheming, the rapid and resolute force of a small group of wealthy capitalists, who are willing and able to apply their own resources in great undertakings to a much greater extent than is the case in England. The ever-shifting conditions of business life in America enable natural selection to bring to the front the best minds for the purpose from their vast population, almost every one of whom, as he enters on life, resolves to be rich before he dies. The modern developments of business and of business fortunes are of exceptional interest and instruction to Englishmen: but their lessons will be misread unless the essentially different conditions of business life in the old world and the new are constantly borne in mind.

[2] A great body of statistics relating to nearly all civilized countries and uniformly tending in this direction is contained in M. Leroy Beaulieu's *Essai sur la*

The inconstancy of employment in modern industry is apt to be exaggerated.

It must be admitted that a rise in wages would lose part of its benefit, if it were accompanied by an increase in the time spent in enforced idleness. Inconstancy of employment is a great evil, and rightly attracts public attention. But several causes combine to make it appear to be greater than it really is.

When a large factory goes on half time, rumour bruits the news over the whole neighbourhood, and perhaps the newspapers spread it all over the country. But few people know when an independent workman, or even a small employer, gets only a few days' work in a month; and in consequence, whatever suspensions of industry there are in modern times, are apt to seem more important than they are relatively to those of earlier times. In earlier times some labourers were hired by the year: but they were not free, and were kept to their work by personal chastisement. There is no good cause for thinking that the mediæval artisan had constant employment. And the most persistently inconstant employment now to be found in Europe is in those non-agricultural industries of the West which are most nearly mediæval in their methods, and in those industries of Eastern and Southern Europe in which mediæval traditions are strongest[1]

In many directions there is a steady increase in the proportion of employees who are practically hired by the year. This is for instance the general rule in many of those trades connected with transport which are growing fastest, and are

répartition des Richesses, et sur la tendance à une moindre inégalité des conditions, 1881 Mr Goschen's Address to the Royal Statistical Society in 1887 on *The Increase of Moderate Incomes* points the same way; and above all so do the very careful and instructive studies of wage statistics made by Mr Giffen in his private and in his official capacity.

[1] One instance, which has come under the present writer's observation, may be mentioned here. In Palermo there is a semi-feudal connection between the artisans and their patrons Each carpenter or tailor has one or more large houses to which he looks for employment; and so long as he behaves himself fairly well, he is practically secure from competition. There are no great waves of Depression of Trade; the newspapers are never filled with accounts of the sufferings of those out of work, because their condition changes very little from time to time But a larger percentage of artisans are out of employment at the best of times in Palermo, than in England in the centre of the worst depression of recent years

On the probable instability of industry in the Middle Ages see Dr Cunningham's *Growth of English Industry and Commerce*, Vol I p. 348

BOOK VI. CH. XII

the representative industries of the second half of the nineteenth century, as the manufacturing trades were of the first half. And though the rapidity of invention, the fickleness of fashion, and above all the instability of credit, do certainly introduce disturbing elements into modern industry, yet, as we shall see presently, other influences are working strongly in the opposite direction, and there seems to be no good reason for thinking that inconstancy of employment is increasing on the whole

But the number of those who are unfit for hard work, does not appear to diminish.

Progress then has done much: but there still remains a great, and—in consequence of improved sanitation—perhaps a growing Residuum of persons who are physically, mentally or morally incapable of doing a good day's work with which to earn a good day's wage, and some of those who are called artisans, together with many unskilled labourers, work hard for over long hours, and provide for others the means of refinement and luxury, but obtain neither for themselves nor their children the means of living a life that is worthy of man.

The temptation to understate the benefits of progress.

There is a strong temptation to over-state the economic evils of our own age, and to ignore the existence of similar and worse evils in earlier ages; for by so doing we may for the time stimulate others, as well as ourselves, to a more intense resolve that the present evils shall no longer be allowed to exist. But it is not less wrong, and generally it is much more foolish, to palter with truth for a good than for a selfish cause. And the pessimist descriptions of our own age, combined with romantic exaggerations of the happiness of past ages, must tend to the setting aside of methods of progress, the work of which if slow is yet solid; and to the hasty adoption of others of greater promise, but which resemble the potent medicines of a charlatan, and while quickly effecting a little good, sow the seeds of widespread and lasting decay This impatient insincerity is an evil only less great than that moral torpor which can endure that we, with our modern resources and knowledge, should look on contentedly at the continued destruction of all that is worth having in multitudes of human lives, and solace ourselves with the reflection that anyhow the evils of our own age are less than those of the past.

§ **13**. We have not yet reached the stage at which we can profitably examine the general effects of economic progress on human well being. But it will be well, before ending this Book, to pursue a little further the line of thought on which we started in Book III., when considering wants in relation to activities We there saw reasons for thinking that the true key-note of economic progress is the development of new activities rather than of new wants; and we may now make some study of a question that is of special urgency in our own generation; viz —what is the connection between changes in the manner of living and the rate of earnings; how far is either to be regarded as the cause of the other, and how far as the effect?

The broader influences of progress

Connection between the manner of living and the rate of earnings.

Let us take the term the *Standard of Life* to mean the standard of activities and of wants Thus a rise in the standard of life implies an increase of intelligence, and energy and self-respect, leading to more care and judgment in expenditure, and to an avoidance of food and drink that gratify the appetite but afford no strength, and of ways of living that are unwholesome physically and morally. A rise in the standard of life for the whole population will much increase the national dividend, and the share of it which accrues to each grade and to each trade. A rise in the standard of life for any one trade or grade will raise their efficiency and their own real wages · it will increase the national dividend a little; and it will enable others to obtain their assistance at a cost somewhat less in proportion to its efficiency.

By the *Standard of Life* we mean the standard of activities as well as of wants

But many writers have spoken of the influence exerted on wages by a rise not in the standard of *life*, but in that of *comfort*;—a term that may suggest a mere increase of artificial wants, among which perhaps the grosser wants may predominate. It is true that every broad improvement in the standard of comfort is sure to bring with it a better manner of living, and to open the way to new and higher activities; while those who have hitherto had neither the necessaries nor the decencies of life can hardly fail to get some increase of vitality and energy from an increase of comfort, however gross and material the view which they may take of it. Thus a rise in the standard of comfort does to some extent involve

A rise in the standard of comfort raises wages chiefly through its indirect influence in raising the standard of activities

a rise in the standard of life; and in so far as this is the case it does tend to increase the national dividend and to improve the condition of the people.

A rise in the standard of wants can consistently be regarded as a chief means of raising wages only by extreme Malthusians.

Some writers however of our own and of earlier times have gone further than this, and have implied that a mere increase of wants tends to raise wages. But the only direct effect of an increase of wants is to make people more miserable than before. And if we put aside its probable indirect effect in increasing activities, and otherwise raising the standard of life, it can raise wages only by another indirect effect, viz. by diminishing the supply of labour.

The doctrine that, merely through its action in diminishing the supply of labour, a rise in the standard of comfort raises wages, and is one of the most effective means for that purpose, can be held consistently by those who believe that population is pressing on the means of subsistence so hardly, that the rate of growth of population exercises a predominating influence on the rate of wages. For if that be true, then it is also true that at least one of the most efficient means of raising wages is to induce people to adopt a higher standard of comfort, in however mean and sordid a sense the term comfort is used: since in order to indulge the new desires rising out of their extended desire for comfort they may probably marry late, or otherwise limit the number of their children. But it cannot be held consistently by those who hold, as most writers of the present generation do, that the new facilities of transport have much diminished for the present the influence which the law of diminishing return exercises on production, that the countervailing influences of the law of increasing return are strong and that an increase of numbers does not tend greatly to reduce the average level of wages.

The influence on wages of a lessened supply of labour of any kind will now be further studied in relation to the hours of work

It is indeed still possible to contend that a mere diminution in the supply of manual labourers as a whole, or of any one class of them in particular, will increase the competition for their aid on the part of the higher grades of labour, and the owners of material capital; and that in consequence their wages will rise. This argument is no doubt valid so far as it goes: but the rise of wages that can be got by any class of labour simply by making itself scarce, and independently of any improvement in its standard of activities is generally not very great, except in the case of the lowest grades. We will consider this problem in some detail with reference to that particular change in the standard of living which takes the form of shortening the hours of labour, and of wise uses of leisure[1]

Too little account is often taken of the wear-and-tear of human beings

§ 14. The earnings of a human being are commonly counted *gross;* no special reckoning being made for his wear-and-tear, of which indeed he is himself often rather careless; and, on the whole, but little account is taken of the evil effects of the overwork of men on the well-being of the next generation, although the hours of labour of children are regulated by law in their own interests and those of women in the interests of their families.

It is wasteful to go without that rest and leisure that are necessary for efficiency

When the hours and the general conditions of labour are such as to cause great wear-and-tear of body or mind or both, and to lead to a low standard of living; when there has been a want of that leisure, rest and repose, which is one of the necessaries for efficiency, then the labour has been extravagant from the point of view of society at large, just as it would be extravagant on the part of the individual capitalist to keep his horses or slaves overworked or underfed. In such a case a moderate diminution of the hours of labour would diminish the national dividend only temporarily; for as soon as the improved standard of life had had time to have its full effect on the efficiency of the workers, their increased energy, intelligence and force of character would enable them to do as much as before in less time; and thus, even from the point of view of material production, there would be no more ultimate loss than is involved by sending a sick worker into hospital to get his strength renovated And, since material wealth exists for the sake of man, and not man for the sake of material wealth, the fact that inefficient and stunted human lives had been replaced by more efficient and fuller lives would be a gain of a higher order than any temporary material loss that might have been occasioned on the way. This argument assumes that the new rest and leisure raises

The gain of a diminution of labour in trades in which there is an injurious strain

provided the rest

[1] Mr Gunton's suggestive writings on the causes that govern wages seem to be somewhat impaired by a lax use of the phrases "Standard of Comfort" and "Cost of Production of Labour."

BOOK VI. CH XII

and leisure are turned to good account

the standard of life. And such a result is almost certain to follow in the extreme cases of overwork which we have been now considering; for in them a mere lessening of tension is a necessary condition for taking the first step upwards.

Exceptional conditions of the lowest grade of workers

This brings us to consider the lowest grade of honest workers. Few of them work very hard; but they have little stamina, and many of them are so overstrained that they might probably, after a time, do as much in a shorter day as they now do in a long one. Moreover they are the one class of workers, whose wages might be raised considerably at the expense of other classes by a mere diminution in the supply of their labour. Some of them indeed are in occupations that are closely pressed by the competition of skilled workers using machinery; and their wages are controlled by the law of substitution. But many of them do work for which no substitute can be found; they might raise the price of their labour considerably by stinting its supply; and they might have been able to raise it a very great deal in this way, were not any rise sure to bring into their occupation other workers of their own grade from occupations in which wages are controlled by the law of substitution[1].

In some trades shorter hours combined with double shifts would be an almost unmixed benefit to all concerned.

§ 15. Again there are some branches of industry which at present turn to account expensive plant during only ten hours a day; and in which the gradual introduction of two shifts of eight hours would be an unmixed gain. The change would need to be introduced gradually; for there is not enough skilled labour in existence to allow such a plan to be adopted at once in all the workshops and factories for which it is suited But some kinds of machinery, when worn out or antiquated, might be replaced on a smaller scale; and, on the other hand, much new machinery that cannot be profitably introduced for a ten hours' day, would be introduced for a sixteen hours' day; and when once introduced it would be improved on Thus the arts of production would progress more rapidly; the national dividend would increase; working men would be able to earn higher wages without tempting capital to migrate to countries where wages were lower, and all classes of society would reap benefit from the change.

[1] See the end of Book VI Ch. III.

The importance of this consideration is more apparent every year, since the growing expensiveness of machinery, and the quickness with which it is rendered obsolete, are constantly increasing the wastefulness of keeping the untiring iron and steel resting in idleness during sixteen hours out of the twenty-four. In any country, such a change would increase the net produce, and therefore the wages of each worker; because much less than before would have to be deducted from his total output on account of charges for machinery, plant, factory-rent, &c. But the Anglo-Saxon artisans, unsurpassed in accuracy of touch, and surpassing all in sustained energy, would more than any others increase their net produce, if they would keep their machinery going at its full speed for sixteen hours a day, even though they themselves worked only eight[1].

It must however be remembered that this particular plea for a reduction of the hours of labour applies only to those trades which use, or can use, expensive plant, and that in some cases, as for instance in some mines and some branches of railway work, the system of shifts is already applied so as to keep the plant almost constantly at work.

But in many trades a diminution of the hours of

§ 16 There remain therefore many trades in which a reduction of the hours of labour would certainly lessen the output in the immediate present, and would not certainly bring about at all quickly any such increase of efficiency as would

[1] Double shifts are used more on the Continent than in England But they have not a fair trial there, for the hours of labour are so long that double shifts involve work nearly all the night through, and night work is never so good as day work, partly because those who work at night do not rest perfectly during the day. No doubt certain practical objections can be urged against the plan, for instance, a machine is not so well cared for when two men share the responsibility of keeping it in order, as when one man has the whole management of it, and there is sometimes a difficulty about fixing responsibility for imperfections in the work done, but these difficulties can be in a great measure overcome by putting the machine and the work in charge of two partners. Again, there would be a little difficulty in readjusting the office arrangements to suit a day of sixteen hours. But employers and their foremen do not regard these difficulties as insuperable; and experience shews that workmen soon overcome the repugnance which they feel at first to double shifts One set might end its work at noon, and the other begin then, or what would perhaps be better, one shift might work, say, from 5 a.m. to 10 a m and from 1 30 p.m. to 4·30 p m, the second set working from 10 15 a.m. to 1 15 p m and from 4 45 p.m to 9.45 p.m., the two sets might change places at the end of each week or month

BOOK VI. CH. XII.

labour would lessen production.

raise the average work done per head up to the old level. In such cases the change would diminish the national dividend; and the greater part of the resulting material loss would fall on the workers whose hours of labour were diminished. It is true that in some trades a scarcity of labour would raise its price for a good long while at the expense of the rest of the community. But as a rule a rise in the real price of labour would cause a diminished demand for the product, partly through the increased use of substitutes; and would also cause an inrush of new labour from less favoured trades.

Origin of the opinion that a general lessening of the hours of labour would raise wages.

This leads us to consider the origin of the common belief that a reduction of the hours of labour would raise wages generally by merely making labour scarce, and independently of any effect it might have in keeping machinery longer at work and therefore making it more efficient, or in preventing people from being stunted and prematurely worn out by excessive work. This opinion is an instance of those misunderstandings as to the ways in which a rise in the standard of comfort can raise wages, to which we referred a little while back.

The fallacy that it would cause a permanent increase in the demand for labour

§ **17.** It appears to rest on two fallacies The first of these is that the immediate and permanent effects of a change will be the same. People see that when there are competent men waiting for work outside the offices of a tramway company, those already at work think more of keeping their posts than of striving for a rise of wages: and that if these men were away, the employers could not resist a demand for higher wages. They dwell on the fact that, if tramway men work short hours, and there is no diminution in the number of miles run by the cars on existing lines, then more men must be employed probably at higher wages per hour; and possibly at higher wages per day But they overlook other consequences, which are more important, though more remote, viz. that tramway extensions will be checked; and that fewer men will be employed in the future in making and in working tramways; that many workpeople and others will walk into town, who might have ridden; and many will live closely packed in the cities who might have had gardens and fresher air in the suburbs. If it were true that the aggregate amount of wages could be increased by causing every person to work one-fifth less than now, then a diminution of the population by one-fifth would raise aggregate wages, and therefore would increase average wages by more than a fifth—a proposition which goes beyond the doctrine of extreme Malthusians.

and that there is a fixed Work-Fund

The source of the error in this argument lies in the assumption that there is a fixed *Work-Fund*, a certain amount of work which has to be done, whatever the price of labour. On the contrary, the demand for work comes from the national dividend, that is, it comes from work: the less work there is of one kind, the less demand there is for work of other kinds; and if labour were scarce, fewer enterprises would be undertaken. Again, the constancy of employment depends on the organization of industry and trade, and on the success with which those who arrange supply are able to forecast coming movements of demand and of price, and to adjust their actions accordingly. But this would not be better done with a short day's work than with a long one; and indeed the adoption of a short day, not accompanied by double shifts, would discourage the use of that expensive plant, the presence of which makes employers very unwilling to close their works; and it would therefore probably tend, not to lessen, but to increase the inconstancy of employment.

It would be at least as likely to increase as to diminish the inconstancy of employment

§ **18**. The second fallacy is allied to the first. It is that all trades will gain by the general adoption of a mode of action which has been proved to enable one trade, under certain conditions, to gain at the expense of others. It is undoubtedly true that, if they could exclude external competition, plasterers or shoemakers would have a fair chance of raising their wages by a mere diminution of the amount of work done by each. But these gains can be got only at the cost of a greater aggregate loss to other sharers in the national dividend[1]. It is a fact—and, so far as it goes, an important fact—that some of these sharers will not belong to the working classes; part of the loss will certainly fall on employers and capitalists whose personal and material capital is sunk in building or shoemaking, and part on the well-to-do

The fallacy of arguing that all trades can gain by making their labour scarce

[1] See Book v. Ch. vi § 2, and Book vi. Ch. ii. §§ 4, 5.

BOOK VI. CH XII

users or consumers of houses or shoes. But a part of the loss will fall on the working classes as users or consumers of houses or shoes; and part of the loss resulting from the plasterers' gain will fall on bricklayers, carpenters, &c., and a little of it on brickmakers, seamen employed in importing wood for building, and others.

One trade can sometimes do so, but a general reduction of output would much diminish the national dividend, and the wage-receivers must bear a large part of the loss

If then all workers reduce their output there will be a great loss of national dividend; capitalists and employers may indeed bear a large share of the burden; but they are sure not to bear all. For—to say nothing of the chance that they may emigrate and take or send their free capital for investment abroad—a great and general diminution of earnings of management and of interest on capital, would lead on the one hand to some substitution of the higher grades of labour for the lower throughout the whole continuous descending scale of employment[1], and perhaps to some falling-off in the energy and assiduity of the leading minds of industry; while, on the other hand, it would check the saving of capital[2]. And in so far as it had this last result it would diminish that abundance of capital relatively to labour which alone would enable labour to throw on capital a part of its share of the loss of the national dividend[3]

[1] See Book VI Ch VII. §§ 2—4.

[2] See Book IV. Ch. VII. § 9, and Book VI. Ch. VI. § 11.

[3] To take an illustration, let us suppose that shoemakers and hatters are in the same grade, working equal hours, and receiving equal wages, before and after a general reduction in the hours of labour. Then both before and after the change, the hatter could buy, with a month's wages, as many shoes as were the Net product of the shoemaker's work for a month (see Book VI. Ch II § 7). If the shoemaker worked less hours than before, and in consequence did less work, the Net product of his labour for a month would have diminished, unless either by a system of working double shifts the employer and his capital had earned profits on two sets of workers, or his profits could be cut down by the full amount of the diminution in output. The last supposition is inconsistent with what we know of the causes which govern the supply of capital and business power. And therefore the hatter's wages would go less far than before in buying shoes; and so all round for other trades

A small part of the loss might be thrown on rent. but it is not necessary to allow for much under this head. Also our argument assumed, what would be sure to be approximately true, that, taken one with another, the values relatively to shoes of the things that the employer had to buy remain unchanged.

It may be well to say here dogmatically, and in anticipation of the results of the next volume, that the influence of foreign trade competition in this connection can be proved to be different from what it at first sight appears. An

Caution against crude arguments from facts: the fallacy *post hoc ergo propter hoc.*

But we must be careful not to confuse the two questions whether a cause tends to produce a certain effect and whether that cause is sure to be followed by that effect. Opening the sluice of a reservoir tends to lower the level of the water in it; but if meanwhile larger supplies of water are flowing in at the other end, the opening of the sluice may be followed by a rising of the level of the water in the cistern. And so although a shortening of the hours of labour would tend to diminish output in those trades which are not already overworked, and in which there is no room for double shifts; yet it might very likely be accompanied by an increase of production arising from the general progress of wealth and knowledge[1]

international agreement to diminish simultaneously the hours of labour in all trades would indeed have the important effect of preventing the workers in any one country from having to fear that capital would leave it for others, and further a reduction in the hours of labour whether by a given percentage, or down to a given minimum, would diminish output in unequal proportions in different trades, and would therefore disturb relative values and relative wages; and these disturbances would be aggravated by competition from a foreign country that was not passing through the same changes. If however the hours of labour could be reduced, not on any rigid plan, but in such a way as not to disturb relative values, the change would not directly affect the course of foreign trade, whether other nations adopted the movement or not. For if it just, but only just, paid to export cutlery and import in exchange sewing machines before the change; then after the change, relative values remaining unaltered, it would still pay, and only just pay, to do the same International agreements are therefore likely to go less far, than at first sight appears, towards lessening the evils of a general diminution of output

[1] We must distrust all attempts to solve the question, whether a reduction of the hours of labour reduces production and wages, by a simple appeal to facts. For whether we watch the statistics of wages and production immediately after the change or for a long period following it, the facts which we observe are likely to be due chiefly to causes other than that which we are wishing to study Firstly, the effects which immediately follow are likely to be misleading for many reasons. If the reduction was made as a result of a successful strike, the chances are that the occasion chosen for the strike was one when the strategical position of the workmen was good, and when the general conditions of trade would have enabled them to obtain a rise of wages if there had been no change in the hours of labour and therefore the immediate effects of the change on wages are likely to appear more favourable than they really were. And again many employers, having entered into contracts which they are bound to fulfil, may for the time offer higher wages for a short day than before for a long day but this is a result of the suddenness of the change, and is a mere flash in the pan On the other hand, if men have been overworked, the shortening of the hours of labour will not at once make them strong the physical and moral improvement of the condition of the workers, with its consequent increase of efficiency and therefore of wages, cannot show itself at once.

General conclusion as to the hours of labour

§ 19. All this tends to show that a general reduction of the hours of labour is likely to cause a little net material loss and much moral good, that it is not adapted for treatment by a rigid cast-iron system, and that the conditions of each class of trades must be studied separately.

Well-spent leisure would be of more real worth than a great part of our material enjoyments.

Perhaps £100,000,000 annually are spent even by the working classes, and £400,000,000 by the rest of the population of England in ways that do little or nothing towards making life nobler or truly happier. And it would certainly be well that all should work less, if we could secure that the new leisure be spent well, and the consequent loss of material income be met exclusively by the abandonment by all classes of the least worthy methods of consumption. But this result is not easy to be attained: for human nature changes slowly, and in nothing more slowly than in the hard task of learning to use leisure well. In every age, in every nation, and in every rank of society, those who have known how to work well have been far more numerous than those who have known how to use leisure well; but on the other hand it is only through freedom to use leisure as they will, that people can learn to use leisure well: and it is true that no class of

And secondly, the statistics of production and wages several years after the reduction of hours are likely to reflect changes in the prosperity of the country, or of the trade in question, or of the methods of production, or lastly of the purchasing power of money and it may be as difficult to isolate the effects of reduction of the hours of labour as it is to isolate the effects on the waves of a noisy sea caused by throwing a stone among them

For instance, when we look at the history of the introduction of the eight hours' day in Australia we find great fluctuations in the prosperity of the mines and the supply of gold, in the prosperity of the sheep farms and the price of wool, in the borrowing from old countries capital with which to employ Australian labour to build railways, &c., in immigration, and in commercial credit. And all these have been such powerful causes of change in the condition of the Australian working man as to completely overlay and hide from view the effects of a reduction of the hours of labour from 10 gross (8¾ net after deducting meal times) to 8 net Money wages in Australia are much lower than they were before the hours were shortened; and, though it may be true that the purchasing power of money has increased, so that real wages have not fallen, yet there seems no doubt that the real wages of labour in Australia are not nearly as much above those in England as they were before the reduction in the hours of labour and it has not been proved that they are not lower than they would have been if that change had not taken place. And it is not certain that the recent commercial troubles in Australia have not been in part caused by over sanguine estimates of the economic efficiency of short hours of labour

workers who are devoid of leisure can have much self-respect and become full citizens: some time free from fatigue and free from work are necessary conditions of a high Standard of Life[1].

A person can seldom exert himself to the utmost for more than eight hours a day with advantage to anyone; but he may do light work for longer, and he may be "on duty," ready to act when called on, for much longer. And since adults, whose habits are already formed, are not likely to adapt themselves quickly to long hours of leisure, it would seem more conducive to the well-being of the nation as a whole, to take measures for increasing the material means of a noble and refined life for all classes, and especially the poorest, than to secure a sudden and very great diminution in the hours of labour of those who are not now weighed down by their work.

Leisure for the young.

In this, as in all similar cases, it is the young whose faculties and activities are of the highest importance both to the moralist and the economist. The most imperative duty of this generation is to provide for the young the best education for the work they have to do as producers and as men or women, together with long-continued freedom from mechanical toil, and abundant leisure for school and for such kinds of play as strengthen and develop the character

The interest of the rising generation in the hours of labour of their parents.

And, even if we took account only of the injury done to the rising generation by living in homes in which the father and the mother lead joyless lives, it would be in the interest of society to afford them some relief Able workers and good citizens are not likely to come from homes from which the mother is absent during a great part of the day, nor from homes to which the father seldom returns till his children are asleep. And therefore not only the individuals immediately concerned, but society as a whole, has a direct interest in the curtailment of extravagantly long hours of duty away from home even for mineral-train-guards and others, whose work is not in itself very hard.

And now we must conclude this part of our study of Distribution and Exchange. We have reached very few prac-

[1] This is well argued by Mr Sidney Webb and Mr Harold Cox in their plea for *An Eight Hours' Day*

BOOK VI. CH XII

tical conclusions; because it is generally necessary to look at the whole of the economic, to say nothing of the moral and other aspects of a practical problem before attempting to deal with it at all: and in real life nearly every economic issue depends, more or less directly, on some complex actions and reactions of credit, of foreign trade, and of modern developments of combination and monopoly. But the ground which we have already traversed is, in some respects, the most difficult of the whole province of economics; and it commands, and, so to speak, holds the key of, that which lies yet before us.

APPENDIX

OF MATHEMATICAL NOTES.

NOTE I. (p 169). The law of diminution of marginal utility may be expressed thus —If u be the total utility of an amount x of a commodity to a given person at a given time, then marginal utility is measured by $\frac{du}{dx}$; and, subject to the qualifications mentioned in the text, $\frac{d^2u}{dx^2}$ is always negative.

NOTE II. (p. 171) If m is the amount of money or general purchasing power at a person's disposal at any time, and μ represents its total utility to him, then $\frac{d\mu}{dm}$ represents the marginal utility of money to him.

If p is the price which he is just willing to pay for an amount x of the commodity which gives him a total pleasure u, then

$$\frac{d\mu}{dm}\Delta p = \Delta u\,; \text{ and } \frac{d\mu}{dm}\frac{dp}{dx} = \frac{du}{dx}.$$

If p' is the price which he is just willing to pay for an amount x' of another commodity, which affords him a total pleasure u', then

$$\frac{d\mu}{dm}\cdot\frac{dp'}{dx'} = \frac{du'}{dx'},$$

and therefore
$$\frac{dp}{dx}\cdot\frac{dp'}{dx'} = \frac{du}{dx}:\frac{du'}{dx'}.$$

(Compare Jevons' chapter on the *Theory of Exchange*, p 151)

Every increase in his means diminishes the marginal utility of money to him, that is, $\frac{d^2\mu}{dm^2}$ is always negative.

Therefore, the marginal utility to him of an amount x of a commodity, $\frac{du}{dx}$, remaining unchanged, an increase in his means increases $\frac{du}{dx} - \frac{d\mu}{dm}$; i e. it increases $\frac{dp}{dx}$, that is, the rate at which he is willing to pay for further supplies of it Treating u as variable, that is to say, allowing for possible variations in the person's liking for the commodity in question, we may regard $\frac{dp}{dx}$ as a function or m, u, and x; and then we have $\frac{d^2p}{dm\,dx}$ always positive. Of course $\frac{d^2p}{du\,dx}$ is always positive.

NOTE III. (p. 179). Let P, P' be consecutive points on the demand curve, let PRM be drawn perpendicular to Ox, and let PP' cut Ox and Oy in T and t respectively; so that $P'R$ is that increment in the amount demanded which corresponds to a diminution PR in the price per unit of the commodity.

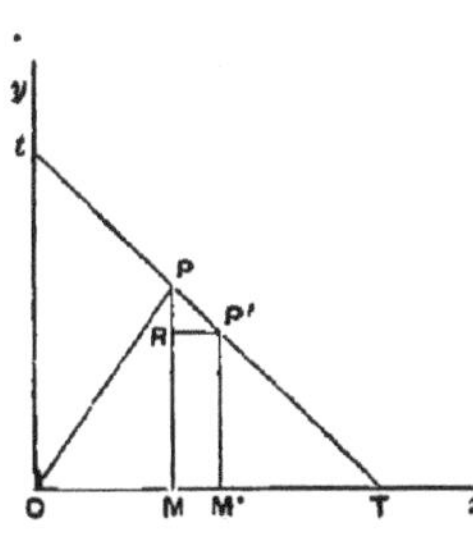

Then the elasticity of demand at P is measured by

$$\frac{P'R}{OM} \div \frac{PR}{PM}, \text{ i.e. by } \frac{P'R}{PR} \times \frac{PM}{OM};$$

$$\text{i e by } \frac{TM}{PM} \times \frac{PM}{OM},$$

$$\text{i e. by } \frac{TM}{OM} \text{ or by } \frac{PT}{Pt}$$

When the distance between P and P' is diminished indefinitely, PP' becomes the tangent; and thus the proposition is proved

It is obvious *à priori* that the measure of elasticity cannot be altered by altering relatively to one another the scales on which distances parallel to Ox and Oy are measured But a geometrical proof of this result can be got easily by the method of projections: while analytically it is clear that $\frac{dx}{x} \div \frac{-dy}{y}$, which is the analytical expression for the measure of elasticity, does not change its value if the curve $y=f(x)$ be drawn to new scales, so that its equation becomes $qy=f(px)$; where p and q are constants.

If the elasticity of demand be equal to unity for all prices of the commodity, any fall in price will cause a proportionate increase in the amount bought, and therefore will make no change in the total outlay which purchasers make for the commodity. Such a demand may therefore be called a *Constant Outlay demand.* The curve which represents it, a *Constant Outlay curve,* as it may be called, is a rectangular hyperbola with Ox and Oy as asymptotes; and a series of such curves are represented by the dotted curves in the following figure.

There is some advantage in accustoming the eye to the shape of these curves; so that when looking at a demand curve one can tell at once whether it is inclined to the vertical at any point at a greater or less angle than the part of a constant outlay curve, which would pass through that point. Greater accuracy may be obtained by tracing constant outlay curves on thin paper, and then laying the paper over the demand curve. By this means it may, for instance, be seen at once that the demand curve in the figure represents at each of the points A, B, C and D an elasticity about equal to one. between A and B, and again between C and D, it represents an elasticity greater than one; while between B and C it represents an elasticity less than one It will be found that practice of this kind

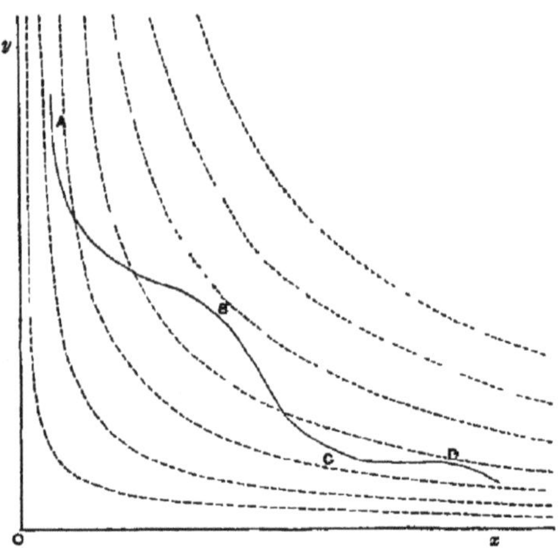

makes it easy to detect the nature of the assumptions with regard to the character of the demand for a commodity, which are implicitly made in drawing a demand curve of any particular shape; and is a safeguard against the unconscious introduction of improbable assumptions.

The general equation to demand-curves representing at every point an elasticity equal to n is $\frac{dx}{x}+n\frac{dy}{y}=0$, i e. $xy^n=C$.

It is worth noting that in such a curve $\frac{dx}{dy}=-\frac{C}{y^{n+1}}$; that is, the proportion in which the amount demanded increases in consequence of a small fall in the price varies inversely as the $(n+1)^{th}$ power of the price. In the case of the constant outlay curves it varies inversely as the square of the price, or, which is the same thing in this case, directly as the square of the amount.

NOTE IV (p. 186). The lapse of time being measured downwards along Oy; and the amounts, of which record is being made, being measured by distances from Oy; then P' and P being adjacent points on the curve which traces the growth of the amount, the rate of increase in a small unit of time $N'N$ is

$$\frac{PH}{P'N'}=\frac{PH}{P'H}\cdot\frac{P'H}{P'N'}=\frac{PN}{Nt}\cdot\frac{P'H}{P'N'}=\frac{P'H}{Nt},$$

since PN and $P'N'$ are equal in the limit.

If we take a year as the unit of time we find the annual rate of increase represented by the inverse of the number of years in Nt.

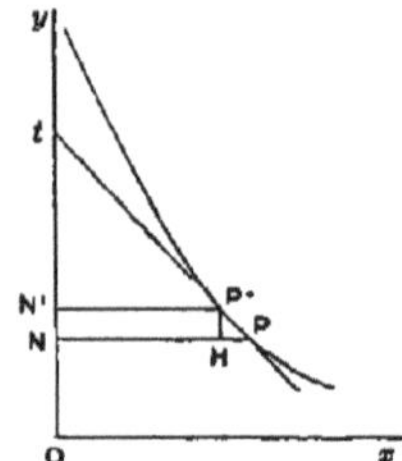

The rate of increase would be constant for all points of the curve if Nt were constant and always $=a$, that is, if $-x\frac{dy}{dx}=a$ for all values of x; that is, if the equation to the curve were $y=-a\log x$.

NOTE V. (p 199). We have seen in the text that the rate at which future pleasures are discounted varies greatly from one individual to another. Let r be the rate of interest per annum, which must be added to a present pleasure in order to make it just balance a future pleasure, that will be of equal amount to its recipient, when it comes; then r may be 50 or even 200 per cent. to one person, while for his neighbour it is a negative quantity. Moreover some pleasures are more urgent than others; and it is conceivable even that a person may discount future pleasures in an irregular random way; he may be almost as willing to postpone a pleasure for two years as for one; or, on the other hand, he may object very strongly indeed to a long postponement, but scarcely at all to a short one. There is some difference of opinion as to whether such irregularities are frequent; and the question cannot easily be decided; for since the estimate of a pleasure is purely subjective, it would be difficult to detect them if they did occur. In a case in which there are no such irregularities, the rate of discount will be the same for each element of time; or, to state the same thing in other words, it will obey the Exponential Law. And if h be the future amount of a pleasure of which the probability is p, and which will occur, if at all, at time t, and if $R=1+r$, then the present value of the pleasure is phR^{-t}. It must, however, be borne in mind that this result belongs to Hedonics, and not properly to Economics.

Arguing still on the same hypothesis we may say that, if ϖ be the probability that a person will derive an element of happiness, Δh, from the possession of, say, a piano in the element of time Δt, then the present value of the piano to him is $\int_0^T \varpi R^{-t}\frac{dh}{dt}\,dt$. If we are to include all the happiness that results from the event at whatever distance of time we must take $T=\infty$. If the source of pleasure is in Bentham's phrase "impure," $\frac{dh}{dt}$ will probably be negative for some values of t; and of course the whole value of the integral may be negative.

NOTE VI. (p. 208). If y be the price at which an amount x of a commodity can find purchasers in a given market, and $y=f(x)$ be the equation to the demand-curve, then the total utility of the commodity is measured by $\int_0^a f(x)\,dx$, where a is the amount consumed.

If however an amount b of the commodity is necessary for existence, $f(x)$ will be infinite, or at least indefinitely great, for values of x less than b. We must therefore take life for granted, and estimate separately the total utility of that part of the supply of the commodity which is in excess of absolute necessaries: it is of course $\int_b^a f(x)\,dx$

If there are several commodities which will satisfy the same imperative want, as e g. water and milk, either of which will quench thirst, we shall find that, under the ordinary conditions of life, no great error is introduced by adopting the simple plan of assuming that the necessary supply comes exclusively from that one which is cheapest.

It should be noted that, in the discussion of consumers' rent, we assume that the marginal utility of money to the individual purchaser is the same throughout. Strictly speaking we ought to take account of the fact that if he spent less on tea, the marginal utility of money to him would be less than it is, and he would get an element of consumers' rent from buying other things at prices which now yield him no such rent. But these changes of consumers' rent (being of the second order of smallness) may be neglected, on the assumption, which underlies our whole reasoning, that his expenditure on any one thing, as, for instance, tea, is only a small part of his whole expenditure (Compare Book v Ch. II. § 3) If, for any reason it be desirable to take account of the influence which his expenditure on tea exerts on the value of money to him, it is only necessary to multiply $f(x)$, within the integral given above by that function of $xf(x)$ (i.e. of the amount which he has already spent on tea) which represents the marginal utility to him of money when his stock of it has been diminished by that amount.

NOTE VII (p. 210) Thus if a_1, a_2, a_3 be the amounts consumed of the several commodities of which b_1, b_2, b_3 are necessary for existence, if $y=f_1(x)$, $y=f_2(x)$, $y=f_3(x)$ be the equations to their demand curves and if we may neglect all inequalities in the distribution of wealth; then the total utility of income, subsistence being taken for granted, might be represented by $\Sigma \int_b^a f(x)\,dx$, if we could find a plan for grouping together in one common demand curve all those things which satisfy the same wants, and are rivals; and also for every group of things of which the services are complementary (see Book v Ch. VI.). But we cannot do this: and therefore the formula remains a mere general expression, having no practical application See footnote on pp 207, 8; also the latter part of Note XIV.

NOTE VIII. (p. 211). If y be the happiness which a person derives from an income x; and if, after Bernoulli, we assume that the increased happiness which he derives from the addition of one per cent to his income is the same whatever his income be, we have $x\frac{dy}{dx}=K$, and $\therefore$ $y=K\log x+C$ when K and C are constants

Let a be the income sufficient to purchase the necessaries of life, so defined that the total pleasure derived from life with an income less than a is a negative quantity; then our equation becomes $y=K\log\frac{x}{a}$. Of course both K and a vary with the temperament, the health, the habits, and the social surroundings of each individual. Laplace gives to x the name *fortune physique*, and to y the name *fortune morale.*

Bernoulli himself seems to have thought of x and a as representing certain amounts of property rather than of income, but we cannot estimate the property necessary for life without some understanding as to the length of time during which it is to support life, that is, without really treating it as income.

Perhaps the guess which has attracted most attention after Bernoulli's is Cramer's suggestion that the pleasure afforded by wealth may be taken to vary as the square root of its amount.

NOTE IX. (p. 211). The argument that fair gambling is an economic blunder is generally based on Bernoulli's or some other definite hypothesis. But it requires no further assumption than that firstly the pleasure of gambling may be neglected, and secondly $\phi''(x)$ is negative for all values of x, where $\phi(x)$ is the pleasure derived from wealth equal to x.

For suppose that the chance that a particular event will happen is p, and a man makes a fair bet of py against $(1-p)y$ that it will happen. By so doing he changes his expectation of happiness from

$$\phi(x) \text{ to } p\phi\{x+(1-p)y\}+(1-p)\phi(x-py).$$

This when expanded by Taylor's Theorem becomes

$$\phi(x)+\tfrac{1}{2}p(1-p)^2y^2\phi''\{x+\theta(1-p)y\}+\tfrac{1}{2}p^2(1-p)y^2\phi''(x-\Theta py);$$

assuming $\phi''(x)$ to be negative for all values of x, this is always less than $\phi(x)$

It is true that this loss of probable happiness need not be greater than the pleasure derived from the excitement of gambling, and we are then thrown back upon the induction that pleasures of gambling are in Bentham's phrase "impure," since experience shows that they are likely to engender a restless, feverish character, unsuited for steady work as well as for the higher and more solid pleasures of life

NOTE X. (p. 217). Following on the same lines as in Note I., let us take v to represent the disutility or discommodity of an amount of labour l, then $\frac{dv}{dl}$ measures the marginal disutility of labour; and, subject to the qualifications mentioned in the text, $\frac{d^2v}{dl^2}$ is positive.

Let m be the amount of money or general purchasing power at a person's disposal, μ its total utility to him, and therefore $\frac{d\mu}{dm}$ its marginal utility. Thus if Δw be the wages that must be paid him to induce him to do labour Δl, then $\Delta w\frac{d\mu}{dm}=\Delta v$, and $\frac{dw}{dl}\cdot\frac{d\mu}{dm}=\frac{dv}{dl}$.

If we assume that his dislike to labour is not a fixed, but a fluctuating quantity, we may regard $\frac{dw}{dl}$ as a function of m, v, and l, and then both $\frac{d^2w}{dm\,dl}$, $\frac{d^2w}{dv\,dl}$ are always positive

NOTE XI. (p. 306). If members of any species of bird begin to adopt aquatic habits, every increase in the webs between their toes—whether coming about gradually by the operation of natural selection, or suddenly as a sport, or (as a minority of biologists still think) partly from the inherited effects of use,—will cause them to find their advantage more in aquatic life, and will make their chance of leaving offspring depend more on the increase of the web.

So that, if $f(t)$ be the average area of the web at time t, then the rate of increase of the web increases (within certain limits) with every increase in the web, and therefore $f''(t)$ is positive. Now we know by Taylor's Theorem that

$$f(t+h)=f(t)+hf'(t)+\frac{h^2}{1\cdot 2}f''(t+\theta h);$$

and if h be large, so that h^2 is very large, then $f(t+h)$ will be much greater than $f(t)$ even though $f'(t)$ be small and $f''(t)$ is never large. There is more than a superficial connection between the advance made by the applications of the differential calculus to physics at the end of the last century and the beginning of this, and the rise of the theory of evolution. In sociology as well as in biology we are learning to watch the accumulated effects of forces which, though weak at first, get greater strength from the growth of their own effects; and the universal form, of which every such fact is a special embodiment, is Taylor's Theorem, or, if the action of more than one cause at a time is to be taken account of, the corresponding expression of a function of several variables.

NOTE XII. (p. 408). If, as in Note X., v be the discommodity of the amount of labour which a person has to exert in order to obtain an amount x of a commodity from which he derives a pleasure u, then the pleasure of having further supplies will be equal to the pain of getting them when $\frac{du}{dx}=\frac{dv}{dx}$.

If the pain of labour be regarded as a negative pleasure; and we write $U\equiv -v$, then $\frac{du}{dx}+\frac{dU}{dx}=0$, i.e. $u+U=$ a maximum at the point at which his labour ceases.

NOTE XII *bis* (p. 415). In an article in the *Giornale degli Economisti* for February, 1891, Prof. Edgeworth draws the adjoining diagram to represent the cases of barter of apples for nuts described on pp. 395–6. Apples are measured along Ox, and nuts along Oy; $Op=4$, $pa=40$; and a represents the termination of the first bargain in which 4 apples have been exchanged for 40 nuts, in the case in which A gets the advantage at starting: b represents the second, and c the final stage of that case. On the other hand, a' represents the first, and b', c', d' the second, third, and final stages of the set of bargains in which B gets the advantage at starting. QP, the locus on which c and d' must both necessarily lie, is called by Prof. Edgeworth the *Contract Curve*.

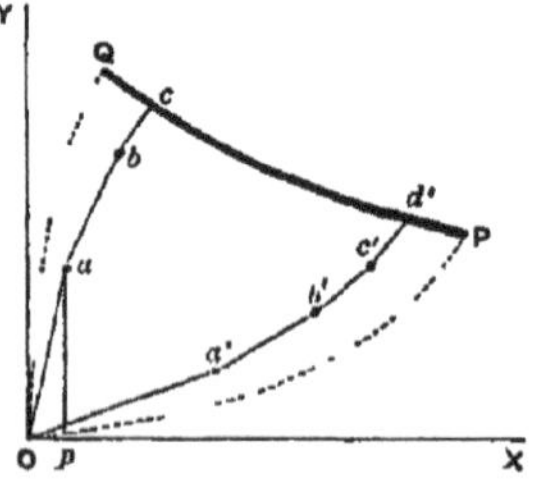

Following a method adopted in his *Mathematical Psychics* (1881), he takes U to represent the total utility to A of apples and nuts when he has given up x apples and received y nuts, V the total utility to B of apples and nuts when he has received x apples and given up y nuts. If an additional Δx apples are exchanged for Δy nuts, the exchange will be indifferent to A if

$$\frac{dU}{dx}\Delta x+\frac{dU}{dy}\Delta y=0\,;$$

and it will be indifferent to B if $\frac{dV}{dx}\Delta x+\frac{dV}{dy}\Delta y=0$. These, therefore, are the equations to the indifference curves OP and OQ of the figure respectively; and the contract curve which is the locus of points at which the terms of exchange that are indifferent to A are also indifferent to B has the elegant equation $\frac{dU}{dx}\div\frac{dU}{dy}=\frac{dV}{dx}\div\frac{dV}{dy}$.

If the marginal utility of nuts be constant for A and also for B, $\frac{dU}{dy}$ and $\frac{dV}{dy}$ become constant; U becomes $\Phi(a-x)+\alpha y$, and V becomes $\Psi(a-x)+\beta y$; and the contract curve becomes $F(x)=0$; or $x=C$; that is, it is a straight line parallel to Oy, and the value of $\Delta y \quad \Delta x$ given by either of the indifference curves, a function of C; thus showing that by whatever route the barter may have started, equilibrium will have been found at a point at which C apples have been exchanged, and the final rate of exchange is a function of C; that is, it is a constant also. This last application of Prof. Edgeworth's mathematical version of the theory of barter, to confirm the results reached in the text, was first made by Mr Berry, and is published in the *Giornale degli Economisti* for June, 1891

Prof Edgeworth's plan of representing U and V as general functions of x and y has great attractions to the mathematician; but it seems less adapted to express the everyday facts of economic life than that of regarding, as Jevons did, the marginal utilities of apples as functions of x simply. In that case, if A had no nuts at starting, as is assumed in the particular case under discussion, U takes the form

$$\int_0^x \phi_1(a-x)\,dx+\int_0^y \psi_1(y)\,dy\,;$$

similarly for V. And then the equation to the contract curve is of the form

$$\phi_1(a-x)\div\psi_1(y)=\phi_2(x)\div\psi_2(b-y)\,,$$

which is one of the Equations of Exchange in Jevons's *Theory*, 2nd Edition, p 108

NOTE XIII. (p. 430). Using the same notation as in Note V, let us take our starting-point as regards time at the date of beginning to build the house, and let T' be the time occupied in building it. Then the present value of the pleasures, which he expects to derive from the house, is

$$H=\int_{T'}^{T}\varpi R^{-t}\frac{dh}{dt}\,dt.$$

Let Δv be the element of effort that will be incurred by him in building the house in the interval of time Δt (between the time t and the time $t+\Delta t$), then the present value of the aggregate of effort is

$$V=\int_0^{T'} R^{-t}\frac{dv}{dt}\,dt.$$

If there is any uncertainty as to the labour that will be required, every possible element must be counted in, multiplied by the probability, ϖ', of its being required; and then V becomes $\int_0^{T'} \varpi' R^{-t} \frac{dv}{dt} dt$.

If we transfer the starting-point to the date of the completion of the house, we have

$$H = \int_0^{T_1} \varpi R^{-t} \frac{dh}{dt} dt \text{ and } V = \int_{-T'}^{0} \varpi' R^t \frac{dv}{dt} dt,$$

where $T_1 = T - T'$; and this starting-point, though perhaps the less natural from the mathematical point of view, is the more natural from the point of view of ordinary business. Adopting it, we see V as the aggregate of estimated pains incurred, each bearing on its back, as it were, the accumulated burden of the waitings between the time of its being incurred and the time when it begins to bear fruit.

Jevons's discussion of the investment of capital is somewhat injured by the unnecessary assumption that the function representing it is an expression of the first order; which is the more remarkable as he had himself, when describing Gossen's work, pointed out the objections to the plan followed by him (and Whewell) of substituting straight lines for the multiform curves that represent the true characters of the variations of economic quantities

NOTE XIV. (p. 430). Let a_1, a_2, a_3 be the several amounts of different kinds of labour, as, for instance, wood-cutting, stone-carrying, earth-digging, &c, on the part of the man in question that would be used in building the house on any given plan, and β, β', β'', &c, the several amounts of accommodation of different kinds such as sitting-rooms, bed-rooms, offices, &c which the house would afford on that plan Then, using V and H as in the previous note, $V, \beta, \beta', \beta''$ are all functions of a_1, a_2, a_3, and H being a function of β, β', β''. is a function also of a_1, a_2, a_3. We have, then, to find the marginal investments of each kind of labour for each kind of use.

$$\frac{dV}{da_1} = \frac{dH}{d\beta}\frac{d\beta}{da_1} = \frac{dH}{d\beta'}\frac{d\beta'}{da_1} = \frac{dH}{d\beta''}\frac{d\beta''}{da_1} = -\ldots$$

$$\frac{dV}{da_2} = \frac{dH}{d\beta}\frac{d\beta}{da_2} = \frac{dH}{d\beta'}\frac{d\beta'}{da_2} = \frac{dH}{d\beta''}\frac{d\beta''}{da_2} = \ .$$

These equations represent a balance of effort and benefit. The real cost to him of a little extra labour spent on cutting timber and working it up is just balanced by the benefit of the extra sitting-room or bed-room accommodation that he could get by so doing. If, however, instead of doing the work himself, he pays carpenters to do it, we must take V to represent, not his total effort, but his total outlay of general purchasing power Then the rate of pay which he is willing to give to carpenters for further labour, his marginal demand price for their labour, is measured by $\frac{dV}{da}$, while $\frac{dH}{d\beta}, \frac{dH}{d\beta'}$ are the money measures to him of the marginal utilities of extra sitting-room and bed-room accommodation respectively, that is, his marginal demand prices for them; and $\frac{d\beta}{da}, \frac{d\beta'}{da}$ are the marginal efficiencies of carpenters' labour in providing those accommodations. The equations then state that the demand price for carpenters' labour tends to be equal to the demand price for extra sitting-room accommodation, and also for extra bed-room accommodation and so on, multiplied in each case by the marginal efficiency of the work of carpenters in providing that extra accommodation, proper units being chosen for each element.

When this statement is generalized, so as to cover all the varied demand in a market for carpenters' labour, it becomes :—the (marginal) demand price for carpenters' labour is the (marginal) efficiency of carpenters' labour in increasing the supply of any product, multiplied by the (marginal) demand price for that product. Or to put the same thing in other words, the wages of a unit of carpenters' labour tends to be equal to the value of such part of any of the products, to producing which their labour contributes, as represents the marginal efficiency of a unit of carpenters' labour with regard to that product; or, to use a phrase, with which we shall be much occupied in Book VI. Ch. I., it tends to be equal to the value of the "net product" of their labour. This proposition is very important and contains within itself the kernel of the demand side of the theory of Distribution

There will be an advantage in developing it with some fulness here, although to do so will partially anticipate later discussions, especially those in the sixth and seventh chapters of Book V. and in the first two chapters of Book VI. and indeed its full significance will hardly be seen until it is read in connection with the last-named chapters

Let us then suppose a master builder to have it in mind to erect certain buildings, and to be considering what different accommodation he shall provide, as, for instance, dwelling-houses, warehouses, factories, and retail shop-room. There will be two classes of questions for him to decide how much accommodation of each kind he shall provide, and by what means he shall provide it. Thus, besides deciding whether to erect villa residences, offering a certain amount of accommodation, he has to decide what agents of production he will use, and in what proportions · whether e.g. he will use tile or slate, how much stone he will use; whether he will use steam power for making mortar etc or only for crane work, and, if he is in a large town, whether he will have his scaffolding put up by men who make that work a speciality or by ordinary labourers, and so on.

Let him then decide to provide an amount β of villa accommodation, an amount β' of warehouse, an amount β'' of factory accommodation, and so on, each of a certain class But, instead of supposing him to hire simply a_1, a_2 . quantities of different kinds of labour, as before, let us class his expenditure under the three heads of (1) wages, (2) prices of raw material, and (3) interest on capital: while the value of his own work and enterprise makes a fourth head.

Thus let x_1, x_2.. be the amounts of different classes of labour, including that of superintendence, which he hires; the amount of each kind of labour being made up of its duration and its intensity.

Let y_1, y_2 be amounts of various kinds of raw materials, which are used up and embodied in the buildings; which may be supposed to be sold freehold. In that case, the pieces of land on which they are severally built are merely particular forms of raw material from the present point of view, which is that of the individual undertaker.

Next let z be the amount of locking up, or appropriation of the employment, of capital for the several purposes. Here we must reckon in all forms of capital reduced to a common money measure, including advances for wages, for the purchase of raw material; also the uses, allowing for wear and tear etc. of his plant of all kinds: his workshops themselves and the ground on which they are built being reckoned on the same footing. The periods, during which the various lockings up run, will vary; but they must be reduced, on a "compound rate," i.e. according to geometrical progression, to a standard unit, say a year

Fourthly, let u represent his own labour, worry, anxiety, wear and tear etc. involved in the several undertakings

In addition, there are several elements, which might have been entered under separate heads, but which we may suppose combined with those already mentioned Thus the allowance to be made for risk may be shared between the last two heads A proper share of the general expenses of working the business ("Supplementary Costs," see p. 434) will be distributed among the four heads of wages, raw materials, interest on the capital value of the organization of the business, (its goodwill etc) regarded as a going concern, and remuneration of the builder's own work, enterprise and anxiety

Under these circumstances V represents his total outlay, and H his total receipts, and his efforts are directed to making $H-V$ a maximum. On this plan, we have equations similar to those already given, viz :—

$$\frac{dV}{dx_1}=\frac{dH}{d\beta}\cdot\frac{d\beta}{dx_1}=\frac{dH}{d\beta'}\cdot\frac{d\beta'}{dx_1}=$$

$$\frac{dV}{dx_2}=\frac{dH}{d\beta}\cdot\frac{d\beta}{dx_2}=\frac{dH}{d\beta'}\cdot\frac{d\beta'}{dx_1}=\ .$$

$$\frac{dV}{dy_1}=\frac{dH}{d\beta}\cdot\frac{d\beta}{dy_1}=\frac{dH}{d\beta'}\ \frac{d\beta'}{dy_1}=$$

$$\frac{dV}{dz}=\frac{dH}{d\beta}\cdot\frac{d\beta}{dz}=\frac{dH}{d\beta'}\cdot\frac{d\beta'}{dz}=$$

$$\frac{dV}{du}=\frac{dH}{d\beta}\cdot\frac{d\beta}{du}=\frac{dH}{d\beta'}\cdot\frac{d\beta'}{du}=\ .\ .$$

That is to say, the marginal outlay which the builder is willing to make for an additional small supply, δx_1, of the first class of labour, viz. $\frac{dV}{dx_1}\delta x_1$ is equal to $\frac{dH}{d\beta}\cdot\frac{d\beta}{dx_1}\delta x_1$; i e. to that increment in his total receipts H, which he will obtain by the increase in the villa accommodation provided by him that will result from the extra small supply of the first class of labour, this will equal a similar sum with regard to warehouse accommodation, and so on. Thus he will have distributed his resources between various uses in such a way that he would gain nothing by diverting any part of any agent of production—labour, raw material, the use of capital, nor his own labour and enterprise from one class of building to another: also he would gain nothing by substituting one agent for another in any branch of his enterprise, nor indeed by any increase or diminution of his use of any agent. From this point of view our equations have a drift very similar to the argument of Book III. Ch. V as to the choice between different uses of the same thing. (Compare one of the most interesting notes (f) attached to Prof. Edgeworth's brilliant address to the British Association in 1889.)

There will be much more to be said, especially in Book VI Ch. I § 8, on the difficulty of interpreting the phrase the "net product" of any agent of production, whether a particular kind of labour or any other agent: but one minor difficulty may be noticed here The builder paid $\frac{dV}{dx_1}\delta x_1$ for the last element of the labour of the first group because that was its net product; and, if directed to building villas, it brought him in $\frac{dH}{d\beta}\frac{d\beta}{dx_1}\delta x_1$, as special receipts Now if p be the price per unit, which he receives for an amount β of villa accommodation, and therefore $p\beta$ the price which he receives for the whole amount β; and if we put for shortness $\Delta\beta$ in place of $\frac{d\beta}{dx_1}\delta x_1$, the increase of villa accommodation due to the additional element of labour δx_1; then the net product we are seeking is not $p\Delta\beta$, but $p\Delta\beta + \beta\Delta p$; where Δp is a negative quantity, and is the fall in demand price caused by the increase in the amount of villa accommodation offered by the builder. We have to make some study of the relative magnitudes of these two elements $p\Delta\beta$ and $\beta\Delta p$.

If the builder monopolized the supply of villas, β would represent the total supply of them: and, if it happened that the elasticity of the demand for them was less than unity, when the amount β was offered, then, by increasing his supply he would diminish his total receipts; and $p\Delta\beta + \beta\Delta p$ would be a negative quantity. But of course he would not have allowed the production to go just up to an amount at which the demand would be thus inelastic. The margin which he chose for his production would certainly be one for which the negative quantity $\beta\Delta p$ is less than $p\Delta\beta$, but not necessarily so much less that it may be neglected in comparison. This is a dominant fact in the theory of monopolies discussed in Book V Chapter XII.

It is dominant also in the case of any producer who has a limited trade connection which he cannot quickly enlarge If his customers have already as much of his wares as they care for, so that the elasticity of their demand is temporarily less than unity, he might lose by putting on an additional man to work for him, even though that man would work for nothing. This fear of temporarily spoiling a man's special market is a leading influence in many problems of value relating to short periods (see Book V. Ch V. VII. XI); and especially in those periods of commercial depression, and in those regulations of trade associations, formal and informal, which we shall have to study in the second volume There is an allied difficulty in the case of commodities of which the expenses of production diminish rapidly with every increase in the amount produced but here the causes that govern the limits of production are so complex that it seems hardly worth while to attempt to translate them into mathematical language See Book V. Ch. XI. and foot-note on p. 584.

When however we are studying the action of an individual undertaker with a view of illustrating the normal action of the causes which govern the general demand for the several agents of production, it seems clear that we should avoid cases of this kind We should leave their peculiar features to be analysed separately in special discussions, and take our normal illustration from a case in which the individual is only one of many who have efficient, if indirect, access to the market If $\beta\Delta p$ be numerically equal to $p\Delta\beta$, where β is the whole production in a large market; and an individual undertaker produced β', a thousandth part of β; then the increased receipt from putting on an additional man is $p\Delta\beta'$ which is the same as $p\Delta\beta$; and the deduction to be made from it is only $\beta'\Delta p$, which is a thousandth part of $\beta\Delta p$ and may be neglected For the purpose therefore of illustrating a part of the general action of the laws of distribution we are justified in speaking of the value of the net product of the marginal work of any agent of production as the amount of that net product taken at the normal selling value of the product, that is, as $p\Delta\beta$.

It may be noticed that none of these difficulties are dependent upon the system of division of labour and work for payment, though they are brought into prominence by the habit of measuring efforts and satisfactions by price, which is associated with it Robinson Crusoe erecting a building for himself would not find that an addition of a thousandth part to his previous accommodation increased his comfort by a thousandth part. What he added might be of the same character with the rest; but if one counted it in at the same rate of real value to him, one would have to reckon for the fact that the new part made the old of somewhat less urgent need, of somewhat lower real value to him (see note 2 on p. 582). On the other hand, the law of increasing return might render it very difficult for him to assign its true net product to a given half-hour's work For instance, suppose that some small herbs, grateful as condiment, and easily portable, grow in a part of his island, which it takes half a day to visit, and he has gone there to get small batches at a time. Afterwards he gives a whole day, having no important use to which he can put less than half a day, and comes back with ten times as great a load as before. We cannot then separate the return of the last half-hour from the rest, our only plan is to take the whole day as a unit, and compare its return of satisfaction with those of days spent in other ways; and in the modern system of industry we have the similar, but more difficult task of taking, for some purposes, the whole of a process of production as a single unit.

It would be possible to extend the scope of such systems of equations as we have been considering, and to increase their detail, until they embraced within themselves the whole of the demand side of the problem of distribution But while a mathematical illustration of the mode of action of a definite set of causes may be complete in itself, and strictly accurate within its clearly defined limits, it is otherwise with any attempt to grasp the whole of a complex problem of real life, or even any considerable part of it, in a series of equations. For many important considerations, especially those connected with the manifold influences of the element of time, do not lend themselves easily to mathematical expression: they must either be omitted altogether, or clipped and pruned till they resemble the conventional birds and animals of decorative art. And hence arises a tendency towards assigning wrong proportions to economic forces; those elements being most emphasized which lend themselves most easily to analytical methods. No doubt this danger is inherent in every application not only of mathematical analysis, but of analysis of any kind, to the problems of real life. It is a danger which more than any other the economist must have in mind at every turn. But to avoid it altogether, would be to abandon the chief means of scientific progress: and in discussions written specially for mathematical readers it is no doubt right to be very bold in the search for wide generalizations.

In such discussions it may be right, for instance, to regard H as the sum total of satisfactions, and V as the sum total of dissatisfactions (efforts, sacrifices &c.) which accrue to a community from economic causes; to simplify the notion of the action of these causes by assumptions similar to those which are involved, more or less consciously, in the various forms of the doctrine that the constant drift of these causes is towards the attainment of the *Maximum Satisfaction*, in the net aggregate for the Community (see above, pp 526–7), or, in other words, that there is a constant tendency to make $H - V$ a maximum for society as a whole. On this plan the resulting differential equations of the same class as those which we have been discussing, will be interpreted to represent value as governed in every field of economics by the balancing of groups of utilities against groups of disutilities, of groups of satisfactions against groups of real costs. Such discussions have their place: but it is not in a treatise such as the present, in which mathematics are used only to express in terse and more precise language those methods of analysis and reasoning which ordinary people adopt, more or less consciously, in the affairs of every-day life.

It may indeed be admitted that such discussions have some points of resemblance to the method of analysis applied in Book III. to the total utility of particular commodities. The difference between the two cases is mainly one of degree but it is of a degree so great as practically to amount to a difference of kind. For in the former case we take each commodity by itself and with reference to a particular market; and we take careful account of the circumstances of the consumers at the time and place under consideration. Thus we follow, though perhaps with more careful precautions, the practice of ministers of finance, and of the common man when discussing financial policy. We note that a few commodities are consumed mainly by the rich, and that in consequence their real total utilities are less than is suggested by the money measures of those utilities. But we assume, with the rest of the world, that as a rule, and in the absence of special causes to the contrary, the real total utilities of two commodities that are mainly consumed by the rich stand to one another in about the same relation as their money measures do: and that the same is true of commodities the consumption of which is divided out among rich and middle classes and poor in similar proportions. Such estimates are but rough approximations; but each particular difficulty, each source of possible error, is pushed into prominence by the definiteness of our phrases. we introduce no assumptions that are not latent in the practice of ordinary life; while we attempt no task that is not grappled with in a rougher fashion, but yet to good purpose, in the practice of ordinary life: we introduce no new assumptions, and we bring into clear light those which cannot be avoided. But though this is possible when dealing with particular commodities with reference to particular markets, it does not seem possible with regard to the innumerable economic elements that come within the all-embracing net of the doctrine of Maximum Satisfaction The forces of supply are especially heterogeneous and complex· they include an infinite variety of efforts and sacrifices, direct and indirect, on the part of people in all varieties of industrial grades and if there were no other hindrance to giving a concrete interpretation to the doctrine, a fatal obstacle would be found in its latent assumption that the cost of rearing children and preparing them for their work can be measured in the same way as the cost of erecting a machine

For reasons similar to those given in this typical case, our mathematical notes will cover less and less ground as the complexity of the subjects discussed in the text increases. A few of those that follow relate to monopolies, which present some sides singularly open to direct analytical treatment. But the majority of the remainder will be occupied with illustrations of joint and composite demand and supply which have much in common with the substance of this note. while the last of that series Note XXI. goes a little way towards a general survey of the problem of distribution and exchange (without reference to the element of time), but only so far as to make sure that the mathematical illustrations used point towards a system of equations, which are neither more nor less in number than the unknowns introduced into them

NOTE XIV. *bis* (p. 455). In the diagrams of this chapter the supply curves are all inclined positively, and in our mathematical versions of them we shall suppose the marginal expenses of production to be determined with a definiteness that does not exist in real life; and we shall take no account of the time required for developing a business with the internal and external economics of production on a large scale And we shall ignore the law of increasing return and all those difficulties connected with it which are discussed in Book v. Ch. XI To adopt any other course would lead us to mathematical complexities, which though perhaps not without their use would be unsuitable for a Treatise of this kind The discussions therefore in this and the following Notes must be regarded as sketches rather than complete studies.

Let the factors of production of a commodity A be a_1, a_2 &c., and let their supply equations be $y=\phi_1(x)$, $y=\phi_2(x)$, &c. Let the number of units of them required for the production of x units of A be m_1x, m_2x, . respectively, where m_1, m_2 are generally not constants but functions of x. Then the supply equation of A is

$$y=\Phi(x)=m_1\phi_1(m_1x)+m_2\phi_2(m_2x)+ \quad \equiv\Sigma\{m\phi(mx)\}.$$

Let $y=F(x)$ be the demand equation for the finished commodity, then the derived demand equation for a_r the rth factor is

$$y=F(x)-\{\Phi(x)-m_r\phi_r(m_rx)\}$$

But in this equation y is the price, not of one unit of the factor but of m_r units; and to get an equation expressed in terms of fixed units let η be the price of one unit, and let $\xi=m_rx$, then $\eta=\frac{1}{m_r}\cdot y$ and the equation becomes

$$\eta=f_r(\xi)=\frac{1}{m_r}\left[F\left(\frac{1}{m_r}\xi\right)-\left\{\Phi\left(\frac{1}{m_r}\xi\right)-m_r\phi_r(\xi)\right\}\right].$$

If m_r is a function of x say $=\psi_r(x)$; then x must be determined in terms of ξ by the equation $\xi=x\psi_r(x)$, so that m_r can be written $\chi_r(\xi)$; substituting this we have η expressed as a function of ξ. The supply equation for a_r is simply $\eta=\phi_r(\xi)$.

NOTE XV. (p. 456). Let the demand equation for knives be

$$y=F(x) \quad \text{..(1)},$$

let the supply equation for knives be $y=\Phi(x)$ . .. (2),

let that for handles be $y=\phi_1(x)$ . . . (3),

and that for blades be $y=\phi_2(x)$ . . ..(4),

then the demand equation for handles is

$$y=f_1(x)=F(x)-\phi_2(x) \quad \text{.... . . . (5)}.$$

The measure of elasticity for (5) is $-\left\{\frac{xf_1'(x)}{f_1(x)}\right\}^{-1}$, that is,

$$-\left\{\frac{xF'(x)-x\phi_2'(x)}{f_1(x)}\right\}^{-1};$$

that is,

$$\left\{-\frac{xF'(x)}{F(x)}\cdot\frac{F(x)}{f_1(x)}+\frac{x\phi_2'(x)}{f_1(x)}\right\}^{-1}.$$

This will be the smaller the more fully the following conditions are satisfied. (i) that $-\frac{xF'(x)}{F(x)}$, which is necessarily positive, be large, i.e that the elasticity of the demand for knives be small; (ii) that $\phi_2'(x)$ be positive and large, i.e. that the supply price for blades should increase rapidly with an increase, and diminish rapidly with a diminution of the amount supplied, and (iii) that $\frac{F(x)}{f_1(x)}$ should be large, that is, that the price of handles should be but a small part of the price of knives.

A similar, but more complex inquiry, leads to substantially the same results, when the units of the factors of production are not fixed, but vary as in the preceding note.

NOTE XVI. (p. 457). Suppose that m bushels of hops are used in making a gallon of ale of a certain kind, of which in equilibrium x' gallons are sold at a price $y'=F(x')$. Let m be changed into $m+\Delta m$; and, as a result, when x' gallons are still offered for sale let them find purchasers at a price $y'+\Delta y'$; then $\frac{\Delta y'}{\Delta m}$ represents the marginal demand price for hops· if it is greater than their supply price, it will be to the interest of the brewers to put more hops into the ale Or, to put the case more generally, let $y=F(x, m)$, $y=\Phi(x, m)$ be the demand and supply equations for beer, x being the number of gallons and m the number of bushels of hops in each gallon. Then $F(x, m)-\Phi(x, m)$ = excess of demand over supply price. In equilibrium this is of course zero · but if it were possible to make it a positive sum by varying m the change would be effected: therefore (assuming that there is no perceptible change in the expense of making the beer, other than what results from the increased amount of hops) $\frac{dF}{dm}=\frac{d\Phi}{dm}$, the one representing the marginal demand price, and the other the marginal supply price of hops; and the two are equal.

This method is of course capable of being extended to cases in which there are concurrent variations in two or more factors of production.

NOTE XVII (p. 458). Suppose that a thing, whether a finished commodity or a factor of production, is distributed between two uses, so that of the total amount x the part devoted to the first use is x_1, and that devoted to the second use is x_2. Let $y=\phi(x)$ be the total supply equation; $y=f_1(x_1)$ and $y=f_2(x_2)$ be the demand equations for its first and second uses. Then in equilibrium the three unknowns x, x_1, and x_2 are determined by the three equations $f_1(x_1)=f_2(x_2)=\phi(x)$; $x_1+x_2=x$.

Next suppose that it is desired to obtain separately the relations of demand and supply of the thing in its first use, on the supposition that, whatever perturbations there may be in its first use, its demand and supply for the second use remains in equilibrium, i.e. that its demand price for the second use is equal to its supply price for the total amount that is actually produced, i.e. $f_2(x_2)=\phi(x_1+x_2)$ always From this equation we can determine x_2 in terms of x_1, and therefore x in terms of x_1; and therefore we can write $\phi(x)=\psi(x_1)$ Thus the supply equation for the thing in its first use becomes $y=\psi(x_1)$; and this with the already known equation $y=f_1(x_1)$ gives the relations required.

NOTE XVIII (p 459). Let a_1, a_2 be joint products, m_1x, m_2x of them severally being produced as the result of x units of their joint process of production, for which the supply equation is $y=\phi(x)$ Let

$$y=f_1(x),\ y=f_2(x)$$

be their respective demand equations. Then in equilibrium

$$m_1f_1(m_1x)+m_2f_2(m_2x)+ \quad =\phi(x).$$

Let x' be the value of x determined from this equation, then $f_1(m_1x')$, $f_2(m_2x')$ &c. are the equilibrium prices of the several joint products Of course m_1, m_2, are expressed if necessary in terms of x'.

NOTE XIX. (p. 460) This case corresponds, *mutatis mutandis*, to that discussed in Note XVI If in equilibrium x' oxen annually are supplied and sold at a price $y'=\phi(x')$; and each ox yields m units of beef: and if breeders find that by modifying the breeding and feeding of oxen they can increase their meat-yielding properties to the extent of Δm units of beef (the hides and other joint products being, on the balance, unaltered), and that the extra expense of doing this is $\Delta y'$, then $\frac{\Delta y'}{\Delta m}$ represents the marginal supply price of beef: if this price were less than the selling price, it would be to the interest of breeders to make the change.

NOTE XX. (p. 461). Let a_1, a_2 be things which are fitted to subserve exactly the same function. Let their units be so chosen that a unit of any one of them is equivalent to a unit of any others. Let their several supply equations be $y_1=\phi_1(x_1)$, $y_2=\phi_2(x_2)$.

In these equations let the variable be changed, and let them be written $x_1=\psi_1(y_1)$, $x_2=\psi_2(y_2)$. .. Let $y=f(x)$ be the demand equation for the service for which all of them are fitted. Then in equilibrium x and y are determined by the equations $y=f(x)$, $x=x_1+x_2+$. , $y_1=y_2=$ $=y$. (The equations must be such that none of the quantities x_1, x_2 can have a negative value. When y_1 has fallen to a certain level x_1 becomes zero; and for lower values x_1 remains zero; it does not become negative.) As was observed in the text, it must be assumed that the supply equations all conform to the law of diminishing return, i.e that $\phi_1'(x)$, $\phi_2'(x)$ are always positive

NOTE XXI. (p. 463). We may now take a bird's-eye view of the problems of joint demand, composite demand, joint supply and composite supply when they all arise together, with the object of making sure that our abstract theory has just as many equations as it has unknowns, neither more nor less.

First, in a problem of joint demand we may suppose that there are n commodities A_1, A_2 A_n Let A_1 have a_1 factors of production, let A_2 have a_2 factors, and so on, so that the total number of factors of production is $\Sigma_1^n a_r$: let this $=m$

First, suppose that all the factors are different, so that there is no composite demand; that each factor has a separate process of production, so that there are no joint products; and lastly, that no two factors subserve the same use, so that there is no composite supply. We then have $2n+2m$ unknowns, viz. the amounts and prices of n commodities and of m factors, and to determine them we have $2m+2n$ equations, viz.—(i) n demand equations, each of which connects the price and amount of a commodity, (ii) n equations, each of which equates the supply price for any amount of a commodity to the sum of the prices of corresponding amounts of its factors; (iii) m supply equations, each of which connects the price of a factor with its amount, and lastly, m equations, each of which states the amount of a factor which is used in the production of a given amount of the commodity.

Next, let us take account not only of joint demand but also of composite demand Let β_1 of the factors of production consist of the same thing, say carpenters' work of a certain efficiency; in other words, let carpenters' work be one of the factors of production of β_1 of the n commodities A_1, A_2 . Then since the carpenters' work is taken to have the same price in whatever production it is used, there is only one price for each of these factors of production, and the number of unknowns is diminished by β_1-1; also the number of supply equations is diminished by β_1-1, and so on for other cases.

Next, let us in addition take account of joint supply. Let γ_1 of the things used in producing the commodities be joint products of one and the same process. Then the number of unknowns is not altered; but the number of supply equations is reduced by $(\gamma_1 - 1)$; this deficiency is however made up by a new set of $(\gamma_1 - 1)$ equations connecting the amounts of these joint products, and so on

Lastly, let one of the things used have a composite supply made up from δ_1 rival sources, then reserving the old supply equations for the first of these rivals, we have $2(\delta_1 - 1)$ additional unknowns, consisting of the prices and amounts of the remaining $(\delta_1 - 1)$ rivals. These are covered by $(\delta_1 - 1)$ supply equations for the rivals, and $(\delta_1 - 1)$ equations between the prices of the δ_1 rivals

Thus, however complex the problem may become, we can see that it is theoretically determinate, because the number of unknowns is always exactly equal to the number of the equations which we obtain.

NOTE XXII. (p. 535) If $y = f_1(x)$, $y = f_2(x)$ be the equations to the demand and supply curves respectively, the amount of production which affords the maximum monopoly revenue is found by making $\{xf_1(x) - xf_2(x)\}$ a maximum, that is, it is the root, or one of the roots of the equation

$$\frac{d}{dx}\{xf_1(x) - xf_2(x)\} = 0$$

The supply function is represented here by $f_2(x)$ instead of as before by $\phi(x)$, partly to emphasize the fact that supply price does not mean exactly the same thing here as it did in the previous Notes, partly to fall in with that system of numbering the curves which is wanted to prevent confusion now that their number is being increased

NOTE XXIII. (p 537). If a tax be imposed of which the aggregate amount is $F(x)$, then in order to find the value of x which makes the monopoly revenue a maximum, we have $\frac{d}{dx}\{xf_1(x) - xf_2(x) - F(x)\} = 0$; and it is clear that if $F(x)$ is either constant, as in the case of a license duty, or varies as $xf_1(x) - xf_2(x)$, as in the case of an income tax, this equation has the same roots as it would have if $F(x)$ were zero.

Treating the problems geometrically, we notice that, if a fixed burden be imposed on a monopoly sufficient to make the monopoly revenue curve fall altogether below Ox, and q' be the point on the new curve vertically below L in fig. (36), then the new curve at q' will touch one of a series of rectangular hyperbolas drawn with yO produced downwards for one asymptote and Ox for the other. These curves may be called Constant Loss curves

Again, a tax proportionate to the monopoly revenue, and say m times that revenue, (m being less than 1), will substitute for QQ' a curve the length of each ordinate of which is $(1 - m) \times$ the length of the corresponding point on QQ', i.e the point which has the same abscissa. The tangents to corresponding points on the old and new position of QQ' will cut Ox in the same point, as is obvious by the method of projections. But it is a law of rectangular hyperbolas which have the same asymptotes that, if a line be drawn parallel to one asymptote to cut the hyperbolas, and tangents be drawn to them at its points of intersection, they will all cut the other asymptote in the same point. Therefore if q_3' be the point on the new position of QQ' corresponding to q_3, and if we call G the point in which the common tangent to the hyperbola and QQ' cuts Ox, Gq_3' will be a tangent to the hyperbola which passes through q_3'; that is, q_3' is a point of maximum revenue on the new curve

The geometrical and analytical methods of this Note can be applied to cases, such as are discussed in the latter part of § 4 in the text, in which the tax is levied on the produce of the monopoly

NOTE XXIII *bis* (p. 544). These results have easy geometrical proofs by Newton's method, and by the use of well-known properties of the rectangular hyperbola. They may also be proved analytically. As before let $y=f_1(x)$ be the equation to the demand curve; $y=f_2(x)$ that to the supply curve; and that to the monopoly revenue curve is $y=f_3(x)$, where $f_3(x)=f_1(x)-f_2(x)$ the equation to the consumers' rent curve $y=f_4(x)$, where

$$f_4(x)=\frac{1}{x}\int_0^x f_1(a)\,da-f_1(x)$$

That to the total benefit curve is $y=f_5(x)$; where

$$f_5(x)=f_3(x)+f_4(x)=\frac{1}{x}\int_0^x f_1(a)\,da-f_2(x);$$

a result which may of course be obtained directly. That to the compromise benefit curve is $y=f_6(x)$, where $f_6(x)=f_3(x)+nf_4(x)$; consumers' rent being reckoned in by the monopolist at n times its actual value

To find OL (fig. 38), that is, the amount the sale of which will afford the maximum monopoly revenue, we have the equation

$$\frac{d}{dx}\{xf_3(x)\}=0;\ \text{i.e.}\ f_1(x)-f_2(x)=x\{f_2'(x)-f_1'(x)\};$$

the left-hand side of this equation is necessarily positive, and therefore so is the right-hand side, which shows, what is otherwise obvious, that if Lq_3 be produced to cut the supply and demand curves in q_2 and q_1 respectively, the supply curve at q_2 (if inclined negatively) must make a greater angle with the vertical than is made by the demand curve at q_1

To find OW, that is, the amount the sale of which will afford the maximum total benefit, we have

$$\frac{d}{dx}\{xf_5(x)\}=0,\ \text{i.e}\ f_1(x)-f_2(x)-xf_2'(x)=0.$$

To find OY, that is, the amount the sale of which will afford the maximum compromise benefit, we have

$$\frac{d}{dx}\{xf_6(x)\}=0;\ \text{i.e}\ \frac{d}{dx}\{(1-n)xf_1(x)-xf_2(x)+n\int_0^x f_1(a)\,da\}=0,$$

$$\text{i.e}\ (1-n)xf_1'(x)+f_1(x)-f_2(x)-xf_2'(x)=0.$$

If $OL=c$, the condition that OY should be greater than ON is that $\frac{d}{dx}\{xf_6(x)\}$ be positive when c is written for x in it, i.e. since $\frac{d}{dx}\{xf_3(x)\}=0$ when $x=c$, that $\frac{d}{dx}\{xf_4(x)\}$ be positive when $x=c$; i.e. that $f_1'(c)$ be negative. But this condition is satisfied whatever be the value of c This proves the first of the two results given at the end of Book v. Chap. VIII. § 7; and the proof of the second is similar. (The wording of these results and of their proofs tacitly assumes that there is only one point of maximum monopoly revenue)

One more result may be added to those in the text. Let us write $OH=a$, then the condition that OY should be greater than OH is that $\frac{d}{dx}\{nf_6(x)\}$ be positive when a is written for x: that is, since $f_1(a)=f_2(a)$, that $(1-n)f_1'(a)-f_2'(a)$ be positive Now $f_1'(a)$ is always negative, and therefore the condition becomes that $f_2'(x)$ be negative, i.e. that the supply obey the law of increasing return and that $\tan\phi$ be numerically greater than $(1-n)\tan\theta$, where θ and ϕ are the angles which tangents at A to the demand and supply curves respectively make with Ox. When $n=1$, the sole condition is that $\tan\phi$ be negative: that is, OW is greater than OH provided the supply curve at A be inclined negatively In other words, if the monopolist regards the interest of consumers as identical with his own, he will carry his production further than the point at which the supply price (in the special sense in which we are here using the term) is equal to the demand price, provided the supply in the neighbourhood of that point obeys the law of increasing return but he will carry it less far if the supply obeys the law of diminishing return

NOTE XXIV. (p 644) Let Δx be the probable amount of his production of wealth in time Δt, and Δy the probable amount of his consumption. Then the discounted value of his future services is $\int_0^T R^{-t}\left(\frac{dx}{dt}-\frac{dy}{dt}\right)dt$; where T is the maximum possible duration of his life. On the like plan the past cost of his rearing and training is $\int_{-T'}^{0} R^{-t}\left(\frac{dy}{dt}-\frac{dx}{dt}\right)dt$, where T' is the date of his birth If we were to assume that he would neither add to nor take from the material well-being of a country in which he stayed all his life, we should have $\int_{-T'}^{T} R^{-t}\left(\frac{dx}{dt}-\frac{dy}{dt}\right)dt=0$; or, taking the starting-point of time at his birth, and $l=T'+T=$the maximum possible length of his life, this takes the simpler form, $\int_0^l R^{-t}\left(\frac{dx}{dt}-\frac{dy}{dt}\right)dt=0$

In saying that Δx is the probable amount of his production in time Δt, we have put shortly what may be more accurately expressed thus —let p_1, p_2 , be the chances that in time Δt he will produce elements of wealth $\Delta_1 x$, $\Delta_2 x$, where p_1+p_2+ cannot exceed unity · then

$$\Delta x=p_1\Delta_1 x+p_2\Delta_2 x+ \quad .$$

INDEX.

[Wherever a reference is given to the contents of a chapter, that indicates that the subject in question is discussed at length in that chapter, and the reader is referred for more details to the analysis of the chapter in the table of contents]

Cambridge:
PRINTED BY J AND C F CLAY,
AT THE UNIVERSITY PRESS

Lightning Source UK Ltd.
Milton Keynes UK
UKHW022021150922
408946UK00003B/81